Wayne Morse
A POLITICAL BIOGRAPHY

Wayne Morse
A POLITICAL BIOGRAPHY

Mason Drukman

The Oregon Historical Society Press
Portland, Oregon

Oregon Historical Society
1200 Southwest Park Avenue
Portland, Oregon 97205

LIBRARY OF CONGRESS CATALOGING-IN-PUBLICATION DATA

Drukman, Mason, 1932-
Wayne Morse: a political biography / Mason Drukman.
    p. cm.
    Includes bibliographical references (p.) and index.
    ISBN 0-87595-263-1 (alk. paper)
1. Morse, Wayne L. (Wayne Lyman), 1900–1974. 2. Legislators—
United States—Biography. 3. United States. Congress. Senate—
Biography. I. Title.
    E748.M76D78 1997
    328. 73'092—dc21
    [B]   97-3380
    CIP

Frontispiece courtesy Wayne Morse Historic Park Corporation.

FOR MY WONDERFUL SONS, SAM AND MAX

Wayne Morse: A Political Biography
was supported in part by generous gifts from

HOWARD GLAZER

REUBEN LENSKE

HOWARD MORGAN

MONROE SWEETLAND

KERMIT AND BARBARA ROHDE

THE WAYNE MORSE HISTORICAL PARK CORPORATION

Acknowledgments

I AM INDEBTED TO THE MANY INDIVIDUALS who helped make the research for this biography possible. I wish in particular to thank Richard Baker, U.S. Senate Historian; Hilary Cummings and Kenneth Duckett, Special Collections, University of Oregon Library; Keith Richards, Archivist, University of Oregon; Penny Krosch, Archivist, University of Minnesota, Professor Neil Sabin, Lewis and Clark College; Eugene Vrana, Associate Education Director, Librarian & Archivist, International Longshoremen's and Warehousemen's Union; and Geoffrey Wexler, Reference Archivist, State Historical Society of Wisconsin. Special thanks also to Pat Cooper, who expertly transcribed the tape-recorded interviews; to A. Robert Smith for his generous encouragement; to Byron Haines, one of the first to suggest doing this book, and to Grey Wolfe for advocating sanity in a world of confusion.

I am grateful to the following board members of the Wayne Morse Historical Park Corporation in Eugene for their unflagging enthusiasm and assistance: Louise Beaudreau, Louise and Harold Bock, Agnes and Hobart McQueary, Laura Olson, Ann Penny, Larry Perry, Charles Porter, Barbara and Kermit Rohde, Monroe Sweetland, and Ethel Villeneuve.

I am similarly grateful to the following individuals in the employ of the Oregon Historical Society: Nancy Trotic, a freelance editor of remarkable skill; book designer and typographer John Laursen, a consumate professional; and OHS Director of Publications, Adair Law, a woman of exemplary patience and good-humor.

Parts of my manuscript were read by Elaine Drukman, George Fasel, Ray Goldstein, Charles Grimes, Elinor Langer, Matthew Perry,

Roger Porter, Sara Shumer, Matthew Stolz, and Trevor Thomas. Their comments were invaluable. As were those of my dear friend Howard Waskow, who gave every word and punctuation mark his thoughtful attention, and who saved me more than once from sins of illogic and infelicity.

I could not have completed this biography without the loving support of my wife, Anne Ide Barrows, poet and teacher extraordinaire, and director of the expository and graduate writing programs at the University of San Francisco. Anne read the manuscript several times over; in the process she taught me to be a better writer.

Contents

PROLOGUE: Morse as Maverick *1*

1 Progressive Beginnings *11*

2 A Maverick's Education *35*

3 Vaulting Ambition *59*

4 Arbitrator Supreme *88*

5 Running Past Rufus *120*

6 Storming the Senate *143*

7 In the Days of McCarthy *174*

8 Leading the Revolution *212*

9 Dick and Wayne *240*

10   Once a Maverick . . .   *301*

11   A Matter of Character   *338*

12   Strong Man of the Senate   *368*

13   Vietnam   *401*

14   A Maverick's Dénouement   *437*

Notes   *465*

Sources   *524*

Index   *533*

PROLOGUE

Morse as Maverick

I am perfectly aware of the fact that in taking the position I do, I take a position contrary . . . to the present prevailing majority opinion in America.
— Wayne Morse, 1947

IT IS A HUMID APRIL DAY IN WASHINGTON. I am interviewing J. William Fulbright in his law office. We are talking about the late Senator Wayne Morse of Oregon. For twenty-four years Fulbright was Morse's colleague in the United States Senate; for eleven years the two men served side by side on the Senate Foreign Relations Committee. Morse has been dead for a decade. Fulbright has been out of the Senate the same length of time.

Fulbright begins by saying, "I am seventy-nine years old, and some things I recall more vividly than others." He seems thinner than he did on television in the 1960s and 1970s—during his days as chairman of the Foreign Relations Committee—almost gaunt, but his eyes are keen and alert, and though his Arkansas drawl may be more languid than I remembered, his voice is vigorous and still resonates with authority.

I am waiting for an appropriate moment to bring up the Tonkin Gulf Resolution, that fateful 1964 measure with which Congress gave President Lyndon Johnson the power "to take all necessary steps, including the use of armed force," to prevent "further aggression" in Southeast Asia—the power, in short, to carry on an undeclared war halfway around the world. As chairman of Foreign Relations, Fulbright was floor leader for the Tonkin Resolution, propelling it

1

through a normally slow-footed Senate in less than two days, winning overwhelming and enthusiastic approval, with only Morse and Ernest Gruening of Alaska voting against it.

I am surprised when, without prodding, Fulbright himself turns the conversation to the Tonkin Resolution. As he does, he takes on that quizzical, apologetic voice the nation listened to during the televised hearings on Vietnam in 1967. He tells me he profoundly regrets his part in carrying the resolution through the Senate. He says he did not believe that the administration would lie to him, and to everyone else, in order to get its way. Then, staring through the window into the hazy morning, he adds,

"I have never understood why Wayne didn't call for hearings in 1964. If he had insisted upon hearings, we could have taken the time to investigate, to check out the facts. But he only made a short speech against the resolution, and while he raised some serious questions, he certainly didn't press the matter the way he had on other issues."

The interview is nearly over. Fulbright has been cordial and, in his wistful mood, helpful in a way I had not anticipated. Vietnam, LBJ, the Foreign Relations Committee—he has been moved by memories that Morse's name has evoked. Haunted by his role in the Tonkin Resolution, he wonders whether events might have gone in another direction. If only Wayne had . . .

In retrospect, Morse appears almost larger than life. As Fulbright contemplates the past, he imagines Morse changing the path of history, an incipient hero who might have saved the nation from a generation of anguish. Of course Fulbright's memory is flawed, the result perhaps of penitent wishful thinking. The truth is that Morse —who did in fact request hearings—could never have altered the outcome of the Tonkin Resolution. His "short" speech consumed four hours of a debate which, in its entirety, lasted only six and a half. He argued strenuously on constitutional and ethical grounds that the resolution should be defeated. "I believe," he said, "that future generations will look with dismay upon a Congress which is now about to make such a historic mistake." And he predicted—with great accuracy, as it turned out—what would happen if the resolution were allowed to pass.

Not only did Morse's remarks go unheeded, but, given the president's call for extraordinary powers in a moment of apparent national crisis, the idea that Fulbright would have considered scheduling hearings is inconceivable, regardless of how hard Morse was pressing for them. Convinced by a guileful administration that U. S. destroyers had without provocation been attacked in neutral waters by North Vietnamese patrol boats, Congress was prepared to give Johnson whatever he requested. Even before the Senate concluded its debate, the resolution had passed the House 416 to 0. Members of the upper chamber were clamoring to get behind it, and it is silly to believe that Morse could have done anything to change the result.

What is interesting here is not so much that it was impossible under the circumstances for Morse to make a difference, but that Fulbright, even in retrospect, can imagine that he might have. This is especially noteworthy because Morse was an avowed senatorial maverick, someone who theoretically stood outside the realm of legislative influence. Fulbright seemed to sense that in matters such as the Tonkin Gulf Resolution, emotional issues on which the congressional rank and file can be easily stampeded, only a maverick has sufficient independence to go against prevailing opinion, to speak from principle rather than ideological convention. Fulbright was right insofar as he believed that if any senator could have persuaded Congress to consider a different course on the Tonkin Resolution, that senator would have been a maverick like Morse.

What does it mean to say Morse was a maverick? Originally used to identify unbranded range cows in the south of Texas, the word *maverick* usually refers to a person who refuses to follow the dictates of a particular group or organization. In politics, mavericks either do not associate with a party or faction or, more typically, if they do join such a group, do not feel bound to honor positions advocated by its leaders. American history records a number (exceedingly small) of mavericks who made their names precisely because they dissented from platforms and deviated from voting patterns set by politicians with traditional affiliations. We think of Robert La Follette, Hiram Johnson, Henry Wallace, William Borah, and especially of Wayne Morse.

The *Oxford English Dictionary* offers an additional meaning of "maverick" that reaches beyond political dissent, beyond the mere resistance to legislative majorities. In the *OED*, a maverick is defined as "a masterless person." Enlarged in this way, "maverick" brings us closer to Morse's essential nature. His maverickness, evident throughout his lifetime but especially during his days in Congress, is expressed most pointedly in a message to a friend in February 1945. "As long as I serve on this job," he wrote from Washington, less than a month after taking his seat in the Senate, "I am going to serve as my own master, under obligation to no one."

Of course, in the strictest sense, no individual can be his or her own master. Choices made in life—vocational, marital, geographic—inevitably rule us, control to a large extent what we can and cannot do, and our room to act in a masterless way is accordingly narrowed. Merely to inhabit organized society is to live under an array of rules and conventions which inhibit one's ability to make unencumbered choices. Masterlessness must be seen as a *relative* condition, realized to the degree that the individual in a given circumstance is able to act as a *relatively* independent agent.

For politicians, a higher level of relativity is involved, since their room to act as their own masters is even more circumscribed. Their foremost task is to get elected and then reelected. To accomplish this—even in America, where party loyalty is weak and ideology weaker—they must be part of a process in which allegiances are formed, debts incurred, and compromises made, a process which invariably involves a large measure of deference, if not outright submissiveness.

Nevertheless, the imposition of obligations does not eliminate the politician's room for masterless action, and mavericks typically seek to exploit and expand whatever space they find available. Even when no such space exists, the quest for masterlessness remains, a persistent and dominating end in itself. To understand mavericks, it is critical to see that, while they may never truly become their own masters, they relentlessly seek such a goal, wish to be "under obligation to no one," and that they *do* have some degree of success, are at various times able to act on their own. Without such a desire, and without at least a modest record of success, we would not know them as mavericks.

Wayne Morse was a maverick *par excellence.* Not only did he dissent and vote according to his own principles much of the time, but his first impulse was to try, whatever the issue, to remain his own master. Like other mavericks, he could not realize his objective in all instances. He joined parties, he courted electorates, he accommodated interest groups—he was, in the ways that matter most, an American politician. However, he was also a maverick, in constant search of masterlessness, and this meant that his life would be filled with conflicting pressures: the politician's external pressure to conform, pledge fealty, be relied upon; the maverick's internal pressure to choose his own path, be his own person, take orders from no one.

Since he was such a maverick, it is not surprising that Morse, forever subject to countervailing forces, has been a source of perplexity to those who have wondered about his apparently patternless behavior. As early as 1947, under the headline "Senator Wayne Morse's Quick Change Tactics Bewilder Party Strategists," a *Kansas City Times* reporter commented that "his inconsistencies sometimes stumble over one another's heels." Ten years later, a *New Republic* editorial complained about his "puzzling behavior" and seemingly "pointless independence." Historian Irving Bernstein speaks for most Morse observers when, in bafflement, he sums up the "eccentric" Oregon senator as an unintelligible "bundle of contradictions."

Wayne Morse could indeed be contradictory. But when he shifted positions he seldom did so out of mere eccentricity. Arising most often out of the desire for masterlessness, his "contradictions" should be seen as the predictable consequences of a characteristic maverick's acting out his quintessential purpose. While confusing to onlookers, such behavior had a logic of its own, a logic born of what it truly means to be an unbranded maverick.

As maverick—political actor *qua* masterless person—Wayne Morse was extraordinarily different from other politicians. If commentators have failed to comprehend exactly why he was so different, it may be because they have missed the point that precisely because mavericks can and do take positions beyond the limits of conventionality, they attain a moral standing which regular politicians typically find unreachable. It was for this reason that Fulbright could imagine Morse (whom on normal issues Fulbright never fully trusted) a paladin, leading the Senate on the path of peace and righteousness. As things were, no one could have carried the Congress on such a path, but only a maverick like Morse, arguing from principle, would have had the moral standing to make a realistic attempt.

Such, however, is not the standing normally granted to Morse in the literature. In *Vietnam: A History*, Stanley Karnow speaks for what seems a near orthodoxy among historians when he contends that Morse could convert no one to his view of the Tonkin Gulf incident because he had lost all credibility in the Senate. He had become, in Karnow's words, "the Typhoid Mary of Capitol Hill. . . . a sanctimonious bore, a garrulous orator whose gravel voice would drone on over trivia. . . . His colleagues would tolerate him for five or ten minutes, since they respected the ritual courtesies of the Senate, but he rarely changed votes. He lacked influence."

Since this assessment runs counter to my own, I asked former Wisconsin Democratic senator William Proxmire what he thought of Karnow's description. In light of his history with Morse, anything Proxmire might say in Morse's favor must be given special weight: after beginning his congressional career as an ally of Morse, Proxmire fell out with him in a bitter dispute over labor legislation in the late 1950s, and the two were never on friendly terms thereafter. Proxmire was, moreover, a consistent enemy of Morse on foreign policy, one of President Johnson's most ardent supporters on Vietnam throughout the 1960s. Here is his response:

> The answer to your question on Stanley Karnow's evaluation of Morse as a "sanctimonious bore" etc., is this: Wayne Morse was recognized during the years we served together 1957 until he left the Senate as having the ablest mind in the Senate. In my mind he never lost his credibility or insight, understanding and logic. Frequently he would take positions which contradicted the President or a majority of the Senate but he would always argue his position with great force. On

these occasions many Senators disagreed with Morse, frequently a large majority disagreed with him but most Senators deeply respected the sincerity of his convictions.

Morse could be remembered by someone like Proxmire with feelings of respect precisely because, as a maverick, he could stake out ground that Proxmire and other legislators could never occupy. They might deride his positions or angrily oppose him, but in the end they also envied his ability to argue from conviction rather than accommodation. Morse never became the "conscience of the Senate." He was in fact too argumentative, too self-centered, too ready to assail his colleagues to be that. But for many years he was the closest thing to a conscience the Senate had. Which is why Fulbright, looking back, could wonder what would have happened if only Wayne had . . .

Today, when mavericks of the Morse variety no longer exist, we may ponder what has happened to Congress and the reasons it is universally held in such low esteem. From the scores of contemporaries interviewed for this book—both those who admired Morse and those who assuredly did not—the most common observation was: "It would be refreshing to have someone like him in the Senate right now." And unanimously from those who follow Washington on a daily basis: "The Senate has been a duller place since Wayne Morse left it."

I FIRST MET WAYNE MORSE IN 1965, during what proved to be his final term in office. I had moved to Oregon from California the previous year to teach political science at Reed College in Portland. One of the extracurricular perquisites of my new job was that it located me in a state where for the first time I felt truly represented by someone in Congress, someone who shared my general political outlook, someone who, most importantly, could express my feelings about Vietnam.

In an attempt to do something about the war from the hinterland of Oregon, I helped to organize a debate on Vietnam in April of 1965. The idea was to make the debate—in which Morse would participate—not just another discussion of the issue, but a dramatic public confrontation, one that would draw significant attention. Once Morse agreed to the idea, my colleagues and I cast about to find another senator willing to come to Portland to defend the administration's position. We had hoped to land one of the leading Democratic hawks in the Senate, perhaps Scoop Jackson of Washington (our first choice) or Gale McGee of Wyoming. The first ten senators we approached turned us down. The eleventh, who accepted, was William Proxmire.

Given that Vietnam was only beginning to penetrate the national consciousness, we were surprised when more than four thousand showed up at Portland's Memorial Coliseum on a damp Friday night to witness the contest. Proxmire began by reporting that fellow legislators had told him he was crazy to try bearding the omnivorous Oregon lion in his own Northwest habitat. He then demonstrated the accuracy of this observation by revealing how ill-equipped he was for the task. It quickly became apparent that he could do no more than parrot the anticommunist propaganda then being spread by the State Department and the Pentagon. Just as quickly, it became clear that Morse had studied the issue and knew far more about it than his adversary.

Morse showed convincingly how the United States was in violation of the Geneva Accords on Vietnam. He argued that there would have been no war in that country had not the United States decided to install a corrupt regime in the South. He quoted President Eisenhower to the effect that Ho Chi Minh, the "father" of his country, would have won 80 percent of the vote in any fair Vietnamese election, but that such an election had never taken place because the United States had opposed it. Along with most of the audience, I applauded in agreement when Morse declared—and this was the first time I had heard him say it—that "our hands are dripping with blood in Southeast Asia." From that moment, I followed Morse's career with increasing interest.

Although I believed that Morse represented my viewpoint while he was in the Senate, and although I counted myself among his supporters, there was much I did not know about him. I knew nothing, for example, of his Midwestern background, of the fact that he had grown up a La Follette Republican Progressive, a member of a poor farming family in the heartland of Wisconsin. I was not aware that in the 1930s he had been the youngest law school dean in the country at the University of Oregon. Nor was I aware of his spectacular record as a waterfront arbitrator and as a member of the National War Labor Board during World War II, or of the role he had played in keeping Harry Bridges from being deported in the 1940s. I did not know that he had been the first U. S. senator to switch parties and be reelected, serving twenty-four years: ten as a Republican, two as an independent, and twelve as a Democrat. I did not know that he had feuded for years with other members of Congress, or that he had steered every Great Society education bill through the Senate in the 1960s. And I was not aware that he had figured importantly, often discordantly, in the careers of presidents Harry Truman, Dwight Eisenhower, John Kennedy, and Lyndon Johnson.

Above all, I knew nothing about Morse's personal characteristics. I had heard something of his vaunted energy, but until I began researching his life in detail, I did not know the extent to which he had thrown himself into his work, so much so that everything else—family, friends, even his beloved horses and prized cattle—could fall out of focus. He was, as I grew to learn, a zealot when it came to his job. It was said that his idea of a good time was a Friday night subcommittee meeting on a holiday weekend.

Because he pursued objectives in his individualistic, outspoken way, irrespective of consequences, Morse often got into trouble, frequently with his own constituents, more frequently with fellow officeholders. Since he could also be prideful, egotistical, and fiercely ambitious, he sometimes found himself making enemies as fast as he could cultivate friends. Controversy followed him throughout his life, wherever he went, whatever he did. But if conflict made his life tumultuous and unpredictable, it also provided him with a source of vitality: he was nourished by it, drew strength from it, even as he painfully suffered the vicissitudes that controversy inevitably brought with it.

I HAVE IN THIS BIOGRAPHY been guided to some extent by *The Real Life of Sebastian Knight*, Nabokov's fictional account of a writer attempting to research and chronicle the life of his dead half-brother. Nabokov warns us that we can never be "certain of learning the past from the lips of the present. Beware," he says, "of the most honest broker. Remember that what you are told is really threefold: shaped by the teller, reshaped by the listener, concealed from both by the dead man of the tale." In preparing this book, I discovered, and more than once rediscovered, the wisdom in Nabokov's advice. I tried to hold it continually in mind: when listening to what others had to say about Morse; when evaluating what Morse on various occasions said, or failed to say, about himself; when thinking about the gloss which I, as biographer, necessarily applied to the events I was writing about.

I have been especially conscious of my "reshaping" role, and have made an effort to keep the glare from my analytical gloss to a minimum. I want the reader to perceive my presence as teller of the tale, but I would have failed in reaching my objective if interpretive reflection on my part served in any way to impair the vision of the tale itself. Morse's history shines forth with a luminosity of its own, and I have tried to present it as straightforwardly as possible, staying out of the reader's line of sight as much as I can.

Elsewhere in *Sebastian Knight*, the narrator tells us he has not written what he calls a *biographie romancée*. Neither have I: that is, I have not tried to explain, in psychoanalytic terms, exactly how or why Morse's earliest years developed as they did. Much less have I tried to show a one-to-one psychogenetic connection between his childhood and what happened in later life, how the boy was somehow father to the man. What I have written is a political biography. My chief interest is in presenting the adult Morse interacting with the people and events of his day. As will be evident, his youth, interesting in and of itself, provides a basis for the more important later narrative. Whether it also provides factors that worked to "predetermine" what afterwards occurred, I made no attempt to discover.

1

Progressive Beginnings

IT WAS NOT A NORMAL CONVOCATION at Madison Central High School. Wayne Morse, the outspoken junior with the protruding ears, viridescent eyes, and slicked-down hair, had risen from his seat in the auditorium. He had a question for Principal Volney G. Barnes. Why was Mr. Barnes interfering in student affairs and imposing unreasonable restrictions on student government? It was the 1917–18 academic year, Wayne was president of his class, and he wanted the student body to know that the principal's office had been overstepping its legitimate authority.

Not a normal convocation, but since it was Wayne Morse who had interrupted proceedings, not that unusual either. Head of his class, president of the History-Civics Club, a star on the debating team, Wayne had long been known as someone ready to speak his mind regardless of circumstances. An anonymous limerick in Central's 1918 yearbook caricatured only slightly:

> There is a young Junior named Morse,
> He can talk till you'd think he'd be hoarse.
> He's always in bad
> But it ne'er makes him sad
> For to him that's a matter of course.

Though it occasionally happened, getting in bad was not a matter of course for the popular "young junior"; but talking at length, questioning authority, and speaking out in defense of strongly held opinions certainly were.

Argumentation, defending one's views, picking apart those of others—these were the ways of the dinner table at the Morse household, and Wayne had been trained in their application long before he entered high school. He absorbed such training almost as easily as he learned to speak. Unlike the Matthew Prior character who "knew better to live than dispute," Morse was one of those people who seemed born to debate, one who from an early age took pleasure in the give-and-take of rhetorical combat. The nightly encounters at the family roundtable provided excellent tutorials in both how to attack an opponent and how to maintain one's position in the face of strong opposition.

Until his sister Caryl was born when he was fourteen, Wayne was the youngest in his family. But being the youngest in no way deterred him from contending on an equal footing with his parents, his sister Mabel, seven years older, and his twin brothers, Harry and Grant, four years older. Jessie Morse, Wayne's mother, usually led the mealtime colloquy, acting as a kind of seminar leader-cum-interrogator, keeping everyone to the point, scolding those who offered insufficient facts to support their convictions. Discussions ranged far and wide and might include Wisconsin crop conditions, animal husbandry, horsemanship, educational reform, or religious beliefs. But politics was always the liveliest topic, and, led by Jessie, the Progressive Morse household spent more time on this topic than on any other.

Jessie Elnora Morse (née White) was an angular, sinewy woman who moved through her days at a bewildering speed, one of those people, according to a granddaughter, whose "feet never seemed to touch the floor." Jessie's vitality was unflagging, so long as her activity could be broken periodically by intervals of rest. After racing through her day and leading the dinnertime discourse, it was her habit to say, "Please excuse me for five minutes," at which point the others retreated from the table while she dropped off briefly, readying herself for a long evening of singing, reading aloud to the family, or preparing foodstuffs for delivery to Madison. Wayne inherited much of Jessie's genetic makeup. Like her, he would go through life at maximum velocity, ever refreshed by instantaneous catnaps taken, in his case, irrespective of where he might be or what might be occurring around him.

While not as quick-minded as Jessie, and fourteen years her senior, Wayne's father, Wilbur Frank "Wib" Morse, also led an active life. Short and powerfully built (he had been an amateur boxer in his youth), Wib usually began his day milking cows at 4 AM and often ended it late in the evening at a gathering of "Fighting Bob" La Follette supporters, or at a meeting of the local school board. Observers would have described Wib as more of a listener than a participant at the family forums, but would have added that when he did contribute, his remarks were usually incisive, especially when the despised corporations controlling Wisconsin's economy were under discussion.

Wisconsin farmers, particularly those in the Madison area, were politically on the move during the early part of the twentieth century, and though he depicted himself as a conservative, Republican, "blue-belted Yankee," Wilbur supported much of their progressive cause. At the same time, his views were not as liberal as Jessie's; seconded by the twins, he would sometimes reach pontifical heights making rambling apologies for the status quo. After listening at length to such discourse, Jessie was apt to interject, "Oh, you Johnny Bull!"—which typically had the effect of bringing Wib's remarks to a rapid close.

Located in Verona, a tiny community eleven miles west-southwest of Madison, the 320-acre Morse farm had been handed down through three generations. Wayne's great-grandfather had originally homesteaded the property in 1848, having migrated from Vermont in a wagon train pulled by Devon oxen. Devon cattle were a mainstay of the farm, and raising them was a tradition which the family proudly traced to bygone Morses in the British Isles. In addition to Devons, which he sold for beef and showed in livestock exhibitions all the way to Chicago, Wib raised Percheron and Hackney horses, dairy cows, hogs, sheep, and poultry, and the feed crops to maintain them. Despite—or perhaps because of—the variety of its products, the Verona farm was always a struggle. It had managed, barely, to survive the 1892–94 depression and the recession of 1896, but it had never been more than marginal, and Wib had to work extremely hard just to keep it in business.

By the time Wayne graduated from high school in 1919, his family had left Verona, probably at Jessie's urging, and moved to a house they owned on Mound Street in Madison. Harry and Grant, then twenty-three, took over the farm's operation. Two years later the Verona acreage, long under the threat of foreclosure, was lost forever in the agricultural depression of 1921. Fortunately for the Morses' survival, Wib had by that time taken a job as gardener at the University of Wisconsin, a position he retained for the next dozen years.

Jessie Morse had grown up in the country. Her father, Myron Renaldo White, owned a farm adjacent to the Morses', the lineage of which went back even farther than Wilbur's. (Stephen White had come west from New Hampshire in 1826.) Unusual as it was for the time, Jessie had been sent away to be educated—to Downer College, a two-year normal school in Milwaukee, from which she graduated in 1892. After she returned at the age of eighteen to marry Wilbur and settle down on his farm, Jessie, needing an outlet for her boundless energy, as well as some means of building on the education she had received at Downer, organized a business of her own, selling smoked ham, dressed poultry, butter, eggs, and baked goods on a regular delivery route in Madison. Money from the business went principally for books, sheet music, and other cultural refinements, such as the purchase of a new piano or singing lessons for Mabel. (Such lessons would have been wasted on Wayne: though an animated vocalist, he was and would always be irredeemably tone-deaf.) In addition to her commercial and household activities, Jessie found time to play the organ for the local Baptist church and take part in the Madison Civil War Veterans Women's Auxiliary.

It was customary on the prairie at the turn of the century to have babies at home, but when Wayne was due, Jessie chose to go to her mother's residence in Madison to give birth; and though her mother, Flora Dickerman White, was an experienced midwife, Jessie also chose to have a doctor present for the delivery. She might even have preferred to lie in at a hospital, but that option was not open to her: there was none in Verona (population 250), and it would be three years before Madison (population 19,000) would have its own hospital, and another seven before inpatient childbirth would become a

Wayne Lyman Morse was born in his maternal grandparents' house in Madison, Wisconsin on October 20, 1900. (Courtesy of Judith Morse Goldberg.)

common procedure. Wayne Lyman was born on October 20, 1900, without complication—but a little precipitately, making his appearance before the doctor could get to the house.

In *West with the Night*, Beryl Markham says of an English acquaintance in British East Africa: "He is a farmer who has farmed for years without crying about it. He likes it. He likes all animals and especially horses." Thus could Wib Morse have been described, going without complaint through his daily regimen in Verona. Thus also could Wayne have been described, as soon as he grew old enough to take his place as a family farmhand. Except that in Wayne's case, the feeling for horses went beyond mere liking.

Wayne had a natural touch with most animals, and was quick to learn their habits and to recognize their individuality. Wib had read the treatises of William Dempster Hoard, Wisconsin's preeminent journalist/politician/farmer, whose motto was "All things shall be added to him that loveth the cow." Hoard believed, as Wib did, that you could pick out a good cow simply by examining its anatomy. He instructed his readers in what to look for in selecting proper specimens for their herds, prescribing everything from correct nostril size to "strong navel development." Wib added his own cow-raising experience to Hoard's and passed both on to his son. The result was that at a tender age, Wayne became expert in distinguishing at a glance cows likely to be healthy and productive—and therefore profitable—from those not up to standard.

But though he did indeed "loveth the cow," Wayne's most ardent affection was reserved for the steed, and he was overjoyed when he was allowed to concentrate on helping Wib with the horses while Harry and Grant tended the other livestock. Horseback riding was his passion—it would be for much of his life—and in this he was encouraged by Wib, whose philosophy held that "the outside of a horse is good for the inside of a boy."

Wayne soon discovered that however much animals were to be enjoyed, on a struggling farm they were a source of income, and had to be valued in dollars and cents. Wilbur began Wayne's business education early. He gave him two Shetland brood mares and a stallion and left him to oversee their breeding. The mares produced several healthy offspring, and by the age of twelve, Wayne was turning a profit as a trader in ponies. He had the same good luck with other marketable animals. From grade school through college he raised chickens and waterfowl, won prizes with them at state and county fairs, and usually made money when he offered them for sale. Over the same period he earned a steady income by raising rabbits and guinea pigs, which he sold in large batches to the University of Wisconsin medical school for experimentation.

Competing at the fair was a family enterprise for the Morses. Not only did Wib and the boys show their livestock and poultry, but Jessie displayed her finest flowers, produce, and baked items. She was famous for her bread and won many prizes for her canned goods. While the competition with other farmers and breeders was always friendly, it was also intense. The Morses enjoyed the participation, with its attendant good fellowship, but they relished the taste of victory even more. They took enormous pride in their successes; and of course the family's prize-winning animals, and their offspring, increased in value as more and more blue ribbons were accumulated.

If a competitive instinct was a Morse characteristic, it somehow ran stronger in Wayne than in other family members. His need to excel was sharpened by his relationship with his brothers. Because they were four years older and closer to his father, and because they shared that protective intimacy characteristic of many identical twins, Harry and Grant constituted something of a self-contained unit. They shouldered their responsibilities, were heavily involved in football (in which Wayne was uninterested), relied principally on each other for companionship, and had little time for their perfervid kid brother. Wayne had to struggle to be seen, to obtain recognition from the other males in his household.

As a consequence of his position in the family, Wayne turned more toward his mother, and she in turn gave him extra attention, perhaps to make up for the exclusiveness of the twins. Moreover, as the youngest child for many years, Wayne was expected to devote a fair amount of time to helping around the house, churning butter, chopping firewood, gathering eggs; and, both because these chores required his being there and because Jessie seemed to want it that way, he spent an unusual amount of time in his mother's company.

He was with her by the wood stove in the kitchen one icy February evening as she waited impatiently for his father and the twins to come home for supper. Wilbur and the boys had been all day on a "hauling bee," carting hogs to market in a caravan of horse-drawn sleighs with several of their neighbors. Such excursions were always slow going, but it was now dark and they had never been this late before. When finally they appeared, Jessie wanted to know what had taken them so long. Wib reported that the roads were a misery and they had had an extra delay because one of the teams had broken down en route. Suspicious, Jessie asked,

"And where did you have lunch?"

"At Hoffman's Saloon," Wilbur answered.

"What did you go to Hoffman's Saloon for?"

"Well, they all wanted to go over and have a beer."

"You didn't have a beer?!"

"How do you think I'd get the free rye bread, baloney, and cheese?"

Wilbur treated the matter jokingly, pointing out that you could get a free lunch at the tavern, but first you had to belly up to the bar for a little something to drink. Jessie failed to see the humor.

"How in the world could you, with a daughter and three boys, even go into a saloon, to say nothing about the glass of beer?"

Wib tried to defend himself, but Jessie was in a temper. She would accept no excuses, and told her husband what she thought of his errant behavior. Wayne had never seen his parents quarrel before. He ran upstairs to his room, crawled into bed, and cried solidly for an hour. Jessie found him there, sobbing, and tried to console him. But she also took the occasion to lecture him at length about the evils of alcohol—a lecture, he later said, that "burned" in his mind forever. When Jessie had finished, Wayne silently vowed that alcohol would never touch his lips.

The details of this incident were recalled by Morse sixty years after the fact and must be read with the usual caveats. However, deciding whether Morse's rendering embellished or even distorted the story is less important than noticing the kind of function this particular memory served in later life. Throughout his academic, administrative, and political careers, Morse insisted on being seen as a man who honored his basic convictions. Teetotalism was one of his more important beliefs. Investing such a belief with portentous family origins was not only natural, but also useful: doing so would make the belief that much more powerful, adhering to it more instinctive. And it seems appropriate to note that Morse did adhere to teetotalism with great fidelity. Though over the years some would contend that they had seen him take a drink, as far as careful research can reveal, with the exception of a medicinal dose or two, he kept faithfully to his pledge for the rest of his life—no small feat for a man who spent twenty-four years in the booze-soaked halls of Congress.

Despite her views on beer and liquor, Jessie could not have been described as a "professional prohibitionist." She did not, for example, join the Madison Temperance Board in publicly attacking the "devil's trinity": alcohol, prostitution, and gambling, all of which were said to be available seven days a week in many, or most, of Madison's ninety-nine gin mills and taverns (one for every thirty-eight adult males). But she was certainly pleased when saloon supporters were forced on the defensive, and even more so when Madison voted itself dry on June 30, 1917, two and a half years before national prohibition went into effect. Jessie simply believed that alcohol did bad things to people: it was bad for your body and bad for your spirit, and if you wished to improve yourself, you should leave it alone.

Improvement, both of the self and of society, was much on the minds of the Morses. One of the cornerstones of Progressivism was the conviction that education, good education, was essential if conditions were to change for the better. Though this idea was championed by Progressive leader Robert La Follette and shared by all who labeled themselves Progressive, its application to grammar and high school levels was promoted most forcefully by women—a more or less natural development in that day, since pre-college education was not then regarded as something in which menfolk properly took an interest. Madison women organized themselves into educational action groups, and because of their strenuous efforts, the brand-new, up-to-date Madison Central High School opened its doors in September 1906, in time for Mabel to enroll in one of its initial classes. Though not, strictly speaking, part of the Madison movement, Jessie shared its outlook: she believed in the necessity of quality education, and she would see to it that Wayne in particular received a full measure of its benefits.

ALL OF THE MORSE CHILDREN began their formal learning in a one-room, one-teacher primary school, half a mile from their home. After the fourth grade, Mabel, Grant, and Harry walked the two and a half miles to the grade school in Verona, and then finished up by going to high school in Madison. Wayne started in their footsteps but completed only first and second grades in the country. Whether because she had become keener in her insistence on a "good" education or because she saw in Wayne a potential she hadn't seen in her other children, or simply because she was closer to him than she had been to his siblings, Jessie decided that Wayne would learn more by attending school in Madison. And though he had left school after the eighth grade, Wilbur shared Jessie's interest in education. Without hesitation, he backed her decision.

And so, beginning with the third grade and before he reached his ninth birthday, Wayne commuted the twenty-two miles—eleven each way—to Madison, riding relay on the family's three little mustangs. With great fondness, the story is told by family members that Wayne made the round trip nine months a year, five days a week; and Wayne himself often repeated the tale, adding that he used the lengthy time on horseback to memorize his multiplication tables. The truth is that during the winter months when the northern winds roared across the plains from Canada, or whenever the journey back and forth was too difficult, Wayne had another option: staying at the Morses' Mound Street house in Madison, being looked after by Grandmother White. (From Mound Street it was less than two blocks to the neighborhood Longfellow School.) However, even if the school commute was not an all-weather, everyday affair, it was nonetheless impressive. Granted that the Verona-Madison route was reasonably flat, covering those twenty-two dusty miles took several hours and would have been an arduous daily task under the best of conditions, even for an experienced adult on a full-sized horse. Only the fact that Wayne had already become an expert rider made the journey feasible.

Much as he loved life on the farm, Wayne was even more taken by the exciting new existence he discovered in Madison. Mound Street ran through a small section called Bowen's Addition, close by a larger district known as "the Bush"—short for Greenbush—a somewhat run-down area inhabited by immigrant families, mostly Italians, with a small component of Russian Jews and a scattering of Romanians and Irish. The Bush was also home to Madison's tiny black population.

If Jessie had it in mind that Wayne needed exposure to a wider variety of people, then the shift to Madison produced immediate results. Wayne palled around with three classmates, his "gang," all of whom lived in the Bush. An active lot, the boys occasionally got into trouble when a little too rambunctious. Six decades after the fact, Morse could recall having incurred the principal's displeasure when he and his friends turned a basketball game with a school from the better side of town into such a rough-and-tumble that athletic relations between the two schools had to be severed. Morse always believed that his enduring hatred of bigotry could be traced to his "cosmopolitan" youth, to life as it was lived on the playgrounds of Longfellow and the streets of the Bush.

The basketball episode notwithstanding, Wayne was not often in the principal's doghouse. Although Miss Lorena Reichert ran the Longfellow School with an unbending discipline, she took an interest in the energetic equestrian from the countryside. She watched out for him and helped him adjust to his new environment. For his part, Wayne had little difficulty with schoolwork. History was his favorite subject, but he did famously in most of his classes. At times, however, his quickness of intellect and his competitiveness got him into hot water. He often sped ahead of classmates and occasionally lost patience with their sluggishness. According to one instructor, he "would interrupt when a slower-thinking student was having trouble reciting." At these moments, she said, "I was hard on him." But such moments were infrequent, and Wayne graduated from Longfellow in 1915 with an outstanding record.

Winters in Madison also meant an intermittent shift in Wayne's religious practices. Grandmother and Grandfather White belonged to a Methodist church near Mound Street, and unless Jessie had come in for the weekend (Wib was a non-churchgoing Episcopalian), Wayne would accompany the Whites to their services on Sunday. But he had been raised a nonfundamentalist Baptist in Verona, and he preferred the uptown First Baptist Church in Madison. He attended it spasmodically during grade school (when Jessie was in town), then more continuously by himself throughout high school and college. Like his mother, he greatly admired the "enlightened" views of the First Baptist's Scottish-born minister, whose sermons, as remembered by Morse years later, smacked just enough of Unitarian liberalism to discomfit the more conservative of his parishioners. Such sermons suited Wayne nicely. Following Jessie, his Christianity was distinctly nondogmatic, and being moved by the rational ideas of a pastor was more in keeping with his idea of religion than paying mindless homage to the established canons of his denomination.

After the eighth grade, Wayne moved on to Madison Central High School, where his record was, if anything, even more outstanding than it had been at Longfellow. Not that he breezed through all of his classes. While history and social studies came easily, languages did not. First-year Latin, for example, was a constant trial. One classmate reported that he gave the teacher "a complete snow job" in an effort to get through the course. Wayne could at times substitute a glib tongue for academic acumen—he was nicknamed "Bluff" in his senior yearbook—but if he did try to snow his way through Latin I, it didn't work. Latin teacher Leah Wilson flunked him, and half a generation later she would chide Caryl Morse for having a "grasshopper" mind like her "stupid" brother before her.

But Wayne did exceedingly well in most classes, especially, in the opinion of one fellow student, in those "where ideas counted heavily." Eventually he even managed to survive two complete years of Latin. And where Leah Wilson found stupidity, the majority of Madison Central's faculty found brilliance. His history teachers were particularly struck by his ability to deal with abstract concepts and by the fact that he could read assignments with both lightning speed and high retention. He earned excellent grades in most of his courses and graduated in 1919 with an honor emblem for finishing in the top ten of his class—a notable accomplishment in light of his innumerable extracurricular commitments.

Of all his instructors, Lynda Webber was the closest to Wayne. He adored her classes; she admired his eagerness to learn. Miss Webber was keen on imparting to her pupils the wonders of science. Wayne was fascinated by the rigorous logic of the scientific method, and tried to incorporate it into his debating technique. It was not unusual to find him lingering after class in Miss Webber's afternoon biology lab until shooed home, past six o'clock, late for supper. Miss Webber grew friendly with Jessie, consulted her often about Wayne's progress, and was available to help him when he got into difficulty in his other courses. Above all, she wanted to be certain that he would go on to the university. When she learned from Jessie that the Morses might not be able to finance his further education, she took out a life insurance policy on him and used it as security to borrow money.

High school biology teacher Lynda Webber took a keen interest in Morse, and helped finance his college education. (Wayne Morse Historical Park Corporation.)

She then lent the borrowed money to Wayne to help defray his expenses. Morse would always insist that he could never have gone to college but for Lynda Webber's generosity.

During the academic year, Wayne's days were consumed by a nonstop regimen of work, study, and school activities. In addition to his animal husbandry business, he held a wide assortment of odd jobs in a never-ending effort to earn extra money. He worked for an uncle who had a package-delivery business and for another who ran a livery stable; he substituted as a newspaper boy; he assisted his mother on her Madison route. Despite his best endeavors, he always seemed to come up short of cash, a condition that would lodge in his memory for the rest of his life.

At Madison Central High, Wayne was a Big Man On Campus: he was involved in student politics, he played intramural basketball and baseball, he was a member of the faculty-student disciplinary committee, he appeared in school dramatic productions, and he was an officer in a number of clubs and societies. But none of his achievements, including his class presidency, brought him the recognition he received as a member of the debating team. Debating was taken

seriously in Wayne's high school days. Crowds came to watch the in-
terscholastic contests, and student orators were given the kind of
adulation reserved today for athletes. In his senior year Wayne was
president of the Forum, the school debating club; he was on the in-
terclub debate committee; and he was toastmaster at the club banquet. But his greatest triumph came in his junior year when he
helped lead the Madison team to victory in an almost unprecedented four of six debates against rival high schools.

Aside from the occasional run-in with Principal Barnes, Wayne's
only consistent problem during high school was his health. A chron-
ic sinus condition left him susceptible to colds, perilously so to attacks of the flu. The whole family was frightened by the epidemic of
"Spanish" influenza that swept North America in 1918. It hit Madison like a Midwestern tornado. Thousands were afflicted, the hospitals were full of the ailing, and schools were closed from early October until November 7. Harry was taken ill on the farm in Verona, and
Jessie forbade Wayne to visit him during his infirmity. She feared
that, given his vulnerability, Wayne could easily become a digit in the
area's mounting mortality statistics. By the time the contagion had
run its course, 268 Madisonians (Harry not among them) had lost
their lives. But Jessie's caution was rewarded: Wayne managed to escape the epidemic without so much as a head cold.

So avid was Wayne's interest in argumentation, so keen was his
willingness to take on all comers, that he carried his enthusiasm into
other arenas—for example, into Madison's first Hi-Y club, which he
joined in 1917. The club's goal was to "maintain high standards of
Christian living" among high school boys, but Wayne, his competitive fires ever burning, turned the organization into something of a
debating society, usually with himself as a minority of one in gleeful
disputation with everyone else. To the outsider, it might have looked
as though the others were ganging up on Wayne, or that they had it
in for him. Which is exactly what Harry thought when Wayne
brought him to a Hi-Y meeting one evening: as the argument grew
heated, Harry, moved to defend family honor, threatened to throw
each of the boys out the window if they didn't let up on his brother
("always get in the first punch" was Wib's fatherly advice). Wayne was

barely able to avert a clubhouse brawl by convincing a dubious Harry that he was witnessing a run-of-the-mill, fun-filled meeting.

The Hi-Y incident occurred when Wayne was living at the YMCA during a brief period after Jessie's mother had died and before the family had moved permanently to Mound Street. In addition to enabling him to sharpen his debating skills, residence at the Y provided Wayne with a new opportunity to garner some cash. He learned to play pool in the Y's billiard room, quickly mastered the intricacies of the sport, and was known thereafter to hustle competitors in a game or two of eight ball. In fact, shooting pool at the Y—another competitive outlet—became a sometime avocation, and remained a handy source of income all the way through college.

Gambling at the Y did not necessarily constitute an act of rebellion against one of Jessie's cardinal commandments. More likely it was regarded as another area where the Morse combative spirit could not be repressed. Competing at the pool table, even for money, could, after all, be seen as healthy recreation, not unlike competing for horse-show honors at the county fair. In each case the outcome depended on the application of intelligence, hard work, and skill, and in each case a prize justifiably awaited the well-prepared winner. However, Wayne's yen for gambling was deep-seated, and probably exceeded Jessie's sense of propriety. He wagered on all manner of things, from "you-wanna-bet" blusterings in support of an argument to the turn of a card in a friendly hand of poker. (Being called "Bluff" in the yearbook may have had as much to do with poker playing as faking it in class.) But while the gambling instinct would hold strong for the rest of his life, it would never become compulsive. The stakes would remain at the small-potatoes level. Jessie's values were too much a part of Wayne; he would be forever safe from the "devil's trinity."

There had been three important women in Wayne's life by the time he reached the midpoint in high school: Jessie Morse, Lynda Webber, and, to a lesser extent, Lorena Reichert. Now there would be a fourth—the daughter of a railroad conductor, a tiny, vivacious, blue-eyed brunette named Mildred Martha Downie, known to everyone as "Midge." The Morses and the Downies first met when Wayne and Midge were in the third grade. The two families frequently went to church together in Madison; their children attended the same Sunday school. Although Wayne and Midge did not go to the same grammar school and did not become "an item" until both were at Madison Central, Midge confessed that while still in grade school, she fell hopelessly in love with Wayne the day she watched him riding his beautiful pony, Queenie, as he proudly led Madison's annual parade on the Fourth of July.

If Wayne was a BMOC, Midge, six months his junior, was his female counterpart. She was active in as many Madison High clubs and societies as he, was class vice president the year he was president, scored her own oratorical triumph by winning the school reading contest as a senior, and crowned four years of outstanding academics by being named class valedictorian. Not only were Wayne and Midge a matched pair, they were involved in many of the same activities:

Morse graduated from Madison Central High School in 1919 with an honor emblem for finishing among the top ten of his class. (Wayne Morse Historical Park Corporation, 90-6-7.)

both were on the student yearbook committee, both had been vice president of the dramatic club, and both had appeared in the school's production of *Twelfth Night*. So much were they together that yearbook editors took to light mockery in commenting on their constant proximity. One edition contained the following specimen of teenage prairie humor:

> One boy . . . : Why don't you shave, Wayne?
> Wayne: I would if I had thirty cents.
> Same boy: Well, you look pretty "Downie."

And a couplet from an earlier edition:

> The parlor sofa holds the twain
> Mildred and her lovesick Wayne. . . .

Mildred "Midge" Downie was vice president of the senior class at Madison Central, graduating in 1919 as valedictorian. (Wayne Morse Historical Park Corporation, 90-6-11.)

By the day of their graduation, it was correctly assumed that Mildred and Wayne had been "twained" for life.

In addition to Midge, there was another significant female presence in Wayne's life. Unlikely as it might have seemed, given how much older he was, Wayne was devoted to his younger sister. Caryl was four by Wayne's senior year, an effervescent spirit, already showing signs that she was cut from the same cloth as Jessie. Wib gave her his attention, but he was now in his sixties, old enough to be her grandfather. Wayne was in some ways as much Caryl's parent as her brother. Caryl tearfully remembered how he found time to play with her, gently teach her about animals, take her with him to local fairs, even tote her on his bicycle when visiting friends. She, in turn, loved him unreservedly, worshipped him as only a younger sister can a heroic big brother. In the coming years, such adoration would not always be appreciated by Midge.

ALTHOUGH WAYNE WAS CONTINUOUSLY ACTIVE in high school politics, he was not much involved in the larger political world beyond the schoolyard. This did not mean that he was unaffected by what Midge would remember as Madison's "wonderful, liberal political climate"—a time, as she put it, of "spiritual and intellectual flux." He was greatly influenced by the Progressive movement, and when he rose in the auditorium to challenge Principal Barnes, his action was in keeping with similar challenges to traditional authority being raised throughout Wisconsin. Moreover, Progressivism in Madison was not a disembodied set of propositions whose leader was a remote ideological figurehead. At least not for Wayne. He knew Bob La Follette to be of genuine flesh and blood. One of his more vivid memories was of the time when as a small boy he went with Wilbur to hear Fighting Bob, the erstwhile thespian, dressed in white shoes, white trousers, and cutaway coat, render Iago's part in a dramatic reading from *Othello*. Furthermore, La Follette, celebrity though he might be, was a neighbor. Wayne knew his sons, and frequently showed his ponies against theirs in county fairs across the state.

In the Madison area the Progressive movement derived much of its strength from the participation of women, and the women's-rights issue was therefore one of its focal points. There may have been many who still felt a woman's place was in the home, but by 1919, when Wisconsin became the first state to ratify the women's suffrage amendment, 33 percent of Madison's adult females were no longer there: they had become part of the city's burgeoning work-force.

The idea of women taking on new roles spilled into the schools. Midge's accomplishments at Madison High were undoubtedly made easier by the new liberalism, and others were equally affected. In Midge's senior year, the spirit of "intellectual flux" generated a minor revolution. Girls suddenly insisted on trying out for debate, and while initially their proposal drew heated resistance, ultimately they were allowed to do so, and three of them made the team.

Wayne could not avoid being influenced by what was happening around him. The pressure for reform was enormous, the movement for change irresistible, and the ideology behind the movement per-meated the atmosphere. Wayne absorbed this ideology, in part by osmosis, but also because much of it was shared by his parents: Jessie was a great believer in getting things done, in taking positive action to improve the world and relieve the suffering of families like her own, which, despite unrelenting hard work, had a difficult time mak-ing ends meet. Wib was one of those Progressive conservatives who believed that the giant trusts and corporations had a stranglehold on Wisconsin's assets, and he looked to the Progressive party to pry the vested interests loose and give everyone a fair chance at economic self-sufficiency.

As far as Jessie and Wib were concerned, Progressivism spoke their language. It championed the cause of the average person, urban or rural, and it ceaselessly attacked the corporate and political ma-nipulators who stood in the way of reform. Progressivism's main-stream ties were also to their liking, especially Wib's. As an indepen-dent farmer and a Republican, he did not wish to turn society on its head. He wanted a "return" to a time when everyone had an equal opportunity to get ahead, when diligence and virtue were justly rewarded. By putting more La Follettes into office, Progressivism could make things come right again.

There was, as it turned out, a noticeable distance between Progressivism's critique of what was wrong and what its leaders, once in power, were prepared to do about it. In remembering the fairly prosaic changes introduced by Progressive reformers—referendum, recall, and the direct primary; the installation of "business" practices in local government—it is perhaps too easy to forget the moral imperatives that motivated those who filled the movement's ranks. The stress was on goodness: good cities, good citizens, good government, good schools, good works in the eyes of one's fellow citizens and of God. If Progressives often settled for such mundane alterations as replacing the strong mayor with the commission form of local government, it was not because they were not outraged at the status quo, but because all but the most radical among them were strongly conservative in some of their basic convictions. They believed in the fundamental rightness of the American system; they felt that by making a few technical changes and, more important, throwing the "rascals" out and replacing them with people of good will, their world would be changed for the better.

In Wisconsin, however, particularly in Madison, changes in the name of goodness sometimes went beyond merely tinkering with the system. Though led for the most part by straightlaced, middle-class Republicans, many of Germanic and Nordic stock, those who wished to improve city life were prepared to insist that individual interests and desires had to give way to the overall needs of the community. The "Madison Creed," adopted by the Madison Board of Commerce in 1915, envisioned a city "where the poor shall be less unhappy, the rich less self-satisfied, for the one shall have a more intelligent understanding of the other; where jails shall be empty of prisoners, streets clear of beggars and neither shall the aged in want be cast upon the charity of strangers; a city where friends shall be true friends; neighbors real neighbors; a city where the strong shall really sympathize with the weak."

Making Madison into such a paragon of cities would, of course, mean throwing the current set of rascals out of office before more

Wayne, Caryl, Wilbur, and Jessie Morse. Like other Progressives, the Morses believed Wisconsin could be a laboratory of democracy. (Wayne Morse Collection, CN 1317, Special Collections, University of Oregon Library.)

fundamental changes could be considered. Madison's rascals were known collectively as "the Bunch," the Democratic old guard who controlled patronage, bought votes, tolerated whorehouses, and gave out liquor licenses to saloons which operated slot machines, served minors, and stayed open on Sundays. Because of a goal held in common, the movement to close Madison's bars included not just Anti-Saloon League types, but those like Jessie who wanted to take power from the undesirables flouting the law and corrupting the city. When Madison went dry in 1915, it not only struck a blow for temperance-movement true believers, it broke the cash connection that had for so long kept the Bunch in power.

Beyond doing combat with the Bunch, Progressives turned Madison into a model of what might be accomplished by dedicated citizen involvement. From 1900 to 1920, Madisonians reduced prostitution and gambling; created a system of parks, playgrounds, and

recreation areas; introduced zoning regulations to control the hap-
hazard development of industry; hired health and building inspec-
tors to clean up the slums; took over garbage collection; fought
against pollution; and built health-care clinics and hospitals—all
while their city's population was growing from 19,000 to nearly
40,000.

Social reform in Madison was aided by having La Follette in the
Wisconsin governor's seat from 1900 to 1906, and then in the U. S.
Senate until his death in 1925. Progressives from around the country
cited Wisconsin as the "laboratory of democracy," and the "Wisconsin idea" was seen as the exemplar of civic improvement on the state
and local levels. With the help of the muckraking *Wisconsin State
Journal*, La Follette worked to regulate the railroads, reduce the influence of special interests, enhance the rights of labor, and promote
academic freedom and women's suffrage, while attacking the exploitation of child labor and the corruption of big business and politics. While by no means everywhere successful, Progressives made
headway on a variety of fronts. Good government, they were convinced, was here to stay.

Although Wisconsin Progressives might, with most Americans,
have believed that government works best when it is governing least,
they also believed that government, when run properly, could make
an important difference to society. And as they enhanced the powers
of government to deal with social problems, they also inevitably enlarged its size. While Madison was doubling in population over two
decades, the city budget increased seventeen times, the number of
city employees fifteen times. For La Follette's followers, these larger
numbers were tolerable; good people were doing necessary work, the
size of the job required adequate manpower, and even if bureaucratic
growth had begun to create problems of its own, no one (save the
Bunch) wanted a return to those dark old days when a small handful
controlled the entire city. If good government meant bigger government, Progressivism, at least in its Wisconsin variety, was prepared
to live with it.

This, then, was the Progressive tradition of which Wayne Morse
was a part, and which was a part of him. It saw a creative role for

political action; it distrusted those who monopolized economic power; it was on the side of "the people," variously defined as the downtrodden, the agrarian, the wage earner, the small businessperson, the disenfranchised, the temperance leagues, and the "city-beautiful" enthusiasts. But since its leadership arose largely from the business classes—"Christian Capitalists," William Appleman Williams has called them—it had a contradictory bias, even as it espoused a radical brand of opposition. It also tended to embody a strict sense of moralism—stricter even than Jessie's—which on certain questions, such as churchgoing and sobriety, bordered on the puritanical. This side of Progressivism was Morse's legacy as well. The day would come when he would enter the political arena, and his Progressive Republican heritage, with all of its fervor, complexity, and internal inconsistency, would serve as a touchstone as he sought to come to his own ideological conclusions.

Morse would also bring attributes of his own into the realm of politics. Beyond symbolically reflecting Progressivism's questioning disposition, Wayne's convocation challenge to Principal Barnes was, importantly, an early expression of the maverick's quest for masterlessness. Though it would change in character, this quest would never diminish. No authority, be it school official, department chairman, university chancellor, party leader, or chief executive, would be followed merely because of the individual's exalted office. Five American presidents would learn that Morse's resistance to *all* authority meant that his vote could never be considered "bankable," that regardless of his position in the past, he might strike out on a heretical path if he felt such a move justifiable.

Morse's innate maverickness would be supplemented by other predilections drawn from his family. Wib's brand of individualism and Jessie's sense of purpose were ingrained in his makeup. More basic still, however, was the desire to accomplish, to succeed, to win. Whether it was billiards bets, blue ribbons, debating trophies, or merely the acknowledgment that he had won the argument, Wayne wanted the fruits of victory, and he would drive himself to see that he got them. Just as he rode Queenie at the head of the parade, he rode his talents with a competitive zeal that knew few limits. But sometimes competitiveness rode him, carrying him beyond the will to succeed to the need for still further self-justification.

That emerging on top could feed a good-sized ego goes without saying, and in Morse's case that ego was seldom satisfied for long, even by the most triumphant of victories. When satisfaction of self was not forthcoming or, worse yet, when criticism from others was, Morse might not react with equanimity. At these times his defenses came up, his tolerance dropped, and his usually pleasant demeanor could undergo drastic alteration. Such occasions would manifest themselves many times in the years ahead.

2

A Maverick's Education

To MATRICULATE AT THE UNIVERSITY OF WISCONSIN in the early decades of the twentieth century was to enter one of the epicenters of American Progressive thought. But not thought alone. From their offices a short walk down State Street, first Robert La Follette, and then his successors as governor, turned to the university—especially to its social science departments—not only for "objective" knowledge and information, but also for practical projects to be put into action. Through expert panels drawn from its faculty, the university provided ideas and programs, brain power and manpower, which produced and carried out much of the state's dramatic legislation during the Progressive era. Nowhere in the nation was there such a vital connection between academic creativity and governmental policy-making, a connection made explicitly for the cause of social reform.

The role of the university as a wellspring for reform did much to animate undergraduate as well as faculty life. Classes were frequently involved in examining public-policy issues, and student government, student traditions, and student associations—political and nonpolitical—were subjected to the same kind of scrutiny given to institutions in the society at large. The stimulating flux that Midge remembered from her high school days was even more pronounced at the college level, and it was made more intense in the autumn of 1919 by those already reared in the ways of Progressivism, like Morse, and by veterans from the war, who brought to their work a sense of maturity not previously seen at the university. There was also the additional intensity produced by an increased female presence, the result of greater enrollment of women students and their greater

involvement in student affairs. It was without a doubt a heady time
to be at Wisconsin.

Much as he might have wished to plunge himself into this exhil-
arating milieu, Morse was initially forced to keep his distance, to concentrate his attention elsewhere. With the exception of rent (he still
resided at the family house on Mound Street), he now had to meet
all of his own expenses—a responsibility that weighed heavily, even
at the outset of classes. Indeed, it is not too much to say that Morse's
first two years at Wisconsin were less influenced by the Progressive
spirit of the campus than dominated by the ceaseless task of finding
the wherewithal to make ends meet.

To keep tabs on his precarious finances, Morse from the beginning maintained meticulous records of every expenditure, as well as
every increment of his meager income. He started his freshman year
$215 to the good, a sum that included $165 from his parents: $100 in
wages for summer work on the family farm and $65 from the sale of
sheep "to Father." But $215, though seemingly substantial, fell short
of seeing him through the year, and like a Dickensian street urchin,
he tried to enlarge his earnings by marketing whatever remnants and
scraps he could lay hands on. Even personal necessities became
vendible commodities: "Sold Shoes to Harry" $1.50; "Sold Mittens"
$.75; "Sold Bicycle" $6.00. Along with his usual animal business—
"Sold Rabbits" $26—such merchandising brought in another $78 by
the end of the school year.

In Morse's financial system, no expenditure was too small to be
recorded ("Gum" $.05; "Weight" $.02) and no possible source of revenue could be left untapped ("Matching Pennies" $.10; "Bet on Pool"
$1.40; "Bet with Mother" $.25). But however scrupulous his accounting or inventive his money-making, he invariably ran into red
ink. Yet, as short as cash might be at any moment, Morse could never
be described as destitute. There were other undergraduates who
managed to get by on less than he had.

Part of the problem was that although in most areas Morse was
frugal and carefully nurtured his cash flow, in a few he was decided-
ly immoderate, if not profligate, in his spending. A minor example
of extravagance was labeled "Treats" in his accounts book. He had

(and would always have) an insatiable sweet tooth: candy, ice cream, desserts of any kind he found irresistible. An unsigned poem from the 1920s, undoubtedly written by Midge, caricatured both his penchant for sweets and his propensity for wagering:

"You owe me a box of candy"
Is his incessant cry.
Twas a bet on this or a bet on that—
Nobody else knows when or why.
But—"You owe me a box of candy.
And when are you going to pay?
Oh don't you remember last summer
I beat you in a game of croquet?"

The most often noted expense went under the heading of "Fussing," which in the local vernacular referred to dating; although in this category outlays were probably kept well below the campus norm. Where Morse did run to excess, particularly given the shape of his finances, was in the area of personal appearance. His pride in being "well turned out" sometimes refused to be limited by an undernourished budget. While not costly as single items, "Hair Cut" and "Shine" appear on his expense sheet with an almost compulsive frequency and must have considerably lightened his wallet, as must the $6.50 manicuring set purchased during his first semester. But these were trifles, even for an ex–farm boy from Verona, compared to the expenditures for clothes—particularly suits, five of which were bought over a three-year period at an average cost in excess of fifty dollars.

It might be argued that since suits were *de rigueur* on campus at the time, especially for a member of the debate team, Morse's wardrobe was not, aside from its price tag, all that extraordinary. However, even if the suit purchases could be thus defended, one would be hard put to make a similar argument for the stylish overcoat with sealskin collar that he coveted. Morse had made no secret either of his longing for the coat or of his inability to afford the seventy-five dollars it was going for. And while he disliked approaching his mother on such matters, so great was his desire that he hesitated only slightly before asking her help. After talking it over with Wilbur, Jessie decided to relax her insistence on her son's "self-sufficiency" and give him the money, justifying her largesse on the grounds that because of his sinus attacks, he needed a quality topcoat to keep himself warm.

As it turned out, neither Morse's sinuses nor the rest of his body received much benefit from the new garment. Shortly after he got it, it disappeared from the coat rack of a Madison eatery while he was deep in conversation over lunch. Though he could be possessive about his property—especially since parts of it might be convertible into income—Morse was in fact less than adept at holding on to even his most valuable items. Those he didn't sell seemed to vanish with alarming regularity, and Wib suggested he put up a sign reading, "I'm your prey. Here, take me."

Both Morse and Midge were thus taken late one night when they made the mistake of walking home through the wrong part of the Bush. As they strode beneath the overpass of the Madison viaduct, an unlit and notoriously dangerous spot, they were accosted by "three large young men" who, ignoring Midge's protest that she and Wayne worked hard for and needed their money, forcibly stripped them of their cash. Morse's only recorded remark on the experience is a single entry in his expense column: "Hold Up" $4.00.

The truth is that both Morse's penchant for fine clothes and his inability to retain possessions were integral parts of his makeup. His "need" for new suits—especially in an environment which, as he saw it, put a premium on appearance—was surely a youngest son's rebellion against a family tradition of big-brother hand-me-downs. (Selling *his* shoes to Harry must have been particularly satisfying.) In any case, cutting a more-than-decent figure in public was a prime concern, and would remain so throughout his lifetime.

A loose hold on possessions also remained a lifelong trait, though one whose display was more unpredictable. Morse would never be driven by the desire for money or for what its accumulation might represent in rank or status. If he was greedy, it was for personal accomplishment and the acclaim that came with it. So focused was he normally on what he wanted to achieve as to be oblivious to what he owned. His bent at such times was to be generous with both his possessions and his money. There would be other times, however— many of them—when he felt oppressed by what seemed to be an ever-shrinking supply of funds. At these times, magnanimity would yield to a more pinched attitude, and he would find himself in heated disputes over what from a larger perspective amounted to the equivalent of nickels and dimes.

In an effort to remain solvent while at the university, Morse tried his hand at various money-making activities. As in high school, he relied heavily on his poultry business, but his "Chicken Account Book" showed a reasonable profit only after 1922. For a while he made a little income driving a mail wagon in the evening between the post office and the train station. In the summer of 1920, he grew a mustache to make himself look older and set out for the Dakotas in search of work on the harvest circuit. After an inauspicious and low-paying ten days as a garbageman on a trash wagon in Aberdeen, South Dakota, he found employment in various hay and grain fields and earned enough to start the following semester with a bit of a nest egg.

At the end of his first year, Morse showed a deficit on paper of $184, a deficit that had been covered by money "Rec'd from Folks."

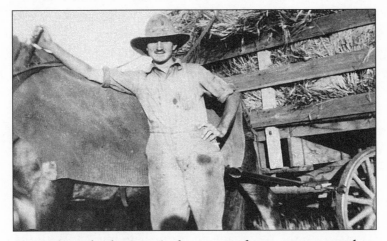

Always short of cash, Morse, in the summer of 1920, grew a mustache to make himself look older and headed for the Dakotas to find work on the harvest circuit. (Courtesy of Judith Morse Goldberg.)

He had worked hard at being self-supporting, but in the end he could not manage on his own. Although he received significant loans from Lynda Webber (as, to a lesser degree, did Midge), his parents, despite their own considerable financial problems, always scraped together enough to cover his ongoing shortfalls and make it possible for him to finish college. It is clear from their readiness with cash that one way or another, Wib and Jessie would not have allowed Wayne to miss out on a university education, regardless of whether Miss Webber's assistance had been forthcoming.

By his junior year, Morse's finances had grown more stable: his poultry business had improved, and his usual sources of income were augmented by giving talks on public affairs to local men's clubs and business associations—usually for ten dollars a speech, but on a few occasions for many times that amount. With increased economic stability, Morse could involve himself more deeply in school activities. He had maintained his interest in formal debating, and now he not only served as a debate-club officer, but also won a place on the varsity debate team. Indeed, rhetorical exposition had become such a central concern that he chose speech as one half of his double major. Speech was originally to be his only major, but, for no good reason that he could later remember, he enrolled in an introductory economics class and was so engaged by its faculty that he decided to earn a degree in that discipline as well.

Morse's junior year also afforded time to become immersed in the tumultuous world of student politics. Morse ran for and won a seat in the student senate, where he immediately found himself confronted by a heated controversy over the propriety of an old campus tradition. A system of hazing had been a long-standing practice at Wisconsin; freshmen were subjected to a series of minor and not-so-minor indignities, one of which included "an official dipping into the waters of Lake Mendota." Though he had passed through his own baptism as a hazing recipient and was now entitled to be on the delivering end, Morse supported those working to eliminate the system. His entry into the fray made an immediate impact. With the help of his friend and fellow senator Ralph Axley, he first moved an antihazing resolution through the senate and then persuaded the appropriate university officials to endorse it.

As another senatorial issue demonstrated, Morse's willingness to join in the radical overturn of tradition was not without limit. Generating even more heat than the hazing dispute was a related question: whether freshmen should be required to wear green caps—the infamous beanies—during their first year on campus. Wearing the caps had been compulsory in the past, and those caught bareheaded were subjected to hazing by an ever-vigilant brigade of sophomores. A campus referendum showed that while students might be open to a measure of reform, most were unwilling to do away with some type of compulsory requirement. Morse was of two minds on the subject. He, too, favored the wearing of beanies, but at the same time felt that the tradition should be enforced only by the freshmen themselves. "My personal conviction," he declared a little pontifically, "is that the voluntary plan would be best for my Alma Mater, and," he added, in the maverick manner already becoming his trademark, "I refuse to vote against my own convictions." In the end, however, he voted for a compromise, albeit one worked out by Axley that deviated only slightly from his stated position.

However significant the green cap and hazing issues, they paled before a problem that arose during the following semester. Swelled by the ranks of ex-servicemen who had enrolled in the university with a vague idea of preparing themselves for a career "in business," the Commerce Department had found itself oversubscribed in the years following World War I. Administered by Fay S. Elwell, a brilliant but authoritarian instructor, Accounting 181 became the course that allegedly winnowed out students deemed not up to standard. Grumblings were heard in the spring of 1922 from those who in the previous term had been given a failing grade, a conditional failure, or a grade of "poor"—three categories that included 127 of the 201 students enrolled in the class.

As the grumblings grew louder, Morse brought the issue before the student senate. He, Axley, and another senator were appointed to investigate. Their committee interviewed everyone involved, including—to the teachers' surprise—Commerce Department faculty, and issued a long report (written in the house on Mound Street) which upheld many of the students' grievances and recommended that the department return to more equitable practices. What was remarkable was not so much the report in itself as the committee's presumed right to investigate in the first place. Occasional freshman-dunking was one thing, and within the putative jurisdiction of the senate, but what went on in the classroom was the province of the faculty, which no student committee had theretofore dared invade. Not only did Morse exceed previous senate boundaries, but his committee's report, reprinted in its entirety in the school paper, found its way to the Wisconsin board of regents. As a result, the university administration was forced to launch an investigation of its own, one that led to departmental changes. Morse was fairly well known before Accounting 181 became a *cause célèbre*; as a successful instrument of academic reform, he had now become a campus hero.

While Morse may have been in the vanguard on certain senate issues, his stand on the beanie dispute could hardly be described as radical, and his politics in general tended to reflect the circumspection of his parents' philosophy. He refused, for example, to join the university La Follette club, not because of any disaffection from Progressivism but because he felt the club, as constituted, was too extremist. His own brand of Progressivism was still confined within Wiblike parameters, and Axley—who in later life would become a steadfast conservative—had to exert considerable effort to nudge him gradually to the left.

At the same time, Morse's personal loyalty to La Follette remained strong. Though he and the rest of his family had disagreed with Fighting Bob's anti-involvement position during World War I, they were not among those who scorned and abused him for taking such an unpopular stand. Because he was one of six U. S. senators to vote against a declaration of war, La Follette had been turned on by much of his constituency: burned in effigy on the university campus, censured by most of the faculty, expelled from the Madison Club, and formally repudiated by the Wisconsin legislature. Though greatly reduced, anti–La Follette feelings persisted in some quarters into the 1920s. To demonstrate how he felt, Morse made it a point to be seen in Madison in the company of La Follette's son, and he spent a brief part of the summer of 1924 working in the La Follette presidential campaign.

Morse wanted it known that he deplored intolerance, a position whose origins also went back to his family circle. Upon the outbreak of hostilities, Wisconsin had succumbed to the national contagion of war fever; one symptom was the state's antagonism toward La Follette, another its manifest hatred of all things German. Madison and the surrounding countryside contained sizeable German settlements, whose inhabitants were maligned and often persecuted by pro-war patriots. Wayne had grown up with German families in both Verona and Madison, and the Morses refused to treat their old neighbors as pariahs or, as some local jingoists did, as enemies. While they supported the war, the Morses did what they could to protect their German friends from humiliation and vilification.

Because of its mixture of liberal and conservative tendencies, Morse's Progressivism often left him with a foot in opposite factions. Though a child of the lower middle class, too poor to afford fraternity rent, he not only pledged Pi Kappa Alpha, but rose to its presidency as a non–house resident in his senior year. On the other hand, and without any sense of self-contradiction, that same year he ran for class president on a maverick ticket whose platform attacked the fraternities for maintaining a stranglehold on student political power through a corrupt system of secret caucuses and behind-the-scenes vote-swapping. Heading a slate of five partisans running for all available offices, he took up the cause of non–frat members clamoring for change.

It was a rough campaign. As anticipated, Morse was accused of being a hypocrite and a turncoat. Fraternity-row strategists, determined to beat him, nominated two rival candidates to run against him. In keeping with how new ways of thinking had swept the Wisconsin campus, the women's vote had become a force to be reckoned with (national women's suffrage had passed the summer before and was awaiting ratification), and regardless of the male candidate's credentials, a balanced male-female ticket was now seen as a prerequisite for election. With this in mind, the fraternity set tried to buy off Morse's potential running mates by promising to make them queens of various campus festivals. When two were lured away in this manner, it looked as though the campaign might have to proceed with an all-male slate, a possible prescription for defeat. At the eleventh hour, however, Midge came to the rescue. Though not particularly eager to hold office, and even less so to spend time buttonholing prospective voters, she agreed to enter as Morse's running mate three minutes before the close of candidate registration.

Unlike Morse, Midge had never been a member of a Greek organization. She therefore had a natural appeal to the nonfraternity/nonsorority electorate. With her on the ticket, and with noncandidate "Sleepy-eyed Axley"—"I was the hatchet man"—managing strategy, the Morse faction ran a high-energy, provocative campaign that transformed a normally bland exercise into a campuswide spectacle. As the *Milwaukee Journal* reported: "The interest taken in this year's election is unrivalled. Hundreds of students waited for hours Friday night for the announcements of the winners to be made from the registrar's office at the top of the 'hill.' After each candidate's standing was read, loud cheers reverberated from the campus down State street, and the henchmen of the successful tickets paraded the streets of the Latin quarter until a late hour celebrating their victory."

One such henchman was Axley, since three of his five candidates, including Midge, had stormed to victory. Although he had campaigned with great vigor, and although he had felt optimistic, realistically Morse never had a chance. As their front man, the fraternities had cleverly settled on a campus hero even bigger than Morse: Rolland F. Williams, captain of the varsity football team. He won by one hundred votes.

While his ticket had done exceedingly well, Morse had tasted electoral defeat for the first time. He was, nonetheless, graceful in losing—surprisingly so, perhaps, in light of his eagerness to win—and content that he had campaigned as effectively as possible. He would have been seen leaving the Latin quarter earlier than Axley, but, while there, would have shared in the happiness of his successful compatriots.

MORSE'S POLITICAL IDEAS were simultaneously reinforced and expanded by his exposure to the University of Wisconsin economics faculty. Though he couldn't remember why he had first taken a course in the subject, it was probably because economics, especially labor economics, figured more prominently than most other disciplines in connecting the university to Progressive forces in the state government. One became involved in the economics department because that was where the action was, where many of the programs that made their way through the legislature were first considered. Of the courses dealing with such material, Morse found those of Edwin Witte and Selig Perlman the most exciting.

From Witte and Perlman, Morse took the proposition that while Progressivism offered a coherent critique of contemporary social problems, its more radical proponents had badly misread reality: contrary to their contentions, present institutions *could* be made to work by enhancing the principle of equal opportunity for all. From this conviction, the economists argued, it followed that labor unions, despite their sometimes excessive militancy, should be seen as legitimate associations representing the workingman's quest for equality; it further followed that legislation in behalf of labor could help to right the balance of economic forces in society. Morse discussed these propositions in his speech classes, defended them in some of his debates, and would remember them in the following decade when called upon to settle labor-management disagreements on the Pacific waterfront.

While enlightening, the teachings of Perlman and Witte were scarcely revelations to Morse, since they were in many ways logical extensions of a perspective familiar to the Morse family dinner table. More novel were some of the materials presented in Professor Arnold Bennett Hall's political philosophy course, which Morse audited during his senior year. Through Hall, Morse was introduced to the writings of Edmund Burke. Burke's conviction that a legislator's first responsibility was not to the temporary will of the voters in his district but to the dictates of his own conscience struck Morse, predictably, as a masterful insight. It was in his maverick nature, even as far back as high school days, to believe that a legislator must be free to vote his conscience. Now he had philosophical underpinnings for that conviction. He would invoke Burke time and again during his senatorial career, especially when he held positions not supported by his constituency.

Though a political theorist by trade, Hall taught his course in the law school, where Morse began taking classes after his sophomore year. Since he already had a double major, studying law meant piling still more coursework onto an already heavy schedule. We may speculate that Morse had already begun to envisage, however dimly, a future where something more than effective public speaking would be called for, where a legal education would be a necessary precondition for both significant achievement and a possible place in the public arena. An extra class burden could be tolerated if such a future might be made more possible.

While Morse learned much from Witte, Perlman, and Hall, his most important mentor, as well as his debating coach, was Andrew T. Weaver of the speech department. Weaver became Morse's friend as well as instructor. He worked extra hours with him on improving his rhetorical technique. He encouraged him to aim for a career in college teaching. He even lent him money from time to time to cover expenses. With Weaver's help, Morse took numerous debating honors, including, in his junior year, the Vilas medal for "excellence in forensic endeavor." According to the student paper, he was known in rhetoric circles as the "Forensic Yankee"—which recalls the "blue-belted Yankee" description Wib had applied to himself, and which perhaps characterized the conservative Progressivism in which both men believed.

As a senior, Morse captained the Hesperia Society team that won the university's major intramural debate by defending a thesis inspired by La Follette: that decisions of the Supreme Court should be subject to override by a two-thirds vote of Congress. Morse personally disagreed with this proposition and originally wanted his side to argue its negative. He and his two teammates—one of whom was the ever-present Axley—decided to visit La Follette at his farm to seek his advice. La Follette persuaded the other two that his was the correct position. Morse held to his viewpoint, but, outvoted by his colleagues, agreed to go along. His team not only won the debate, but did so on the strength of Morse's brilliant closing speech.

Morse used an identical speech to win an audition a few days later. As a result, he was selected to represent Wisconsin in the annual contest of the Northern Oratorical League, the debating society of Midwestern universities. With the encouragement of Weaver, he reworked the speech—the only one he had ever made defending a position he did not endorse—and used it a third time in the Oratorical League competition, in which he distinguished himself by finishing second and winning fifty dollars.

Although La Follette persuaded the Hesperians to go contrary to their captain, Morse found the visit to his farmhouse otherwise instructive. Sitting in a rocking chair, sipping lemonade on his front porch, La Follette drew a distinction between arguing to educate and arguing to win, a distinction new to Morse. He insisted there was merit, indeed honor, in making an argument for educational purposes, even if you didn't win the argument. If you are right, he said, your audience will eventually come to understand the issue properly and support your position. He suggested that one should of course speak to win, if possible; but one should always speak to educate, to inform, and to enlighten, even if victory is beyond one's reach. Morse would have numerous occasions to recall this instruction when, in the U.S. Senate, he took positions violently opposed by the majority. And it is apparent that when in later years he thought back to his early encounters with La Follette, he found in Fighting Bob the consummate model of maverick independence: "He was a very versatile man, and he knew how to grip young people . . . he was a man of great principle. You realized when you were in his presence and listening to him, whether people agreed or disagreed with him, this man couldn't be bought, he couldn't be kept, he was dedicated to serving what he considered to be the interests of the people."

Morse's academic and extracurricular activities were certainly demanding, but as the "Fussing" entries indicate, all was not work and struggle at the university. Though not a great one for night life, Morse attended his share of social functions, usually in the company of Midge. He even went to occasional dances, though one suspects that Midge had to prod him vigorously in their direction. Given his exhausting workload, however, there were many moments when being with Midge was something less than a social event. Axley recalled several instances when the three were together at Midge's house, Morse prostrate on the sofa, so deeply asleep that they had trouble awakening him.

Because he was a serious student and an undeviating teetotaler, Morse was not a participant in the Roaring Twenties, even in Madison's muted expression of that decade. Nor was the more adventurous Midge, though she was active in those campus dramatic circles where the university's version of undergraduate flappery was sometimes displayed. But Midge saw nothing wrong in the occasional sip of bathtub gin, and a mildly chiding notation by Morse probably arose from one such experience: "Thanksgiving 1921 and Midge had to go and get sick. Dissipation don't agree with tummies."

Dissipation was *not*, however, Mildred Downie's usual style. Although a home economics major, she was interested generally in the arts and humanities. Unlike Morse, whose reading was confined largely to his assigned subjects, she read in a wide variety of areas, and it is fair to say that she emerged from Wisconsin with a broader education than her future husband. In her last year she was awarded the first annual Edna Kerngood Glicksman prize of fifty dollars, given "in recognition of intellectual attainments, high womanhood, and service in the college community." (Caryl Morse would win the same award several years later.)

MORSE LEFT THE UNIVERSITY OF WISCONSIN in June 1924, having stayed on an extra year to get a master's degree in speech and to take courses in the law school, while he assisted Weaver in coaching the debate team. Midge spent that year teaching high school in Sparta, Wisconsin. After a nine-year courtship—during which they had dated no one but each other—the couple had become betrothed the previous month when Morse had purchased an engagement ring. In all likelihood the engagement would have been made official earlier, and would have run longer than three and a half weeks, had

After a nine-year courtship, Wayne Morse and Mildred Downie were married on June 18, 1924. The couple immediately drove their Model T to Minneapolis for a brief honeymoon. (Wayne Morse Collection, CN 1318, Special Collections, University of Oregon Library.)

Morse been able to afford it. As it was, he had to borrow $60 from Miss Webber and another $104 from Midge herself to pay for the ring.

The couple exchanged vows at three o'clock on the afternoon of June 18, 1924, at the First Baptist Church in Madison, where Morse was now a deacon. Morse, it must be said, was less than a lively groom, having that morning written a four-hour exam to complete his degree work. Nevertheless, the newlyweds drove immediately to Minneapolis in their Model T to begin a brief honeymoon. The honeymoon was not only brief in duration, but also short on romance, since Morse spent a good deal of it looking into a possible teaching job at the University of Minnesota. He ultimately landed the position—with Weaver's support and assistance—and in September would begin working as an instructor of speech and argumentation and coach of the debating team.

Morse earned additional income during July and August of 1924 by teaching summer school at Wisconsin, but after paying off some old debts and covering their transportation costs, the couple had only ten cents between them when they arrived in Minneapolis in September. A kindly landlady rented them a tiny apartment, with no money down, and fed them until they could obtain a $150 bank loan to tide them over. And in a stroke of good fortune, Midge was hired as a one-term replacement to teach courses in the home economics department on Minnesota's St. Paul campus. The Morses were suddenly in a position to save money for the first time since they had started college five years earlier.

During his years at Minnesota, Morse worked a schedule that made his Wisconsin program appear insubstantial by comparison. He immediately asked for and received permission to study at the university law school in his "spare" time. He did his law assignments while carrying a full teaching load and spending extra hours with the debate team. In his third and fourth years he devoted three nights a week to criticizing sermons delivered by students at a nearby seminary. Whenever he could, he offered extension courses at the St. Paul

Morse worked on his law degree at the University of Minnesota while teaching an extra-heavy load in the speech department and coaching the varsity debate team. (Courtesy of Judith Morse Goldberg.)

campus; he never missed an opportunity to teach summer session, as many classes as possible; and he frequently appeared as a speaker at campus events and at high school convocations throughout the state.

One year Morse earned extra money working for the La Follette family. Bob La Follette had died in 1925, and the following summer his widow, who was preparing a biography, hired Morse to tour Wisconsin's smaller towns to collect stories that had been printed about her husband. Morse visited most of the local newspapers and gathered a vast amount of material, much of which ultimately found its way into Belle La Follette's book. From this work he would remember best those oft-repeated stories about how the senator would start talking at 3:30 in the afternoon and still have his audience captivated at 7 PM, while "every cow in the township was 'bellerin' to be milked." Similar stories would be told about Senator Morse in the years to come.

Midge, meanwhile, returned to high school teaching. She had hoped to continue in the home economics department after her one-term appointment, but the university refused to waive its nepotism rule even though she worked on a separate campus from her husband. The closest job she could find was in the suburb of Bloomington, and because its school board required teachers to live in town, she took a room there and came back to Minneapolis on weekends. Though not the happiest of situations, the dual residency did not much alter the Morse mode of existence. From a vantage point half a century later, Midge could suggest that the arrangement scarcely made an impact: "I hardly saw him during the week anyway," she recalled, without apparent bitterness. "He always carried the workload of three men, and it was no different then."

If Morse's workload was heavy, he was good at what he did. His boss was Professor Frank Rarig, a gentlemanly administrator and a noted scholar. Rarig especially admired Morse's enthusiasm. Many years later he recalled an example of that enthusiasm: "We wanted a human larynx and sent him over to the professor of anatomy in the Medical School to get one. To his request, the professor replied: 'There is a new cadaver out there on a dissecting table. Cut off the head and take out his larynx.' He performed the operation and came back with a fresh larynx. Morse let no grass grow under his feet and had no use for teachers who did." Because of Morse's effectiveness with students, Rarig recommended that he be given a raise at the end of his first year's teaching. He also suggested that Instructor Morse "be encouraged to do further graduate work with the understanding that in due time he may expect promotion to an assistant professorship."

Morse's success in the classroom was equaled by his accomplishments with the university debate team. He revolutionized customary practice by expanding the size of the team. Instead of the usual two- or three-man squad, he chose a group of twelve, and gave each student the intensive coaching and experience normally reserved for the designated top debaters. According to one of his colleagues in the speech department, part of Morse's method involved getting his boys intensely worked up in defense of their arguments: "He liked to see them get so mad in debate practice meets that they'd actually swear. Morse liked that." To the surprise of many, Morse's twelve-man team won the Northern Oratorical League competition during his first year, defeating a visiting delegation from Oxford University in the process, and finished second only to Northwestern University in the following year. Drawing on his Wisconsin experience, Morse also organized a regular intercollegiate debating conference for women, and his own female team typically defeated all comers.

Morse's effectiveness might have been at least partially the result of his approach to speech instruction. He had been influenced by Dr. Smiley Blanton's mental-hygiene theories, which were then gaining currency in the field. Blanton, with whom Morse had studied in Wisconsin, eschewed the traditional elocutionary methods of speech preparation in favor of a system that took into account the emotional condition of speakers and their state of adjustment, or lack of adjustment, to their immediate environment. Morse, following Blanton, stressed the psychological aspects of rhetoric and, to better equip himself in the area, took psychology courses along with his classes in law. He wrote papers in defense of mental-hygiene techniques, and became known in speech circles as something of a zealot in their application.

Morse completed law school and was awarded an LL.B. in 1928. He had by then been promoted to assistant professor and was acting chairman of his department during the 1928 summer session. As he accepted his degree, he and Midge were already planning to spend the following year on leave in New York City. Morse had applied for and been awarded a $1,500 fellowship to Columbia University Law School to spend nine months studying toward a doctorate of jurisprudence. It would prove to be a telling nine-month period, at the end of which Morse's career would undergo a dramatic change.

IN MOST WAYS NEW YORK made a deeper impression on Midge than on Morse. The change in location was a powerful tonic, one that she badly needed. That summer, tragedy had struck when her sister and her sister's baby daughter were drowned in a boating accident. New York helped her to deal with her loss. The crowds, the shops, the subway, the Bronx Zoo, eating at the Automat, swimming for the first time in salt water—such novelties served to divert her from her sadness. And, once she landed a job as a home-appliance analyst for *The Delineator* magazine, she began to think more cheerfully about the future. Moreover, though Morse spent long hours at the library, he was far less distracted than at Minnesota, and Midge, for the first time since she had known him, had him more or less to herself. "Never before," she reported to Mrs. Rarig, "have we attained such a perfect companionship; we've always been too busy to enjoy each other."

Midge, in fact, had as busy a schedule as Morse, but she found time to describe for Mrs. Rarig her impressions of living in America's largest city. She felt both stimulated and oppressed by New York's crush of humanity—its "wilderness of people"—and the galloping pace of its existence. Most of those she met were different and interesting, but "full of defenses to hide their fears." She marveled that she and Wayne, like everyone else, were "living in layers," in little crannies carved out of huge apartment buildings. "Sometimes," she said, "in the subway particularly, I have the feeling of dried peas being shaken around in a pan."

For Morse, New York was Columbia Law School. The rest scarcely existed. He shared Midge's experiences, but not her insights. "Midge & I spent the day at Bronx Park," he joked in a letter to Rarig. "It was very interesting but I have seen all the zoos, outside of a mirror, that I want to see for sometime." Morse was preoccupied by the demands of his J.D. program, which required one year of intense residence work and a research project that culminated in nothing less than the publication of a full-length book. Only one such degree had been awarded at the time of Morse's candidacy.

Morse plunged into his work with his usual élan. His favorite class was a seminar, Logical and Ethical Problems of the Law, that was codirected by Columbia's most famous pedagogue, John Dewey. Of all his instructors, Dewey clearly became his intellectual hero. In letter after letter to Rarig, Dewey is depicted as "more than a philosopher—he's a scientist as well"; a "droll fellow" whose "mind is a catalogue of knowledge." Morse was uncharacteristically moved to almost literary expression in his image of Dewey: "His appearance is somewhat rustic, and as he sits slouched in his chair one can imagine his counterpart riding a corn plow out in Iowa."

Morse found Dewey's way of looking at problems congenial with his own mental-hygiene perspective, and although he never mentioned it, he must have also found congruence between Dewey's pragmatic politics and his own Progressivism. He could report to Rarig that the great man "had a good chuckle the other day when I remarked that the Law could administer Justice better as soon as it freed itself of religious impediments. . . . We punish the criminal who suffers from emotional disturbances but we revere the religious fanatic who is suffering from the same type of emotional disturbance. Our Criminal Law is just as logical as orthodox religion and no more."

Morse's one-semester exposure to Dewey was clearly a broadening experience, but it seemed to have little lasting effect. Under Dewey, Morse stretched his mind to consider philosophical issues which theretofore had been beyond his ken. As soon as he left Columbia, however, he would be drawn back to a narrower focus, to the concentration on precedent and procedure emphasized by most professional law schools. Morse would eventually earn his doctorate of jurisprudence; but jurisprudence per se, the philosophy of law and its theoretical implications, would be left for the more academically inclined to contemplate.

While his other classes were not as riveting as Dewey's, Morse did well in every one he took. Of his twelve grades over two semesters, he received eleven A's and one B, a far better record than he had achieved either as an undergraduate or as a law student. Toward the end of his second term he began to work closely with Professor Raymond Moley, a connection that would prove a mixed blessing in the years to come.

Soon after he completed his Minnesota degree, and even before going to New York, Morse started to think about shifting his teaching vocation from speech to law. Having made good at Columbia— though the book was still to be written—he was faced with a crucial question: was now the time to change his future? He had been moving, however uncertainly, toward the law over the past few years, and a return to Minnesota at the age of twenty-nine might mean that he would be stuck in speech forever. On the other hand, he had a secure position at Minneapolis, he had built a name for himself, and other Midwestern speech departments had been making offers—should all of this be abandoned to start a new career at the bottom, even if that career might open important doors later on? Was this the moment for boldness or for caution?

The fact is that for one of the few times in his life, Morse could not decide what to do. He did not so much choose boldness as compel boldness to choose him. He "resolved" his dilemma by making a demand on Minnesota that was impossible for the school to meet. He said he would consider, but not promise, a return to Minnesota if offered a salary of $4,000 and the rank of associate professor. Since Rarig, after twenty years on the job, made but $4,500, such a demand had no chance of a favorable hearing. So when Rarig offered $3,500 and the prospect of an associate professorship at some unspecified time in the future, *after* Morse had done further research "within the discipline," Morse insisted that he had no honorable choice but to resign.

The negotiations with Rarig were anything but pleasant. Whether he would return or not, Morse, once he had made his proposal, came to feel he deserved both the extra money and the elevated title, and did not hesitate to let Rarig know the reasons why. Rarig had to worry about what others would think if he argued Morse's ambitious case to the administration. Morse was little concerned with such niceties. As his colleague Bryng Bryngelson put it, "I liked the guy but he obviously didn't care whether a lot of people here liked him or not." Morse had developed a reputation for being quick on the trigger. Bryngelson thought of him as "a fighting cock, volatile and potentially explosive. He could get mad as hell in a short time and didn't always keep his balance."

Whether it was a mad-as-hell Morse in the dispute with Rarig is difficult to say. Morse did in fact use provocative language in a rapid-fire series of letters to his chairman: he accused Rarig of "glandular" thinking and of feeling threatened by the advancement of underlings within his department, and he claimed that Bryngelson had been opposing him behind his back. Morse would write such angry letters again and again throughout his lifetime when he felt he had been wronged or misunderstood, and he continued to gibe at Rarig for a time even after the dispute had been settled. But though his anger was real, Morse also seemed, as he would so often in later years, to have engineered the explosion at Rarig for maximum effect. Righteous indignation could be a powerful debating tool, and Morse learned early how to use it to full advantage. In this case it may have been utilized to force a decision that he had wanted to make anyway but could not reach on his own, without having something or someone to react against. Whatever Morse's motivations, Rarig handled the matter with diplomacy, all wounds inflicted were healed within a reasonable period, and the two men remained friends for life.

Nevertheless, Morse had cut his ties with Minnesota and, with doctorate not yet in hand, had placed himself in the position of having to cast about for a job.

IN HIS 1951 EDITION OF *INSIDE U.S.A.*, John Gunther offers the Morses' law school period as prototypical Americana: the heroic young couple struggling to fight their way out of inherited poverty. Gunther writes: "Mrs. Morse was a crack student . . . and while her husband was studying law, she taught home economics in a Minneapolis high school. This . . . is part of a familiar American pattern, that of the brilliant-but-poor young student ably assisted by a young woman with her own job as well as the job of raising a family and washing dishes." Aside from getting the location of Midge's high school wrong, Gunther's rhapsodic analysis neglects to mention that Morse was earning a full academic salary at the time and children were nowhere in the picture. The fact was that together, the Morses were able to meet their expenses, pay off their debts, and sock away considerable capital during their five years in Minneapolis and New York. Except for outlays for the occasional horse show or riding expedition, they recorded few expenditures for social occasions, and they had more than $10,000 on hand as they prepared to depart Minnesota.

Such a substantial cash reserve provided a useful cushion, for, after what seemed to be a welter of possibilities, genuine job openings came down to only two: at the law schools of George Washington University in Washington, D.C., and the University of Oregon in Eugene. Undoubtedly the paucity of offers was due partly to the fact that Morse's heavy teaching load at Minnesota had kept him from earning better than a B average in his legal studies. Morse and Midge preferred the Eugene position—they had a longing to see what lay beyond the Dakotas—but even that job might not have been forthcoming had not Oregon's president been Arnold Bennett Hall, Morse's old political theory professor at Wisconsin. However, Hall did not clearly remember Morse at first, and initially wanted to fill the slot with Orlando Hollis, an outstanding local graduate who would later join the faculty and become Morse's closest colleague. Undaunted, Morse kept the pressure on with a flurry of telegrams to Hall; and Hall, on the advice of Charles Carpenter, dean of Oregon's law school, eventually offered him the position, at a salary of $3,000 —the same as he had been making at the University of Minnesota.

Morse was elated. His immediate acceptance showed that pay had never really been the issue at Minnesota. Had money mattered most, he could have made more of it at one of the Midwestern speech departments that had been courting him. The appeal of both Oregon and GWU was the opportunity each afforded for changing disciplines. What gave Oregon the edge was the added attraction of living somewhere west of the Rockies.

As soon as the summer session ended, Morse and Midge headed out of Minneapolis for what they hoped would be their great adventure in the Pacific Northwest. It would prove to be more of an adventure than either had bargained for.

3

Vaulting Ambition

NESTLED AMONG THE CONIFEROUS HILLS at the southern edge of
the Willamette Valley, Eugene, Oregon, was in 1929 a world apart
from what the Morses had known in their Midwestern environs. The
city of nearly 19,000 dealt in two main products, boards and bac-
calaureates, but it was the former that gave the area its character. As
a community, it had little of the diversity peculiar to a progressive
state capital like Madison, and nothing comparable to the energy of
a fast-growing metropolis like Minneapolis-St. Paul. Despite the
presence of the university, Eugene had the rough-hewn personality
of a Pacific Northwest lumber town.

The thoughtful diaries of John Laurence Casteel, a cultivated
speech instructor who migrated to Eugene shortly after Morse's arrival, provide an east-of-the-Rockies perspective on what it was like
to come to the University of Oregon at the turn of the decade. New
to the Northwest, the youthful Casteel was first taken by the "almost
idyllic" nature of Oregon's sylvan terrain. His initial glimpse of the
university, however, produced a more mixed response. "The campus," he noted, "is somewhat beautiful, the main effect arising from
heavy firs that stand here and there on the lawn. These are tall and
dense enough to conceal the horrors of the old university buildings
—but the new structures stand unshadowed on base plots."

Casteel was horrified by more than the campus architecture.
Oregon, he said, musing on the university's undergraduate student
body, "is the kind of land that harbors the dull, the indolent, the stupid class who flourish in the backwoods country." Where, he wondered, thinking similarly about his faculty colleagues, might one find
in such country men who "can be called educated, in the liberal,

broad, rounded sense—men who have inner gentility and outer comprehension?"

Casteel's observations are cited not merely to suggest that Morse had forsaken a more stimulating intellectual context for a post in an educational backwater—although that to a large degree is what had occurred—but to make the point that because he tended to be so absorbed by work and driven by ambition, Morse, unlike Casteel, typically remained impervious to his immediate surroundings (recall the narrow focus of his year in New York). Reflecting from retirement on his university situations, he said he had "found no difference between Eugene, Oregon, and Madison, Wisconsin, or Minneapolis, Minnesota, as far as the social, academic and economic environment was concerned." Preoccupied by other matters, Morse could feel as comfortable or uncomfortable in one place as he could in another.

In the case of Eugene, Morse might anyway be forgiven a lack of Casteelian awareness, for scarcely had he arrived when he was forced to confront the insistent and seemingly endless demands of his new employment.

FIRST CAME TEACHING, which proved to be far more of a chore than anticipated. Though Morse was unhappy about it, Dean Carpenter assigned him all of the classes on property, an area he hadn't studied since his undergraduate years. At the outset he had to do considerable cramming just to keep a step ahead of his students.

In addition to classroom preparation, Morse was much involved in completing his doctor of jurisprudence requirements for Columbia University. His collaboration with Raymond Moley was based on an elaborate nationwide survey of judicial attitudes toward grand-jury prosecutions. It had been Moley's idea, but Morse was doing the tedious compilation and correspondence, and it was his task to write up most of the results. He had worked hard on the project, and as the new decade was beginning, the end was finally in sight.

However, the survey was *not* the idea that Morse had originally proposed for his thesis; he therefore had to spend time and energy convincing his dissertation committee in New York not only that he had switched topics legitimately, but also that doing the survey was equal in scholarship to carrying out his previous proposal, an analysis of psychiatry and the law. While all of this was occurring, he further crowded his schedule by embarking on a related but separate survey of crime in Oregon. The relaxed days of New York City were gone forever.

Nevertheless, Morse could carve out just enough time to return to his first love and main source of recreation: horseback riding. At the beginning of the term he managed to saddle up two or three times a week. As the semester wore on and his program became more manageable, he could be seen riding nearly every day, including Sundays—"while," he exulted, "the preachers in town are stirring up the fires of hell." Wib Morse's philosophy still obtained: if, as Wib had insisted, the outside of a horse was good for the inside of a boy, it would, as far as Wayne was concerned, be even more so for the man.

Following this philosophy, Morse drew on his savings to buy two saddle horses during his first semester. Although not an insignificant expenditure, purchasing two horses scarcely depleted household reserves, what with that $10,000 securely tucked away in a bank account. Unfortunately, as it turned out, the money was not in safe keeping. In fact, it was not in a bank. It was on deposit with a Minneapolis building and loan society, an institution which, like so many of its kind, lost all of its assets in 1930—including the Morses' $10,000.

The loss was a calamity. Money, or rather the absence of it, had long been a concern. When they had possessed none, Wayne and Midge had amused themselves in their Minneapolis apartment imagining what it would be like to have a million dollars. Now, after all those years of scrimping, they were back to penny-pinching as a way of life.

As crushing as the blow was, however, it was far from fatal. In the first place, the couple could take solace in the fact that they were not alone: losing one's fortune was by no means unique at the beginning of the Great Depression, and other nest eggs in the Eugene community had also vanished overnight. Moreover, the Morses had much to fall back on. Not only was Wayne employed while millions were out of work, but he had just learned of his promotion to associate professor, effective the following autumn, with a $300 increase in pay. The Morses might be down, but they were certainly not out.

Morse was promoted even though he had had some difficulty with his course in real-property law during his second semester. According to those who attended them, his classes were normally open and relaxed, with considerable give-and-take between instructor and students. At the same time, he quickly became known as the law school's toughest grader, and he had been especially hard on his first-term students in Real Property, giving almost half of the class D's or F's. What happened the following term is open to dispute.

As Morse remembered it, the class started the trouble by going on strike: at the second meeting, he said, every student answered "not prepared" when asked to discuss the very first case they had been assigned. Interpreting these responses as a "work stoppage" prompted by his severe grading of the previous semester, he announced that the class was "in contempt of court" and that no further meetings would be held until the final examination.

William East, one of Morse's former students (who because of Morse's support went on to become a federal judge), recalled this part of the story differently. According to his version, what occurred had no connection with first-semester grades. Morse, he said, normally assigned a large number of cases which the class was to brief and have ready for discussion. For their part, students had grown used to the fact that Morse never got past analyzing the first one or two—"he would just belabor a case until it was a dead horse well kicked"—and it became their custom to prepare only those cases at the top of the list and ignore the rest. Without warning, Morse changed his approach one day and went "boom, boom, boom" through a series of cases, giving five or six minutes to each. Once the first were disposed of, the class fell dumb. When no one could discuss even one of the other cases, Morse "slammed his books on the podium and stomped from the classroom." In East's rendition, the class decided to go on strike only when Morse failed to show up at their next designated meeting. They formed a committee and took their grievance to Dean Carpenter.

Regardless of who went on strike when and for what reason, a situation had developed in which a law school professor was refusing to meet with his students. Carpenter tried to persuade Morse to relent, but Morse insisted he would not return until the student committee had apologized in writing on behalf of the entire class. The controversy ultimately reached the desk of President Hall, and while Hall extracted a promise from Morse that he would never take such unilateral action again, he publicly supported the ultimatum. In the face of such a firm line, the students gave in, Morse got his apology, and the class returned to something approaching normal.

Some time after this incident, but apparently not in connection with it, Carpenter announced that he was leaving Eugene to replace Justin Miller as dean at the University of Southern California Law School. (Morse had known Miller in Minnesota, and Miller had supported his application to Oregon.) Because Carpenter was going and, more precisely, because the governor had severely cut the university's budget, Morse also began to think about moving on. He wrote to former professors seeking "a position which would be an advancement over the one which I now have."

Whether or not Midge was aware of Morse's thinking is unclear. The loss of the $10,000, which she had taken harder than her husband, was now but a memory. She was pregnant with their first child, excited about becoming a mother, and content to be settled in their "dear little home." "Sometimes," she confessed to friends, "I wonder if there isn't some awful catastrophe in store for me because it doesn't seem right that one person should have so much happiness." Relocating at that moment to some other city would have constituted just such a catastrophe.

If Midge did fret about moving, her worries were soon over. To his delight, Morse discovered that he was being considered by President Hall as Carpenter's replacement. Early betting, however, favored someone from the outside, while the inside front runner was thought to be Carlton Spencer, a law professor in his forties who had formerly been the university registrar.

Hall sounded Carpenter out, and Carpenter at first gave Morse a mixed review. "Morse," he said, "is a finished speaker and makes a fine public impression. He has plenty of vitality, energy, and ambition." But, he added, Morse also had problems, which Carpenter attributed to his background in rhetoric. "Students complained to me that Professor Morse was a bluffer and that they had lost all confidence in him. . . . I have had to work with Morse to secure more masterful preparation." Of the four instructors in the law school (not counting himself), Carpenter felt that students would rank Morse third. Furthermore, there was his personality to worry about: "He is a fighter you should know, but with all that, excessively sensitive to criticism. Should you make him dean, you would need to be careful in selecting your committees and avoid any possible appearance of neglect. Otherwise, he would be in a slough of despondancy [sic]."

Carpenter sent his assessment to Hall on March 23, 1931. Two weeks later he did an about-face. On April 8, he told Hall that his views had been "too unfavorable," based as they were on Morse's earlier performance. Of late there "has been a great change as Professor Morse has grown in teaching method and knowledge of the law." It was Carpenter's revised opinion that "the students would welcome his appointment as dean enthusiastically and it is my own impression that if you appoint someone from the faculty he would be the most desirable choice."

Why Carpenter reversed himself is impossible to say, unless he sensed that Hall in the intervening fortnight had fixed his mind on Morse and that it would be unwise to depart Eugene in disagreement with his president. Whatever the reasons for Carpenter's endorsement, Hall came down on Morse's side, sending him a coy, confidential message that put the one-year appointment in writing. He referred to the new dean as "your friend," and told Morse that he hoped "your friend will make good and earn a permanent appointment." Morse's "friend" eagerly accepted the job, and in so doing became the youngest dean of an accredited law school in the country.

Why Hall opted for Morse is also difficult to say, except to note that an uninspiring Spencer was never really in the running, and that both of Carpenter's evaluations, however contradictory, contained elements of the truth. It *was* true that Morse had had problems with his teaching, and that he was sensitive to criticism and susceptible if not to "sloughs of despondency," then at least to periods of morose-ness. But it was equally true that he was far and away the most in-teresting member of the faculty and had become the law school's most popular instructor. And though his scholarship could not have been described as distinguished, it was certainly productive, and his survey-research methodology involved him in what at the time was one of the frontiers of social science. All in all, President Hall could satisfy himself that in Professor Morse he had made a judicious, if unorthodox, selection.

One other factor, of which Morse was not unaware, had played a part in the promotion. It would have been difficult (though per-haps not impossible) to obtain someone from the outside with a reputation equal to Carpenter's for the maximum stated salary of $5,500. Morse was not just an appropriate choice, he was a bargain: he would be paid $4,250, and if he did poorly during his probation-ary year he could always be replaced. But though the salary was a bargain for the university, for Morse it represented an increase of 27 percent. Which, as many of his colleagues noted, was not bad for a

As dean of the University of Oregon law school, Morse was, at thirty-one, the youngest law school head in the United States. (Wayne Morse Collec-tion, Special Collections, University of Oregon Library.)

man of only thirty who had served less than nine months as an associate professor.

Morse's raise was greatly appreciated at home, for, three weeks before it became effective, a new arrival, Nancy Fay, was added to the Morse family. She did not come easily. Midge was in intermittent labor for nine straight days before the doctors decided to perform an emergency caesarean section. The birth was successful, but Midge's life hung in the balance for three days until the bleeding could be arrested. By summer vacation, however, mother and daughter could both be described as enjoying excellent health.

Morse moved quickly to consolidate his position by tightening his connection with Orlando Hollis. One of his first acts as dean was to get Hollis, a fellow horseman in his late twenties who had been a half-time faculty member for less than two years, elevated to full professor. The quiet, hard-working Hollis became Morse's in-house confidant, and was assigned the role of acting dean whenever Morse was away from Eugene. Their opposite personalities were nicely balanced, and Morse felt he could count on Hollis to support him in even the boldest of his proposals. Before long he would need such support, from Hollis and from anyone else he could rally to his side.

MORSE HAD BECOME DEAN of a financially strapped law school that was part of a university desperately short of funds, in a relatively poor state under siege by the Depression. To save money, officials in the state capital of Salem had slashed the higher-education budget to the barest of bones, and had given the choicest of these to Oregon State College (as it was then known) in Corvallis. Oregon State had been under the strong hand of President William Jasper Kerr, a former Utah educator who had spent nearly twenty-five years amassing influence in Salem. Only in recent times had Eugene sought to catch up with Corvallis, under the leadership of Arnold Bennett Hall.

It was Kerr's ambition to consolidate the two schools under one roof in Corvallis. Thus, in 1932, in the name of "economy," an initiative to that effect, known as the Zorn-MacPherson bill, was put before the Oregon electorate by a group of Corvallis citizens. Eight weeks prior to the vote, Kerr and Hall announced their resignations. The State Board of Higher Education accepted both, but, as part of a prearranged deal, Kerr was then appointed chancellor of higher education, a newly created office which would have authority over both campuses. The initiative, known in Eugene as "the Grab," was roundly defeated, thanks to vigorous action by pro-university interests throughout the state. Morse, who sent present and former law students far and wide to work against the initiative, was part of a near-unanimous Eugene which believed, correctly, that its viability was being threatened. Among those community members who campaigned beside Morse were three who would soon play significant roles in his career: William Tugman, editor of the *Eugene Register-Guard*; James Gilbert, dean of the School of Social Science; and Richard Neuberger, outgoing editor of the student paper, the *Oregon Daily Emerald*, who would one day be Morse's colleague in the U. S. Senate.

To celebrate the defeat of Zorn-MacPherson, the university canceled classes for a day. For Morse and his friends, however, the celebration could be only half-hearted: despite the victory, the much-despised Kerr was now entrenched in his new chancellor's office, wielding power theretofore unknown in Oregon education. That Kerr came out of the contest with his own position vastly improved was not that surprising. He was, to quote acid-tongued E. C. "Eddie" Sammons, then Board of Education finance chairman, "the goddamnedest finagler you ever saw." To show "impartiality," Kerr set up headquarters in Eugene rather than Corvallis. This was probably a mistake.

Led by Gilbert and Morse, and spurred on by Tugman, the faculty was openly hostile to the new chancellor, resisting and delaying Dr. Kerr's every suggestion for change. Morse went even further. He asked his friend and former Minnesota colleague Joe Smith, who taught speech at the University of Utah, to investigate Kerr's credentials. Smith reported that he could find no evidence of a Kerr doctorate, save an honorary Doctor of Science and Didactics degree awarded by the Mormon Church. Morse passed this information to allies on the Board of Education, who elected to do nothing with it

William Jasper Kerr was the longtime president of Oregon State College; but, because of pressure from Morse, he was a short-term chancellor of higher education. (University of Oregon Archives.)

—perhaps because they knew that Kerr, though universally addressed as "Doctor," had made no claim to a Ph.D. on his contractual documents.

Kerr, meanwhile, arbitrarily involved himself in administering the Eugene campus—much to the annoyance of senior faculty, who, unlike their counterparts in Corvallis, were used to a fair amount of self-governance. Tensions simmered over the summer of 1933 and were reaching a boiling point as school opened in the fall. Morse heated things up in late October by giving a Dad's Day speech before 1,700 students and parents in which he took issue with statements made by Roscoe Nelson, the newly appointed Board of Education chairman and an ardent Kerr supporter. The entire speech was reprinted in the *Emerald*, and formed a backdrop for Nelson's first visit to Eugene as chairman ten days later.

Addressing a student assembly, Nelson, with the chancellor seated behind him, tore into those "self-appointed few" who, moved by "unsated ambition," were secretly "sabotaging" Kerr at every turn. In the auditorium, Morse bristled, even though he had been exempted from the charges by name because, Nelson said, Dean Morse had at least made his criticisms publicly.

Morse decided that he, Hollis, Gilbert, and a secretary should drive up to Oregon State, where Nelson was to speak later that day. Nelson reiterated his accusations in Corvallis, in even stronger language, to a wildly cheering, pro-Kerr audience. Morse moved from heated indignation to cold fury. "Orlando," he promised, "I'm going to get that son of a bitch."

From his out-of-character profanity, Hollis knew that Morse was not making an idle threat, but he had no idea how he planned to "get" Nelson. "Only when Wayne managed to insinuate himself as speaker at the Saturday Homecoming luncheon," Hollis said, "did I realize what he was up to."

In a large dining hall packed to capacity with students, faculty, and alumni, and with Chancellor Kerr at the head table, Morse delivered a blistering attack on Nelson. He labeled Nelson's remarks "insulting, insinuating, unfair and vicious," and said that Nelson had been "duped" by a chancellor who had been selected in a "plot so rotten that it stinks to high heaven." Morse wanted Nelson to know that Kerr, aided by certain local townspeople, whom Morse referred to by name, had been violating academic freedom by interfering with long-established faculty procedures. Because he had falsely accused university employees of subversion, and because he had brought "disharmony to Oregon education," Nelson, Morse insisted, had no choice but to resign forthwith.

Morse's own words colorfully describe the effect of his speech: "The meeting ended in pandemonium. . . . members of the faculty all over that room, as well as alumni, rose to their feet. All the dishes were tipped off of the tables and crashed to the floor. I saw some members of the faculty with tears running down their faces." Amidst the tumult and applause, Kerr fled the hall in a towering rage. That night, John Casteel wrote in his diary: "No one knows where this will lead us, but at least now those on the faculty who are against Kerr will stand or die in the fight. . . . Exciting, but unsettling."

Unsettling it was. Morse's address—which came to be known as the "Rotten Plot" speech—made headlines across the state. The following Monday the faculty, with Gilbert in the chair, passed without dissent a resolution calling for Nelson's resignation. A petition promoted by Neuberger endorsing the resolution gathered more than a thousand signatures, representing nearly a fourth of the full-time student body. One day later, Nelson handed in his resignation. True to his promise, Morse had "gotten" his man, and it had taken him less than a week to do so.

Riding the wave of popular sentiment, Morse then called for Kerr's resignation. But Kerr was a tougher proposition than the gentlemanly Nelson, with whom Morse, astonishingly, maintained a decorous private relationship during the worst of their public dispute. Kerr persuaded the Board of Higher Education to charge Morse with insubordination, and the board appointed a committee to look into the matter. But Morse had anticipated this move: even before the board acted, the Eugene chapter of the American Association of University Professors—of which Morse was conveniently president —produced a fifteen-page bill of particulars enumerating Kerr's various malfeasances. Additionally, at Morse's request, Raymond Moley (who had recently relinquished his appointment as Under Secretary of State in the Roosevelt administration) commented from his new position as editor of *Today* magazine that Dean Morse was being victimized by the "encroachment of politics." After the insubordination investigation was begun, the national AAUP was called in to do an investigation of its own, to see whether Morse's academic freedom was being violated. Morse's job hung on the outcome of these parallel inquiries.

Morse held up reasonably well under the pressure, but there were moments of severe strain. The University of California professor who headed the AAUP probe initially contended that justice and injustice could be found on both sides and that larger interests had to be considered. To Morse he argued: "You take the position that the Chancellor is a crook and that nothing will satisfy you but his summary dismissal. Concede that he is a crook.... The work of the world must go on, and it always has and always will involve dealing with crooks." As if this attitude from the outside were not appalling enough, similar sentiments were sometimes expressed on campus in informal faculty gatherings.

Morse came home from such a session so tense one evening that

Midge had to ask a doctor who lived nearby to give him something to make him sleep. The doctor made the mistake of prescribing a shot of whiskey: it was only the second Morse had ever taken (the first had also been medicinal), and this one had the singular effect of winding him all the tighter. When friends came by to discuss strategy, he became slightly hysterical and broke into a fit of nonstop talking. The doctor had to be called again. He was able to calm Morse, but only by injecting him with two vials of morphine. Morse fell into a stupor and slept through the night and the following day, finally awakening at four in the afternoon, unable to remember anything after the moment he drank the liquor. His one-day absence immediately gave rise to rumors that he had suffered a nervous breakdown.

Part of the problem was that, given the high personal stakes involved, Morse felt perpetually on the spot, and though he generally acted as his own best advocate, he could, when put on the defensive, alienate even some of his closest allies. Six weeks after the whiskey episode, Casteel recorded the following: "Today brought another quarrel in faculty meeting, but Morse's argument grew so absurd that most of the faculty went away somewhat provoked. . . . I listened to the discussion, and realized again that the nerve to speak up is not at all correlated with the wisdom of what one has to say. I think I would not be guilty of argument as flimsy as that used by Morse today."

Fortunately for Morse, the days were few when he provoked the faculty with flimsy argumentation. Not only was most of the faculty behind him, but he had the reassurance of knowing that his faction on the State Board of Higher Education, though a minority, was unwavering in its support. Vice President Charles Brand pledged, "I am with you heart and soul." And without meaning to be ironic, he added, "I know it is enough to drive one to drink. Well, take a good drink, and then be patient, for we are surely going to win."

However inappropriate Brand's advice on drinking, he was correct in his prediction. On January 15, 1934, the board voted to reestablish presidencies at Eugene and Corvallis. At the same time, it decided to drop its investigation of Morse, saving face by saying that in the future it would punish anyone who aired criticisms publicly before first going through channels.

The board's majority caved in for two reasons. The AAUP had swung to Morse's side and was preparing a strong statement in his defense; and Morse refused to participate in a private meeting where he would be essentially unprotected. For its part, the board feared to tangle with Morse in open forum. With the press and public in attendance, Dean Morse would surely bring up the question of "Doctor" Kerr's title, and would very likely overwhelm the majority with his powerful rhetoric. He was, after all, as board finance chairman Eddie Sammons described him, "a masterful orator. . . . the damnedest guy I ever knew. He could make black look white."

Recognizing the inevitable, William Jasper Kerr announced on April 17 that he would resign as soon as a replacement could be found. Having heard the announcement, a few guilt-ridden faculty members wanted to throw the departing chancellor a farewell banquet. Morse saw the suggestion as blatant hypocrisy. His slogan for Kerr was "No gangster's funeral."

Morse was taking no prisoners. In the space of six months, he had engaged in battle and annihilated the two most powerful men in Oregon higher education. He had, as far as most of Eugene was concerned, "saved the university," and his exploits were recounted in newspapers throughout the state.

Despite the good press, Morse did not feel entirely secure in his victories. He had made important enemies, and he wondered how long he could keep them from exacting revenge. In fact, before the board decided in his favor, he felt reasonably certain that he would be fired. Coincidentally, earlier in 1933, he had an unexpected chance to go elsewhere. One day he answered his telephone and on the other end was the redoubtable Senator Huey Long of Louisiana, calling from Washington. Though they had never met, Long asked Morse to take over the deanship of Louisiana State University's law school, at double whatever he was then making and including all moving expenses. Once past the initial surprise, Morse was inclined to accept the dramatic offer. But after consulting Moley, who had apparently recommended him in the first place, he decided that moving into Louisiana's political jungles as Long's ostensible factotum could, however much it satisfied ambition, prove even more perilous than enduring the continuing uncertainties of Oregon. Moley later wondered, as we might today, "Now what would have happened had Wayne Morse gone to Louisiana?"

Although Morse would not accept Long's proposition, he used it as leverage on his own behalf before he turned it down. Moley had helped to bring Morse's doctoral committee around on the matter of the thesis: two articles on the grand-jury survey, which first appeared under Morse's name in the *Oregon Law Review*, were bound in booklet form and, as such, accepted by Columbia as a published "book." Morse received his doctorate of jurisprudence in 1932. Despite that lofty degree, and despite his deanship and promotion to full professor, he had never been given tenure. Whether this was due to an oversight on Hall's part or to his continued cautiousness regarding Morse is not clear. Whatever the case, Hall was in no position to resist Morse's further advancement. Buoyed by his recent celebrity and with Long's offer in hand, Morse whipsawed Hall and the university into not only a grant of tenure, but also a raise of $500.

Nevertheless, since his tryout as dean had dragged on for two years, probation ending only because he had forced the issue, Morse continued to explore other possibilities. He was contacted about law school deanships at the Universities of Indiana, Missouri, and Kansas and American University in Washington, D.C. He might have taken the prestigious Missouri job—the others he never really considered —but when a Missouri offer failed to materialize, he decided that, at least for the time being, it would be best to stay put.

One of the factors in considering relocation was a pending increase in the Morse family: Midge was pregnant again. As with her first, she was not having an easy time of it, and her pregnancy was complicated by something that had happened during her fourth month. She and Nancy, now two and a half, were returning in late January from a visit to Salt Lake City and were scheduled to change trains in Davis, California. When the Southern Pacific limited they were riding overshot the Davis terminal by a quarter of a mile, they and their baggage were deposited by the side of the tracks outside of town, from which point they had to walk back to the station in the dark of night. Midge was still so upset by the episode when she reached Eugene that her doctor ordered her to bed for a week, and everyone feared the worst for her pregnancy. But though another caesarean was required, the delivery went without complication, and a healthy Judith May was born on June 26, 1934.

Though the Morses now had a second daughter, few beyond Eugene heard the news. Wayne neglected to send out announcements, which he was supposed to do during Midge's confinement. Midge suggested that he had "forgotten" the chore because the baby had not turned out to be the boy he had wanted; and Morse admitted that "in my own dreams, I never even thought about the possibility of having a girl." But, he insisted, "after they arrive it doesn't make a bit of difference." Furthermore, though now approaching her mid-thirties, Midge was prepared, despite Morse's opposition to having a third child, to make yet another attempt at conceiving a boy.

Whether the next Morse would be born in Eugene was another matter. Morse had won crucial conflicts for the university, but the overall war appeared endless. The AAUP report of the previous year had not been released; and though Kerr had theoretically resigned, his replacement had yet to be found, and he still retained his office. Adding further gloom, the new president of the university was C. Valentine Boyer, former chairman of the English Department, whom Morse regarded as an educational opportunist who would advance the interests of his favorite academic departments and neglect, among others, those of the law school. Although prepared to do battle with Boyer on an almost daily basis—including, as he had done with Kerr, secretly investigating his academic record—Morse feared that the university had lost its "moral vigor," and he yearned to escape the unrelenting field of combat. As he told one correspondent in early 1935, "I am doing everything I can to get out of here."

His best avenue of escape was to a possible job in Washington, where he would, he said, be content with even a temporary position while on leave from the law school for a year or two. Justin Miller had been appointed to the U.S. attorney general's office, and he hoped Morse could join him there. When Miller asked what kind of work he preferred, Morse said he would take any legal job, anything that "would provide me with an enriching experience and training"—anything, that is, that would take him out of Oregon, if only for a while.

Since Congress did not provide the necessary funding, however, Miller was unable to make Morse an offer, at least for the time being. Meanwhile, Morse's outlook began to brighten—the AAUP report was at last made public, Kerr finally vacated his office, Boyer was on the defensive, and Morse was once again enjoying the heat of the fray. "Things are going along just fine up here," he gloated to a former secretary who had moved to San Francisco. "We are averaging two good fights a day and no one knows when he comes to the office in the morning just what keg of dynamite is going to explode before night." By mid-December 1935, Morse could describe the past term as "the best one that I have experienced since I have been in Oregon."

Morse also owed his uplifted spirits to a new enterprise in which he was involved. Through a former student, he had gotten the job of arbitrating a waterfront labor dispute in Portland. He single-handedly settled the dispute and a number of ancillary disagreements on terms acceptable to both sides, thereby preventing an impending strike of the Ferryboatmen's Union. Ecstatic at the outcome, he said of the Portland settlement (at the risk of seeming immodest): "I am satisfied that it is the best piece of work that I have ever done."

Despite mounting satisfactions derived from both the arbitration work—more assignments followed the Portland case—and the improved situation on campus, Morse was still eager to get away. Boyer's minions, or "the Brotherhood of Faculty Engineers," as Morse called them, could be counted on to continue the fight over educational policy within the university; and Morse hoped that Miller might swing something for the 1936 spring quarter, even though it would mean that he would be away when Midge was due to produce that long-awaited boy in February. While Miller was again unable to offer anything, Midge delivered on schedule, except that once again the boy of Morse's dreams turned out to be a girl: Amy Ann arrived on February 18.

With the family enlarged again, Morse seemed more committed to remaining in Eugene for the foreseeable future. He purchased twenty acres in the hills in the south of the city (he had been leasing the acreage and keeping animals on it), and he engaged an architect to design a "modest" house and barn to be constructed on the property over the summer. Though Midge was anxious to move into larger quarters, Morse convinced her that for their requirements, the barn deserved first priority. However, the barn-raising went quickly, and the house itself, complete with four bathrooms and split-level lower floor, was finished by the end of the summer; the family moved in at the start of the fall quarter. Morse named the property (to which another eight and a half acres had been added) Edgewood Farm after his prize stallion, Edgewood Bourbon.

As the house was nearing completion, news came that Wilbur Morse had died. Wayne did not return to Madison for Wib's funeral. The house-building needed his oversight; he was in the middle of teaching summer school; the trip was too long to make on short notice—for perhaps all of these reasons, he decided to stay in Eugene. But even without these deterrents, it is doubtful that he would have gone. Wib had been failing for some time, and his death did not come as a surprise. And Wayne's connection with his father had grown increasingly remote over the years as his attention was consumed by his family in Eugene and by what it would take to advance his career.

WHETHER IT WOULD CONSTITUTE AN ADVANCE remained to be seen, but the appointment in Washington finally came through in January 1937. Morse was originally slated to assist Miller in completing a WPA-funded Parole, Pardon and Probation study, which was under the auspices of the Justice Department and was known as the "Attorney General's Survey of Release Procedures." But just prior to Morse's arrival, Miller was appointed an appellate tax judge, and Morse, as the newly named administrative director, suddenly found himself responsible for supervising the whole four-hundred-person project. He took a one-year leave from the university and moved to

Washington. After first deciding that Midge and the children would remain in Eugene, he changed his mind and brought them east in February, when affordable housing became available.

Morse was determined at the outset to enjoy his respite, concentrate on his new obligations, and stay out of any controversy that might develop back on campus—especially since, as he told a Eugene colleague, "I am not there to defend my views." With the exception of one speech critical of the university administration given before an alumni group in New York, he was able to hold to this resolve for nearly six months. However, an unexpected shift in campus politics in early June instantly drew him back onto the old battlefield.

"Two-gun" Boyer (so labeled because he fancied dude-ranch vacations) had, to everyone's surprise, announced his resignation. Fearing that everything he had worked for was suddenly in peril, that if things went wrong, some incarnation of William Jasper Kerr might be visited upon the campus, Morse sprang into action. With a government stenographer at his disposal, he deluged correspondents with a massive outpouring of letters, giving advice, plotting strategy, promoting interests from three thousand miles away.

Along with Tugman, Morse argued that Boyer's successor should be a university faculty person, and that Gilbert was the perfect man for the job. Though close to Morse in educational politics and a forceful speaker, Jim Gilbert was an unprepossessing soul who made it clear that under no circumstances would he be a presidential candidate. Grudgingly, Morse took Gilbert's "no" for an answer, but kept insisting that he should reconsider. "If you are not interested in the presidency," Morse inquired, "what the hell is going to happen to us?"

Though he continued to press Gilbert to change his mind, Morse allowed as how his friends could, if they wished, put his own name forward, especially if Gilbert remained adamant. The longer Gilbert resisted, the more Morse came to believe that despite obvious barriers, he should be the one to make the run. He thus placed himself in the peculiar position of wanting to be president, being certain in his own mind that he was qualified for the job, and feeling that he had a reasonable chance of landing it, all the while stating for general consumption that (1) he was not really a candidate, and (2) he was aware that he hadn't a prayer of getting appointed. Furthermore, he told his friends that they owed it to him to act in his behalf, if only to protect his status as dean of the law school.

It is highly unlikely that the deanship was in jeopardy. But from faraway Washington, Morse began to imagine that it might be, and just thinking about such a possibility caused him to speak openly about embarking on another kind of career. If, he told Hollis, he were to lose control of the law school, he would start a legal practice in either Portland or Eugene and then "throw my hat into the political arena." While this remark—the first of its kind—may have revealed Morse's innermost ambition, the reference to politics was largely for emphasis, for, the law school aside, Morse had convinced himself that with a disciplined mustering of the troops, the presidency could be his.

The fact was, however, that Morse greatly overestimated his chances. There were those on the State Board of Higher Education, including some who admired his pluck, who were dead set against him. Opposed also were those Eugene businesspeople (the "Willamette Street crowd," as Morse referred to them) who had been named in the "Rotten Plot" speech and whose feelings for Morse ran from qualified contempt to unmitigated hatred. Even Tugman, while an enthusiastic Gilbert supporter, had serious reservations about installing Morse as president.

Knowing that he had formidable opposition, Morse relentlessly pressed his campaign. To one colleague he wrote:

> Let me whisper this in your ear. You might suggest . . . that they write to Attorney General Cummings and find out what sort of job I have done back here. I am not in a position . . . to say anything about it in Eugene. You know what my enemies would say. They think I am a damn boaster anyway and that my ego knows no bounds. However, I have had to toot my own horn for publicity reasons because . . . the moment my enemies thought I was losing power they would have taken courage and proceeded to decapitate me.

To his friend and fellow horseman Paul Washke of the Physical Education School, he suggested that the Willamette Street faction was "plenty scared. The thing to do is keep them scared by talking it up and talking it up and talking it up." In a follow-up message, he promised Washke that his "interests [would] not suffer" if the right person became president, and then instructed him to "burn this letter immediately after reading it."

As the weeks went by, Morse gradually reconciled himself to the fact that he might not be selected. He was alarmed, however, that sentiment seemed to be shifting toward hiring an unknown quantity from the outside. As each new name was submitted, he made it his business to conduct private investigations into the candidate's background. He suggested that if outsiders had to be considered, Justin Miller might be the best man for the job. His fallback candidate was Hollis, his man Friday; and when no one responded to the Miller recommendation, he tried to gather supporters behind Orlando. Barely thirty-three, Hollis had few enemies and the respect of much of the faculty, but his youth and bland disposition worked against him. In the end, Donald Erb, a onetime Eugene economics professor who had been teaching at Stanford, was chosen. Initially opposed to Erb, Morse was eventually forced to accept and even work for his appointment.

Morse's feverish attempts to orchestrate from afar were destined to cause embarrassment. A year earlier he had advised a colleague to "be very careful about what you write, even to your friends." But despite sending many letters "in strictest confidence" and requesting that others be incinerated, Morse himself was not nearly careful enough: his voluminous communications were widely circulated and invariably taken by those who received them as part of his campaign to get himself chosen, even when he was genuinely taking up the cause of some other candidate.

If Morse's relatively selfless letters were subject to misinterpretation, those in which he was on the attack were potential sources of disaster. In the latter he seemed incapable of exercising caution. To take one example, he had become irritated with Gilbert, who would neither seek the presidency nor support Morse's candidacy. In a letter to a Board of Education member, Morse felt compelled to commit his irritation to paper. "I am exceedingly fond of Jim Gilbert as a personal friend," he wrote, "but permit me to tell you in confidence that he is not a liberal. . . . Gilbert is a liberal when he is among liberals and a conservative when he is among conservatives. As a result of his flop-jack [sic] tendencies, I have learned not to take him into confidence on matters involving liberal causes."

Whether the Gilbert letter got into the wrong hands is impossible to say, but similar ones certainly did. According to the usually reliable Tugman—who came to Eugene in 1927 and would remain as managing editor of the *Register-Guard* until 1954—Morse was driven into backing Erb by a group of pro-Erb Eugenians who threatened to make his correspondence public if he refused to go along. Morse had failed to heed his own advice. Recklessness through the mails had cost him. It would do so again.

But it was not mere recklessness that had eroded Morse's position. There was about his behavior throughout the presidential quest an almost compulsive single-mindedness. He was, like Macbeth, prone to "vaulting ambition, which o'erleaps itself and falls on others," an ambition whose force is as obvious in retrospect as it was to those "others" in 1937 who might have been standing in his way. While in this instance vaulting ambition may have driven Morse imprudently to pursue the university presidency, at other times his ambitiousness, however powerful, might be checked or at least tempered by the limitations of reality. Indeed, given normal circumstances, we might expect that he would have seen the folly of his candidacy once the waters had been tested and found uninviting. That he did not suggests that circumstances were other than entirely normal.

Under certain conditions, Morse sometimes exhibited what can be called, for want of a better concept, a siege mentality. This typically occurred when he was functioning at the limits of endurance, unable to deal effectively with the manifold pressures about him. At such times, he could lose sight of the larger picture and see himself, to use his own imagery, in perpetual danger of decapitation by his enemies. By way of response, he might lash out at those involved, often failing to distinguish adequately between friend and foe. In the case of the Eugene presidential contest, the siege mentality that impelled him to entreat with and attack supporters and opponents alike was related not just to a continuous embroilment in crucial events back home, but to a simultaneous involvement in bureaucratic difficulties in Washington.

The parole survey was not so much completed as brought to a close when its WPA funding ran out. Morse would return to Oregon in late July, having been promoted to Special Assistant to the Attorney General; he would be in charge of analyzing and writing up the collected data, a task he could presumably accomplish from Eugene. But before he left Washington he had to deal with another labor-relations case, this time not as an arbitrator but as a representative of management.

Survey workers had gotten word that the project was running out of money, and in mid-June they threatened to occupy the Great Hall of the Justice Department if, as seemed likely, they were going to lose their jobs. Though sympathetic to their economic plight, Morse felt it his duty as project director to confront and neutralize those Workers' Alliance of America members who were organizing the protest. From the balcony of the Great Hall he delivered what he called "the most vigorous speech I have ever made." At a time when he was heavily pressuring associates in Eugene to back his candidacy, he told departmental workers they would be ashamed as Americans if Justice gave in to their strong-arm tactics, and he warned that they would be cleared out "in record time" if they persisted. In the face of his tongue-lashing, the workers departed, and when Morse spoke again two weeks later, reporting that the project was indeed being wound up, they listened meekly, applauded when he finished, picked up their final paychecks, and dispersed without incident. Such a forceful handling of the situation received press attention in Washington, and would be remembered by administration labor officials in the years ahead.

While in many ways Morse flourished in his leadership position in Washington, he had begun to weary of the sheer detail involved in the survey. He had also come to see that the job, because it distanced him from important concerns on the home front—thereby raising his frustration level—was perhaps more taxing than it was worth. Suddenly he yearned to be back among the Douglas firs of South Eugene, saddled up on Edgewood Bourbon, stealing a moment for relaxation. To Gilbert he wrote, "I shall be leaving the Department with a lot of recognition for having put the Survey on a sound organizational basis and if they let it flop after that, it will be no skin off my back." He informed Washke, who hardly needed to be told, "I have decided that I am crazy about horses." So crazy, in fact, that he felt moved to explain to Boyer, of all people, how much he missed his favorite pastime—"more," he reported, "than one who is not horsey can imagine." Morse was of course nothing if not horsey, and as if to emphasize this trait, he spent several extra days on the road returning from Washington, with Midge and the kids in the car, pulling a trailer containing the latest addition to his stable.

No sooner was he back in Eugene, however, than he began to feel restless. The truth is that Morse had long since outgrown his deanship; the experience in Washington only confirmed this fact. Now, neither the most tractable of campuses nor the happiest of bridle paths would be enough to make him feel satisfied with Eugene; and no one was surprised when, in December of 1937, the survey drew him east once again—making the sixth straight year he would not be with the family for Christmas.

As it turned out, the survey's editorial work required more of Morse's on-site supervision than expected. Thus, the following April he took another leave of absence and again shipped the Morse clan to Washington. In June, with the survey report apparently being put to bed, the Justice Department offered him a further twelve-month appointment, and the university expressed willingness to grant yet another leave. Morse debated the possibility, then decided against it. Because the appointment was for only one year, because it would involve switching to the wholly new area of criminal appeals, and especially because more-stimulating arbitration work awaited in the West, it seemed to Morse that, at least for the present, his future would be better secured by returning to Eugene.

Morse was officially back in residence during the 1938 autumn term, but this did not mean that he could be found on campus at any given moment. Arbitration hearings entailed frequent trips out of town—including several to San Francisco and Seattle—as did the chairmanship of the Special Commission on the Improvement of Oregon's Parole, Probation and Sentencing System. As usual, Midge and the girls were upset that Morse was gone so often—Christmas of 1938 found him once more in Washington, putting what would, it was hoped, be the finishing touches on the survey—but now students were beginning to complain as well.

Being away from campus so regularly, Morse had to fit his classes into whatever time slots he could find that did not conflict with students' schedules. This sometimes meant teaching two weeks worth of classes in daylong sessions or holding marathon meetings at night or on Saturdays. Student reaction was predictable. Late in 1938, against Morse's better judgment, Hollis distributed questionnaires to law school students to get their opinions of professors. Morse, once the school's most popular instructor, received miserable ratings. From the class of 1936: "Too often absent from classes"; "lack of concentration on job of teaching." The class of '37: "Leaves too much for the last couple of weeks of the term"; "his 'extra curricular' activities and his duties as dean don't harmonize." The class of '38: "Is so busy with other activities that he must rely too much upon his ability to 'throw the bull'"; "obvious—doesn't devote enough time to law school."

Perhaps, as the last student put it, it *was* obvious that Morse was devoting insufficient time to teaching. Obvious or not, it would in no way change his priorities. In the coming years he would spend more, not less, time away from campus as his areas of interest grew wider and more diverse. Off-campus activity had become a necessity, needed both to satisfy an appetite for meaningful work and to provide increased possibilities for recognition. And it might even be said that Eugene's "indolent" students—to borrow John Casteel's characterization—could only profit from what such real-life experience contributed to the classroom. Morse argued, moreover, that the university's reputation was enhanced when, as was frequently the case, his participation in important outside activities received widespread coverage in the press.

More salient, perhaps, is the observation of Morse's former student Judge William East: "As the years progressed, Morse's ability as a teacher did not increase as much as his ambition." On the other hand, Morse did have a point. As he sought out larger worlds to conquer, the university was always happy to bask in the glow of his celebrity. For this reason it usually tolerated, and sometimes encouraged, his ever-growing involvement in nonacademic affairs.

As if his innumerable professional and teaching obligations were not enough, Morse was, at various times during the 1930s, president of the Eugene Rotary Club, a member of the Eugene Power Board, and president of the Eugene Hunt Club, a group whose male and female posses met weekly to train members and their horses in the finer points of equestrianism. Morse's connection with horses was,

Morse in a roadster on the drive leading away from the family home at Edgewood Farm. During the 1930s, Morse was president of the Eugene Hunt Club, a group interested in the finer points of equestrianism. (University of Oregon Archives.)

as always, as constant as he could make it: not only did he participate frequently in regional shows, parades, and expositions, but, fancying himself a shrewd deal-maker, he ran something of a private trade out of his dean's office in the buying and selling of horseflesh. His stable was domiciled at Edgewood Farm, an enterprise he tried to manage in his "spare" moments. When time allowed, which was seldom, he worked long-distance with Moley to turn their now-aging judicial survey into a textbook.

Morse's life seemed simultaneously to revolve around and be consumed by his innumerable activities. The extent of his absorption in these activities may be judged by the content of his mountainous correspondence over the course of the decade. This was an era of momentous events—the Great Depression, the New Deal, the outbreak of war in Europe and Asia. Though former students report that such events might come up in the course of conversation with Morse, discussion of them almost never appeared even in the most private of Morse's letters from the 1930s; and historians today would get a meager return trying to probe these letters for material reflective of that turbulent decade.

While certainly astonishing in light of a later career that showed a sophisticated grasp of the most difficult domestic and international problems, Morse's lack of attention to the wider world of the thirties can be attributed to one factor: his immersion in those activities that extended from his professional life. One is tempted to say that such an immersion was more apparent than real, that someone of Morse's background and temperament could not help having and expressing ideas on the issues being discussed by most intellectuals of his generation. But it was precisely his temperament—always purposeful, relentlessly goal-oriented—that made the immersion in work so all-encompassing and left so little time for considering questions of more transcendent importance. If, in the Marxian sense, you are what you do, Morse was unsurpassably what he did; and, with but a few exceptions, what he did did not involve voicing thoughts on life in the larger world around him.

Morse's preoccupation with what he did could also be so great as to distract him from significant problems close to home—not only his home in Eugene, but also his parental home in Madison. Though it had been more than two years since Wib had died, most of his funeral bill was still outstanding. Jessie, who no longer had the house on Mound Street, was hurting financially, and her own health had deteriorated rapidly since her husband's death. Morse had paid part of Wib's funeral charges, but he said he could not afford to pay the remainder *and* be expected to contribute to Jessie's living expenses. He felt that his brothers and sisters should be able to do more. Under the pressure of time, he had taken to dictating the monthly letters he sent to Jessie, and had clearly lost most of the closeness he had had with her as a child.

He could even justify his dissociation when Jessie suffered a stroke in mid-December and was on the verge of dying: "I have been expecting it," he wrote to Washke, "and therefore have more or less steeled my nerves so that I can take the loss in stride. It is one of those things that a person should not brood over or permit himself to reflect on unduly, because after all it is an inevitable eventuality and I think the greatest respect that one can show for the loss of one so close to him is to take it when it comes."

If this sounds like rationalization, it probably was. Despite Jessie's critical condition, Morse felt compelled to remain in Washington, and was there when she died a few days later. He had hoped she would not emerge from her post-stroke coma, but he learned from Caryl that she had been conscious at the end and had wanted badly to see him. "That makes me feel awful," he informed Hollis, "because had I known that, I would have just gone, survey or no survey. I didn't go because I thought there wasn't anything I could do, and I am not very much good in such situations anyway. . . . I feel very badly about my not being there but it can't be helped now."

Despite the additional rationalizations, there is no reason to doubt that Morse truly did feel rueful about not being there to say good-bye to Jessie. However, as usual, the press of business would not allow for the further examination of such feelings: in the very next sentence (of a letter that went on for two more pages covering law school affairs) Morse announced: "I shall be back in Eugene not later than January 5, so go ahead and schedule extra classes through that date. . . . The only change in the winter term schedule that I made was the one for Personal Property." And if the demands of professional life at the close of 1938 could work to prevent Morse from pondering his reaction to his mother's death, there would be even less room for matters of this sort in the years just ahead—years which would be, if possible to imagine, even busier than those Morse had previously experienced.

4

Arbitrator Supreme

ON A SUMMER DAY IN 1934, a day that came to be known in the
Bay Area as "Bloody Thursday," a twelve-week dockworkers' strike on
San Francisco's Embarcadero reached a climax when two strikers
and one bystander were killed and 115 people were hospitalized—all
casualties of the day's open warfare between five thousand pickets
and a heavily armed police force. In the aftermath, 1,700 National

*As the result of violence that erupted after a twelve-week dockworkers' strike, Cal-
ifornia National Guard troops barricaded San Francisco's Embarcadero waterfront
in 1934. (Anne Rand Memorial Library of the International Longshoremen's and
Warehousemen's Union.)*

Guard troops barricaded the Embarcadero with barbed wire, posted machine-gun nests, and patrolled the streets in armored vehicles with orders to shoot to kill. The unions responded by calling a general strike that paralyzed the entire Bay Area for more than two days, before being crushed in a series of brutal raids by police and paid vigilantes.

It was into a labor scene with this tumultuous recent history that Morse entered following his well-publicized 1935 success in the Portland Ferryboatmen's case, a case that led to a growing number of arbitration assignments along the Pacific waterfront. Fortunately for Morse, tensions had eased by the mid- to late 1930s, and though the memories of 1934 remained strong and occasional corpses were still known to wash up at harbor docksides, the violence had largely given way to an interest on the part of all concerned in trying to settle differences through negotiation.

However, while the waterfront had become more peaceful than in the past, antagonisms had scarcely disappeared. For example, between January 1, 1937, and August 1, 1938, more than 350 work stoppages were recorded on the West Coast. Yet despite their large number, these interruptions were for the most part amenable to collective bargaining between the main protagonists, the CIO-affiliated International Longshoremen's and Warehousemen's Union (ILWU) and the Waterfront Employers' Association (WEA). All that was wanting was a neutral party to oversee negotiations, someone both sides could rely on to grant an honest hearing and issue fair and objective rulings. Morse proved to be, *par excellence*, the man for the job.

Whereas Morse's conservative brand of Progressivism had caused him difficulty in undergraduate politics, this ideology served him well in his role as arbitrator. He was not so much neutral as bipartisan. He remembered the lessons of Selig Perlman and Edwin Witte: he accepted as fact that the profit motive was the vital engine which drove the economy, and he rendered decisions that allowed entrepreneurs to make reasonable profits on their extensive investments. But he did not believe that profit-making in any way precluded an equitable return for the workingman. The latter, he insisted, had every right to organize in his own interest. Such a right was not only inherently justifiable; it had, whether management liked it or not, been guaranteed by the Wagner Act of 1935.

Irrespective of the Wagner Act, however, waterfront laborers had seldom been recognized as holders of economic rights. Historically, they had worked on a casual, day-to-day basis, hired in what was known as the shape-up system—or, as Morse called it, the shape-up/shakedown system: "shaping up" by reporting every morning to a company gang boss in the hope of being assigned work loading or unloading a freighter; shaken down when they had to pay that same boss a bribe for every assignment received. Through numerous arbitration awards, Morse helped to abolish this system by ensuring that the hiring hall would be institutionalized as a place where, free of the gang boss, everyone would have an equal chance to obtain work on a rotating basis.

Morse brought to the arbitration process an approach that was unique on the waterfront. While he became friendly with many of the participants, he kept all parties at a respectful distance, studiously avoiding even the appearance of cronyism. Unlike most of his predecessors, he ran his hearings strictly according to judicial procedure. Evidence was taken in chronological sequence, always with a court reporter present, and attorneys were seldom allowed to stray from the point. Sessions were extended until all relevant facts had been heard; questions of law were ruled upon immediately; awards were usually issued within seven to ten days.

Morse's decisions were normally so tightly argued and so logically derived from the terms of whatever contract was in question that even when they disliked his conclusions, disputants almost always accepted them as dispassionate and reasonable. As a result, within two years of the Ferryboatmen's decision, Morse was acknowledged as the leading arbitrator on the West Coast, a dockside Solomon in demand in every port from Puget Sound to Long Beach Harbor.

Many wondered how Dean Morse had risen to such heights so quickly. That his ideological outlook and the needs of the historical moment were a good fit was certainly the case; but given his repu-

Morse goes over the terms of a contract (with George R. Stuntz, right, represent-
ing the unions, and C. W. Deal representing the shippers) during a waterfront strike
in Puget Sound. (University of Oregon Archives.)

tation for being combative and uncompromising, he might have
been expected to be too zealous, too incendiary, to earn the trust of
hostile parties highly resistant to persuasion. The fact is that Morse's
normal fervor in dealing with issues stood him in good stead on the
waterfront. For once, he could devote himself to an endeavor in
which he had no immediate interest other than the combined one of
dispensing justice and doing a good job. He could thus direct his
enormous energy and sharpness of mind toward one overriding purpose, defending the sanctity of *the contract.* Once an agreement was
signed, he would protect it against assault from either side, defining
terms so that neither could use its language to tyrannize the other.
As an arbitrator, Morse was no less zealous than he was as an advocate, the difference being that as arbitrator his goal was the promotion not of himself, but of fairness for everyone appearing before
him.

Morse thrived on such work. Unlike a mediator or conciliator,
an arbitrator operates on the understanding that parties to a controversy have agreed beforehand that all rulings will be binding, so
that when the arbitrator makes a pronouncement it effectively has

the force of law. Morse reveled in the exercise of such power. He found interpreting labor contracts and making precedent-setting awards far more satisfying than teaching conventional criminal procedure to aspiring litigators. Once he reached a decision, he paced his office, dictating from sketchy notes to his secretary, Norma Frazee. He hovered while she typed, and refused to rest—or let her rest—until all drafts were completed and the entire opinion recorded, even if that meant working until one or two in the morning. Frazee reports that when Morse came to a conclusion on a case he could not contain himself: "He had to get it out. He'd be so excited and relieved. Dean Morse was so, so [Frazee has trouble reaching for the appropriate phrase], so full of words."

So authoritative were his words, so generally accepted were his decisions in so many significant cases, that in January 1939 Secretary of Labor Frances Perkins named Morse Pacific Coast Arbitrator of all disputes between the ILWU and the WEA. His job was to supervise arbitration in every port along the coast, making him, in the words of labor economist Charles Larrowe, "a kind of one-man longshore industry supreme court." In addition, as time allowed, Morse would be responsible for handling personally those cases arising in the still highly charged Port of San Francisco. It was Perkins's hope that through his work, Morse could prevent a recurrence of 1934.

MORSE'S FIRST IMPORTANT CHALLENGE as Pacific Coast Arbitrator arose not from a San Francisco dispute, but from a disagreement between factions in Oregon. Four months after his appointment, Morse intervened in a quarrel that had closed the Port of Portland. He forced the local arbiter to step aside, immediately reopened the port—declaring its closure by employers illegal—and speedily found the union's picketing, to which employers had been objecting, entirely legitimate and in keeping with a contract that was binding on both parties. Impressed by such decisive action, Secretary Perkins added Portland to Morse's personal portfolio.

A few weeks later came the first critical test in San Francisco.

Again there was a port closure, again the closure was the result of a lockout by employers in response to union action. But since in this instance the union involved was the Ship Clerks—a Longshoremen affiliate not covered by the ILWU-WEA contract—the case was not within Morse's normal jurisdiction. Nevertheless, both sides agreed that Dean Morse should be called in.

Although the port had been idled for eight successive days and the union was threatening to tie up the entire coast, Morse was able to "settle" the dispute at once, not by resolving outstanding differences, but merely by entering the picture. As soon as he consented to arbitrate, the port was opened, and all parties said they would resume operations as usual as long as they could be assured that Dean Morse would be the one to hear their grievances in the weeks to come. Morse had overcome a potentially dangerous situation through the sheer force of his reputation. No other arbitrator could have had such an impact.

But San Francisco was never peaceful for long, and though the lockout/closure dispute had been at least temporarily defused, barely four months later Morse's authority was put to a more difficult test. The issue was whether Longshoremen could, in order to unload a waiting vessel, be forced to cross picket lines set up by the Ship Clerks. The working agreement between the employers and San Francisco's eight waterfront unions was due to expire on October 1, 1939. All except the Ship Clerks had agreed to a sixty-day extension, pending discussions on a new contract. Claiming a breakdown in negotiations, the Ship Clerks threw a picket line around a Panama Pacific freighter on October 6. Contending that their personal safety was in danger, members of the Longshoremen's union refused to cross it.

Morse discovered that Harry Bridges, the pugnacious president of the Longshoremen, had been consulted beforehand about the plan to establish a picket line, and that officers of his San Francisco local were directly involved in setting it up, even though the pickets were from another union. Morse labeled this arrangement "collusive," ruled that no one's safety was in jeopardy, and ordered the Longshoremen to unload the vessel.

Bridges was on the spot. He had theretofore worked closely and cooperatively with Morse and was reluctant to cross swords with him; but his union had taken a stand and he did not want it to be seen as backing down under pressure. He announced that his men would not act as "strike breakers" and that the Ship Clerks' picket line would not be violated.

Morse had been handing down rulings for four years; he had issued forty-one written and numerous oral decisions, and this was the first to be defied by anyone. His authority was being challenged, and he was not about to stand for it. As soon as Bridges made his announcement, Morse, who was in San Francisco at the time, declared that he could not and would not arbitrate without the guaranteed acquiescence of all parties. Bridges's action, he said, left him no choice but to quit as Pacific Coast Arbitrator, effective immediately. He turned in his resignation and caught the next train for Eugene.

Morse's departure was the last thing wanted by *any* party, since his work had benefited everyone. On the owners' side, he had issued countless orders disallowing capricious or illegitimate union activity —especially jurisdictional strikes by competing unions, which he regarded as unfair to management—and his vigorous enforcement of contractual obligations had allowed WEA shippers to realize predictable earnings on what had theretofore been highly chancy investments. He had advanced the dockworkers' cause by consistently protecting their right to a just return for work performed (granting in one instance—to the employers' horror—holiday pay to casual laborers) and by ruling steadfastly against the WEA's regular attempts to regain control of the hiring hall. As far as the government was concerned, Morse had brought order and calm to a coastal situation that could easily have degenerated into the violent turbulence of 1934.

Since the pro-Morse sentiment was so overwhelming, and since the Longshoremen had so much to lose by Morse's withdrawal, Bridges lost no time in ordering his men back on the job. But he was too late. Morse said he would not return as arbitrator—several more cases were pending—unless he were officially reappointed by the Labor Department and unless he received absolute assurance that the ruling in question, *and all future rulings,* would be unequivocally obeyed. On President Roosevelt's instruction, Perkins dispatched John Steelman, director of the Department of Labor Conciliation Service, to Eugene to move things along. Meanwhile, since the WEA refused to enter into further negotiations with the Longshoremen until Morse was reinstated, Bridges was forced, hat in hand, to accept Morse's conditions. Only after Bridges had thus relented and his concession had been made public did Morse agree to return to San Francisco.

Morse had not only won a signal victory over one of the most powerful labor leaders in America, he had also used the crisis to solidify his position on the home front. He had attached a further condition that had to be met before he would resume arbitrating, one that had nothing to do with problems in San Francisco or anywhere else on the waterfront: he would require the "consent of his superiors" to devote further time to arbitration work. Thus, at Morse's request, Steelman spent part of his stay in Eugene extracting such consent from University of Oregon president Donald Erb.

Under the circumstances, and with heat being applied from Washington, Erb could hardly stand in the way. He had, in fact, always supported Morse in his extracurricular endeavors, but he had become disturbed of late by his dean's increasing absences—on the average, Morse was hearing a case every ten days—and by the disruption these caused in the law school. Erb wanted to know, in financial and organizational terms, exactly how Morse went about separating his professorial duties from his arbitrating work. (Rumors on campus had it that Morse was getting rich doing labor negotiating on university time.) Morse's response was a thirteen-page, single-spaced letter detailing how his affairs were arranged. He argued that he kept his professional spheres entirely apart, that his outside income was inconsequential by industry standards, and that he used his office and his secretary for arbitration business almost exclusively after hours.

Morse's contentions were only partially accurate. His customary fee—fifty dollars a day, plus expenses—might have seemed astronomical to hard-pressed campus colleagues in the depths of the

Depression, but it was significantly lower than that charged by arbiters of lesser standing. On the other hand, the delineation of spheres of activity was anything but clear. The truth was that Morse ran most of his life from his office, an office in which professional and private concerns were hopelessly entangled. Thus, in addition to dealing with deanship, teaching, and arbitration matters, Mrs. Frazee's duties included keeping tabs on the horse trade, corresponding with insurance agents, maintaining records on Edgewood Farm, and baby-sitting Nancy, Judy, and Amy while doing paperwork on Saturday mornings. If ever an office was guilty of violating categorical boundaries, that office was Morse's. Nevertheless, whether he knew better or not, Erb accepted Morse's explanation, leaving his dean at liberty to take on even more arbitration work than before.

Harry Bridges, president of the International Longshoremen's and Warehousemen's Union, was keen to have Morse stay on as arbitrator in West Coast labor disputes. (Anne Rand Memorial Library of the International Longshoremen's and Warehousemen's Union.)

BRIDGES WAS HAPPY to have Morse back on the job, and not just because Morse could be relied on to do justice by his union. Harry owed him one. Earlier in 1939, Morse had appeared as a character witness on Bridges's behalf at a deportation hearing in San Francisco. After years of harassing Bridges, federal authorities were attempting to exile him to his native Australia. Perhaps the most militantly outspoken labor leader of his day, Bridges was accused of being a communist, or a communist sympathizer, whose presence in the country constituted a clear and present danger to the United States government.

For security reasons, the deportation hearing was held at U.S. Immigration Service offices on Angel Island in San Francisco Bay. Under a subpoena from defense lawyers, Morse testified that in the forty to fifty times the union president had appeared before him, Bridges had done nothing unethical. Harry, he said, had a good reputation on the waterfront, and Morse had no reason to believe he was a communist. How important Dean Morse's observations were is difficult to tell, but coming from a person of his standing—the trial examiner was a fellow law school dean (from Harvard)—his views may well have contributed to the favorable decision Bridges ultimately received.

Morse was called upon to repeat his testimony when the government made a second attempt to get rid of Bridges in 1941. By then Morse had become fed up with what he saw as an unmitigated witch hunt. At the behest of the Bridges Defense Committee, he wrote a letter to Senator William King of Utah, which he released to the press, attacking those in the Senate who were sponsoring a bill requiring Bridges's deportation. While saying he in no way supported Bridges's political views, he contended that the movement against the Longshoremen's president was "charged with emotionalism, hysteria and much misinformation," and added that in his opinion Bridges was "more sincere in his convictions concerning democratic processes than many of his critics who seek to deport him."

Morse took considerable flak from conservative shippers for his support of Bridges. He took even more from the International Longshoreman's Association—the American Federation of Labor union whose origins predated those of the more radical ILWU—when, during this same period, he ruled against a strike it had called for Tacoma, Port Angeles, and Anacortes, Washington. The ILA had little love for Bridges or his ILWU, and even had Morse ruled in its favor, his pro-Bridges testimony would have alienated the rank and file of the Washington locals. The ILA passed a resolution declaring Morse a "Dictator," editorialized that what "he doesn't know about industry and its ethics would fill . . . a fifty volume encyclopedia," and blatantly ignored his ruling. Because the strike could be defined as a wildcat affair not governed by the contract covering Washington's ports, Morse on this occasion did not resign as arbiter. But he was not pleased at having a rebellious union thumb its nose at him.

Any public diminution of Morse's status was particularly painful at this moment, because behind the scenes he was maneuvering for a seat on the U.S. Maritime Commission and needed all the good will he could muster. The idea for getting him on the commission had originated not with Morse, but with progressive journalists on the *San Francisco Chronicle* who wanted to get behind someone from their own part of the country who would "do an honest job" as commissioner. Once under consideration, however, Morse worked hard to line up influential contacts to speak on his behalf.

Secretary of Labor Perkins informed Roosevelt that Morse was seeking the position, adding to her memo: "He is a sound person." While others wrote more elaborate recommendations, Morse never seemed to be truly in the running. He felt that part of the reason the job went to another candidate had to do with partisan politics. Trying as usual to have it both ways, he said in a letter to one of his supporters that he had "always been a registered, progressive Republican"—which meant, of course, that he had merely been a Republican, a member of Herbert Hoover's party. In light of this, Morse may have been correct in thinking that party affiliation had been enough to cost him the appointment. On the other hand, Roosevelt had been known to name the occasional Republican to federal openings—Interior Secretary Harold Ickes, for example— and in all likelihood he decided that, however useful Morse might be on the Maritime Commission, it was more important to keep him exactly where he was, maintaining order on the unpredictable Pacific waterfront.

If FDR was happy to have Morse stay on the job, those on the waterfront were desperate to have him do so. In December of 1940, ILWU and WEA negotiators reached accord on a long-term contract. So anxious were both sides to have Morse's continued involvement that in an unprecedented arrangement, they included a clause in their contract specifying him by name as their full-time, Pacific Coast arbitrator, at a staggering annual salary of between $20,000 and $25,000. Morse was flattered by such a tribute, and gave the offer serious consideration. But since Erb insisted that he would have to give up his deanship in order to take it, and since the job would not have the most secure tenure in the world—if either side declined to honor an award, he would be out—Morse refused to go beyond his old, part-time commitment. Such being the case, the ILWU delayed signing until it could at least be assured that he would be available to review, in the manner of an appellate judge, every arbitration case he did not personally decide.

Morse agreed to accept this authority, an authority which, because it was bestowed by the contractual parties themselves, was even more far-reaching than the similar power previously conferred by Perkins. After the contract was signed, *The Coast* magazine described the new appointee in terms befitting his exalted situation: "Wayne L. Morse . . . Boss of the Waterfront."

WHILE ROOSEVELT FELT SECURE in knowing that the "Boss" was keeping West Coast harbors open for business, in the autumn of 1941 he decided to utilize Morse's skills in yet another area of labor unrest. Though still ostensibly uninvolved in World War II, the United States was by late 1941 in a condition of semi-mobilization, daily increasing both its external involvement and internal preparedness. The railroads formed the critical transportation link which allowed both internal and external defense operations to function. This link was broken when in early September, roughly ninety days before the bombing of Pearl Harbor, contract talks between the railroad

workers and management broke down, and an industrywide strike
was called. Under the Railway Labor Act, Roosevelt suspended the
walkout and turned to Morse to head an emergency five-person fact-
finding team to investigate the stoppage and discover a way of avert-
ing its resumption once the suspension period ran out.

Thus Morse suddenly found himself in Chicago, holding hearings before huge audiences in Kimball Auditorium, while ILWU and
WEA attorneys waited impatiently for him to return to San Francisco to arbitrate their latest contract. It was a stiflingly hot September
in Illinois in 1941, "suffocating" in the packed auditorium. "As I look
out," Morse wrote in a letter to Hollis, ". . . all I can see are members
of the audience fanning themselves. Most everyone has his coat off,
although I am pleased to report to you that to date I have kept mine
on." Morse not only maintained proper attire, he did his best to keep
the hearings at a high level of decorum, and was not amused when a
smart-aleck reporter asked him if he would provide striptease intervals to liven up the duller periods of testimony.

Heat or no heat, Morse kept to his schedule, and at the end of six
weeks the Emergency Board, as it had come to be known, presented
a series of recommendations to the president. While the board went
some distance toward meeting the demands of the railroad brotherhoods, it did not go as far as Morse wanted, and he was not surprised
when the unions rejected the recommendations and renewed their
call for a strike. Under the pressure of a more favorable settlement
just reached by the United Mine Workers, and with concurrent
strikes threatened in the airline and telephone industries, Roosevelt
was eager to reach a compromise. He persuaded the board to reopen
its investigation to hear "new evidence," and then allowed its members to act as mediators in an attempt to head off the strike.

To carry out his mediation role, Morse, who had been back in
Eugene for less than a month, reconvened his board at the Raleigh
Hotel in Washington at the end of November. He ran the mediation
sessions nonstop for thirty-four hours, in six different rooms, with
participants catnapping on the floor as the negotiations progressed.
At times Morse relieved his own tension by pitching pennies with reporters in the hotel press room. Under his iron fist, the marathon

ended successfully on December 1, six days before the proclaimed strike deadline (and six days before America's entry into the war). But the agreement between the carriers and the unions covered only an overall wage figure; all parties had to return to Chicago to work out the thorny particulars that would go into the final contract. It was not until December 18, after a further series of twenty-four-hour-a-day meetings—during which Morse went without sleep for sixty consecutive hours—and only after he had been given arbitrator's powers over certain difficult issues, that a contract could be signed and Morse could proclaim, "It is all over! Believe it or not, that's the God's truth."

Now that it *was* all over, Morse suffered a letdown. His reaction, he told Hollis, was "entirely different from what I anticipated. I thought I would be real jubilant and ready to go out and do the town. On the contrary I find myself in a rather irritable mood and anything but ready to celebrate. That probably is due to the fact that I'm just about dead on my feet, although I won't admit that even to myself." As such logic chopping revealed, Morse was in fact totally spent. He said that he hoped Hollis had been collecting all the campus gossip for him and would "be ready to regale it to me upon my return." But when he did get back to Eugene shortly before Christmas, he was put to bed for a week with an illness, which, though diagnosed as flu, was probably complete exhaustion. This was neither the first nor the last time that Morse would become ill because of an acute case of fatigue.

Morse's paranoia quotient frequently went up when, as in this instance, he drove himself beyond endurance. The more tired he grew, the more anxious he became over what might be happening behind his back. His recently appointed secretary, Elma Doris Havemann, was given the task of protecting his stern while he was tied up in Washington and Chicago. In letter after letter, Morse admonished her to stay on the alert. "Keep the fences up," he told her, "and remember my oft repeated statement that a confidential secretary is chiefly her employer's standing alibi." Miss Havemann was especially enjoined to reveal nothing of Morse's affairs to anyone, and that included Orlando Hollis—who was, as ever, filling in as acting dean.

"Keep the fences up," Morse told his secretary Elma Doris Havemann, "and remember . . . that a confidential secretary is chiefly her employer's standing alibi." (University of Oregon Archives.)

Morse instructed her to "keep your own counsel. My absence does not call for or justify your taking up with Hollis or any other member of the staff."

Morse was particularly concerned that increased resentment might have developed because the Emergency Board was now keeping him away for weeks on end. In addition, President Roosevelt had appointed him an alternate member of the National Defense Mediation Board. He was convinced that his enemies would take advantage of his absences, and he pleaded with Miss Havemann to send him all relevant gossip: "One with your wits and diplomacy certainly ought to produce more results than you have sent me up to now.

Surely," he insisted, "the ex-administrative crowd must think that I should be fired for being off the campus."

Once America entered the war, however, Morse, tired as he might become, could relax his rear guard and let the internecine struggles of Eugene fade from consciousness. The ink was scarcely dry on the railroad pact when he was again pressed into service in Washington: having recuperated from the Emergency Board ordeal, and having finally found time to arbitrate the waterfront contract in San Francisco, he was appointed by the president to the newly formed National War Labor Board. Now he would be engaged in vital wartime work for his government. Now no one could argue that he should be fired, no matter how long he stayed away from the law school.

FOLLOWING THE TYPICALLY AMERICAN THEORY which holds that parties to be regulated should be represented among the regulators, the National War Labor Board was composed of four members drawn from labor (two CIO, two AFL), four from industry, and an additional four, including Dean Morse, acting in behalf of the general public. This twelve-person group, sitting as a super-arbitration agency, was charged with seeing to it that workers and employers pulled together to provide the materials needed to wage the war. Aside from a general understanding that for the war's duration there should be no strikes by labor and no lockouts by management, the board was largely left to establish its own policies in the pursuit of this objective.

Morse's work on the WLB was hindered at the outset by a series of West Coast complications. He moved to Washington in January 1942 (the family followed a few months later), but did not at first take official leave from Eugene. Instead, he compressed most of his quarter's instruction into less than a week in early March, teaching twelve classes in criminal law and two in legal ethics in one four-day visit to campus. Similarly, he did not relinquish his job as Pacific Coast Arbitrator—both labor and management insisted that he stay on—which meant that he had to be ready to leave for the coast whenever the situation there required his attention.

*President Franklin D. Roosevelt had
trouble deciding whether Morse's talents could be best used on the West
Coast, the East Coast, or in Washington, D.C. (Anne Rand Memorial Library of the International Longshoremen's and Warehousemen's Union.)*

Despite the fact that the WLB's docket became crowded almost
immediately and demanded Morse's full involvement, the pull of the
West Coast threatened to make it impossible for him to do his job
properly. Immediately after Pearl Harbor, Roosevelt appointed Ad-
miral E. S. Land as War Shipping Administrator to ensure the smooth
functioning of the nation's ports. Land knew of Morse's previous
work, and wanted to take him out of Washington entirely and appoint him chairman of the newly formed Pacific Coast Maritime Industry Board—to make him, in the words of the press, wartime
"czar" of the West Coast waterfront. Morse did in fact serve in this
capacity, but only on a time-available basis; and since he was intent
on staying in Washington and Roosevelt had not been keen on
Land's idea in the first place, he was allowed to resign from the Maritime Industry Board after a few months and concentrate exclusively on WLB obligations.

Curiously, Roosevelt seems to have changed his mind more than
once about where Morse might best make his contribution. After first

deciding that he needed him full-time to keep peace on the Pacific Coast, he chose to bring him to Washington once America was in the war. Then, after opposing Land's attempt to return him to his home territory, he toyed with the idea that Morse would make an excellent "Coordinator" on the *East* Coast: "This," the president stated, "is even more important than the work he is doing now." Now it was Land's turn to join Morse in disagreeing, and as a result of their combined resistance, nothing ever came of Roosevelt's East Coast suggestion.

To say that Morse was the most powerful figure on the WLB would be a gross understatement. Though the board had a chairman —William H. Davis, former head of the National Defense Mediation Board—Morse, by dint of experience, personality, intellect, and energy, took over the board's most important work. He wrote three times as many opinions as the other public members combined; he was made Compliance Officer, responsible for enforcing all board decisions; and he headed the panel which traveled around the country hearing appeals arising from cases that originated with the board's regional offices. If many mistook him for the board's official head, they might be forgiven, for it was difficult to believe otherwise. When the WLB spoke for public consumption, it typically did so in Morse's voice; and when Morse spoke to the general public, he usually had the board's majority behind him.

Morse threw himself into his WLB work—"this is a great job," he wrote Hollis—spending twelve to fifteen hours a day at it, six and sometimes seven days a week. Although he quickly came to dominate the board's proceedings, he had eleven other members to deal with, and he did not find it easy to move his colleagues in the direction of unanimity. In the interest of their supposed common objective—getting maximum effort out of the industrial sector—Morse felt that the members should ignore the board's tripartite division and act as impartial arbiters in every dispute that came before them. But he had a hard time convincing the labor and employer contingents that they had a responsibility to something over and above their traditional economic interests. The employer group, led by Roger Lapham, president of the American-Hawaiian Steamship Company (and later mayor of San Francisco), and Walter Teagle,

board chairman of Standard Oil of New Jersey, proved to be especially uncooperative at the outset.

Morse was convinced that if given the chance, employers would
use the exigencies of wartime to engage in wanton union busting.
To defend the unions against this possibility, and also to reward
them for their no-strike restraints and (he hoped) for limiting their
wage demands, Morse felt they should be granted "membership-
maintenance" clauses in their contracts with management. Membership maintenance was a euphemism for an arrangement that
closely approximated the union shop. Under such an arrangement,
if the majority of the employees at a given facility elected to establish
a union, this facility became the workplace exclusively of dues-
paying union members for the duration of their contract. Anyone
refusing to join or remain in the union once the vote was taken and
the contract signed would not be allowed to work.

The vehicle for establishing this policy was a 1942 case involving International Harvester, a giant producer of defense materials.
Morse wrote an opinion requiring International Harvester to accept
membership maintenance as part of a contract with its unions. He
naturally had the four labor members behind him, but he also had
the support of the other public members. However, the employer
quartet was adamantly opposed, and Teagle kept finding ways to
block the opinion from being issued. Having suffered Teagle's delaying tactics for several weeks, Morse decided in mid-April that if the
opinion was not released, he would, using one of his favorite tactics,
resign and issue a statement bluntly explaining why he had been
forced to quit. In the face of such a challenge, Teagle withdrew his
objections. The International Harvester decision was handed down,
and membership maintenance became government policy until the
end of the war.

The application of this policy had a profound impact on the
trade-union movement. Under membership-maintenance contracts,
unions for the first time were guaranteed security of existence, and
could function over the long term without having to spend time and
energy in relegitimizing themselves on a month-to-month basis.
Ultimately, only 20 percent of those covered by union agreements

enjoyed the benefits of membership maintenance. But this 20 percent worked in the largest and most vital manufacturing sectors,
whose mode of operation was used as a general guideline for union-
management relations throughout American industry. Organized
labor had temporarily given up the right to strike, but in return the
WLB had provided it with a system within which it could flourish.
And flourish it did, growing more than at any other time in U. S. history, before or since. Though he has never received credit for it,
Morse was instrumental in promoting this development.

Morse supported his defense of membership maintenance with
ideological as well as economic reasons. He argued that a prospering
union movement was vital to the well-being of the nation:

> Following this war we shall be faced . . . with movements
> against our form of government by internal forces of Com-
> munism and Fascism. I consider organized labor to be one
> of the great strongholds of national defense against both
> such movements. I think American employers should rec-
> ognize that it is in their selfish interests, as well as in the in-
> terests of our country as a whole, that organized labor be
> kept strong. It is a conviction of mine that the average union
> man is basically conservative and a staunch believer in our
> democratic form of government.

As to the government itself, Morse believed that its democratic
form was subject to wartime modification: the war, he contended,
constituted an ongoing emergency, and under emergency conditions
the president had virtually unlimited powers. When FDR asked
Morse's opinion about possible legislative restrictions on his authority in labor-management matters, Morse said that given the present circumstances there were none: "Congress can pass all the laws
it wants to," he insisted, "but if you decide that a certain course of action is essential as a war measure, it supersedes congressional action."

Morse also believed that by extension, when the WLB acted, it
was invested with presidential prerogative. Thus, when General Motors refused at first to abide by a WLB ruling, Morse accused the be-
hemoth corporation of standing "in defiance of the President of the

United States." He urged Roosevelt to order a federal takeover of companies that had disobeyed legitimate decisions of the board. Roosevelt complied with this request in just enough cases—the most notable one involving the Toledo, Peoria & Western Railroad—to throw a scare into corporate management. Thereafter, Morse had only to brandish the federal-takeover sword to bring most recalcitrant corporations into line.

If Morse was hard on intractable corporations, he could be equally hard on organized labor when, in his judgment, it failed to do its part. The no-strike understanding was simply that, an understanding, and it was increasingly ignored by wildcat locals as the year wore on. Morse felt that no work stoppage could be justified during wartime, but he was especially impatient with those resulting from jurisdictional disputes between the AFL and the CIO. He told union representatives that if such stoppages continued once the board had ruled on them, "drastic action" would be taken—"even," he suggested, in a statement that caused a nationwide furor, "to the applications of the laws of treason."

The wire services picked up Morse's treason remark and carried it across the country. Newspaper editorials responded immediately, most with unstinting praise. The *Memphis Commercial Appeal*: "Mr. Morse talked turkey." The *Evansville* (Indiana) *Courier-Press*: "Mr. Morse is everlastingly right." The *Knoxville Journal*: "To the sentiment expressed by Mr. Morse, a hearty amen will ring out through the whole country."

A hearty "amen" had indeed resounded throughout the country, but not in every publication. The *New York Times*, for example, said that "a costly mistake could be made by expanding the theory of treason beyond all sensible and constitutional boundaries." Naturally enough, industry board member Roger Lapham answered the *Times* with a letter supporting Morse's position. But Morse was quite prepared to argue his case himself. He informed the editor of the *Wilmington* (Delaware) *News* that "as a teacher of Constitutional Law, I would not hesitate to stand before any court in the country and defend the proposition that ... such a stoppage of work would amount to giving 'aid and comfort to the enemy.'" As far as Morse was concerned, the fact that he had never actually taught constitutional law in the classroom was beside the point. He saw himself now as teacher in a larger academy. The nation was his student body, and he had one important lesson to drive home: it was wartime, and in wartime the usual parameters of constitutional constraint do not apply. Let union leaders and industrialists alike take this lesson to heart.

There were those in both categories who refused to accept Morse's instruction on the Constitution. One was Sewell Avery, the obdurate president of Montgomery Ward & Co. On November 7, 1942, the WLB, by unanimous vote, directed Avery's company to accept a union contract containing a membership-maintenance clause. (Avery was undoubtedly unhappy that the board's employer members had voted against him, but had he been following WLB decisions, he could not have been surprised. Morse's persuasive powers had had their effect. Of the several hundred cases that had come before it, the board, to the astonishment of many, had reached unanimous opinions in more than 65 percent. In the remainder, the public members had voted roughly half of the time with labor, half with industry.) Despite the board's unanimity, Avery balked at the decision. On November 17, Montgomery Ward took out large advertisements in 850 papers saying that the WLB had no power to impose membership-maintenance requirements. The ads concluded, however, by stating that if the president, as Commander in Chief in time of war, ordered the company to comply, "we will respectfully obey." Roosevelt promptly directed Montgomery Ward to accept the WLB ruling.

But instead of conceding to the president, Avery demanded a clause in the contract stipulating that the company considered the provision "illegal and unsound" and that it was complying with the government only under duress. The board refused, though it did agree that Montgomery Ward might say it accepted the board's terms "after protest." This offer was rejected, prompting Morse to describe Avery's position as "one of the most unpatriotic . . . any citizen could take in time of war." The board issued a second order for compliance. Avery ran further advertisements, continued to drag his feet, and insisted on receiving yet another command from the White House before he would do anything.

Morse was asked to consult with the president on how to handle Avery's latest ploy. He had told a friend that he might recommend denying Montgomery Ward the use of the post office for the war's duration, thereby shutting down the mail-order house by cutting it off from its customers. He and board chairman Davis visited the White House early on a Saturday morning to find Roosevelt not yet up and about, but conducting business as usual from his bed. Morse was greatly moved by the president's manner: "It was an inspiring thing to see him so completely buoyant in light of the tremendous problems he had on his calendar for that day.... He was so informal and human about it all that we were never conscious, during our conversation with him, we were talking to probably the most powerful figure in the world."

Impressed as he was, Morse was not so awestruck that he didn't see fit to disagree with his president. Roosevelt wanted to bring Avery into his office and tell him face to face what he thought of him. Morse explained that a reactionary like Avery would get considerable mileage out of a White House appearance, and that "the best thing to do was to hit him right between the eyes with a one sentence letter." Following this advice, Roosevelt sent a second commander-in-chief message, described by Morse as "a peach," directing Montgomery Ward to comply fully with the WLB order "without further delay." Having received the directive, Avery capitulated, at least for the time being. As a result, the authority of the WLB remained intact, and Morse did not have to resort to his extreme—and clearly unconstitutional—suggestion that Montgomery Ward be deprived of access to the mails.

Although engaging in important government work could be seen during these years as contributing to the war effort, standing highest on the patriotic ladder, treated as heroes by a grateful public, were those referred to as "our boys," men and women "doing their part" by serving directly in some branch of the military. The pressure to participate in this "higher" patriotism, to be among those "in uniform," was enormous, and like so many American males under fifty, Morse attempted to enlist. He had never lost his early interest in military science, but he had allowed his ROTC second lieutenant's commission to lapse in 1929. He had tried in the late 1930s to earn a reserve captaincy in the Judge Advocate General's office, but never finding time for the required coursework, he was twice dropped from the program for failing to complete assignments. In mid-1942, he reapplied to the Judge Advocate's office for a wartime commission, but was told by the Army there were no openings. He made one final attempt toward the end of the year to obtain a commission— "particularly," he said, "if I can be assigned to duty in connection with industrial relations." He was optimistic that, given his record in the field, this request would be honored; but in March 1943 he was forced to report to Hollis, "I got a letter from the Army today blasting my hopes of getting a commission." At least for the time being, Morse's contribution would be confined to the WLB.

The board was put to a severe test in 1943 by John L. Lewis and the United Mine Workers on one side and Secretary of the Interior Harold Ickes on the other. The UMW had gone out on strike for higher wages, and the hardheaded Lewis had kept his men out even after the government took control of the mines. Morse wrote an opinion for the WLB ordering the union back to work under a contract that called for less than the pay increase requested, and which promised a quick return to management control of the mines. A 1942 decision by Morse known as the Little Steel Formula had set anti-inflationary guidelines for wages, guidelines which were supposed to last for the war's duration. "Fair" increases were to be allowed, but wage hikes would not be tied, as some labor leaders thought they should, to advances in the cost of living. If met, Lewis's demands would render the Little Steel Formula obsolete.

In Morse's view, the UMW strike had "no parallel in American history." He told the president that it constituted a "serious threat to the maintenance of Government by law and order," and he advised that Lewis should be made to accept nothing short of unconditional surrender. Ickes—who had long regarded the WLB as "unnecessarily foolish and priggish about its own authority"—felt there was room to maneuver. He was responsible for the mines while they were under federal control, and he believed that a compromise might be struck with Lewis, even if that meant continuing government operation of the mines for the foreseeable future. Assisted by his skillful under secretary, future Supreme Court justice Abe Fortas, Ickes worked to convince Roosevelt that he was right and Morse was wrong. The question became whether the WLB order was to be enforced or whether the Department of the Interior would be given leeway to negotiate.

Both sides presented their cases before the president in a confrontation on June 2, in which Fortas and Morse not only disagreed on policy, but called into question the validity and even the honesty of each other's arguments. Fortas followed up with a memorandum to FDR dated the following day. Morse came back with a letter to Roosevelt restating the WLB position and accusing Ickes of engaging in "subterfuge." When Fortas replied in ironic tones, Morse responded with heat, and the two launched into a series of attacks through the mail—the kind of written exchange that Morse was to be involved in for the rest of his life. What follow are some of the more choleric extracts.

> *FORTAS, JUNE 5:* I am not bothering the President with a copy of this comment upon your trivial letter, nor am I discussing it with the press.

> *MORSE, JUNE 7:* I think that you and the Secretary of the Interior have written a disgraceful page of American Industrial History by adopting the methods which you have followed in handling the Coal Case. . . . It was only because the War Labor Board considered your tactics to be of the trickster type that it decided to authorize me to file an answer to your memorandum with the President.

> *FORTAS, JUNE 7:* Your letter of June 7 is as intemperate as has been your entire conduct in the handling of the coal case. After reading it, no one can doubt that you are completely unsuited for any position which requires the exercise of judgment and balance. . . . If and when Secretary Ickes and I feel that we need guidance as to our responsibilities to the President or to the Government, we certainly will not consult a person who is so obviously irresponsible as yourself.

MORSE, JUNE 8: Your letter is most amusing and it displays your own weaknesses in an unmistakable manner. . . . I am particularly glad to stand on the record which I have made in defending the position of the National War Labor Board in the coal case against your "fixing" tactics.

At this point Fortas apparently saw the futility in such intercourse, and with what may or may not have been genuine sincerity, he sought to bring the exchange to a halt.

FORTAS, JUNE 8: I have not opened your letter of today and I do not propose to do so. I am sure that if I opened it, I would find that you had excoriated me, my motives, intelligence, character, and habits of life. . . . I am sure that if I read your letter, I would feel it necessary to reply and to attempt to match, if not excel your own effort.

I am sure that neither of us, try as we might, could convince the other that he is a worthless thus and so, absolutely lacking in essential decency and unworthy of the position that he holds or any other. So I propose to let the matter stand.

And there the matter might have stood, except that Fortas had shown the correspondence to Ickes, and the "Old Curmudgeon" felt moved to get in some licks of his own.

ICKES, JUNE 11: My first, as my last, reaction to the sticking out of tongue in which you have indulged is an image in my mind of a street urchin of not particularly good manners who tauntingly assures his disputant that "my dad can lick your dad." . . . I know of no circumstance in which a subordinate is justified in undertaking to deceive his superior officer, especially when his superior officer happens to be the President of the United States. . . . I note with amusement the minatory finger that you wiggle-waggle in my direction in your letter of June 7 to Mr. Fortas. Time will show whether Mr. Fortas and I "have written a disgraceful page of American industrial history." At any rate, we will not be found to have written a comic strip.

If Ickes's letter was meant to put Morse in his place, it failed to do so.

MORSE, JUNE 14: Thank you very much for your letter of June 11, 1943. It is in keeping with and supports my low esteem of you. The attempt of you and Mr. Fortas to try to convict me, without justification, of deceiving the President in order to divert attention from your gross mishandling of the Coal case should be beneath you as a Cabinet officer. ... I welcome the opportunity to tell you that I consider your conduct in the Coal case ... all the evidence I need as to your emotional instability. . . . I am perfectly aware of the fact that for one in my subordinate position to express his complete lack of respect for and confidence in men in such high positions as you and Mr. Fortas is not in accordance with Government protocol, but I could not have done less and kept faith with myself.

Morse may have kept faith with himself, but his exchange with Fortas and Ickes, which found its way into Roosevelt's hands, probably hurt him otherwise. He had grown weary of the bureaucratic bickering in which the WLB was continually engaged and would have preferred a position of more clear-cut authority, similar to that he had enjoyed as Pacific Coast Arbitrator. "I suppose," he had informed one correspondent in 1941, "that the only selfish desire I have ... is an appointment to a federal judgeship, if and when my public-service record would seem to merit it." Morse applied for just such an appointment, to the Ninth Circuit Court of Appeals, in September 1943. Roosevelt asked various aides, "What do you think of this idea?" It is not clear whether the Old Curmudgeon was one of those asked, but if he was, his reply would have been predictable. In such an event, FDR would have stood by his Interior Secretary. It is thus not surprising that when the position was ultimately filled, a non-controversial Californian was named instead of Morse.

To make matters worse, Ickes ultimately had his way on the coal case. He signed a contract with Lewis in November, granting most of the UMW demands. Then, as a final insult, the WLB, under pressure from a White House desperate to get the mines fully functioning again, approved the agreement by a vote of 11 to 1. In casting the sole dissenting vote, Morse angrily pointed out that the decision not only scuttled the Little Steel Formula, it marked the first time the board had agreed even to rule on a contract dispute while the workers involved were on strike. Whatever the merits of his argument, as 1943 drew to a close, Morse found himself painfully out of step with his WLB cohorts.

IF 1943 PROVED A DIFFICULT YEAR FOR MORSE, it was a calamitous one for Midge. In early summer, about the time Morse was having his contretemps with Ickes and Fortas, Midge was kicked by a horse and lost the use of her arm for several weeks. Later in the summer she returned to Wisconsin for her father's funeral, and while she was in Madison her forty-five-year-old brother dropped dead from a heart attack. Finally, in November, after the girls had one after the other come down with the flu—Amy with a most serious case— Midge slipped in the cramped Morse apartment and cracked the lower end of her spine on a bedroom baseboard. She spent more than a week in the hospital and a considerable period at home recuperating in bed.

The fact was that Midge had been having a hard time for several years trying, in Morse's words, to be "both father and mother to the three 'Indians.'" Morse was keenly aware that he had become an absentee parent. "How is your family?" he asked an acquaintance in mid-1942. "I haven't seen enough of mine for the past eight months to qualify as the male member of the group." Even his friends noted his lack of familial involvement. Earlier that year a Eugene colleague scolded him, commenting that Midge "certainly is a swell little dame, and you are lucky to have her stay loyal to you when you gad around so much all over the country, and only peek in for a short moment, over a week-end, once in three months!" This depiction was only slightly exaggerated. Morse mentioned to a friend that he was taking his "first real vacation" since joining the WLB by visiting the girls in August of 1942 at their summer camp in Virginia. "We leave tonight at five o'clock and arrive there late tonight. The horse show is at ten o'clock tomorrow morning and we expect to catch the afternoon bus in time to get back here for a staff meeting tomorrow night." In other words, the Morses' "vacation" would amount to little more than half a day at their daughters' camp.

Morse's absences from home predated his work with the WLB. By 1939 Midge had come to refer to herself as a "law widow," and her husband's nonpresence had become customary long before that. Morse's life was consumed by his work, whatever it might be at any given time. As he wrote to one friend in 1940, "I have worked and worked and worked and if I filled up the rest of the sheet with the word 'work,' I still would not be able to give adequate emphasis to what I've done." Such work not only took him away from home, it also left him little time to touch base with Midge while he was away. When out of town he frequently relied on others to keep her posted, even to the point of letting her know when he would be returning to Eugene. As he was completing work on the Railroad Emergency Board, he wired Hollis on law school business and, almost in passing, asked him to "call Midge. Tell her I expect to be home sometime next week." After taking the WLB job but before bringing the family to Washington, he instructed his Eugene secretary to maintain contact with home. "Keep in touch with Mrs. Morse," he told Miss Havemann, "and if there is anything you can do for her from time to time by supplying her with information be sure to do it. She apparently is very lonesome, and when you hear from me . . . it would be a good idea to just call her up and chat with her about the news."

While he was still at home with the family in Eugene, Morse on the farm tended to run at the same relentless pace as Morse in the professional world. By the early 1940s, Edgewood Farm's menagerie had expanded to include sixteen Romney sheep, fifteen Angora goats, and seven American saddle horses, along with a "yard full of chickens, number unknown." Though he employed a hired hand from time to time, and while he always found the work relaxing, Morse invariably had more to do than he could handle. The horses, in particular, required considerable attention. There were the Eugene Hunt Club sessions to supervise, and much time was spent preparing Spice of Life, the prize-winning stallion Morse had personally bred, for various state and county horse shows.

Beyond horses, Morse had another long-standing interest to which he was devoted while still in Eugene, one that occupied his mind when he was out of town and part of his time when he was at home: he loved to play poker. He often wrote to Eugene friends from other cities to ensure that their usual game would go on as scheduled upon his return. From Washington, in the midst of Emergency Board negotiations, he took the time to rib Hollis for playing cards with some other group: "I don't mind your participation in another organization . . . but I shall register a vigorous howl if you have decided to throw our august body overboard." As always, Morse enjoyed winning even more than playing—and he usually did win, if only because he remained sober while fellow players drifted into inebriation. In 1940 he gloated to a friend in California that on one such occasion, he had had "one of my big nights to the tune of $17.45."

While Morse's poker playing was in itself a minor indulgence, the general neglect of family to which it contributed was not. Although Midge was not happy about his frequent absences, she had long since accepted their necessity. She took the greatest pride in Morse's accomplishments and, like most women of her time, saw it as a matter of duty to help further her husband's career. For the girls, it was another matter.

From the perspective of middle age, Nancy, Judy, and Amy recall their father with affection, respect, and admiration. He was and is their hero. But as they reflect on their youth, it is apparent that their memories are also tinged with resentment. When they were young, they simultaneously idolized Daddy and were unhappy that they saw so little of him. When they lived in Eugene, they were ecstatic when he was around. On the farm they trailed after him like ducklings, straining to keep up with his rapid strides. They rode with him on mounts of their own through the hillside trails of South Eugene. They especially loved to go with him to the local fairs and expositions, where, when they were not helping out, they were allowed to wander on their own among the other stalls and display booths, without the supervision they usually received from Mother. Midge,

The Morse girls—Nancy, Judy, and Amy—tended to see less of their father once he joined the National War Labor Board and moved the family to Washington. (Wayne Morse Historical Park Corporation.)

meanwhile, had the responsibility of applying family discipline, occupying a role which did little to endear her to her daughters.

Even though the girls were delighted when they had their father's attention, they never felt they had it in sufficient quantities. This situation was exacerbated after the family moved to Washington, for though Morse was now in town most of the time (and not, for example, out of reach overseas, as were so many fathers during the war), he was somehow even more unavailable than he had been in Eugene. And when school vacation came, the girls were shunted off to summer camp, if only to give Midge some time to herself; indeed, to give her as much time as possible. As Morse explained in a letter to the camp director, "We are very anxious to keep the girls there an extra two weeks if you keep the camp open that long."

The summer-camp experiences of 1942 and 1943 were fraught with tension. While Amy seems not to have been a problem, Nancy, now eleven, did not want to go the first year, and Judy, three years younger, was equally reluctant the next summer. Both girls had trouble adjusting once they arrived at Camp Strawderman in Columbia Furnace, Virginia. Morse was forced to write several letters to the camp director in an attempt to sort things out. Nancy, he explained, was "a very negative child [who] suffers from a terrible inferiority. As a result, she compensates by pouting and quitting when she fails to have her own way." In a similar vein, he wrote that Judy "over compensates for a sense of inferiority that we just have not figured out. . . . rather than stand up to competition, she withdraws from a group of children, goes off by herself, and tends to live in a dream world in which she is successful."

It was Morse's opinion that the answer to most of his daughters' problems could be found in an increased application of his favorite panacea: horseback riding. He felt that success in the saddle would improve their overall self-confidence, and he enlisted the director's assistance in overcoming whatever resistance they might offer to his prescription. "I am afraid," he said, "that they may need a little urging in order to get them to ride as much as I want them to, and I shall appreciate it if you will do whatever you can to help."

As far as his parental role was concerned, Morse would continue to need all the help he could get. He understood that his absences contributed to the family's difficulties, but he also knew that such absences were not likely to diminish in the future. His work would soon make even greater demands on his time. Even before Ickes's triumph in the coal case, he had begun to lay the groundwork for extricating himself from the WLB. But he was not planning to leave the board merely to return, as Midge hoped he would, to the sedate life of a law school dean in Oregon. Such a life had long ago lost its appeal. Morse had finally found an opportunity to do what he had been thinking about doing since the mid-1930s, perhaps since the mid-1920s: he was at last throwing his hat into the political arena.

5

Running Past Rufus

JUDGE WAYNE LYMAN MORSE. As one of Morse's former students had observed as early as 1937, such a title "would sound kind of nice." Not only would "Judge Morse" have had an agreeable ring, but wearing the jurist's mantle would have bestowed upon Morse the kind of prestige he had long been seeking—a fitting role for a man whose skills were so well suited to the job and who had already made significant "legal" contributions with arbitration opinions that had been widely cited throughout the country.

At the same time, the federal courthouse would have sealed Morse in something of a safety chamber, protecting him from the maelstroms that had seized so much of his previous career. In such a setting, displaying the objectivity and brilliance of mind he had shown as an arbitrator, he would almost certainly have become a distinguished appellate judge, the sort who, under the right set of circumstances, might one day have succeeded to the U. S. Supreme Court.

But if, after a reasonable interval, a Supreme Court seat had not been forthcoming, could Morse have remained content as an appellate judge the rest of his life? Like others who start on the judicial path and later abandon it for a life of action, Morse surely would have tired of the law's built-in restraints and inherent lack of excitement. He *desired* the elevated status of a federal judge, and he had more than enough talent to fill the position. But he *needed* another kind of existence, one where confrontation, rhetorical exchange, and the public spotlight are inherent to the enterprise. He was, as Midge had always feared, bound to find politics his natural métier, and when Roosevelt failed to name him to a judgeship in 1943, he turned instinctively in that direction.

Morse had begun toward the end of 1943 to investigate the possibility of running for the U. S. Senate in the Oregon Republican primary against the incumbent Rufus Holman. He was cautious at first, noting to friends that "there is nothing more ineffective than an ex-candidate for Senate. I fear that I am too young to destroy my future usefulness in that way." When, however, he learned how much opposition there was against Holman—and how much support he could hope to count on—he made up his mind by Christmas, and announced his candidacy in January of 1944.

When Morse decided to take the political plunge, he left little to cushion the fall in the event that he failed. He simultaneously gave up his $10,000-a-year job on the War Labor Board and resigned his position at the law school. Departing the university after so long a tenure disturbed him not at all: he had de facto left years before. But there were others who were sorry to see him go. President Erb had died suddenly in 1943, and with the university suffering an apparent lack of direction, Morse's old supporters hoped he might step in and take over.

Nothing at that moment could have persuaded him to do so. Once his cherished objective, a university presidency—in Eugene or anywhere else (the University of Iowa also wanted him)—now held no interest. Facing the happy possibility of holding office in the United States Senate, he could hardly contain his excitement. "Wowie!" he exclaimed to neighbor Ruth Washke. "I have been trying to find time to write you for weeks. . . . My hat's in the ring for the Senate race. I am probably jumping from the frying pan into the fire, but I can assure you there will be plenty of sizzling and I don't expect it to be my flesh."

As someone who had never held or even run for political office, Morse might have been seen as more than presumptuous with his candidacy—a brash political novice reaching for the Senate in his very first campaign—but his eagerness to run happily coincided with an equal eagerness on the part of many Oregonians, Republicans included, to rid themselves of Holman. For them, the lubberly

Rufus C. Holman, the incumbent Republican senator in 1944. Though ridiculed in the press as "Raving Rufus," Holman commanded a large following and had never lost an election. (Oregon Historical Society, OrHi 48437.)

incumbent was at best an embarrassment. Alluded to editorially as "Rattling," "Rampant," "Raucous," "Roaring," "Raving," or "Right Honorable" Rufus, Holman had the misfortune not only of having a first name that lent itself to alliterative ridicule, but of seeing his unbending isolationism, which had won widespread support in the 1930s, carry him to the far right of Oregon politics by the mid-1940s.

In the thirties and early forties, Holman had ceaselessly preached that the United States must in no way become involved in events overseas, and on the eve of the bombing of Pearl Harbor he was still insisting that Americans should "mind our own business." And though he had come around to supporting the war effort, he had never recanted his earlier views. At a time when American troops were fighting on four continents and patriotic fervor was at its highest, Holman continued to refer disdainfully to those who had "maneuvered us into war."

Morse would be not just the candidate of forward-looking Republicans—led by E. Palmer "Ep" Hoyt, an old ally from Zorn-MacPherson days and publisher of the *Oregonian*, the state's most powerful newspaper—but also the candidate of those from both parties who wished to force Holman out of office. Chief among these were Oregon Jews, who had good reason to believe that Holman was anti-Semitic. For starters, he had been an officer in Oregon's active Ku Klux Klan movement in the 1920s. More recently, he had voted in the Senate against a liberalization of immigration laws aimed at making it easier for persecuted Europeans to come to America. Oregon's small but influential Jewish community, centered in Portland, was determined to see him defeated, and since in 1944 winning the state Republican primary in May virtually guaranteed winning the general election in November, Jews, regardless of party affiliation, decided to put their efforts behind Morse in the primary.

That Republicans controlled Oregon's statewide and national offices was no surprise; they had been doing so for years. Though it had been steadily increasing in registered voters, the Oregon Democratic party in the mid-1940s was in disarray. In 1942 only 30 percent of its eligible members voted in the primary, and in the general election of that year Democrats running for governor and for the Senate received only 22 percent of the ballots. This moldering condition had obtained for over a decade. In the 1930s, party activists had split over the issue of public power, with the entrenched conservative factions usually winning out. As a consequence, while Democrats everywhere were galvanizing behind the New Deal, reactionary party regulars in Oregon were growing more and more unpopular.

Even the trade unions, normally stalwart in their Democratic support, more often than not endorsed Republicans for statewide or national offices, all the while backing Roosevelt for the presidency. Nowhere was this more the case than in Portland's Multnomah County, Oregon's most populous. During the 1940s, Republican congressman Homer Angell continually won reelection in Multnomah County over one conservative Democrat after another, never failing to garner the endorsement of labor in the process. In 1942, for example, with the unions behind him, Angell was elected to a third term even though Democrats had by then possessed a registration majority for nearly four years. If Holman could be beaten in the 1944 primary, it was a foregone conclusion that Morse would duplicate

Angell's success by defeating whichever Democrat ran against him in the autumn.

Morse came to the forefront an unknown quantity. Aside from the Zorn-MacPherson ballot-measure contest in 1932, he had never taken even a minor part in an Oregon campaign. Politically speaking, what did he stand for? Although he had been widely quoted on labor and educational issues, he had said almost nothing about parties, programs, or larger public policies. Even many of his associates were in the dark about his positions, for, with the exception of private discussions in the early 1930s with a few of his students—Steve Kahn and Dick Neuberger, to name two—he usually kept his political opinions to himself.

Because Kahn had seen strong indications of Morse's liberal side while in law school, he grew impatient after graduation waiting for his former instructor to bring his politics into the open. He wrote Morse in 1937 asking him to be more forthcoming. But Morse was far from ready to embrace active liberalism without reservation. He saw himself, as he had in his college days, in an in-between position. He informed Kahn that "we need liaison men between the conservative forces and liberal forces, and as long as I can be of service . . . in the liaison capacity, I shall do so." Furthermore, he argued, the uncertainties of his deanship made it unwise at that moment to be overly conspicuous. "I have had to watch my step for the past three years," he said, "and as soon as I feel that I am sufficiently secure in [my] job, I can become more active in connection with certain interests that coincide with my philosophy."

What these "certain interests" might have been is not entirely clear. In keeping with his "liaison" status, Morse sometimes showed his liberal colors, and sometimes kept them camouflaged. In 1936, Gus Solomon, a Portland lawyer who in 1944 would be instrumental in raising campaign funds among Oregon Jews—and who, with Morse's assistance, would later become a federal judge—invited him to become a sponsor of the state branch of the American Civil Liberties Union. Morse declined, saying he was "interested, of course, in the liberal movement," but could not "take as active a part in the official liberal groups as some of my friends would like."

One such liberal group was the Oregon Commonwealth Federation, an alliance of left-leaning farm and labor interests. Morse eschewed membership in the Federation despite entreaties from its president, Stephenson Smith, one of his colleagues at the university. On the other hand, he did join the even more radical National Lawyers Guild in the late thirties, a rather daring act in that witch-hunting period. But he left the Guild after two years, probably because he found it too extreme for his tastes.

Like Dwight Eisenhower eight years later, Morse appeared on the scene with no definite identification with either party. Those who thought about it at all assumed him to be a Democrat, since he had worked for some years under Roosevelt in Washington. Indeed, many Democrats hoped he might in fact become their candidate. Some interviewed for this book argue to this day that Morse could have gone in either direction, that he aligned himself with Republicans only because they, and not the Democrats, had the wherewithal to finance his campaign. There is, however, no evidence to support this contention. Morse had been a lifelong Republican, and though he sought advice and support from several Democrats before making his decision to run, he never considered entering the lists under their insignia, regardless of the money they might have provided.

There were one or two individuals with whom Morse had corresponded about politics prior to 1944, and they were among the few who caught glimpses of his overall outlook. In 1938 he wrote to his former speech student, Minnesota governor-elect Harold Stassen, explaining why his loyalties had been divided over the years: "I have always retained my membership in the Republican party because it has been impossible for me to swallow a good deal of the New Deal. At the same time, I have been unable to take to bed with me Hoover Republicanism, with the result that I voted for Roosevelt in 1932 and again in 1936, and I shall vote for a Democrat again unless our party can be cut loose from the Hoover-Hamilton influence."

True to his word, Morse voted for Roosevelt in 1940—winning election bets of $38.50 in the bargain—and he described FDR's convincing victory as a "good, swift kick in the pants for Willkie business men." He believed that progressive elements, though in the minority, were important to the Republican party. Thus he could explain to Democratic activist Monroe Sweetland, "I have not been the least bit moved to change my party affiliation, although my record is perfectly clear as to where I stood in the campaigns of '32, '36, and '40."

Fortunately for Morse, his record on presidential campaigns prior to 1944 was *not* "perfectly clear." As a Republican candidate, he could not win his party's nomination without substantial backing from nonliberal interests. But since his support for Roosevelt was known only to a handful, he could appeal to conservatives reasonably secure that his earlier apostasies would go undetected. Nevertheless, Morse's work on the War Labor Board under FDR, when added to his testimony for Harry Bridges, aroused considerable suspicion, convincing many—even if they did not know he had voted for the president—that he was a sympathizer of organized labor and a covert New Dealer.

Morse went to great lengths to convince potential supporters that he stood proudly as a middle-of-the-road Republican. To refute the pro-labor charge, he pointed to his dissent in the John L. Lewis coal case, a case still fresh enough in the public mind to provide persuasive evidence. He explained that his testimony at the deportation hearings had not amounted to an endorsement of Bridges, but was simply a statement of the truth as he saw it, and in this he was backed editorially by Hoyt in the *Oregonian*, by his old confederate Bill Tugman in the *Eugene Register-Guard*, and by other editors throughout the state. The charge of being a New Dealer was more difficult to handle: it stood to reason, after all, that Roosevelt would not have continued to appoint someone to positions of power unless that person was in ideological agreement with the administration. But Morse had ammunition with which to counter this notion as well.

His one political speech prior to 1944, which was the only exception to his public silence in this area, was delivered at a 1940 Lincoln Day gathering of Republicans in Klamath Falls, a logging town in south-central Oregon. Though he would vote for Roosevelt in November, Morse, speaking in February before a rabidly partisan election-year audience—perhaps with his future candidacy already in mind—used the occasion to express his unqualified opposition to the policies of the Democrats: "The New Deal, by its program of confiscating savings through taxes and of stifling private enterprise, has in a real sense created a general financial panic. We cannot confiscate the private wealth of our country and preserve at the same time the economic opportunity of our people through individual initiative to create wealth under our profit-motive economy." Morse went on to score the administration for its "centralization" and "regimentation" and its method of "building up alphabetical pressure blocs in the interest of perpetuating the regime of the party in office." Aside from its self-serving, bureaucratic nature, the New Deal "plan" for running the country was, in Morse's opinion, devoid of logic. "You make sense out of it," he told his fellow Republicans. "I can't."

Morse in 1944 thanked his lucky stars that he had made this speech in 1940. He alluded to it almost as if he hadn't remembered giving it, calling it "the greatest godsend that has come my way in this

President Roosevelt addressing workers at Puget Sound Naval Shipyard in mid-1944. By this time Morse was running for the Senate as a member of the Republican party. (Oregon Historical Society, OrHi CN 014525.)

campaign." He told a labor leader from the East that if he did not have it to point to as a precampaign record of his beliefs, he would have "about as much chance of winning the primary election as a snowball would . . . of turning into an icicle in a blast furnace." Morse and his campaign workers exploited the speech to the fullest, referring to it time and again, whenever anyone leveled the Morse-as-New-Dealer accusation.

The Klamath Falls address also served to enhance Morse's reputation as a man expert in the understanding of foreign affairs. He had lectured his audience in that area as well, arguing that Roosevelt was correct in his internationalist outlook. "We must," he had said, "cease to be a party dominated by an outworn theory of isolationism." This perspective, which when delivered had run counter to conventional Republican wisdom, was warmly received in 1944, even by the most conservative GOP members: engrossed as they were in events occurring halfway around the world, and swept up in the anti-Axis chauvinism of the day, they had long since discarded their once-popular isolationist convictions.

Morse might need the votes of conservatives to win the primary, but to run his campaign he required money, lots of money, and for that he sought out an assortment of progressive Republicans and friendly Democrats. Among the former were Hoyt, who had been in Washington at the same time as Morse, serving as National Affairs Director in the Office of War Information (and who for a time had considered running for the Senate himself); E. B. McNaughton, president of the First National Bank of Portland; Aaron Frank of Meier & Frank, Oregon's largest department store, who had connections to Jewish financial interests; and Eddie Sammons, Morse's old defender on the State Board of Higher Education, who was soon to become president of the U. S. National Bank of Oregon.

Morse's chief Democratic connection was Jim Landye, one of his favorite students from the mid-1930s. It was Landye (pronounced Landee) who, as a young attorney just beginning his association with organized labor, had gotten Morse his first arbitration case in 1935. Since that time Landye had become the primary legal counsel to labor in Oregon, representing locals of both the AFL and CIO. Landye was one of many Portlanders who in late 1943 had encouraged Morse to run—Hoyt had done the same in Washington—and it is doubtful whether Morse would have considered making the effort without his enthusiastic support.

With all of his various contacts, it appeared that Morse would have little trouble generating funds for his campaign. Initially he insisted, as beginning politicians are apt to, that he would not spend a cent of his own money, and that unless an adequate war chest were put together *beforehand,* he would not enter the race. But, excited by the prospect of a successful contest, he retreated from this position, deciding to rely on the promise of significant sums to be raised by various parties in the immediate future. As a result, the campaign began with a badly underfinanced treasury and a hope that as momentum was established, accrued indebtedness could be taken care of on a charge-now, pay-later basis.

So inadequate was Morse's funding that he immediately had to turn—as liberal Oregon politicians would from that day forward—to sources outside the state. Of these, by far the most important was E. D. Conklin of San Francisco. Craggy, plain-spoken Ed Conklin had been Morse's court reporter in almost all of his important arbitration cases. Over the years the two had developed a close working relationship—each had frequently boosted the other for assignments—and though Conklin had only a little money of his own, his devotion to Morse was such that he was prepared to borrow on his assets and lend whatever he could raise to the Morse campaign. He sent $7,500 in early February, a huge infusion which meant, among other things, that a campaign headquarters could be opened on schedule. Morse was enormously grateful. He told Conklin that "although of course Midge would take care of it even without such protection," he was adding a codicil to his will guaranteeing repayment of the loan in the event of his death.

Though short of capital, Morse enjoyed certain advantages as he embarked on the campaign trail. To begin with, for a political neophyte he was reasonably well known by much of the electorate. In one way or another he had been in the public eye since his dispute with William Jasper Kerr more than a decade earlier. In addition to name familiarity, he had a ready-made cadre around the state composed of former students from the law school. Some of these men and women had fought alongside their dean against the Zorn-MacPherson bill; many had risen to positions of prominence in their own communities—a number had become district attorneys—so that Morse always had someone who could open precinct doors as he traveled from one locality to another.

Although he did not get exactly the men he wanted to run his campaign, for a first-time candidate Morse put together a fairly competent organization, headed by logging-company owner Ralph Moores as campaign manager and Charles Ohling, an experienced PR man, as publicity director. He was helped no end by his younger sister, Caryl, who, while her husband was in the service, came west to lend her considerable energies to the effort. To save money, Caryl shared a Portland apartment with the ever-faithful Elma Doris Havemann, who, though not wild about the job, had taken on the onerous task of managing her boss's endless stream of correspondence.

However capable its organization, the success of the Morse campaign would depend finally on the candidate's own ability to capture votes. Morse knew almost intuitively how to go about establishing effective contact between himself and his constituency. Not necessarily *person-to-person* contact, however—though he would get better at it, he never was and never would be adept at pressing flesh, patting backs, and mixing easily with voters on an individual basis. He was most effective dealing with people en masse, speaking from the lectern, expounding his views and convincing nonbelievers through the persuasiveness of his oratory.

Morse was an undeniable presence, both in his person and in his voice. He still possessed the lean, penetrating visage of his earlier days, but now he peered at his electorate from beneath eyebrows grown thick and bushy, making him seem, if possible, even more intense than he had been in the past. From a series of throat infections—and perhaps also from an excess of speech-making—his voice, once clear in tone, had taken on a gravelly quality, which gave it a ring of rugged, Western authenticity and made it an unmistakable trademark.

Morse's years as debater, instructor, and public speaker had prepared him well for a tour on the hustings. He knew how to lecture, and lecture he did, addressing his audience more as teacher than politician, providing information and analysis in a confident, nononsense style that was utterly convincing. Not given to humorous interjection, Morse tended to win converts through a masterful command of the facts and the sheer power of argument, skillfully blended with the debater's ability to hit the enemy at the weakest point. Many who came to the hall committed to his opponent left at the end of the evening spellbound, their allegiances transferred. Early in March, in what was billed as a "nonpolitical" speech, he moved a capacity meeting of the Oregon City Kiwanis Club to applaud with such vigor that he was forced to take what the press referred to as an unprecedented "curtain call." Such experiences were repeated again and again throughout the campaign.

As he warmed to his task, Morse grew increasingly outspoken in his attacks on the administration. In another Kiwanis address, this one in Albany, he went beyond his earlier delineation of the New Deal as overly regimented, suggesting in a pharmaceutic metaphor that no "matter how soothing the new deal economic syrup may be represented by the quacks who concoct it, analysis shows it is doped with the ingredients of totalitarianism." A few weeks later, New Deal "totalitarianism" became a front-page issue. Sewell Avery had again reneged on his deal with the War Labor Board. This time the government responded by seizing Montgomery Ward, and newspaper photos in late April showed soldiers carrying a resisting Avery bodily from his office. While Holman pondered whether to issue a statement, Morse, speaking once again in Klamath Falls, jumped at the opportunity. He described the seizure as a "high-handed and arbitrary use of power," one more intolerable example of "administrative tyranny."

Most of the Oregon press, which largely supported Morse, failed to point out that his attack directly contradicted what he had advocated only months earlier as a member of the WLB. This was, after all, the same Wayne Morse who had told FDR that presidential power was effectively unlimited in wartime, who had been prepared to punish the "unpatriotic" Avery by denying him access to the U. S. mails. Morse himself chose to regard his new stance not as a contradiction, but as a recasting of perspective before the demands of a less-than-liberal electorate.

In the course of requesting speech-writing assistance, he explained his situation to Steve Kahn, at that time an Army private stationed in Texas: "Steve, I need help in writing some hot speeches. My style is too heavy. . . . you can do it in a style that will attract attention and still not alienate the conservative vote. I can't win without the conservative vote and must count on my friends in the professions and labor to stay with me, knowing they can count on me to be fair and impartial in deciding the merits of any specific questions that may arise concerning their interests."

A similar point about alienating votes, this time labor's, was made in a letter to another former student, Bill Berg, who had worked for Morse on the WLB: "I must get the conservative Republican vote in the primary. I want to do this honestly and not misrepresent my stand. I can honestly oppose New Deal domestic policies, for I have done this for many years. However, in courting the conservative vote, I do not want to alienate the labor vote."

Morse had to toe dance a political tightrope, simultaneously appealing to opposing factions while trying to alleviate the concerns of both about his ideological purity. He felt he was particularly deserving of support from the national labor movement. He wrote to George Meany of the AFL (Meany had sat with him on the WLB) and the CIO's Philip Murray, asking them to solicit funds on his behalf. But given the nature of the election, he said, such funds must not carry the imprint of any particular union. As he stated to one labor leader: "I can't accept money directly from the unions as a union donation because that would be politically unwise in view of the fact that the opposition is carrying on a very effective whispering campaign charging me with being a labor stooge and what not. Then too, as a matter of principle, I don't want money directly from the union treasury because I don't want to be under obligation to unions or employers' associations."

But there were other possible ways of raising the money:

The matter of making contributions for my campaign simply calls for the use of some imagination. For instance, any
union or employers' association that seek my legal advice
on any pending labor case can get it and pay a reasonable fee
for same. I shall not hesitate to use my own money to win
this campaign if I have the money. . . . I am sure it is unnec-
essary for me to make more suggestions to you as to how
contributions can be made without placing me under any
obligations.

If Morse had imaginative suggestions to give labor leaders as to
how they could help him, he was equally ready with advice to management. On the same day that he wrote to Meany and Murray, he
sent a letter marked "VERY URGENT" to Almon Roth, an employer member of the WLB. He wanted Roth to organize a Washington
group which would send someone out to spend three or four days
with Portland employers, someone who would "tell them that I have
a record of service in labor cases which entitles me to support. Tell
them that you think I would bring to the United States Senate qual-
ifications for fearless public service that are needed there. Tell them
that my ability to analyze facts and reach decisions on the evidence,
and my strong trait of judicial independence further entitles me to
their support."

For all of his letter-writing and arm-twisting, Morse got little
help from Washington that was in any way decisive. Winning the
election would come down to his own ability to catch on with the
electorate, and in this area he was supremely confident. As he told
one correspondent: "My greatest opponent in this campaign is 'time'
and not Holman. If I can only get around the State fast enough and
appear before enough groups, I can win this campaign hands-down."
If this assessment was correct, then Morse had good reason for optimism, for he staged a whirlwind campaign across the far reaches
of Oregon the likes of which had not been seen before. The same
tirelessness he had exhibited in his previous work now went into pol-
iticking. He averaged two and a half speeches a day for thirteen consecutive weeks, with question periods often lasting hours past the

*Crowds watch Morse parading through Portland on a "Republican"
elephant. (Wayne Morse Historical Park Corporation.)*

end of his address. As he barnstormed from town to town, large
crowds unfailingly came to hear him, and from the way they responded—even when he was at his most long-winded, which was
frequently—it was clear that the more often he was able to speak, the
more votes he could add to his column.

The campaign did not, however, proceed without its share of set-
backs. To take a minor example, Gus Solomon early on set up a gathering with the press, a relaxed social affair in which, it was hoped,
Morse would score points with media people from around the state.
Score he did, but not in the way Solomon had planned. Morse sat in
on a poker game that a few reporters had started, and not only did
he become so absorbed in the playing that he ignored everyone else
in the room, but, to Solomon's chagrin, he was thoughtless enough
to win, emptying the wallets of some of the state's leading journal-

ists. Solomon feared that campaign press relations had been irreparably damaged.

Of more serious consequence was the constantly irritating shortage of money. Whatever Morse's talents might be, raising significant contributions seemed not to be among them. Those who were helping him to tap the local community had been only moderately successful, and by late spring everything that had been raised—much of it from Seattle and San Francisco businessmen—had been spent. As the campaign was heading into the home stretch, Morse was fearful that because stations were demanding payment in advance, a radio blitz scheduled for the closing days would have to be canceled. Into the breach stepped Conklin, this time with loans of $4,000 and $5,000, which, when added to an $8,000 loan from Landye, allowed the campaign to meet expenses temporarily.

Morse's task was made easier by the increasing ineptness of his opponent. The years had obviously taken their toll on Senator Holman. He could not comprehend why some Oregonians had turned against him. He expressed his bitterness in 1943 in a handwritten letter to his friend Henry Hanzen: "It certainly is discouraging to work as diligently as I have in the five years I have been in the Senate and to have accomplished as much as I have since becoming a Senator, and then to be rewarded by the efforts of some people back home to defeat me. Do any of them ever demonstrate wherein I have been incompetent, or neglectful or unpatriotic . . . ?" Insofar as he understood it, which was apparently not at all, Holman found the anti-Semitism charge particularly befuddling. "Anti-Semitic?" he said, in a wondrous remark that was quoted as far away as London. "Now why should I be anti-Semitic? My own father was an Englishman. I have relatives in England."

When Holman first learned of Morse's candidacy, he could only assume that FDR supporters and others of equally low repute were behind it: "Undoubtedly Wayne Morse—I do not know him or really anything about him—is the *New Deal* candidate. His choice . . . undoubtedly originated here [i.e., in Washington], although local strike-masters and racketeers of labor and other interested corporations and individuals are in co-operation with funds and services."

Holman hoped he could spend the period of the primary doing his "patriotic" duty in the Senate, riding above the turmoil of partisan politics, leaving it to others to carry him through the reelection process. By late April, however, it became clear that he must come home to campaign or run the risk of losing his seat by default.

Holman might have been better off following the example of certain other senators—mostly those with unassailable seats—by remaining in Washington. Being away from the Senate while critical wartime decisions were being made could only make him look bad, since he already had a reputation for senatorial absenteeism—a reputation Morse's supporters were enlarging every day. When he finally did appear before the voters, he made the mistake of giving voice to the peculiar ideas he had on his mind.

No sooner had he returned to Oregon than he accused Morse of being a dissembling New Deal carpetbagger whose objective was not to capture the election but simply to split the Republican party so that a Democrat could win in November. When no one took this observation seriously, he charged that as part of an insidious, Washington-directed plot, Henry J. Kaiser had imported into his Portland shipyards a hundred thousand workers whose sole purpose was to register Republican and vote for Morse. This accusation was so outlandish that editors around the state had a field day. One referred to Holman as "the Halitosis of Oregon Politics," while another stated that the "trouble with Holman is that, like the ants, he has misplaced the center of the universe."

It might be easy for the press to portray Holman as a rattlebrain, but there was no guarantee that such portrayals could be translated into votes for Morse. Holman had risen progressively from Multnomah County commissioner to U. S. senator, and he had never lost an election. He had a large mass of loyal followers, some of whom remembered his liberal public-power positions during the thirties. He was an incumbent with important committee assignments in Congress, and despite his innumerable gaffes, he could be counted upon to pull a sizeable vote on May 18.

Morse had also assured himself of a large bloc of voters. He had added endorsements from labor organizations to those he had received from the press, many Democrats were crossing over to vote for him in the primary, and everyone agreed that his campaign had been highly effective. Had it been effective enough? Two weeks before the election, a private poll showed him carrying Multnomah County, Holman's home territory, by nearly 5 percent. That was good news, since winning there—and in his own Lane County—would be crucial, for it was prudent to assume that Holman would do well in the more conservative outlying counties.

The only imponderable was a third candidate in the race, an isolationist Beaverton horseradish farmer by the name of Earl E. Fisher, who, if possible, stood to the right of Holman on international affairs. One of his campaign slogans was "Relocate all Japs back to Japan." Would Fisher, who had spent little money on his campaign, have a serious impact on the election?

The outcome was close. Morse went to bed on May 18 believing he had won, but because the downstate vote was still trickling in, he could not be certain. By the following morning, the result was no longer in doubt. Holman had taken twenty of Oregon's thirty-six counties, but Morse had won every significant one, including Multnomah and Lane by huge majorities. The final tally showed Morse with 70,716 votes, Holman 60,436, and Fisher 12,241. Morse was a clear-cut winner, although, having garnered less than 50 percent of the vote, he could probably thank Fisher—most of whose ballots would surely have gone to Holman had he not been in the race—for his margin of victory.

With euphoria running high in the Morse camp, little attention was paid to how important or unimportant Fisher's participation might have been. Instead, there was much self-congratulation on a campaign well run. If the campaign had in fact been well-organized, the reasons may have been largely financial: its official cost was placed at between $23,000 and $27,000 (it certainly ran much higher), nearly two and a half times the amount Holman reported spending and a huge figure for Oregon at that time. When the exultation subsided, Morse realized that because so few large contributions had been made and so much of the money had come in the form of loans, he would have to set up a special committee to deal with the debt—mostly owed to Conklin—even as a separate committee was being established to raise funds for the general election.

Some feeling was expressed that, for all its enthusiasm, the Jewish community had not come through to the degree anticipated. Even before the primary was over, the *Astorian-Budget* bluntly commented that an "audit will show that Wayne Morse has had very little Jew finance in his campaign, far less than one might expect." How an audit would show this the paper did not explain. (It did, however, observe with Christian charity that "it is no more of a crime for Jews to back their political views with their money than for others.") Whatever an audit might have demonstrated, Morse himself was of the opinion that Jewish support had been inadequate. In a note to McNaughton he pointed out that, contrary to rumors heard around the state, "the Jews contributed a very small proportion of my funds." Aaron Frank had been particularly disappointing: he had, in Morse's view, promised much, but by the end of July he had "yet to give me a dollar."

As it turned out, the problem with Frank was based on a misunderstanding that McNaughton was eventually able to clear up. Ultimately, Frank did much toward helping with the debt, and thereafter there was seldom talk of insufficient contributions on the part of Jews. Indeed, by the time both the primary and general elections were over, Morse had established a close connection with liberal Jewish financial interests, a connection that would grow even closer over the years and be of invaluable assistance for the rest of his career.

Although he tried to be philosophical about it, Morse was less than pleased that well-heeled Republicans had kept their purses zipped during the primary. As he had indicated he would, he raised a fair amount of money by giving "advisory opinions" on labor matters to an assortment of interests—ship owners, Alaskan salmon packers, small companies in Portland and Eugene, the Meat Cutters and Teamsters unions—an onerous exercise (even if he had suggested it) which he might have been spared had his treasury been more abundant. At the same time, however, because so many business leaders made contributions only *after* he had taken the primary, Morse could more easily maintain the independent status he had insisted upon. The important election was over. Those coming late to the party would discover they had less leverage with their future senator than they might otherwise have expected.

With the primary behind him, Morse sought to mollify those who felt he had gone too far in cultivating conservatives. He complained to Bill Berg that he was "at a loss to understand why so many of my liberal friends are so excited about the stand I took in the primary. I have not sold out any of my liberal principles." But he had a hard time convincing some that they had no grounds for excitement. So difficult was his tightrope act that he sometimes danced himself into ideological amphigory. To a correspondent who had argued at length that the two-party system should be changed so that one party could represent conservatives, the other liberals, he wrote, "I think that my thinking on that score simply needs a lot more thinking and our debate on the issue will have to wait until I am convinced that I am ready to really disagree with you."

For a time, at least, Morse felt it important to keep his various coalitions in place. Holman was taking his loss badly—so badly that he was considering running as an independent in the general election. To oppose Morse, the Democrats had nominated Edgar W. Smith, a wealthy, conservative wheat rancher and businessman who, ironically in light of Morse's past experience, was also a member of the State Board of Higher Education. Holman agreed with Smith's general outlook, so that if running on his own turned out to cost his party the election, that, as far as he was concerned, was perfectly acceptable. However, Holman's threat was never carried out. Eventually he was persuaded to drop out of the contest, and in the end he contented himself with a public endorsement of Smith.

But Holman wasn't Morse's only worry: there was the possibility of yet another independent candidacy. At a union convention in July, Morse publicly praised the CIO Political Action Committee, whose endorsement he was seeking but which was much hated by conservatives. In response, angry GOP leaders talked not only of setting up a Republicans-for-Smith movement, but also of finding a "partisan of unquestioned regularity" to run in the autumn, and they had a group of county chairpersons ready to stand behind them. In a closed-door meeting at the Multnomah Hotel in Portland, it took all of Morse's persuasiveness to convince members of the rebellious faction that he had been victimized by "a vicious smear campaign" and that he was sufficiently "regular" to warrant their continued backing.

Once the threat of independent spoilers was quelled, Morse could concentrate on building the widest possible support. Not only did he line up the state's leading labor groups—some of which were slow to come around because he insisted on endorsing Republican Thomas E. Dewey for president—but he also had inside influence in the *Oregon Labor Press*, a newspaper that billed itself as the "Official Organ of Organized Labor in Oregon." In "an unusual departure from our policy," editor S. Eugene Allen, a registered Republican, gave the Morse campaign free advertising space in his publication —a departure which, Allen cautioned, had to "be kept strictly in confidence."

Morse felt comfortable enough about how things were going that in early September, when the campaign would otherwise have begun to heat up, he took time out to show his beloved Spice of Life at consecutive fairs, first in Myrtle Point on the central Oregon coast, then in Eugene. Of course displays of his riding skills, while ostensibly nonpolitical, did little to detract from his popular appeal. During the primary, he had countered Holman's caricature of him as a "bureaucratic professor" by showing his fine horsemanship astride the regal Spice at the annual Pendleton Round-Up, a performance that received wide publicity and which played well with farmers and ranchers throughout the state.

For all that it mattered, Morse might just as well have spent the rest of the campaign at horse shows, expositions, and fairs. Or, more profitably, at home. As might have been expected, the campaign had only made Midge's situation more acute: instead of a law widow, she was now a political widow. Morse urged his Salt Lake City friend Joe Smith to write her. She was alone much of the time, Morse reported, "because I am just never home. We meet each other at various towns where she can be with me for some meeting. Then she has to rush back to the youngsters and I have to rush on to the next campaign

A victorious Morse soon to be sworn in as the junior senator from Oregon. (Oregon Historical Society, OrHi 93518.)

speech. Don't ask me if it is worth it, because I am in it now and I intend to see it through."

Morse never really believed that his goal wasn't worth the candle, but if he had possessed any doubts, they were dispelled by the gratifying results on election day. Not only did he trounce Smith 269,095 to 174,140, carrying every county and more precincts than any senatorial candidate in Oregon history, but he led the Republican ticket statewide and outpolled Roosevelt by more than 9 percent. The victory was greater than even the most optimistic forecasts had anticipated.

Any reservations Midge might have had vanished, or nearly vanished, in the face of her husband's great elation. She would take her pleasure in his satisfaction, even if their new life was not the one she would have chosen. As she confessed to a friend, "There are a thousand other things I would rather have him be, but I could not be selfish as I feel that he is now exactly where he belongs and that he will be supremely happy in this new work for which he is so eminently qualified. I am proud of him, but I didn't need this to make me so."

Whatever Morse's later fate would hold, he was indeed supremely happy at the moment of his triumph. He had catapulted himself
into the United States Senate in his first try for political office, and
he was uncharacteristically ready to share his festive mood with any
and all who might wish to participate. The Morses held open house
at Edgewood Farm on election night, and more than a hundred well-
wishers came by. The party lasted until the couple turned in at 4 AM.
Morse was up at dawn laying plans for his move to Washington.

6

Storming the Senate

MORSE HAD MADE IT TO THE SENATE, and although to get there he had been forced to do some fast talking to make his liberal Republicanism acceptable to both liberals and Republicans, in other ways his victory was a natural product of Oregon's unique style of politics. The state had always been conservative—which meant that it usually voted Republican—but its conservatism was of the Northwest, open-air variety, demanding little in the way of discipline, accepting new, even radical ideas when the occasion warranted. Morse's progressive, internationalist outlook, tempered by his insistence on governmental restraint, made good sense to an electorate not overly given to ideological conformity.

Even if Morse's views had been seen as inconsistent, however, the electorate, for its part, might have been described in identical terms. Oregon actually sent two new senators to Washington in 1945. While Morse was winning a normal six-year term, Guy Cordon, a right-of-center Republican, was defeating a pro–New Deal Democrat in a race to complete the tenure of the recently deceased Charles McNary. McNary, another former law school dean, had in his own right been a voice of independent Republicanism in the Senate for more than twenty years. Given that fact, perhaps the voters had *not* been so inconsistent in their selection of Cordon. Perhaps they were saying, "We're progressive enough when we have to be. Morse is our replacement for McNary, and one progressive in the Senate is as far as we are willing to go."

Whatever the voters' motivation in 1944, political independence of the Morse-McNary variety had always held a secure place in Oregon politics, where party commitment had historically been weak and party organization weaker. Democrat Oswald West, one of the state's more colorful politicians, won the governorship in 1910 in the face of a three-to-one Republican edge in registration by convincing voters that he was first and foremost a "nonpartisan progressive." In 1930, Julius Meier, Aaron Frank's department-store partner, became Oregon's first Jewish governor, running officially on an Independent ticket and soundly defeating both of the regular-party candidates. Morse might arouse suspicion as a liberal in conservative's clothing, but, as a self-styled independent, he could expect to find a receptive constituency. It is doubtful, however, that anyone knew just how fiercely independent he would turn out to be.

MORSE EMBARKED ON HIS SENATORIAL CAREER still in debt to Ed Conklin for primary expenses. He made arrangements to repay Conklin in unspecified installments (Conklin refused the offer of a second mortgage on Edgewood Farm), but the mere existence of that "god-damned deficit" made him even more determined to go his own way, unbeholden to powerful interests. He took it as given that Oregon business leaders had conspired to deprive him of funds so they could keep him under their influence. The "fat cats," he told Paul Washke, are putting "a squeeze play on me, but it will never work." Adopting what he described as a "go-to-hell attitude," he insisted that "as long as I serve on this job, I am going to serve as my own master, under obligation to no one, financial or otherwise"; "I am not going to . . . lick anyone's boots."

"To serve as my own master": the maverick's motto and Morse's watchword as he began his life as a legislator. But going the maverick's route would be difficult for any freshman member of Congress. For Morse it would be even more so.

In the first place, though the election was over, Morse's tightrope act was not. He still had the problem of reconciling opposing camps, and he would spend much of the next six years explaining to liberals and conservatives alike why he was taking positions that satisfied neither. More importantly, unlike the typical beginning senator, he was not content to play the obedient backbencher, deferring to his seniors,

Morse's creed as a freshman senator: "As long as I serve on this job, I am going to serve as my own master." (Oregon Historical Society, OrHi 90702.)

spending the usual learning period in on-the-job apprenticeship. Had he followed customary first-year rules, building visibility slowly and strategically, he might have made things easier for himself.

But it was not for Morse to take things slowly, and his cautionary resolution to himself—to keep his mouth shut for the entire first session—never had a chance of being kept. He plunged immediately into senatorial give-and-take, speaking his mind when and as he saw fit, attacking those whose positions he disagreed with. His performance was especially conspicuous not only because he was a freshman legislator going beyond the normal bounds of decorum, but also because he was a member of a party that had been in the minority for a dozen years. Indeed, Congress as a whole had been dominated by the White House throughout Roosevelt's presidency, and though the war was winding down and Republicans could hope for better things in the future, the situation as the 1945 session began was as it had been: FDR making policy, the Democratic leadership in Congress seeing that his policy was enacted into law. Congressional Republicans, many of whom had served all of their legislative lives under Roosevelt, had grown accustomed to reaching accommodation with the Democratic majority. Taking his own course, Morse saw no reason to seek accommodation with anyone of either party merely in order to get along.

As the following from an August edition of the *Washington Post* indicates, his assertiveness did not go unnoticed.

> He has bearded the formidable Senator Kenneth McKellar, President Pro Tempore of the Senate; baited the veteran Senator Tom Connally, touchy chairman of the Senate Foreign Relations Committee, and made Majority Leader Alben W. Barkley fighting mad.
>
> He has lambasted the leadership of his own Republican Party, crossed swords with Senator Robert A. Taft (R., Ohio) and ignored the counsels of Minority Leader Wallace H. White of Maine.
>
> In the few short months he has been here, freshman Senator Wayne L. Morse, Oregon Republican, has laid about him with a broadsword. . . .
>
> Morse has made more speeches in the six months he has been in the Senate than all the other freshmen put together.

Many of Morse's innumerable speeches were on topics of national importance. His maiden address on April 2 was a powerful defense of his own amendment, which the Senate accepted, establishing fair appeal procedures for the War Manpower Commission. But, as he would in the future, he logged much of his time dealing with narrower issues. It was on this level that he often laid about with broadsword, extracting cries of anguish from those within polemical striking distance.

From early June to the end of July, he staged a one-man campaign in behalf of the soft-lamb ranchers of Oregon. Because there was a glut on the market of soft lamb, a milk-fed variety that spoils rapidly, Morse wanted the Office of Price Administration to remove it from the wartime rationing list. He addressed this subject so frequently—late every afternoon, it seemed—that the press gallery tagged him "The Five O'Clock Shadow." When the OPA lifted rationing on utility-grade lamb but continued it on soft lamb, he responded by accusing OPA bureaucrats of being "cheap little politicians" whose methods were "stupid" and "asinine" and by calling for the resignation of the agency's director, Chester Bowles, one of FDR's favorites.

An unnamed Washington wag reduced the issue to verse:

Wayne Morse has lots of little lambs
That people wish to eat,
But Bureaucrats have drawn up rules
That keep them in retreat.
They want to go to meet the need
For food to feed the masses,
But cannot go 'cause silly rules
Are made by O. P. Asses.

Even a Senate member, identity unknown, was moved to try his hand:

Mary had a little lamb
And so did Wayne L. Morse
But OPA—a-lack-a-day—
Is even rationing horse!

Such attempts to lighten the dialogue were lost on many of Morse's colleagues. More than a few were vexed by his bulldog tactics, none more so than Foreign Relations Committee chairman Connally, the "touchy" Texan, who was beside himself when Morse interrupted debate on the United Nations Charter—which Morse ardently supported and had spoken eloquently for—to return to the soft-lamb issue. As Morse began discoursing on price controls,

Connally stormed from the chamber to the Senate cloakroom. There he fumed and sputtered, chewing savagely on an unlit cigar, refusing to return until told that Morse had concluded. Though Connally and others were infuriated by Morse's tactics, it must be said that such tactics produced results: the OPA soon gave way and lifted the rationing requirements for soft lamb.

Morse took other positions that irritated at least some of his brethren. In late May he blew the whistle on a quiet Senate attempt to pass a nontaxable $2,500 increase in members' expense allowances. He argued that such an increase actually constituted a raise in salary—an unconscionable raise, since the paychecks of most American workers were severely limited by the Wage Stabilization Act. Because Morse had thrown the spotlight on it, the proposed raise, seen as meritorious by many in and out of Congress, failed to pass. For the next several days, members retaliated by solemnly depositing their luncheon checks on Morse's table in the Senate dining room.

Along these same lines, Morse drew attention to what might be called the privileged status of Washington solons. In an attempt to speed up action on foreign-relief appropriations, he read the Senate restaurant menu into the *Congressional Record*—a necessary act, he said, because what was eaten on Capitol Hill was "a matter of historical interest showing how well-fed the Senators were while at the same time they delayed fulfilling their humanitarian responsibilities to the starving peoples of Europe."

Flamboyant as it was, such a maneuver was not without its point: most Europeans in 1945 were existing on between 1,000 and 1,500 calories a day, while the average American consumed nearly 3,500 in a country where obesity was beginning to be seen as a national problem—a problem highlighted by some of the wider-waisted members of Congress. Morse was aware of this invidious situation, and though not a member of the Foreign Relations Committee, he felt free to pronounce on such issues when he deemed it necessary. Indeed, almost as soon as he arrived in the Senate, he revealed a sophisticated grasp of international policy, which was surprising given his sporadic attention to that area in the past.

Although in his prepolitical days he had spoken only occasion-

ally on foreign affairs (recall his unusual 1940 Lincoln Day address),
Morse had always been an anti-isolationist (recall, earlier, his family's split with La Follette over entering World War I), and he had held
consistently to the idea that the United States must be involved in
what happens in the rest of the world. Once seated on Capitol Hill,
he quickly became known as one of the best informed and most outspoken Republican analysts of international issues.

Two INTERRELATED QUESTIONS dominated the diplomatic sphere
when Morse entered the Senate. The first involved U.S. participation
in the United Nations. The second grew out of America's apparent
monopolization of atomic energy.

Morse initially followed the lead of Senator Arthur Vandenberg
of Michigan on most foreign-policy matters. It was Vandenberg, a
rehabilitated isolationist, who persuaded dubious fellow Republicans
to get behind Roosevelt and, after Roosevelt's death in April, behind
Truman to promote ratification of the UN Charter. Morse spoke in
support of the charter in late July. Then, going beyond Vandenberg,
he introduced a resolution to place the United States under the UN-
sponsored International Court of Justice, better known as the World
Court. While the Senate voted almost unanimously to ratify the
charter, Morse's World Court resolution was sent to Connally's Foreign Relations Committee, where its fate was at best unpredictable.

Morse had become convinced that a world court, or something
very much like it, had to be established to resolve international disputes. He believed that, while the country was showing intelligence
by joining the UN, it was at the same time acting foolishly by thinking it could retain exclusive control of atomic weaponry. Though
conflicting signals were being given by various administration spokesmen, it had become clear that President Truman's foreign policy, especially as it related to the Soviet Union, was to be based upon U.S.
military superiority, and that such superiority would depend on having sole possession of the bomb.

Like other Americans, Morse was greatly relieved when the
Japanese surrendered in August of 1945, bringing World War II to a

successful conclusion. But he saw with stunning clarity that what had happened at Hiroshima and Nagasaki had ushered in a new era of unparalleled danger. He understood, as few around him did, that the United States could not monopolize the secret of atomic power forever, or even for very much longer. While Vandenberg, Connally, and Senator Scott Lucas of Illinois (all members of the new Joint Committee on Atomic Energy) were privately urging Truman not to "give away our secrets," Morse was insisting—and for a time he was the only senator to do so—that "the atomic bomb does not belong to the people of the United States but . . . to mankind."

Although Morse strenuously argued his position on the bomb in public, he used his private correspondence as a testing ground, and his most complete statement on the subject is contained in a series of letters to former university associates in Eugene. He was particularly anxious to change the thinking of his friend Paul Washke, who believed that because of its atomic preeminence, the United States could take as tough a line as it wished with the conventionally armed Soviet Union.

Morse greatly feared such an attitude, which in its extreme form could reach the kind of demagoguery being voiced by the likes of Edwin Johnson, Democratic senator from Colorado. Johnson's stance was, in Morse's opinion, frighteningly stupid: Johnson had said that America had the "opportunity" of offering its enemies a simple choice—"adopt the policy of lasting peace on the basis of justice and equality, or be burned to a crisp." Morse was determined to show Washke why, in this new day and age, such a proposition was unthinkable: "Never before in the world's history have we ever had anything analogous, or even remotely analogous, to the situation which has been created by our harnessing atomic energy. It has changed the world. It has changed the entire history of mankind and I am afraid that we, as a people enjoying the comforts of our present preferred position, do not grasp the implications of what has happened. . . . We have got to think in terms not of a few years but of a century."

In this light, from the perspective of a century, it could be seen that the Soviet Union would have its own atomic capability within a few ticks of the scientific clock, and that the United States could do nothing to prevent it. In a comparison he knew Washke would understand, Morse suggested that you "might just as well try to keep a divorce of a couple of faculty people a secret in Eugene as to keep the innermost facts of the atomic bomb secret, not only from Russia but from the scientists in other nations."

As far as Morse was concerned, the crucial moment was at hand, and the United States should not allow it to pass without making every effort to reach a lasting settlement: "I say, Paul, we will never survive as a nation if we miss this chance to internationalize atomic energy." Internationalization could be realized through an agreement—one hammered out in the UN that would be in everyone's best interest, including that of the USSR: "If she will enter into such an agreement then we have nothing to fear from Russia, nor incidentally she from us, because the police machinery that would go along with such an agreement gives us our best chances of checking outlaw nations."

Morse was advocating nothing less than the abandonment of traditional national self-interest in favor of looking at the world as one interrelated legal system. He indicated that in reality "all of our thinking about national sovereignty is passé. What we should be doing is holding an international peace conference continuously, with all of the world's problems on top of the table for solution by an organization which would correspond to the international court."

He was appalled that some not only failed to see the need for such an organization, but were actively moving against it: "The powerful Military and Naval forces of this country," he wrote, had given "no indication that they are desirous of working [things] out." He was even more appalled that certain military leaders believed that war with the Soviet Union within the next fifteen years was a foregone conclusion.

In a letter to chemistry professor Adolph Kunz and his wife, Morse made clear just how far he was prepared to go with the UN Charter: "Right now," he said, "we have the greatest chance that any nation in all history has had to direct the United Nations Organization into a world government. It requires . . . that the general assembly must be allowed to evolve into a legislative branch of a world government, with the World Court empowered with jurisdiction on a compulsory basis."

The World Court, equipped with decision-making authority, stood as the linchpin in Morse's system. Such a court would serve to provide the "police machinery" he had mentioned earlier. Morse believed that, at least for the interim, during the transition toward a world government, there would be no need to establish a traditional police agency, one that relied on coercive power to enforce acceptance of preexisting laws and agreements. While he did not say so, it is clear that he envisioned a world legal order that followed the methods used in labor arbitration, where disputants agree beforehand to relinquish their "sovereignty" and be bound by decisions of a neutral third party. If a commitment to binding arbitration could bring an end to savage warfare on the Pacific waterfront, could it not, in the common need for survival, work equally well in resolving disputes among nations?

Given the political realities of the day, there was little reason to believe that Morse's maverick vision, for all its creativeness, could be made to work. While the General Assembly might evolve into something of an international legislature, standing apart from it, and designed so that the trickiest international problems would be placed on *its* agenda, was the UN Security Council, where, at the insistence of the United States, each of the Big Powers had been given the right to veto decisions of the majority. It was apparently Morse's hope that—again, over the long run—the World Court might transcend *both* branches of the UN in certain critical cases, that nations would agree to place their most incendiary disagreements before it, thereby substituting the administration of justice for the exercise of power in settling disputes. Morse knew that for any chance of realizing this hope, American participation in the court would be vital.

There was no strong opposition to his World Court resolution; neither was there organized support. If it were to get through the Senate, Morse would have to develop backing in the right places. In something of a coup, in November 1945 he lined up a bipartisan group of senators—including his usual enemy, "Mr. Republican" Robert Taft—to join him in adding a World Court requirement to a

UN implementation bill. The fact that the conservative Taft was among its cosponsors made certain that the proposal would receive attention from the Republican side of the aisle.

Despite initial resistance from Vandenberg and Democratic majority leader Alben Barkley, Morse was able to schedule floor debate on his resolution by mid-1946. As written, the legislation left the decision whether to participate in the World Court to the president (Truman had earlier in 1946 said he would participate), but once that decision was made, submission of *all* relevant disputes to the court's jurisdiction would thereafter be compulsory.

Morse encountered no difficulty in the Senate until Connally rose to offer a six-word amendment. The resolution contained a clause stipulating that the court could not decide matters falling "within the domestic jurisdiction of the United States." To this clause, Connally added the words "as determined by the United States." Despite Morse's heated opposition, the Connally "reservation" carried: the Senate was willing to swallow the compulsory requirement, but it wanted no outside authority telling the United States what did or did not constitute a domestic dispute. Once that question was out of the way, however, the resolution passed 60 to 2.

Even with the loophole provided by the Connally reservation, passage of a World Court resolution, having the binding effect of an international treaty, was a significant event, and one that probably would not have occurred without Morse's persistence. And though the realization of world government might still seem remote, Morse was satisfied that an important step toward the preservation of international order had been taken. In his handling of the resolution, he had shown once again that he was someone to be reckoned with —a member of Congress who knew how to get what he wanted, whether in the realm of international law or in dealing with the price of four-legged provender.

As events would soon indicate, however, the court, despite being a useful instrument from time to time, would never live up to Morse's expectations. Regardless of the compulsory requirement, it would be utilized or ignored by the major powers as it suited their interests. And it would play no role whatever in universalizing the control of nuclear power. Indeed, despite a belated display of moderation in mid-1946, the Truman administration stuck largely to its dependence on what came to be known as "atomic diplomacy," a strategy that generated a nuclear-arms race that would last another forty-four years. This strategy also contributed to the eruption of the Cold War with the Soviet Union—a war that would turn many progressives, Morse included, into ideological foot soldiers.

Although Morse shifted his thinking over the next few years, becoming a supporter of bigger and bigger military expenditures, his maverick starting point allowed him, at least temporarily, to reach an analytical clarity that seems astonishing even today. Moreover, he never entirely lost his belief that the UN was an important institution, one which law-abiding nations should work through whenever possible. At a later time, at what might be called his personal Cold War coda, he would return to the conviction that the UN was humanity's best hope—its *only* hope—for controlling armaments and preserving peace through the application of international law.

EVEN BEFORE THE WORLD COURT VOTE, Morse had begun to receive increased national attention. For its issue of December 25, 1945, the editors of *Look* magazine polled eleven American "leaders" on their predictions for the future. Morse was the only senator selected, appearing with such luminaries as his recent *bête noire*, Chester Bowles; Donald Douglas, president of Douglas Aircraft; Philip Murray, CIO president; and Colby Chester, chairman of the board of General Foods. In 1946 he gained even greater renown in a direct confrontation with President Truman.

Another crippling railroad strike had hit the country in the spring of 1946. On May 25, Truman addressed a joint session of Congress requesting, in light of the continuing postwar "state of emergency," authority to draft striking workers directly into the army. In mid-speech, Truman was interrupted and handed a piece of paper by the Senate secretary. He looked over the message, paused dramatically, then announced to a hushed audience that the strike had been settled moments earlier at the White House. "That," said Morse, after the cheers had died away and Truman had departed the chamber, "was one of the cheapest exhibitions of ham acting I have ever seen."

Morse was not necessarily objecting to the content of Truman's position; after the railroads had been functioning for four and a half years under what amounted to presidential fiat, a request from the Commander in Chief for the power to draft railroad workers so they could be ordered back on the job did not seem all that extraordinary. What was bothering him, said Morse, was that Truman and his aides had orchestrated the whole event, that even before coming to the Hill, Truman had known of the railroad brotherhoods' readiness to settle. Union officials, Morse declared, had been set to sign an agreement, but had been kept cooling their heels in a White House waiting room—all so that Truman could indulge in an extravagant bit of showmanship. The administration indignantly denied the charge, and produced a chronology of events "demonstrating" that Truman had acted in good faith.

But the question of who was right or wrong was lost in the furor caused by Morse's remark. How much support Truman would have had for what might have been an unconstitutional proposal was unclear. But it was extremely clear that Morse had gone beyond the bounds of decorum. No one in those more delicate days would support the use of such demeaning language when applied to the president, and Morse took considerable heat from around the country for his outburst. Colleagues tried to pressure him into striking his words from the *Congressional Record*. But, having published his own chronology of events, he adamantly refused.

Although the "ham acting" accusation temporarily soured relations between Morse and the president, the affair ultimately had a positive ending. On March 12 of the following year, Morse stated for the record that he regretted having been "unkind in the language I used in expressing my disapproval." Truman read this as an apology, and three days later he sent a handwritten note from the Flying White House stating that he appreciated "what you said very much. I'll admit that my feelings were somewhat ruffled by your comment on the Rail Strike Speech. I've always been an admirer of yours.

Honest men may differ but they may still be friends." With the disagreement behind them, Truman and Morse grew increasingly close
over the next few years.

Part of the reason for Truman's renewed friendliness was that
Morse was turning out to be a vital supporter of the president's legislation. He backed Truman's program even though he had been
quoted as saying that "the man in the White House is head of one
of the most corrupt political machines in this country," and that as a
Republican he found much to dislike about Truman's presidency.
The problem was that he found even more to dislike in what his own
party had to offer. When in January 1946 congressional Republicans
followed Taft in opposing an increase of ten cents in the minimum
wage, Morse, in a statement quoted by the *New York Times*, declared
that his party had "demonstrated in a frightening manner why the
common men and women of America cannot look to the reactionary republicans . . . to protect and improve their standard of living."
The following April, the Republican National Committee held a
strategy meeting in Washington's Statler Hotel. Morse issued a press
release describing the first session as "a grand flop." "We listened," he
said, "to the same old clichés and reactionary nostrums *ad nauseum*
which have produced Republican defeats since 1932."

Meanwhile, Morse was having problems with the Democrats as
well. Over his objection, Senate Democratic leaders had sent emergency strike legislation proposed by the administration to the Interstate Commerce Committee; more logically, it should have gone to
the Labor and Public Welfare Committee, of which he was a member. Adopting one of his oft-used tactics, Morse resigned from the
Labor Committee in protest, saying he had "better things to do with
my time than spend it on a catch-as-catch-can committee which is
evaded whenever it suits Senate strategists to do so." A short time
later, however, he rescinded his resignation when fellow senators,
Democrats especially, prevailed upon him to reconsider.

Though Morse was characteristically unhappy with both parties,
his heaviest artillery was saved for Republican reactionaries. Yet he
found himself supporting just such reactionaries in the autumn of
1946. Party elders asked him to campaign for Senate hopefuls run-

ning in the West, but so effective was he that the Republican National Committee decided to send him to fifteen different states, in support of all manner of candidates, from mainstream moderates to right-wing conservatives.

Morse justified such indiscriminate participation on the ground that as an elected Republican legislator, he had to answer when his party called. But Northwest progressives were outraged when he decided to speak in Washington state in behalf of the reactionary Harry Cain, a renegade Democrat who was trying to unseat the incumbent, liberal New Dealer Hugh Mitchell. He told a Tacoma labor rally that "Harry Cain will be a great asset in the Senate in support of those things which we middle-of-the-road liberals in the Republican Party must fight for."

Morse drew even more heat when he appeared for Henry Dworshak, a Republican senatorial aspirant from Idaho who stood, if possible, somewhere to the right of Cain. Dick Neuberger, who had again become active in Democratic politics, and many others wrote Morse to protest. In speeches delivered in Boise and Portland, Idaho's senior senator, Democrat Glen Taylor, accused Morse of "prostituting" his liberal standing. Taylor proclaimed that under similar circumstances, he would not even consider campaigning for reactionaries from his party, and that it was inexcusable for Morse to endorse men like Dworshak.

Morse defended himself in typical fashion. He advised Paul and Ruth Washke not to "worry about . . . the frothy attacks on me that are being circulated . . . by guys like Neuberger. I'm proud of the part I played in the 1946 campaign, and before 1950 comes around the ones who are criticizing me . . . are going to recognize that I have an understanding of political ethics and moral principles that entitle [sic] me to their support." Despite its evocation of ethics and principles, Morse's counterattack was less than convincing.

It is apparent that, once again, he felt the need to have it both ways: he wished to retain his liberal standing while simultaneously strengthening his credentials with establishment Republicans, especially those who made committee assignments in the Senate. He informed Neuberger that "in each instance, I campaigned for men who, I am satisfied, will prove to be very able Senators." At the same time, he told C. C. Chapman, conservative editor of the *Oregon Voter*, that "some of my old guard Republican critics . . . have finally become wise to the fact that my determination to bring the Republican Party back into power is even more deep-seated than theirs because I am really doing something about it, whereas, they just sit and spit."

Morse had certainly not been content just to sit and spit. In subjecting himself to party discipline by supporting reactionary candidates, he acted both in and out of character as a maverick. It was certainly in keeping with maverickness that he should support whomever he wanted, whether political progressives liked it or not. But it weakened his masterless status to do so at the behest of a Republican hierarchy which routinely exacted such fealty from its rank-and-file members. Morse, whose membership had been anything but rank-and-file, had temporarily given up his prized independence. But only temporarily. All references to supporting questionable candidates because of "political ethics and moral principles" would be dropped as soon as the next session of Congress got under way. Both Cain and Dworshak won their contests, and Cain in particular showed immediately that he was by no interpretation a "middle-of-the-road liberal," or any kind of liberal. Morse had to admit that he was "very much disappointed" in Cain; but he suggested to Jim Landye, apparently by way of minimizing his mistake, that "for the most part this job is a chain of disappointments." Thereafter he would be more selective about those he supported, and except for the special case of endorsing fellow Oregonian Guy Cordon's reelection in 1948—for which he was again attacked by Neuberger and "guys like" him—he would never again associate himself with reactionary candidates.

It was ironic that Glen Taylor should have been one of Morse's chief critics in 1946, for he would be one of his chief allies in 1947 in the battle over labor reform. The demand for such reform was the result of the seemingly endless series of strikes that had plagued the nation in the postwar era, at a time when the country was anxious to "get back to normal." Because of the strikes and the anti-union attacks they generated in an unsympathetic American press, the public turned angrily against the trade-union movement and its apparent benefactor, the Democratic party.

In the first six months of 1946 alone, in what the Bureau of Labor Statistics called "the most concentrated period of labor-management strife in the country's history," nearly three million workers walked off their jobs. Virtually every industry was hit: electric power, steel, the railroads, meatpacking, municipal services, public utilities, transportation, communications. The soft-coal miners went out on April 1, causing a nationwide brownout. They were followed by the railroad engineers and trainmen, resulting in what one authority has described as "an almost complete shutdown of the nation's commerce." But of all the walkouts, the most unpopular with a postwar public ravenously hungry for new vehicles was the 113-day strike against General Motors by the United Automobile Workers.

Pressure to curb labor by "improving" the 1935 Wagner Act had become overwhelming. The GM strike ran through the autumn elections of 1946 and had much to do with Republicans' gaining control of Congress for the first time in fourteen years. It was certain that, once in control, they would produce some kind of legislation affecting the union movement. The Senate Labor and Public Welfare Committee, which was responsible for working up such legislation in the upper house, was chaired by Taft. Having long since dropped his resignation threat, Morse was still a member of that committee.

Bowing to popular sentiment, President Truman was prepared to accept a modicum of labor reform. But he was against scrapping the protections of the Wagner Act, and though it might prove politically dangerous, he promised to veto any effort from Taft and his followers in that direction. Truman's chief lieutenants in the Senate were expected to show the way in resisting Taft wherever possible. However, as the editors of *Newsweek* were surprised to discover, it was not Democratic minority leader Alben Barkley, or even minority whip Scott Lucas, "but a maverick Republican, Sen. Wayne Morse of Oregon . . . leading the fight to take Mr. Truman off the political hotspot."

Morse could exercise such leadership not just because of his forcefulness and acknowledged expertise in labor matters, but because he was joined in his efforts on the Labor Committee by Republicans George Aiken of Vermont and Irving Ives of New York and by the four liberal Democratic members. Taft complained that this coalition had snatched the committee from his hands, and his observation was only slightly exaggerated. Though Morse's group accepted the fact that because of public pressure some kind of bill would have to be reported out of their committee—one would surely emerge from the corresponding committee chaired by conservative Fred Hartley in the House—they were able, through a series of 7 to 6 votes, to save the unions from the more draconian of Taft's reforms. The result was a bill which contained many restrictions on union activity, but which did not go nearly as far as Taft would have liked.

When the Taft-Hartley bill reached the Senate floor, it was divided into four parts. Morse moved to convert each of these into separate bills, which would be voted up or down by the Senate. The strategy was to have Truman receive several distinct pieces of legislation, allowing him to veto the worst one or two while appeasing reformers by signing the others into law. Taft, however, insisted on one omnibus bill, and by a vote of 59 to 35, the Senate saw it his way.

Having won on the omnibus approach, Taft then moved to restore most of what he had lost to Morse in committee. He offered four amendments, each of which tightened federal controls on labor. Morse was able to beat back one, which would have outlawed industrywide collective bargaining, but Taft persuaded the Senate to support him on the other three. The result, as far as labor was concerned, was catastrophic. Among other things, the bill:

> permitted injunctions against secondary boycotts and jurisdictional strikes;
>
> required union leaders to take an oath that they were not communists;
>
> outlawed *closed* shops, in which only union members could be hired; permitted states to outlaw *union* shops, those requiring workers to join a union if a majority of their fellow workers so voted;

allowed the government to get eighty-day injunctions against "national paralysis" strikes, as in a transportation or coal-mine tie-up;

permitted injunctions making unlawful any union activity deemed harmful to "national health or safety";

forbade federal employees from striking.

After passing through a Senate-House conference committee, the bill was sent to Truman, who, as anticipated, exercised his veto. The House easily overrode the veto, 331 to 83, and there seemed to be enough votes to allow the Senate to follow suit. On the other hand, the bill had originally passed the Senate 68 to 24, so a change of mind by just a handful of members could mean that the necessary two-thirds to override would not be available in that chamber. The vote was to take place late on Friday, June 20, or early Saturday. But Morse felt that his side would have a better chance if the decision could be postponed until the following Monday, and he threatened to organize a filibuster if Taft refused to go along. Taft refused. Morse filibustered.

Leading off for Morse's team was his former critic, Glen Taylor, a onetime roadshow performer still referred to in the press (without apologies to Gene Autry) as "The Singing Cowboy." Taylor began speaking on Friday just before 5 PM. Morse took over at 6:25 the next morning, spelling Harley Kilgore of West Virginia, who had relieved Taylor after the latter had talked for over eight hours. Morse spoke for nine hours and fifty-nine minutes, the Senate's longest uninterrupted oration since Huey Long had filibustered for more than fifteen hours in 1935. He stopped only because Taft had finally given in, not just to the Monday vote, but also to allowing three hours of debate, evenly divided between proponents and opponents, before the vote was taken.

For all of his hard work, Morse was to be disappointed at the outcome. When the votes were counted, they added up to the identical number by which the bill had passed in the first place. Not one senator had been moved to switch. The Taft-Hartley bill was now the Taft-Hartley Act. Morse had fought the good fight, but he had lost, and with his defeat the enormous wartime gains by organized labor

—many of which Morse had promoted through his War Labor
Board rulings—began to be eroded in a process of union bashing
that has continued to this day.

The battle between Morse and Taft was of epic proportions, and
it drew national attention for a period of weeks; the filibuster captured headlines everywhere. Along with a packed Senate gallery, reporters covering it were astounded that during his nearly ten hours
of continuous talking, Morse never deviated from his subject. Taylor, in time-honored Senate fashion, had run the oratorical gamut—
from a discussion of his impoverished youth, when he had been
forced "to eat jack rabbit," to an attack on the present-day evils of
Wall Street.

Though Morse had come out of the Taft-Hartley battle with increased prominence, he had not escaped injury. The use of the filibuster confused many. Almost from his first day in the Senate, Morse
had been an outspoken critic of filibustering, and he had taken the
lead in beating down the filibuster launched by Southern Democrats
against the Fair Employment Practices Commission in January 1946.
He argued that his Taft-Hartley talkathon was not comparable to
that of the Dixiecrats because, unlike them, he was not trying to
thwart the wishes of the Senate—he merely wanted to defer a decision for a couple of days, "until the democratic will of the people
could manifest itself." To many, however, perhaps to most, a filibuster
was a filibuster, a deplorable device which, whatever its ultimate purpose, brought legislative action to a maddening halt.

Because he fought Taft-Hartley from a defensive position, conceding much before moving to the attack, Morse was pictured by
some on the left—those who felt that no concessions whatever
should have been made—as having sold out the cause of labor.
To them, his preservation of industrywide collective bargaining
seemed but a small saving when measured against the afflictions they
had suffered at the hands of their enemies. From this perspective,
Morse, however valiantly he had struggled, could be seen as weak
and ineffective.

At the same time, conservative Republicans in Oregon could say
that in the Taft-Hartley contest, Morse had finally revealed his true

colors, that he was, as they had always suspected, a mouthpiece for labor, a clandestine New Dealer masquerading as one of their own. They saw him not as weak and ineffective, but as a demonic force wreaking havoc within the ranks of their party.

Morse was thus caught in an impossible situation. Although he had enhanced his nationwide reputation and earned increased respect in the Senate, he would have to redouble his efforts back home to keep his coalition of diverse activists from coming apart.

But for those who were not activists, i.e., for the general Oregon public, the Taft-Hartley episode merely confirmed what they already knew: that their hero was a hard-fighting maverick who stood up for his beliefs. They seemed to care little that he was inconsistent or that he voted with his own party only 30 percent of the time—wasn't that, after all, how independent members of Congress were supposed to act? Furthermore, as illustrated by an event that occurred just before Taft-Hartley, they knew that Morse was prepared to defend himself with more than just his vote.

The Senate had been debating the confirmation of David E. Lilienthal as head of the Atomic Energy Commission—debating it heatedly, since the appointment was being vehemently resisted by reactionaries who felt that former Tennessee Valley Authority director Lilienthal was too radical to hold *any* government post, let alone one so sensitive. At the end of a grueling night session in early April, acting Republican leader Kenneth Wherry of Nebraska, who opposed Lilienthal, pushed through an adjournment motion while Morse, who strongly favored the nominee, was trying to get the floor. Morse had no great love for Wherry to begin with—Wherry had contributed to Rufus Holman's campaign in 1944—and he protested angrily as he and the Midwesterner were leaving the chamber. Wherry, a licensed embalmer known in the cloakroom as "The Merry Mortician," responded with a few choice words of his own, and then, to the amazement of those witnessing the scene, he collared Morse and attempted to yank him through the door into the hallway. Morse broke free, slammed down an armful of documents he had been carrying, and, remembering Wib's advice about getting in the first punch, directed a haymaker at Wherry's jaw. Whether it would have found its mark is unclear, since colleagues and the sergeant-at-arms separated the two men before blows could be landed. The next day Morse released a statement which, though it made light of the altercation, did nothing to diminish his home-front image as a two-fisted scrapper who would hold his ground against all comers. "We Westerners," he stated, "can't be pushed around very easily, even by a plainsman from Nebraska."

ALTHOUGH MORSE HAD LOST ON TAFT-HARTLEY in the open arena, behind the scenes, in a totally different area, he was in the process of making a little-known but critical contribution to governmental practice, one that would last nearly a generation. Along with Labor, his other important committee assignment was Armed Services, and this committee had to deal with a complicated problem that had arisen after the war: how to dispense the millions of acres of acquired property no longer needed by the military.

The most valuable acreage was coveted by state and local authorities, by a variety of organizations, and, in rare cases, by individuals. Title to these parcels was typically transferred from the federal government to designated recipients, without charge, through private bills introduced by members of Congress whose districts would benefit from the transaction. When such bills came before the Senate, they were scrutinized by Armed Services, and this gave Morse an opportunity to study them.

Study them he did, and he did not like what he found. He was incensed by what he described as these "grab bag" bills, which allowed members of Congress to take for their localities, without compensation to the United States, something of value belonging to the entire nation. Morse was appointed to a three-member subcommittee to review the problem, and from that subcommittee emerged a plan known thereafter as the "Morse Formula." The Morse Formula brought to an end the free distribution of surplus military property. It stipulated that when state or local public bodies acquired land for a public purpose, they had to pay the government fifty cents on the dollar, after the property's fair market value had been established.

If the property was being acquired for private use, then a full 100 percent of market value had to be paid.

Once this formula was established, Morse insisted on its broadest possible application. As a result, what started as a method to prevent avaricious raids on excess military real estate became, as the years went by, a means of regulating the disposal of federal surpluses of any kind, irrespective of previous use. Morse took it upon himself to dissect *every* surplus-disbursement bill to see that it conformed to his formula. And it became customary for colleagues, in order to avoid trouble down the line, to clear their bills with his office before placing them for consideration on the Senate unanimous-consent calendar.

Because of the rules governing operation of the consent calendar, Morse was able to force acceptance of his formula on reluctant fellow senators. Having moved through relevant committees and been approved by designated members of both parties, private bills are normally placed on the consent calendar to be passed en masse on a given day, usually without debate and frequently without attention. Should only one senator object to a bill, however, it automatically fails and cannot be reconsidered until the consent calendar is again before the chamber. Prior to the Morse Formula, senators seldom challenged other members' private bills. The conventions of logrolling—A votes for B's bill, B votes for A's—usually obtained, so that when unanimous consent was requested, it was invariably granted.

In true maverick fashion, Morse ignored this convention. He contested every private bill dispensing surplus federal property that did not meet the test of the Morse Formula. This meant that unless senators were willing, and able, to carry the issue through the labyrinths of normal Senate procedure, Morse had an absolute veto over their bills.

Though disinclined to change a system that seemed to serve everyone by providing free resources for home-state constituencies, the Senate grudgingly accepted the formula, and Morse took great pride in its application. Over the many years of its use, it earned the government millions of dollars, though often at the expense of some county authority or municipality. It also earned for Morse a fair amount of derision. He told President Truman in 1950 that "the pressure and heat has been tremendous as various Senators have attempted to get me to make an exception to the policy." The occasion for this comment was one of those rare instances when a House-Senate conference committee deleted the formula, allowing the army to cede Fort Des Moines to the state of Iowa free of charge—an action Morse labeled "The Fort Des Moines Steal." But defeats of this sort were uncommon. The formula usually exacted its toll, whether fellow senators liked it or not. A day would come, however, when it would also exact a toll of its author. (We will pick up that story in chapter 9.)

DURING MORSE'S FIRST TERM IN THE SENATE, the year 1948 was unusual: except for the Cordon endorsement, which perturbed liberal supporters while delighting conservatives, Morse managed to escape controversy for the entire twelve months. Though his voting record still deviated sharply from the Republican norm, and though he was far ahead of his time as a civil-rights advocate (he was now on the board of the NAACP), Morse by 1948 had become a veteran of Senate procedure, and fellow party members had grown accustomed to, if not accepting of, his maverick ways. Moreover, on at least one issue—military policy—he was now taking a line identical to that of the congressional majority.

Like Vandenberg, Morse supported the Marshall Plan and its design to send millions of American dollars overseas in an effort to strengthen Western Europe and return it to some measure of prosperity. Along with Marshall Plan aid, he continued to support participation in the UN as an effective means of exercising foreign policy. But, seeing things as he did in 1948, he accepted the popular administration contention—proclaimed the previous year in the Truman Doctrine—that neither the Marshall Plan nor the UN could be depended upon to deter Soviet expansion. Six weeks after the Czechoslovakian Communist party took control of the government, Morse proposed a massive increase in U.S. military spending, so that, he said, "we will be able to enforce the peace at a moment's notice if Russia should decide to extend her policies of aggression."

Standing behind the call for a massive enlargement of the military was a reliance on yet another mainstream position, atomic diplomacy. Only a few years earlier, Morse had advocated sharing American atomic knowledge with all of humanity. Now, falling victim to the anticommunist hysteria of the period, he argued for maintaining the scientific status quo. As he told one of his constituents: "I am opposed to sharing A-bomb secrets with any country—be it the English or any others. I think that one of the ace cards we have in the hole, so to speak, is our A-bomb secret. I recognize that in due course of time other nations will develop their own atom bombs, but I see no reason for giving away our atom bomb secrets in the meantime." Like most politicians of his time, Morse had become a Cold War yeoman of the guard.

Nineteen forty-eight was also an election year, and Morse, whose own seat was not up until 1950, was once again in great demand on the campaign circuit. In addition to Oregon, he appeared in Massachusetts, Kentucky, Pennsylvania, Ohio, Indiana, West Virginia, New Jersey, Michigan, Illinois, Wyoming, and Montana, speaking principally in behalf of Republican presidential candidate Thomas E. Dewey. His appearances were welcomed not only because he was an effective speaker, but also because his national popularity had been growing steadily—in fact, rumor had it that if Dewey won the presidency, he would appoint Morse Secretary of the Interior.

The evidence of Morse's increased popularity was impressive. In December, even after the Republicans had been upset in the election, NBC radio carried coast-to-coast his speech to the Salem, Oregon, Chamber of Commerce entitled "The Elephant's Future." His mail at that point was approaching an astonishing one thousand pieces a day, much of it from non-Oregonians. And, as testimony to his having arrived as a national figure, his name appeared in a "Joe Palooka" comic strip, where he was mentioned as one of those "great men" who, like Tom Dewey, Earl Warren, and Omar Bradley, had been newspaper carriers in their youth.

With his additional prominence, Morse in 1949 felt he could

renew a request he had first made of his party's leadership in January of 1946. Then he had asked, now he was demanding, to be appointed to the next Republican vacancy on the Foreign Relations Committee. He had previously—and in his eyes, unfairly—been passed over in favor of two conservative members from the class of '44, and he had also lost out to Henry Cabot Lodge of Massachusetts when the latter returned to the Senate in 1946. He had been a good soldier in the '46 and '48 campaigns and was determined to get his reward, even if that meant carrying his appointment fight from the Republican caucus to the entire Senate.

He had Vandenberg on his side but, as ever, was opposed by Taft, who apparently wanted the opening for John Foster Dulles, the conservative Republican from New York who had only recently joined the Senate. Morse kept the pressure on throughout 1949, and his chances seemed to go up when, because of his ability to attract votes from labor, people began to talk of him as a potential candidate for vice-president in 1952.

But even with Vandenberg in his corner, Morse had an uphill battle. There were those within the Republican caucus who wanted nothing better than to see him defeated, not only because of his maverickness, but also because he had berated them so often on so many issues. One such was Indiana's abdominous Homer Capehart, who would be Morse's enemy for as long as both served together in Congress. From the floor of the Senate, Capehart accused Morse of being one of "those who know everything about everything": "It doesn't make any difference what the subject is; he knows it all; and he jumps to his feet and talks and talks and talks, and takes the time of the Senate."

Capehart's observation was not without foundation. A survey by the Senate librarian demonstrated that for the first six months of 1948, Morse far outdistanced all other Westerners of either party in occupying space in the *Congressional Record*. He spoke sixty-three times, and his words (including inserts) covered 162 pages; meanwhile, to take but one example, Utah's Elbert Thomas, the most verbose of the Western Democrats, spoke thirty-three times, using up a mere fifty-eight pages.

In the course of vying for the Foreign Relations seat, Morse and Dulles had a verbal exchange that was ironic, given the positions each would take in later years. At issue was whether the North Atlantic Treaty Organization required the expenditure of American dollars for European rearmament. Morse contended that although the treaty did not say so, until Europe was able to protect itself, the United States had a "moral obligation" to contribute "huge sums of money" to that area's self-defense. Dulles, taking a position he would largely abandon when he became Secretary of State, insisted that the treaty in no way "meant that we had to build upon the continent of Europe a military establishment sufficient to withstand an all-out assault by the Soviet Union."

Whether Morse could, under other circumstances, have gained a Foreign Relations seat in 1949 is impossible to say. The Democrats, who had won a huge victory in 1948, decided to place eight of their own number on the committee; this meant that only five slots were allotted to the Republicans, and these were filled by five returning minority members—leaving Morse *and* Dulles out in the cold. Morse continued to press his case into the 1950s, but with the death of Vandenberg in 1951, he lost his chief supporter; and after the 1952 election, his claim to membership on *any* Senate committee would be challenged, by Democrats and Republicans alike.

IF 1948 HAD BEEN RELATIVELY QUIET, two events, one happy, the other painful, would bring Morse increased attention in 1949. The first occurred on a sultry day in late July, when President Truman invited Morse to accompany him to Leesburg, Virginia, to visit the grave of Colonel Edward Dickinson Baker, Oregon's first senator and a hero in the Civil War Battle of Ball's Bluff, Virginia. The trip was noteworthy for a number of reasons. To begin with, despite the nervousness of the Secret Servicemen in the back seat, and though he hadn't driven in nearly two years, Truman decided to take the wheel of the open Lincoln convertible. After motoring casually, if unsteadily, through suburban Virginia—to the astonishment of gawking pedestrians—the party was hit by a cloudburst on a remote country road and had to get out of the car in the driving rain to put up the top. Finally, after picking up Secretary of State General George C. Marshall in Leesburg, and crawling through prickly berry bushes and under a barbed-wire fence to reach the supposed gravesite, the men learned, as Morse had already suspected, that Baker's body was not there—it had been carried back to the West Coast for permanent interment. Despite their misadventures, all had an enjoyable time (with the possible exception of Marshall, who felt that Baker, as a good soldier, should have been where he was supposed to be).

Morse, doing what he often did when he wanted his views or actions publicized, reported the outing to his favorite journalist, Drew Pearson; and Pearson, as he usually did when fed material by Morse, recounted what had happened in his widely read "Washington Merry-Go-Round" column. This was the sort of publicity that politicians dream of, and with a reelection campaign looming in the not-too-distant future, Morse, with Pearson's help, extracted maximum mileage from every word.

Though he also benefited from publicity surrounding the second 1949 event, Morse would have preferred an experience less traumatic in its impact. He had returned to Oregon in September to compete in the state fair in Salem, as he did every year. During a midweek horse-and-wagon race, his buggy skidded on a curve and tipped over, spilling him to the ground. Unhurt, he righted his wagon, continued with the race, and was the ultimate winner in his class. He had had a lucky escape, for the moment. In a second race on the following Saturday, the noseband of his horse's bridle snapped, and the horse broke free and tore down the track so fast that the buggy careened off the ground, trailing behind "as though it were an airplane." When the horse abruptly stopped, Morse crashed to earth. This time he did not get up. Unconscious, he never felt the wagon as it landed on his back, badly lacerating spinal ligaments and muscles.

Morse spent a week in a local hospital, and then, after a trip across country—in the course of which he was dropped from a stretcher by inattentive orderlies—he was transferred to Bethesda Naval Hospital outside of Washington. Though he lay there in considerable pain for another eight days, he was cheered greatly by a

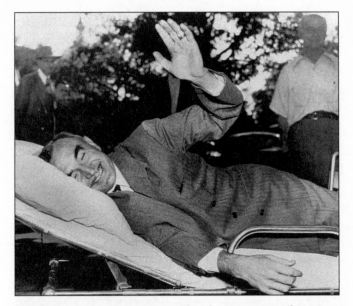

Recovering from an injury incurred at the Oregon state fair, Morse waves from an abulance cot as he is wheeled into the Senate to cast a vote. (Wayne Morse Collection, CN 1316, Special Collections, University of Oregon Library.)

wire from Truman saying, "I hope you are not seriously hurt and that you will be able to win the prize before the show is over." The accident generated a fair amount of publicity in its own right, but nothing compared to that attending Morse when newspaper photographers caught him being wheeled, prostrate, onto the Senate floor to cast his vote on a defense-appropriations bill.

WITH THE REELECTION PROCESS ABOUT TO COMMENCE, Morse was pleased to receive all the publicity he could get, even though, like most incumbents, he hoped to be spared a contest in the 1950 primary. While he felt secure about his renomination, he knew that liberals from both parties were unhappy with him—not so much because of Taft-Hartley, which he was pledged to amend as soon as possible, but because of a regional issue: the proposal to establish a Columbia Valley Authority in the Pacific Northwest.

The idea of harnessing the mighty Columbia River by setting up a federally financed system of power generation, flood control, and crop irrigation, similar to that established in the Southeast by the Tennessee Valley Authority, had been at the top of the Oregon liberal agenda for more than a decade. Time and again Morse had been asked to endorse the idea. Time and again he had put off making a definitive decision, saying in each instance that he needed more facts. Finally, as 1949 moved toward a close, he announced that while the notion itself had some good features, overall he was against it.

Critics took it for granted that Morse, an avid TVA supporter, had attacked CVA in order to mollify Oregon Republicans, who, like Republicans everywhere, were intractably opposed to all such "socialist" initiatives by the federal government. Not that they objected to the further taming of the Columbia—everyone in those days believed in the exploitation of the nation's water power; they merely wanted it done by a consortium of state and private interests and not by Washington. Morse argued along similar lines. He insisted— without benefit of supporting evidence—that conditions in the Northwest were not comparable to those in the Southeast, and for this reason he favored some kind of interstate, regional development for his corner of the country.

Since it faced entrenched opposition in Idaho, CVA might have been in serious trouble anyway. But whatever chance it had was killed when Morse announced his position. No large-scale regional system could be built without federal money, regardless of who controlled the system, and such money could be obtained only through the unanimous agreement of every Northwest delegation. Morse's stance ensured that such agreement could not be reached.

Assistant Secretary of the Interior C. Girard "Jebby" Davidson was so enraged by Morse's action that he threatened to run against him in 1950. Davidson, a drawling Southern New Dealer, had worked as an attorney for TVA in the 1930s and had strongly boosted CVA when he filled a similar role for the Bonneville Power Administration in Portland from 1940 to 1946. Equally upset was another CVA enthusiast, Oregon's outspoken Democratic National Committeeman, Monroe Sweetland; he, too, considered taking on Morse in 1950.

But even before the primaries came around, both men withdrew from consideration—neither believing he had a reasonable chance—leaving Morse, as in 1944, with only his own party to worry about.

Morse's position on CVA apparently did serve to eliminate the most serious of his intraparty rivals. Word was that had he gone the other way, he would have faced a challenge from William Walsh, a well-heeled Coos Bay radio-station owner and reigning president of the Oregon state Senate. But even without Walsh, the party's right wing was not about to give Morse a free ride. They mounted a heavily financed campaign behind an unknown dairy farmer from the tiny town of Deadwood, one David Hoover, whom the press immediately labeled "Deadwood Dave." Although the Hoover forces received large quantities of antilabor money from in- and out-of-state business interests, Morse, with a minimum of effort, cruised to an easy victory, taking 60 percent of the primary vote and all but two of the state's counties. With Deadwood Dave out of the way, and with Republicans still having a stranglehold on statewide offices, the general election seemed a mere formality.

And for the most part, it *was* a formality. As they had in 1944, the Democrats nominated a conservative: in this instance, Howard Latourette, a political warhorse who had served a short term as speaker of the Oregon House. Also as in 1944, Morse's Republican opponent in the primary came out for his Democratic rival during the fall campaign. But a good word from Deadwood Dave was scarcely enough to carry Latourette even to a decent showing. When the votes were tallied, the result was even more decisive than in 1944: Morse had garnered more than 75 percent, winning by one of the widest margins in Oregon history.

His reelection secured, Morse could now return to Washington with enhanced power, with a constituency that had shown itself solidly in his corner. Though still a confirmed maverick, now he could operate with six years of seniority under his belt, from a position significantly above the lower ranks of his chamber. Now, fortified by his added political strength, he was prepared to renew his battle with the Tafts and the Wherrys and the Lucases, the reactionary captains of the Senate minority, for the heart and soul of his party.

7

In the Days of McCarthy

THE FEELING ON CAPITOL HILL IN 1951 was a far cry from what it had been in 1945 when Morse first entered the Senate. Gone was that end-of-the-war, hail-to-the-victors sense of euphoria. Gone, too, was the idea that the future might bring a world of international peace and harmony. A ferocious wave of anticommunism had swept the chambers, washing away the earlier sense of hope and expectation. The world was once again a perilous place. The "red menace" and the rabid emotions it provoked lay beneath every important debate, and to avoid being labeled "soft on communism," members outdid each other in demonstrations of ideological purity.

The emotional response in Congress was generated in part by the seemingly endless series of communist victories in the late 1940s, first in Eastern Europe, then in China. Decisions affecting overseas interests were measured by their contribution to combating communism wherever it existed. On the domestic front, where hordes of subversives were alleged to be lurking in bureaucratic corridors, union hiring halls, and faculty lounges, the imposition of internal security procedures and loyalty oaths and the investigation into citizens' political beliefs became accepted as the price that had to be paid for "protecting" democracy. This was the period of McCarthyism, when a manifest hatred of all things communistic became the minimal test of political legitimacy.

Morse's reaction to anticommunism, to its belligerent diplomacy and assault on civil liberties, was mixed. Having discarded his dream of a world order based on international law, he had become an avid supporter of a bigger, more powerful military machine to meet the ominous threat from the East. At the same time, he had moments of doubt, periods when he worried that "the military establishment" (he was one of the first to use that term) was exceeding its legitimate authority. The Korean War provided a prime example.

President Truman's policy on Korea was to fight a limited war, with limited objectives. Far East Commander General Douglas MacArthur insisted that there was "no substitute for victory," by which he meant unconditional surrender; to achieve this end, he sought to expand the war into China. When Truman relieved MacArthur of his command on April 11, 1951, and recalled him to the United States, and when eight days later the general bade his emotional "Old Soldiers Never Die" farewell to a joint session of Congress, the disagreement between the two precipitated a constitutional crisis of monumental proportions. MacArthur intensified the crisis by making a cross-country tour to tell his side of the story.

Millions turned out to hear the "Old Soldier" espouse the cause of victory and decry the government's policy of "appeasement." Everywhere the general received hysterical acclaim and a hero's adulation. As MacArthur himself described it: "My welcome throughout the entire land defies description. America took me to its heart with a roar that will never leave my ears."

Congress also heard that roar. Both houses were bombarded by messages expressing vehement anti-Truman sentiment. "When," wired one constituent, "an ex–national guard captain fires a five-star general, impeachment of the national guard captain is in order." Similar observations were being made in every corner of the nation. In Milwaukee, where he was addressing a gathering of six hundred furniture dealers, Senator Joe McCarthy put it more succinctly. That "son of a bitch," he told reporters, "should be impeached."

Amidst the tumult, Morse rose in the Senate to defend Truman's right to dismiss MacArthur. "God help the American people," he shouted, "if the day ever comes when we fail to retain civilian control over the military establishment." He scored those demanding the instigation of impeachment proceedings even before the incident had been looked into by the proper investigating body, which was then being established by Congress. As it happened, Morse was to be a part of that body, being put together in the Senate from the

members of the Foreign Relations Committee and his own Armed
Services Committee.

During the joint committee's closed-door inquiry, Morse carefully tried to build a case in support of Truman. In so doing, he found
MacArthur, who was questioned over the first three days, to be an especially slippery witness. As he reported to Ed Conklin, "Every time
we pressed MacArthur to answer a question which had to do with
global defense of our country, he ducked by saying that he was not
qualified to pass judgment." To illustrate Morse's point: the Joint
Chiefs of Staff had been worried that extending hostilities into China
could produce the worst of all scenarios, the entrance of the Soviet
Union into the conflict. When Morse, with great deference, asked
MacArthur about this possibility, the general replied that the question "goes far afield," involving "policies I wouldn't care to discuss."

Morse doggedly repeated his question until he extracted something akin to a direct response. "There is," MacArthur said, "no certainty that Russia will come in. There is no certainty that she will not
come in. . . . You have to take a certain degree of risk on these things,
one way or another." While not entirely satisfactory, this answer was
the sort that Morse had hoped to elicit. For it was, as he later indicated, precisely such a risk that Truman and the Joint Chiefs had
wished to avoid.

The hearings ran on for seven weeks, the Democrats calculating
—correctly, as it turned out—that with the passage of time the situation would be defused somewhat. Unable to come to a coherent
consensus after completing its work, the committee voted, with three
dissents, not to issue a report of its conclusions. However, eight of its
twelve Republican members signed a declaration drawn up by the
ever-present Harry Cain, which said among other things that Mac-
Arthur's had been the only positive plan for victory in Korea and that
there had been no "serious disagreement" between MacArthur and
the Joint Chiefs of Staff as to overall strategy.

Morse released a statement in reply to Cain's. He pointed out
that MacArthur had for months been at odds with both the Joint
Chiefs and the Secretaries of State and Defense, and that Truman finally had no choice but to act precisely as he had. As Morse had stat-

ed earlier, not to "have done so would have been tantamount to sur-
rendering the White House to the military brass."

Since the Democrats adhered to the committee's agreement and
remained silent, Morse became, as A. Robert Smith pointed out in
The Tiger in the Senate, the only one "of the twenty-six-member
panel to render a formal and firm judgment that President Truman
was both constitutionally proper and strategically wise in taking the
bold political step of recalling modern America's most legendary
military figure."

Morse came under intense fire because of his resolute stand. He
confessed to Conklin, "My mail on the MacArthur issue is the worst
that it has ever been since I have been in the Senate." But he was convinced that the public would come around, that it would "come to
understand that MacArthur's removal not only was justified but that
he should have been fired long before he was." Though the public
may never have reached that level of understanding, unhappiness
with Morse did begin to lessen, just as it did with Truman. While the
aging MacArthur would remain a five-star savior to much of the
electorate, the MacArthur crisis appeared—to quote the general's
own prediction about himself—to "fade away" as the Korean conflict dragged on and the nation became preoccupied by other aspects
of the war on communism.

Not all of the support for MacArthur had stemmed from spon-
taneous public outrage. Neither had all of the condemnation of Truman. Much of both had been orchestrated by an obscure right-wing
group which came to be known as the China lobby. During the
course of the MacArthur hearings, Morse asked Secretary of State
Dean Acheson, General Marshall's successor, to turn over any material his department had compiled on this group. Later, after Acheson had failed to produce anything of substance, Morse called upon
the Senate to launch its own probe into the workings of the lobby.

What exactly was the China lobby, about which so little was apparently known? To begin with, it did not operate as an official lobby,
in the way that the National Teachers Federation or the American
Tobacco Institute function as lobbies. It was a loose association of
like-minded ideologues who disbursed huge amounts of money to

those who would promote the interests of the Chinese Nationalists and frustrate those of the Chinese Communists. It was the lobby's position that China had been delivered into the hands of the radicals by subversive intellectuals hidden from scrutiny in the bowels of the State Department. Lobby adherents saw to it that this position became the gospel of the House Committee on Un-American Activities and Joseph McCarthy's Permanent Investigating Subcommittee in the Senate.

Morse was concerned that the China lobby was de facto making policy for the Republican party. His old sparring partner, Senator Wherry, was one of its spokesmen, as were Senators William F. Knowland of California and Styles Bridges of New Hampshire (both of whom signed Cain's MacArthur declaration). Taft's China position was virtually identical to that of the lobby, and even Vandenberg, supposedly more liberal on foreign-policy matters, made similar arguments. Furthermore, in back of these senior Republicans marched a parade of heavyweight writers and business and military leaders who worked to generate a pro–Chiang Kai-shek consensus in America. Henry Luce, for example, who ran frequent heroic illustrations of Chiang on the cover of *Time* magazine, was a lobby supporter.

The lobby's pendragon was Alfred Kohlberg, a wealthy textile dealer who had made millions by importing Irish-made linen via slave-wage embroidering factories in China. Kohlberg bankrolled the American China Policy Association, an organization led at various times by such anticommunist zealots as Clare Boothe Luce, Henry's wife, and William Loeb, the extremist publisher from New Hampshire. Using this and other organizations, Kohlberg led a relentless attack against groups he regarded as sympathetic to the enemy. One of these was the Institute for Pacific Relations, an international study association which, he charged, had slavishly followed the Communist party line on China.

Morse was a member of IPR and had been since 1934. This fact was used as the basis for a series of smears appearing in the *Chicago Tribune* and on the *Tribune* wire service in September and October, *after* Morse had called for investigations of the China lobby. The *Tribune* and its publisher, Colonel Robert McCormick, crusaded for the lobby's cause, and McCormick was livid that Morse, a Republican, had supported Truman on the MacArthur issue. The articles pointed out that, unlike others who had joined IPR "in good faith" and later left the organization, Morse had chosen to retain his membership. They mentioned as well that such left-wing figures as Alger Hiss, Owen Lattimore, and Earl Browder were "associated with" IPR, and that the confessed communist spy Elizabeth Bentley had testified to the McCarthy committee that the institute was as "Red as a rose." Almost in passing, it was noted that Morse's prime objective, getting the China lobby investigated by Congress, was also "the No. 1 item of the communist party program for action on China."

While many public figures ran for cover when attacked by stories less virulent than these, at this point, at least, such smears could do little to frighten Morse into silence. He was, to put it simply, a "clean liberal" and a poor target for red-baiting. For one thing, he was militantly anticommunistic in his own right. He could even find points of agreement with some of the goals of the China lobby. In summary, these goals were:

> preventing U. S. recognition of "Red China";
>
> preventing China's seating in the UN;
>
> ousting those in the federal government who were opposed to financing Chiang's return from Taiwan to the mainland;
>
> helping to elect those friendly to Chiang.

Though he would later change his mind, in 1951 Morse was neither for recognizing China nor for seating it in the UN. Before MacArthur's recall, he even declared that "we should not hesitate to bomb the principal supply depots and military bases within Red China" (a position that, ironically, MacArthur was taking at the time and that ultimately helped to get him fired). Moreover, Morse saw nothing wrong in "freeing Chiang" and arming Nationalist forces so that *they* could carry on guerrilla warfare on the mainland.

But he did have three basic arguments with the China lobby. The first was that many of Chiang's supporters saw the U. S. treasury as a bottomless reservoir for personal financing. Morse had in mind

Chiang's brothers-in-law, who had amassed fortunes in China, fled to the United States with their booty when the Nationalist government was overturned, and now acted as conduits for American funds sent to the Nationalists.

Second, he objected to the clandestine nature of the lobby's operation, and to the secret channeling by "a foreign power" of funds —much of which had come from American taxpayers in the first place—to U.S. politicians and others who favored the interests of that power.

Finally, he feared that if the lobby had its way, the United States would be dragged into a land war on the Asian continent in an attempt to retake China from the Communists. He regarded any such attempt as suicidal and not worth "the life of a single American boy."

Morse originally offered his resolution for investigating the lobby in the spring of 1951. A year later, the Senate having taken no action on his request, he brought the matter up again, this time with supporting evidence that he placed into the public record. He had gotten his hands on a series of secret messages that had been sent from the Nationalist embassy in Washington to Chiang Kai-shek on Taiwan. Among these were references to "secret information" obtained at great expense by the Chinese from "the highest levels of the proper authorities," information relating to confidential U.S. governmental proceedings. The messages also intimated that the embassy was doing everything in its power to see that the "strongly prejudiced" Dean Acheson was removed from his job as Secretary of State.

Morse's revelations of foreign interference in U.S. government matters, however sensational they might have been under other circumstances, attracted little interest at the time they were made. While the *New York Times* ran a long article on the documents, the rest of the media, either through neglect or because of tacit ideological agreement, did little with the story. National attention was focused on the upcoming presidential nominating conventions and on finding a way to end the Korean War.

Morse's attack was not entirely fruitless, however. If nothing else, it alerted the nation, or at least those who cared, to the existence of what the *St. Louis Post-Dispatch* referred to as the "Chinese Dragon

That Eats Our Dollars." Thereafter it would be more difficult to accept at face value all the propaganda put out by pro-Nationalist factions. To that extent, Morse had weakened the ground under those seeking to accomplish what the Nationalist embassy had cryptically alluded to as "our ultimate aim" in Asia: to bring America into open combat on the Chinese mainland.

DESPITE HIS ALMOST UNRELENTING INVOLVEMENT in policy debate, Morse always managed to find time for his favorite pastime. Given his keenness, he could not rest content waiting for trips to Oregon to compete in horse shows and fairs. He entered the greater-D.C. equestrian scene almost as soon as he came to the Senate, and on those weekends when he wasn't competing, he could be found cantering down the bridle paths of Rock Creek Park on one of his blue-blooded mounts. In fact, because of his interest in horses, newspapers in 1944 had singled him out from other freshmen coming to Washington to begin their tenure in the Senate. They showed photos of the horseman from the far Northwest arriving with Nancy on Christmas night at the Meadowbrook Saddle Club in Chevy Chase, after the pair had driven across the country, slipping and skidding for thirteen wintry days, pulling a trailer containing the beloved Spice of Life and Oregana Bourbon. Why, asked the press, had he and his daughter endured such a trial? (Others wondered where the wartime gasoline coupons had come from.) "It's my only hobby," Morse explained.

By 1951, Morse had become a fixture at the biggest of the mid-Atlantic competitions. On August 4 of that year, his new stallion, Morse's Chief, took the blue ribbon in the Orkney Springs, Virginia, grand championship for American saddle horses. In the barn, after the show, Morse walked into the stall of Missie, a mare belonging to his friend, Mrs. Jerry Johns. He awoke hours later in a hospital bed in nearby Harrisonburg.

Missie, for no discoverable reason, had delivered a sudden kick which hit Morse flush on the mouth with such force that had it found the point of his chin, it would, in the doctor's opinion, have killed him on the spot. As it was, it tore his lips nearly off, fractured his jaw in four places, knocked out most of his upper teeth, and loosened several others. After a short stay for emergency treatment in Harrisonburg, he was moved once again to Bethesda Naval Hospital for surgery and rehabilitation.

Morse was kept at Bethesda well into September, lips stitched in place, jaws wired shut, taking nourishment through a straw and enduring, mostly with good humor, days and nights of extreme discomfort. Few outside of the family knew how serious the accident had been. Many, especially in the Senate, treated it with humor, as did Morse himself when speaking through clenched teeth—what was left of them—to the press. Republican senator William Jenner of Indiana reportedly raised forty dollars passing the hat to buy hay for Missie, and there was much guffawing in the cloakrooms over the thought that the voluble Oregonian had finally been muzzled.

But if the Senate believed it was on a Morse-free holiday, it was mistaken. Even with jaws clamped tight, Morse was not about to keep his peace. He began dictating letters from his hospital bed soon after the accident, and by the end of August he was permitted to leave Bethesda every afternoon for the Hill, where, to the chagrin of his enemies, he participated in debate with defiant vitality. "It is surprising," he wrote Conklin, "how much a fellow can talk through his teeth without moving his jaw." By October, that very jaw, now fitted with dentures, was almost back to normal, and so was Morse's involvement in Congress. But the accident was not forgotten. Eight years later, it would play a part in a political fight between Morse and Clare Boothe Luce over the latter's appointment as ambassador to Brazil.

When Morse had suffered his earlier accident at the Salem fairgrounds, President Truman had told him he hoped he would get better and "win the prize before the show is over." Now, in December of 1951, with Morse fully recovered from his latest misfortune, the president had a prize of his own to bestow, one that would present Morse with a difficult decision.

Truman had taken a terrific battering in the press in 1951. Beyond the MacArthur issue was the still more serious problem of corruption in the bureaucracy. An Internal Revenue Bureau collector in San Francisco had been fired for inefficiency and then indicted for tampering with tax returns. So had a second collector in St. Louis. Then a Nashville agent was fired because of drug addiction. The entire bureau was said to be in disarray. Stories were circulating that malfeasance was rampant, and that neither the bureau's directors nor the Justice Department was exercising adequate oversight.

Truman did what he could to limit the damage, sacking both the assistant attorney general and the bureau's general counsel. Next he tried to set up a panel composed of the FBI director, the attorney general, and the chairman of the Civil Service Commission to look into the matter and clean it up. When he met resistance from these parties, he opted for an independent commission of nongovernmental officers, but because of personality disputes, that body also failed to get off the ground.

Morse was opposed to the idea of involving any sort of commission, even an independent one. In a speech in southern California and then in a radio debate from Washington, he said that what was needed was a change at the top: a new attorney general. Whether Truman took his cue from Morse or reached this position on his own, he came to the same conclusion. He decided, moreover, that Morse himself was the man for the job. As he wrote in a memo in Kansas City on the day after Christmas, he was taking an entirely "new approach. Give the Atty. Gen. an ambassadorship and put Wayne Morse, Senator from Oregon, in as Atty Gen. and have the clean-up from that angle."

Truman had called Morse to the White House four days before Christmas and secretly offered him the position. Morse at first thought the president was kidding. Assured that the offer was serious, he agreed to think it over and give his reply within twenty-four hours. He spent much of that period agonizing over the decision with Midge and, by telephone, with a few of his longtime advisors.

What should he do? This was an offer that would propel him into the center of the national limelight, bring him the kind of recognition he had always craved, the kind he might never receive as senator from the small state of Oregon. Furthermore, it was an offer that

The Morses exchange greetings with President Harry S. Truman and Bess Truman (as Democratic National Committeeman Monroe Sweetland, left, looks on). Truman wanted to appoint Morse attorney general in 1951, though Morse was then a Republican. (Oregon Historical Society, OrHi 73855.)

might never be repeated. And if he turned it down, he wouldn't even enjoy the publicity of having received it in the first place—for obvious political reasons, its secrecy had to be protected.

After mulling things over for the full twenty-four hours, Morse decided to say no. He had planned to see Truman in person on December 22, but, bedridden by the flu, he had to break the news via letter. He told the president that "a Democrat could do a much better job for your Administration in this post than any Republican could possibly do. . . . Let me assure you that I deeply appreciate the trust and confidence represented by the proposed appointment. My decision to decline it has not been an easy one for me to reach because of the great challenge presented."

It would be the grossest understatement to say that Truman was disappointed by Morse's answer. "Dear Wayne," he responded,

Your letter of the 22nd was handed to me by the White House Usher last night. I had a premonition that it contained bad news—so I didn't open it until after dinner. My appetite wouldn't have been so good if I had. I appreciate your arguments, and understand—but I wish you could have done the job—not for me but for the country. Political considerations were not a part of my suggestion. What is needed is a tough, unbiased approach to a situation which is rampant in the country. . . . What we need is an Isaiah or a Martin Luther to put us back into the "straight and narrow path". . . . I came to the conclusion that another approach with you the spark plug would do the business. Well all I can do is to start again.

While there is no record of their conversation, Truman must have used this same kind of language when he first tendered the job to Morse. Why, in the face of such persuasion, and with apparently so much to gain from the appointment, did Morse turn it down?

Despite its seeming attractiveness, being attorney general at that moment was fraught with danger for Morse. The risk of failure was great: why should a Republican rush in where so many Democrats feared to tread? Assuming he was confirmed by the Senate—by no means a sure thing—joining a Democratic administration ran the risk of alienating his Republican brethren, both in Washington and at home, even more than he had in the past. He might be burning bridges before he had to. Finally, and most important, the timing was wrong, even for an ambitious maverick. Truman was entering the last year of his term, and given his dismal showing in the polls, it figured also to be his last year in the White House. He was already exhibiting terminal lame-duckness, and the odds were that any attorney general he might appoint would within short order be politically dead in the water. Morse could, as he had told the president in his letter, make his "greatest [read "safest"] contribution" by continuing his work in the Senate.

MORSE ENTERED THE 1952 ELECTION SEASON still a senator, still working, at least on paper, as a legislative member of the Republican party. But his closeness to Truman began to make even moderate Republicans feel nervous. He came to Truman's defense yet again when, after a labor dispute had closed down the nation's steel industry, the president seized control of the fabrication mills, an act which nearly all Republicans, many Democrats, and ultimately the Supreme Court saw as a blatant usurpation of power. Morse supported Truman's action—as he had supported similar action by Roosevelt in World War II—justifying it under authority derived from the declared Korean War "state of emergency," authority which, he contended, superseded the normal limitations imposed by the Constitution. This time, however, no one in the Republican party agreed with him.

As if the steel-seizure controversy were not enough, Morse announced in a May 28 speech in Washington before the Electric Consumers Conference that he would effectively desert the Republican party in the event that it nominated someone from its "isolationist wing" for president. He was serving notice, he said, that he would never again ask voters to support a candidate just because he was a Republican. If the machine bosses who ran both parties would not come up with better candidates, then, he declared, "it is about time we set up a real people's party that will." At this, the audience of five hundred, liberals all, gave him a standing ovation.

It was against this backdrop that the Oregon delegation met in Salem in early June to organize for the July Republican convention in Chicago. Morse was occupied in Washington with Armed Services Committee business and did not attend; he was represented by his alternate, Clay Myers, Jr., the eager new president of the Oregon Young Republicans. Given his senatorial status, the thousands of votes he had amassed in the delegate election (finishing second only to Governor Douglas McKay), and his expressed interest in the area, it was expected that Morse would be chosen as one of Oregon's two representatives to the convention platform committee. But, angry at what they regarded as his continued apostasy, McKay and his friends had other ideas.

Prior to the meeting, the governor's group had organized a faction in opposition to Morse and in favor of a twenty-nine-year-old Willamette University political scientist named Mark O. Hatfield. Though he had also been a Morse supporter, and though he had apparently not been solicited beforehand, Hatfield was ambitious in his own right, and accepted the nomination when offered it. And with the votes stacked against them, there was nothing Myers or the other Morse backers could do about it.

Adding insult to effrontery, not only was Morse kept off the platform committee, he was not elected to *any* delegation post. McKay won the chairmanship, and numerous resident Republicans were selected for the other positions of importance. Morse had to suffer the indignity of going to Chicago as a delegate without portfolio, unable to participate in any of his party's formal deliberations. He may have been the only U. S. senator at the convention in such a demeaning position.

Despite his humiliation, Morse wore a proper political face during the proceedings. He was pleased when his man, Eisenhower, defeated Taft for the nomination, and to Myers's surprise, he even joined the convention-hall parade to celebrate the naming of Richard Nixon as Eisenhower's running mate. It took great effort, however, to put on such a show of solidarity. He was furious over his treatment at Salem, he had long despised Nixon, and he made no secret of his distaste for the traditionally conservative platform that his party had written.

Although he had his reservations, and they were serious ones, Morse left Chicago promising to do everything he could to ensure success in November. However, his less-than-ecstatic attitude was made clear in a "Dear Dick" letter sent a few weeks after the convention. He informed Nixon, who was surely already aware of the fact, that Leverett Saltonstall had been his choice for vice president. But, he added,

> you may be sure that you and Eisenhower will receive my active support not only in the campaign but my cooperation in the Senate after you are elected, reserving to myself of

course the right to express an honest difference of opinion
on the merits of issues as I see them.

I trust you will not think me presumptuous for making
one suggestion in regard to a major problem which I think
confronts us in the campaign. I refer of course to the platform, which I think is the worst Republican platform since
the time of McKinley. It is my judgment that you and Eisenhower can strengthen our party's position in regard to the
reactionary weaknesses of the platform if you will speak out
boldly on specific legislative issues and not hesitate to lay
down some specific legislative proposals.

Nixon could not have thought such a letter other than presumptuous. From its cautionary, even disrespectful tone, it was apparent that
the Republican ticket was going to have trouble with the junior senator from Oregon.

Whether or not that trouble was unavoidable is a matter of conjecture. Smith argues that Eisenhower could have minimized Morse's
unhappiness by being seen to consult with him on significant policy
questions, by taking him into the campaign and making him feel important—in short, by massaging his ego. When he failed to do this,
Smith contends, he made Morse's ultimate disaffection a foregone
conclusion.

After the campaign was well under way, the Eisenhower forces,
fearful that an alienated Morse could hurt them with labor, finally
did invite him out to campaign headquarters at the Brown Palace
Hotel in Denver. But Morse said he could not afford the trip on his
own, and he would not accept a ticket paid for out of campaign
funds. At the urging of advisors, Eisenhower intervened personally:
he wrote directly to Morse requesting his support. The letter reached
Morse in London, where he was on the first stop of a Senate inspection tour of NATO installations.

From the nature of Morse's reply, copies of which he proudly sent
to newspapers all over the country, it is apparent that Smith's point
about flattery is well taken. Morse was clearly pleased by the general's attention. "I deeply appreciate receiving your letter," he wrote.

You may be sure that upon my return to the United States
. . . I shall throw myself into your campaign with all of my
vigor, and do whatever I can to help you and Nixon. . . .

It is unimportant that I disagree with you on certain
specific issues, because as to those issues, only time will tell
what is the correct solution. What is important is that our
people have as a President a man such as you, in whom they
can place their complete confidence.

While it is true that flattery could get you a fair distance with
Morse, it would be wrong to think it could get you anywhere you
wanted. As subsequent events demonstrated, differences over policy
were ultimately compelling, too compelling finally to be mitigated
by the most assiduous attempt at personal blandishment. Despite the
pledge of support from London (which had been followed by a
warm note of appreciation from Eisenhower), Morse, after returning
to the United States on September 9, became increasingly upset at the
moves to the right that Eisenhower and Nixon seemed to keep taking.

*During an inspection tour of European NATO installations, Morse (pictured here
with Senator Russell Long, Dem., La.) promised General Eisenhower that he would
"do whatever I can to help you and Nixon." A month later, Eisenhower's campaign
policies had driven Morse out of the Republican party. (Wayne Morse Collection,
CN 1315, Special Collections, University of Oregon Library.)*

First there was Ike's endorsement of William Jenner, the Hoosier senator who had referred to General Marshall as a "front man for traitors" and who frequently outdid McCarthy in his persecution of political dissenters. Then there was Nixon's endorsement of Mc-Carthy himself—McCarthy was up for reelection—at the Wisconsin Republican state convention. Finally, there were the campaign speeches of both Eisenhower and Nixon, which had begun to sound as though they had been turned out by hired hands from the China lobby.

What pushed Morse over the edge was a meeting between Eisenhower and Taft at Morningside Heights in New York on September 12. Out of that conclave came an agreement advancing nearly every item on the conservative agenda that Taft had for years been promoting in Congress. As Democratic contender Adlai Stevenson put it, "Taft lost the nomination but won the nominee." And with the nominee ensconced in Taft's parlor, Morse headed for the nearest exit. The Republican party had lost him forever.

Though total, the break took place in stages. First Morse announced that he could not in good conscience work any longer for Eisenhower's election: he would, as an "Independent Republican," sit out the rest of the campaign. A newspaper cartoon showed him wearing a button reading "I Liked Ike." Soon he dropped the term Republican entirely and began to refer to himself simply as an Independent. On October 18 he summoned the press to his office, and with cameras flashing, he put an X on his absentee ballot beside the name of Adlai Stevenson. "The Eisenhower I supported for the nomination," he told reporters, "is not the Eisenhower who is dangling ... at the end of political puppet strings being jerked by some of the most evil and reactionary forces in American politics." A week later, Morse officially resigned from the Republican party. He had already begun appearing on behalf of Stevenson.

The moment, so long in coming, had finally arrived. The stormy relationship with the Grand Old Party had played itself out. No longer would Republicans have to listen to Morse's lectures on liberalism, a maverick's disquisition on how and why the party had gone so hopelessly wrong. No longer would Morse have to define himself and what he stood for according to contradictory constituencies. Now, *truly* independent, he could call his own shots. Now he was free. Now he would discover whether Oregonians were ready to accept yet another test of their open style of politics.

AT FIRST, IT DID NOT LOOK AS THOUGH THEY WERE. While many Democrats applauded Morse's move, Republicans, almost without exception, exploded in fury. The sharpest criticism came, predictably, from former supporters. Eddie Sammons stated publicly that Morse was "morally dishonest." The state GOP chairman described him as a "Judas," a "Benedict Arnold," and said he looked "pathetic." Henry Corbett, a Portland financier who had contributed to his coffers, suggested that the "recent kicks of his horse have evidently addled his brains." And the *Salem Capital Journal* assailed him as an "egomaniac" and a "blatant double crosser, publicity seeker and opportunist."

Not only was Morse raked over the coals, but his family was abused as well. One aggravated acquaintance wrote not to Morse but to Midge, using language which she—obviously quoting her husband—labeled as "snide" and "calumnious." Judy and Nancy, attending school in Eugene, suddenly found themselves cut dead by people they had known all their lives. Like their parents in Washington, they began receiving insulting phone calls in the middle of the night.

Morse handled most of the criticism with a display of equanimity. But while he quietly extricated himself from his old law "partnership" in Eugene when he heard that the firm's clients had been complaining, and while just as quietly he severed connections with other erstwhile supporters, he could do little when sensitive broken relations became public. For example, when Genevieve Cooper, his private secretary since his first day in Washington, resigned, stating to the press that "the senator felt I had been of no help in this crisis," he could say nothing that would repair the damage.

As the attacks raged on, Morse, despite his outward good humor, began to wonder privately whether he had committed political suicide. Jim Landye's former law partner, B. A. Green, tried his best to cheer him up. "The only thing that disturbs me," Green wrote in one letter, "is that . . . you seemed quite depressed. Forget it! Many things can happen in the next four years." In a follow-up note he advised: "Keep calm! Keep your chin up! It takes time for these things to jell. I am more worried about your worrying and about your getting discouraged than anything else."

The break with Eddie Sammons, whom Morse had known and worked with since the early 1930s, was perhaps the most difficult to overcome. Although the two continued, briefly, to exchange polite correspondence, Morse was aware that Sammons, along with most of the Republican establishment, had turned violently against him. He had undoubtedly learned through the grapevine that Sammons had been referring to him as "a lying sonofabitch" and had told a mutual friend, "I wouldn't piss on him." And he also knew that while other ex-backers might have been using more delicate terminology, their pronouncements were no less execratory.

HOWEVER WORRISOME THE OPPOSITION in Oregon might be, Morse could not dwell on it for long. As soon as the new Congress commenced in January 1953, he had more immediate things to think about. What would his new role be? Where, as the Senate's sole Independent, did he fit in? Indeed, where—since he was neither Democrat nor Republican—would he sit in the upper chamber?

He showed up on opening day carrying a folding chair, ready to situate himself in the center aisle, conspicuously apart from either party. But he accepted his old desk when offered it by the Republican elders. Their generosity may have been prompted by his announcement that he would vote with his former party so that it could organize the Senate and control its committees. Had he chosen to go with the Democrats, the two parties would have been dead even, and the Republicans would have been forced to start the session from what might have seemed a position of weakness: having to call upon the vice president to break the tie before they could assume organizational power.

Returning Morse to his desk may have saved the Republican hierarchy a slight embarrassment, but it stretched their generosity to its limit. Morse believed that, following the precedent set in the case of La Follette after his Progressive presidential race in 1924, he might have to forfeit his seniority but would surely retain his membership on the Armed Services and Labor committees. However, since he was now a man without a party, Taft took the opportunity to bounce him from Labor: when the Republican slate of committee nominees came out, Morse's name appeared on the Armed Services roster and nowhere else.

Morse reacted immediately, insisting that he would accept committee nominations from *neither* party and citing Senate Rule XXIV, which, if strictly interpreted, required the Senate as a whole to elect committee members by ballot. But Rule XXIV had rested for generations in obscurity, and had never been so interpreted. The Senate had always organized itself on two-party lines, and the party leaders had invariably appointed every member of every committee, even in those cases when independents of one kind or another had served in the chamber. Until Morse did so, no one had ever called for Senate-wide elections.

Would he have made such a call had he not been dropped from the Labor Committee? Perhaps. Though he prized his old assignments, he also reveled in his newly achieved independence, and he was in no mood to incur obligations either to Taft on the Republican side or to Lyndon Johnson, Taft's Democratic counterpart. Furthermore, he felt that if Rule XXIV were enforced and his peers were free to vote on the issue, he would have sufficient support to retain his seat on *both* of his committees.

Honoring Morse's request, neither Taft nor Johnson assigned him to any committee when they released their final lists, although Taft did leave open slots on the minor Public Works and District of Columbia committees. Morse accused the Republicans of utilizing "punitive measures," and said that Taft's move was "a terroristic device . . . to compel compliance and insure subordination."

The unprecedented situation drew national interest, especially when Morse demanded that he be treated as *the* Independent party, with all of a political party's rights and privileges. In a January 14 story, the *Philadelphia Bulletin* stated that he had "received more public attention in the last month than any other member of the Senate, excepting only the majority leader, Robert A. Taft."

Attention was one thing; victory was another. In a front-page article on that same day, the *New York Times* reported that the Senate, having agreed to follow Rule XXIV, had voted 81 to 7 to keep Labor and Armed Forces exactly as Taft and Johnson had drawn them up, i.e., minus the services of Senator Morse. Morse had been wrong about how much support he would have in an open contest (he had been denied a secret ballot, under which he probably would have done better). He might be generating headlines across the country, but he was losing his battle on the Hill.

Morse took his lumps well enough, but refused to hide his displeasure with those liberal colleagues—"gutless wonders," he called them—who, in his opinion, should have risen to his defense. Many so designated cringed at his wrathfulness. Hubert Humphrey, for example, who had *not* been among the seven voting for him, sent an unctuous letter pleading for forgiveness. "Wayne," he wrote,

> I want to talk with you. I have been disturbed because there may be a misunderstanding between us. Just believe me when I tell you that no man in America admires you more than I do, and has more affection for you and your family. You are truly a great man. I feel honored to be associated with you. I know of no person more courageous nor, at the same time, one with more intellectual integrity and brilliance and the ability to make that courage meaningful and effective. I hope you do not feel that I have let you down, Wayne. I haven't; at least not in my own heart. Possibly I have exercised bad judgment; if I have, I ask your understanding.

Morse responded coldly to the future vice president's overtures, and continued to press his case throughout the winter and into the spring. He even turned down the generous offer by New York's Herbert Lehman to yield his own Democratic seat on Labor. Instead, he proposed a compromise resolution which called for placing him, along with an additional Republican to ensure a GOP majority, on

Armed Services and Labor. Pending a vote on that resolution, he received permission to leave suspended what he called Taft's "garbage can" appointments to the Public Works and District committees. He was, at least for the time being, the only man in the Senate without a committee to call his own.

Morse stuck to his guns until the middle of May, when the Senate finally took up and, after four and a half hours of debate, turned down his "extra Republican" proposal, 56 to 19. Bereft of further parliamentary maneuvers, he finally acknowledged the inevitable and accepted the minor committee assignments. But not without his usual flair for the dramatic.

The *Washington Daily News* described him as "Glum but Game" —glum over his defeat, game to make the most out of his new positions. He had previously introduced a bill that would bar segregation in the District of Columbia in all places of public education, accommodation, entertainment, or amusement, a bill the Eisenhower administration was anxious to see buried. As the District Committee's newest member, he promised—whether the administration liked it or not—to call for hearings on that bill without further delay. He might have been relegated to the bottom of the committee barrel, but the Senate and the nation would know that even from that lowly position, Wayne Morse was still capable of fighting for what he believed in, was still someone they could not ignore.

Sitting among Republicans though no longer one of their number; keeping the Senate in session after hours every Friday with lengthy "committee meetings" of the Independent party; voting more often than not with the Democrats; carrying on a running battle with Majority Leader Taft—such deportment did nothing to endear Morse to GOP regulars. Syndicated columnist George Dixon reported that Morse's nearest neighbor on the Senate floor, Irving Ives of New York, had taken to harassing him at every opportunity. Whenever Morse rose to speak, Ives, according to Dixon, would, in a whisper that Morse alone could hear, deliver such barbs as "You silly jackass! Just listen to that asinine drivel you're spilling! Why don't you shut your silly mouth and go out and drop dead?" At the same time, Ives's accomplice, Herman Welker of Idaho, would stroll through the chamber, apparently without aim, but when he came abreast of Morse he'd hiss: "You stupid ass! Everybody knows you're a dope! Do you have even the faintest idea what you're yapping about?" Dixon wrote that in the face of these attacks, Morse had asked to be shifted to the Democratic side of the aisle.

Morse did in fact request a change in location. And in all probability the reason for his request—which he said was personal—*was* related to problems he had had with Ives. But it is doubtful that the Ives-Welker whispering campaign described by Dixon ever took place, or, if it did, that Morse was fully aware of it. His actual conflict with Ives, a former ally on the Labor Committee, was much more direct, though no less provocative.

In the course of Senate business one day, Ives accused Morse of having campaigned against him in New York during the previous election. Morse denied it, insisting that while he had opposed Eisenhower in New York, he had never said a word against Ives. Ives interrupted, told Morse to keep his "goddamned big mouth shut," and said that he never wanted Morse to speak to him again. Responding in writing to Ives's "profane, insulting and abusive remarks," Morse promised to oblige.

Moving his desk to the other side of the chamber would facilitate keeping such a promise, and that is why Morse asked to be moved. But he changed his mind once his request was leaked to the press. He did not, he said, "want the public to get the impression, based on the Dixon story, that I was being driven out of my seat by Ives and Welker." At least for the moment, he would remain at his old station, directly in front of the senator from New York.

IT SURPRISED NO ONE that Morse had proposed a bill for desegregating the District of Columbia. He had long been on the frontier of civil-rights activism, not only on the Senate floor and the board of the NAACP, but on a personal level as well. Though minorities made up a minuscule percentage of Oregon's voters and Morse was in no way dependent on their backing, he was among the first of the postwar senators to give a patronage job to an African-American constituent. He loved nothing better than to bring blacks to lunch in the Senate dining room—an almost unheard-of practice at the time— and to table-hop with them, pausing at length at those occupied by Southern reactionaries (James Eastland of Mississippi was his favorite), insisting in his friendliest manner on formal introductions and gentlemanly handshakes all around.

If, however, Morse had always been strong on civil rights—i.e., in the fight for racial equality—he had not been as forceful on civil *liberties*, in defending those freedoms enumerated in the first eight amendments to the Constitution. When it came to such issues as free speech and assembly and the right to political dissent, his views tended to be inconsistent: on occasion courageously protective of individual freedom, often plainly and profoundly illiberal. He might have been outraged by the persecution of Fighting Bob La Follette during and after World War I, but in subsequent periods he would find other kinds of political persecution entirely acceptable.

Though he always professed an expertise in the area and had very much wanted to teach the subject, Morse had never found an opportunity to offer a course in constitutional law while at the University of Oregon. Perhaps if he had, and had grappled with, for example, the sedition legislation enforced during World War I, he might have arrived at a more coherent position. As it was, he expressed a deep-seated commitment to civil liberties, but it was a commitment of the most abstract variety, imperfect in its logic, inconsistent in its meaning, unreliable in its application.

Morse's problematic approach to civil liberties went back to his days in Eugene. He was quick to claim a violation of academic freedom when he was being attacked by Chancellor Kerr and the Board of Higher Education, after he had publicly attacked them in 1932–33. But in a remarkably similar case, he was utterly unsympathetic when his ultraliberal colleague, Stephenson Smith, a Rhodes scholar and, in Morse's own words, "the most outstanding teacher" in the university, had his job threatened because of views expressed in public on Oregon political personalities. Indeed, unable to see the similarity, he successfully argued against having the faculty intercede on Smith's behalf—the same faculty that had defended *him* against

Kerr; he contended that once a professor became "embroiled in State politics," he could expect no help when politicians went after his hide. Academic freedom, he said, was limited to those instances where an individual was pressured for having voiced opinions "on a subject in which he is an expert."

It was a short jump from this anemic understanding of academic freedom to the view that teachers might be banned from the classroom because of their political beliefs. Morse made this jump in 1949, holding that keeping "communists and fellow travelers" off of college faculties was entirely justifiable. When one of his old friends, the noted legal scholar Arthur J. Freund, took exception, Morse insisted that since in his opinion communists promoted internal subversion, they were not covered by the protections of academic freedom. He did, however, admit that he shared one or two concerns with Freund:

> What I fear is that in the name of getting rid of Communists in our schools, "witch hunts" will be conducted to the damage of innocent people. Furthermore, there is the danger that students may be encouraged to follow Communists much more than would be the case if an attempt were not made to get rid of them. Nevertheless I believe those two dangers can be minimized if the utmost fairness is exercised by school administrators in presenting proof against teachers who either admit they are Communists or can easily be shown to be Communists.

It was an even shorter jump from proscribing communists on campus to endorsing congressional investigations of possible subversive activities in America's universities. As a March 1953 story in the *Chicago Tribune* indicated, Morse made this leap as well. At a meeting of the National Education Association, he said that educators could not consider themselves immune from such investigations, that in fact they should welcome them as opportunities to inform the public about their work. The next edition of *I. F. Stone's Weekly* carried the headline "Morse Truckles to the Witch Hunters." Arguing against Morse at the Chicago NEA meeting, and directly challenging the legitimacy of the investigating committees, was a man who would figure large in Morse's later political life: the president of the Rockefeller Foundation and future Secretary of State, Dean David Rusk.

It was doubly ironic that the right-wing *Tribune* should run a story in which Morse, one of the Trib's favorite targets, was taking the paper's usual side against a militant anticommunist like Rusk, a man who, in little more than a decade, would be accusing Morse of giving aid and comfort to the nation's communist enemies. Far from ironic, however, was Morse's contention that the purge of the universities was a necessary and even useful process, one that could be administered properly without annihilating the traditional safeguards of the classroom. Like most legislators of his day, Morse failed, refused, or was afraid for political reasons to acknowledge that McCarthyism was from beginning to end a witch hunt, and that witch hunts by their nature cannot be controlled by even the fairest of procedures.

Though he went his maverick way on most important questions, Morse was a product of his times when it came to civil liberties. However broad-minded and even unorthodox he might otherwise have been, his perspective on such issues was limited, in his early Senate years by the American anticommunist consensus, before that by the equally strong consensus on the idea that the imperatives of warfare overrode the usual constitutional restraints on the chief executive.

In 1942, Frank Graham, a close colleague on the War Labor Board, had asked Morse to respond to an American Civil Liberties Union challenge to the powers of the presidency. The ACLU opposed the wartime executive order requiring the relocation and incarceration of Japanese-Americans living on the Pacific Coast; it contended that such an order constituted a gross violation of civil liberties.

What the WLB's interest in the matter was is not clear, but whatever it was, Morse complied with Graham's request. He stated that (1) the ACLU would be making a mistake by resorting to "a lot of technical legal procedures which would be bound to interfere with the action of the President's officers"; (2) from his own point of view, as "a liberal and a staunch defender of civil liberties, I am enough of a realist to recognize that these are times when we have to

expect liberties to be abridged"; and (3) he had a number of Japanese friends on the Coast "who are citizens and who have been moved
into evacuee or concentration camps for the duration, and with one
exception they have accepted their plight without criticism." He concluded with the following: "My answer to the American Civil Liberties Union is simply 'Why take a chance?' of endangering our safety
by insisting upon fighting over a theory of civil liberties when that
theory does not make a constructive contribution to a successful
prosecution of the war?" If the measure of any such theory was
whether it contributed to a successful war effort, not many would
stand the test. All could be seen as relying on technicalities and interfering with the effective operation of the executive branch.

Possessed of this mentality, Morse was even driven into partial
agreement with jingoist sentiments from back home. A future constituent, a county judge from Hood River, wrote in 1944 reporting
that voters in his part of Oregon were "demanding the return of these
bestial ideaoligists [sic] to their home land. We would be pleased," he
added, "to know what your conviction may be covering the return
and exclusion of the Japanese from America, at the conclusion of the
war with these barbarians, an early reply will oblige."

Morse obliged within the week, suggesting that while the popular tack would be to advocate deportation of all Japanese, the Constitution simply would not allow such an approach and he would not
pursue it. However, he believed that there should be no further immigration of Japanese into the United States after the war, and that
those Japanese who were already here and were loyal citizens could
be resettled once the hostilities were over, so long as they could be
"spread out very thinly over large sections of the country and not be
allowed to concentrate in colonies, so to speak."

A year later, with the war drawing to a close, Morse was prepared
to be more generous to citizens of Japanese ancestry—accepting the
idea of uncontrolled resettlement—and less responsive to "the prejudiced bigoted letters" he said he had been getting. But by then the
nation was already falling into the grip of a militant anticommunism, and new targets for political prejudice were coming quickly
into focus.

In general, Morse's position on the red menace was illustrative of how most politicians thought from the late 1940s forward: the spread of communism had to be stopped, and it was incumbent upon Congress to do the job. Unlike many around him, however, Morse did not enroll in the anticommunist crusade a mindless true believer intent on achieving his goals regardless of the cost. He thus became distressed by what he saw as McCarthyism's undesirable extremes. Communists, he believed, were fair game, but as he repeatedly tried to indicate, witch hunts were totally unacceptable.

Morse became increasingly fed up with McCarthy's trials by accusation and with the fact that a never-ending parade of witnesses were systematically smeared, browbeaten, and broken on the rack of adverse public exposure. On June 1, 1950, he joined with six other Republicans in issuing the "Declaration of Conscience," written by Maine's Margaret Chase Smith, which condemned the lack of judicial due process in the probes of alleged communists. A few weeks later, he refuted one of McCarthy's most often repeated charges: that he, McCarthy, had proof showing that a high-ranking official, whom

Morse shares a platform with Senator Margaret Chase Smith (Rep., Me.) at the Waldorf-Astoria in New York. (Oregon Historical Society, OrHi 48580.)

he labeled "Mr. X," was a card-carrying communist secretly making anti-American policy from the heart of the State Department. Morse revealed the mysterious Mr. X to be one Edward G. Posniak, a low-level economist he had known in Washington in the late 1930s, a man whose loyalty he said there was no reason in the world to question. He told reporters that the investigations had degenerated into "kangaroo courts," depriving those appearing before them of their "constitutional guarantee of a fair trial in America."

Despite such strong language, Morse always stopped short of condemning McCarthy's ultimate goal: spotlighting communists everywhere and eliminating them from positions of authority. He was barraged by messages from Oregonians who felt that only Joe McCarthy stood between them and a communist takeover of America. In responding, he continually sought to distinguish praiseworthy ends from malevolent means. "I do not," he told one constituent, "question the sincerity of Senator McCarthy's motives nor do I his laudable objectives, but I do decry the methods he has used." "It is my personal judgment," he told another, "that there are some people in the State Department who are ... of such a liberal tinge in their political philosophy that the public interest demands that they be removed. However, it requires proof to remove them.... McCarthy's strategy simply handicaps us in getting the proof."

"Of such a liberal tinge"—if Morse could employ a phrase as vague as that to justify purging the State Department, then he could just as easily flow with the tide when it came to legislating against potential communist subversion elsewhere. He had supported the repressive Smith Act in 1948, and in September of 1950 he was one of the many liberals who voted both to pass the McCarran Act (officially, the Internal Security Act) and then to override President Truman's veto. The McCarran Act required the registration of so-called Communist-action groups; it used political beliefs, rather than action, as grounds for denying aliens admission to U.S. territory or for deporting them; and it set up concentration camps for detaining subversives "in time of national emergency." As one historian put it, not "since the bleakest days of World War I had American civil liberties been as seriously compromised."

Morse, as the following note to Eddie Sammons indicates, may have felt slightly guilty over not joining Hubert Humphrey, his old friend Frank Graham (now a Democratic senator from North Carolina), and eight others in voting to sustain Truman's veto—but not so guilty that he regretted his action.

> I would be the first to admit there are some rough spots in the McCarran bill, but the goals of the bill are sound and we can amend it later if experience with its administration shows that such amendments are needed.
>
> It seemed to me it would be a terrible thing to adjourn without passing some anti-Communist legislation because our failure . . . would have been a show of weakness on the part of the Congress and would have given aid and comfort to subversive elements within our country.

The existence of such "subversive elements" was a constant worry to Morse (and would be for much of his career), even as he also worried about the excesses of McCarthyism. The possible presence of such elements brought him into consonance with the anticommunist agenda of J. Edgar Hoover and the Federal Bureau of Investigation. He not only commended Hoover on "the great work which you and your organization are doing" in dealing with "communistic developments in this country," but he spoke on more than one occasion to the graduating class at the FBI Academy, applauding the bureau's unrelenting vigilance against internal subversion.

Such is the nature of anticommunism, however, that no one is beyond incrimination. So it was that when Morse (like most liberals) received letters from the public accusing him of being a communist, he would turn these over to Hoover to investigate for possible charges of slander. Meanwhile, the FBI was surreptitiously amassing its own files of potentially damaging material on *him*. Among other examples of Morse's dubious behavior, the bureau saw fit to record information from the attorney general of Georgia which said that Morse had engaged in (unspecified) "Un-American activities"; memoranda from field agents detailing his opposition to capital punishment in the District of Columbia; data describing his interest in opening up government records to defendants in federal court cases; and, apparently most serious of all, reports that he had been connected with a number of groups named on the U. S. attorney general's list of subversive organizations. According to McCarthyist precepts, such evidence could, from the bureau's perspective, be seen as grounds for casting suspicion on any man or woman in public life, even anticommunists like Morse who were otherwise regarded as "clean."

On one point Morse refused to compromise, red menace or no. He was firmly against the use of wiretapping, and he did not care who knew it, including the FBI. Of course the FBI did know, and duly noted his position in its files. The issue came up in 1954, when Attorney General Herbert Brownell asked Congress to pass legislation allowing evidence gathered through wiretapping to be admitted into court cases involving espionage or sabotage. Previously, it had been legal to obtain such evidence but illegal to use it as a basis for prosecution. Even before the question reached Congress, the bureau was tracking it, following the debate before the American Bar Association. Official notice was taken of Morse's statement to the ABA that wiretapping "is a police state method and members of the American bar should be in the forefront of those resisting totalitarian devices."

Throughout 1954, Morse made speech after speech attacking the wiretapping proposal. It was, in his opinion, a device that was worse than the evil it was supposed to correct. "I am shocked," he said at one point, "that an attorney general of the United States should believe Gestapo methods are needed in detecting Gestapo elements." On another occasion he contended that the practice—a "lazy policeman's tool," he called it—constituted "real subversion of the same class as Communist subversion," and he stressed that having to get a magistrate's warrant before installing a wiretap afforded no real protection of the citizen's overriding right to privacy. It seems that his ceaseless criticism had an effect on the outcome in Congress. Expected to sail through the Senate, the bill ultimately died in the Judiciary Committee, one of the few measures of its kind to fail during the McCarthy era.

If Morse stood stalwart on the wiretapping issue in 1954, he went in the other direction that same year on the question of political association. The Communist Control Act, passed in August, contained a key clause that had first appeared as an amendment offered by Humphrey. The amendment, which Morse had cosponsored, defined the Communist party as "an agency of a hostile foreign power" and declared that membership in the party was in and of itself a prosecutable offense. Civil libertarians fought the amendment bitterly, arguing that it effectively denied individuals the right to vote, was an abridgment of free association, and constituted both a bill of attainder and an *ex post facto* law.

Up for reelection in November, and perhaps eager to show his anticommunist colors after his McCarran Act vote, Humphrey, with the help of Morse, Lyndon Johnson, and a young senator named John F. Kennedy, pushed his motion through the Senate by a vote of 41 to 39. The final bill, deprived of enforcement powers as the result of a conference with the House, passed unanimously. With or without enforcement powers, Morse proclaimed it a triumph of congressional solidarity.

Morse's inconstancy on civil liberties was evident in a great many areas, nowhere more so than in dealing with the congressional investigative power itself. By February of 1954, McCarthy's abuses had generated a groundswell of reaction. Morse and Herbert Lehman offered a resolution setting out guidelines for bringing some semblance of judicial fairness to all Senate inquiries. Quickly labeled the Morse-Lehman Code, the resolution guaranteed witnesses:

> the right to counsel;
>
> the right to know the subject to be discussed, and the date and place of the inquiry;
>
> the right to confront and cross-examine accusers;
>
> that no hearing could take place without a majority of the committee present;
>
> that closed-hearing testimony could not be published without majority approval.

Though the resolution had wide support, it was, according to customary procedure, referred to the Senate Rules Committee. There,
under pressure from Jenner, it was shelved indefinitely.

However useful the Morse-Lehman Code might have been in
curbing abuses, it and other proposals like it were, in the opinion of
civil libertarians, not the most effective means at hand. The one thing
that McCarthy, McCarran, Jenner, and their ilk depended upon was
money. Without adequate financing, their committees could not
function. How much, or even whether, a given committee was funded was the prerogative of the Senate as a whole; it could, if it voted to
do so, put a runaway committee out of business by denying it the
dollars it needed to operate. This is precisely what many had hoped
the Senate would do a year earlier, at the outset of the Eighty-third
Congress.

At that time, the Internal Security Subcommittee, formerly
chaired by McCarran but now by Jenner, had asked for a budget of
$150,000. Morse, to the surprise and disappointment of many, said
he would under no circumstances join in the move to deny the committee its funding. He even volunteered the opinion that Jenner was
probably not asking enough. In the course of debate, in a legislative
recitative of a kind heard only in the U. S. Senate, he and Jenner conducted a theatrical interlocution aimed at getting the committee
every dollar it had requested.

> *MORSE.* Does the Senator from Indiana agree with me that
> there is in the body politic . . . a great deal of concern over
> the question as to whether there exist in our country sub-
> versive elements which, in case of an all-out war with Rus-
> sia, would work to the detriment of our security?
>
> *JENNER.* I do not think there is any question about that. . . .
>
> *MORSE.* Let us be frank, as I know the Senator from Indiana
> always is. I am referring to no Member of the Senate, but
> does the Senator agree with me that there are those in this
> country who seem to be in opposition to the granting of any
> increase in funds for the investigation of subversive activities

to which the Senator has referred, because for their own reasons, none of which is good, they do not want the Congress
to put itself in a position where it will have the funds to de-
tect subversive activities in this country.

The "always frank" Senator from Indiana was extremely happy
to agree, and even happier to thank the Senator from Oregon for his
final benediction:

> MORSE. To the Senator from Indiana, I say I wish him well
> in the investigation. I think the attitude of the Members of
> the Senate should be to judge the Senator on the basis of the
> procedures which he follows. I have no reason to believe that
> those procedures and the conduct of the committee will not
> be in keeping with the high standards of American justice
> and fair play.

Of these remarks, I. F. Stone wrote: "It is hard to believe that this was
Wayne Morse of Oregon talking."

Morse might have been more believable had he limited himself
to his usual principle that investigations are essential to the work of
the Congress and that an attempt to emasculate any one committee
could potentially endanger the viability of all of them. By itself, such
an argument would, under the circumstances, have sounded merely a discordant note rather than a false one, and at least would have
struck Morse followers as not unfamiliar. But for Morse to make that
argument and then go on to red-bait the opposition and state that
he expected nothing but "fair play" and "justice" from a committee
he had previously described as a kangaroo court made clear that the
exchange with Jenner was entirely disingenuous.

Why had Morse gone so far? However ardent he had been about
rooting out communists, he had always kept some distance between
himself and the leading red-bashers. Indeed, a few years earlier he
had courageously protected Anna Rosenberg, a Truman Defense Department nominee, from senatorial witch hunters who sought to de-
fame her. Why had he now become a defender of those very same
huntsmen? A. Robert Smith contends that in this instance, he may

himself have succumbed to the fear of McCarthyism. Smith is probably right.

Precisely at the moment Morse was singing Jenner's praises, an
Oregon constituent, one Russell W. Duke, was being investigated by
McCarthy's subcommittee. Duke was what might charitably be
called a freelance entrepreneur, or, in the parlance of the day, a promoter. He was a combination fixit man and influence peddler who
set himself up in "public relations," representing individuals having
tax troubles with the government. When McCarthy subpoenaed
Duke (he was actually after one of Duke's contacts) and took possession of his records, he made public mention of the fact that Duke
had had dealings with Morse. Duke had contributed to Morse campaigns, and Morse's office had done occasional favors for him, apparently in the normal course of constituency business.

Assuming that Morse had done nothing wrong in his connection
with Duke—and there was no evidence to the contrary—would the
mere mention of his name in association with a McCarthy investigation have been enough, as Smith suggests, to move him to support
someone like Jenner? Normally, it would not. Morse, however vac-
illating he might have been in confronting McCarthyism, would normally have come down on the side of preserving the judicial integrity
of congressional investigations. But in this instance, he may have
been frightened of becoming himself an object of the witch hunt.

This was, after all, the period (early to mid-1953) when Morse
was at his weakest—a time when he was on the receiving end of
enormous abuse from former friends and present colleagues; when,
committeeless and seemingly without allies, he was depicted by
Collier's as "The Loneliest Man in Washington." Under these conditions, isolated during the reign of terror that was McCarthyism,
tagged in the best-selling *U.S.A. Confidential* as an "ideological Socialist" and a "Marxist apologist," he may have taken the easy way
out. By defending and even praising Jenner, he may have deflected
McCarthy—who later stated for the record that Morse was blame-
less in the Duke affair—and thereby saved himself from a charge of
guilt by association from which he could not have defended himself.

If Morse did cave in to McCarthyism in 1953, by the following year, when the Senate finally came around to the question of disciplining McCarthy, he was ready to join forces with those who wished to bring the witch hunters to bay. Even then, however, his methods raised eyebrows. When, in a tension-filled evening session in late July, Republican Ralph E. Flanders of Vermont introduced his historic motion to censure McCarthy, Morse immediately called for a seven-point bill of particulars providing grounds upon which such a censure could rest. His motion helped to crystallize debate by focusing on an itemized list of offenses committed by McCarthy. At the same time, however, it shifted the focus by calling for the whole issue to be sent to committee before being decided by the Senate as a whole. Coincidentally, but for different reasons, this was the very position being advanced by Guy Cordon of Oregon, William Knowland of California, Herman Welker of Idaho, and most of the conservative coalition. They hoped that at best the motion would die in committee or, at worst, languish there until after the November elections.

Was Morse once again rallying to the side of McCarthyism? The answer in this instance is a definite no. In supporting the censure motion, he made no bones about his feeling that severe punishment was in order. He accused McCarthy of "political thuggery" (a description Barry Goldwater would later apply to Morse) and said that he must be stopped; but he insisted, as he had in his labor-arbitration work, that proper procedures must be followed. Especially in this case, he argued, it would be hypocritical to violate normal Senate procedure in an attempt to discipline one of the members for committing that very kind of violation.

Though his stance might have been procedurally sound, Morse knew it would irritate those who wanted to pounce on McCarthy without parliamentary delay. As he informed Jim Landye, "I realize that a good many liberal groups misunderstood my position on the issue but [had I not called for committee action] . . . I would have had to walk out on the sound principles that I taught for fifteen years in a course of criminal law procedure."

Morse's advice was followed, and as part of the larger censure motion, his bill of particulars was sent to a designated committee for deliberation. While that was happening, Morse and McCarthy met head-to-head on the floor of the Senate. Their confrontation was in a sense a delayed playing out of an event that had been scheduled the previous year: the two were to have had a televised debate sponsored by the AFL—the topic being "the fairness of Congressional investigations"—but the debate was canceled when McCarthy backed out at the last minute.

The Communist Control Act was at issue, and McCarthy was livid that Morse would stoop to supporting such an abstract measure while simultaneously pointing the finger at someone—namely, McCarthy—who was fighting subversion where it really counted, in the frontline trenches. He complained that "nice little boys" like Morse and his friends were pleased to pass grandiose resolutions condemning "skunks," but steered clear of the "dirty, unpleasant business" of digging them out. "They do not," McCarthy shouted, "like the odor that goes with skunk hunting." Morse angrily rejected the skunk metaphor, charging that McCarthy's procedures involved "blackmailing innocent people" and constituted nothing short of "lynch law."

> *McCarthy*. I think the junior senator from Oregon is guilty of the most fantastic, dishonest name calling. . . .
>
> *Morse*. I love these kisses of death.

And so for forty-five minutes the argument raged, until Morse pointed out that it was foolish to continue since the Senate would have the final say when it considered the censure motion and resolved to impose a code of fairness on all investigations.

Though Morse's bill of particulars played a role in McCarthy's ultimate demise, it cannot be said that he was one of the leaders in the anti-McCarthy movement. Indeed, the two legislators—one a maverick, the other soon to become an outcast—had, on some undefinable level, a kind of understanding and perhaps even a modicum of mutual affection. Both had grown up in rural Wisconsin (in fact, it was once predicted that McCarthy would follow in Morse's progressive footsteps) and both were used to going their own way, regardless of the consequences. Clay Myers reported that when he visited his dispirited senator just after he had bolted the Republican party, Morse took him into the Senate dining room, where, to Myers's astonishment, the only senator he introduced him to was Joe McCarthy. Perhaps Myers would have been less surprised had he known that Joe and Wayne had long indulged in the whimsical practice of swapping neckties in the Senate chamber whenever either decided he didn't like the one the other was wearing.

Yet when all is said and done, Morse came out where he did for ideological rather than personal reasons. When the Communist Control Act passed, Morse said it demonstrated that in the Senate "there is no division of opinion among liberals, conservatives and those in between when it comes to our utter detestation of the Communist conspiracy." These remarks prompted historian Robert Griffith, looking back, to observe that because "the Senate remained transfixed by this anti-Communist consensus, the problem of dealing with Joe McCarthy became an exercise in circumvention—to strike McCarthy while leaving intact the issues and assumptions upon which he had built his political career."

Such circumvention was, and would continue to be, part of Morse's mixed approach to the problem. It should be emphasized that his approach *was* mixed. As a maverick progressive, he would not conform to *any* ideological dogma. In addition to his fight against wiretapping, he had also been outspoken in attacking another facet of McCarthyism, the federal loyalty program, which he described in 1949 as "insulting" to every government worker ever forced to sign a loyalty oath in order to retain his or her employment. And by 1961 he would come to suggest that the really serious communist threat was to be found overseas, that the Communist party–USA was scarcely a danger to anyone, made up as it was largely of FBI infiltrators. Nevertheless, he remained, in Griffith's words, "transfixed by the anti-Communist consensus," and it would be late in life before he would see this question from a broader perspective.

8

Leading the Revolution

THE FIRST SEVEN MONTHS OF 1956 are seldom thought of as a watershed in American political history. Yet two decisions made during that period would prove to have transcendent significance. First came the news in early March that, despite the serious heart attack he had suffered six months earlier, President Eisenhower would stand against Adlai Stevenson for a second term in the White House. This was followed by the eleventh-hour announcement that Eisenhower had, against the wishes of many in his party, chosen to retain Vice President Nixon as his running mate. Together, these decisions would influence the direction of American political life, not only for the ensuing four years, but for the next two decades and beyond.

As for the more immediate future, which is what concerns us here, the Republican party—out of power those thirty long years prior to 1952—was, with or without Nixon on the ticket, overjoyed at the probability of another Eisenhower term. Republicans were also hopeful that given the broad sweep of Ike's coattails, they might again control the Senate *and* its key committees, as they had during the president's first two years in office. Since Senate Democrats held only the slimmest of majorities in 1956, the Republicans could regain superiority merely by retaining the number of seats they currently held—a likely prospect—and winning a single additional seat in November. The seat they had in mind above all others, the one they would move prodigiously to capture, belonged at that moment to Senator Wayne Morse of Oregon.

Morse was targeted in 1956 for several reasons. First, there was the natural desire to take revenge against a man regarded not only as a deserter, but as a turncoat now seeking reelection as a registered member of the opposition. (The story of Morse's switch to the Democratic party will be related shortly.) Beyond vengeance, getting rid of Morse would also eliminate the GOP's *bête noire* on Capitol Hill. More than any other Democrat, Morse had used the Senate floor as a forum for berating the president and his policies. He had especially irritated the administration by delaying, "on principle," Senate approval of nearly every cabinet appointment sent up for consideration, even that of his old friend and former student Harold Stassen. Most unforgivable of all was the fact that while still an Independent, in January 1955, he had cast the tie-breaking vote that transferred organizational control of the upper chamber from Republican hands to those of Lyndon Johnson and the Democrats.

While the thought of retribution was enough to place Morse at the head of the Republicans' hit list, there was an equally important reason why he was marked for defeat. Previously, no one in American history had been able to switch parties and be reelected to the Senate, and it seemed unlikely, especially given his bridge-burning over the preceding four years, that Morse would be the first to do so. Republicans would pour huge anti-Morse resources into Oregon in part because they regarded him as vulnerable, a weakened incumbent ready to be taken.

Weakened or not, Morse could be counted upon to run a tireless campaign. Knowing this, GOP strategists in Washington thought they could turn clear advantage into certain victory by choosing a candidate who could, by reputation alone, generate massive support at the polls, regardless of how effective the Morse campaign might prove to be. They selected a man closely identified with President Eisenhower, a man whose name would at least rival Morse's in popular recognition among Oregon voters: the current Secretary of the Interior and former two-term governor of Oregon (1948–53), the Honorable Douglas McKay.

Such a choice might have been masterful just a few years earlier, but in 1956 that choice, made with little consultation on the home front, was potentially a disaster. In their eagerness to defeat Morse, Republican leaders in Washington had failed to take into account the extensive changes that had occurred in Oregon politics over the preceding half decade. Not only had registered Democrats grown to outnumber their Republican counterparts, but with two congressional victories in 1954—Edith Green's in the House, Richard Neuberger's in the Senate—Oregon Democrats had decisively broken the traditional Republican stranglehold on the state's national elective offices. And since Morse had played a crucial role in these victories—campaigning effectively and raising money for both, actually making the difference in the case of Neuberger—he would come to his own campaign far stronger than Republicans in Washington imagined. McKay, on the other hand, despite significant residual popularity, was a holdover from the past, representing an older Republicanism now under attack throughout the state.

ALTHOUGH THE FULL STORY of the Oregon Democratic party's rise from oblivion is too long to present here, there is room for a brief telling of a tale whose beginnings have, with the passage of time, taken on legendary proportions. As the story goes, a plot for nothing less than a political revolution was hatched during the Second World War in the remotest reaches of the South Pacific by two young Oregonians, one a naval lieutenant, the other a Red Cross field secretary. Both envisioned a postwar Oregon liberated from Republican conservatism, embracing a Democratic leadership not only enlightened and progressive, but wise in the ways of electioneering.

The truth, as Howard Morgan (the Navy lieutenant) remembered it, was slightly less spectacular. "At various times and places during the Pacific war," he wrote, "I enjoyed long sessions with Monroe Sweetland [the Red Cross worker] . . . on the general subject of Oregon politics and what might be done after the war to revive the moribund Democratic party." For his part, Sweetland's most dramatic political effort while in the Pacific involved getting thirty-four Oregon GIs, nearly all Democrats, registered to vote via absentee ballot in the 1944 Republican primary for senatorial candidate Wayne Morse against incumbent Rufus Holman.

Nevertheless, while far from a revolutionary conspiracy, the Morgan-Sweetland meetings provided an important starting point

*Oregon Democratic chairman How-
ard Morgan (here with Congresswoman Edith Green) and national
committeeman Monroe Sweetland
led the state Democratic party's re-
surgence in the 1950s. (Oregon Historical Society, OrHi 91000.)*

for the postwar work to which each was committed. The energetic
Sweetland had been national president of the leftist League for Industrial Democracy during the latter days of the Depression. He had
spoken at Reed College in Portland, where he met tough-minded
Morgan, then president of the Reed student body. Their friendship
grew as a result of their wartime conversations, and this, more than
any commonly held strategy, allowed them to cooperate in their attempt to revitalize the state Democratic party. On one idea, however, there was firm agreement: revitalization would have to take place
from bottom to top, would have to include precinct, district, and
county organizations as well as those which, like the Oregon Young
Democrats and the party Central Committee, operated on a statewide basis.

One cannot say that the Morgan-Sweetland program was everywhere triumphant. Party organization would never become consistently powerful on the state level, and in some counties the party remained as moribund as Morgan had known it in the old days. But in
large measure, and where it mattered most—at the polls—the reforms were enormously productive. Along with Dick Neuberger and
a host of younger activists, Sweetland, who was elected Democratic

National Committeeman in 1948, and Morgan, who after a tour running the Oregon Young Democrats became Democratic state chairman in 1952, were able to infuse into their party's electoral politics a
renewed sense of dedication and purpose. Many county committees,
and for short periods even statewide organizations, were greatly
strengthened and suddenly in a position to mount campaigns which
Republicans could ignore only at their peril. The stunning victories
in 1954, which also included significant gains in the state legislature,
demonstrated just how great that peril could be.

Looking back from the end of the decade, Morgan graphically
described what he saw as his accomplishment:

> The party was fatally burdened by crooks, drunks, has-
> beens, never-wases and stumble-bums. Our party was not
> taken seriously by the voters in those days. Too many of
> them knew that it served as an auxiliary to the Republican
> Party, drawing its financial backing from moneyed Republi-
> cans, who thus guaranteed themselves a docile adversary
> which could be either defeated or managed. . . . My job as
> state chairman from 1952–56 consisted mainly, then, of rid-
> ing the bums out, recruiting first-rate candidates and giving
> the public competing points of view to choose between. The
> merit of this approach shows in the election results.

Although Morse had labored heroically with Morgan in the 1954
election, he had remained an Independent, his nominal status since
the end of 1952. Even at that earlier date, when Republicans were blistering him for deserting their party, Democrats were already wel-
coming him as one of their own. By 1954, liberals like Sweetland and
Morgan were more than anxious to enlist him publicly into their
ranks. Sweetland had been acquainted with Morse since the early
forties and was one of those Democrats who had urged him to oppose Holman in the Republican primary of 1944; he was especially
hopeful that Morse might quickly register as a Democrat and, incidentally, bring to his new party the support of organized labor that
he had always enjoyed.

Morse, on the other hand, found it convenient to bide his time.

He listened, though never seriously, to innumerable overtures to start a new, national third party; and while hinting in 1954 that he might run as an Independent in 1956, he repeatedly indicated that he did not know how his name would finally appear on the ballot.

Oregon Democratic party activists regarded the addition of Morse to their 1956 ticket as monumentally important. The sooner they knew his intentions the better, for a successful Morse campaign would not only mean a Democratic monopoly in the U. S. Senate; it could, some believed, also pave the way for a sweep of statewide and congressional offices. Sweetland had wanted a declaration from Morse soon after the '54 campaign so that organizing for '56 could begin in earnest. While everyone was still celebrating the Neuberger and Green victories, he applied pressure by suggesting publicly, without discussing the matter with Morgan, that Morse might lose party support in 1956 unless he announced as a Democrat within the next few months.

For his part, Morgan was happy to have Morse's electoral assistance and was content to play a waiting game as far as formal party designation was concerned. Having already begun to discuss with Morse the when rather than the whether of a registration announcement, he responded angrily, and also publicly, to Sweetland's

National committeeman Monroe Sweetland at his desk in 1959. (Oregon Historical Society, OrHi 90997.)

ultimatum, describing it as "unfortunate" and in no way representative of the Oregon Democratic party; he also implied that because of his actions, Sweetland was not a "responsible member" of that party. Though Morgan and Sweetland had had disagreements in the past, none had generated such open animosity. Morse's continued independence had inadvertently driven a wedge between the state's two most important Democratic functionaries.

There was also increasing friction between Morse and Sweetland. Morse took at least as much exception as Morgan to what were perceived as Sweetland's strong-arm tactics. Although he had had a long association with Sweetland, and although as a national party figure Sweetland had gone to bat for him in his Senate committee quest and had helped to place him on the board of Americans for Democratic Action, Morse never quite trusted him again. Thereafter he would turn first to Morgan for political advice and consultation.

It is not hard to imagine why Morse delayed his decision for so long. He enjoyed the attention derived from his senatorial standing as a freewheeling, one-man Independent party—the maverick beholden to no one—and, other things being equal, he would have gladly continued thus unencumbered, especially since he was about to regain some of his seniority in the Senate. He also enjoyed playing to the limit his hard-to-get act in Oregon, if only because it left him a significant creditor in the political-debt department. However, it was clear to all who understood the situation that it *was* an act, that Morse had no home except in the Democratic party, that he had no chance of winning as an Independent in 1956.

Morse also knew he had no real choice in the matter. His resolute work for Democratic candidates was done not merely to advance the cause of liberalism, but also to secure his potential standing in the party (and perhaps to atone as well for supporting reactionary candidates in 1946). Charlie Brooks, who worked with Morse during the 1954 campaign and then became his Oregon representative in 1956, recalled that a Democratic candidacy was simply taken for granted. "I didn't even talk to him about it," Brooks said. "It never occurred to me, and I don't think to him, that he wouldn't run as a Democrat. I certainly knew he was not going to run as an Independent."

After more than two years as an independent, Morse (with a pleased party chairman Morgan looking on) registers as a Democrat in early 1955. (Wayne Morse Historic Park Corporation.)

When Morse finally registered as a Democrat in February 1955, it was no surprise to anyone, Sweetland included. Given the potential importance of the act, however, the *St. Louis Post-Dispatch* found it newsworthy to run a summary of reactions from eleven Oregon newspapers, most of which, although unable to resist a derisive jab or two, were at least accepting of what had become the inevitable. The *Bend Bulletin* offered a fairly representative opinion:

> This is Morse's third political affiliation in less than two and one-half years. He wasn't happy in the Republican party. He wasn't happy in the Independent party even though he was its only member. It is doubtful that he will remain happy with the Democratic party forever.

It's a new party label for the senior Senator from Oregon. But it's nice to see it's the same Wayne.

That "the same Wayne" would conduct a formidable campaign
in 1956 was not in doubt. His health was good and his energy level
was, as ever, extraordinarily high. Just a few years before, however,
there had been questions about his condition. In early 1953, after finishing a two-hour speech against the nomination of General Motors'
Charles E. Wilson as Secretary of Defense, Morse stepped into a
lobby just off the Senate floor and fainted. Though quickly revived
and able to return to cast his vote against Wilson, he was sent home
on the advice of a physician.

It was widely believed that Morse had suffered a heart attack or
stroke, a belief he found ridiculous. He insisted that the "blackout,"
as he called it, was the result of an overdose of codeine, which he had
taken to relieve the pain of some dental work (part of the continuing treatment made necessary by the horse kick he had received the
previous year). "I am tip-top in all departments," he told a concerned
Jim Landye. "I can lick my weight in Republican reactionaries and
lick triple my weight in phony Democratic liberals." A few months
later, he would demonstrate that such a self-appraisal was not all that
extravagant.

TODAY, IT IS THE POSITION of environmentally concerned liberals
that coastal states should have the right to decide when, how, and
whether their offshore oil reserves will be utilized. Most liberals oppose a federal policy that at times has sought to exclude the states
and give giant petrochemical companies a free hand in exploiting,
and probably desecrating, the Atlantic and Pacific continental shelves.
In the 1950s, however, liberals took an opposite stand. They believed
that underwater lands, whose rich potential had only recently been
discovered, could be better preserved and more prudently managed
by federal agencies, which, they were certain, would be more resistant than the states could be to the massive pressure for development
exerted by the oil companies. Debate on the "tidelands" issue raged

especially hot in the Senate in 1953, revolving around an administration bill that gave individual states effective decision-making power over all offshore resources.

With a small group of Democrats, Morse began a filibuster on April 1 against the administration proposal. On April 24, with the filibuster holding strong, he took his regular turn in the speakers' rotation, prepared if necessary to talk almost as long as he had in his ten-hour Taft-Hartley filibuster in 1947. As it turned out, he went considerably past his anticipated deadline. Indeed, holding forth for an astonishing twenty-two hours and twenty-six minutes, he broke by five hours the Senate's previous nonstop-speaking record, which had been set by his idol, Fighting Bob La Follette, in 1908.

Morse's feat, which made headlines throughout the country, was notable in many respects. First, there was the sheer endurance he had displayed. Though given occasional speaking breaks when fellow filibusterers put friendly questions to him, Morse was denied the extended rest periods senators usually enjoy while lengthy quorum calls are taken. He was denied these because Senate leader Taft ruled such calls out of order. As the *New York Times* indicated, Taft kept Morse glued continuously to his spot on the Senate floor. When at one point Morse started to sit down, the *Times* reported, "Robert A. Taft of Ohio, Majority Leader of the Senate, called him to order. Senate rules require a speaker to stay on his feet, behind his desk, or lose the floor. . . . Senator Morse was permitted to prop himself against the face of the desk behind him at times but otherwise was held strictly to Senate rules."

For nourishment, the *Times* continued, Morse "sipped sparingly from cups of bouillon and tea and once in a while took a swallow of ice. This was supplemented by a few crackers and a chocolate bar donated by a colleague." The *Times* reporter apparently missed the occasional glass of orange juice, a notable omission if only because the juice preparation was personally supervised in the Senate kitchen by either Bill Berg, Morse's administrative assistant, or Merton Bernstein, his chief legislative aide. Morse had heard tales of Senate orations having been summarily aborted because the speaker of the moment had been slipped a mickey, and he was taking no chances that one of his beverages might be similarly spiked.

More amazing to many than either Morse's endurance or his meager food intake was his apparent bladder control. Morse stood on the floor of the Senate for more than twenty-two hours without relieving himself. Furthermore, after finishing speaking, he immediately held a press conference, and only when it concluded did he return to his office to use the bathroom. Was such a thing possible? Many, including some physicians queried, believed it was not. Even Morse's sister Caryl thought he had worn a type of adult diaper. Others opined that he had had a "motorman's friend" or some similar contraption strapped to his leg. But those who, like Bernstein, were there throughout the filibuster, insisted, as did Morse himself, that no such device was used, that he had relied on his self-control and good physical condition to get him through the ordeal. And since Morse had not known beforehand that he would not be allowed to leave the floor, there is every reason to accept this explanation.

If Morse's physical accomplishment was remarkable, his oratorical performance was equally so. Like his Taft-Hartley filibuster, this speech was notable for its consistent relevance to the subject at hand. While filibusters are notorious for ornamental blather—Huey Long liked to give recipes for Southern "pot liquor"—Morse seldom deviated from his topic. His tidelands speech did include parentheses on why he left the Republican party, his latest stand on Taft-Hartley, his committee-assignment problems, the worthiness of World Court membership, and the virtues of the rural electrification program. But relative to the whole, these were minuscule departures, and Morse could note with justifiable pride that "there is much comment in the Senate about the fact that all of my filibuster speeches have been germane to the subject." And not only germane; they were for the most part extemporaneous. Of the entire tidelands filibuster, less than 25 percent was read from prepared material. In other words, Morse spoke for more than sixteen hours without benefit of written text.

Of such deeds are legends made. And as the following somewhat gabbled exchange indicates, it did not hurt in legend-building that Morse could retain parliamentary acuity even after remaining on his feet for such a protracted period.

THE PRESIDING OFFICER. The Chair would remind the Senator from Oregon that it is now tomorrow.

MR. MORSE. No; it is still today. Most respectfully I say that I think the Presiding Officer is referring to yesterday, but I am talking about today. I know where I am. This is today, 6 minutes old.

By way of adding to the legend, Morse wore a red rose in his lapel during most of his speech. A Portland schoolteacher was among those in the gallery when he began to speak; so taken was she by his argument—he supported an alternative tidelands bill that would earmark offshore-oil funds for education—that she purchased a rose from a florist near the Capitol and sent it to Morse with a note of support. He acknowledged the gift and wore the rose (with a fresh replacement provided by aides every few hours) for the rest of his speech. Thereafter, it became a custom for the Senate to expect a lengthy oration whenever Morse appeared on the Hill, rose *en boutonniere.*

INCREASED PROMINENCE resulting from the tidelands debate probably helped Morse's efforts to improve his standing in the Senate, but not much, especially since in the end his side lost and the administration bill prevailed. Of far more importance in an institution where holding power means everything was Morse's January 1955 vote that allowed the Democrats to take over the Senate. Two years earlier he had voted with the Republicans because, he said, he had only just resigned from their party and owed it to his constituents to cast such a vote. While not insignificant, his vote in 1953 was not crucial: had he supported the Democrats, he would have created a tie that Vice President Nixon would have broken in favor of the GOP. In 1955, Morse had the deciding vote in an otherwise evenly divided chamber. Everything depended on which way he would go.

Morse always maintained that no quid pro quo had been involved in making his decision. He argued that as far as backing the Democrats was concerned, he "never had a single conference with

Lyndon Johnson or the Democratic leaders with regard to any committee assignments"—and there is in fact no indication that such a conference ever took place. But the truth is that it never had to take place. Morse had announced six months earlier that he would vote with the Democrats to organize the Senate. Johnson, Morse, and the entire Democratic caucus knew he must be rewarded for this. Indeed, Johnson, who became the youngest Senate majority leader in history as a result of Morse's vote, made no secret of his intentions when he told the *Washington Star* the previous November that Morse would receive his due: "What he wants," Johnson asserted, "he's going to get. If I have it [to give]." Because of what *each* man wanted and expected, each had become, in the words of Johnson biographer Alfred Steinberg, "the most important man in Washington to the other."

So much was riding on Morse's vote that Johnson—who, rather more than Morse, never forgot that today's political enemy may be tomorrow's ally—could ignore the fact that just eleven months earlier Morse, angry at Johnson's tidelands position, had stormed into Texas and denounced him for being too cozy with the Republicans. The *Houston Chronicle* quoted Morse as saying:

> I can't reconcile certain action[s] of your senior senator (Lyndon Johnson) except upon the basis of the fact that he is afraid he is going to be defeated.
>
> Texas ought to elect itself two senators. It doesn't have any now. One (Price Daniel) represents the oil interests and the other (Johnson) represents Lyndon. When I say this I have engaged in the height of senatorial courtesy. It is a very polite statement.

Even though Morse's salvo—which received a huge press in Texas—may have hurt Johnson's reelection chances, Johnson not only saw fit to ignore it but, by the end of 1955, could describe himself as one of Morse's most ardent supporters. In October he sent Morse a birthday note, telling him that "way down here deep in the heart of Texas, you have got at least one vote for Wayne Morse in almost anything that he wants. That vote belongs to Lyndon Johnson who thinks that you are one of the ablest men in the United States

Senate and who counts you among his closest friends." While Johnson's sentiments, expressed in his typical down-home smarminess,
cannot be taken at face value, they nevertheless show how far Morse's
star had risen in the Democratic party.

For his pro-Democratic (pro-Johnson) vote, Morse was awarded some of the committee assignments he most desired. The long-
coveted seat on Foreign Relations was finally his, as was a slot on the
powerful Banking and Currency Committee. In addition, while retaining his seat on the D.C. Committee, he was named to the Select
Committee on Small Business, making him, in LBJ's words, "one of
the very few members of the Senate who is serving on four Committees" and, in Johnson's eyes, one of the "few men who can take
on such a heavy work load and perform all of the work ably and
thoroughly."

The new positions brought with them a new stature. At last
Morse had come in from the cold of committee exile. Now he could
take his rightful place among the veteran leaders of his chamber.
Now, entering the 1956 election season, he could accurately be described as a Democrat with clout in Congress, someone who, as he
saw it, the Oregon press would "have difficulty in belittling."

While the press might stop short of belittlement, that was about
the best Morse could expect. His connection with former ally Bill
Tugman had long since been broken; and there would be no other
editorial support in a state whose major newspapers were entirely in
the hands of Republicans, many of whom had never forgiven Morse
for leaving their ranks. Moreover, Morse had recently had to endure
the attacks of his old mentor, the onetime New Dealer Raymond
Moley, now a syndicated conservative journalist whose column appeared in many Northwest dailies and who regularly received anti-
Morse bulletins from a network of Oregon informants.

Morse was fortunate to get any kind of hearing in the press, for
he had previously had serious difficulties with individual papers,
with particular reporters, and even with one of the wire services. So
angry had he been at one point that for a single, minor transgression
he had barred from his office A. Robert (Bob) Smith, Oregon's leading political journalist (and future Morse biographer), and Roulhac

Hamilton of the *Oregon Journal*, accusing both of consciously misrepresenting the facts in a particular story to make him look bad.
Because of another alleged distortion, he similarly banned *all* representatives of the Associated Press; the organization's copy, he
stated, was so biased and misleading that whenever he saw the AP
byline, he read it as "Always Polluted." However, by election time the
differences with Smith, Hamilton, and the AP had been more or less
patched up, and as the 1956 campaign moved ahead, the Morse
forces would discover that the working press would treat them with
a reasonable degree of fairness—as reasonable, that is, as one could
expect given the pro-McKay sentiments of most editorial offices.

THOUGH FIRMLY AGAINST MORSE, those who controlled the media
were far from ready at the outset to open their arms to McKay. Neither they nor the other stewards of local Republicanism had been
sounded out on his selection. Had they been, they might have
warned McKay—who filed his candidacy at the absolute deadline—
that he should think twice before running. Many had been backing
McKay's successor, Governor Paul Patterson, and when Patterson
unexpectedly died a few months before the primary, had moved
their support to a popular former state senator, Phil Hitchcock.

With superior money and manpower, McKay defeated Hitchcock in the primary, 123,281 votes to 99,296—a solid enough victory, except that his total was actually less than the sum accumulated
by Hitchcock and two also-rans. In other words, McKay would enter
the general election having failed to win a majority in his own party.
He could perhaps console himself with the thought that the total
votes for all Republicans exceeded those for the two Democratic con-
testants by more than 14,000.

On his side, Morse cruised to the Democratic nomination by
trouncing a little-known, small-town gas station owner named
Woody Smith, at a campaign cost of less than $10,000. He had re-
mained in Washington during most of the primary attending to Senate business, and paid scant notice to the 39,000 votes Smith managed to attract. His mind on McKay, he saw the real campaign about

to commence, and he was ready to give the former governor the fight of his life.

In fact, he was more than ready. According to Charlie Brooks, the Morse camp had hoped all along that McKay would choose to run. Mert Bernstein went even further. "We were absolutely jubilant," he said, "when McKay filed at the very last minute. We were only afraid he might not make it in time."

Why so much eagerness to have McKay as an opponent? First, as Secretary of the Interior, McKay had been on the front line defending administration natural-resources policies, many of which were unpopular in Oregon. This not only provided Morse ammunition he might not have had against other candidates, it also gave him an opportunity to begin his campaign the way all politicians dream of beginning: decisively and unreservedly on the attack. Second (and at least as important), Morse's people regarded McKay as an easy mark, a man who was, in Bernstein's words, "very wooden, quite inept, and not too bright. . . . a small man in every sense, with no personal

Secretary of the Interior Douglas McKay, former governor of Oregon, heeded President Eisenhower's call to run against Morse in 1956. (Oregon Historical Society, OrHi 88328.)

appeal." In sum, a man who, despite his renown, was unlikely to measure up to the presence and *éclat* of a Senator Morse.

However, considering the 39,000 primary votes against their
man and the 14,000 surplus pulled by the Republicans, there was a
danger of early overconfidence at Morse headquarters. Whatever
Morse and his followers believed, a Multnomah County poll in early
July showed Morse in front by only three percentage points, with 15
percent undecided. A statewide poll a month later gave Morse another half percent, but in light of the attitudes expressed, it was clear
that support for both candidates was thin and potentially volatile.
For example, many who described themselves as Morse backers also
said they greatly disapproved of Morse's opposition to Eisenhower
(the man, not his policies); nearly half of those supporting McKay
did so not because they liked him, but because they disliked Morse;
and a substantial number felt that, at bottom, the election provided
Oregonians with a "bad choice situation."

To consolidate or improve their standing with voters, the candidates would have to run effective, professional campaigns. For this
there would have to be money, and given the importance of the
race—the *New York Times* assigned two reporters to cover it—
money in large quantities. If money was needed, money there would
be. It came from everywhere, especially the coffers of both parties in
Washington. GOP national electoral committees sent McKay more
than two and a half times the amount sent to any other Senate candidate. Large McKay donations also poured in from the chief executives of such wealthy corporations as Tidelands Oil, Republic Steel,
General Electric, and Seagrams (as well as from Morse's old Republican standbys throughout Oregon—Eddie Sammons, Aaron
Frank, et al.).

Oregon's high-powered campaigns did not go unnoticed in the
rest of the nation. The *New York Times* asserted that "the Oregon
Senate seat is a top-priority target of both parties this year. Each has
invested more prestige, high-level effort, and possibly even cash, in
the Oregon outcome than in any other Senatorial race in the country." The Washington-based *AFL-CIO News* agreed with the *Times*
on the magnitude of the race, but saw the forces at work from a more

partisan perspective. As the *News* described it, the election had been turned "by outside influences into a matter of nationwide significance"; and it was the paper's opinion that these reactionary "influences" intended to defeat Morse "at all costs."

If anti-Morse factions beyond Oregon had loosened their purse strings in an all-out effort to control the election, organized labor, local and national, was prepared to meet them head-on, dollar for dollar. Morse was thus the beneficiary of large contributions sent by most of the important unions in the country, from the Steelworkers and Machinists to the Hatters, Cap and Millinery Workers. His treasury was also increased by considerable funds from the Committee on Political Education of the AFL-CIO. As a bonus, labor-movement supporters who normally gave only in their own areas made significant donations from such faraway cities as New York, Miami, Philadelphia, and Chicago.

Measured by today's campaigns, with costs running into the multimillions, Oregon's 1956 Senate-race totals seem less than impressive. Seen against the norms of the day, however, the amounts were staggering. Just two years earlier, Dick Neuberger had spent $104,000 to Guy Cordon's $138,000 in a Senate campaign thought to be shamefully expensive. At the end of their contest, Morse reported expenditures of $266,431, McKay $229,680. And in light of the huge quantities of unaccounted-for cash that flowed through both offices, it is likely that the reported figures, high as they were, were grossly understated.

The election brought not only big money into Oregon, but also the biggest names in each party. Both presidential candidates, who otherwise might have skipped Oregon with its meager supply of electoral votes, made an appearance to support their man. Drawing huge crowds, Vice President Nixon came not once but twice, the second time when McKay's campaign fortunes seemed to be sagging. For Morse, along with Democratic vice-presidential candidate Estes Kefauver (who drew poorly), there was a parade of Democratic dignitaries, including Eleanor Roosevelt and Senators Paul Douglas of Illinois and Albert Gore of Tennessee. Lyndon Johnson, remembering Morse's intrusion into his Texas race in 1954, promised, only half

Adlai Stevenson and Dick Neuberger with Morse at a Democratic rally in Portland in 1956. (Oregon Historical Society, OrHi CN 014737.)

facetiously, to "come out and campaign for or against you, whichever you deem best."

Given that neither candidate could buy the election with a superior war chest, what was needed—more than the backing of visiting luminaries, which locals tend to discount anyway—was an edge in the campaign itself, a solid issue that citizens could base their votes on. At various times, each candidate believed he had such an issue.

The Morse camp was convinced that McKay was vulnerable on natural resources, and public sentiment in Oregon, reaching new heights of Democratic populism, seemed to support this conviction. Morse relentlessly assailed McKay, both for the inexcusable "giveaway" of the tidelands oil rights and for the equally indefensible "giveaway" of Hells Canyon. The canyon had been making explosive front-page headlines for years. In May 1953 the Eisenhower administration, speaking through McKay, reversed a policy of the Truman administration and announced a plan to allow the Idaho Power Company to erect three small hydroelectric dams on the Snake River in Hells Canyon along the Oregon-Idaho border. With fellow liberals from the region, Morse had attacked this plan, calling it a "shocking abandonment" of public power, an idea whose only aims were to enhance the profits of a private monopoly and drive up the price of electricity in the Northwest. He proposed instead—as Truman had, following the example of the highly successful Bonneville project on the Columbia—one large dam to be built and operated by the federal government. Although still alive in Congress, Morse's proposal suffered a major defeat in the Senate on the eve of the campaign, which made him all the more determined to flay McKay with the issue.

Whether McKay reacted too quickly at times to Morse's forceful rhetoric or whether the wealthy ex–Chevrolet dealer merely gave random expression to a mindlessness he was sometimes noted for, the result was the same: instance after painful instance of declaiming first and thinking later. For example, rather than respond to the Hells Canyon attack by simply presenting the administration's position, he chose to wax patriotic. "I represent the American free enterprise idea," he declared. "Morse represents the left-wing Socialist idea." Morse, he added, stopping just short of red-baiting, was like those other senatorial socialists, Herbert Lehman, Hubert Humphrey, Estes Kefauver, and Dick Neuberger: "They're the worst of those left-wingers—and they're always all together." Such ideological cant was ignored or ridiculed by Oregonians well schooled in natural-resources issues and served only to make McKay sound silly. He would sound even sillier later in the campaign making gaffes of a more serious nature.

Part of the problem was that, whatever his intelligence quotient, McKay and the campaign were not a happy fit. As his last-minute entry suggests, the sixty-two-year-old Interior Secretary was a reluctant torchbearer, agreeing to answer his party's call only because the president's closest advisors had thus persuaded him. Moreover, the initial reception he received from the local hierarchy did little to improve his attitude. "You'd think I was a carpetbagger coming here from Washington," he complained to the *Wall Street Journal*, "instead of the grandson of a Hudson's Bay Co. trapper who settled in Oregon in 1842."

McKay's less-than-full measure of enthusiasm made it all the more difficult to overcome his customary low-key campaigning style. Folksiness, wherewithal, and a leg up in registered voters had been enough to win two gubernatorial races against undistinguished, underfinanced opponents. But now everything had changed. Now, as the nominee of the minority party, he was up against a well-heeled candidate who, in McKay's own wistful words, had "a wonderful speaking ability," a candidate who, as the *New York Times* put it, was a most "intense personal campaigner."

Just how intense was summarized by an obviously bedazzled *Times* reporter: "He was on the road at 5:30 AM for a 6:30 breakfast meeting fifty miles away. He made four other small meetings by mid-afternoon, drove 150 miles at speeds up to eighty miles an hour to catch a plane into Portland, arrived just in time to introduce Mrs. Franklin D. Roosevelt at a Jefferson-Jackson Day dinner, then drove seventy miles back eastward to spend the night and be on hand for a 7 o'clock breakfast the next morning." Against such a daily onslaught, McKay—described by the *New York Post* as a man "with the benign and agreeable air of a small-town druggist"—would have to fight with everything at his disposal.

For McKay there were from the beginning but two issues: one was Morse, the other Morse's opposition to the president. When he

Eleanor Roosevelt came to Oregon in 1956 to raise funds for both Morse and Bob Holmes (right), the Democratic candidate for governor. (Wayne Morse Collection, CN 1312, Special Collections, University of Oregon Library.)

first announced his candidacy, the ex-governor said it was his great pleasure to give Oregonians a chance "to choose between honor and the objectives of the Eisenhower administration and the slippery philosophy of Wayne Morse." Morse's "slippery philosophy" was his special target, and to highlight it, his campaign published a 250-page book (later expanded by a hundred pages) entitled *The Documented Record of Senator Wayne Morse*. The book contained Morse's eleven-year voting record, excerpts from his public utterances (including his most savage attacks against Ike), and selected extracts from what others had said about him.

By relying on direct quotation and ignoring context, the book's compilers were able to put Morse in a bad light. They showed that he not only had changed positions on certain issues over the years, but had typically defended new positions in the name of principles described as inviolable, even when doing so contradicted previous positions based on principles that had also been pronounced inviolable. The book thus provided a running catalogue of oratorical inconsistency, some apparent, some real. Perhaps worse, it also contained negative commentaries by Dick Neuberger, who in his pre-senatorial period as a freelance journalist had written critical pieces about Morse's days as a Republican.

While it made an initial impact, the effect of the *Documented Record* fell far short of what its authors had hoped. More interested in live campaign events, most news people simply skimmed the volume and reported its highlights. And although the book did provide fodder for editorial columns, since most of these were anti-Morse to begin with, it accomplished little in the process. In fact, Morse managed to turn the *Documented Record* to his advantage. Because the general public was not inclined to spend time reading such a lengthy treatise, Morse could attack it with impunity, indignantly labeling it—not entirely without justification—as part of a smear campaign aimed at diverting voters from more important questions.

Having failed once, the McKay forces tried a second publication, a sixteen-page pamphlet carrying the awkward title *The Record Wayne Morse Would Like to Have You Forget*. In the middle of the pamphlet was a double-page photo showing Morse orating to a legislative chamber devoid of occupants; accompanying the picture was a caption reading in part, "Wayne Morse empties the Senate with his long-winded speeches." Rerun in papers throughout the state, the photo was an effective piece of propaganda. It ostensibly offered graphic proof of what the *Documented Record* had claimed: namely, that Morse's endless speeches, especially his Independent party "committee reports" on Friday afternoons, were systematically ignored by fellow senators.

It soon became clear, however, that McKay's people had botched things again. The photo depicted not, as implied, a normal Senate speech, but a filibuster being delivered at a late hour when most senators were home asleep. Even worse, it turned out the photo had been cropped from a larger picture that had appeared earlier in *Life* magazine. Immediately there were charges of "tampering" and "smear tactics," charges for which McKay had no answer. The fact that even the uncropped original had shown only one additional senator in attendance was lost in the clamor, and so was the argument about Morse's general lack of listeners. A crafty ploy had been transformed into yet another instance of campaign bungling.

The more mistakes McKay made, the more Morse seemed to turn up the volume of his attack—so much so that Montana's Mike Mansfield, Morse's colleague on Foreign Relations, felt it necessary to counsel less stridency and more reason: "A high-level, idealistic approach . . . will get you just twenty times as many votes in Oregon as a 'Give 'em Hell' fighting speech, however much more the latter might be to your personal liking. . . . you are speaking *for* the people of Oregon to the nation, and you want to make them *proud of you*, not mad at either you or the Administration." But since Morse was himself mad at the administration, as well as caught up in the tenseness of the campaign, he was neither interested in nor capable of taking a more "idealistic approach."

At times, especially after a particularly grueling stretch, Morse could become tired, depressed, out of sorts, and convinced that regardless of objective evidence, things were going poorly, McKay was edging ahead. On such occasions, words of encouragement, even from those closest to him, could have an effect opposite to that intended. Mert Bernstein remembered a night at the Roosevelt Hotel in Portland when he tried to counter one of Morse's gloomy predictions with an optimistic forecast of his own. Suddenly he found himself the object of his boss's wrath: "'Goddam it, Mert,' he shouted at me, 'I don't want to hear that kind of thing.' And he flung a mechanical pencil against the wall with such force that it shattered. It was as close as he ever got to physical violence, and I felt that, in effect, he was striking me. That was one of our lowest points."

While such low points were rare, there were other, more nagging sources of tension that had to be dealt with. The Sweetland-Morgan breach had never been healed, and there had been complaints from around the state that Morgan had become increasingly high-handed in his style of leadership. Whether as the result of such criticism or not, Morgan decided during the summer to take a position with the Stevenson presidential campaign; among other things, this meant that he would be less available to assist in Morse's. Yet even with intraparty rivalries swirling about him and without confidant Morgan's full involvement, Morse was able to keep his campaign moving in a positive direction.

At the outset, he had had the good fortune of bringing aboard a competent, reliable chairwoman. Since most of the activists with whom he had had ties were Republicans, he did not now know where to find such an individual. On the recommendation of party leaders, he hired Jean Lewis, a member of the legislature with solid Democratic connections throughout Oregon. Reputed to be the first woman ever to manage a U.S. Senate campaign, Lewis proved to be especially effective in working with the indefatigable Charlie Brooks in coordinating Morse's barnstorming schedule.

Rivaling Lewis and even Brooks in overall importance was the powerful crew Morse had brought with him from Washington. Along with the exuberant Bernstein were Bill Berg, who came to run the Portland office with a steadying hand, and Phyllis Rock, a stalwart legislative assistant whose job it was to prepare position papers and help with strategy. Morse's obvious dependence on this team of "outsiders" could and did give rise to a certain degree of factionalism; and it was indicative of the extent to which all participants were committed to the cause that resentments arising out of D.C.-Oregon jealousies were kept to a nondisruptive minimum. When resentments did arise, their prompt settlement owed much to the calming influence of Berg.

Anyone who has looked closely at Washington life knows that every successful senator has someone upon whom he or she relies to help shoulder an otherwise impossible burden, someone who not only is an effective silent partner but, when the occasion demands, can speak authoritatively for "The Senator" to members of the staff and to the outside world. In Bill Berg, Morse had one of the best.

Born in Chehalis, Washington, Berg had been one of Morse's favorite students at the University of Oregon law school. Having enrolled the year Morse arrived in Eugene, Berg went on to earn a doctorate of jurisprudence at a time when that degree meant producing extra work as well as a dissertation. In 1937, he joined Morse's staff at the attorney general's office in Washington. After a teaching stint at the University of South Dakota, he went back to work for his old boss at the War Labor Board in the early 1940s, stayed on when Morse left to run for the Senate in 1944, and was a professor of law at the University of Colorado when Morse lured him to Washington in the spring of 1952.

In doing historical interviews, it is rare to find consistent opinions about any given individual. In the case of Berg, however, the recollections of those who knew or worked with him are astonishingly close to unanimous. In a high-pressure job that could have been for some a continual nightmare, Berg was noted for keeping his composure, for dealing straight with all comers, for never misrepresenting his boss's intentions. He was probably the only person in Washington Morse ever fully trusted, and the only staff member who addressed him by his first name. (When the ambitious Bernstein asked for the same privilege, Morse told him that it wouldn't be appropriate.)

There is no question that Berg, as administrative assistant, had control of the office. His ability in this area was described by former Morse employees as "brilliant," "artful," and "truly wonderful." His relationship with Morse was in some ways similar to the jocular connection Morse had enjoyed with Paul Washke in the old days in Eugene. A great deal of banter arose over Berg's fastidiousness. For example, Morse liked to make him uneasy by occasionally resting a crate of live chickens on his desk. Then there was Bill's Catholicism, another of Morse's favorite targets. And while Berg's admiration and respect for Morse were obvious, he had no difficulty disagreeing with him, gave as much as he took in the ragging department, and, unlike many in the office, always understood that his boss was a mere mortal. His secret code name for Morse was "Windbag," which he sometimes affectionately invoked when passing on instructions "from W. B." to Charlie Brooks.

In election campaigns, Berg's contribution would be less in the area of political tactics—he did not, in Bernstein's words, "have much taste for politics"—than in keeping things on an even keel, making sure everyone was pulling together. He was especially skillful at maintaining Morse's personal equilibrium, so that it would probably have fallen to him to lift Morse from the kind of depths described by Bernstein in the pencil-throwing incident.

In the 1956 campaign, however, even if Berg should have failed in his efforts, McKay could be counted upon to do or say something to bring Morse back to normal. During his first visit to Oregon, Nixon held a strategy session for McKay supporters in Eugene. When one worker complained that Morse had been scoring big with natural-resources pronouncements, Nixon, by way of a pep talk, assured the group that issues were not really that important. "It's the votes that count," he said, and then admonished his listeners to "go out and get the votes." That night, giving Nixon's words his own special spin, McKay told a huge public audience that "the issues don't amount to anything. It's the votes that count."

It was as if McKay had invited Morse to jump down his throat. Morse was quick to oblige. Campaigning in Eastern Oregon, he told the press, which had splashed McKay's assertion across the state, that he was "not surprised" by such a cynical remark, one that "describes McKay's philosophy perfectly." From that moment forward, Morse seldom delivered a campaign speech without flailing McKay with his "issues-don't-count" sentiment. And since such attacks were typically well received by audiences, the press, whether it wanted to or not, was forced to quote McKay's words every time Morse attacked them. Similarly, when at subsequent appearances McKay tried to qualify or amend what he had said, he invariably reiterated his original remark, thereby making matters worse. There was no escaping the blunder.

Years later, Morse would look back at 1956 and pinpoint the Morse-McKay debate in Portland three weeks before the election as the campaign's turning point. (A. Robert Smith would follow him in this view.) Morse did in fact emerge from that long-awaited, oft-delayed event stronger than he had been, but the truth is that by that time the electorate had already made up its mind. An early October poll showed Morse significantly ahead in three of Oregon's four con-gressional districts and hugely ahead (49 to 39 percent) in populous Multnomah County. The poll also showed him to be more favorably viewed by members of his own party than McKay was by Republi-cans. Only the memory of Truman's upset of Dewey in 1948, plus a Republican press that preferred not to give up the ghost, kept alive the question of who would ultimately win.

Given Morse's lead, the Portland debate could help McKay only if Morse stumbled badly. Since nothing close to that happened, the rest of the campaign, though fought to the wire, was anticlimactic. On election night there were the usual last-minute jitters at Morse headquarters, but the voting trend became clear almost as soon as the polls closed, and thereafter the only uncertainty was how big Morse's edge would be. The final tally gave him 54.2 percent to McKay's 45.8, a truly astounding victory in the face of Eisenhower's statewide margin over Stevenson of 55.2 to 44.8 percent. In his first race as a Democrat, Morse had smashed his opponent and had near-ly equaled the votes of one of the most popular Republican presi-dents in U.S. history.

"Well, we did it," Morse exulted to a friend a few days later. But rather than gloat over having routed the enemies who had sought to crush him, he struck a more objective note. "I'm glad it is over," he told his friend, "although at the same time I am glad that I was able to be the vehicle through which the Democratic Party was able to beat the type of campaign that was waged against us." And if using the first person plural and picturing himself as a "vehicle" through which others might achieve their goals seemed a bit pretentious, Morse could be forgiven a moment of excess. Whereas Eisenhower's celebrated coattails had shown little carrying power, just the opposite could be said of Morse's. In addition to the Senate victory, Oregon Democrats had taken three out of four congressional contests, plus the governor's race, while earning a majority in the lower house at Salem and an even split in the upper. The Democratic revolution had reached its zenith, and it was understood by all that Morse was its man of the hour. It thus seemed entirely natural when, shortly after the election, Dick Neuberger issued a press release advancing Morse as a most likely vice-presidential nominee for 1960. After all, if Wayne Morse could lead Oregonians to such a famous victory, there was no telling what he might do for the national ticket.

(We may reflect for a moment on how different our world would now be had Morse (1) captured the vice-presidential nomination, (2) been part of a victorious campaign with John F. Kennedy, and (3) succeeded JFK to the presidency: no Lyndon Johnson as Commander in Chief, no military escalation, no Tonkin Gulf Resolution, no Vietnam War, and in all probability no Richard Nixon in the White House.)

At the crest of his popularity, Morse could be even more relaxed than he had been after his crushing defeat of Howard Latourette in 1950. With the election behind him, he could look forward to the last third of the decade confident of both his standing at home and his status in Washington. Out of such confidence, he could even depart from the immediate past and magnanimously promise to rise above partisanship and "extend to President Eisenhower my full cooperation in the great crisis that confronts not only our country but the world." Morse being Morse, however, and politics being politics, such promises would prove easier to make than to keep, especially when the moment of electoral triumph had faded and new grounds for disagreement had arisen. Controversy, with Eisenhower as well as others, with Democrats as well as Republicans, would be, as it always had been, a part of Morse's career for the rest of his life.

9

Dick and Wayne

WITH MORSE'S VICTORY IN 1956, Oregon Democrats could celebrate not only their occupation of both U. S. Senate seats for the first
time since 1914, but also the knowledge that many regarded their delegation as the most outstanding in the upper chamber. Like Morse,
Dick Neuberger had wasted little time once in the Senate making a
name as an extremely bright and promising legislator. Oregon might
occupy a little-known corner in the far Northwest, but its team of
dynamic Democratic senators commanded respect and admiration
throughout the country.

By the late 1950s, however, respect and admiration had, at least
in Oregon, given way to wonderment and confusion. Once seemingly so close that the press referred to them jointly as "Morseberger,"
Wayne and Dick were now openly at each other's throats, attacking
one another almost daily, and Oregon Democrats, for all their electoral achievements in the fifties, were beginning to feel demoralized.
The Morse-Neuberger relationship had deteriorated to such a degree
that the two men were now engaged in American history's most extraordinary public feud between two senators from the same state
and the same wing of the same party.

That their relationship could be described as extraordinary was
nothing new: going back thirty years, it had always been extraordinary. But only those who knew something of its history—and there
were few who did—could understand why all attempts to end the
feuding would be doomed to failure.

MORSE FIRST MET NEUBERGER IN 1931. This in itself was an out-of-the-ordinary occurrence, since Morse, who had just become dean of the University of Oregon law school, would in the normal course of events not have encountered the nineteen-year-old freshman. He was introduced to Neuberger by Ep Hoyt, editor of the *Oregonian*. Dick had worked for Hoyt as a sports reporter while in high school in Portland, and he would continue as the paper's campus correspondent in Eugene. Morse was impressed by Neuberger's intelligence and felt almost immediately that he would make a significant mark on the university.

Neuberger did not so much matriculate at Eugene as descend upon it. Tall, curly-headed and broad-shouldered, with an engaging smile and an effusive manner, he began his collegiate life with an air of supreme self-confidence. Despite his freshman status, he was given control of the sports desk on the student newspaper, the *Oregon Daily Emerald*. The following year he became the first sophomore in university history to be elected editor in chief, beating out upper-classman and future roommate Stephen Kahn for the position.

Neuberger's initial semester in the editor's seat was conspicuous for its ideological orthodoxy, as when he announced in a front-page column just before the 1932 election that he was voting for Herbert Hoover (gratuitous testimony, actually, since he was not yet old enough to vote). Neuberger had grown up in a protected environment, a pampered son in a well-to-do Jewish family—his parents owned a chain of eight bakeries and three restaurants—and his political views, when in fact he thought about anything other than sports, probably reflected those of his strong-willed, conservative-minded mother.

Politics aside, Neuberger's impact on the paper was powerful. He knew instinctively how to sell a story. "He had," according to Kahn, "a gift for embroidering the news to make it more interesting: if there were two hundred people there, the crowd would swell to six hundred."

Kahn, like Neuberger, came from a well-off, educated Jewish family; unlike Dick, though, he arrived in Eugene with a highly developed political consciousness—a consciousness raised by *his*

As fellow undergraduates and roommates at the University of Oregon in the 1930s, Dick Neuberger and Stephen Kahn fought for a program of liberal reform, on campus and off. (Oregon Historical Society, OrHi CN 021261.)

mother, who had long been a liberal activist in New York. Kahn began to influence Neuberger even before, but notably after, they became roommates in 1933. Neuberger quickly converted to Kahn's perspective—especially after being introduced to the poorest parts of Eugene, where for the first time he saw families wracked by poverty, disease, and hunger—and immediately embarked on a feverish journalistic crusade to combat social injustice.

Neuberger and Kahn aimed their guns in all directions—sometimes collaboratively, sometimes separately—with editor Neuberger in the position of point man and Kahn, who was not on the *Emerald* staff, operating behind the scenes. One of their ideas, the "Oregon Daily Emerald plan for reduced living costs for hard-pressed students," dominated campus discussion for nearly a semester. Every *Emerald* issue for a month and a half headlined their proposal, which maintained that if the university would turn one or more of its half-empty dormitories into cooperative living and dining facilities, students could eat for $1.62 a week and live on fourteen dollars a month. The fraternities, charging thirty to forty dollars a month for room and board and worried about maintaining occupancy at those prices, were appalled by so "radical" a proposal. The Interfraternity Council condemned the plan and its creators as "detrimental to the best interests of the student body and the University in a year of unrest and readjustments." Neuberger, in turn, described the fraternity stand as "the meaningless gibberings of davenport scandal-mongers." Frat members nailed up collection cans to send him "back" to Harvard, where all such radicalism was presumed to originate.

Once unleashed politically, Neuberger seemed to be everywhere at once. He ceaselessly excoriated student waste and frivolousness in the face of nationwide deprivation. Like Morse a teetotaler for life, he further alienated fraternity row by supporting a ban on 3.2 percent beer in campus living organizations. (Drinks with a higher percentage of alcohol were already forbidden.) In addition, he mounted a strenuous campaign against compulsory ROTC, testified before the state legislature, wrote letters to governmental officials at all levels, became heavily involved in off-campus campaign work, and turned out articles for publications with coast-to-coast audiences. All the while he was becoming more closely involved with Dean Morse.

Which came first is impossible to say, but it is clear that Morse took a shine to Neuberger and that Neuberger cultivated Morse's patronage. It was a cultivation so unabashed that its public expression might have drawn attention, except that readers of the *Emerald* had grown accustomed to regular doses of editorial hero-worshipping. For all his apparent radicalism, Neuberger lavishly praised selected authority figures from around the state. Morse he depicted as a "Roscoe Pound of the future," a man of "militant fearlessness," cut from "the same legal stamp that produced men like Louis D. Brandeis, Benjamin N. Cardozo, Harlan Fiske Stone and Oliver Wendell Holmes." In return, Morse, always susceptible to flattery, provided the paper with a pipeline into the inner circles of campus power. Neuberger was a frequent visitor to the dean's office, where the two would talk long and intimately about on- and off-campus politics, where they would, as Morse put it, "sing together songs of hate" directed at common enemies.

By the time he completed his one-year editorial stint, not only had Neuberger come to take for granted his influence with Morse, but, depending on circumstances, he seemed to see himself as prized

Neuberger took his influence with Morse for granted, and saw himself alternately as Morse's intimate associate or as his favorite nephew. (Private collection.)

student, intimate associate, favorite nephew, or spoiled son; and Morse was sufficiently indulgent to let him play these roles with impunity. At the end of the summer of 1933, Neuberger thought nothing of writing Morse from Portland and asking him to see that an F he had received in a speech class was changed to an incomplete. The following week he wired Morse to meet his train when it arrived in Eugene.

Neuberger entered the University of Oregon law school after his junior year, a move not uncommon for students in those days. However, he had not given academics a high priority as an undergraduate and, with a record of incompletes and dropped courses, had failed to fulfill three years of credited work. Although he had strongly encouraged Neuberger to major in law, Morse tried to persuade him to attend summer school to make up earlier coursework before commencing legal studies. Neuberger refused. "I only want to know the law," he insisted. "Aside from that, to heck with the degrees!"

Morse then tried to persuade him to spend his first year at the University of Washington law school, where he would be free from the extracurricular distractions that had kept him from his class work in Eugene. This advice Neuberger also rejected, explaining that he saw his future in Oregon politics and prominent liberals had told him that he could not in later years afford to have it said that he had been driven from the university. Morse found this argument ridiculous. He urged Neuberger to "face facts. . . . You do not know what it is to grind upon a course of study, and I predict for you a very poor record in this law school unless you do devote every hour of your time to the study of the law." Neuberger ignored the counsel, held to his decision to return to Eugene, and soon had occasion to test the accuracy of Morse's prediction.

Morse made one last attempt to get Neuberger to see the light, but mixed as it was with admiration for Dick's growing reputation as a journalist, it was scarcely convincing.

> I cannot begin to tell you how proud I am of you, because when you stop to think of it, Dick, you have published more articles in this last year in outstanding national magazines and newspapers than many prominent academic men are able to publish in a lifetime. In spite of my tendency to beat you over the back, which I assure you I am going to keep on doing, I do want you to know how pleased I am about your writings. They show an ability which I don't want you to destroy by moving ahead too fast in the matter of getting your law school training.

Morse finally resigned himself to the inevitable, but he cautioned, "If you do return to this school . . . remember that I am not going to accept any alibis for a single grade below B, nor shall I give you any time to help you out of any controversy that you get into, because if you return here your job is to study law and not to crusade." Morse would find it difficult to maintain such determination.

Although he left the *Emerald* editorial board early in the fall quarter, Neuberger, as Morse had feared, found little time for class work and did just enough to scrape by with a C-minus average. His attendance was sporadic, and Morse had to reprimand him more than once for cutting so frequently. The crunch came in Carlton Spencer's course, Legal Bibliography, a required class in elementary research. For "Legal Bib," students had to hand in written responses to a series of questions at each class meeting. Reflecting back on Legal Bib fifty years later, Kahn (who had entered law school a year before Neuberger) remembered that no one, least of all he and Dick, took the course seriously. Not only were the assignments trivial in the extreme, but, Kahn recalled, "you had to turn in your homework, like in grade school." Kahn dutifully did his homework, and before turning it in, he, like every class member, compared his answers with others to ensure that he hadn't listed incorrect page numbers or case citations. His mind elsewhere, Neuberger had no patience even for this procedure. He skipped all but one class, and to save time, he simply copied appropriate answers for every assignment from one or another of his classmates.

It happened that the upperclassman who graded papers for Spencer was a fraternity man, and when he noticed that Neuberger invariably came up with answers identical to someone else's, he brought charges before the law school honor committee. Composed exclusively of "frat rats," the committee was overjoyed at this unexpected opportunity to go after their nemesis. Likening what he did to cribbing on a midterm, the committee voted unanimously to find Neuberger in violation of the honor system, recommending that he be failed in the course and lose twelve hours of academic credit. Neuberger professed to be dumbfounded. "Those sons of bitches," he exclaimed to Kahn, "have found me guilty of cheating!"

Those "sons of bitches" did not have the final word, however. At Kahn's instigation, Neuberger appealed to the law school faculty, which agreed to hear the case and then make a recommendation to the university Student Advisory Committee. Though Kahn, representing the defense, argued "like a Philadelphia lawyer," and though Neuberger testified "absolutely honestly" that he had had no intention of "doing a wrong"—he would not, he said, have copied the assignments so openly had he felt he was cheating—the faculty, with one exception, voted to uphold the student committee and confirm the guilty verdict. The one exception was Dean Morse, who, while admitting that he might be "yielding to sentimentality," and while finding the defendant "*motivated by thoughtlessness, carelessness, lazi-*

ness, and a lapse of ordinary good judgment," could not bring himself to conclude that he was fundamentally dishonest and in violation of the honor system.

Unknown to Kahn, before the procedure began and throughout the nine days of deliberation by the faculty and the Student Advisory Committee, Neuberger deluged Morse with what must be one of the most remarkable series of letters ever written by an undergraduate to a university professor, let alone to the dean of a graduate-level professional school. Many composed in the small hours of the night, the letters alternately beseech and command Morse to deliver Neuberger from his "enemies." They show a desperate young man in mortal fear that his professional life had been ruined; they also show a familiarity with Morse that allowed Neuberger to press his demands to extraordinary limits.

Over and over again, Neuberger gave instructions as to strategy and tactics, including long paragraphs of specific language Morse should use in defending him. As far as the law faculty was concerned, if Morse could not get one or two colleagues to vote with him, he should simply preempt the proceedings and make his own conclusive finding in Neuberger's favor: "Dean, what are you going to do? . . . You have the power to prevent this injustice. You have veto powers in the law school. . . . You have the power of God today—you can make or break my reputation. What are you dean for, if it's to sit by as merely one of five? You can save me. It might make a few of your colleagues perturbed for a short time; but, Dean Morse, it is better that they be perturbed than I be wronged." If vetoing his own faculty was not strictly kosher, Morse should remember that Neuberger had "never adhered to rigid newspaper ethics" in writing pro-Morse stories for the *Emerald*: "I think the time has arrived for you to repay that favor."

Neuberger appealed to Morse's sympathy: "It would break my parents' hearts if I was penalized for this." To his loyalty: "Please, please, please, save this situation. I'd do it for you. I'd do anything for you. . . . I've always dreamed of you and I doing something great for the people of the state someday." To his conscience: "Can you lie easily on your pillow in the night watches of the years to come if you know that I was humiliated and my honor stained, without you doing every solitary, possible, obtainable, act WITHIN EVERY BIT OF POWER YOU CAN COMMAND to prevent it?" "I returned to this hell largely because of my faith in you." To his vanity: "Dean Morse, you are a man of unimpeachable intellectual integrity. . . . you are a man of courage, character and conscience." And, with a narcissistic touch, to Morse's political convictions: "The reason I pray you can get me off without a flunk on the record for Spencer's course is that . . . [they would] be able to go around and say, 'Dick was penalized for cheating.' It would set me back years and damage irrepably [sic] the Progressive cause in Oregon."

Neuberger was not above turning political screws if he had to. He argued that if what he had done constituted cheating, it was also cheating for everyone else to compare answers with classmates before turning them in. His actions, he said, were not that unusual; he had simply been singled out for punishment, he was being persecuted. The university certainly could not prosecute everyone, but, he declared, if he alone were convicted when all about him were equally guilty, he would "have a basis for complaint and protest, and all hell will break loose." He threatened to call for an American Civil Liberties Union investigation and to make the whole affair a statewide political issue: "God knows I'd hate to quit here and start an attack throughout the state," but if his persecution continued, he would do precisely that.

He threatened a more portentous act if all else failed—"one card," as he described it, "no one can play except myself." He said that

> no one can repudiate the honor of a departed martyr to class persecution and religious bigotry, and it is better that I live a short life with honor and integrity than a long one with an unjust stain hanging over my head, ready to be used against me every time I assert the intellectual honesty which no one in the school possesses except myself and you. . . . There is a way out—a way they never dream I would take. But I have the nerve, I have had it all along, and I am not afraid. I believe every man lives for a certain cause, and when I believe

he can best aid that cause by aiding it no longer, he should do so. . . . Unless you can save my character from an unjust stain, I shall conclude this last letter to you with

So long, dean.

There are times when passionate young persons under stress must be taken seriously when they threaten suicide. Given his other attempts to turn up the pressure, however, it is difficult to see Neuberger's outburst as anything more than emotional blackmail. How Morse saw it is impossible to say. He did not provide written responses to any of these letters, and there is no record of his having discussed them with anyone.

Court of last resort, the university Student Advisory Committee was composed of various deans and administrative officers. The law faculty decided to submit to the committee both the majority opinion, written by Orlando Hollis, and the minority opinion, prepared by Morse. But at Morse's request, he and Hollis were allowed to read their opinions in person. Hollis, a man of solid mind and stolid manner, tended to be tight-lipped and perfunctory in speech—some students found him boring—and in rhetorical exposition he was no match for Morse. As events developed, however, Morse had more than oratorical mastery going for him; he was not alone in working for Neuberger's acquittal.

A behind-the-scenes lobbying effort had been mounted to swing the committee to Morse's view. The intermediary was Cornelia Pierce, the wife of former governor Walter M. Pierce and an influential member of the State Board of Higher Education. In a hand-delivered letter, Roscoe Nelson, former board chairman and a friend of the Neuberger family, had urged her to use her influence on Neuberger's behalf. At the same time, Kahn had gone to Portland to persuade her to intercede directly with the committee member most responsible for student discipline, Karl W. Onthank, dean of personnel administration. In Kahn's presence, Pierce called Onthank and told him to "stop tormenting that boy." Shortly thereafter, the committee announced its decision: it reversed the law faculty and voted unanimously to find Neuberger not guilty.

Morse had saved Neuberger's neck—without his minority opinion there would have been no grounds for reversal—but the victory was not without its price. In defending Neuberger, he had used up
valuable good will with his faculty. Indeed, at one point Morse himself was subject to censure for exceeding accepted rules of confiden-
tiality. While the Student Advisory Committee was considering the
Neuberger case, Morse indiscreetly discussed both his position and
that of the law school majority with his senior class in Wills. Word of
his discourse got out immediately, questions were raised in a special
faculty meeting that afternoon, and he was forced to defend himself
before dubious colleagues. He emerged from the meeting unscathed,
but just barely. According to the recorded minutes, "After Dean
Morse's discussion it was agreed by the members of the staff that his
remarks [had been] within the proprieties."

Before Neuberger's final verdict had been rendered, Morse repeated his suggestion that even if he won his case, Dick would be
wise to withdraw from the university and start elsewhere with a clean
slate. Neuberger, however, would have none of it. In his first communication to Morse, one day after the Advisory Committee had exonerated him, he stated flatly:

> I do not intend to leave Oregon; I am going to stay here and
> fight it out. I like you and I think you have a good law school;
> so I'm staying; that's final. In your heart you know that the
> solution to this situation is not for me to withdraw from the
> field of combat; the solution is for you to get law school of-
> ficers who will not use their positions to advance their per-
> sonal grudges and hates. . . . Listen, Dean, face facts. . . . you
> have a bad situation on your hands. I think if you do not
> clear it up you will face all sorts of trouble from future sim-
> ilar situations in the years to come. Probably this seems like
> a pretty bitter letter after all you've done for me. Well . . . I
> feel that you should recognize the undeniable fact that your
> law school student body is headed by students motivated by
> personal prejudice and that because of them, your honor
> system is on the rocks.

If the sheer arrogance of this response did not disturb Morse, Neuberger's reference to prejudice, which he had raised many times before, certainly did. Morse fired off a telegram the next day telling Neuberger, who was in Portland for Thanksgiving, to stop making alibis. To Roscoe Nelson, who occupied a leadership position in Oregon's Jewish community, he explained that Neuberger had developed a persecution complex. "Any Gentile," he said, "who would conduct himself as these boys [i.e., Neuberger and Kahn] have, would make enemies to the same extent. . . . There are other Jewish boys in the law school and they are well liked, and I wish that somehow we could stop Dick from taking refuge under the skirts of racial prejudice every time some student tells him a thing or two." (Kahn felt that anti-Semitism *had* played a role in Neuberger's honor case, but he had no evidence, real or circumstantial, to support that feeling.)

Meanwhile, there was the autumn term to complete, and though Neuberger claimed he was "studying now as I never studied before," Morse remained unconvinced. He was furious when Neuberger petitioned Acting Dean Hollis to take his final exam in Criminal Law (Morse's course) in a campus location of his own choosing. From Wisconsin, where he was attending a conference on crime, Morse wrote that he hoped Hollis "had unloaded on him because I do not appreciate his asking such a request . . . in view of the fact that I told him before I left that he would not be permitted to write his papers outside of the building." Was Morse now concerned about Neuberger's integrity as well as his "laziness" and "lapses of judgment"? Neuberger worried that he might be. "I hope," he said, "you never had in mind the fear that I'd get help. . . . You know darn well that regardless of anything else, I play the game square."

Morse had in fact come to have doubts about how square Neuberger was willing to play the game. He had grown weary of what he called Dick's "cheap dramatics." He gave him a D in Criminal Law, and when Neuberger complained, he went over the final exam with him and decided that the original grade had been too generous. He lowered it by ten points, thereby flunking Neuberger in the course. The message was clear: if Neuberger would not leave the university voluntarily, Morse would force the issue. He had already telephoned

Neuberger's parents, whom he knew slightly, advising them to discontinue financing their son's education in law school.

Neuberger started the next term but officially withdrew from school at the end of February, with neither a law degree nor a bachelor's degree to his credit. Kahn reports that Neuberger never forgave Morse, either for the flunking grade or for the unsolicited advice to his family.

It is apparent that after a certain point, Morse simply gave up on Neuberger. But why did he work with such diligence to protect him in the first place, especially when doing so pitted Morse against his friend Hollis, to say nothing of the rest of his faculty? We may surmise that at least part of Morse's motivation, a small part, was connected to the identity of the law professor involved in the dispute. Carlton Spencer, though known as an intellectual lightweight, was for Morse an enemy. An earlier rumor on campus had it that Morse would be demoted by university president Valentine Boyer and replaced by Spencer, who was, as Morse described him, "safe, sane and conservative, and willing to take orders without question." Coming from behind, as it were, to defeat a Boyer favorite would have been highly pleasing, for it could also be seen as a defeat for Boyer himself.

Beyond the prospect of winning one over an enemy—always a source of satisfaction—Morse was probably moved by what might be called the invidious class distinctions involved in the case. He could recall his own challenge to the student establishment at the University of Wisconsin; thus, the prospect of Neuberger being brought to book by the fraternity crowd in so trifling a circumstance —cheating or no cheating—could easily have aroused his sympathy.

However, neither enmity toward Spencer and Boyer nor upset over the manner in which Neuberger was being attacked seems sufficient to have caused Morse to risk so much by taking the stand he did. Clearly, the major factor was the emotional hold Neuberger had on him. Morse had allowed—in many ways *encouraged*—Dick to become his intimate, and Neuberger had worked enterprisingly to enhance that status. Thus, though the intimacy was never as close as Neuberger had imagined, when he made demands in the name of "friendship," with or without histrionics, Morse had reason to feel the pressure of obligation. Dick had been *his* boy, and he had no choice but to go to bat for him.

But Dick was his boy no longer. However amicable or paternal Morse's feelings had been, those feelings had drastically changed in the course of events. He now had fundamental doubts about Neuberger's character, and it may have been a mark of residual affection, mixed perhaps with belated embarrassment, that Neuberger's presumptuous and erratic behavior had not alienated him entirely. Morse's attitude toward Neuberger over the ensuing years would continue to be avuncular, but it would also be heavily qualified. What happened in 1934 was crucial, and Morse would have reservations about Neuberger for the rest of his life.

Similarly, Neuberger's feelings were not as they had been. He had lost his confederacy with Morse; the easy camaraderie was gone forever. Though he had been saved by his mentor from dishonor, he had been cast out by that same mentor, by the man he had most admired, and he would never get over the experience. He would spend the rest of *his* life trying, by every means in his possession, to reestablish the privileged relationship to which he felt entitled.

AS IT TURNED OUT, MORSE WAS CORRECT about Neuberger's future as a writer. In many ways that future was upon him. The year before he entered law school, he had already reached a significant audience with an article in the *Nation* on Nazi Germany. By 1935 he had become a stringer for the *New York Times*, and his subsequent output was truly astonishing. Kahn described him as "a very adept writer, and the fastest two-finger typist I have ever seen." He did articles for all manner of publications—in some cases, in a process he called "shingling," rewriting the same material for up to seventeen periodicals—from obscure trade magazines to *Reader's Digest*. And unlike many others in the field, he made a good living as a freelancer. By 1954 *Time* would estimate his journalistic earnings at $30,000 a year, a decent freelance income today, a staggering figure for that time.

After his debacle in Eugene, Neuberger took up law again at night school in Portland; but, as Morse had surmised, his heart was

not in it, and the effort was short-lived. Instead, along with his journalism, he became increasingly involved in Oregon politics. After
failing in 1936, at the age of twenty-five, to win a seat in the Oregon
state Senate, he was elected in 1940 as a Democratic state representative from his Portland district.

Morse and Neuberger kept in touch over the next several years.
Their exchanges were friendly enough, but without the closeness of
earlier days. In the fall of 1939, Neuberger did a highly favorable piece
for the *Oregonian* on Dean Morse's waterfront labor-arbitration
work, for which Morse was exceedingly grateful. The following year
Morse encouraged Neuberger in his legislative candidacy and, after
his election, congratulated him and made bold to mention how far
he thought he had come since his undergraduate days. He would not
be surprised, Morse said, if "University honors are offered to you.
How times do change! 'From the Doghouse to the Citadel' would
make a good title for any account of your University career."

In this congenial spirit, Morse and Neuberger met in Portland
late in 1943, when Morse was leaving his post on the War Labor
Board and trying to make up his mind about running for the U.S.
Senate. Neuberger urged him to do so. In 1944 Morse wrote in support of Neuberger's unsuccessful application for an appointment to
the U.S. Boundary Commission. (Neuberger's political career had
been interrupted by a tour in the army—he made captain.) From
this point forward, correspondence between the two grew more frequent, and was marked for the most part by a kind of informal cor-
diality. Nevertheless, both men remained cautious.

Morse had an extra reason for reticence: he was now a politician
seeking election to office. Though Neuberger himself had been an
elected official (and would be again), he was in 1944 first and foremost a member of the press, that singular institution about which
politicians feel most ambivalent. Journalistic relations with Neuberger were particularly sensitive, since he immediately developed a
minor specialty in writing articles about Senator Wayne Morse.
Whatever the promise of Morse's politics, the aspiring progressive
from Oregon made good copy, and Neuberger would, as he had on
the *Emerald*, get maximum mileage out of him.

His first effort was for a late 1945 edition of the *Progressive* in which Morse was set in the tradition of La Follette, Borah, Hiram Johnson, and Huey Long and was lauded for his first year's performance: "With his movie-villain mustache and lean stride, Morse presents a vigorous and forceful appearance as he walks onto the Senate floor. He looks like a panther ready to strike." But Neuberger also noted weaknesses which, he maintained, Morse's "friends" were concerned about: the senator's tendency to talk too much, to "fire on too many targets," to be overly solicitous of the Portland Chamber of Commerce. While less than ecstatic over the criticisms, Morse seemed largely pleased with the *Progressive* piece. The image of the sleek Morse panther prowling the Senate floor seemed to catch his fancy.

A revamped and enlarged version of the *Progressive* article ran two months later in the *Brotherhood of Locomotive Firemen and Enginemen's Magazine.* Appearing shortly thereafter, a similar piece for the *Signalman's Journal,* equally bestowing of praise, contained one sentence to which Morse took exception. Of the senator's days teaching rhetoric at the University of Minnesota in the 1920s, Neuberger wrote: "He used to stand in front of a mirror in his college bedroom, hold his lapels in statesmanlike fashion and imagine himself delivering a great speech in the United States Senate or British House of Commons." To which description Morse responded: "I don't object to editorial license but sometime I want you to explain to me what there is about a literary artist that causes him to go temporarily cuckoo as you did in that sentence."

Though Neuberger wrote about Morse continuously, it would be four years before another story gave rise to friction. In the meantime, they would maintain their correspondence. In early 1946 Morse congratulated Neuberger on the announcement of his marriage to Maurine Brown, whose uncle, Paul Kelty, had been one of Neuberger's editors on the *Oregonian.* Two months later, on the first of March, without warning, Neuberger asked Morse to advise him on a series of critical questions: Should he consider running for governor of Oregon? Would he make a good race? A good governor? Did Morse think he could make more of a contribution as a writer or an officeholder?

If Morse was startled by the precipitance of the inquiries, he gave no indication of it. To the first two questions his reply was negative. Dick would run "a swell campaign" but would have no chance of unseating the incumbent. Would Dick be a good governor? Yes and no —and here Morse seemed to sense a consonance of character between himself and Neuberger, one of the traits that had attracted him in the first place. As governor, Dick would be a good administrator but "too much of an individualist" to be a good lawmaker. Politician or writer? In Dick's case there was no question: "There is practically no limit to the influence you can exercise as a writer whereas you have many limitations as a candidate for office. I am not saying that you should never be a candidate for political office but I am saying that . . . it is political suicide for you to become such a candidate now." Morse reinforced his argument by reporting that he had lunched that day with noted columnist Marquis Childs, and the two had agreed that Neuberger "should not, at least for now, dissipate [his] energies by even thinking about political office."

Neuberger's response to Morse's advice is unknown, though he did not in fact run for governor. Instead, he ran for the state Senate and lost. Morse may have been quick to discourage Neuberger for the reasons he gave, but there may have been another reason as well: he could not help but see that with a successful gubernatorial campaign behind him, his former student could mount a forceful challenge to his own Senate seat in 1950. He must have been pleased when Neuberger decided not to enter the governor's race (and perhaps secretly pleased when he lost in the legislative contest).

Two years later the subject of Neuberger's political ambitions came up again. This time the inquiry was directed to Childs rather than Morse, and this time Neuberger had in mind running not for governor but for the U. S. Senate against incumbent Guy Cordon, a conservative Republican whom Morse had already endorsed. But, as in 1946, Childs and Morse talked the matter over, and although this time his counsel was unsolicited, Morse volunteered the same opinion: it would be folly for Neuberger to run. Morse said his advice had nothing to do with the Cordon endorsement; he was only concerned with Dick's best interest. Whether or not Neuberger found Morse's views persuasive, he decided to forgo a U. S. Senate race, and instead captured a seat in the Oregon Senate.

Persuasive or not, Neuberger surely must have been put off by Morse's unasked-for advice. Morse, after all, had burst into politics to become a U. S. senator in his first try for elective office, whereas Neuberger had already paid his dues in previous campaigns and had served a term in the state legislature. Couldn't his journalism—which he planned to continue even if elected—be seen as a useful and legitimate jumping-off point for a political career? Shouldn't Morse have been more sympathetic to his aspirations? If such questions were on his mind, Neuberger never raised them. His next communication with Morse concentrated on a difference over issues, one that had been building since 1946.

Along with most Oregon liberals, Neuberger looked to Morse for political leadership, and like other liberals, he was disappointed when Morse refused to endorse the proposal for establishing a Columbia Valley Authority. He continually brought the matter up and Morse continually shot it down. "Off the record," Morse told him, "it isn't doing you any good to keep dangling Columbia Valley Authority bait before me. . . . I am no King Arthur's knight. I can't fight a lot of dragons at once." But CVA was not just another dragon; for many Oregonians it was a burning question, and to the extent that Morse refused to join the issue he might be seen as a knight in tarnished armor. So Neuberger described him in a 1947 letter to *American Mercury* editor Charles Angoff: "brilliant in debate but short on constructive accomplishment, a great orator but a trimmer in some respects."

By 1950, Neuberger's dissatisfaction had become more intense. "To what extent," he asked, "should a man in public office compromise his principles to stay there?" This query he raised as the lead sentence in an article entitled "Morse versus Morse" in the January 14, 1950, issue of the *Nation*. The article had been provoked by Morse's announcement some months earlier that he had finally made up his mind on CVA: he was against it. Neuberger accused Morse of political expediency. And it wasn't just CVA. He charged that in 1948, Morse had endorsed Cordon, a man who would oppose him in fifteen out of sixteen key votes in the next session of

Congress, simply in order to curry favor with conservative Republicans whose support he would need when his own seat was up in 1950. And for the same reason, Neuberger wrote, Morse had said he would campaign for Governor Douglas McKay's reelection, despite the fact that McKay was a rock-ribbed reactionary, opposed to everything Morse had ever stood and fought for. As for the senator's public condemnation of CVA, it was "difficult to believe that Morse, in his heart, meant these words" when, after all, he had been an undeviating supporter of TVA. Instead, Neuberger suggested, Morse had heard talk that a possible opponent who was rabidly anti-CVA was getting ready to challenge him in the primary; by coming out against CVA himself he had cut the ground from under his potential rival. As Neuberger saw it, Morse had compromised his progressive principles to ensure his reelection.

"Morse versus Morse" attracted considerable attention, especially in Oregon, where election-year politics were beginning to heat up. When Morse returned to his state briefly in early February, he was beset by reporters wanting his reaction to the article. To their disappointment, he casually dismissed it as "an interesting piece of Democratic political writing by a Democratic state senator." Toward the state senator himself Morse was positively convivial. He assured Neuberger that he took no offense despite what he saw as the article's obvious inaccuracies. Such was Morse's overt demeanor. Beneath the surface tranquillity, however, he was livid.

He let off steam to his former rhetoric mentor, Andrew Weaver of the University of Wisconsin. But instead of addressing the arguments—which would have been difficult, since he *did* have to worry about conservative support in 1950—he questioned Neuberger's motives. To the charge that he had supported Cordon out of mere expediency, he countercharged that Neuberger was "one of those Democrats who thinks that a liberal in the Republican Party should foul his party's nest." Actually, he said, the Neuberger article should be seen for what it really was: a put-up job by Oregon Democrats who hoped Morse would be defeated in the primary. He believed that Neuberger had his own eye on a Senate seat and that there was "at least a 50-50 chance" that Dick would be the Democratic opponent come autumn. Seen from that perspective, as a potential rival, the "old," unreliable Neuberger makes a sudden reappearance. Oregonians, Morse stated, knew that Neuberger had "great difficulty in distinguishing imagination from fact. He had the same difficulty when he was a student."

Four months later, *Frontier* magazine published an article— "Jekyll and Hyde in Politics: Oregon's Wayne Morse"—in which Neuberger argued that because of the great geographical distance between Morse and his constituency, the senator could pontificate out of both sides of his mouth and get away with it. In a dubious comparison, Neuberger wrote that "no Parisian *roué* ever dashed more expertly between boudoir and counting house than does Morse between the dinners of ADA and the annual banquets of the West Coast Lumberman's Association."

If Morse was irritated by Neuberger's further dissection of his politics, he did not show it. In fact, he did not hesitate to come to Neuberger's aid in the course of his state Senate reelection campaign when gossip was spread about Neuberger's old problems at the law school. With the evidence in the case either unknown or ignored, many came to understand that Neuberger had been summarily dropped from the university for cheating. To the several people who sent him inquiries on the subject, Morse, speaking for the record, gave an abbreviated recapitulation of the facts, stressed that Neuberger had been fully exonerated of all charges, omitted any mention of the preliminary guilty findings, and insisted that Neuberger "did not care to continue with the study of the law because of his preference and greater liking for journalism." In sum, he provided Neuberger with a valuable vote of confidence which, coming as it did from a member of the opposition in an election year, carried a fair degree of political clout.

Was Neuberger grateful? Did he feel uncomfortable being in Morse's debt once again? From available evidence these questions are impossible to answer, at least as far as the late 1940s are concerned. But they would come up again, for at a later time, with a U. S. Senate seat at stake, Morse would again come to Neuberger's defense against the cheating accusation, and later still he would remember the law school incident with a good deal less charity.

If Neuberger was ambivalent about Morse in print, in private he was more so. To a journalist friend he said, "I swing back and forth like a pendulum on my views on Morse. One moment I think he is a great liberal in the Norris tradition, and the next minute I feel that he is only an opportunist and a mountebank." Regardless of Neuberger's vacillations, he and Morse continued to exchange courteous correspondence. Then, on June 30, 1953, Neuberger, who was on a first-name basis with many of the nation's leading journalists, received a short note from Childs mentioning that he had tried to discuss Neuberger's *Frontier* article with Morse, "but he is so bitter that it just drew another tirade from him." On the basis of this remark, Neuberger came to the conclusion that Morse had been denigrating him to the press all over Washington. He told Helen Fuller of the *New Republic* that Morse had "indulged" in "'diatribes' against me" and hoped she would give little credence to whatever the senator had been saying.

As of mid-1953, the Morse-Neuberger relationship could be summed up as follows: uncertain appreciation—respect for each other's politics qualified by uneasiness about each other's motives and ambitions—reinforced by a kind of mutually beneficial interdependence. For Neuberger, Morse was a never-ending source of marketable stories; for Morse, Neuberger could be relied upon to provide a continuous stream of national publicity.

Beneath this reciprocity, however, each harbored memories of the other from earlier days. Whatever his accomplishments, Neuberger was to Morse a man flawed in character. From Neuberger's end of things, the matter was more complicated. His feelings about Morse were deeply ambiguous. He was still a hero, the man whose powerful hand had once saved his reputation, and Neuberger felt compelled to seek his advice and to write about him, again and again. That their politics were largely in harmony made it all the easier.

But because the two men had never confronted their past, allowing it merely to fade into the background, Neuberger was left

with a double resentment: he could not forgive Morse either for propelling him out of law school (whether he was serious about the law
was irrelevant) or for having had to protect him in the honor proceedings. The honor case—during which Neuberger had shown
himself to be weak and vulnerable—created a debt he could never
repay, a debt that would grow larger every time Morse was called
upon to defend him anew against the charge that he had been
thrown out for cheating. Owing such a debt, he would remain in a
distressingly subordinate position, possessed of all those resentments
combative persons inevitably feel toward their moral creditors.

By late 1953, however, the context for the Morse-Neuberger
relationship had begun to change. And as the context changed, so did
the relationship. Oregon's Democratic revolution, which would register its first statewide triumphs in the following year, was well under
way, and among already-elected Democrats the name of Neuberger
—Maurine was now also a state legislator—stood at the vanguard.
Morse perceived that times were changing, and while he was not yet

*The "Dick and Maurine Show" played successfully in Salem during the
early 1950s, when he was a state senator and she was a state representative. Many were convinced that the couple wanted to rerun their act
in Washington after Dick became a U.S. senator. (Oregon Historical Society, OrHi 72505.)*

ready to shed his Independent mantle for that of the Democrats, he realized that he must seek accommodation with those who not only were in control of the party's future but, in the final analysis, were ideologically closer to him than any prominent Republican in the state had ever been. Having burned his Republican bridges in 1952, Morse had now to establish firmer connections to those who were leading the forces of displacement. Neuberger was high on his list.

On October 10, 1953, Neuberger again sought Morse's help in making a difficult decision: should he run for governor or the U. S. Senate? If he ran for the latter, where would the campaign funds come from? Once again Morse did not hesitate to give counsel. The governorship idea should be dismissed out of hand. Neuberger's liberalism was needed on the national scene; that is where he could make his greatest contribution. Moreover, understood properly, the choice was not really Neuberger's alone:

> Where in the world and how in the world did you ever develop the idea . . . that your personal interests are of first importance? Dick, I think that is an unsound premise. You have made a record of liberalism, and there are thousands upon thousands of the so-called little people of the country that have the absolute right to expect you to place their interest above yours. . . . Let it never be said about you or any of the rest of us in the liberal movement that we are afraid to be defeated.

As for campaign contributions (the assurance of which may have been Neuberger's main reason for contacting Morse), more would come in than Dick anticipated. Morse concluded by urging him not to wait until he had money enough to make the race—there never is enough—and to "stop worrying about being smeared, lied about and abused." Such, as Morse saw it, was the unavoidable fate of all liberals.

Why was Morse now so eager to have Neuberger run? One of the reasons was, obviously, tactical. A Neuberger victory in 1954—a genuine possibility—would mean that Morse would be free to run as the liberal and, most likely, as the Democratic candidate in 1956, unopposed by an increasingly popular Dick Neuberger. In addition, such a victory would break the Republican stranglehold on national representation in Oregon and make it easier for all statewide Democratic candidates in 1956. And finally, Neuberger did agree with Morse on most political issues; he could be expected to add powerfully to the voice of liberalism in Congress. Notwithstanding his reservations about character, Morse had come to believe that Neuberger would make an effective U. S. senator. He was both ready to welcome his candidacy and prepared to turn his Senate office into a campaign center East (and some of his chief aides into campaign workers), to give the candidacy every chance to succeed.

Though he had sought Morse's opinion and received his encouragement to run, Neuberger, once in the Senate race, worried about how closely he would be associated with the Morse name. He wanted—and needed—Morse's access to funding outside Oregon, but he preferred to keep him at a distance in all other ways.

It was widely believed that Neuberger's wariness stemmed from Morse's reputation for volatility and unpredictability. Morse had deserted his own party and had shown a fondness for attacking Dwight Eisenhower, a hugely popular president. He was said to have alienated adherents and could therefore be seen as a political liability. But there was more to Neuberger's apprehensiveness than concern over Morse's uncertain reputation. State Chairman Howard Morgan remembers organizing a Democratic dinner sometime before the 1954 election. To stir up interest, he scheduled Independent Morse as the featured speaker. Neuberger was horrified, and though the dinner had already been announced to the press, he tried to get Morgan to cancel it. When Morgan refused, Neuberger at first said neither he nor Maurine would come. He finally relented, but only on the condition that he and Maurine be seated at opposite ends of the head table, as far away from the speaker as possible.

This seating arrangement was symbolic of what was really bothering Neuberger. While he may have worried about Morse's negative image, above all he wanted to be regarded as his own man, not as a Morse disciple. He believed that "outright indorsement [*sic*] of me might well be misinterpreted and subjected to a good deal of

distortion." Morse, in turn, had a friendly tip for Neuberger, one with
a very sharp point: "May I say good-naturedly and by way of 'Dutch
uncle' advice, Dick, there is a rule of life that applies in the field of
politics as elsewhere; namely, it's never a mistake to stand in public
for and with your friends."

The point was received, the recipient wounded. Dick wanted no
Dutch-uncleing from Senator Morse. "Really," he wrote, reverting to
the voice of the petulant student, "I don't think you should scold me
so much. Undoubtedly I have my share of frailties, but I think my
record for integrity and consistency is pretty good. . . . I want you to
do what comes naturally in the campaign. If that includes speaking
for me and trying to raise some financial help for me, go right ahead.
You certainly are a sovereign citizen and have that privilege."

After further prodding from Morse, Neuberger finally owned up
to what was bothering him: "I only believe you should back me in
such a way as to make clear the truth—that I am my own candidate
and that, as a Senator, I would be my own man. They are using
against me all over the states [sic] that I would be your 'stooge' and
your 'man Friday.' We know that isn't true, but I believe your indorsement of me should be in such a way as to give the lie to these
charges." Morse agreed to endorse Neuberger precisely on the terms
suggested, if for no other reason than "the simple fact that it is impossible for me to imagine anyone thinking that Dick Neuberger
could be anyone's stooge or that I would want one."

But Neuberger had raised one other matter, and on this Morse
wanted to set the record straight. Neuberger had mentioned that he
had been under heavy pressure "for many months, to forsake my
Senate ambitions until 1956—pressure from your mortal enemies."
In short, he was threatening to take Morse on in the following election unless Morse played it his way in this one. Morse was unmoved
by the threat. He said his backing for Neuberger had no strings attached: he would run in 1956 on his own record; any and all liberals, Neuberger included, were free to support, oppose, or run against
him as they saw fit.

For his part, Morse also had a complaint, followed by a threat of
his own. He informed Neuberger that according to mutual friends,

"when you are involved in discussions concerning me you are inclined to make general statements of approval, but they are usually followed by reservations or qualified criticisms which destroy any favorable impression that your words of general approval might otherwise convey." Morse suggested that although he was not personally bothered by such assertions, Neuberger should be careful. "You should not overlook the fact that ardent Morse supporters in the state (and I have my share of them) are not going to react to you with enthusiasm if they feel you are trying to play up to ultraconservative critics of mine by making . . . veiled detractions of me." In other words, watch what you say about me or the Morse "machine" will be turned against you.

Having delivered his warning, Morse threw himself fervently into the campaign, more fervently than Neuberger might have wished necessary. He contributed his own money to the campaign treasury, raised thousands more from around the country, dispatched legislative assistant Merton Bernstein from his Washington office to lend a hand, and (depending on who is telling the story) made anywhere from 70 to 150 speeches on the stump. And when the law school cribbing charge was exhumed, he recirculated his earlier letter defending Neuberger's integrity.

The narrowness of Neuberger's victory—a mere 2,462 votes out of 569,088 cast—showed how important Morse's contribution had been. And whether Neuberger liked it or not, the widespread celebration that followed gave Morse equal billing. *Time* ran the smiling faces of both men on the cover over the caption "The Senators from Oregon" and, in smaller type, "Two chips from the same timber." The article inside went even further, referring to the duo as "Morseberger," men who might not "match Oregon's mountains, but like mountains they fill the eye." Richard Neuberger may have become a United States senator in his own right, but to his dismay, many found it impossible to distinguish him clearly from Senator Morse.

Though Neuberger was unhappy over sharing the headlines, he was openly grateful for Morse's help; he knew he could not have won without it. As a quid pro quo, he let it be known early in the campaign that he and Maurine would support Morse's reelection in 1956 whether he ran as Democrat or Independent. Morse, in turn, was pleased by their endorsement, and so the "Morseberger" alliance in the Senate was off to a positive start. But Neuberger lost no time in establishing a claim to independence when, less than two months into the session, he supported the president and opposed Morse on the Formosa Resolution, delivering a well-received speech on the floor of the Senate in defense of Eisenhower's foreign policy.

Morse used the occasion to write to Maurine, who, having retained her seat in the Oregon House, was still back in Salem. He wanted her to know that "reaching a different conclusion on some issue will never make the slightest difference to me in my loyalty to him and my determination to always strengthen his hand. . . . One thing I do not intend to let happen, and that is to permit evildoers to drive any wedges of discord between us."

It would not, however, take evildoers to create divisions between Morse and Neuberger. Despite the sugarcoating, Morse was clearly annoyed, if not over Neuberger's position (Morse was in fact nearly alone in opposing the Formosa Resolution, which called for possible U.S. military action against mainland China) then over the speed with which Neuberger had moved to stake it out, and the fact that he had spoken against Morse on the Senate floor. Writing a "friendly" letter to Maurine instead of to Dick was simply a way of making the point without getting directly into a struggle with Neuberger himself.

Meanwhile, Neuberger clearly chafed, not only under the media's "Morseberger" appellation, but at what he perceived as the secondary status to which observers had permanently relegated him. Morse's style did little to soothe his irritation. However generous Morse might try to be, he inevitably expected a degree of deference from his former student. But Neuberger was not inclined to be deferential; he despaired at having to listen to Morse's persistent references to himself before Oregon audiences as "your senior senator," knowing that as long as they were congressional colleagues he would always be the junior.

At the same time, it would be wrong to characterize the Morse-Neuberger relationship at this point as wholly frictional or lacking in cooperation. Morse was soon to become a registered Democrat, and with his own reelection on the horizon, he could ill afford to alienate that party's leading actor in Oregon. And as a Senate neophyte, Neuberger, who after a rebellious start would turn out to be something of an acolyte in his party's authority structure, knew better than to take on a veteran of the Hill like Morse. Furthermore, Morse and Neuberger actually did function well together at the outset; their staffs combined brilliantly, and the result was a two-man delegation which Americans for Democratic Action rated as the most liberal in the Senate. More important, in this heady period of cooperation, Morse could, at least temporarily, consign his old feelings to the back of his mind: the day had arrived when he and his former student could in fact do "something great for the people of the state," and he could honestly report to his sister Caryl that he and Dick enjoyed "very fine working relations as well as personal relations."

Their most notable collaboration was in the area of public power, especially on the question of damming Hells Canyon. This was Oregon's leading political issue in the 1950s, and Morse had introduced Hells Canyon legislation well before Neuberger's arrival in the Senate. But Neuberger was by no means new to the subject: he had written many articles on it and was active in groups resisting the Republican plan to let a privately owned power company have its way in building dams in the canyon. And since Neuberger had been appointed to the Senate Public Works Committee (as well as the related Interior Committee), leadership on Hells Canyon naturally fell under his jurisdiction. Morse was content to give Neuberger his head. The staffs of the two senators worked as one in pursuit of their common objective, and when the Senate finally passed a pro-public-power canyon bill in 1957, the offices of both could justifiably take pride. Ultimately they were defeated when the House bottled up their bill in committee; but if they lost the Hells Canyon battle, they won the public-power war on virtually every other front.

Before the Eisenhower administration, dam building in all of its aspects on the Columbia River had always been a function of the federal government. The Republicans under Eisenhower promoted a "partnership" concept, which meant that in harnessing water power, private utility companies would install electricity-generating equipment while the government would provide financing for such unprofitable aspects of water engineering as flood control, navigation, and fish conservation. Morse and Neuberger were able to kill every administration bill setting up federal partnerships with Oregon's utilities. And with the help of other Northwest members of Congress, they appropriated funds for exclusive government construction on the Columbia, most notably for the million-kilowatt dam at John Day. If you wanted to traffic in power construction in the Northwest, you had to deal first with the Morseberger coalition.

The alliance was still at work in 1956—first at the Democratic national convention, where both men worked for Adlai Stevenson's nomination (Morse as Neuberger's alternate); then in Oregon, in Morse's hard-fought reelection campaign against Douglas McKay. True to his word, Neuberger, along with Maurine and much of his staff, labored long and hard for the Morse campaign. From his position on the Interior Committee, Neuberger was especially helpful in providing valuable ammunition for use against McKay. Since Morse won by a sizeable margin, however, such efforts were not seen as making a critical difference. The score was not even. Neuberger owed his election to Morse, but Morse did not owe his to Neuberger. Morse, as ever, remained in a dominant position.

But Morse was genuinely appreciative, and the good feelings carried into the new congressional session and beyond. Morse had taken to referring to Neuberger as "Mr. Conservationist," continually praising his undertakings in wildlife and forest preservation. In a San Francisco speech just after the election, Neuberger proposed that the Democrats nominate Morse for the presidency in 1960. Then, in January of 1957, on his own initiative, he announced the formation of the National Friends of Wayne Morse, a group dedicated to securing his colleague a spot on the 1960 national ticket. He followed that with a lengthy piece in the April issue of the *Progressive*, entitled simply "Morse for President," in which he first advanced ten arguments in support of his thesis, and then sought to calm those who might be frightened at the prospect of Senator Morse as the Democratic standard-bearer:

People ask if he is not too harsh and strident and arrogant—an opinion perhaps inspired by his fiery, pounding political speeches. My own experience as Morse's junior Senate colleague is the best refutation of such an impression. . . . I never have felt the slightest envy because of Senator Morse's greater fame and prestige. He has not tried to impress upon me his longer experience and service. We have worked together as harmoniously as two Senators could. . . . We have yet to quarrel or have a single sharp word.

Despite its apparent good intentions, "Morse for President" again displayed Neuberger's ambivalence: the article managed to promote and cast doubt upon Morse at the same time. If one is seriously arguing the case for a presidential candidacy, one does not raise the charge that the candidate is considered to be "harsh and strident and arrogant." Neuberger may have felt compelled to say *something* about Morse's reputation for belligerence, but cataloging his alleged faults, even if only to "refute" the allegations by citing personal experience, was a dubious way of going about it (akin to, say, Hubert Humphrey promoting the cause of Lyndon Johnson by claiming that Johnson's reputation for ruthlessness was false, since LBJ had never been personally ruthless to him). At any rate, three months after "Morse for President" appeared, not only had quarrels between the two senators come to be commonplace, but "sharp words" had become their primary mode of communication.

ONCE AGAIN THERE WAS A CHANGE in the context of their relationship. The near sweep of statewide offices by Democrats in 1956 brought with it the sweetness of victory—*and* a myriad of problems. It also further entrenched Congresswoman Edith Green, who was reelected by a large majority. There had never been much affection between Green and the Neubergers, and many, Green more than most, believed the Neubergers wished to reopen in Washington their "Dick and Maurine Show" that had played so famously in Salem when Dick was in the state Senate and Maurine in the House. If Maurine

actually harbored congressional ambitions, she could fulfill them
only by directly challenging Green. Green, on the other hand, was
said to have eyes cast on the upper chamber in Washington, and
since Morse was now seen as virtually unbeatable, her target would
of necessity have to be Neuberger. Neuberger, who according to one
of his assistants "saw possible challengers under every rock," certainly regarded Green as a more-than-potential rival. Whether based on
fact or not, the distrust between Green and the Neubergers was so
great that it occasionally bordered on paranoia.

At Green's instigation, Morse called a meeting of the entire Oregon Democratic congressional delegation—which also included
newly elected representatives Al Ullman and Charles Porter—in an
attempt to smooth things over. The result was an "Open Letter to the
People of Oregon," drafted by Green and signed by all five members,
asserting that "there is no personal rift within this delegation" and
that none of the signers coveted a seat held by a colleague. Whatever good this compact did, it was short-lived. Three months later it
was Neuberger's turn to press Morse for a delegation meeting, citing
his continuing difficulties with Green. But Green refused any such

*Oregon's Democratic delegation toasts the new Congress in January 1957. Morse, Edith
Green, and Neuberger welcome freshman representatives Charles Porter (second from
right) and Al Ullman (right). (Oregon Historical Society, OrHi 90999.)*

meeting, and in the end Morse was able to satisfy neither side. In a mélange of metaphors, he complained that

> Dick Neuberger and Edith Green are annoyed with me because I am a devotee of the Nehru philosophy of neutralism. . . . Charlie Porter, Al Ullman and I had breakfast Friday morning in an endeavor to try to figure out how we can get the boiling teapot off the hot stove, but we can't find any handle to take hold of. I have been proceeding on what I always thought was an immutable physical law that fires finally burn out, but I am afraid this one is fueled by a natural gas field.

Neuberger by this time imagined Morse in collusion with Green, at least in part because his own relationship with Morse was beginning to break down, personally as well as politically. After the debate on the Formosa Resolution, Morse had opposed the administration on a number of key bills and amendments, and in each case Neuberger had voted the other way. But it was the indirect effect of a domestic-policy dispute that accelerated the deterioration. When Morse, on the Senate floor, charged his usual allies with "parliamentary expediency" and "phony liberalism" for their handling of the 1957 civil-rights bill (see chapter 10), Neuberger took it personally, especially when Morse sent copies of these charges to many of his constituents. Neuberger retaliated by getting Senator Paul Douglas of Illinois to write a letter to Oregon voters extolling the Neuberger civil-rights record, a letter that pointedly made no reference to any work done in that area by Senator Morse. Morse was livid and let Neuberger know about it, in writing.

Thus began the first in an extraordinary—that word again—series of exchanges which saw the two senators, separated only by one floor and at opposite ends of the same building, firing charge and countercharge almost daily via missives hand-carried by messenger to each other's office.

Morse opened fire on August 5, 1957, by forwarding to Neuberger the text he had sent to those who had inquired about the Douglas letter. He said that such people were keenly disappointed because they saw Douglas's letter as "a snide attack upon me. . . . As you know, there are those who are constantly trying to create the impression in Oregon that there is a personal split between Dick and me because we have differed in our votes on some major issues. Nothing could be fartherest [*sic*] from the truth."

On the following day, in a letter marked "Personal," Neuberger said he didn't know what Morse was talking about: "Because I had sided with Senator Douglas, he mentioned in some letters to Oregon that he approved of my stand on the civil rights issue. I cannot regard this as a 'snide attack' upon you."

Morse's rejoinder came a day later. He said he didn't like this sending of letters back and forth, preferring instead to sit down and discuss their honest differences "man to man." Nevertheless, he had to point out that Douglas had described Morse's conduct as dishonorable. "He made those bitter personal attacks prior to sending his letter into Oregon. The language of his letter is a snide reference to those criticisms and you are only kidding yourself and not me if you try to deny it."

On the same day, Neuberger came back with a letter marked "Personal and Confidential." He accused Morse of sending "enormous" amounts of material back to Oregon which contained implicit criticisms of *him*, especially materials referring to liberals who had played into the hands of the anti-civil-rights forces: "Of course, I was among this group. Wayne, I have never resented this at all. I feel you had a complete right to uphold your position with your usual vigor. . . . It is my hope that people who have ulterior motives will be unable to drive a wedge between us. I admire you and I think you are a great Senator." Neuberger echoed Morse in hoping that they could "talk over this entire unfortunate misunderstanding in the usual friendly fashion which has typified our pleasant working relationship." It had been a long time, however, since their working relationship had been pleasant, and in the next forty-eight hours it would grow distinctly worse.

Neuberger was told that Morse had been saying things to the press about him behind his back. He dashed off an angry letter on August 9, Morse responded in kind, and the forensic crossfire increased in intensity.

NEUBERGER, AUGUST 9, 1957 [copies, indicated only on Neuberger's carbon, to Senator Humphrey and journalists Drew Pearson and Robert S. Allen]: I was stunned and shocked yesterday to be called off the Senate floor by several newspapermen, who said to me that you had gone to them with a story about how I had collaborated with Senator Douglas in foully and unfairly attacking you. . . . Needless to add, I am deeply disturbed that you evidently feel so keenly against me that you would deliberately seek wide publication of material which would damage me greatly and reduce my effectiveness as a Senator.

MORSE, AUGUST 12, 1957: I am sure you appreciate the fact that your letter contains clear charges reflecting upon my friendship for you, my integrity and my loyalty to the political cause which we both serve. I do not intend to permit gossip mongers, whether newspapermen or Senators, who have misinformed you to destroy the personal and political relationship which exists between us. . . . I feel that you and I are so much together in political ideology, in personal philosophy toward life and in close bonds of friendship that it is a dirty shame that these frictions of the last two or three weeks should have arisen.

Again, Neuberger answered on the day he received Morse's letter. He reiterated his accusation but rephrased it slightly, saying that if Morse doubted its validity, he was "regretful. I will not mention it further because I do not think you and I should charge each other with lack of honesty." Morse chose to read the change in language as an overture to peace. "I am," he said, "a great believer in the healing value of the passage of time." He repeated his interest in having "a friendly conference," but meanwhile he wanted to carry on in a way "that demonstrates that our friendship is bigger than the relatively minor differences which have developed between us over the civil rights fight."

Despite the self-serving rhetoric and disingenuous prose used by both men, the matter might have been put to rest, at least for the time being, by Morse's reinterpretation of Neuberger's argument and his renewed declaration of friendship. The two might even have sat down, as both continually insisted they should, and come to some kind of agreement, however temporary. But those possibilities were made unlikely when Neuberger informed A. Robert (Bob) Smith, Washington correspondent for most of the Northwest's leading dailies, about the exchange of correspondence (giving him a peek at some of the letters) and Smith then described what had transpired to his readership.

The face-to-face meeting finally did occur on August 27, and though Neuberger said the session "served a very useful purpose," by then it was much too late. Stopping in Portland two days later on his way home from Washington, Morse repeated his attack on "civil rights liberals" and said that Neuberger was one of those who had been "sucked in" on the various Senate compromises. Neuberger rushed out a press release saying he was "bewildered" by Morse's accusation, and privately complained that he had done nothing to provoke Morse and said it was "a shame that we have this cross to bear."

On September 14, Neuberger fulfilled a long-standing obligation he had to the Washington County Democratic Central Committee to introduce their featured speaker for the evening, Senator Wayne Morse. "Lately," he said,

> there has been a good deal of comment in the press concerning the fact that Senator Morse and I have voted differently on such issues as civil rights, foreign aid, reciprocal trade, Eisenhower doctrine and the like. Had we voted identically on these issues, there might have been somewhat different comment—then we would have been accused of being "stooges" for each other. . . . I have no quarrel, and I am not going to quarrel with a man whose brilliance and ability I admire as much as I do these qualities in Senator Morse. . . . Oregon is fortunate to be represented in the Senate by so able and illustrious a citizen.

Washington County's Democrats were cheered by such commendatory words, and there was just enough truth in them to give

Neuberger's monotone delivery a ring of conviction. There *was* a part of Neuberger that had a residual admiration for Morse, even as it was mixed with resentment and envy—the same part that had written laudatory articles about his progressive liberalism in their pre-senatorial days; so when he applied words like "brilliance" and "illustrious" to Morse, he undoubtedly meant them. Similarly, when Morse said that he and Neuberger were "together in political ideology" and "personal philosophy," he could do so sincerely because a part of him believed it to be true. But more fundamental aspects of each man's psyche regarded the other with suspicion and doubt, nurturing feelings that had been festering for two and a half decades and which could not be overcome by public pronouncements, no matter how conciliatory.

Neuberger's enumeration of policy differences with Morse was accurate, and these differences also helped to widen the gulf between them. With the passage of time, Neuberger's positions were becoming more and more accommodating to mainstream Senate opinion. Not only did he want to be perceived as a figure separate from Morse, but he was also ambitious to achieve status within the inner circles of senatorial power. He would come to Majority Leader Lyndon Johnson's defense when a group of younger senators, supported by Morse, attacked Johnson's conservative control of Senate business. He had his staff compile and then circulate a list of twenty-five roll calls in the Eighty-fifth Congress where he and Morse had voted on opposite sides. Ultimately, he defended his support of Eisenhower in international affairs by resorting to the conventional shibboleths of Cold War patriotism. He told one constituent that "Mr. Eisenhower is my President, even though I never voted for him. If you think I should attack him on foreign policy when he is representing us in the free world, then you are totally at liberty to seek a new Senator from the state of Oregon." In this spirit, in May of 1957, he cast the sole Democratic vote in the Senate for funding the much-criticized U.S. Information Agency.

As Neuberger moderated his stands and further distanced himself politically from Morse, his stock with Oregon's Republican press began to rise, just as he hoped it would. As one editorial put it:

"Admiration for Neuberger—grudging in some cases but neverthe-less admiration—has come into the picture [and] we'll wager if Neuberger were forced to run again tomorrow, against much of the Republican opposition now on the scene, fully half of the state's daily newspapers would support him." No Oregon editor would have risked an equivalent wager on Morse.

By the end of 1957, the Morse-Neuberger estrangement was be-yond remedy. But because their rift was not completely understood by others, hope for reconciliation persisted over the next two years, as colleagues and admirers worked to bring about an accommoda-tion. Public misperception resulted in part from the two men's ef-forts to keep up appearances, to the degree that was possible. But those closest to Morse knew where he stood, or if they didn't they soon found out.

Although Merton Bernstein had recently left his job as Morse's legislative assistant, he continued to give him the benefit of his ideas. When in late December he sought to downplay the conflict with Neuberger, Morse wrote him a scorching reply:

> You tried to alibi for Neuberger, Linde [Neuberger's legisla-tive assistant] and the rest of them. In fact I seriously doubt if at any time you fully appreciated the extent of the intrigue and back-knifing tactics to which Neuberger, Hans Linde, and the others had stooped during the many months that I repeatedly warned you about their course of conduct. The fact is that we were dealing with Neuberger and his staff and Porter and his staff over a period of many months when be-hind the scenes they were doing what they could to politi-cally destroy me. They may have succeeded.
>
> Only time will tell. But let me assure you mine isn't going to be the only political funeral. . . . At the present time the political situation in Oregon for me is very bad, but it is beginning to become very bad for one Dick Neuberger. . . . Let me assure you that I intend to see that it gets worse for him.

In fact, it got worse for everyone.

BORN OF THE EXUBERANCE OF THE 1956 ELECTIONS, weekly break-fast meetings of the Oregon Democratic delegation were held in Washington to coordinate legislative strategy among the two sena-tors, the three representatives, and their chief assistants. Although the chairmanship of these gatherings was theoretically rotated among the five elected officials, those who attended remember Morse being permanently in charge. For a while the breakfasts were friendly and even productive occasions, generating a united front on a variety of policy matters, but even then they were not everyone's cup of tea. Lloyd Tupling, Neuberger's administrative assistant, recalled them without affection: "We used to have to get up at the crack of dawn on Mondays and have breakfast. . . . And everybody was so damned tired. . . . When you meet at seven o'clock [Morse's favorite meeting hour]. Oh, god. And usually at one of the Senate dining rooms. Scrambled eggs or something. It was terrible." Though seen as an af-fliction by some, and though held amid mounting tensions within the delegation, the meetings continued throughout 1957 and into the early months of 1958. Inevitably, however, the weekly breakfast could not escape the rancor that had come to characterize so much of the delegation's other interactions.

At a January 1958 breakfast there occurred an off-the-cuff dis-cussion of Oregon governor Bob Holmes. Morse in particular ob-served that Democrat Holmes had more Republicans in his employ than seemed necessary or desirable. Word of the discussion was ob-tained by Bob Smith, he dutifully filed a story on it, and everyone ran for cover. Morse had chaired the meeting and had the responsibili-ty for minimizing public damage. He issued a press release saying he was "amused" by the "rumor stories" and pledged his full and ener-getic support to Holmes's reelection. Privately, he was more irate that someone in the delegation had broken confidence than concerned that the story might cause problems with Holmes. He sent a mem-orandum to Neuberger, Green, Ullman, and Porter voicing his irri-tation and recommending that all subsequent meetings be held in strict executive session.

Neuberger sent out a memo of his own to the delegation, main-taining *he* had no need to issue a news release because he was not the person "who spent approximately half an hour criticizing Governor Holmes, his personal staff, and many of his appointees." He also told Smith—and Smith then reported in his column—that he, Neuberger, was being blamed for the leak. Morse, meanwhile, said he was prepared to accept the fact that none of the principals had been responsible for the leak and that therefore one or more on their staffs were. Neuberger argued that the principals should not be exonerated unless they were at the same time willing to exonerate all of their staffs.

Nearly four weeks later, with the question still unresolved, Morse wrote to Bud Forrester of the *East Oregonian* explaining that the leak had to have come from the staffs because each delegation member had denied being the source "and their word is their bond with me." Having seen the letter, Neuberger wrote to Morse (with copies to Porter, Green, and Ullman) saying the charge was unfair since the staffs had never had a chance to issue denials of their own. At this Morse exploded (with copies to all concerned), calling Neuberger's position "nonsense" and an insult to him, Green, Porter, and Ullman. "Al, Charlie, Edith and I each told you . . . that we did not leak any story to Smith. One or more on the staffs obviously did. It is just as simple as that, and your grandstanding in defense of the staffs leaves me cold, as does so much of your snide conduct these days."

Because Smith would later write a book about Morse, the question of who leaked the story to him takes on added interest. It seems likely—and not just because of his "grandstanding" for unspecified staff members—that Neuberger did the leaking. Smith, an old friend of Neuberger's who had previously been banned from Morse's office for three years because of a disagreement over one of his stories, is himself illuminating on the subject. Interviewed in his Virginia office in 1984, Smith confessed that his 1962 volume, *The Tiger in the Senate*, attributed the feud with Neuberger too much to Morse. In hindsight, he felt he had been somewhat manipulated by Neuberger and should have made more of his exploitation of Morse. Neuberger was, in truth, genuinely pleased at Morse's use of intemperate language—pleased to turn it to his own advantage and, when circumstances permitted, especially pleased to feed the juiciest details to

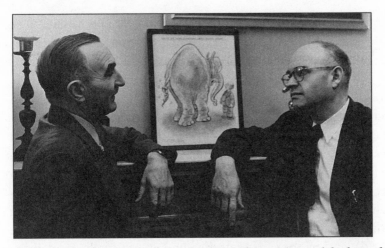

Morse and Neuberger regarded each other with suspicion and doubt; each nurtured feelings that had been repressed for two and a half decades. (Oregon Historical Society, OrHi CN 020846.)

Smith for distribution throughout Oregon. Smith could be counted upon to pounce on and develop every new twist in what was, for an industrious political reporter, an irresistible story. In many ways his book would be a continuation of that practice.

Though he may not have highlighted it as he later wished he had, Smith did spell out Neuberger's modus operandi when he summed up the feud in *The Tiger in the Senate*: "In the political quarrel . . . a contrasting feature was that Morse tried to hush it up and Neuberger deftly nudged it into public view. Morse wanted to spank his junior colleague, but in the privacy of the U.S. mails. Neuberger knew the only gain in a quarrel with Morse was to be derived from the sympathy it would arouse for him among Oregon's many Morse haters —among them many newspaper editorial writers."

And speaking of a later period, when the dispute had reached epic proportions, Smith wrote: "Neuberger may not have altogether relished the depths to which his relationship with Morse had plunged, but the last thing he now wanted was to hide his difficulties with Morse behind some new façade of party unity. With each new expressed difference he had become a greater hero to many Oregonians. He especially cherished the backing of those editorial writers who loved to take sides against obstreperous Wayne Morse." The more Morse exploded, the more Neuberger maneuvered so the world could hear the detonation. Smith was a useful, if partially unwitting, ally in this endeavor.

The Morse-Neuberger feud—or "Rumpus," as it was labeled in Neuberger's files—reached its cataclysmic finale in a seemingly trivial disagreement over a piece of surplus federal property. Beginning in the early 1950s, Oregon's Douglas County Historical Society, headquartered in Charlie Porter's congressional district, made efforts to acquire a piece of federal property for the city of Roseburg. Members of the historical society hoped to get the parcel with Morse's blessing and without charge, under an exception to the Morse Formula (see chapter 6); and by 1958 they felt they had an especially good argument. Just a year earlier Morse had granted an exception when Roseburg had reacquired part of a tract it had originally donated in 1932 for a veterans' hospital. The society now wanted Roseburg to take possession of another surplus parcel, this one donated to the government by a private party.

The Lillie Moore house was an old downtown residence which had been willed to the United States by Mrs. Moore, who had died in 1940. According to the society's plan, the city would take possession of the Moore building, move it to a public site, and use it for a historical museum, leaving the lot in the hands of the government. A bill to this effect passed Congress in 1956 (without objection from Morse); but when it was discovered that the house could not be shifted without severely damaging it, Porter introduced a second bill to convey both the house and its original lot to Roseburg at no cost to the city.

Porter's bill cleared the House without difficulty and was given to Neuberger to carry through the Senate. Porter, who because of his closeness to Neuberger had had little recent contact with Morse, wrote to Morse on March 3, 1958, to sound him out on the bill. Morse replied a week later that his formula undoubtedly had to be applied, but he would reserve final judgment until he could analyze the report of the Government Operations Committee. Neuberger testified for the bill before that committee in late July; it cleared Operations the following day and came to the Senate for a vote in early August. When the required unanimous consent was requested, Morse refused to give it. The bill, he said, violated terms of the Morse Formula.

Greatly embarrassed by Morse's veto, Neuberger immediately dispatched an angry note, and the two senators were off again, hurling explosive missives from opposite flanks of the Senate Office Building, with carbons to Congressman Porter. Neuberger started things on August 5, saying he did not want to argue the merits of the case since he did not know enough about the intricacies of the Morse Formula. But, he pointed out, "there was ample time and opportunity to inform Charlie Porter, the Senate Committee on Government Operations and me of your views with respect to this bill."

It had been "Dear Dick" and "Dear Wayne" heretofore, but it would be "Dear Neuberger" from this point forward; and if that salutation sounded unfriendly, Morse meant it to. "You have a lot of guts," he said the following day, "to write me the message contained in your letter of August 5th." He insisted that Neuberger had been aware of his steadfast opposition to the Lillie Moore bill: "The cowardly attempt in your letter to pass the buck to me for your failure . . . is but further evidence of your complete untrustworthiness as a colleague."

Before the sun had set, Neuberger was back with a rejoinder in which he said he refused to trade insults (he would continue to open his letters with "Dear Wayne"), though he "regretted" Morse's "abusive and intemperate tone." He repeated his assertion that since neither Morse nor one of his staff had appeared before the Operations Committee, he was perfectly justified in assuming there was no objection. He indicated his willingness to join with Morse in amending the bill to square it with the Morse Formula.

On August 7, Morse was back on the attack, noting that Neuberger's letter was "in keeping with your record of trickiness in your relations with me." He said he had had no knowledge of the hearings, and that Neuberger and Porter should at the very least have brought the Lillie Moore question up at one of the delegation breakfasts: "Apparently you thought if you could get the bill to the Senate calendar then you could get by with this violation." Morse said he would agree to no amendments to the bill, but would accept it only when it came over from the House with the Morse Formula already a part of it. He was, in short, insisting that Neuberger and Porter start all over and do it his way from the beginning.

Again, Neuberger responded the very day he received Morse's letter. He continued to regret the "abusive nature" of Morse's correspondence. There was, he felt, no reason for it: "Neither Charlie Porter nor I ever has resorted to trickery in sponsoring the Lillie Moore bill and you know it. We have been open and above-board about the entire matter." What was more, they did "not have to consult with you about everything that we do, any more than you must consult or confer with us. There are not enough hours in the day for that." Neuberger had only one wish above all: "that, somehow, you can subdue the terrific personal resentment you seem to have against me, so we can work together in the best interest of our state and nation."

As the following excerpts show, no amount of exposition by either party could ever prove convincing. Morse would continue to be outraged; Neuberger would continue to seek vindication.

MORSE, AUGUST 8, 1958: I understand very well why you are upset over my letters because at long last you now realize that I have had my fill of your deceit, trickery and completely untrustworthy tactics as a colleague.

It is obvious that you do not know what the word teamwork means. . . . My disrespect for you has become so complete that there is no basis on which you and I can work together.

NEUBERGER, AUGUST 8, 1958: I am completely at a loss to account for the venom contained in your letters to me.

Let us suppose that Charlie and I were derelict in not notifying you about the Lillie Moore bill. Is that any reason for you to accuse me of every abysmal quality which words can describe? . . .

You are a brilliant man with wide knowledge of public affairs. I urge you not to damage yourself by harboring personal malice against me which can only damage you far more than it damages me. I bear you no ill will. I bear you no malice. If I have done anything to offend you in this Lillie Moore legislation, I apologize and I hope you will forgive me.

Before considering Morse's next salvo, it will be helpful to dwell for a moment on what was going on behind the battle lines. It was the summer of 1958 and a fearful nation was transfixed by the latest developments in the Cold War: American troops were in Lebanon and the Soviet Union was threatening reprisals; war with China loomed over the disputed islands of Quemoy and Matsu; Senator John F. Kennedy announced that American defenses were imperiled because of a massive "missile gap" between the United States and the USSR. Such momentous issues might rivet a nation, but not a Neuberger or a Morse, all of whose attention was focused on the personal struggle nearer to hand.

Each new letter was pounced on as soon as it arrived. In his office, Morse paced the floor "for hours," grimly dictating further denunciations of his colleague's treachery. In his, Neuberger pounded away at his typewriter, heatedly defending his integrity and honor and counterattacking at every possible opening. Neither would spend the few minutes it took to negotiate the one set of stairs and hallway to reach the other's office, or call the other on the telephone.

To Phyllis Rock, one of Morse's legislative aides, such compulsive behavior by "two supposedly intelligent people" was "ridiculous and disgusting. I just thought—what a terrible waste. You couldn't get to Senator Morse about anything else." Nor, according to Lloyd Tupling, could you interest Neuberger in other pressing matters. "I swear to god," he said, "we'd go in and talk to Dick about something, and we'd go out and be doing our work. Ten minutes later we'd be back in [laboring on yet another letter]. It just about drove us nuts. We were trying to do our jobs, and here Dick was spending way more of his time than he should have trying to get in the last word."

Self-justification was more important, and perhaps more satisfying, for both men than settling the problem, and in the last analysis the correspondence was written as much for posterity as for either senator's edification. Morse had a relentless enthusiasm for setting the record straight. In this case, however, Neuberger had an even stronger concern. Though prepared to capitalize on the feud, Neuberger, high-strung by temperament and in failing health, had difficulty handling the strain; he was fighting a powerful antagonist of very long standing and the contest tended to get on his nerves. At certain points he would vacate his typing chair and turn the letter-writing over to legislative assistant Hans Linde, whose job it was to give each criticism a measured response, in subdued language, demonstrating always Neuberger's unassailable reasonableness in the face of what could be seen as extreme provocation. Thus Neuberger's letters often leave the impression of having been written for a wider audience, even as they are directed to answering Morse's every argument.

Morse was not unaware of Neuberger's intentions. The relatively moderate tone of his next communication suggests that he wished to reply in kind.

> Your letter of August 8, 1958, apparently seeks to leave the impression with anyone who reads it that my differences with you are based on the procedures you followed in connection with the Lillie Moore legislation. Apparently you fail to appreciate the fact that your handling of the Lillie Moore legislation was just the straw that broke the camel's back so to speak.
>
> What has hurt me so deeply over the many months has been your many actions of inexcusable disloyalty to our friendship. No one could have tried harder than I have tried to teamwork with you. The saddest thing about this unpleasant experience is that I started my service with you in the Senate after the historic election in 1954 with deep personal fondness for you. . . . It certainly would make me very pleased and happy if after the passage of a year or two such a new relationship between us might re-establish the personal regard that once existed.

However modulated the sentiments expressed in this letter might have been, the assignment of guilt for both devotion betrayed and gratitude withheld, and the promise of a possible reprieve pending future repentance, reveal at last the classic struggle the two men had been waging since 1931: that of dominating father and rebellious son locked in the age-old fight for supremacy.

This aspect of their relationship neither man had been able to escape. Neuberger had never overcome his inferior footing. Morse had held the symbolic power of life and death over him in the incident of 1934, and had exercised it first in extricating him from punishment, then in forcing him to leave the law school. Though a bitter pill for Neuberger to swallow, the exile from law school probably made the subsequent parent-child struggle possible. If Neuberger had stayed, he would have been left powerless in the face of Morse's authority, carrying only the enormous burden of obligation derived from Morse's having saved his reputation, a burden reinforced and multiplied by political debts incurred in 1950 and 1954 and further reinforced by the memory of those law school letters—those feverish, arrogant, beseeching letters, whose writing Neuberger must have rued a thousand times over. If he still resented Morse for driving him out of Eugene, he could at least extract energy from that resentment to take him on in political combat. He would try, however indirectly, to carve out a territory of his own, distinct from that controlled by the imperious senior senator. He would try, but would he ever succeed?

As a member of the Oregon delegation, Neuberger had to live with both the possible permanence of his junior senatorial role and, after 1956, the fact of Morse's paternal status in the delegation. The flinty Green made no secret of her deference to Senator Morse. He had assisted her in her successful campaigns of 1954 and 1956, and she would honor her political debts. And even if that had not been the case, her dislike of the Neubergers was sufficient to put her—at least during this period—in Morse's corner.

For Ullman, Morse was a figure larger than life. Hells Canyon was Al's issue, the main plank in his campaign platform, and Morse, who he hoped would someday be president, was in his eyes the principal champion of that cause. It would be fair to say that Ullman (who named his first male child after Morse) had come to Congress a Morse disciple. Thus Morse could make free to chastise him when, in his opinion, one of Ullman's first votes in the House was cast incorrectly. In a handwritten note of January 31, 1957, Morse said he was "very sad this morning to read in the Congressional Record of your vote yesterday and your statement in support of it. I shall always defend your duty and right to follow the dictates of your conscience. However, I cannot defend your position on this issue and shall not."

Ullman, who would go on to become one of the most powerful men in the House, replied contritely that Morse's message added to "an already heavy burden of conscience on this matter." He said he was trying to find his way in Washington and hoped that Morse would continue to offer advice and assistance.

As he was for Ullman, Morse had long been a hero for Charlie Porter: while in law school, Porter had studied and been impressed by Morse's labor-arbitration decisions and had later, in 1947, applied for a job in his Washington office. Moreover, though Porter had not been Morse's first choice as a Democratic congressional candidate, Morse had been exceedingly helpful in raising money for his campaigns, including two successive $1,000 contributions of his own money. When Porter voted as Ullman had in his first month in office, Morse sent him an almost identical note. Porter replied that "I do have a lot to learn. . . . It is my hope that, with guidance from experienced friends like yourself, I'll get organized before long and have a better opportunity to reflect on the pertinent facts of these great issues coming before Congress. I certainly don't want to be a disappointment to you."

Given Porter's concern about Morse's approval, and given the fact that his House reelection campaign was already under way, it is not surprising that he made up his mind to yield on the Lillie Moore issue. At approximately the same time Neuberger was telling Morse he was "completely at a loss to account for the venom contained in your letters," Porter wrote to Morse in quite a different spirit:

> I have, on thorough consideration, come to the conclusion
> that I made an error in judgement in not having consulted
> you prior to the introduction of the bill and that I com-

pounded the error by my failure to consult with you in person regarding the legislation at any time subsequent to its introduction. However, you will believe me when I tell you that
there was no intent on my part to be pernicious or even dis-
courteous. There was no malice in my mind and no thought
on my part of achieving by circumvention what might have
been resolved by direct discussion. . . .

For the errors of judgement I have made in connection
with this matter I can only plead brevity of experience and
offer a sincere apology. I have made many other mistakes and
will make many more, but none that I will regret more. . . .

As a campaigner you have no peer and whatever effort
you may be free to expend in my behalf during the next few
months could well mean the difference between my return
to Congress in January and my resumption of private life.

Porter's extensive apology returned the congressman temporarily to
Morse's good graces. As a consequence, Neuberger was returned to
where *he* had been vis-à-vis Morse: alone, without the support of a
political "stepbrother," left, as the following excerpts from his next
letter indicate, petulantly defending himself against the severe judgment of Morse's patriarchal authority.

I am glad to note from your letter of August 11 that you recognize that your utterly abusive, venomous and defamato-
ry letters of August 6, August 7 and August 8 could not stand
as the final record of your views. . . . I do not care to leave
unanswered all the self-serving, special pleading that is also
again contained in your letter of August 11. Upon review, you
will find that your recent series of accusations against me
have been so vague, unspecific and rhetorical that it is hard
for me even to understand what, precisely, I am supposed to
have done—let alone to meet your nebulous allegations
with factual answers. . . .

You have accused me, without specification, of "undercutting" you. You have repeatedly accused me of "character
assassination." You have referred to completely vague "over-

whelming evidence against me;" but you have specified only
one alleged conversation with an unidentified radio com-
mentator concerning equally unidentified representations I
am alleged to have made to him about you. I deny it; I do not
know either whom, or what representations you could mean.

It has been your letters, not mine, that have contained
the terms "disloyal," "untrustworthy," "amoral," "cowardly"
and "snide." It has been your letters, not mine, that have
hurled accusations of "trickery" and "deceit."

I shall gladly concede, without contest, your preeminence
in the use of personal invective and imprecations.

If Neuberger's previous behavior had provided straws to break
the camel's back, this letter would leave the animal dead in the sand.
On the following day, August 13, Morse reiterated his previous
charges and finally reached back to the law school incident to re-
affirm his present convictions. And in a move he would soon come
to regret, he also gave a green light to the possibility of going public
with the correspondence, a prospect Neuberger relished.

I am amused by your letter of August 12 which reflects again
your sanctimonious holier than thou attitude. I am perfectly
willing to have you make public our correspondence and let
the public be the judge of our differences. . . . When you were
a student of mine, I found you amoral. I had hoped over the
years that you would mature and develop a character of
moral responsibility. Your relations with me in the Senate
have proven that I was mistaken in placing that hope in you.
. . . I fully expect that you will continue to write me letters as
long as I answer yours. Therefore, I wish to notify you that
this is the last personal letter you will receive from me.

And it was—at least for the next several months. Morse even took to
monitoring the mail from Neuberger's office and accepted only that
which he knew called for routine staff cooperation.

There was some truth to the contention that Morse gave few examples of Neuberger's supposed "snide undercutting." What exactly

had he done that was so deceitful and cowardly? Others who saw the letters could not understand what Morse was getting at. LBJ assistant George Reedy was shown the correspondence by Neuberger, and it left him mystified: "I read it and reread it and reread it and reread it, and I never found what in the devil they were fighting about." "Dick would write him a nice letter, and, wham, back would come this sizzling denunciation." Reedy and the many others to whom Neuberger revealed the letters failed to understand that given Morse's ingrained suspicions, Neuberger would inevitably fall from grace. The immediate cause would not have mattered: misunderstood intentions, offhand remarks to a third party, perceived attempts at monopolizing attention; any of these could have proved sufficient, and taken together over time, they were more than enough. In the end, even a supplicatory letter like Porter's could not have saved Neuberger from Morse's contempt.

This is not to say that Neuberger was innocent of Morse's accusations. His need to break free of Morse's dominion and his inability to confront him directly forced him to carry on his fight obliquely, subtly maneuvering to be seen in his own light as Morse's light appeared to be dimming. As the following incident demonstrates, he could carry such maneuvering to imaginative extremes.

National headlines in the first half of 1958 were dominated by the Sherman Adams "vicuña coat" scandal, an exposé of high administration officials accepting expensive gifts in return for political favors (see chapter 10). Neuberger used the scandal as an illustration of why it was necessary to institute reform in a related area: congressional campaigning. In a Senate speech in late June 1958, he compared the receipt of expensive gifts by those in the executive branch to the receipt of large campaign contributions by legislators, and said the two practices were equally evil: each left the individual beholden to wealthy economic interests.

Neuberger was speaking here in behalf of his bill, of which Morse was a cosponsor, to provide federal funding for congressional election campaigns. In the course of his argument, most of which Morse would normally have endorsed, he asked, "Is it morality for a senator to collect $500 or $1,000 speaking fees from many labor unions or liberal groups and then to oppose a federal right-to-work law, but immorality for Harry Vaughn at the White House to be given a deepfreeze or Mr. Adams a coat?" While not mentioned by name, Morse was the obvious referent of this comparison, and everyone knew it. He had for years been supplementing his income with such speeches (though typically for less than the fees cited by Neuberger) and was the chamber's foremost practitioner of the art.

A gibe in the Senate by Neuberger was bad enough, but in its next edition the *Washington Post* editorialized in support of his contention and carried a column by Roscoe Drummond which went even further, accusing Congress of "moral finger-pointing" at Adams to divert attention from its own scandalous conflicts of interest. In this connection, Drummond quoted verbatim Neuberger's remark about speaking fees. Morse hurried to the Senate floor and, with Drummond's column in hand, declared he was "a little weary of snide attacks on the Congress without a bill of particulars backing up the attacks." Warming to the argument, he insisted that the present system of campaign financing did not control the way congressmen voted. Despite this assertion, he said he would continue to support Neuberger's bill.

Neuberger had clearly engineered the *Washington Post* coverage; the next-day appearance of both the editorial and Drummond's column defy coincidence. Neuberger had been able to score points for himself and make Morse look bad, all in the context of arguing for a bill both were supporting. Morse was left with the choice of either assaulting a principle he normally endorsed or keeping silent: he couldn't very well focus on the extramural speech-making without bringing an unwanted kind of attention to himself. Characteristically, he eschewed silence, thereby placing himself in the illogical position of attacking critics of Congress while defending a bill based on the validity of their criticism.

Moreover, Neuberger knew that paid speaking engagements were not logically pertinent to the campaign-financing bill and were not in the same category as influence peddling or political slush funds. He also knew, and had even said publicly, that Morse was less influenced by economic-interest blocs than any other man in the

Senate. Likening the ethics of speaking for money outside of Congress to those of accepting expensive gifts was simply a means of casting aspersions on his senior colleague under the aegis of promoting liberal reform.

The purpose here is not to belabor Neuberger's deviousness, but to point up his need to employ such deviousness. He had never been able to develop a mutually satisfying relationship with Morse, who remained in an exalted position, not only seeming to demand a measure of deference, but actually expecting it. His professed affection for Neuberger in the mid-fifties may have been genuine, but if so, it was the affection of a mentor for an unmanageable pupil who has never quite grown up. In that context, suspicion and mistrust— well-known constants of political life in the best of circumstances— would lie always just beneath the surface.

There may be truth in Francis Bacon's dictum that one can find "little friendship in the world, least of all between equals." But establishing some level of parity is crucial if friendship is to have even the slightest chance of arising between those who were once involved in the superior-inferior mold of a professor-student relationship, to say nothing of a relationship whose beginnings were as bizarre as in this case. Morse and Neuberger had become United States senators, but they had not become equals. Neuberger's circuitous method of trying to even things up merely evoked the earlier period of inequality, when others had called him "deceitful" and "tricky" and Morse, from on high, had been forced to come to his rescue.

ALTHOUGH BICKERING IN PRIVATE HAD CEASED because Morse had halted the correspondence, public evidence of the feud was increasing. Neuberger had been among those many Democrats who in the 1958 gubernatorial election had disowned Morse's eleventh-hour assault on Republican candidate Mark Hatfield's "intellectual honesty" (see chapter 10). In mid-November, Governor-elect Hatfield invited the Oregon congressional delegation to meet with him to discuss problems of mutual concern. Morse refused the invitation, describing the proposed gathering as "political window dressing." Neuberger then criticized both Morse and Hatfield for ignoring Oregon's real problems while they "jockey[ed] politically for 1962." Troubled waters had become more agitated. Morse's own metaphor involved a different liquid. He wrote to Mert Bernstein: "During your six years with me, my office on many occasions was a bloody battleground. However, that blood flowed in mild skirmishes compared with the war that is now on. Both time and our limited supply of stationery make it impossible for me to give you the gory details. . . . The Hatfield incident has smoked Neuberger out so that I have been able to answer what I call his snide political back knifings in public."

In a private conversation, Morse was quoted as calling Neuberger a "political prostitute" and saying that he would work to defeat him in 1960. Predictably, these remarks got back to Neuberger, who, at least for the benefit of his informant, treated them lightly. "Senator Morse," he said, "ventilates a lot of malice and hatred merely by bragging privately as to what he is going to do to me or against me. . . . He is the little boy grown up who is going to eat the tiger alive if he ever saw a tiger on the way home from school." But with his intimates, Neuberger was less breezy. To Lloyd Tupling he described an evening he and Maurine had recently spent with Edith Green as "very unsatisfactory": "She is intransigent and very pro-Morse. Even her friends were disgusted and revolted with her lack of desire to make peace. . . . All most distressing."

Neuberger had far more than Green's intransigence to cause him distress. A routine medical examination in August 1958 had revealed a case of testicular cancer. He underwent surgery in the autumn, began a regimen of radiation therapy, and was forced to cut back his schedule. The illness would play a part in the next development of the "rumpus": publication of the senators' correspondence.

During the second week of December, excerpts from the Morse-Neuberger letters appeared simultaneously in Robert S. Allen's column, which was carried by the *Oregonian* and other Northwest papers, and in *Newsweek*. The impact was sensational. No one had ever seen in print such vituperation between two senators from the same state, *and* from the same faction of the same party. Predictably, Morse took a beating in the press: his strong language was cited again and again as exemplifying his arrogance and intolerance, whereas Neuberger was portrayed as put upon and abused. Even the *Coos Bay World*, previously one of Morse's few supporters among the Oregon press, depicted him as "carried away by fits of jealousy and his deep persecution complex," and found it "a mystery" that Neuberger, usually "extremely thin-skinned to personal attacks," had kept "down his temper and his own talent for cutting words."

Morse moved quickly to defend himself. In a news release, he said he had tried on several occasions over the past summer to reconcile his differences with Neuberger. At the time, he stated, "I was not aware that my colleague, Dick Neuberger, was seriously ill. . . . his illness explains psychologically even more than he may know his conduct toward me." The press release made headlines, and the apparent unseemliness of Morse's observation about Neuberger's mental health might have made further headlines if the question of who leaked the correspondence in the first place had not taken center stage. Morse had Bob Smith to thank for diverting public attention.

The feud had been Smith's story for several months, and now he had been scooped on its most spectacular development. He rushed into print with a confused dispatch which ran in the *Oregonian* under the headline "Morse Leaks Senatorial Spat Letters"; he attributed responsibility for the "calculated leak" to Morse, but did not clearly describe exactly who showed the letters to whom. Not only did Morse fire off a telegram denying Smith's allegation, but Samuel Shaffer, author of the *Newsweek* story on the letters, charged that Smith's mistaken description was the result of professional jealousy. Though he tried to defend what he had written, Smith had in fact gotten it wrong—Tupling had released the correspondence at Neuberger's instruction—and his error took some of the heat off Morse.

Nevertheless, the publication of the letters did Morse considerable harm. Shaffer had ended his article with a patently anti-Morse observation: "Since then [the last letter from Morse], Neuberger has described Morse as 'a brilliant man with one of the most brilliant minds in the Senate,' and added: 'I would be happy to shake him by the hand tomorrow.' But from Sen. Wayne Morse there has been no answer." A week later the *Oregonian* ran a poll showing that 95 percent of the voters rated Neuberger "satisfactory," "good," or "excellent"; only 44 percent placed Morse in the same categories, and 56 percent rated him "poor" or "very poor." In Washington, Senator Barry Goldwater cited the Morse-Neuberger correspondence as evidence of Morse's "political thuggery."

Morse was also losing credibility among some of his diehard supporters. Tom Enright, for example, who had worked in Morse's Washington office in 1954, wrote to Neuberger in December, describing Morse's letters as "nothing short of ridiculous. And when he started blaming everything on to your illness, he left himself wide open to the charge that if anybody is emotionally unbalanced it is him."

Riding the crest of his increased popularity, Neuberger ventured a letter to Morse on January 2, 1959, his first since Morse had broken off communication the previous August. He wrote as if doing so were entirely natural and included a newsy update on his medical condition: the doctors were optimistic but advised him to stay in Portland for radiation treatments until the end of the month. He said he was looking forward to working with Morse again, and then

Green, Neuberger, Morse, and Ullman at the 1959 celebration of Oregon's centennial. Despite the outward congeniality, behind-the-scenes tensions had grown increasingly serious. (Oregon Historical Society, OrHi CN 020847.)

added: "I trust we can resume our breakfast meetings for discussion of Oregon projects and general legislative affairs, perhaps following the practice which has been used by the Maine delegation of including all members, regardless of party.... such breakfast sessions might prove even more beneficial than in the past. I hope that a breakfast meeting can be scheduled soon after my return so we can bring each other up to date on events in Congress and in Oregon." Neuberger concluded with "best wishes for the New Year."

Since Neuberger had the political upper hand for the moment, what did he hope to gain by risking reopening the correspondence with Morse? The recitation of his medical situation may have been meant to play on Morse's sympathy, but that is not likely. Nor is it likely that he was worried lest Morse get the wrong idea about his absence from Washington. His main thought was his own political survival: it was not too early to be concerned about 1960, and writing Morse in a friendly manner was the start of an effort to neutralize his opposition to Neuberger's renomination. However, bringing up the ill-fated delegation breakfasts was something else again; consciously or unconsciously, this could only have been intended to antagonize Morse anew. And it probably did, though if Morse was agitated, he saw fit to conceal his anger.

He addressed his reply "Dear Senator Neuberger"—not the "Dear Dick" of old, but an improvement on the "Dear Neuberger" of more recent vintage—and said the optimistic health forecasts were "good news." As for the breakfasts, he felt they would be subject to the same leakage problems experienced in the past, and though he indicated he would give the idea further consideration, he concluded by virtually dismissing it as not being "of momentous importance anyway." Nevertheless, he signed off politely with "best wishes for a speedy recovery."

With this renewed attention to social amenities, one might have wondered whether the protagonists were ready to sheathe their blades and establish a more peaceful environment. Such a question would not have been entirely rhetorical, since at times Neuberger seemed to desire a safer arrangement by which at least the pretense of amity could be possible—thus his proposal for including Republicans at

delegation breakfasts. He said he was "very distressed" when Drew
Pearson's column mentioned that he and Morse no longer said hello
to each other, and he took pains to correct Pearson's wrong impression: "*This is not true, Drew.* Wayne and I have not seen each other
for over five months." A technically accurate, if disingenuous, distinction: if you haven't seen someone, you cannot be accused of not
saying hello to him. Such clarifications were of no interest to Morse.
He continued to remind correspondents (hundreds wrote to plead
for reconciliation) of Dick's "old law school cribbing habits," and as
a recent case in point he cited a bill that he had introduced in the
previous Congress with Neuberger as cosponsor and that Neuberger
had *re*introduced under his own name in the new session, with
Frank Church as cosponsor. Morse justifiably saw this as an "act of
legislative thievery."

Neuberger was scarcely unaware of Morse's continued hostility.
Despite that knowledge, and despite his apparent wish to reduce the
level of tension, he could not resist one final shot on the Lillie Moore
issue. In what would be his last correspondence with Morse, he noted
on April 13, 1959, that Morse had waived his formula for two parcels
of federal land which had been ceded to Indian tribes in New Mexico. In light of this fact, he wondered if Morse might reconsider his
position on Lillie Moore.

Morse replied the following day: "I am sorry you still do not
understand the Morse formula. It was not waived in the two cases
referred to in your letter of April 13; it simply didn't apply to them
because of the Federal interest involved. . . . Also, may I say most respectfully that because you can't see a distinction it does not follow
that a distinction doesn't exist." And that, as far as available records
indicate, was the last letter Morse ever wrote to Neuberger. He attacked Neuberger's foreign-policy positions in a number of speeches, and in mid-May he announced from Washington his intention in
the coming campaign to "point out to the voters of Oregon the sorry
record he has made on issue after issue."

For his part, Neuberger was of two minds about Morse's opposition, and this, apart from his deeper ambivalence about Morse, explains why he found ways to increase provocation even as he sought

a reconnection in 1959. He told Herbert Lundy of the *Oregonian* that, while confident of reelection, he feared that Morse could give him trouble by backing someone else for the nomination: "Morse has the vitality of a water buffalo. . . . It might be that I could not keep pace." On the other hand, Neuberger reveled in Morse's opposition and felt that it could only help him at the polls; he reportedly told a friend that his worst nightmare would be Morse embracing him during the 1960 campaign.

It is easy to see that Neuberger could take either approach at various times because either might produce positive results at the ballot box. The option of keeping Morse's dander up was frequently irresistible: in what could only have been an attempt to incite exasperation, Neuberger proposed over the summer to have the Green Peter Dam in the Willamette Basin renamed after the recently deceased Douglas McKay, Morse's Republican opponent in the bitter campaign of 1956.

Morse flirted with the idea of either finding someone to run against Neuberger in the primary, or campaigning against him, with or without a capable competitor in the race. But Charlie Brooks had made a careful analysis of political currents on the home front and reported that support among the party faithful for an all-out attack was lacking. Morse's strong feelings had in no way abated: "My opinion of Neuberger," he told a friend, "can best be stated this way, 'If you and I were in the same room with Neuberger, and you asked him the time of day, I would look at the clock.'" Nevertheless, he accepted Brooks's analysis, deciding not to campaign against Neuberger should he be renominated, but to work in behalf of other candidates in the general election. In a short time, however, all such considerations would become irrelevant. Morse's antagonist would suddenly be removed from the contest.

ON THE NIGHT OF MARCH 9, 1960, Neuberger died in a Portland hospital. He was forty-seven. His death was attributed to a massive cerebral hemorrhage, but cancer, the malady that had first struck him in 1958, was the root cause. The announcement of his passing caught almost everyone, and especially Morse, by surprise. What had seemed to be improvement had been merely a temporary remission. Neuberger had known for some weeks that he was dying. And so had several members of the Oregon press, but such was his relationship to editors around the state that they had agreed to keep the seriousness of his illness a secret. He had hoped to live to the end of his term and then be succeeded by Maurine.

Morse officially announced Neuberger's death to the Senate on March 10. He paid homage to his fellow Oregonian's record as a great conservationist and concluded his eulogy by saying, "We will all be lonesome because this fallen leader is no more in mortal flesh."

Whatever Morse felt at Neuberger's passing, it could not be described as loneliness. However, other members of the Senate would genuinely miss him. He had gained favor with his colleagues in a way that Morse seldom could. He had curbed much of his brashness and had clearly been marked for a leadership role within the chamber.

Still, Neuberger rivaled or outdistanced Morse in his sensitivity to criticism; and when the criticism came from Morse, that sensitivity knew no measure. Unlike Morse, Neuberger could not handle critical give-and-take with equanimity. He wanted badly to be liked, and there is no reason to doubt him when time and again he states that the controversy left him "greatly distressed." Morse may have been distressed as well by the continual conflict, but as the letter to Bernstein about blood and gore suggests, the feud also provided a source of vitality; and one imagines Morse's psychic battery reading positive as the polarities became more permanent and the interchange more highly charged.

Despite his perpetual willingness to risk defeat at the polls by taking unpopular positions, Morse loved his seat in Congress. With whatever heartache it might hold, the Senate had become his life. He was *Senator* Morse, and no one could think of him otherwise. The Senate was not Neuberger's first love, and almost as soon as he had known the satisfaction of rising to its heights, he began to think about leaving. In January 1957, after serving only two years of a six-year term (and at a time when his relationship with Morse was still amiable), he admitted his feelings in a confidential letter to Morse.

Never before have I said this to anybody, but I am by no
means clear in my own mind that I will be a candidate again.
I have enjoyed my service here, and I especially have appreciated the privilege of working with you. But I value my ability and talents as a writer, and I feel that this ability has scant
chance to show itself now. I am not becoming any younger
[he was forty-five], and if I am to write some of the things
which I aspire to undertake, it can only be done by making
literary work my sole career and leaving full-time political
activity to others. This is something I have yet to face up to,
but it confronts me quite often in my thoughts.

Neuberger's commitment to journalism was genuine. Those who
worked for him say that although he was skillful at both vocations,
he never stopped thinking of himself as a writer first and a politician
second. Why, then, since politics caused him no end of pain and frustration and kept him from pursuing his primary objective, was he
prepared (before he knew of his impending death) to serve another
six years in office? There was, of course, the post-Eisenhower agenda to be fought for; all competent hands would be needed, and Neuberger was more competent than most. But it is arguable that, as
Morse had argued years before, Neuberger could do the progressive
cause more good outside the Congress than he could within. Whatever the validity of that argument, couldn't it be that Neuberger was
driven by impulses stronger even than those which moved him toward political accomplishment or journalistic productivity? Didn't
he imagine that somehow, through some twist of fate, he might
reach that day of ultimate triumph when he, and not Morse, would
head the state delegation, when he, and not Morse, would be Oregon's senior senator? Wouldn't Dean Morse then have to show him
the respect he so manifestly deserved?

THE WORD "TRAGIC" WAS FREQUENTLY USED to describe the dis-
solution of the Morse-Neuberger coalition. Most Democrats found
tragedy in the inability of two men of superior intellect and pro-

gressive outlook to get along, particularly since their beginnings in the Senate had held such great promise. Oregon liberals wondered if they would ever again enjoy such an extraordinary consolidation of senatorial power. Had they known more about the Morse-Neuberger history, how much each man had had to repress in order to come together even temporarily, they might have been grateful for the two fruitful years that had somehow been provided.

If political tragedy marked the relationship, there was psychological tragedy of a deeper dimension. Neither man could forget his earliest resentments toward the other, and subsequent resentments merely enlarged the store. For Morse, letting go of resentment was never an easy proposition. He informed Samuel Shaffer—who, despite the article in *Newsweek,* hoped he could stay on Morse's good side—that "when one suffers such a disappointment in a friendship as I have suffered in our case it is impossible for me at least to pretend that no hurt was done. . . . I am very forgiving but not a forgetting soul." In truth, Morse could not forgive unless he could first forget, especially when he took the "hurt" personally. And since he and Neuberger had never confronted their law school difficulties, let alone resolved them, forgetting Neuberger's transgressions was beyond his reach; forgiving him was out of the question.

Morse's life overflowed with those he disapproved of, those he felt suspicious of, those he held in contempt, those he had attacked at one time or another. Sometimes, even in the worst of cases, rapprochements were later possible—made feasible by a sufficient passage of time, made necessary by the imperatives of the moment. But with some there would be no rapprochement, whatever the cost in popular support or political status.

Such was the situation with Neuberger. Had he lived, Dick might have found a way to reestablish some small ground for accommodation, but he would never have regained Morse's good will. Wayne had judged him, finally, as unpardonable. As such, he would be an outcast forever.

10

Once a Maverick . . .

Compromise used to mean that half a loaf was better than no bread. Among modern statesmen it really seems to mean that half a loaf is better than a whole loaf.

> —G. K. Chesterton
> *What's Wrong with the World*

WHEN MORSE RETURNED TO WASHINGTON IN 1957 after his electoral victory, the political situation in the capital was as he had left it: Democrats still controlled both houses of Congress; the Republicans, with Eisenhower swept back into office, still occupied the White House. Majority Leader Lyndon Johnson, as he had in the previous Congress when legislative and executive power were similarly divided, took it as his statesmanlike duty to foster not the traditional politics of loyal opposition, but a politics of consensus, a politics "geared," in his words, "to the best interests of our people." He consequently exerted his considerable influence on fellow Democrats to accommodate administration proposals to the greatest possible degree so that, in a spirit of compromise, both parties could get something of what they wanted.

Morse was more than a little suspicious of Johnson's approach. He believed that all too often, Johnson consensualism was indistinguishable from the program being promoted by the conservative coalition in Congress. He could see no reason to cooperate with an administration most of whose positions he regarded as both wrongheaded and reactionary. Not only was he unprepared to be a two-party consensus builder, he was unwilling to moderate even slightly the critical stance he had taken against the GOP since he bolted that organization in 1952. Thus, despite the conciliatory tone struck in Eugene during a moment of postelection euphoria, once back in the trenches of Washington, he immediately resumed his broadside attacks on the Eisenhower administration and on the president himself. And as had so often happened in the past, one such attack caused serious repercussions.

Appearing on Mike Wallace's ABC interview program in late May, Morse described Eisenhower's Hells Canyon "giveaway" as ethically equivalent to Teamster president Dave Beck's thievery of union finances. Morally speaking, he said, he could not differentiate Eisenhower's granting the Idaho Power Company millions of interest-free taxpayer dollars to build dams on the Snake River from Beck's dipping into union-member pockets in order to fill up his own. (He had made the same statement a few days earlier in a speech in Detroit.) When outraged Republicans contended that if uttered within the halls of Congress, such pejorative remarks would subject their speaker to disciplinary proceedings, Morse rushed to the Senate floor and repeated his assertion.

The charge of immorality was not all that new. Morse had been excoriating Eisenhower in similar language for years. But associating the president with an alleged felon like Beck *was* new, and it moved some Republicans to the highest of dudgeon. According to the *Philadelphia Inquirer*, a furious Homer Capehart of Indiana declaimed in the Senate that Morse was guilty of intellectual dishonesty. Iowa's Bourke Hickenlooper hit even harder, characterizing Morse's statements as "far more odious . . . than anything Joe McCarthy ever said." Along with others, Capehart argued that Morse, like McCarthy, should be formally censured by the Senate for what amounted to presidential character assassination. When, however, Morse dared Capehart—whom, to the delight of the press, he referred to as "a tub of rancid ignorance"—to introduce a resolution of censure, the Republican hierarchy decided it would be unprofitable to wage parliamentary warfare against the Senate's "Stormy Petrel" (the *Inquirer's* metaphor), and saw to it that the matter was dropped. When asked why they had backed away, Senator Alexander Wiley of Wisconsin replied, "Do you think I'm crazy? [Only] a bunch of jackasses" would take Morse on. Thus unencumbered by the fear of Republican retribution, and at the same time unmoved by the bipartisan "statesmanship" of LBJ and his cadre, Morse would continue to berate the president in whatever terms he felt appropriate.

But the rancor had left an acrid taste in many senators' mouths, not excluding Morse's. He was especially disturbed that neither Johnson nor Democratic Whip Mike Mansfield had risen to defend his right of free speech in the face of what he took to be a jugular assault by Republican enemies. He dispatched an angry letter to both accusing them of failing to carry out their prescribed responsibilities. Mansfield replied apologetically that he had been off the floor during much of the debate or would certainly have entered the fray. In his reply, Johnson also offered an apology of sorts, but he was clearly rankled that Morse had stirred up such a partisan furor. "I am not," he said,

> in the habit of writing hasty and impulsive letters for the present edification of my friends and for the future regret of Lyndon Johnson. I do not intend to make an exception in this case.
>
> The debate yesterday took place mostly while I was away from the Chamber. . . . I assumed that you had the situation well in hand and that an organized counter-attack would merely lend some dignity to an obviously contrived and somewhat childish attack.
>
> For my assumption, I apologize. I stand by my judgment, however. . . . The next time you feel you are out of your depth, let me know and I will organize a group of Democrats who can handle a Republican attack.

Normally, such condescension would have elicited an equally caustic rejoinder from Morse. In this instance, however—perhaps because Johnson had so recently granted his long-held wish for a seat on the Senate Labor and Public Welfare Committee—Morse merely indicated that *his* letter had been neither hasty nor impulsive, reiterated disappointment in his leaders' dereliction of duty, and concluded by assuring Johnson that "our differences over this matter will in no way impair my continued cooperation with you and Mansfield in the Senate of the United States." One imagines Johnson reading this last sentiment and wondering, "What-in-hell cooperation is that?"

And well might he have wondered, for Morse's reluctance to enter the compromise game had more than one antecedent. His philosophical differences with the Eisenhower administration (especially over foreign policy, which we will examine in detail in chapter 13) would have been grounds enough to prevent collaborating with the opposition, but there was also a compelling force making cooperation within his own party problematic. That force emanated, as ever, from the maverick's quest for masterlessness. Morse may have found in the Democratic party a place to hang his ideological hat, but he had not necessarily found a political home, not if such residence meant unquestioningly taking direction from Lyndon Johnson and the other doyens of the upper house. However indebted he might feel toward Johnson for his assistance, Morse was incapable of evening accounts by playing the obedient foot soldier in Senate combat—even, as the contest over civil rights would show, when an issue close to his heart was at stake.

THE SUMMER OF 1957 MARKED NEARLY THREE YEARS since the Supreme Court had declared in *Brown v. Board of Education* that segregated education was unconstitutional. Many hoped Congress would follow in the wake of *Brown* with a program of its own, one that would vigorously attack segregation and provide remedies for the many other aspects of racism rampant throughout the country. Because of Southern recalcitrance, however, which typically took the form of interminable filibustering in the Senate, Congress had been unable to pass such a program, which meant that a near-century-old record of legislative inaction in the field of civil rights had been maintained. Would 1957 keep this record intact, or might it go down as the year of change, the year when Congress began at last to correct the manifest wrongs of racial injustice?

Optimism was in the air. The antisegregationist movement had been building steadily since *Brown*; some Southern Democrats were feeling pressure for change from local "progressive" business interests fearful of losing national revenues; and the Eisenhower administration seemed serious in wanting to get some sort of civil-rights bill through Congress. But the biggest cause for optimism was a shift in the thinking of the Senate majority leader: "Lyndon Johnson," according to the slightly inflated prose of one writer, "made the move of his political life." Having voted segregationist his previous twenty years in Congress, Johnson, with sights already on the White House, decided that the moment for at least minimal action on civil rights was at hand. And though *action* there would be, *minimal* it would also be, for Johnson, as always, had in mind a compromise bill, one in this instance that would slide through Congress raising the least possible resistance from the formidable coalition of conservative Republicans and Southern Dixiecrats. Morse went along for a time, as Johnson appeased opponents by stripping from the bill one empowering provision after another. When, however, a point of "unconscionable compromise" had been reached, he refused to go any further.

The administration's civil-rights bill, passed on to the Senate from the House, contained three key provisions. Under the firm instructions of Johnson and the irresolute leadership of Senator Paul Douglas of Illinois, two of these provisions—one to establish a commission on fair employment practices, a second to support the Supreme Court's desegregation decision—were dropped almost immediately. Even more telling was a trade-off on the third provision: how voting-rights violations would be dealt with. Originally, the bill specified criminal contempt-of-court prosecution before a federal judge for those accused of failing to obey a voting-rights enforcement order. Southerners insisted on jury trials for all alleged violators, a provision the bill's supporters strongly opposed because they feared that Southern juries would never bring in convictions. The compromise took the form of reclassifying violations from *criminal* to *civil* contempt of court. Under this arrangement jury trials were eliminated, but interfering with a citizen's voting rights was reduced to a minor offense, punishable merely by a petty fine imposed by a magistrate. Thus divested of meaningful enforcement provisions, the civil-rights bill became, in the words of Senator Joe Clark of Pennsylvania, "a pallid little measure," or as Joe Rauh of Americans for Democratic Action put it, "a piece of shit that isn't worth saving."

Despite his initial revulsion, Rauh, then president of ADA, and Clarence Mitchell, president of the NAACP, deemed it important to show the nation that a civil-rights bill, even such an excremental one, could be enacted, and they pressured Senate liberals to settle for the compromise. Most agreed with Rauh and Mitchell that something was better than nothing. Morse took exactly the opposite position: conscientiously doing nothing was, he felt, far preferable to passing a do-nothing bill and pretending it added up to something important. When the Civil Rights Act of 1957 was passed into law toward the end of summer, he cast the only non-Southern vote from either party against it.

Hubert Humphrey defended his capitulation to the Dixiecrats by proclaiming that "compromise is not a dirty word." For Morse, it could not have been dirtier. He was incensed when B'nai B'rith's Anti-Defamation League honored the Eighty-fifth Congress for passing the act. He told Jewish colleague Herbert Lehman of New York, "It disgusts me. . . . It is my opinion that Jewish leaders . . . have never learned that their just causes are not strengthened by honoring compromisers of principle." He was especially appalled that Democrats had acted so as to give the Eisenhower administration a boost for seeming to take dramatic action in a field in which it had a minimal interest at best. He believed the Dixiecrats were "laughing up their sleeves" because liberals had been "sucked in" by both Lyndon Johnson and the administration.

That Morse was going to take a maverick position on the civil-rights bill was clear as early as a month before the final vote was taken. At a time when the *New Republic* was headlining him derisively as "Oregon's Lone Ranger," he wrote to Governor G. Mennen Williams of Michigan that

> I think we Democrats in the liberal wing of the party should
> make up our minds as to what we think a good civil rights

bill should contain, and then we should . . . just go ahead and fight for that bill. If we continue to follow the strategy of . . . Democratic liberals now being managed by Douglas we will end up with a civil rights bill that will not meet the needs of the country, but . . . many people will be fooled by it and the country, as a whole, will believe that the Eisenhower administration is the political savior of the colored people. I do not intend to be a party to such a short sighted civil rights program.

Morse knew that not being a party to enacting the civil-rights bill would bring down criticism from many quarters, but he was, as ever, more than ready to hold his ground. When his old University of Minnesota boss Frank Rarig chided him for being so obdurate and for castigating Douglas and other fellow liberals, he delivered an extensive treatise on the absolute correctness of his actions. Contained within was the following lecture on how a maverick of his stripe survived in the Senate: "I would point out to you that being a liberal in the Senate is not easy traveling. There are many unpleasant personal experiences connected with it. It is not pleasant to have to be tough and rough, but it has been my observation that any liberal who follows the old maxim 'you can catch more flies with honey than with vinegar' will soon find himself devoured politically."

Toughness, roughness, and a vinegary attitude certainly helped sustain Morse throughout the Civil Rights Act drama. Subjected to considerable abuse, he gave at least as well as he took, and, solitary though it was, his depiction of the act as nothing less than a "hoax and a sham" was indelibly etched on the record. A reasonable argument could be made that the act served as a useful progenitor for future, more compelling legislation in the civil-rights area. Equally reasonable was Morse's argument that passage of the act was merely an exercise in cynicism which misled the public and increased its frustration. Whichever was more valid, it is clear in retrospect that, in and of itself, the act effected no meaningful change in the law. In his 1971 memoirs, Douglas himself looked back on what he and LBJ had accomplished, and found little worth remembering. "The 1957

Civil Rights Act," he wrote, "proved ineffective." Reading these words, Morse might have inquired, "Isn't that what I predicted fourteen years ago?"

IF THERE HAD BEEN UNCERTAINTY as to how Morse would comport himself once elected as a Democrat, the civil-rights debate of 1957 erased all doubt. It again confirmed him as an unreformed, unrepentant, unpredictable maverick. At the same time, it renewed his reputation as an intrepid man of action, one willing to risk political disfavor to defend strongly held principles. Because of this reputation, he was, and would always be, besieged by individuals and groups espousing a variety of unpopular causes. Among those soliciting support were some who could only be described as fanatical true believers with lunatic axes to grind. But there were others— conscientious public servants, agency whistle-blowers, institutional reformers—who turned to Morse precisely because he was seen as invincibly unbeholden to the Washington establishment. One such individual was Professor Bernard Schwartz of New York University.

The thirty-four-year-old Schwartz had been hired as chief counsel by the House Commerce Committee in 1957 to look into the Federal Communications Commission and other independent regulatory commissions, bodies which, rumor had it, were being manipulated by the very industries they were supposed to control. In a memorandum to the committee, Schwartz reported that not only were the rumors true, but individuals close to the president were, in return for various kinds of consideration, breaking the rules for specified corporations. However, because it was chaired by Arkansas's Oren Harris—who hoped to be named by the administration to a federal judgeship and who was himself involved in a regulated business—the Commerce Committee refused to launch a congressional investigation.

Information from Schwartz's memo implicating both business executives and bureaucrats materialized in a series of Drew Pearson "Washington Merry-Go-Round" columns. The entire memo then appeared in the *New York Times.* The resulting clamor forced the reticent committee to open an investigation, but, under the guileful hand of Harris, its first substantial act was to fire its chief investigator, Professor Schwartz. Fearing that without his presence his findings would be doctored or buried by the committee, Schwartz took the precaution of emptying his files upon vacating his office, escaping the building just minutes before committee staff arrived to commandeer his records.

Schwartz hoped that somehow his material could be used to prevent the committee from whitewashing the whole investigation. Clark Mollenhoff of the *Des Moines Register*, who later emerged as a Nixon undercover man, pressured him into showing it to Republican senator John Williams of Delaware. But Pearson and his associate Jack Anderson interceded, persuading Schwartz to take the papers from Williams (who wasn't that interested anyway) and deliver them into safer hands, those belonging to one of Pearson's most trusted allies in the Senate. Thus, around midnight on a cold February night in 1958, a pajama-clad Morse received the documents—either one or two suitcases or several cartons full, depending on who is telling the story. He kept them for a day and a half, returning them to Harris only when requested to do so by the venerable House Speaker Sam Rayburn.

It was believed that Morse had copied Schwartz's work before handing it back, especially since he announced that it revealed an Eisenhower administration "honeycombed with immorality." In fact, he hadn't made copies, but he *had* allowed Anderson to spend several hours taking notes on the most critical portions. Along with other liberal senators, Morse had earlier tried to exert pressure on the House committee from the floor of the Senate. As described by Anderson, Morse, "erect and pugnacious, with the visage of an offended eagle . . . led off with a blistering attack on the House cover-up, demanding that the Senate take on the regulatory investigation if the House continued to shirk its duty." While such provocative oratory had worked to keep the issue alive, it was only after Morse's temporary possession of the documents and the attendant publicity it generated that Schwartz could at last rest easy: not only was his material secure, but, not knowing what Morse and others might have discovered, the committee would now have no choice but to use it as the basis for a full-scale investigation.

The resultant hearings ran on for several weeks, exposing rampant wrongdoing in what had theretofore seemed a scandal-proof Republican administration. The inquiry culminated in the firing of Eisenhower's esteemed chief assistant, Sherman Adams, who, the evidence clearly indicated, had accepted luxurious gifts (including the headline-making vicuña coat) in return for interceding with the Federal Trade, Interstate Commerce, and Federal Communications commissions on behalf of powerful corporate interests. In Pearson's mind, the Republicans' defeat in the 1960 presidential election was due in large measure to the embarrassing revelations of 1958.

It was clear that Schwartz had been led to Morse by the omnipresent Pearson. Just as clear was the fact that Schwartz, who would go on to become one of the nation's most distinguished legal scholars, was attracted to Morse because of his reputation for fierce independence. According to Anderson, they believed that no one but Morse had both the reputation and the courage to take possession of what many lawmakers, Rayburn included, regarded as stolen property. Without Morse's part, the entire investigation might have been derailed and the malfeasance of federal officials in high places never exposed.

Morse's maverickness often carried him down the road to disappointment and defeat. This time it helped bring about if not a historic victory, then at least a significant setback for the opposition. And personal vindication as well: Morse had been dilating on the administration's ethical shortcomings for over half a decade, endeavoring to educate a public that had been largely indifferent when not openly antagonistic. Now everyone, even the most ardent among Eisenhower's devotees, could see at least the possible validity of his previous accusations. Ike was, after all, merely a Republican chief executive. George Washington he was not. Chalk one up for maverick tenacity.

IT IS THE NATURE OF THE MAVERICK not to look back with regret. Having second thoughts about past decisions is but a short step from fretting about future consequences the way ordinary politicians do. Indeed, perpetual worry about the limits of acceptable opinion and behavior is a defining characteristic of the ordinary politician. Morse seldom succumbed to such ordinariness. His normal mode was to follow his own path, defend with vigor whatever move he had made, and proceed to his next concern free from self-recrimination. There came a moment in 1958, however, when he was forced to have second, even third thoughts about a particular step he had taken. What he had done had, as usual, led him into heated controversy, but on this occasion the controversy was one which even he might have preferred to avoid.

The Oregon Democratic revolution led by Morse in 1956 was reasonably well entrenched in 1958: neither Morse nor Neuberger was up for reelection; Edith Green, Al Ullman, and Charlie Porter seemed to be having little difficulty holding on to their congressional seats. The only gloomy race was the governor's, where Bob Holmes was facing a strong challenge from thirty-six-year-old Republican Secretary of State Mark Hatfield. As election day approached, the chance that Holmes would retain his Salem office appeared slim. Just before the end of the campaign, Morse, who had been touring the state in support of Holmes and other Democratic candidates, tried to reverse the momentum by attacking Hatfield in a series of widely reported speeches.

Eighteen years earlier, Hatfield had run into and killed a seven-year-old girl in a car accident. A civil lawsuit ensued in which a trial court found Hatfield liable for $5,000 in damages, payable to the girl's family. On appeal, the Oregon Supreme Court reviewed the facts in the case, declined to accept Hatfield's version of events, and upheld the trial court's judgment against him. Although criminal charges were never brought, Morse told audiences that Hatfield's testimony—which, according to the court, was totally unsubstantiated by available evidence—revealed him to be thoroughly unreliable and intellectually dishonest. These same characteristics, he contended, were plainly reflected in the maliciously misleading campaign

*Republican candidate Mark Hatfield (left) was roundly at-
tacked by Morse, who supported Democratic incumbent Bob
Holmes in the Oregon gubernatorial race of 1958. (Oregon
Historical Society, OrHi CN 010819.)*

Hatfield had been waging against Holmes. Immediately after one
such speech, Morse was quoted as saying, "I don't intend to let a man
run for public office who lies to a jury. I don't intend to let a man lie
to a jury and get away with it."

From the historical perspective of the 1990s, when a candidate's
sexual proclivities and living arrangements are commonly regarded
as relevant "issues," Morse's exhumation of a painful episode from
an aspirant's teenage past seems a routine exercise in negative campaigning—surprising, perhaps, but scarcely worth a second look.
Even in 1958, his remarks drew little attention outside Oregon. Within the state, however, up and down the Willamette Valley, along the
coastline, beyond the Cascades, his observations set off the equivalent of a political H-bomb. Unfortunately for Morse, most of the fall-
out rained exclusively on him.

When it hit the wire services that Morse had gone after Hatfield
with a personal tragedy nearly two decades old, Oregon's Democratic
leaders (most of whom had known about the court case and had advised against using it) rushed to distance themselves from his views.

Porter, Green, and Neuberger issued statements saying they either "deplored" or "regretted" Morse's remarks, and Holmes himself followed suit; the head of the Multnomah County Labor Council referred to Morse's charges as "goofy"; a candidate for state representative suggested that "Sen. Morse was too long in the Republican party. That's Republican party tactics, not Democratic"; Keith Skelton of Eugene, a member of both the legislature and the state Central Committee, publicly repudiated Morse's position and privately decried his remarks as "ill-timed, ill-tempered, and stupid"; and a filmed "unity" appearance for television featuring Morse, Green, and Neuberger scheduled for the Saturday before the election was shelved in favor of a live presentation by Holmes and Green. So great was the negative reaction that Morse's office had to prepare a form letter responding to constituents who had either telephoned or forwarded criticisms through the mail.

Critics were scarcely confined to Morse's party. The Salem Chamber of Commerce, which prided itself on nonpartisanship, canceled Morse's luncheon talk on election eve; a Portland voter called the *Oregonian* to express sorrow "for the mother of that little girl" now forced to relive her agony, while another reflected the opinion of many by suggesting that the mere reprinting of Morse's accusation was "inexcusable. . . . He's a dirty dog, with apologies to the dogs."

In *The Tiger in the Senate,* A. Robert Smith writes that Morse took his usual forceful stand in the face of mounting opprobrium: "No regrets, no backing down, no apologies to the sensibilities of others." This, as far as it goes, is a correct assessment. In his constituent letter, in press releases, in a TV address the night before the election, Morse ardently defended his position and insisted that his judgment of Hatfield was unassailably accurate. Moreover, he was livid that his Democratic colleagues had deserted him with such celerity. His severest reproach was reserved for Green, for whom he had campaigned in three consecutive elections. To Mert Bernstein he wrote:

> Not even Edith Green came through on this one. . . . She tried to talk to me about it over the phone but I wasn't very helpful and she fell into tears. She didn't succeed in washing

away my views on the issue when she tried to tell me that her office was flooded with bitter criticism the day after I made my first attack on Hatfield. . . . I informed her that we were receiving some such mail also, but we were also receiving a great deal of mail . . . that asked the question, "What happened to Edith Green's guts?" That upset her even more. . . . I said, "Of course, Edith, now that you have crawled into a bed of political prostitution with Neuberger, Holmes, Davidson, Sweetland, Porter, Skelton, et al., I hope you enjoy it." Needless to say that opened the flood gates further.

Despite his staunch self-defense and his fury with others, Morse *did* have moments, albeit private ones, when he seemed to question the wisdom of his campaign tactics. In the letter to Bernstein, he acknowledged that he was "in a very deep political slump in Oregon, probably the deepest one I have ever been in. It may be the last one, in that I may not climb out of it." But he was less worried about his personal future than about the harm he might have caused Holmes, who had lost to Hatfield by nearly eleven percentage points—a thumping margin no one had predicted. In a postelection letter, he tried to both explain and justify to Holmes the approach he had taken, and although he had located the governor in Green's "bed of political prostitution," he also expressed in this letter what seemed to be genuine concern for the man and for the difficulty he had caused him. He was, he said, "heartsick over the turn of events caused by my speeches"; he apologized for not discussing strategy beforehand directly with the candidate; and he concluded by saying, "You have been a very fine Governor, and when I think of the loss of your services and any responsibility I have for the loss of those services as Governor of the State, I feel terribly blue."

Could Morse have avoided the blues, prevented his political slump from occurring? There were some who believed that his whole attack on Hatfield had been part of a prearranged plot to get rid of Holmes, a possible rival in the next senatorial race, by causing him to lose to Hatfield through an imprudent act seemingly done out of friendship. Even if Morse had been capable of such duplicity, this scenario seems highly improbable, especially considering the danger of permanent damage and given Morse's very real rage at his Democratic brethren after the fact. More likely is Smith's view that Morse did what he did with reckless disregard for consequences, out of his own egocentric capacity to attack first and check for casualties later. But even this analysis is more wrong than right, or, more accurately, partially right but for the wrong reasons.

Why *did* Morse bring up the accident when the risks of its backfiring were so great and when so many others refused to touch it? It is tempting to find the reason in the maverick's penchant for doing things precisely *because* the risks are too high for the less audacious. While maverick propensities are part of the tale, the whole story is more complicated. Morse said he was encouraged to use the court records by Harry Hogan, Holmes's campaign chief, who had reached a point of desperation and felt that nothing less would work against Hatfield. Smith, however, accepts the statement Hogan made at the time that while he gave Morse the records to examine, he told him not to use them. Yet when I later asked Hogan to confirm his statement, he was unwilling to do so. But even if Hogan had *begged* him to use the case, Morse was assuredly free to say no. In the end, he made the decision on his own, and found going forward irresistible.

For one thing, Morse had no cause to regard Hatfield as anything *but* dishonorable and unscrupulous. Recall that it was Hatfield who had replaced him as a presidential-convention delegate in the anti-Morse coup in Salem in the summer of 1952, shortly before Morse left the Republican party forever. Although Hatfield always contended that he was merely the beneficiary of what happened in Salem and had nothing to do with the humiliating ostracism of Morse, there is no reason to think that Morse had come to believe him. Jebby Davidson had correctly predicted late in the summer of 1958 that "when Wayne Morse gets home there may be some fireworks. Morse apparently nurses a tremendous bitterness about Hatfield, stemming from the 1952 convention, when Hatfield euchred him out of a seat on the Platform Committee." With "incriminating" court records as further evidence, Morse could view Hatfield much as he viewed Oregon's other ambitious young man on the rise, that unprincipled one who had offended and continued to offend by his very existence.

Thus, in his constituent letter and in his election-eve address on Portland's Channel 5, Morse could as well have been denouncing Dick Neuberger as Mark Hatfield. The script was the same. "In my speeches," he said, ". . . I only pointed out as an old teacher that it had long been my experience that when intellectual unreliability is present in the mind of a student it usually carries forward into adult life." (In a note to a political ally a few days later, he said he knew of "one prominent Democrat in the State who was particularly upset about my . . . observations as a teacher." In his latest letter to Neuberger, written less than three months earlier, he had said, "When you were a student of mine, I found you amoral. . . . I had hoped [in vain] over the years that you would mature and develop a character of moral responsibility.") Morse also told the electorate that Hatfield had (just as Neuberger had) been "evasive, equivocal and all things to all people," and he therefore considered it his "duty" (as he had with Neuberger) "to forewarn the people of Oregon of this pattern of behavior."

As Dick Neuberger in Republican trappings, Hatfield was as much personal *bête noire* as political target. Having seen the Supreme Court report, Morse must inevitably choose to use it. He could tell himself that if it worked, Hatfield would be defeated, which would certainly be good. He could also tell himself that as a practical matter, if it didn't work, Holmes would be no worse off, since he stood to lose anyway. The latter thought he found less consoling once the results were tallied. Even though most believed that Morse's attack had affected the outcome only by adding to Hatfield's percentage, Morse was left with the nagging idea that he might in fact have cost Holmes the contest. For that possibility, remote as it was, he was truly sorry. He had no great affection for Holmes, but he certainly preferred him to the Neufields and Hatbergers he found in ascendancy everywhere he turned. As for Democratic leaders in general—those who had jumped ship when he was the man overboard—affection was in short supply anyway, since, as Morse saw it, most had long ago sided with Neuberger in the ongoing Morse-Neuberger feud. Toward them, as the letter to Bernstein amply demonstrates, there would be a lingering sourness that would not soon be dissipated.

MAVERICKS, BY THE LOGIC OF THEIR SITUATION, are normally denied the largest of triumphs. When visible at all, their achievements can most often be seen in the form of modest successes in limited areas: discrediting Capehart, dislodging Sherman Adams, enforcing the Morse Formula. Thus it made perfect sense for Morse to raise unceasing questions about key presidential appointees as they paraded before the Senate, not just to irritate the president by delaying confirmation—satisfying in itself—but to expose, if possible, how each prospect occupied a place in the Republican old guard, that wing of the party to which, in Morse's judgment, Eisenhower was hopelessly wedded. The most notable such case during Ike's second term involved Clare Boothe Luce, nominated in the spring of 1959 to be ambassador to Brazil.

Each of the many books written on the celebrated Luce family contains a section on Clare's Brazil nomination and Morse's resistance to it. Similarly, every person past a certain age interviewed for this biography remembered the rudiments of what happened in 1959: (1) Morse resolutely opposing Luce's nomination; (2) Luce being approved by the Senate; and (3) Luce being forced to resign because of remarks about Morse's having been kicked by a horse. While not inaccurate, such a recapitulation captures only partially an end-of-the-decade series of events as fascinating and unusual as any in the 1950s.

Before Brazil there was Italy, where Luce had been Eisenhower's ambassador from 1953 to 1956, the first American woman to hold such a prestigious diplomatic post. Before Italy there had been an eminent, often glamorous career as actor, dramatist, critic, magazine editor, war correspondent, and two-term congresswoman. And accompanying this career, making much of it possible, had been an opulent, jet-set existence, first as wife to Wall Street millionaire George Brokaw, then as the high-profile spouse of media magnate Henry Luce, impresario of the Time-Life publishing empire.

Before being considered by the Senate, Luce had to clear the Foreign Relations Committee, as she had in 1953. As chairman of the Latin America Subcommittee, Morse formally put her name before the whole committee, and decided initially to go along with chairman William Fulbright and the rest of the members, most of whom seemed eager, even without benefit of testimony from the nominee, to recommend her to the full Senate. But Morse grew uneasy after a story appeared in her husband's *Time* magazine quoting an unnamed American official in Bolivia to the effect that the only solution to that nation's plight was to "abolish Bolivia and let its neighbors divide the country and its problems among themselves." Reacting to the story, ten thousand Bolivians stoned the American embassy, burned the U. S. flag, and rioted in the streets of La Paz. Two Bolivians were killed, and hundreds of Americans evacuated to safety. Many believed that someone at *Time* had made up the quote, presumably meant as a wisecrack, and although Henry denied the charge, the Bolivian foreign minister officially inquired what the American government planned to do "if it proves that the statement attributed to an American official was forged by the magazine."

U. S. diplomacy expressed via "Lucepress," as W. A. Swanberg has called it, was of special concern to Morse, whose subcommittee had to attend to the interests of Bolivia, Brazil, and the other nations of South and Central America. If the Bolivian incident had given him pause, information provided by *Reporter* magazine editor Max Ascoli caused him to rethink the whole nomination. Ascoli suggested that it might have been the acerbic Mrs. Luce herself who had authored the Bolivian quip. In addition, he reminded Morse how controversial her position in Italy had been. Notorious as a person who had difficulty keeping observations to herself, she had commented in a speech before the American Chamber of Commerce in Milan that if the wrong people gained power in the upcoming Italian elections, it would have "grave consequences for the intimate and friendly cooperation between Italy and the United States." This was interpreted as a threat to cut back vital U. S. aid to Italy if the Communist party were voted in, and Luce was accused by an irate Italian press of meddling in the country's internal politics. The fear of funding reductions was lent credence by the fact that before she came to Rome as ambassador, Luce had been a strong financial supporter of right-wing Christian Democrats and an unabashed enemy of the Communists, a party which, unbeknownst to most Americans at the time, was one of Italy's most popular.

Having reconsidered, Morse pressed Fulbright to hold a hearing. It didn't take much pressing. Although he would vote for her in the end, Fulbright relished the opportunity to bring up old business he had with Luce. She was thus called to appear in the New Senate Office Building on April 15 to answer questions from the committee. When, adorned with expensive jewelry, mink stole, and cerise fingernails, she entered Room 4221, the committee, more accustomed to conventional male applicants in bureaucratic business suits, seemed positively awestruck. Except, that is, for Fulbright and Morse.

Fulbright had delivered his maiden speech in the House in the mid-1940s in response to the very same Luce (both were then congressional freshmen), who had accused Democratic vice president Henry Wallace of spewing what she called "globaloney" in his advocacy of internationalism. Now, fifteen years later, Fulbright wanted to know whether she still believed, as she had previously stated, that Franklin Roosevelt was "the only American President who ever lied us into a war," or that the ranks of the Democratic party were, as she had claimed, infested by the nation's "mortal enemies." Regarding the latter question, Luce was willing, however unconvincingly, to reformulate her conclusion on more general lines: everyone knew there were highly placed subversives throughout the country, ergo there must have been highly placed subversives within that party—the Democratic—which had so long run the country. As to a mendacious FDR, however, Luce would not budge, insisting that the historical record supported her judgment.

Morse followed Fulbright's line of questioning, but in a more confrontational manner. He told Luce that unless she could document her charge about Roosevelt's lying the country into war, he not only would oppose her nomination, but would have to consider her assertion to be subversive. "There are," he growled, "all sorts of subversion, you know." Luce tried to argue that her remarks had merely been those of a private American citizen freely voicing her opinion, but Morse reminded her that when she made them in 1944, she was in fact a member of Congress.

Morse grilled her for over an hour—the hearing lasted two—dwelling at length on the *Reporter's* analysis of her Italian tenure. And although it was apparent that his examination had made her uncomfortable (she began chain-smoking Italian cigarettes from her lacquered cigarette case), it was just as apparent that she had the committee solidly behind her. John F. Kennedy, for example, asked no questions whatever, but said he had known Luce for twenty years and supported her nomination "wholeheartedly." Fellow presidential aspirant Hubert Humphrey missed more than half of the hearing, and when he asked a question, it tended, by his own admission, to be "in the form of a statement," the sort Luce could and did answer with, "Oh, yes, Senator" and "I think the Senator is altogether right." It was clear that whatever they felt privately, with the 1960 campaign only months away, Kennedy and Humphrey would do nothing which might turn Lucepress power against them. The committee voted 16 to 1 to recommend the nomination. The nay vote was Morse's.

As with the committee, so with the Senate. Apart from a three-and-a-half-hour speech from Morse, there was little opposition, and Luce was confirmed by a vote of 79 to 11. On the following day came Luce's infamous response. After thanking the chamber for its over-whelming endorsement, she stated, "My difficulties of course go some years back and began when Senator Wayne Morse was kicked in the head by a horse." Morse pulled this quote from the Senate's AP ticker and reportedly showed it first to Paul Douglas, remarking, "That explains me, but what accounts for her?" He then interrupted Senate business to read it to his colleagues, adding that Luce's "slanderous" remarks showed, as he had indicated in his speech, "an old, old pattern of emotional instability." The backlash against Luce was instantaneous. Senator after senator rose to say that had they a second opportunity, they would reverse their votes. Even Kennedy reacted, requesting the State Department to get Luce to issue a retraction.

But Luce would not retract. (Indeed, to friends she embellished her retort: Morse, she said, had actually been kicked on the *right* side of the head, which accounted for his "thinking left" ever since.) Instead she tendered her resignation, informing Eisenhower that "the climate of good will was poisoned" and implying, with a skillful bit of red-baiting, that Morse, "the American author" of the attacks against her, had planted "seeds of hostile suspicion. All through the course of my mission these seeds could be watered carefully, either by their author for unknowable motive or by any political element with the clear motive of discrediting America by the simple device of disparaging an American Ambassador." Exactly two weeks after the Foreign Relations Committee hearing, Eisenhower accepted her resignation.

The preceding material covers the essential details of the Luce episode. There were, however, a number of sidebars to the story, ranging from the humorously unusual to the enterprisingly bizarre.

When Morse brought up Luce's "Roosevelt-lied-us-into-war" pronouncement on the Senate floor, the pontifical Everett Dirksen asked, "Why beat on an old bag of bones?" To which Humphrey, adding his own brand of buffoonery, immediately responded, "I must rise to the defense of the lady. . . ."

From Missouri came ex-president Harry Truman's possibly intentional confounding of gender: "What a nice thing it is to have Mr. Clare Boothe Luce in the grease in Bolivia. He spent a lot of time trying to put me in the grease but never succeeded."

Democrat Stephen Young of Ohio, one of the eleven anti-Luce votes, inserted into the record a bit of pointed verse from Victorian poet William Watson, the first few lines of which were:

> . . . In truthful numbers be she sung,
> The Woman with the Serpent's Tongue;
> Ambitious from her natal hour
> And scheming all her life for power;
> With little left of seemly pride;
> With venomed fangs she cannot hide.

Sometime before the hearing, Morse learned that Luce had undergone psychiatric care (hence the "emotional instability" remark)—a potentially explosive piece of background information, as Senator Thomas Eagleton would discover thirteen years later. After the hearing but before the vote in the Senate, Morse telephoned her doctor in New York to follow up this lead. When the *Chicago Tribune* revealed that Morse had made such a call, he was accused by many of a serious breach of ethics. His defense, paltry at best, was that the initiative had been the doctor's, not his: the doctor had told a reporter (unnamed) that he had something important to relate and wanted Morse to get in touch with him. When Morse finally tried, he discovered the doctor had died two weeks earlier.

There was another reason for the suspicion of emotional instability. Luce's health had deteriorated while she was in Italy. Her symp-

The cartoonist Yardley made this parody of a Time *cover for Morse. (Wayne Morse Historical Park Corporation.)*

toms—lethargy, disorientation, loss of appetite—were apparent, their cause was not. Doctors could find nothing physically wrong, but a urinalysis revealed a minute trace of arsenic in her system. The CIA suspected poison. A year after the fact, the Luces explained that arsenate of lead in the form of flaking dust had been falling from painted stucco roses on her bedroom ceiling into her coffee cup, not enough to be lethal, but sufficient to make her continuously ill. This diagnosis was disputed by the Italian architect who had decorated the villa and by observers who pointed out that her room had been used by her two ambassadorial predecessors with no deleterious effects. The incident prompted the following comment from Luce's friend and biographer, Wilfrid Sheed: "I was quite willing to believe that something bad had indeed come down from the embassy ceiling. . . . But I wished it had happened to somebody else. Because her long-dormant record for self-dramatization came rushing back. . . . As I recall, there were pictures of a ceiling and a sofa, proving I'm not sure what, and newspaper stories presumably written by men who believed that women, especially Clare, are subject to hot flashes."

Sheed argues that Henry wanted Clare to persevere and go to Brazil regardless of the problems involved and that he was furious when she resigned. (He had already set up an office there, as he previously had in Rome, and was planning to spend six out of the next twelve months in South America.) Another Luce biographer, Stephen Shadegg, suggests that in the end Henry really did not want her to go, which is what he indicated in a statement released *before* her resignation. To his request that she give up the ambassadorship, he added: "For twenty-five years in the course of her public life my wife has taken not only the criticism provoked by her own views and actions, but also many punches which were intended for me or for the publications of which I am editor-in-chief. The attack of Senator Wayne Morse is perhaps the most vitriolic example of this."

There are still more sidebars deserving of attention. For example, the Morse-Neuberger feud inevitably became involved: Neuberger would naturally not be found among those recanting support because of

Luce's ill-timed impropriety; he wrote to her to say that he had "no regrets for having voted for your confirmation" and to deplore the "bitter and abusive attack . . . made upon you." But however intrinsically interesting, such sidebars must be understood as precisely that—marginalia to a story that is centrally Morse's, a maverick's relentless pursuit of, and gratifying victory over, an ideological adversary.

The ideological component was crucial. Not that Henry's accusation was without merit. Morse certainly could remember rough treatment from *Time* over the years—on the occasion of his leaving the Republican party, for example, or over his stubborn opposition to the Eisenhower-Dulles foreign policy. He might even have recalled, and been irritated by the memory, that his one appearance on the cover of *Time*, in 1954, had to be shared with Neuberger. (When *Time* celebrated its fortieth birthday in 1963, Morse, like Fidel Castro and Chairman Mao, was not on the guest list of former cover personalities, although other political enemies who had graced the cover —Adlai Stevenson, Norman Thomas, even Henry Wallace—*were* invited.) More important than personal animosity or a craving for revenge, however, was a fundamental disagreement with what the Luces stood for: their particularly virulent kind of superpatriotism which involved moral, financial, and editorial support of people like Joe McCarthy, Richard Nixon, Douglas MacArthur, Chiang Kaishek, and the paid apologists of the China lobby. To defeat the Luces and their brethren, even in the smallest way, to have one less ambassador like Clare abroad in the world, even in a country of little significance, was surely worth the effort.

And worth the risks, the kind only a maverick would dare to take. Like Kennedy and Humphrey, Morse also stood to lose by turning the Lucepress irretrievably against him. For, like them, although no one knew it at the time, he also harbored wider ambitions, dreamt that dream that bemuses so many Washington politicians. Like his colleagues, Morse contemplated running for the presidency, perhaps as early as the following year. But unlike Kennedy and Humphrey, he could not allow such ambition to deter him from his more immediate mission; and if that mission should cost him badly needed media support, that was a price that had to be paid, the sort of price all mavericks must pay in quest of a masterless independence.

TWO QUESTIONS OF CONSEQUENCE: Should a maverick run for president? If he does, will anyone take him seriously?

To the first question Morse had always had an answer, and, at least as far as his own career was concerned, it was no. A practical, not a categorical answer. He did not, for example, fault La Follette for his effort in 1924, but he repeatedly told those who urged him to seek higher office—many had—that his long history of political dissent made him a very unlikely prospect and that he could best serve his state and country as a progressive-minded member of the United States Senate. Even after the then-friendly Neuberger and others established the National Friends of Wayne Morse to promote his candidacy—selling five-dollar stock certificates as "Investment(s) in Oregon's Future"—he did nothing on his own to move in that direction.

Indeed, in 1959, as nominee hopefuls were gathering momentum for the 1960 run, Morse took steps to discourage activity on his behalf. These were the days of "favorite son" candidates, when states nominated governors or legislators for the presidency, normally to gain national publicity or increase leverage at party conventions. In April, the Oregon Young Democrats, on a motion by Edith Green, voted to advance Senator Morse as a favorite son in 1960. But in July, Morse filed an affidavit in Salem proclaiming he was not, and did not intend to become, a presidential candidate. Most took the affidavit to be Morse's final word. Green, soon to be state chairwoman of the John F. Kennedy campaign, claimed that, just to be sure, she asked Morse on three further occasions whether he planned to run, and on each he said he did not.

As it turned out, Morse's negative answer to the question of a maverick presidential candidacy was not irrevocable. The key word in Green's query was "planned." If by that we mean an intentional effort to muster party support, raise a war chest, and assemble a campaign organization, then it is clear that no such arrangement was contemplated. But if the term can include letting others act in one's interest while one waits quietly for positive developments, then it may be applied to what subsequently occurred. What is needed if one wishes to orchestrate such a sequence is the ability to conduct from the audience with an unseen baton.

Fortunately for Morse, the basis on which such an idea could be played out (as opposed to the idea itself) originated not with him but with a retired logger named Gary Neal, who—assisted by Portlander Jack Churchill, one of the few party activists to side with Morse against Neuberger—circulated statewide petitions from his Salem address to get Morse's name on the ballot. Neal was successful, and when enough petitions were declared valid, Morse announced that whatever his personal wishes, he could not ignore the will of the electorate: he had no choice but to become an active presidential candidate. He formally entered the primary race two days before Christmas 1959. By so doing, he immediately raised the question of whether anyone would take his candidacy seriously. From Oregon's best-known Democratic leaders an answer came in almost as soon as the petitions were counted, and to Morse's great chagrin, the answer was no.

A *resounding* no. Green, Porter, Holmes, Jebby Davidson, Monroe Sweetland, even Al Ullman (and of course the Neubergers): most were already committed to one of the "real" candidates, Kennedy or Humphrey; all said they saw no necessity to unite behind Morse, as he insisted they should. He might be someone's favorite son, but he would not be theirs—some felt his entry would diminish the primary's national importance—and their refusal to back him, following similar refusals in the Hatfield episode, drove Morse to a renewed state of fury. In public he barely concealed his vexation. Privately he referred to Green, Porter, et al. as enemies, "Morse back-knifers," spineless politicians the Oregon Democratic party would be better off without.

Despite the leadership's response, Morse not only persevered in Oregon, but entered primaries in Maryland and the District of Columbia, and would have done the same in Wisconsin if not for a lack of funds. Money was of course a critical consideration in whatever state he entered, and he was extremely short of it. The Teamsters pro-vided a little. They had, as most labor organizations had, always given to Morse campaigns, and now, because of their hatred of the Kennedys (who had gained renown investigating mob influence in their union), they were happy to support anyone running against a member of that family. But in light of the amounts needed, the Teamster contribution was a pittance; other unions—many of which were backing Kennedy—gave even less; the Friends of Wayne Morse raised next to nothing; and according to Charlie Brooks, the only other donations of significance came from a few liberal Jewish supporters in Los Angeles and New York. Obviously, where it count-ed most in the run-up to an election, Morse was *not* being taken seriously.

With or without adequate funding, Morse threw himself into the campaign. Kennedy was the main target—in Oregon, where Hum-phrey's support was tepid, and in Maryland, where Humphrey was not entered—and Morse did not hesitate to go after him. His chief issue was the recently passed Landrum-Griffin Act, which Morse re-ferred to as the *Kennedy*-Landrum-Griffin Act: a labor "reform" mea-sure, contrived in the aftermath of the celebrated union-racketeering probes, that had passed the Senate with only Morse and Republican William Langer of North Dakota voting against it. The Senate's orig-inal draft of the act was entitled Kennedy-Irvin, a bill that Morse, along with a majority of the Senate, had supported. In conference, led on the Senate side by Labor subcommittee chairman Kennedy, the Kennedy-Irvin bill was, over Morse's strenuous objection, heav-ily compromised in favor of the far more restrictive House bill. Thus modified, the bill emerged as Landrum-Griffin and was passed large-ly with the concurrence of union leaders, who feared the imposition of more draconian measures if it wasn't.

Given his shortage of funds, Morse was forced to get his labor message out via a campaign motion picture, purchased at forty dol-lars a print and distributed by the Teamsters and Machinists unions. With an American flag and a set of law books as backdrop, Morse gave a twenty-eight-minute bravura performance, sans script, ex-tolling his own labor record, accusing Kennedy of "political opportunism," and noting that Kennedy, as the conference committee's "chief architect," "apparently thinks so little of the bill that he doesn't want to have his name associated with it." So much in demand was this film that the original negative wore out and Morse had to return to the studio for an impromptu second filming.

Although Morse reached a number of voters and raised good money with his film, it was clear that the odds were running increasingly against him—except perhaps in Washington, D.C., where because of all those years on the District Committee he had an established base to work from and, in his own words, "an exceptionally good chance to win." Kennedy did not bother to enter the District, but for either Morse or Humphrey, picking up its few delegates would constitute a momentum builder for more important primaries to come. Morse campaigned feverishly. The *Washington Post* pictured him working the District "like an alderman who fears that he is going to be defeated in the next election." However, the same paper tagged him repeatedly with the "not-a-serious-candidate" label, and try as he might, he could not convince them that he was. Perhaps because voters agreed with the *Post*, or perhaps because his opponent was better organized—Joe Rauh ran the Humphrey campaign—Morse was defeated in a dismal election in which fewer than twenty thousand D.C. Democrats chose to cast their ballots. Morse not only lost 7,831 to 5,866, but because of the vote distribution, Humphrey took seventeen of the eighteen delegates, the other one going to Adlai Stevenson.

Commentators pointed out that Morse's loss in the District was attributable in part to the atrocious turnout, but Morse, writing to his brother-in-law Hibberd Kline two days later, admitted that "if our campaign did not inspire people to go out to vote, then we have no one but ourselves to blame." He was quick to add, however, "that this defeat will, in no way, diminish my efforts in Maryland and Oregon. In fact, I am going to campaign all the harder in those two places."

Morse did intensify his efforts in both states, especially in Maryland, where he had done little and where the Kennedy forces were exceptionally strong; but the hardest campaigning could not make up for a paucity of resources. When the Maryland votes were tallied on

John F. Kennedy (shown here speaking in Portland)
reached election week in Oregon in the 1960 Democ-
ratic primary with six consecutive victories behind
him. (Oregon Historical Society, OrHi CN 012309.)

May 17, Morse had accumulated roughly 49,000—not bad considering he had filed at the last possible moment, but minuscule compared to the 199,000 (a whopping 70 percent of the total) amassed
by Kennedy. Months earlier, the irrepressible Mert Bernstein (an
early Kennedy backer) had asked, "Why, in God's name, go into the
Maryland primary? You are wasting your time and talent." To which
Morse had replied: "You seem to be concerned about the fact that I
may get beat in Maryland. I probably will. So what! When I get
through with the campaign in Maryland, a record will have been
made as to the differences in my political philosophy and Kennedy's."
To which Bernstein could justifiably have responded with his own
"So what!" And, had he had the nerve, with "A lot of good that will
do you the following week in Oregon."

Kennedy reached election week in Oregon with six consecutive
victories behind him, Morse nursing embarrassing defeats in the
only two he had entered. Morse was poorly organized, Kennedy was

anything but. Campaign recruiter Walter Spolar and the other Kennedy workers refused to view Morse as a genuine rival—a point, Spolar recalled, made with "constant repetition . . . from hamlet to hamlet"—but still they worried about the harmful effect of a late loss to a favorite son on their growing image of invincibility. According to Monroe Sweetland, even though Humphrey had withdrawn from the Oregon contest, the Kennedys were leaving nothing to chance. "They sent in Rose. They sent in Teddy. They concentrated time and effort and money." Morse also concentrated time and effort —Midge for the first time made campaign speeches—but if in politics, as in *Ecclesiastes*, "money answereth all things," he was conspicuously short of answers. When the postcampaign financial reports were filed, his totaled around $9,000, Kennedy's more than $54,000. The election itself surprised only Morse's truest of believers. The final count gave Senator Kennedy 142,850, Senator Morse 90,049. Morse had been trounced in his own home state. His presidential race was over.

Why, we might wonder in retrospect, did Morse decide to run in the first place? At the time he recorded it, he surely meant what he said in his Salem affidavit. There *were* those who believed that Morse never intended to honor his pledge, that he engineered the petition drive from beginning to end in order to enter the race without directly confronting opponents in his party. But the evidence suggests that Neal developed the plan on his own and that Morse came on board only after Neal had initiated the process. Once the drive was under way, however, Morse clearly became captivated, if not obsessed, by the idea of running and began to think of how to capitalize on what the retired logger had started. The petition route had the dual advantage of being extremely inexpensive and of creating the compelling image of a reluctant candidate seemingly unable to resist a surging groundswell of popular support. During the drive, Morse held at least two secret meetings with Neal (from which even the true-blue Charlie Brooks was excluded) and knew exactly how things were proceeding well before the counting was completed. Thus, when the petition results were in and the anticipated "draft" from the grass roots was authenticated, he was more than prepared to accept it.

Assuming the above analysis to be accurate, that a preconceived grand strategy had not been concocted, other factors must have caused Morse to embrace the petition drive once it had commenced. One important influence was a perceived change in the roster of potential candidates. As the summer of 1959 wore on, Morse became convinced that Adlai Stevenson, whom he had enthusiastically supported in '52 and '56, would not be a candidate in 1960. (It was thus wrong to believe, as some did, that Morse came in as a stalking horse searching for votes to be used in a Stevenson coup at the convention.) Sadly, from Morse's perspective, Democratic center stage had been left to Kennedy and Humphrey, with long shots Lyndon Johnson and Stuart Symington in the wings. Morse could live with the idea of the unspectacular Symington, former Air Force secretary and present Senate colleague, as president, but the thought of one of the others, *any* of the others, occupying the White House was dreadful enough to make his own entry into the race seem increasingly urgent.

While Stevenson's departure, along with disappointment with the remaining candidates, might have aroused thoughts of competing, it took a second, more powerful factor to propel Morse officially into the contest: the astounding idea that he might in fact be able to win it! From Neal's petition drive Morse's mind took flight, imagining an elaborate scenario in which Kennedy and Humphrey, each with insufficient votes to secure the nomination, fought to a draw, while Morse won handily in Washington, made a good showing (at least 35 percent, with a "fighting chance" for victory) in Maryland, and carried Oregon by a comfortable margin. In this fantasy, a stalemated Democratic convention would turn ultimately to Senator Morse, who, with added support from adherents in other states— both Jack Churchill and Morse claimed they were numerous—would be nominated for the presidency.

Morse kept the extent of his dream to himself, which is why, even as he campaigned strenuously, no one believed him when he repeatedly declared himself a "dead serious" candidate, or understood the intensity of his irritation at not being believed. Those paying careful attention, however, might have noticed the occasional revealing admission. At a mid-May gathering of Coos Bay Democrats, for example, he forecast a convention hopelessly deadlocked on the tenth ballot: "Even a Wayne Morse," he remarked offhandedly, "can be nominated in such a situation." With the possible exception of Midge, the only person interviewed for this book to whom Morse expressly confided his plan was Raoul "Joe" Smith, son of Professor Joseph Smith, Morse's old Salt Lake friend and former rhetoric colleague. Joe worked for a time in the Senate, courtesy of Morse's patronage, and on his Poolesville, Maryland, farm; lived several weeks with the Morse family in Washington; and considered himself a Wayne Morse disciple. He recalled his mentor telling him, "'It's a long shot, but I'm damn well going to take it.' The senator really felt he had a chance to become president," Smith added, "and so, I think, did Midge."

A timely acceptance of the Young Democrats' invitation would certainly have benefited Morse, at least in Oregon, and since Kennedy stayed out of every other favorite-son contest, it might even have left him effectively unopposed in his home state. As it was, even with Kennedy and the others committed to Oregon, Morse saw indications after his pre-Christmas announcement that gave him more to go on than the mere beguilement of ambition. In January, for example, a nonscientific *Oregon Statesman* poll showed him leading Kennedy 50 to 22 percent, with Stevenson at 18. Three weeks later, no less a figure than syndicated columnist Mary McGrory informed the nation that Morse was unbeatable in Oregon and that "second best is all that anyone [else] can hope for." Even as late as April, a poll conducted by Charlie Porter had Morse still ahead. Porter mailed out postcard ballots to all of his congressional constituents. Among the 10,423 Democrats who responded, Morse nosed out Kennedy by slightly more than two percentage points. By the first of May, however, with the Kennedy campaign at its peak, it was apparent to impartial observers that Morse had no chance for victory. But by then the dream had been nourished by enough straw polls and punditry to keep it alive, and like Cardinal Wolsey in *Henry VIII*, Morse could still imagine today's "tender leaves of hope" becoming "tomorrow's blossoms" of victory. When the dream was dashed and tomorrow brought only the dead leaves of defeat, Morse had a difficult time accepting reality.

For the second time in his professional life, Morse had been blinded by the glare of flaming ambition, unable to see that the prize he craved lay far beyond his grasp. The parallels between 1960 and 1937 were remarkable. Just as he had sought the University of Oregon presidency in 1937 when the man he would have supported (Jim Gilbert) declined to run, Morse entered the contest in 1960 only when his man (Stevenson) similarly declined. In 1937, as in 1960, he came in obliquely, encouraging others to advance his candidacy while he seemingly watched from the sidelines. In both instances, he argued that friends must necessarily rally behind him, if only to protect his present position—the deanship in '37, his Senate seat (up in a short two years) in '60—and he was irritated at those who refused, so irritated in 1960 that he voiced what must have sounded like a threat of future reprisals: "Don't forget," he told an April campaign meeting in Eugene, "what we do now will have a great bearing in 1962. . . . If your senior senator goes down, then a great many will go with me." If he couldn't personally achieve his goal, Morse had in mind, both in 1937 and 1960, backup candidates who might stand in his stead—Orlando Hollis in '37, Symington in '60—but because he so grossly overestimated his ability to carry the day against his opponents, he failed to see that even his ostensible surrogates never had a realistic chance of succeeding.

It wasn't that Morse could not learn from earlier defeats. His ultimate willingness to work his way up the Senate seniority ladder a second time shows that he could see what was and was not within his grasp under given conditions. But in 1960, with the enticement of the presidency itself before him, he was impervious to the edification of previous experience. He would thus reenact at a higher-stakes level the drama played out in 1937: vaulting ambition would o'erleap itself once more, leaving Morse once more confused and angry, especially angry at those who had stood in his way.

However negative his attitude, Morse said he would do nothing to derail the Kennedy bandwagon at the national convention (in fact, so incensed was he at Oregon's Democratic leaders for their lack of support that although elected as a delegate, he chose to stay home with Midge and watch the proceedings on TV), but he saw no reason to close ranks behind the man who had so roundly beaten him. There was, he said, too much about the Kennedy candidacy that filled him with gloom. To Harry Hogan, to Mert Bernstein, to a long list of correspondents, he expressed his reservations about the rising star from Massachusetts. His most pointed letter, written two weeks after the Oregon election, was sent to Jason Lee, a youthful Salem attorney who had augmented Neal's efforts and had worked tirelessly for six months in Morse's behalf. Morse provided Lee with a sweeping inventory of Kennedy's foibles.

> Jason, I serve on the same two major committees Kennedy serves on—Foreign Relations and Labor and Public Welfare. I know this man Kennedy. I know how dangerous he is behind this glamorous front. I am deeply convinced that the destiny of my country cannot run the risk of Kennedy as President. . . . You have never seen Kennedy lose control of himself. I have, many times. You have never seen Kennedy confronted with controversies that he has never faced up to before, with no one to prepare material for him, but faced with the immediate necessity of responding to the question. He does not have intellectual depth, and he shows it under such circumstances. . . . I shall not campaign against my Party in the 1960 election, but I do not see how I can campaign for Kennedy in view of my great fears about him.

In a letter to Mert Bernstein, Morse put the matter more succinctly: "Let me assure you that you will never witness my backing Kennedy in or out of the White House. Some day you will wake up, I hope, to a recognition of what a dangerous person he is." And as if Kennedy were not bad enough by himself, there on the television screen was Lyndon Johnson, arms raised at the convention, anointed as JFK's running mate. In a follow-up letter, Morse offered Bernstein a one-sentence review of his party's national ticket: "Neither Kennedy nor Johnson is a liberal, neither is a man of principle, neither will be good for our country."

Given his long and fractious history with Johnson, Morse might not have surprised correspondents with his attitude toward the

Texan, but many must have wondered about his feelings toward Kennedy. Why (aside from a fathomable measure of postelection sour grapes) were these feelings so deep, so passionately held, so uncompromisingly negative, especially since Kennedy had run a reasonably positive campaign in Oregon, free of mudslinging and finger-pointing? What *specifically* had Kennedy done to cause such heated opposition?

Some observers believed that Morse had been motivated from the start by an anti-Kennedy animus and had come into the race as Oregon's contribution to the nationwide "stop Kennedy" movement that the Teamsters were supporting. This view was partially correct. Though Morse in fact belonged to no one's movement to stop anybody, he had always ranked Kennedy dead last among Democratic presidential aspirants, behind even Humphrey. The question remains: why? While there may be many answers to this question, at least one goes back to events surrounding the Landrum-Griffin bill.

Midge Morse is asked in the mid-1980s how her husband regarded Senator Kennedy prior to 1960. She muses for a moment, then replies, "Wayne thought he was lazy." Midge has few details to provide, but it is clear that Morse's view grew out of the subcommittee work leading up to Landrum-Griffin. According to labor leader Alexander Christie, who closely monitored the bill's progress, Chairman Kennedy was frequently absent during the long hours of testimony taken at a series of subcommittee hearings. Much of the load thus fell on Morse, the subcommittee's second-ranking Democrat, with Kennedy resuming control at the final House-Senate conference. Kennedy scheduled a strategy session for Democrats just prior to the conference—a session that, we are told by Samuel Merrick, a subcommittee staffer at the time, began earlier than announced and concluded before Morse could get there. Thus, when the conference met, Morse was confronted by a compromise he not only found abhorrent, but about which he had not been fully consulted.

Had Kennedy purposely conducted the strategy session early to avoid dealing with Morse's anticipated objections, or had he merely been under such time pressure that he inadvertently neglected to wait for his number two committee member? In light of Kennedy's polished political skills, the latter is hard to believe, but in either case Morse would have felt shabbily treated, especially since so much of the hard preliminary work that was sacrificed in conference had been done under his direction. Invariably opposed to the younger man's hawkish foreign-policy positions, Morse now had reason to question both Kennedy's position on labor and his ethical character as well.

That the issue would not be allowed to die Morse made clear almost at once. He publicly attacked Kennedy and other Senate progressives after Landrum-Griffin's enactment, hurling the same epithets—"phony liberals," "gutless wonders"—that he had in the civil-rights dispute two years earlier. Senator William Proxmire of Wisconsin took it upon himself to defend Kennedy, insisting that "Morse couldn't have been more wrong. Kennedy did a magnificent job in the 90 per cent of the bill that was drafted in the Senate." Whereupon Morse revealed that immediately after the bill's passage, Proxmire had chosen to congratulate him for his vote and had asked Morse if he was "willing to shake hands with a coward." When, from Wisconsin, Proxmire denied this assertion, Morse wired the *Madison Capital Times* stating that "no matter how frequently Proxmire tries to lie about what he said to me, he knows in his own conscience that my statement is the truth."

The rupture with Proxmire—for whom Morse had expressed "a tremendous admiration" and whom he had described in 1958 as "the liberal who has exceeded my expectations many times over"—would never be fully healed. However, circumstances being what they were, the same would not be the case with Kennedy. Even though Morse told correspondents over the summer that "we are certainly in a sorry state in our country when we have to make a choice between Kennedy and Nixon," since such a choice was unavoidable, Morse, for all his antipathy toward Kennedy, would not hesitate to select his fellow Democrat over a Richard Nixon he knew to be irretrievably corrupt, pernicious, and depraved. Indeed, the more Morse contemplated the appalling possibility of Nixon running the nation, the less heinous seemed the sins of Kennedy. Thus, as autumn wore on, Morse, on temporary assignment from the Foreign Relations Committee to the UN, saw fit to make himself available to the Kennedy campaign, which gladly used him as a frontline spokesman at rallies in Manhattan, Harlem, Queens, Brooklyn, and New Jersey. And by the time the general election was over and Nixon had been defeated, Kennedy's manifold defects had faded to insignificance. Senator Clinton Anderson of New Mexico sat beside Morse at Kennedy's inaugural address. Anderson recalled him listening rapt to Kennedy's oration and, when it was over, stating, "This guy is going to be a wonderful President."

In the prologue to this biography, I indicated that because of the constraints of reality, maverickness must be understood as a *relative* condition in which independence of action is achieved only to the degree allowed by the boundaries of the political arena. Morse spent his life pushing reality's constraints to their limit and beyond. Whether his dramatic about-face on Kennedy in 1960 (even without Nixon in the picture, one senses he would eventually have supported his party's ticket against *any* Republican) constitutes the recognition and acceptance of boundaries or whether it is one more example of a maverick unpredictably exercising his unfettered right to change his mind, I do not know. Whichever is true, the reversal would pay enormous dividends. Morse had helped the new president to victory in a very close election. As an appreciated ally, and with elevated committee rankings forthcoming in the Senate, he would enter the decade of the sixties as one of Kennedy's more valued guides to the New Frontier. Maverick he would continue to be, but for the first time he would be a maverick operating from the inner sanctums of senatorial power.

11

A Matter of Character

"CHARACTER," WRITES AUTHOR CAROL BRIGHTMAN (*Writing Dangerously: Mary McCarthy and Her World*), "is always the starting point . . . of biography." An "interesting character," she adds, is "one who acts outside the norms of society but whose work or deeds survive to illuminate that society." Morse was, in every sense of this definition, never less than interesting. But he was also interesting in quite another way, unusually so.

With some politicians—one thinks especially of the Kennedys—the character exhibited in open forum or before the cameras may differ greatly from that perceived behind closed doors. What you think you see in public is not always what you get. Morse, on the other hand, drew his great strength in politics from being exactly who he was at all times, regardless of where he might be or who might be watching. Phil George, who coordinated every Morse campaign from 1967 until Morse's death in 1974, reported that he found "very little difference between the way the Senator was as a private person and the way he was publicly." Though characterizing only the last several years of Morse's life, George's observation fits the preceding decades as well.

Displayed openly in the political limelight, Morse's public character was well known to friend and foe alike. His maverick disposition was necessarily that of a competitive, individualistic, self-reliant loner. In many respects, and for some of the same reasons, he was similarly disposed in private life: just as competitive, just as individualistic, and in the ways that mattered most, just as much the self-reliant loner.

IF ONE DID NOT KNOW THAT MORSE worked overtime every day on the Hill, one would surely deduce from his voluminous correspondence on horses and cows and chickens and sheep that he was a professional trader of livestock who spent *all* of his time competing at fairs, expositions, and roundups while maintaining commercial farm operations on opposite sides of the continent. Morse did in fact give a significant part of his life to these activities, and he did so with a *joie de vivre* that at least rivaled the enthusiasm he had for politics. Indeed, those who visited his Senate office remembered him being prouder of the colorful prize ribbons bedecking his wall than of the obligatory political cartoons and VIP photos.

In the late 1940s, Morse leased a seventy-five-acre farm in Poolesville, in Maryland's Montgomery County, to house his formidable stable of horses. He purchased the property in the mid-fifties and rented hundreds of acres nearby, as he added a herd of cattle along with a collection of chickens, goats, peacocks, donkeys, and other barnyard creatures. Thus stocked, the Poolesville farm was a source of enormous satisfaction. There Morse could relive the life he had loved in his youth. Always tastefully (if a little unfashionably) attired in the Senate, he was never more at home than on his slightly ramshackle property, clad in battered straw hat, logger's shirt, grimy pants, and Western boots, a self-described "dirt farmer" whom Frank Rarig remembered emerging from the chicken coop "hair flying, shirt-tail partly out, hands and face dirty."

While everything about country life attracted Morse, it was his passion for horses that moved him to purchase the farmland needed for them wherever he located. "I have always owned horses," he informed a journalist in 1945, "ever since I was a little boy. I bought my first horse in Oregon a few days after I arrived in Eugene, and during the fifteen years that I have lived in the state I have owned approximately one hundred eighty saddle horses." Morse was so possessed by the horseman's spirit that even his prescribed hospitalization after the jaw-kicking incident was insufficient to keep him from the paddocks. He couldn't resist gloating to Jim Landye, who had advised giving such activity a long rest, that "last Saturday afternoon Judy and I slipped away from the hospital and showed my horse at the Montgomery County Annual Horse Show. . . . I drove the horse in the fine harness class and won the blue ribbon. That didn't hurt my jaw any. . . . When I got back to the hospital that night I sure felt cocky."

Cocky Morse was, and cocky he had a right to be, for his accomplishments at breeding, showing, riding, and racing horses (trotters) were enough to inflate any horseman's ego. Featuring the handsome Spice of Life for showing and Sir Guy Laurel for racing, he had a continuous run of success, which meant that he was able to recoup some of his considerable investment by charging stud fees above the going rate. Regardless of return, however, Morse would draw satisfaction merely from competing, immense satisfaction from coming in first. Typical of his sentiments were those expressed in a 1946 letter which recounted in minute detail Spice of Life's triumph at a Fourth of July show in Virginia, a triumph that left him "as tickled about the way Spice is going . . . as a kid with a new toy." And if winning with Spice provided such delight, racing ahead of the pack with Sir Guy was even more thrilling. According to one printed story, Morse had a rep-

With "his famous big brown stallion," Sir Guy Laurel, Morse had a continuous run of success in trotter competitions. (Courtesy of Mildred M. Morse.)

utation for riding "hard, fast and energetically, exactly like he talks," a reputation confirmed by a second story which noted that "the Senator has a habit of yelling 'I'm coming through' during roadster [i.e., trotter] competition. . . . His competitors have learned the Senator will get through, [even] if it means driving right over the top of another buggy." In the same vein, a third article described Morse—resplendent in lemon and green satins, with checkered hat and green goggles—capturing an important stake race behind Sir Guy, as he "howled and yipped . . . his famous big brown stallion" past all challengers at the Pacific International Horse Show of 1950.

Morse could also be heard howling and yipping while driving cows from field to field in Poolesville; and as the years went by, his renown as a buyer, seller, and breeder of Devon cattle—that same short-legged, sorrel-colored line raised by his ancestors in Europe and his father in Wisconsin—began to surpass his reputation as a horseman. Like his forebears, he had always taken pride in Devons (the horns of an 1880 champion had adorned his Madison bedroom), and he became a zealous promoter of the breed in those parts of the United States, especially Maryland and Oregon, where Devons had been little known or appreciated. As always, his interest ranged beyond animal husbandry to the competitive realm, but initially he was as much a maverick among cattlemen as among politicians: there was no Devon association to manage expositions, nor were there enough local owners to compete against, and for a considerable period managers refused to allow Morse and his odd-looking creatures to enter their shows. Morse's solution was first to form an association, installing himself as president, then to create competitors by persuading nearly everyone within the reach of his voice to buy stock from his farm and join him as friendly rivals in the Devon-breeding business.

As a salesman for Devons on the hoof, Morse was indefatigable. His enthusiasm for the breed was contagious, and he was able to persuade an astonishing variety of individuals, some who previously had never kept so much as a milk cow, to purchase selected specimens from his ever-growing herd. Among his customers—most of whom became association members—were Poolesville neighbors like syndicated columnist Drew Pearson; former Wisconsin class-mate and editor of *U.S. News & World Report* Owen Scott; and Gladys Uhl, who often fed Morse breakfast on Sunday mornings (and who agreed to be secretary of the association), along with a number of fellow politicians—even old "rancid tub" himself, Homer Capehart. Once Devons were accepted for showing, Morse, as the premier breeder in the area, naturally became the region's foremost competitor, a status he maintained even when experienced rivals began to appear. He had taken to naming his bulls after senatorial colleagues, and nothing amused him more than to hear the show an-nouncer call out "Barry Goldwater" or "Hubert Humphrey" as the prize-winning bull of the day.

Due to Morse's entrepreneurial vigor, Humphrey (the senator) was more or less involved in some cattle raising of his own. In 1960 he, Senator Eugene McCarthy, and Oscar Chapman, former Secretary of the Interior, were, to use McCarthy's word, "induced" by Morse into forming a partnership and buying eight Angus cows from the Poolesville operation, at $300 a head (Morse wanted the partners to buy Devons of equal quality, but they balked at his asking price of $400–$500 each). The arrangement was that Morse would care for the cows and their hoped-for offspring—meeting all expenses save veterinarian fees—until they were ready for market; in return, he would get half the calves or the proceeds from their sale.

The deal was a disaster for the partnership. One cow, the oldest, lost mobility during the first year and had to be auctioned for a third of her cost; a second cow died in year two; some incipient mothers failed to produce calves, and one that did gave birth to a stillborn; and all the while, bills from the vet ran far beyond expectation. De-spite such adversity, exchanges among the contractual parties were never less than good-natured. Morse began his letters to the partners with "Dear Cowboys"; the one reporting the second cow's demise opened with a dramatic "Death stalks the range." On the more seri-ous side, Morse kept reassuring everyone that handsome profits were still achievable, especially, he said, if the partners would pony up another several hundred dollars each to add a number of robust Devon females to their inferior Angus herd. The triumvirate resist-

Under Morse's direction, a cattle investment by Senator Eugene McCarthy (Dem., Minn.) and two other partners went badly awry. (Courtesy of Mildred M. Morse.)

ed this counsel, and Chapman decided to cut his losses and drop out of the partnership altogether by contributing all of his remaining interest—two healthy cows and one calf—to the Morse 1962 reelection campaign.

Morse urged the others to go their defunct partner one better. He again invited them to enlarge their stock by adding Devon females, the purchase of which, he argued, would assuredly protect their initial investment and, by a happy coincidence, greatly enhance the Morse-for-Senator treasury. To this invitation McCarthy responded: "If the United Nations agenda is light this year, we might suggest that they take up our case. At this writing, I suggest that you not plan to finance the remainder of your campaign on any good that might come to you from our mutual cattle venture." Morse dutifully accepted "Rustler" McCarthy's retreat, and after paying his fellow senators the little that was left of their capital, he terminated the undertaking in late 1962.

As an example of amateur speculation gone awry, the cattle-investment saga makes an interesting vignette. But it also calls attention to important aspects of Morse's life. Whether originating with this undertaking or not, the idea of generating sub-rosa campaign funds via the sale of range cattle became fixed in Morse's mind, and, unknown to the public, this doubtful practice would be followed in all campaigns thereafter. More importantly, negative balance sheets at this time were scarcely confined to the intrepid Washington "cowboys." Midge often complained about a paucity of family funds, a legitimate complaint—as letters of alarm from Morse's accountants frequently attested—based on a repeated history of serious budgetary shortages. Midge observed that "Wayne was a frugal man, except when it came to horses and cows." The problem was that it always did come to horses and cows, and the effect was to keep the Morse bank account perpetually in distress. To those who raised eyebrows over the speech-making stipends he earned—more than anyone else in Congress—Morse always insisted that such non-senatorial income was necessary merely to meet ordinary living and travel expenses (including the costs of private school and college for the girls). But it is more likely that the extra funds were regularly required to offset the never-ending outlays for the farm operations in Eugene and Poolesville. The day would come, after the girls were largely on their own, when Wayne and Midge could be described as comfortably off, but until that day (in the mid- to late sixties), pinching pennies would be required practice in the parsimonious Morse household.

Morse sometimes pinched quite tightly. His papers are replete with examples of the felt need to exercise the strictest economy. Illustrative is an unabashed Christmas 1948 instruction to a Portland supplier to send "to Mrs. Paul R. Washke . . . the cheapest winter blanket for her colt that you carry in stock." A decade later, Morse spent $100 to purchase a beat-up old Ford that had been sitting idle in the Uhls' back forty. He drove the car for six months, but when it began to leak oil, he decided he no longer wanted it. The Uhls agreed not only to take it back, but to repurchase it at Morse's requested price of $125, a price which, Gladys recalled, "we thought very amusing because the car was in much worse shape than it had been." Earlier that same year, Morse found himself "burning with embarrassment" when his Poolesville hired man (an illiterate known in the office as "Ph.D.") mistakenly delivered a load of firewood to John F. Kennedy's house—but not so burning as to keep him from charging Kennedy thirty-four dollars "for two cords of wood, duly delivered."

Even more of an embarrassment, perhaps, was an incident involving another hired hand, the one employed as caretaker of the Eugene property. In late 1958, the press picked up the fact that sixty-six-year-old D. F. Pickert, who had worked part-time at Edgewood Farm for twenty-five years, had been fired by Morse over a political disagreement: having theretofore kept such opinions to himself, Pickert, a Republican, had for some reason begun letting people know that he opposed Governor Holmes and continued to support President Eisenhower. Being condemned in the press for firing an elderly worker solely on partisan grounds was bad enough; making matters worse was the revelation that Morse had been paying his longtime caretaker a meager one dollar an hour.

Morse sought to cut costs wherever he could. He saved a few dollars by unashamedly drafting Monday-through-Friday office staff into a weekend work force for Poolesville. However dubious, this practice was generally accepted by most personnel as part of what it meant to work for Senator Morse. Some, like Joe Smith, loved toiling in the rustic countryside and looked forward to doing it. One or two of the senior staff cheerfully resisted Morse's earnest solicitations and, as in the case of Bill Berg, either stayed away from the farm entirely or showed up wearing unsuitable business attire. The younger patronage staff, most of whom were more than a little awestruck by *the Senator*, usually felt honored to be asked to labor alongside their eminent chief.

But even some of the younger employees occasionally wished for more time to themselves. Hugh Cole, Jr., a youthful staff member from Bend, Oregon, who normally didn't mind the trek to Poolesville, tried to beg off one morning after a boozy Saturday night, citing the need to attend Sunday mass. "The cornfield," Morse insisted, "is the greatest cathedral God has ever made, and you can never be closer to Him than by worshipping there." Another staffer, whose out-of-office duties seemed always to involve him in cow manure, was distinctly *not* pleased to spend his Sundays shoveling out stables in Montgomery County. "I lived on a farm all my life," he complained to Gladys Uhl. "I wanted only to get away from there. I worked hard to go to college. I worked hard to get my law degree, and now look at me." Morse was so much in his element on the farm that such lamentations were beyond his comprehension. Cole felt that the younger staff could be overwhelmed by their boss's enthusiasm: "And then we'd go out to that damn ranch and we'd plough around in the mud and the guy used to just astonish me because, if anything, he'd speed up on the weekend. I'm eighteen, nineteen, twenty years old during this time, in relatively good condition; he's in his late fifties, and I couldn't keep up with the guy. At the end of a day my ass was dragging, and he was just going full bore. It used to rev him up just to be out there."

Like most senators, Morse saw no reason to confine his staff to a narrow definition of congressional business. Unlike many, however, he was entirely candid about his mode of operation, especially when it came to mixing Senate responsibilities with electoral politics. Indeed, as far as Morse was concerned, in his office legislation and electioneering were part of everyone's function. In a July 1961 memorandum, he reminded his staff that "a job in a Senator's office is a political job," a job with a heavy workload and long hours, especially during election periods. "It is only fair," the memo continued, "for me to give notice now that my campaign for re-election in 1962 starts now. This means that the work load of the office is going to be heavy and the hours long. It is my hope that the political objectives for which I stand in the Senate will cause each member of the staff to want to enlist in my campaign for the duration. However, unless you possess the necessary zeal for this political contest, then you should voluntarily resign from my staff now."

Where Morse tended to deviate from other members of Congress was in the *extent* to which he engaged his help in extracurricular activities. Keeping batteries of secretarial assistants late into the night to do correspondence had been normal procedure going back to law school deanship days; and in Washington, as he had in Eugene, he dictated letters covering not just official matters, but everything from saddle purchases and hay allocations to house insurance and requests for pocket money from his daughters. While a case might be made for utilizing secretaries for such purposes—it is, after all, not always easy to draw a line between official and unofficial correspondence—it is more difficult to make a case for the employment of office personnel in the livestock business. Morse's use of Charles Lee may represent the most egregious instance of such employment. Lee was Morse's efficacious assistant on issues pertaining to education: from 1960 forward, each of the numerous bills that left the Subcommittee on Education did so only after Lee had worked on their language, negotiated their terms with interested parties, and marked them up for final passage by the Senate. Not only did Lee put in considerable time at Poolesville, but he also accompanied his boss on various occasions hauling cows to the Carolinas and horses to Oregon. Furthermore, it could not even be said that Lee's salary was attributable to Morse's office budget. He was in fact paid out of funds from the Labor and Public Welfare Committee.

How in general Morse treated his staff is very much a matter of opinion. Bob Smith argues that Morse, like certain other liberals, ran a clerical "sweatshop," a "hardship post" in which only "phlegmatic" or "passive" types were able to last more than a few years. There is some evidence to support this view. At times, staff turnover in the Morse office was high, and some of those who stayed the longest more or less fit Smith's description. Moreover, Morse's behavior may have exacerbated whatever conditions of hardship employees did have to endure. By far his least phlegmatic staffer over the years was legislative assistant Mert Bernstein, who, despite being widely admired for his considerable ability, was told by Morse that he might more profitably seek his future elsewhere. According to Lawrence Hobart, Bernstein's counterpart in Neuberger's office,

> Morse was unmerciful on his staff. He really used them up in a fierce way. . . . Mert Bernstein was an excellent person,

very intelligent. He was really lucky to have a guy of that cal-
iber. . . . We used to have these joint meetings between the
Neuberger and Morse staffs, with the principals present.
He'd attack his staff. He'd attack Mert in front of the whole
group. Accused him of not doing his job. . . . I also saw Morse
do that with lower-echelon people, secretaries, and people
like that.

Hobart was very much a Neuberger man and admittedly not a great
Morse admirer; however, there is just enough corroborating opinion
from certain other former staffers—including Phyllis Rock, who was
promoted to fill Bernstein's position—to lend some credence to his
description.

On the other hand, *most* ex-staffers interviewed for this book,
and Rock in particular, looked back with great fondness on their
time with Morse. Even Bernstein, who went on to a distinguished career as a professor of law and public affairs, never ceased to think of
himself as a trusted associate, one who saw fit to advise his old boss
on policy matters years after his legislative assistant's tenure was over.
Several staff members reported that because of the positive atmosphere in their office—fostered by *both* Morse and Bill Berg—they
were the envy of other senatorial personnel. Many simply liked working in a setting where exciting things happened, for a man who could
not be bought at any price by any interest, for a senator willing to
fight for what he believed in, even if he risked his job (and theirs) by
so doing. Juliane Johnson, who advanced from file clerk to recep-
tionist during Morse's third term, recalled that everyone was more
than eager to give their all for the senator: "There was an attitude in
the office that by gum, you busted your fanny and got the work done.
I didn't know about coffee breaks or going home at five o'clock."
Penny Gross, Johnson's successor, probably spoke for the vast majority of Morse's employees when she stated, "It was the kind of thing
where he was our leader, we were inspired by him, and there was
nothing we wouldn't sacrifice for him."

MORSE'S FAMILY WAS ALSO CALLED UPON to make sacrifices—
many. Among the volumes of collected news clippings in the Morse
papers is one from a June 1948 edition of the *Eugene Register-Guard*
headlined "Morse Family Home Again." Featured is a quarter-page
photograph of Nancy, Judy, and Amy (ages 17, 14, and 12), gathered
cozily with their mother before a console radio, listening intently to
Morse, who, we are told, is moderating a broadcast of "Town Meeting of the Air." This depiction—Midge and the girls at their residence, Wayne involved elsewhere—accurately reflects the familial
situation the Morses had known at various locations since the mid-
1930s. The accompanying story updates the girls' recent school year
in Washington, D.C., summarizes Midge's household schedule
for the vacation season, and notes that because the senator is "planning a tour of the state when he returns from Washington," he "will
be at home very little" over the next few months. For the summer
of 1948, the Morse family would, as usual, be without its husband
and father.

A charitable observer might suggest that 1948 was, after all, an
election year, and Morse, though not himself running, had no choice
but to go where his party directed him to support fellow Republicans
campaigning for office. Such an observer might further note that the
demands of political life are notoriously ceaseless and that part of the
high cost of being involved in politics is to be pulled away from
friends and family for impossibly long periods. In Morse's case, however, such separations were as much self-imposed as not. During
most holiday periods as well as other times, in election years and off
years, Morse, when not at work in Congress, typically committed
himself to activities which so monopolized his time and attention
that little of either was left for his family. A journalist once asked
Amy—then a nursing student at the University of North Carolina—
why her father had dashed in and out of Chapel Hill on a speaking
engagement without spending more than a fleeting moment with his
youngest daughter. "This isn't unusual," Amy responded. "At home
I never got to see him much either. . . . He was always up before
breakfast and headed for the office. We didn't see him again until
midnight or later."

Morse's Capitol Hill calendar was an almanac of political meet-ings, committee hearings, and legislative sessions that seemed to run on without end; whatever spare time could be managed was spent chiefly not with the family, but working on the farm in Poolesville. Morse was, as Amy indicated, always up before breakfast, but first light often found him not in his office but thirty-five miles away in Montgomery County, herding cows or feeding fowl, *before* scurrying in for a quick bite at the Senate dining room and the eight o'clock appointment that usually followed. On weekends, when he wasn't away at a speaking engagement, in town on political business, or participating somewhere in a horse show or animal exposition, he was back in Poolesville at the break of day, ready, with the assistance of one or more office staff, to put in ten to twelve hours of arduous labor.

The girls would occasionally journey to the farm to work with their father, but their interest was primarily equestrian, and, along with their mother, they found plodding through the multi-gated Poolesville terrain far inferior to what they had known earlier on the bridle paths of Rock Creek Park or the picturesque trails in South Eugene. Moreover, as Morse turned increasingly from raising and riding horses to breeding and selling cows, the farm became yet a further extension of a world that belonged to him, not the family— a world he dearly loved, a world they chiefly endured.

In the Morse family, Wayne had his life and his daughters had theirs, and, as epitomized by the visitation to Chapel Hill, the two intersected only intermittently. It was not that Morse was indifferent toward his daughters or lacking in love for them. At times he could show them the greatest affection and consideration. But so con-sumed was he by his own interests, his own activities and ambitions, that the girls tended to drop out of focus. It was Midge's opinion, ex-pressed ten years after her husband's death, that "Wayne was a good father when he had the time, but he never had the time. The girls," she added, "always resented that, and they still do."

As Charlie Brooks saw it, Morse was immersed in other matters to such a degree that "even when he was with the family, he wasn't really there." Thinking of Morse and the girls, Brooks recalled a time when his boss and an old friend were driving across country from Washington to Oregon, with Judy in the back seat. So engrossed was Morse in a discussion with his companion that when they stopped at a Midwest service station and Judy went to the restroom, Morse had the tank filled, paid for the gas, and departed the station without noticing that Judy had not yet returned. "They just started the car," Brooks exclaimed, "and drove off! This really happened! They got forty miles down the road—still talking—before he came to and saw that Judy wasn't there."

Midge's comment about her daughters' resentment is supported by feelings expressed by the daughters themselves as adults. Interviewed in London in 1985, Judy stated that Morse "would pull away from responsibilities as a parent. I sometimes asked myself, 'Who is this stranger?'" As pointed out earlier, however, the girls' resentfulness, though keen, was combined with an equally keen adoration of their father. Morse was for them a heroic parent, revered not just because he was famous and a hero to others, but precisely because he *was* a part-time father, one treasured for those adventurous moments when he was available to pal around with at horse shows or on cross-country junkets, one whose paternal preeminence remained undiminished by the routine dailiness of life at home.

The Morse girls, especially the older two, tended to be rebellious as they were growing up. Perhaps an indication of their resentful side, they often used the family car with a reckless disregard for the rules of the road, and the Morse sedan, with "Oregon 1" on the license plates, became well known to Police Chief Murray and units of the D.C. traffic squad. Where the girls took the car was also a matter of concern. Despite admonitions to the contrary, they were known to frequent undesirable parts of the District, which caused Morse at one point to remodel the basement of a newly purchased house in the hope that they might entertain and "have a good time at home" and thereby stay out of trouble. The "volatile Judy," as Morse referred to her, gave her parents the most difficulty. She liked to conceal caches of alcohol and tobacco around the Morse residence —items strictly forbidden by her father—and while still in high school threatened more than once to leave home forever.

Morse's irregular contact with his offspring meant that he was frequently out of touch with their growth and development, and he therefore seemed to have trouble accepting the reality of their approaching adulthood. When Amy was seventeen, she wrote home from a camp in Virginia asking if her colt Flirt could be brought down for the summer. Morse wrote back, refusing on the grounds that the move would be too dangerous given the value of the animal. The letter had been dictated to a secretary, and its language, even more than its message, made clear that whatever the merit of Amy's entreaty, Morse—who regularly carted *his* valuable horses back and forth across the country—still regarded her as a little girl. "I am sorry to disappoint you," he said, "but your request really is not a wise one, and I hope you will accept the fact that Daddy's judgment is better than yours when it comes to horses." (Flirt would remain in Poolesville, and as far as can be determined, no horse of lesser value was sent as a substitute.)

Morse was not unaware that he was an absentee parent, but he adopted a kind of sanguine fatalism that allowed him to avoid dwelling on how things might have been better. To his Eugene friends, the Washkes, he admitted in 1953 that there was "no doubt about the fact that my political life has denied them in many ways a normal home environment, and I have always felt sad about that. However, Midge and I have tried to make it up to them in other ways, and only time will tell whether we have given them the training and support which they need for pre-marital adjustments." What those "other ways" might have been is anyone's guess, and as far as the girls' "pre-marital adjustments" were concerned, it was Morse who had the greatest difficulty making them.

Looking back, Nancy complained that the men she and her sisters became interested in were, in their father's eyes, never good enough for one of the Morse girls. (Judy described Morse as "a very possessive father.") Morse had disapproved of Nancy's 1950 betrothal to Bruce Chase, a college classmate, and was pleased when Chase broke off the engagement the following year. In 1954 Nancy, then teaching dance at Coker College in Hartsville, South Carolina, fell in love with Hugh Campbell, a young man from a traditional Southern business family. In true Dixie fashion, Campbell went to Washington to ask Morse for Nancy's hand. Morse refused to see him and, according to the *New York Daily News*, replied to a subsequent letter from Campbell by telling him that he would never be welcome as a member of the Morse family. Nancy, the *Daily News* reported, "took matters into her own hands. She personally announced her engagement—without benefit of her parents' names—in the local paper," and she and Campbell were married within the month.

Had Nancy married someone *because* her father disapproved of him? The Rarigs concluded that each of the girls had rebelled in precisely this way. Rarig wrote the following to a friend in 1958, after all three daughters had been wed: "Eta says if you see Wayne and Midge, give them her sympathy. Nancy married into a rich conservative family down South; the second daughter married an Episcopal minister, and now Amy has married a Catholic. We knew that these daughters had reacted against politics and had vowed never to marry politicians, but it is disconcerting to have them react so far back into the ancient shades of conservatism." Rarig's analysis may be correct, but given the exalted view Morse had of his girls—"he worshipped his daughters," reported Nancy—it is likely that, ideology aside, marriage to any man would have felt to him like an overt act of rebellion.

Morse undoubtedly did worship his daughters, but because of its persistent remoteness, his adoration tended to lack the unqualified acceptance and understanding that had long been second nature to him when it came to animals. The following (dictated) letter was sent to Nancy in July of 1942, when, at the age of eleven, she was having trouble at summer camp (see chapter 4) and very much wanted to return to Washington.

> Mother and I felt very badly when we read your letter in which you said you wanted to come home because of some little difficulty you had over riding. . . .
>
> You are a fine girl and you can live above your difficulties, just as Daddy has to face his every day. You must remember not to run away from your troubles. It would be

cowardly for you to come home, even if you could, and I wouldn't be proud of you if you didn't conquer your troubles there. . . .

It would make us very unhappy to think that you are not taking advantage of the fine opportunity which you have to be happy this summer in that camp. It is a very fine camp and you should be very happy there. If you aren't happy, you must learn to be happy there, even though troubles develop from time to time. . . .

Now, Nancy, be sure and hold up your chin and smile and do your part in helping make everyone around you happy.

Such homilies from a busy parent to a difficult daughter may be contrasted with the sentiments Morse typically voiced when speaking of his farm animals, especially his horses. When Spice of Life won a grand champion's ribbon in Arlington, Virginia, in 1947, Morse issued a press release saying, "It was . . . a very hard week for me and taught me again the lesson that even though friends will let you down now and then a good horse never will." Eight years later, he told a freelance reporter for the *Saturday Evening Post* that few people "understand the relationship that develops between man and horse after one raises a colt and trains him." As the following letter to the Washkes indicates, such a relationship could be extremely heartfelt.

The Morse stables has [*sic*] a little tragedy. . . . Yesterday morning Frances York was either kicked by Patsy, or in trying to get away from Patsy's heels twisted her right front leg. It is swollen to at least twice its normal size clear to her shoulder and she cannot put her foot on the ground. . . . last night I put liniment on it and bandaged it. The liniment seemed to give her some relief although she is in great pain.

This morning I gave her another application of liniment and that soothed her. I am inclined to believe that she twisted the leg because there is no sign of a kick, although it is sore as a boil. . . .

I am satisfied that there is nothing a veterinarian could do that I have not done, and I think that what the mare needs more than anything else right now is hot applications and rest. I have your winter blanket on her and that keeps her nice and warm. Her ears are warm, her eyes are bright, and this morning she ate a quart of oats, so I think that's a good sign, especially in view of the fact that last night she would not touch feed. The poor old thing is a wonderful patient. When I massage her leg she holds it forward and puts her nose on my back and seems to get a great deal of relief from the rubbing.

The above correspondence is quoted at length not to imply that Morse had an affection for his horses that he hadn't for his children, but rather to suggest that, unlike his attenuated fatherly sentiments, his feelings—one might say his *maternal* feelings—toward animals came to him naturally, a product of his earliest years in Verona, and needed little further cultivation to reach their full expression. Thus, one is not surprised when Midge, remembering her husband's involvement in the Eugene Hunt Club in the 1930s, observes that "Wayne usually preferred the horses to their owners" (recalling J. D. Salinger's character in *The Catcher in the Rye* remarking, "I'd rather have a goddam horse. A horse is at least *human* for God's sake"). Nor is one surprised when Midge adds: "The only time in my life I saw Wayne stand absolutely still, perfectly motionless, was when he was leaning on a fence one day looking into the chicken yard. 'Come here, Mama,' he said. 'Just look at that chicken.'"

Midge hated chickens—"especially their smell"—just as she hated politics. But she so loved and admired her husband that she was willing to subordinate her life and interests to his. "It was," she said, "what women did in those days." If Wayne was an absentee spouse as well as father (one who dictated letters to his wife as well as his children), Midge did all she could to optimize whatever time he might have available. Often this meant coming to the Capitol to eat with Wayne, who was almost always too busy to return to the house for dinner. Just as often it meant waiting up and fixing a meal

Morse loved chickens and most other farm creatures. Said one staffer, "I honestly think that the senator did relate better to animals than he did to human beings." (Oregon Historical Society, OrHi CN 013761.)

when he came home hungry, having eaten nothing since lunch. Many a midnight found Midge crating Wayne's redolent chickens for competition at a fair the next morning.

While being married to a famous senator was always a source of great pride for Midge, it held little glamour for a wife who found day-to-day household obligations somehow unrelieved by her husband's exalted station. As she told one reporter after ten years in D.C., "Housekeeping is just the same in Washington as anywhere else —if you don't do the dishes, they'll pile up." Morse had no taste for the capital's endless cocktail circuit, which meant that the couple's social life was confined to the occasional dinner party, largely with the horse and cattle set or members of the bureaucracy. Midge in truth was sorry to have given up the comfortable life the Morses had enjoyed in Eugene for the difficulties of raising a family on limited funds in Washington, difficulties compounded by their frequent changes of address—ten moves in their first twelve years in the District—and by the fact that despite faithful promises of assistance, Morse always discovered vital business to do on the Hill whenever the moving van arrived. Columnist George Dixon quoted Midge telling the girls in 1957, "Your father came up with another moving-day excuse—as he's done 19 of our 22 moves" (in thirty-three years of marriage).

Those closest to the family knew that, as Rarig put it, "Midge has had to suffer as the wife of Wayne Morse," even as she readily did whatever it took to keep the family afloat and Wayne in the Senate. Charlie Brooks saw Midge as an "intelligent, well-organized woman. Outwardly calm, inwardly boiling all the time." Nancy described her as a "bantam hen" who was defensive about her shortness of stature, who had to fight to emerge from Wayne's shadow, and who, over the years, came to lose her sense of humor.

To say that for Midge the world began and ended with Wayne during his lifetime would not be to overstate the case; and Midge was not reticent about telling others how she felt. "I have long thought that Wayne is wonderful," she informed a reporter in 1956. "I thought so . . . before anyone else did." But "wonderful" fails to do justice to the strength of Midge's adoration. Hal Gross, a Washington veteran who worked on Morse political campaigns in the sixties, came closer in suggesting that "Mrs. Morse sometimes confused Wayne Morse with God."

Whether or not such adulation was, like that of the daughters, intensified by Morse's perpetual unavailability, the result was that Midge was greatly distressed about having to share so much of him with the rest of the world. Her animus was directed chiefly against women, many of whom she seemed to think had romantic or lascivious intentions toward her mate. While it is true that women found his charismatic personality a powerful attraction, and while Morse clearly enjoyed female company, according to every person interviewed for this book who knew him more than slightly, his connubial faithfulness was beyond question. Orlando Hollis: "Not once in forty-five years did he show awareness of the opposite sex." Charlie Porter: "Wayne never even recognized when the most gorgeous woman was coming on to him." Joe Smith: "I don't think the Senator ever looked at another woman. His women were politics." For Midge, however, the reality of Wayne's actions seemed irrelevant; she would, regardless of his decorous behavior, remain intensely suspicious.

When he suffered so severely from the infamous horse kick to the jaw, she tenderly helped to nurse him back to health. But she later permitted herself to divulge to Hollis, "The accident wouldn't have happened, you know, if Wayne hadn't been doing a Boy Scout act for a female."

Once the girls were gone from home, Midge began to spend an increasing amount of time at Morse's office, taking on among other things the job of updating the constituency mailing list—much-needed work which, by all reports, put her organizational skills to ex-tremely good use. There were those, however, who questioned her motives. Morse had had as his secretary a charming and efficient Southerner named Nan Burgess, whom Charlie Brooks described as "a real doll." Morse had been forced to let Burgess go because in Midge's eyes, she had become too much the senatorial office wife, if not her husband's sexual partner. Most Morse staffers were convinced that although there was no validity to the idea of a sexual liaison, Midge put in her time at the office to see to it that nothing even re-motely like a Nan Burgess situation could emerge there in the future.

The consensus of those interviewed for this book was that de-spite an overabundance of suspiciousness, Midge was not only a competent wife and mother but, as Mert Bernstein discovered in traveling to the West Coast and back with her, also an interesting and adept conversationalist who had informed opinions on a variety of subjects. Midge would have preferred holding absorbing conversa-tions with her husband, but getting him to sit still long enough to en-gage in one was not easy. "I never asked him a question at bedtime," she reported. "He was always asleep before his head hit the pillow." In an effort to have Wayne all to herself for an entire two weeks, Midge somehow persuaded him in the late 1960s to rent a cottage on Cape Cod, for what would be their first real vacation in nearly fifty years together. Cut off from his usual world—the only phone was down the road—with nothing to do but relax in the sunshine, Morse stood it for three days, then announced that he had to "get the hell out of here." Before nightfall, the Morses had returned to their "normal" existence in Washington.

One time when he was sitting here he told me, much to my
amazement, that he could count the friends he had on the
fingers of one hand. And here he was, a man whose name
was known throughout the world.

— Ed Conklin, 1983

I don't think anyone really has a very large number of real,
intimate friends.

— Wayne Morse, 1973

WHEN *COLLIER'S* MAGAZINE headlined its April 1953 Senator Morse
story "The Loneliest Man in Washington," it did so to highlight
Morse's *public* isolation, a consequence of his nonaffiliation with either political party. But the headline might have been applied as well
to Morse's private life, which was characterized by isolation of a more
personal nature. Something about Morse stood between him and
those with whom he came in contact, kept others at a discernible and
respectful distance. From Hugh Cole's perspective, that something
was Morse himself. "I honestly think," he said, "that the Senator related better to animals than he did to human beings."

Charlie Brooks made an even stronger observation. "There's no
question about it," he reported. "Taken individually, the Senator
didn't like people." Even those Morse did seem to like could be put
off by his general demeanor. What Cole recalled most clearly was
Morse's "stern manner" and the fact that he always seemed "super serious." Morse at his best was Morse on the dais, lecturing audiences
on the rightness of his position, an approach that proved enormously successful so long as everyone agreed on the gravity of the
issue at hand. On rare occasions everyone didn't; and at such times
Morse had little to fall back on. As he told a supporter in 1951, "I seldom use humor in my speeches because apparently I never have developed the ability to transmit to people my meaning when I am kidding them." If Morse lacked such ability from the lectern, he could
be similarly wanting on the personal level, where his kidding often

took the form of needling—pointed barbs which, depending on the strength and status of the recipient, could be interpreted as friendly teasing or as biting sarcasm. Someone of Berg's stature could take Morse's worst and breezily reply in kind. But those of lesser rank might feel put down or intimidated. Remembering "that gravel voice and bushy eyebrows," Stephen Wasby, a Congressional Fellow who worked with one of Morse's committees in the mid-sixties, believed that "many people found [Senator Morse] if not terrorizing at least someone of whom one was in awe."

As for intimate friends—the kind who might exchange barbs on an equal basis—one wouldn't need an entire hand's worth of fingers on which to count them. Over Morse's lifetime, only labor attorney Jim Landye and neighbor Paul Washke, both of whom went back to the days in Eugene, fit the description. But Landye died suddenly during Morse's second senatorial term, and with Washke there was always a modicum of mistrust, even when the two were collegial confidants at the University of Oregon. After Landye's death, most of those referred to as "friends" could more accurately be labeled followers—the "true blue," as Midge tagged them on the office mailing list—leaving Morse in private as he typically wished to be in public: largely on his own.

While Morse could be an extraordinarily receptive listener when he had to be, instantly digesting and committing to memory the most complicated and lengthy reports and briefings, his first impulse was to lecture, regardless of who or how many he was talking to, and this also had the effect of distancing him from others. Nothing captures this predilection more than the description of Morse standing in his Eugene bedroom, clad only in undershorts, delivering "as if ... on the floor of the Senate" a twenty-five-minute disquisition on Vietnam, "complete with gestures [and] inflections," to an audience of one campaign worker. Morse could get so caught up in impromptu declamation as to lose awareness of what was happening around him. He and Midge were dining one day with former staffer Tom Enright and his wife. As Morse was explicating a point to Enright, he dug into his acidic grapefruit in such a way as to squirt Mrs. Enright in the eye, causing her some distress. When he went on without pause, Midge said, "Wayne, you've just squirted grapefruit juice into Mrs. Enright's eye!" "That's very nice," he replied, and continued talking. On another occasion he spent a night with Gerald Robinson, a Portland attorney and longtime supporter. In honor of their distinguished guest, Mrs. Robinson prepared her special *coq au vin* for dinner. The next morning, as he was taking his leave, Morse thanked her for her warm hospitality and for "that wonderful steak you served us last night."

Occasionally Morse seemed aware, sometimes poignantly so, that he was perceived as a remote figure, operating, in Hugh Cole's words, "on an entirely different plane from the rest of us." In 1965 Orlando Hollis, still occupying Morse's old seat as law school dean, wrote to inquire why Morse's full name did not appear on Foreign Relations Committee stationery. Specifically, Hollis wanted to know "what the hell has happened to your middle initial?" To which Morse replied: "I really have no good reason for not using it except a psychological one. It has been my observation that people are more inclined to call me Wayne Morse than they are when my middle initial is used. In the latter instance, they are inclined to be more formal and call me Senator Morse. I prefer the more informal approach, particularly when in the minds of so many, I am supposed to be a cold fish anyway."

Perhaps by 1965 Morse did wish for less formality in address. If so, it was a departure from the past—as his earlier refusal of Bernstein's request to be on a first-name basis indicates—and much too late, after twenty-one years in the Senate, to be taken seriously. Most acquaintances, even fellow legislators like Al Ullman and Edith Green, continued to refer to him as *Senator* Morse, and the absence or presence of a middle initial had nothing to do with it. Juliane Johnson would never have agreed with the "so many" who characterized her boss as a cold fish; but when I mentioned his response to Hollis's query, she said without hesitation, "You don't call the Pope by his first name, do you?"

As an iconoclastic maverick, Morse was, of course, far from popish in either purpose or deed, but his tendency to pontificate made Johnson's analogy understandable. Bill Tugman was fond of quoting a mutual acquaintance in Eugene to the effect that Morse was the way he was because he had "never played marbles with the boys." Others said they could never imagine going out with him for a beer, and not because he wouldn't touch alcohol. The fact was that the same abstemiousness Morse displayed regarding alcohol could also be seen in his attitudes about social behavior in general. Midge described her husband as "very straightlaced as far as personal morals were concerned." After a single visit to Finnochio's, San Francisco's famous transvestite cabaret, he remembered it as so totally "disgusting . . . that psychologically it has become very deeply submerged in my experience"—a reaction which any Roman prelate might applaud (and psychologist ponder).

It was not, however, prudishness that created the most difficulty. In the course of interviewing those who knew and worked with Morse, the word heard most frequently was "ego," a word applied with equal frequency to Morse's public and private worlds. That his ego was always large, whatever the circumstance, there is no doubt. That it required continual reinforcing is also beyond question. According to Joe Smith, who made the case more plainly than most, it was not friends that Morse needed but followers, the kind of followers who would give him "total attention, unquestioned fealty . . . a support system of fairly large proportions. He had to have that, and while you can say it was too bad and a great flaw that he had to have so much, how else could he take on the wrongs of the world and make them right, slay the dragons and win victories against his enemies?"

Smith's explanation returns us from the private to the public realm, a realm filled to overflowing with intractable enemies—"Wayne's shit list," as Joe Rauh called it. Morse constantly preached the necessity of distinguishing between issues and personalities and seems to have worked hard to maintain such a distinction, so that regardless of how heated things got, today's bitter foe might conveniently become tomorrow's friendly ally. In reality, however, especially before 1961, this distinction broke down more often than not; differences over issues were frequently interpreted as personal attacks, attacks whose scars might never be healed. As fellow Demo-

Morse could be heard expressing irritation at incompetent Senate colleagues by paying them his "disrespects" every weekend in Poolesville, with an audience of younger staff personnel in attendance. (Courtesy of Judith Morse Goldberg.)

crat Jebby Davidson put it, "One thing we all agree on is that when Morse hates, he hates well and long."

In Morse's case, animosity was also a consequence of impatience with a political universe populated by inferior intellects. Thus he could be heard ventilating irritation at incompetent senatorial colleagues by paying them his "disrespects" every weekend in Poolesville with younger staff members in attendance. Thus he could also be heard, as he was by Pat Holt (a 1960s aide for Morse's Latin America Subcommittee), telling one functionary after another what a wonderful job he was doing—with "the silly bastard just sitting there, glowing"—then exclaiming after the person's departure, "What a nincompoop!" Indeed, Morse might have been diagnosed as having a superiority complex, except that, objectively speaking—"in fairness to myself," Morse would have said—it was probably no complex. Republican senator Mark Hatfield, whose relationship with

Morse spanned two and a half decades, believed it inevitable that a man of such "sheer, absolute brilliance," a man with "the Senate's greatest gift of debate and rhetoric," would find difficulty in the realm of party politics, where, in Hatfield's view, "the majority of people are very average intellectually."

Whether it was inevitable or not, Morse never went long without finding himself in contentious disputation, feeling in many cases a sense of outrage at what he saw as betrayal on the part of opponents. Tugman believed that Morse was at his worst when he had endured "long periods of overwork and strain"; at such times, Tugman argued, he would be under "spells of . . . self-hypnosis during which he might lose all perspective." While impossible to document, this view has at least some basis in logic. Laboring sixteen out of every twenty-four hours at whirlwind velocity was bound to exact a toll, regardless of the many regenerative catnaps taken during breaks in the schedule. It is therefore not surprising that Morse experienced numerous intervals of exhaustion—typically diagnosed as "flu"—during which he was often put to bed for days at a time; and it is fair to surmise that quarrels and controversies could only be exacerbated in the periods leading up to such intervals.

(Also worth mentioning, but even harder to document, was the view held by some that Morse's psychological generator was fueled largely by sugar, a fact presumably demonstrated by his insatiable desire for sweets. Answering a query from a journalist in 1959, Morse indicated that "next to T-Bone steak my favorite dish is really a dessert—Mrs. Morse's Pecan Pie." From nearly everyone who knew him came further tales of confectionary cravings that could take hold at any time of the day or night: ice cream; root beer; chocolates—he once ate a two-pound box in one evening at Ed Conklin's; apple pie; ginger ale; lemon balls and licorice, which at various times were kept in abundance at his office front desk; and an additional assortment of sugary concoctions, not excluding selections from the "greasy pastry shelf" [Mike Kopetski's description] at Denny's restaurants, all of which gave his sweet tooth at least temporary satisfaction. If the theory that Morse's psychic engine ran heavily on sucrose is unprovable, so is its implied corollary: i.e., that the *lack* of sugar at strategic moments could cause him to be morose and cantankerous. His medical record sheds little light on such conjecture.)

As "a layman trying to psychoanalyze" his former colleague, Mark Hatfield thoughtfully described the impact of Morse's ego as it was felt on the floor of the Senate.

> I would sit there and watch and listen to him. And I really feel the man would soar with such intellectual analysis and passion . . . that he moved into a whole other world. And anybody and everybody around him would totally disappear. There was none of the old conviviality that existed maybe at the lunch table. Now he was so committed, so carried into the subject, that personalities and relationships just didn't exist. Therefore, he could attack or counterattack or advocate or defend with the fierceness of a Genghis Khan because his ego or self had been confused with the issue. He became the embodiment of the issue. Therefore, your counterview was immediately interpreted as a personal attack and would be responded to by a counter–personal attack.

Hatfield acknowledged that he saw Morse orating in this fashion on only a few occasions, but heard about many more such instances before his own arrival in the Senate in 1966. The fact was that as Morse's legislative influence increased in the 1960s, his speeches, though never less than stalwartly independent, grew far less personal and, with the exception of speeches on foreign policy, far more conciliatory than in earlier years.

Although, as Hatfield suggested, Morse's ego often carried him into an attack/counterattack mode, that ego was also the source of his maverick strength. Quoting an unnamed observer, an *Atlanta Constitution* reporter wrote in 1953: "Wayne Morse . . . is at one time the most courageous man in the Senate of the United States and also the member with the most egotism. But I do not criticize the latter because I consider a great deal of egotism sustains him in his unrelenting courage." Joe Smith spoke of Morse in almost identical terms —"his strength came from the ego and the constant reassurance that he was right"—and he cited Nan Burgess, voicing the opinion of most Morse associates, in the same vein: "She said she didn't like his temper or his ego, but she was afraid if you took those away you'd take away the guy, and no one wanted that."

Not only did no one want to lose the essential Wayne Morse by stripping him of his ego, there were many who simply accepted the fact that big egos are part of what politics is all about and who were in no way put off by them. For example, Hal Gross, who worked on the staffs of Senators Frank Church and Alan Cranston as well as on Morse's, said he knew all about egotism and politicians and remembered having little trouble dealing with Morse on a basis of mutual respect and recognition. "I realized," he said, "that to be on any kind of footing with Morse you had to be thoroughly prepared and you had to be mentally alert. But if you met those two tests, he was a hell of a human being. He was warm, public-spirited, with that penetrating intelligence."

Perhaps it took such a combination of preparation and alertness, plus sufficient intelligence and self-confidence of one's own, to appreciate fully the unique qualities Morse brought to his work. When he thought back on it, tough-minded Howard Morgan—former Oregon Democratic party chairman, state public utilities commissioner, and member of the Federal Power Commission—expressed surprise that he and Morse had had such a positive relationship, since, as Morgan wrote, "each of us had a deserved reputation as a man who was hard to satisfy." "I don't want to give the impression," Morgan continued,

> ... that Wayne was a perfect candidate—my view has always been that there never was, or ever will be, such an animal. But in the half-dozen or so Oregon elections in which I participated ... and four national campaigns, Wayne was the easiest candidate to work with, the least troublesome and the most dependable and predictable. He had an ego at least as large as Dick's [Neuberger's]—nothing wrong with that, and anyone who aspires to be a U.S. Senator had better be equipped with one—but he also had maturity and genuine self-assurance to match it. I never knew him to be afraid of

anything or anybody, he knew exactly who he was, what he wanted to do, how to do it with the minimum of outside help, and *did it* without fuss or flap. He had brains, guts, skill and energy in abundance and he shot square with everyone who shot square with him—and with many who didn't.

It may be that, with the exception of how his family felt, Morse could never have been similarly admired in his private life; but as John F. Kennedy's New Frontier passed into Lyndon Johnson's Great Society, and as Morse's public stature increased in the process, more and more of his colleagues came to share Morgan's opinion. By 1965, Morse's legislative successes in the field of education would prompt the following from no less a figure than New York's Senator Jake Javits, a member of the opposition party: "It is extraordinary that a man of so many abilities in so many fields becomes the most adroit, intelligent, wise judge, conciliator, and friend when he is in charge of a bill that any committee could ever have. It is most extraordinary." To which Democratic senator Thomas Dodd of Connecticut, speaking for his side of the aisle, saw fit to add: "The Senator from Oregon is one of the great Members of this body."

12

Strong Man of the Senate

I WRITE THIS IN THE MID-1990S, a time of great political change. The Republican majority in Congress, swept into power in 1994, is strenuously at work trying to undo much of what the national government has sought to accomplish over the past several generations. Near the top of a very long hit list is federal aid to education, a thirty-seven-year-old program based on the idea that the U.S. government must use its offices to help provide a good education for all of its citizens. Except for mandating prayer in public schools, the Republican leadership has rejected this idea.

Important political change was also in the air three and a half decades earlier, when John F. Kennedy moved into the White House. After eight years of relative inaction on the domestic front, Kennedy and the Democrats had in mind revitalizing and enhancing federal authority, especially in the area of education. Indeed, nothing more strikingly distinguishes JFK's New Frontier from mid-nineties Republicanism than the ideology of each as revealed in its position on education. For today's congressional conservatives, federal policy is so thoroughly perverted that no genuine reform can take place unless and until the U.S. Department of Education is demolished and all decision making transferred to the states. For the New Frontiersmen, federal aid to education—overseen by an *enlarged* Office of Education—was an indispensable part of national renewal and progress. For Kennedy himself it was, as Theodore Sorensen has written, "the one domestic issue that mattered most."

Like President Kennedy, Morse had long believed that only through large-scale, federally administered programs could the country's educational system be raised out of a sorrowful condition of impoverishment and neglect. As early as 1955 he had called (unsuccessfully) for President Eisenhower to convene a special congressional session on education to face the "emergency situation about which something must be done." Five and a half years later, with Eisenhower at last out of office, he was suddenly in a position to see that something was in fact accomplished.

KENNEDY'S DEPARTURE FROM THE SENATE provided Morse with an opportunity to move to a higher rank on the Labor and Public Welfare Committee. It was an opportunity Morse was not about to miss; and while education may have been a primary concern, he let it be known that he was equally interested in promoting labor legislation, as long as in either case he was given the chairmanship of the relevant subcommittee. Historian Irving Bernstein has written that "Morse ... was eager to get the [Education] job," but the truth is that even before the new Congress opened for business, Morse had informed Labor and Welfare chairman Lister Hill of Alabama that what he chiefly wanted was to "move onward and upward to *either* the Labor Subcommittee or the Education Subcommittee"; and while in the past Morse had repeatedly attacked the seniority system as antediluvian and undemocratic, now, as Labor and Welfare's third-ranking Democrat (behind Hill and Pat McNamara of Michigan), he would not hesitate to use it to his own advantage. Thus he announced to Hill that "until the Senate chops down that worm-eaten [seniority] tree, I insist on the right to my share of the fruit, wormy as it may be." Since the influential trade unions—which had not forgotten Morse's independent stand on Landrum-Griffin—insisted on the more tractable McNamara managing "their" legislation, Morse's share of the fruit would necessarily be the Subcommittee on Education.

As it turned out, Morse and Education proved an ideal match. At the outset, however, there were those who had their doubts. Morse had never chaired such a consequential Senate panel, and many were nervous about whether he could cooperate effectively with colleagues or get along with Kennedy's high-powered bureaucrats.

Samuel Halperin, then a deputy secretary at the Department of Health, Education and Welfare, fretted about Morse's reputation for being "cantankerous and irascible" and regarded him initially as "a bull in a china shop, or worse." Even Morse's adoring sister Caryl was holding her breath. "We all hope," she wrote in early January, "that . . . you will strive to get along with the new administration as much as possible. . . . We do not suggest that you sacrifice your high principles . . . but if those principles are to become part of the fabric of this government then you have to win support and you can't do it by alienating people. Even Jefferson and Hamilton had to give and take a little to get their major principles accepted by the majority."

Caryl Kline was one of the few people on earth who could lecture Morse with impunity, but given his own understanding of what his new role would entail, it is far from clear that he needed such instruction, from her or anyone else. He was busy on his own trying to dispel the idea that he couldn't conform to congressional mores, that he had placed himself permanently in legislative limbo. In mid-January he wrote to Ken Johnson, editor of the *Capital Press* in Salem, disputing those in the media who typically portrayed him as standing "all alone on various issues without any support behind me"—a portrayal, he pointed out, that perpetuated the myth "that I am a maverick and that I don't teamwork and all the rest of the malarky which you know is used against me."

For Morse to describe as "malarky" the maverick label—which he had previously worn with pugnacious pride—suggested a turnabout of enormous proportions, a shift to a whole new way of doing business. It was one thing, however, to eschew maverickness verbally; acting as a nonmaverick would be quite another. It would soon become apparent that Morse was incapable of performing as a Democratic regular in all respects, on every issue, obediently following the line prescribed by either the White House or the party's congressional caucus. And yet when it came to the one area of education— where admittedly as subcommittee chair he would be calling many of the shots—that is exactly how he acted. Although few historians have credited him sufficiently for his accomplishment, during the next eight years Morse would be the Democrats' man-in-the-Senate

Morse and President Kennedy in the Oval Office discuss New Frontier education legislation pending before Congress. (Wayne Morse Historical Park Corporation.)

on education, dutifully carrying every New Frontier and Great So-ciety bill through the upper chamber; doing so with unprecedented bipartisan support and, to the amazement of many, with an under-stated brilliance that was at the time unequaled in the Congress.

The Kennedy administration faced a difficult task in getting Congress to move on education. Since 1940, it had passed only three pieces of educational legislation of any significance: the "impacted areas" laws, which helped to fund schools in localities with heavy fed-eral employment; the GI Bill, which gave direct support to students who were veterans of World War II or the Korean War; and the 1958 National Defense Education Act (NDEA), the Sputnik-inspired law, which, with an emphasis on the sciences and foreign languages, pro-vided grants and loans to institutions of higher learning. Given so many decades of so little done, it may have been inevitable that year one of the New Frontier would turn out more successful for Morse than for the administration.

As soon as he took office, Kennedy asked Congress for massive federal aid to public schools and to universities (public and private), largely for classroom construction. In the face of heated opposition from the Catholic establishment, upset because aid to parochial schools had not been included in the bill, Morse skillfully maneuvered the proposed legislation through the Senate. Once passed, it was sent to the House "suffused," as one writer later put it, "with triumph and hope." Morse and his staff even worked behind the scenes with New York's controversial congressman Adam Clayton Powell to move the bill through Powell's House Education and Labor Committee, only to see hope vanish when the House Rules Committee killed the proposal by a one-vote margin. Despite Morse's best efforts, as far as Kennedy's education program was concerned, "the year 1961 was," in the words of Irving Bernstein, "a total loss."

Or nearly so. Morse was at least able to retain support for some of the earlier programs, including NDEA. Artfully micromanaging the NDEA legislation, he took great pains to see that nothing went wrong. In language he had rarely used in his seventeen years in the Senate, he told Lister Hill that he did "not want to weaken our chances of passing the NDEA bill by including amendments that will not be absolutely defensible on the floor of the Senate." To the *Washington Post*, the exercise of such prudence on Morse's part was "the biggest surprise of the session."

Though not widely covered outside Washington, Morse's assiduous handling of all education bills that year, NDEA included, impressed everyone who knew about it. Even Maurine Neuberger— who had succeeded her late husband in 1960—had to acknowledge "the great skill displayed by the senior senator from Oregon." Majority Leader Mike Mansfield stated simply that "in 1961 Morse was the strong man of the Senate."

The following year was in many ways a repeat of 1961. Despite unsteady signals from a White House weakened by staff reorganization, on February 6 the Senate passed a higher-education bill under Morse's direction that provided loans for constructing college facilities, public and private, and scholarships for needy undergraduates. Having cleared the Senate, the bill had to be reconciled with the

House version. A conference committee worked out a compromise, but because the normally supportive National Education Association lobbied hard against the proposal (the NEA, made up mostly of grammar and high school teachers, opposed aid to all private institutions, even universities) and because conservative resistance had grown stronger over the summer (Southerners especially feared that "needy students" was administration argot for blacks), the House rejected the compromise on September 20. With November elections in the offing, nothing further could be done before the end of the year. As Irving Bernstein saw it, "In round one (1961) Kennedy had taken a severe pounding and had dropped briefly to his knees. Round two (1962) was worse and he had gone down for an eight-count."

Kennedy might have been down for the count—as the nation's first Catholic president, he would lose standing in some quarters however the issue of aid to parochial schools came out—but Morse stood taller than ever. This time it remained for Bob Smith to offer praise for a job well done. Writing in the *Oregonian*, Smith reported that for "the second successive session, Sen. Wayne Morse has completed a legislative assignment in the Senate in a remarkable fashion which is altogether unique in the annals of his maverick career. . . . What has caused considerable remark among senators and newsmen was the skill displayed by the Oregon senator in fending off unwelcome amendments which might have drastically altered the provisions of the legislation." Even more remarkable, Smith might have noted, was the fact that, with Morse steering it through the chamber, the bill had passed the Senate by an astounding vote of 69 to 17.

Having developed such a senatorial majority, Morse could realistically expect to build on the work of 1961 and 1962, with the hope that the entire Congress would come around to passing an acceptable bill in 1963. Meanwhile, however, he had to ensure that he would himself be around in '63 to see it happen.

TRUE TO HER NAME, Phyllis Rock was a solid and dependable member of Morse's staff, one who worked on a variety of issues, including education. Toward the end of 1961, while Morse was putting together his 1962 subcommittee agenda, Rock began to worry about her chief's reelection chances. A mid-December poll showed him slightly behind announced Republican rival Sigfrid "Sig" Unander. Rock took one look at the poll and fired off a memo to Charlie Brooks in Oregon. "Is this clipping as alarming as it sounds?" she inquired. "For such a lightweight as Unander to be ahead at this stage only makes me wonder how far ahead he will be by next November, after he has gotten himself better known in the state." Rock feared that Morse would want to base the 1962 campaign exclusively on his legislative accomplishments. "The boss talks only about what we should do to compile his 'record,'" she complained, "but I think he is misjudging somewhat the real weakness we have to overcome. Of course, he won't admit it, but I think our biggest problem is still going to be his fights with other politicians."

Rock knew that many of these fights, including the one with Neuberger, would be reprised with the publication of Smith's biography of Morse, due out the following month. Her hope was that even if *The Tiger in the Senate* opened old wounds, it could end up being a considerable asset to the campaign. In an earlier memo to Brooks she had stated:

> The boss refuses to believe it, but I think that on the whole, the book will be favorable to him. It will have some criticisms, probably, and this will make him think it is "an attack" on him, but I still believe it will be generally sympathetic and will give our campaign a boost. It will do so just because it is bound to be reviewed, read, and discussed all over the state. The Smith book will center attention on Senator Morse, most of it for the good, for the early months of next year.

Although the biography was more critical of Morse than Rock had anticipated and could in no way be regarded as "generally sympathetic," her assessment of its impact was nonetheless correct.

Smith dropped a copy off at Morse's office, personally inscribed:

For Wayne Morse

With gratitude for your cooperation and admiration of your courage, I offer this unfinished record of your adventure-orous [*sic*] career, at its mid-point, with the prayerful hope that you will attain the very summit of legislative effective-ness, political wisdom and public statecraft in the era of great opportunity which beckons.

Affectionate best wishes
your unbiased friend
    Bob Smith

Morse's response was "Get that the hell out of my office!"

How much of the book Morse actually read is unclear, but he did, as Rock predicted, regard it as a personal attack, describing it publicly as premeditated "character assassination" sponsored by "political en-emies" who wished to see him defeated in the fall. The book received enormous press coverage, as did Morse's reaction to it; and despite its negative depiction, it had exactly the impact Rock had hoped for, placing her boss center stage once again in the Oregon political arena.

Thus spotlighted, Morse cruised to victory in the primary, de-feating crane operator Charles Gilbert, a member of the Hoisting and Portable Engineers Union, 174,402 to 44,441; he remained most-ly in Washington during the campaign and spent less than $19,000 promoting it. (Edith Green, who would be returned to the House in the fall, had an even easier time, spending a total of $310 on her cam-paign.) But the general election would be another matter, and if Unander was, as Rock had described him, a political lightweight, he was a lightweight with clout, one who knew how to raise money and capture votes. Big of frame and slow of speech, the forty-eight-year-old former GOP state chairman had been Oregon's treasurer for two terms, garnering 416,410 ballots in his 1956 reelection—to that point the biggest vote ever accumulated by a Republican in a contested race. One of his weak spots, however, was that he had made an enemy of Mark Hatfield while running unsuccessfully against him in the 1958 gubernatorial primary, and he would therefore receive lit-tle support from the popular governor.

Unander was weak in other respects as well. While his plodding style might befit a candidate for state treasurer, it appeared lackluster beside Morse's more "senatorial" persona, which had retained its old appeal to the public despite the bad press resulting from Smith's biography. And though at least one indisputably heavyweight Oregonian, Ernest Swigert of the Hyster Company, raised funds for Unander by warning fellow industrialists that "if we really believe . . . capitalism is a better choice than socialism, we must act now," the Unander campaign appeared unable to translate money thus accumulated into increased support from voters. Nevertheless, a confidential poll taken in late July showed Morse ahead by only four percentage points, a finding that prompted a panicky letter to Kennedy asking for concerted and immediate assistance. "Unless steps are taken quickly . . . giving proof that you want me re-elected," Morse wrote, "you are going to be faced with dealing with Unander as my replacement in the next session of Congress." It is doubtful that Kennedy was much alarmed by Morse's warning, since the general feeling in both Oregon and the White House was that unless something unforeseen occurred, Morse would continue to pull away from his opponent.

Part of Morse's strength in 1962 could be attributed to his solid standing with the timber industry. Since Unander was the scion of a wealthy timber family, it might have been thought that timber interests—tree growers, loggers, forest-products manufacturers, and lumber merchants—would unify behind a candidate demonstrably one of their own. However, like every successful Oregon politician, Morse had accepted as given that the economic health of his state and the well-being of its largest industry were coterminous. He knew better than most that Oregon led the nation in lumber production and that one out of every ten jobholders worked directly in the industry. Morse may have loved cantering through the majestic forest trails of Lane County, but he had also learned to love the surrounding Douglas firs for the millions in income they generated annually, and for that reason he seldom missed a chance to advance the interests of timber throughout his state. During the 1956 campaign, the *New York Times* quoted one Republican lumber broker as saying, "I don't like Morse or anything he stands for. But when any of us go to Washington with a request, Wayne will see us and turn Washington upside down to get us what we want, if he's convinced we're right."

While Morse could be counted on generally to help constituents in the industry, the "if" in the preceding quote was crucial. Early on, he chose to ally himself with the smaller operators, usually the buyers of timber, rather than such giants as Weyerhaeuser, Crown Zellerbach, and Georgia-Pacific, each of which owned or controlled many thousands of acres of lucrative forest and considered Morse their enemy. As a supporter of small companies, Morse necessarily championed maximum competition within the industry, which meant constructing publicly funded logging-access roads wherever feasible and following the philosophy of sustained-yield production so that predictable quantities of timber would be available for future exploitation by everyone. Although by today's standards those who, like Morse, endorsed the sustained-yield mentality must be seen as having put product development ahead of environmental protection, by the norms of the day they were true conservationists, working diligently to preserve and replenish the natural resource they depended on. In this same spirit, Morse did much to educate mill owners, large as well as small, to the principle that in the long run, genuine competition could not flourish if all parties thought only of maximizing short-term profits.

One cannot say that operators were invariably pleased to be so educated, nor that they always understood or appreciated what their senator was trying to do in their behalf. On timber legislation, Morse had the assistance of Bob Wolf, a perseverant Senate Interior Committee staffer who probably knew more about timber policy than anyone in Washington. In 1958, with the help of other Western senators, he and Morse slipped through an amendment to the Small Business Administration Act which had the potential of revolutionizing the purchase of government-owned timber. Joe McCracken of the Western Forest Industries Association remembered "eating breakfast one morning in Portland, and there in the *Oregonian* was an article mentioning that Senator Morse had inserted an amendment allowing small firms to bid on timber *preferentially*, and the big boys would be excluded. And I said, 'Jesus Christ! Are they talking about free competition? Where in hell did this come from?'"

What had happened was that small outfits, most of which were represented by McCracken's organization, had complained bitterly that they were in danger of going under because they were being systematically outbid by the large companies for logging rights on Department of Interior or Bureau of Land Management parcels. Morse's amendment sought to protect the small companies by allocating a percentage of annual timber sales exclusively to them—a guaranteed "set-aside," as it was known—to be supervised by the Small Business Administration. However, because McCracken's members had not been in on the idea (Morse, McCracken later realized, knew the plan would be crushed by Weyerhaeuser et al. if its existence became known beforehand) and didn't fully grasp what it meant, they actually lobbied against it; and because they refused to support it even after it became law, the plan never really got off the ground.

By 1962, however, most of the smaller operators had become aware of how valuable Morse had been to them. "We had begun to grow up," said McCracken, "to catch up with what Senator Morse had been doing for us." Morse further solidified his standing by pressuring the Interior Department to reform its regulations regarding rights of access through privately held forestlands. Most private acreage was owned by the giant companies, and as things stood, these companies could prevent small outfits from reaching significant enclaves of national-forest timber by charging exorbitant fees to cross their property. The new policy, announced in early March of 1962, would require all private owners who were themselves logging on government lands—as all were—to provide access through their property free of charge. This change would lead to the "unlocking" of fifty-five billion board feet of timber that could now be affordably bid for, harvested, and processed by small operators as well as large. Morse, who had ceaselessly badgered the Interior Secretary's office to rewrite administrative guidelines to effect this change, properly received credit for the government's shift in policy.

With Morse unassailable on timber issues, with more than enough money in his reelection coffers—a single luncheon in D.C.

had netted $15,000—and with Unander unable to gather momentum, the race became, in Charlie Brooks's words, "a walk in the park for all of us." It did not hurt that two weeks before election day, with the nation terrified by the possibility of a nuclear confrontation, Morse dramatically canceled a campaign appearance because he had been "called back" to Washington to consult on the Cuban missile crisis (during which he fully supported Kennedy). The final tally gave Unander 291,587 votes (46 percent), Morse 344,716 (54 percent). Indicative of how smoothly things had gone, the campaign had cost Morse $110,000 *less* than had the effort against McKay six years earlier. Furthermore, though he outspent Unander by $22,000, his post-election bank account showed a surplus of over $30,000. For the very first time, Morse could return to Washington after a contest free from the nagging obligations of campaign debt, free to give total attention to his legislative agenda—and free to lead the Democrats' 1963 education program to triumphant passage.

ALTHOUGH THE EDUCATION SUBCOMMITTEE was Morse's prime concern, its chairmanship in no way inhibited him from taking positions on non-education issues, and if these positions ran counter to those of his party, his party would, as usual, have to endure it. Morse had resumed his "five o'clock shadow" speeches, pointing out the foibles in American foreign policy, especially as it was applied to a little-known corner of Southeast Asia referred to as—depending on which wire service carried the story—Viet Nam, Viet-Nam, or Vietnam. On the domestic front, even as he was shepherding the 1962 higher-education bill through the Senate, Morse filibustered against the administration proposal placing the ownership of American communications satellites in private hands. At one point during the satellite debate, he responded to a provocative Mansfield maneuver against the filibuster by informing fellow senators: "So far as I am concerned, [Mansfield] will never represent me as my Majority Leader. . . . He is the Majority Leader, but not with the support of the Senator from Oregon. Get that clear."

A week later, Morse sat through a long, private meeting of Senate

Democratic chieftains in which speaker after speaker agreed that the party should exercise caution in proceeding with the more controversial New Frontier proposals they had before them, including Medicare for the aged. Vice President Johnson, acting as Kennedy's emissary, summed up the session by saying, "As I gather it, the consensus of this meeting is to advise the President that these measures should be laid over until the next Congress." At this, Morse, who had been listening in what was described as "brooding silence," exploded, accusing his colleagues of stalling, pussyfooting, and backsliding while the American public was calling for action. According to one press report, Morse's blast left his fellow Democrats so startled that they were unable to offer "a word in reply."

Being stunned into silence by Morse's scolding may in fact have felt like a relief to colleagues driven to near shock by his earlier attack on a custom greatly cherished by both parties. Without prior warning, he had presented a resolution banning hard liquor in all public rooms of the Senate and in both Senate office buildings. "Morse Uncorks 'Dry Senate' Bill," blared an April *Washington Post* headline. To sharpen the point of his proposal, he timed its introduction to coincide exactly with a cocktail party for President Kennedy being hosted by Mansfield in the New Senate Reception Room. Morse had long been disgusted by the sight of drunken members in the halls of Congress and especially by the spectacle of legislators quaffing lobbyists' booze in quarters paid for by the public. (At his behest, the Senate dining room had begun serving "Oregon's new fresh fruit dairy drink. Compliments of Sen. Morse.") No senator dared in open forum to oppose a call for sobriety, so the proposal was quickly moved to the Senate Rules Committee. There, behind closed doors, it was immediately "postponed" by unanimous vote. For the next several months, alcohol served under the Capitol dome would be referred to as "Morse water."

Morse's colleagues may have been periodically agitated by his irrepressible boat-rocking in so many channels; but senators are nothing if not masters at compartmentalizing issues, and they had no difficulty continuing to look to him for direction on education. As indicated earlier, Morse's leading role in that area was made immeasurably easier by the capable assistance of Charles Lee. Lee, a chubby, chain-smoking Reed College alumnus with a background in public administration, joined the Morse team as a volunteer in the 1956 campaign and then, with a good word from Caryl Kline, was taken on by Morse, first as an aide to the District of Columbia Committee and then as the sole professional staff assigned to the Education Subcommittee. Historian Norman C. Thomas has written that "Lee had a 'confidential relationship' with Morse that enabled him to act as an alter ego. Repeatedly, I was told that Morse's thinking could be ascertained by talking to Lee and that Lee's acceptance of a point at issue would ensure its approval by Morse." That one often had to deal with Lee to get Morse's views tended to rankle Edith Green, who recalled a moment of irritation in a meeting when she snapped, "If Senator Morse doesn't know the answer, maybe Senator Lee does."

Morse might have fought for the Labor Subcommittee chair had he known that the other important congressional player in education policy-making would turn out to be fellow Oregonian Green. Ten years Morse's junior, Green had also had a career in education,

Morse in a friendly chat with Carrol Kearns (Rep., Pa.), ranking minority member of the House Education and Labor Committee; Charles Lee, Morse's chief assistant on education is in the rear. (Courtesy of Charles W. Lee.)

spending eleven years in the 1930s teaching sixth grade and junior high school in Salem before entering politics. The 1962 elections had boosted her seniority as well as Morse's, and shortly after Morse took over his Senate subcommittee she became chairwoman of the House Special Subcommittee on Education. If Morse was education's key figure in the entire Congress, Green was not far behind. Looking back from 1968, HEW's Halperin could say that "next to Senator Wayne Morse, whose imprint exists on all the education statutes since 1961, no single member of the Congress has had more lasting impact . . . than Mrs. Green."

Distrust lingered between Morse and Green—a residue of the Hatfield-accident issue in 1958 and the presidential primary in 1960 —but at least at the outset, both were sufficiently committed to the New Frontier education program to work harmoniously toward a common goal. There were indications, however, that fissures might appear in the future, and though it was Morse who carried the reputation for dissidence, the signs suggested that in this case Green might be the one to cause trouble—and not just for Morse. She refused, for example, to have anything to do with HEW Assistant Secretary Wilbur Cohen. She wouldn't let him into her office, reported Kennedy aide Jim Grant Bolling: "She simply didn't like him." Green's likes and dislikes would become increasingly problematic as the decade wore on.

Whatever the future might hold, in 1963 Morse and Green were able to suppress some of their differences and present a near-united front to the Congress. Morse introduced an administration-backed, 182-page omnibus package—the National Education Improvement bill—in the Senate, and Adam Clayton Powell dutifully did the same in the House. But when Green (and Powell) openly expressed reservations about such a catchall plan, it became clear that despite the fact that both Green and Morse had held marathon hearings on the omnibus approach (the Senate subcommittee had produced 4,429 pages of testimony filling seven huge volumes), the bill would have to be divided into smaller measures. Of these, Morse was forced to give top priority to the Higher Education Facilities bill because unyielding conservative opposition at that moment meant it would be

*Morse and others look on as Congresswoman Green receives
a pen that President Johnson used to sign an education bill
into law. Although she was known as "Mrs. Education,"
Green often stood in the way of Great Society legislation
sponsored by the Johnson administration. (Oregon Historical Society, OrHi 37442.)*

useless to offer an even more needed bill covering aid to elementary
and secondary schools.

For a bill like Higher Education Facilities—which expanded the
proposals of 1962 while eliminating the controversial provision for
student scholarships—the time at last seemed ripe. As political
analyst James Sundquist pointed out, "people *do* learn from experience. . . . The NEA and its public school allies now knew that an all-
or-nothing attitude would mean, for the public schools, nothing.
Likewise, Catholic leaders now understood that an equal-treatment-
or-nothing position would mean, for the Catholic schools, nothing."
Nobody wanted nothing, but a diminution in resistance did not
mean that the bill would sail through Congress without the usual
quota of hard work and negotiation.

Surprisingly, in light of its inaction the previous two years, the House, prodded by Green, passed its version by mid-August, while Morse's bill was still under study in his subcommittee. When it finally reached the Senate floor, Morse was unable to fight off a Republican-Dixiecrat anti-Catholic amendment that would give individual taxpayers the right to test in court whether the law violated the constitutional separation of church and state. What Morse lost on the floor, however, he regained in conference with the House: the conference committee deleted the amendment, and then Morse, by cleverly coupling the revised bill with another that many conservatives supported, persuaded the Senate to vote it up or down in early December. The chamber voted up, and the recently installed President Johnson signed it into law on December 16.

Lost in his pugilistic metaphor, Irving Bernstein wrote that "in round three (1963) the tide of the fight turned. [Kennedy] not only kept his feet but also won going away"—an unfortunate choice of words, perhaps, since Kennedy, as all the world knew, went down for the last time when he was assassinated in November, before the bill had been approved. Nonetheless, one can justifiably say that with Morse leading the way, the Higher Education Facilities Act was in fact a victory for Kennedy, one that, despite being earned posthumously, was among his most significant. The act was important for both what it accomplished and what it represented. It provided:

> an infusion into higher education of nearly two billion dollars, to be administered by the states over a three-year period;
>
> grants to construct graduate schools and libraries—at public and private, secular and church-related institutions—in math, science, engineering, and foreign languages;
>
> allotments to construct community colleges and technical institutes;
>
> low-interest loans for general academic construction.

As far as church-state boundaries were concerned, the act more or less maintained traditional distinctions that had been upheld by the courts; it was thus stipulated that federal funds could, for example, cover building a science lab at Holy Cross but could not be applied toward facilities to be used for sectarian instruction, religious worship, or divinity studies.

Passage of the Higher Education Facilities Act, along with the passage of four related bills—the Vocational Education Act (the one supported by many conservatives), the Health Professional Educational Assistance Act (the only one signed by Kennedy before his death), and the Mental Health Facilities and Community Mental Health Centers Construction Acts—and the extension of two more (NDEA and impacted areas), marked a radical departure from previous postwar politics. The legislative bottleneck in education had finally been broken. For the first time since 1945, a general education law had been based not, as with NDEA, on the needs of national security, but on merit, on the idea that improvement in education was, in its own right, vital to the well-being of the nation.

The *Oregonian* reported that "Sen. Wayne Morse had the most successful year of his long political career in 1963," but neither the newspaper nor the Oregon public truly understood what their senator had accomplished or how he had contrived to do it. With Lee's help, Morse had carried the art of compromise to a new level, accommodating a vast assortment of divergent views while resolutely maintaining the integrity of his legislation. According to Lee,

> Morse was a master at retreating on a bill's language in order to retain its substance. He was also a master—this went back to his labor arbitration days—of small group dynamics. In mark-up sessions he could sense intuitively where somebody had gotten off the tack, and he would carefully back up until it got back to the basic agreements, and then, without being obtrusive, gently probe to find out what this person's real agenda was and why he was holding up progress. You could always find room for compromise on the details that do not really affect the principle involved. For example, you will give up two or three years of authorizing [funds for] a program because you know damn well that three years down the road you will re-authorize the thing.

Irving Bernstein wrote that Morse "had a cast-iron behind" because he was willing to sit through endless hours of committee hearings. Lee indicated there was method to Morse's endurance:

> Morse was very liberal on hearings. He knew that this is the
> ore you mine for everything you do thereafter; so you put as
> much in the hearings as possible. One thing: you're the only
> one that will ever read it, and your senator will read the
> salient portions that you mark for him, and that will equip
> him to handle nine-tenths of the questions that come up
> from left field. Whatever was asked, Morse would always be
> ready to answer: "Now if the gentleman will turn to page 389
> of volume five of the hearings he will see that . . ."

Morse, Lee reported, was always ready to respond because he prepared himself to be: "He was wax to receive and iron to retain. When
you had your briefing session with him, he'd read the language, and
if he didn't get it the first time, he would hammer at you until you
had explained it so that he felt comfortable with it. And because he
had the ability to hold so many things in his mind, he'd just push the
button and out it came. Which is why he was so effective in conference: he knew his legislation."

If Morse worked hard to know precisely what was at issue, he insisted that others do so as well, especially those sent from the administration to testify on the government's behalf. As he informed
a meeting of school administrators: "I conduct my hearings in the
form of a seminar, with term papers assigned to the Administration
witnesses. So I told the Commissioner [of Education, Francis Kep-
pel], more in sorrow than in anger, that, in my judgment, he had
flunked the course. . . . But I held out hope. I told the Commissioner
that he could repeat the course for make-up credit in this session."
While this description slightly exaggerates what Morse had said
to Keppel, it was well known throughout the Office of Education
that to appear before Morse's subcommittee inadequately prepared
could subject bureaucrats to a pointed rebuke from the chair, to say
nothing of an embarrassing homework assignment for their next
appearance. Keeping Education staff thus on their toes helped con-

siderably to move the legislative process along once specific bills
came up for consideration.

While most of the 1963 education bills had been enacted, four
outstanding problems remained: aid to primary and secondary education, undergraduate scholarships, the parochial-school issue, and
Edith Green. The first three were being worked on; the last was cause
for growing concern. When he signed it into law, President Johnson
had referred to the Higher Education Facilities legislation as the
"Morse-Green Act," and it was certainly the case that Green's efforts
had been crucial to its passage. However, at the final Senate-House
conference, she nearly derailed the whole year's work by siding with
Republicans in an effort to divest the bill of some of its key provisions, and it took all of Morse's negotiating skill to keep the session
from disintegrating. His successful effort prompted an extraordinary
letter from one of Green's House colleagues, Carl Perkins of Kentucky, chairman of the General Education Subcommittee (as opposed to Green's Special Subcommittee on Education). Perkins felt
that "Mrs. Green's stand . . . made our task most difficult. But for
your outstanding leadership in uniting our House Democratic Conferees, in my judgment both bills would have gone down the drain."
It would not be the last time that Morse would have to forge majority support for education legislation in his own chamber and then
do "an end run" (Lee's term) around Green to produce a similar result in the House.

WHEN ONE THINKS OF LYNDON JOHNSON'S GREAT SOCIETY, one is
apt to think first of the War on Poverty and the related civil-rights
struggle, typified respectively by the Economic Opportunity and Civil
Rights Acts of 1964. But when LBJ presidential aide George Reedy
reflected back on the sixties, he opined: "You know, the thing I think
Johnson was the most serious about was doing something about
education." Whether education ranked as Johnson's very top priority is difficult to say, but it clearly was high on his list. And in his eagerness to build on the start made by Kennedy, Johnson reached out
even more directly to Morse to get his program through Congress.

Whereas Kennedy was cautious at first about acknowledging Morse's pivotal role, Johnson didn't hesitate. Special assistant Joe Califano quoted his boss as follows: "On [an] education bill he might say, 'Look, I want you to talk to Wayne Morse about that. See whether he thinks it's a good idea because if he doesn't like it . . . you might as well forget it.'"

No one had to tell Stewart McClure that Senator Morse ran the education show in the Senate. A rough-hewn Midwesterner who had worked on the Hill since 1949, McClure was a staffer on the Labor and Welfare Committee, a situation that put him in frequent contact with Morse's subcommittee and even more frequent contact with Charles Lee. Sometime in 1964, over a bottle of Kennedy brand Irish whiskey, McClure and Lee fell to talking about how federal aid to public schools might be made acceptable to more members of Congress. As the bottle's contents diminished, the two men had a sudden inspiration: since senators hate to embrace totally new ideas but seem receptive to repackaged old ones, why not redefine impacted areas to include effects *other* than those caused by the presence of government workers? The principal effects McClure and Lee had in mind were those produced by poverty: "If *impacted* could be made to include *poverty-stricken*," said McClure, then every truly needy school district in the country could become eligible for federal assistance. Without revealing its alcohol-soaked origins, the two aides took their idea to Morse, and he immediately ran with it.

But not very far. Morse held hearings on an expanded impacted-areas proposal and tried to persuade Commissioner Keppel and Secretary Cohen to support it, but because 1964 was an election year, the administration was not eager to move aggressively on any educational front that might prove controversial with voters. Morse therefore had to settle for further expansion of NDEA and for the creation of Upward Bound, a program providing students from underprivileged backgrounds with the skills and motivation needed to attend college. Because he was optimistic about moving forward in 1965, Morse was also philosophical about marking time in 1964. To a late-October educational conference in Nebraska he quoted the motto over the entrance to the National Archives building in Washington:

"What is past, is prologue"—a motto, he said, that would guide him in "the opening semesters" of the next Congress.

Morse could not have asked for a more propitious political moment than the beginning of 1965. In trouncing Barry Goldwater, Lyndon Johnson had not only consolidated his presidency, but also led his party to a smashing victory in Congress: Democrats now had a 62 to 38 edge in the Senate and, with a gain of thirty-eight seats, a 295 to 140 margin in the House. With such irresistible majorities in hand, the administration was eager to get new education legislation quickly before Congress. Even before the new year, Vice President-elect Hubert Humphrey told a New York audience that a "massive investment" in education would be the "single most important step toward building the Great Society." Morse would see to it that as far as the Senate was concerned, that step would be determinedly taken by the time the first congressional "semester" had reached its halfway point.

A contentious thesis the previous year, the revised impacted-areas concept had, with the Democratic electoral sweep, become accepted doctrine in 1965. Aid to education was now seen as a central front of the War on Poverty, a front whose engagements could mark success or failure for the entire Great Society. It was Morse's responsibility to capture this front for the administration. Even before the old year had passed, he was ready with a strategic battle plan: the proposed Elementary and Secondary Education Act (ESEA) would first be carried through the House, where, hopefully, opponents could be beaten back; then, accepting no amendments—a tactic made possible because the Democrats had such a huge majority—the Senate would pass the House version in toto, thus avoiding a Senate-House conference, a death chamber for previous education bills.

Rough waters had been forecast for ESEA in the House, and rough waters were encountered—mostly whipped up not by Republicans, but by the Democrats' own Edith Green. Known as "Mrs. Education" to her admirers (and "Madame Nhu" in Morse's office), Green raised serious objections to the bill. (Because ESEA was seen as an across-the-board approach, Powell gave it to Perkins's General

Education Subcommittee rather than Green's Special Education Subcommittee.) Republicans were delighted to have such a prominent Democrat take on her own administration. As one minority-party staffer put it, "We made the decision to let her carry the ball for us whenever she wanted to." Looking on from the Senate, Morse was appalled at Green's behavior. Mike Manatos, in a memo to fellow presidential aide Larry O'Brien, reported that "Morse had commented on Congresswoman Edith Green expressing the hope that the White House was now convinced that she is a dangerous individual who will avail herself of every opportunity to throw roadblocks in our way in the Education Bill."

There were those who hoped Green would confront directly the constitutional issue of federal aid to parochial schools—ESEA would go even further than previous acts to assist students in religious schools. Green's opposition was said by some to be based on anti-Catholicism, an absurd idea given her avid support of Kennedy in 1960. But even if Green had wanted to raise the traditional church-state question, she would have found little support among the usual interest groups: Catholics were for the most part pleased that more would be coming their way, while the Jewish community—previously united in opposition to such legislation—was now divided on the question, the more orthodox having rallied behind the bill because it promised assistance for *their* students as well.

Green objected principally to the formula Morse and Lee had devised for distributing funds among the nation's poverty-impacted school districts. (Some thought she objected *because* they were the authors of the formula.) She argued that their system, which gave funds to districts on the basis of numbers of children from low-income families, gave too much to the richest states and too little to the poorer ones. ESEA proponents countered that not only did it cost more to educate children in the richer states (mostly in the north), but the proposed formula provided greater *percentage* budget increases to the poorer states. Green first offered an amendment that would allow individual districts to sue on the grounds that the allocations were constitutionally unequal. When this failed, she moved an amendment to provide a flat $200 per low-income-family child, which would have raised the allotment for thirty-five states and reduced it for fifteen. Under normal circumstances, Morse could have lived with the latter arrangement (he would in fact move to equalize funding in the following session). But he and other supporters feared that *any* significant change at that moment would risk splintering the national coalition behind the bill—"this tenuous alliance," as Paul Douglas called it—that had been so long in coming together, a risk Green seemed for whatever reasons willing to take.

Along with the administration, Morse was greatly relieved when Green's second amendment was also defeated, especially since the process had been further delayed in Powell's full committee when the flamboyant New Yorker decided in the middle of deliberations to take an extended holiday at his Bimini retreat in the Caribbean. While Powell, a Baptist minister, eventually opened debate on the House floor with one of the more imaginative prolegomena in congressional history—"Let us not forget the words of the great brooding father when he said that this Nation 'will never perish from the earth' as long as we maintain a government of the people—black and white—for the people—Jew and Gentile—and by the people —Protestant and Catholic"—it was left to Perkins to get the legislation through the House intact. This he was able to accomplish; the bill passed the House on March 26 by a vote of 263 to 153 and moved on to the Senate.

President Johnson announced that he wanted to sign the bill before the Easter break, which meant that Morse had less than two weeks to steer it through the Senate, and to do so without deviating from his no-amendment strategy. Since he had held extensive hearings earlier in the year, his initial task was to get a favorable report first from his subcommittee and then from the full Labor and Welfare Committee. What he got was unanimous approval from both, a coup seldom realized on any significant legislation and almost never on such a highly charged, partisan issue. Eugene Eidenberg and Roy D. Morey, authors of the definitive study of ESEA, explained that the

unanimous vote was indicative of Morse's harmonious relations with the Republicans on the subcommittee rather than of their attitude on the bill. The unanimous vote also reflects a respect and admiration held for Morse by his subcommittee colleagues. The public image of Morse is often that of an outcast and troublemaker.... But when he is out of the spotlight of publicity and working with his fellow senators as a chairman and colleague, his relations are warm and cordial. In the words of a Southern Democrat, he is regarded as "a man of high integrity who is fair, open-minded, honest, and reliable."

With such a unified, bipartisan committee behind him, Morse was able to limit debate to three days, soundly defeating eleven proposed amendments in the process—a feat the *New York Times* described as "one of the year's legislative miracles." (As LBJ remembered it, Morse had convinced his colleagues that "the stakes are too high for the children of America for us to run the risk of jeopardizing this legislation in conference.") The bill passed the Senate 73 to 18, and Johnson signed it on April 9. Amid the subsequent euphoria, the *Washington Star* described a meeting on the Senate floor of what it labeled "the Wayne Morse Fan Club," during which "bouquets were flung at him from both sides of the aisle" by senator after senator, including Mike Mansfield. "Busy, successful, and happy," the *Star* concluded, "Wayne Morse was ... the first clear beneficiary of the education bill of 1965."

The *Star* might have added that the real beneficiaries of ESEA would be the millions of schoolchildren mentioned by Morse who had been forced for generations to endure decrepit, overcrowded, unsafe, and ill-equipped classrooms presided over by instructors grossly underpaid for heroic teaching efforts. The act distributed $1.3 billion among the following categories:

TITLE I—grants to school districts with low-income students (including private-school students) to broaden and strengthen elementary and secondary school programs;

TITLE II—grants for library resources, textbooks, and other instructional materials;

TITLE III—grants for supplemental services and centers in the arts, languages, music, counseling, and educational media;

TITLE IV—grants for cooperative research;

TITLE V—grants for strengthening state departments of education.

Columnist Walter Lippmann described the Elementary and Secondary Education Act as "a great innovation," one that constituted "an epoch-making advance towards the improvement of American education." Said Stewart McClure: "ESEA was the best goddamned thing we did in the sixties."

An encore meeting of the Wayne Morse Fan Club was held the following autumn to celebrate passage (79 to 3) of the $2.5 billion 1965 Higher Education Act. Riding the momentum of ESEA, Morse had engineered legislation that would pump still more money into colleges and universities (including continuing-education programs and community colleges) and, overriding conservative objections, would make funds directly available to needy undergraduates in the form of scholarships, student loans, and work-study grants. The act also established the National Teacher Corps, which would allow thousands of teachers to assist in instructing the nation's poorest schoolchildren. In short, the act included nearly everything that for political reasons had been left out of the Higher Education Facilities Act of 1963. Small wonder the *Oregonian* found Morse near the end of the congressional session "accepting the encomiums heaped upon him by his colleagues." Had Irving Bernstein continued his narrative beyond the Kennedy years, he could easily have crowned Morse in 1965 America's "Heavyweight Champion of Education."

In many ways, 1965 was the high-water mark in Great Society education legislation. Thereafter, all domestic programs would compete for funding with the ever-escalating requests of the military. In a tortured reminiscence of the mid-sixties, LBJ insisted: "If I left the woman I really loved—the Great Society—in order to get involved with that bitch of a war on the other side of the world, then I would lose everything at home." As the record indicates, Johnson did not abandon his first love, nor did he lose his domestic program; but as his involvement with that "bitch" in Southeast Asia continued to grow, he became increasingly less able to manage things on the home front. It is one of the ironies of recent American history that it fell to Morse, Johnson's severest critic on the war, to maintain the impetus on education, despite the budgetary sinkhole that the conflict in Vietnam was becoming.

By keeping the pressure on in 1966, Morse managed to re-fund at increased levels both ESEA and the Higher Education Act, the latter by unanimous vote. But the International Education Act—a program designed to improve high school and college instruction in international affairs—constituted the year's only major piece of new legislation; and while Morse remained hopeful that more could be done, he worried that the exigencies of Vietnam might bring educational reform to a dead stop. As he told an Oregon Democratic state convention, "We may find that an America called upon to organize for war abroad, inflamed into the natural passions of supporting fighting men overseas, to destroy in the name of creating, can lose its zeal and its capacity for internal regeneration."

The war and its budgetary demands were in fact major deterrents to education legislation in 1967, but probably no more than Mrs. Education herself, who was again making trouble in the House. Again the issue was ESEA, but this time the act was up for full reconsideration; and this time, with an administration wounded by dissent over the war, it would be harder to subdue ideological differences or avoid an interchamber conference involving Green. This meant that the tactical end runs around Green that had worked in the past might now be impossible to execute. In 1968, Mike Manatos would predict that "Morse will never do anything which gives the impression he will take direction from 'that woman.'" But a year earlier Morse might, in the interest of keeping a functional education program alive, have to accept the dictates of "that woman" as well as her direction.

Carl Perkins, who had succeeded Adam Clayton Powell as chair of the House Education and Labor Committee, tried to limit Green's impact by holding hearings in the whole committee rather than giving them to her special subcommittee. However, as Mrs. Education (and second-ranking member of the full committee), Green carried enormous authority, so that even though she was not presiding over the ESEA hearings, her good will was regarded as vital to the passage of *all* education bills. The administration tried at the outset to line up her support. However, White House aide Douglass Cater was forced to send a bleak memo to President Johnson stating that "Congresswoman Edith Green is coming to have lunch with me at 1 PM today. As you know, she has been dragging her feet on the Teacher Corps and is now making strange noises of discontent about the Elementary and Secondary Education Act. . . . She is a most difficult woman but I decided to have one more try at reasoning with her. Do you wish to shake hands while she is here? I can't find it in my heart to recommend that you do." Cater appended the following query: "Shake hands with Congresswoman Green? Yes __ No __." Johnson put a huge check mark after "No."

Green's "strange noises" ultimately took the form of amendments, backed by Republicans and conservative Democrats, giving states greater control over key parts of ESEA at the expense of the Office of Education. She also moved to delete the Teacher Corps reauthorization from the House bill, thereby placing its fate in the hands of her subcommittee. Green argued that such changes were necessary to gather enough votes to pass the bill. Critics charged that more state control would mean less civil-rights enforcement, especially in the South, and a less creative approach to new modes of instruction. Stewart McClure felt that, while real, such policy disputes served to conceal darker motivations. "Green," he declared, "was pulling a Neuberger. She was vicious, vindictive, and sought ways to screw things up. And to hear those House members referring to her as 'the gentle lady from Oregon.' As gentle as a hungry snake." Despite much heated debate over her amendments, as Norman C. Thomas wrote, "When the smoke had cleared, only Mrs. Green could claim victory." The amendments of the gentle lady from Oregon had passed the House, as did the bill itself on May 24.

Because it had a June 30 expiration date, Morse had to deal first with the Teacher Corps before revisiting ESEA. And since Green had not obtained passage of a House version until June 20, Morse was forced to accept that version as it stood rather than risk losing the Teacher Corps entirely by passing separate Senate legislation and then having to endure the danger of yet another Senate-House conference. Although Morse put on an amicable public face, and Bob Smith informed readers that Senator Morse and Representative Green had effected a "political reunion" and were now "working harmoniously" (in a letter to the *Oregonian*, Morse had praised Green's "fine record . . . on education"), those on the inside, like Joe Califano, knew that Morse had sacrificed his own agenda to the larger interest of protecting the Corps. Califano reported to Johnson that "on the Teacher Corps, Morse receded on his amendments late this afternoon and agreed to take Edith Green's House bill to the Floor of the Senate tomorrow afternoon. . . . As you know, this was a bitter pill for Morse to swallow (coming from Edith Green) and you may wish to call him this evening and thank him." One assumes that LBJ made the call.

Although Green's bill gave almost total control over recruitment and training of Corps teachers to local authorities and recommended only half the funds the administration had requested, it otherwise expanded the Corps's work in ways that Morse and other liberals could readily accept. Nevertheless, Morse had to fend off several amendments and convince balky senators that they were not being stampeded by the House. He managed to get the bill through by voice vote and then rush it to the White House for Johnson's signature, just beating the expiration deadline—which prompted a relieved Cater to express his "deep admiration for the way you saved the Teacher Corps. It took a lot of doing, but you did it." (At appropriation time, Morse tried to salvage the full $33 million originally asked for, saying he would "get down on both knees" if that would help; but despite an offer some found tempting, his proposal was defeated 45 to 43.)

Whereas only a short time earlier Morse could count on carrying education legislation through committees and the Senate itself with a minimum of opposition, now there would be a parade of impediments. ESEA emerged from the House with several amendments, the two most important of which were turning over total financial control of Title III to the states (sponsored by Green); and requiring a hearing and a finding before funds could be withheld from a school district for not following a desegregation plan, as required by the 1964 Civil Rights Act (offered by L. H. Fountain, a Democrat from North Carolina, with Green's strong support).

Morse worked out clever compromises on both issues, and both squeaked through the chamber. But then senators began to intrude with their own amendments. First, the Senate accepted a proposal by Democrat Sam Ervin of North Carolina making it legally easier to challenge federal assistance to parochial schools. Then Richard Russell, a Democrat from Georgia—speaking for Southerners who coveted federal education money but were still resisting desegregation of their schools—reworked the Fountain amendment, stipulating that once HEW told a school district how much money it was going to get, that district could not have any taken away even if it violated the Civil Rights Act. Morse headed off Russell's effort by getting a letter from HEW Secretary John Gardner assuring Southerners that districts would be informed by the previous spring of possible civil-rights action, and that notice of violations would be given on or before September 1. Acceptance (38 to 35) of what appeared to be a half-hearted compromise was, in the words of Norman C. Thomas, "more a tribute [of] respect for the integrity of Morse and Gardner than any kind of vote of confidence in HEW or the administration"—but since the compromise *was* accepted, there was only the need to reconcile the Senate's ESEA bill with that of the House to pass it into law.

Morse didn't just lead the Senate into conference with the House, he did so with proxies in his pocket from all Democratic and two of the four Republican members of his subcommittee. Thus fortified, and facing a somewhat disorganized collection of fourteen House members, he was able to work out two further compromises. With the first, the Senate gave up Ervin's judicial-challenge amendment in exchange for the House accepting Gardner's letter and dropping the Fountain amendment. According to the second, the states would, as Green wished, take over administering Title III funds, but only on a gradual basis, with Education retaining important civil-rights oversight until 1970. With these provisions agreed to, both houses overwhelmingly passed the conference report, and Johnson signed a revised and renewed (for three years) $9.3 billion ESEA on January 2, 1968.

Morse had done it again. Yvonne Franklin, who was the education correspondent for most of Oregon's leading dailies and who had followed the ESEA debate from the beginning, provided a Greek chorus to his exploits. She depicted Morse as "the never defeated long-distance runner" besieged by "Southern Senators, their togas girded about their withered loins, [trying] to trip Morse . . . by thrusting gnarled toes at him labeled civil rights amendments for white folks." But the senator, she wrote, "waved a baton of mesmerizing sweet reasonableness at them and, one by one, they collapsed by the wayside, their amendments withdrawn or defeated." Further extending her labored metaphor, Franklin went on to chronicle the compromise Morse worked out with Green, whom she saw as a sagacious warrior, "girt in her armor like Minerva herself." Finally, stretching trope to travesty, Franklin concluded that "Morse, his baton held high, sprinted to victory. The education bill was saved, and Wayne Morse did it. As is their wont, the Senators piled garland upon garland of praise upon the victorious Morse. Smiling happily, his bristling eyebrows slowly disappearing under the increasing weight of the garlands, Morse sank quietly through the Senate floor."

If Morse sank through the Senate floor at the end of 1967, he rose quickly enough to enter the next educational marathon in 1968. But while he may have been ready for another sterling race, the Great Society—with Vietnam daily consuming the equivalent of Oregon's entire annual budget—seemed to have lost its heart. Morse was prepared to push for as much as he could get, but he could only express outrage when at the beginning of the year the administration requested a mere $3.7 billion for federal education programs when $6.4 billion had already been authorized by Congress (and when the military budget had skyrocketed to more than $80 billion). Yet however incensed he might be at administration shortsightedness, Morse would do all he could to keep the momentum of the earlier years from being totally squandered.

For the most part, he had to settle for enacting amendments to previous legislation, including the Higher and Vocational Education acts. He sped the former through the Senate in near-record time, but then had to negotiate nearly a hundred points of difference with the House, a process that took until the end of September. Reflecting the temper of the times, the most troublesome difference concerned severe House-proposed penalties to be imposed on federally supported students who engaged in campus disruptions. Overcoming considerable resistance, Morse convinced House conferees that such penalties should be applied only to certain disruptions, those vaguely defined as being "of a serious nature." As for amendments to the Vocational Education Act—also accepted by both houses in September—these were more housekeeping than substantive, but nonetheless important. They had to do, for example, with the disposition of Upward Bound and the future of Head Start, the highly praised preschool enrichment program begun in 1965, which Morse was anxious to see succeed.

Morse was in fact eager to see that not only Head Start, but also Upward Bound, ESEA, Higher Education, and the rest of the breakthrough programs enacted during the preceding several years —nearly sixty separate pieces of legislation—would continue to flourish. But though he took great pride in what he had accomplished during the 1960s—knowing he had opened educational opportunities to impoverished schoolchildren and university students throughout the country—as the leading congressional critic of the Vietnam War, he more than anyone else could see that the Great Society was in political disarray. By the time the 1968 education amendments passed in mid-July, the war had come to dominate the daily headlines, and the national unrest it produced had already caused Johnson to forswear another possible run at the presidency. The future did not look bright.

AFTER NEARLY THREE FULL TERMS as ideological gadfly, Morse had, as far as educational policy-making was concerned, risen to become the Senate's undisputed, unchallenged leader. As such, what he said

and did had come to matter, to have wide-ranging consequences—
not only in Washington, but in statehouses, school districts, and
classrooms across the nation. He had devoted himself unflaggingly
to the education struggle, a struggle whose success he had placed
ahead of his own continuing need for personal recognition. While
working their way through Congress, many of the education bills
had carried Morse's name—the "Morse-Green bill," the "Morse
Higher Education bill"—but none would bear his imprimatur at
final passage. There would be no momentous "Morse Act" inscribed
in the annals of American history. Yet for Morse, accomplishment
in the struggle—getting effective bills through Congress, improving
the nation's educational system, making the world a better place—
seemed to outweigh all narrower considerations, and in a display of
selflessness rarely exhibited before, he appeared to content himself
with the increased respect received from colleagues and the plaudits
of the small circle of educational activists who truly grasped the
magnitude of his achievement.

But now, in 1968, Morse felt that everything he had worked so
diligently for had been placed in jeopardy. Would the federal government continue to care about the education of America's youth?
Could it afford to? Would the progress made in the sixties be con-
veyed at least into the next decade? The answer, in Morse's opinion,
was a melancholy no—not unless Johnson's "bitch," that "God-awful
bloodbath" in Vietnam, was immediately terminated.

In April of 1964, Morse had forecast that if unchecked, the war
would "engulf the resources and manpower of the American people."
In 1968, as a distracted Congress tried to focus on the Higher Education amendments, he offered a new prediction: unceasing approval
of the billions upon billions requested by the military would, he said,
"reduce the domestic advances of the last five years to a memory." In
a degenerative process that continues to this day, history has shown
his prediction to have been distressingly accurate.

13

Vietnam

The protesters against the Vietnamese war are in good historical company. On June 12, 1848, Abraham Lincoln rose in the United States House of Representatives and made a speech about the Mexican War worthy of Wayne Morse.

— J. William Fulbright
The Arrogance of Power

IN HIS 1971 BOOK *THE PRESIDENT'S WAR*, Anthony Austin argues that although Morse's speech opposing the 1964 Tonkin Gulf Resolution was constitutionally sound, it lacked effectiveness because it ran on too long. If, Austin contends, Morse had sat down after stating his central proposition, "the blunt directness of his view, agree with it or not, would have had an impact. But Morse was just warming up. For another hour or more he would smother his major points under a weight of prolixity, amplification, digression, repetition. 'Senators will remember that in 1955 and again in 1957 the senior Senator from Oregon made clear that . . .'." While not as severe as the criticism leveled by Stanley Karnow (see page 6), Austin's reproach implies, as Karnow's does, that with sufficient "impact" Morse could have influenced colleagues to vote against the resolution. Both Austin and Karnow are wrong. In light of the implacable anticommunism of the day and the Johnson administration's manipulation of evidence, no one, in or out of Congress, could have exerted such influence. Blaming Morse for being unpersuasive about impending catastrophe in Vietnam is like blaming Noah for convincing no one of imminent diluvian disaster.

It was certainly true that Morse usually spoke longer than necessary, often far longer. But if ever there was a moment when he was
entitled to extended exposition, the Tonkin Resolution provided it.
Along with the gentlemanly Ernest Gruening of Alaska, Morse saw
what other senators could not or would not see: that giving the president *carte blanche* to commit American military might to Vietnam
was dangerous in the extreme as well as unconstitutional. He had
already agreed with fellow Democratic senator Joe Clark of Pennsylvania that, whatever any member of Congress might say, the
resolution would be unstoppable. Thus he saw it as his obligation to
lecture the chamber—the historical record demanded no less—not
only on the wrongheadedness of the proposal, but also on the critical issues raised by its consideration: the ongoing abuses of military
power by the chief executive and the continual presidential support
of dictatorships abroad.

While Morse's own record on such issues was that of a maverick,
it was nonetheless consistent and clear. It rested on three basic principles: Congress has constitutional responsibility for the power to
make war, a power that must not be relinquished to the White
House; the United Nations must be used, honestly and forthrightly,
as the world's arbiter of international disputes; and under no circumstances should the United States become involved in a land war
in Asia. Standing on such principles, Morse found himself frequently alone in a Cold War world in which the executive branch and the
Pentagon had, in the name of national security, been granted an unprecedented degree of independent power. The Tonkin Gulf Resolution could be seen as one more example of a policy imperative that
had obtained since the end of World War II.

Six months before his death in 1974, Morse observed: "Many
people seem to think that because the Senate passes something, that
makes it constitutional. Well, the Senate can't make something constitutional which is unconstitutional in fact. The authority they
sought to give the President in the Formosa Resolution and the Gulf
of Tonkin Resolution and the Middle East Resolution . . . is just an
unconstitutional act on the part of the Congress as well as on the
part of the President." As the following will indicate, Morse saw the

policies underlying these resolutions as not only patently unconstitutional, but also based on ideas that were ill-considered, irresponsible, and perilously militaristic.

THE FORMOSA RESOLUTION, JANUARY 1955. Spurred by the China lobby and Secretary of State John Foster Dulles, President Eisenhower asks Congress to allow the president to support the Chiang Kai-shek regime against a perceived threat from China, by employing "the armed forces of the United States as he deems necessary for the specific purpose of protecting Formosa [Taiwan] . . . against armed attack." Such authority would include "the taking of such other measures as he judges to be required or appropriate." The resolution passes the House 409 to 3, the Senate 85 to 3, and provides, in the words of D. F. Fleming, a "blank check authorizing the President to make war at any time for Formosa" or its nearby islands.

MORSE'S RESPONSE. Morse has opposed American intervention in Formosa at least since 1950, when, while still a Republican, he debated the issue in the Senate with his party leader (and China lobbyist) William F. Knowland. He votes against the resolution, first at the hearing level as the newest member of the Foreign Relations Committee, then with Herbert Lehman of New York and Republican William Langer of North Dakota to provide the three no votes on the Senate floor. Formosa, he declares, is "a completely dictatorial government," an American "satellite" whose differences with the mainland should be brought before the United Nations. The resolution, he says, allows the president, at his own discretion, to engage in a "preventive war," which "trigger happy" elements have been advocating for years.

Morse warns those senators pressing for the use of atomic bombs on China that "we could not subjugate China by atomic action." He counsels, much as he later would on Vietnam, that "in the last analysis we could not subjugate China by any means except manpower, and that would mean American manpower, with foot soldiers—American foot soldiers. . . . no matter in what language it may be couched, any proposal for a preventive war means not a little war, not a police action, but a total war."

MIDDLE EAST RESOLUTION / EISENHOWER DOCTRINE, 1957–1958.
In early 1957, the president, seeking to broaden the language of the
Truman Doctrine to apply to the Middle East, declares that the United States will, with the approval of Congress, henceforth follow the
Eisenhower Doctrine in foreign affairs. To this end, Eisenhower asks
Congress for the authority to use military force to help nations "requesting assistance against armed aggression from any country controlled by international communism." A "Middle East Resolution"
incorporating such authority passes the House 350 to 60 and the
Senate 72 to 19. In July of the following year, Eisenhower invokes the
doctrine to send thousands of marines into Lebanon to intervene in
a civil conflict against the side that is, he claims, "under the domination of Moscow."

MORSE'S RESPONSE. Morse's is one of the nineteen votes in the Senate against the Eisenhower Doctrine. In a floor debate with John F.
Kennedy he states, "I am not going to vote to give the President any
power to make war in the Middle East by a predated declaration of
war." He describes Eisenhower's ensuing actions in Lebanon as "unconstitutional and authoritarian," insists the conflict is entirely internal to that country, and notes that in reality it "is oil our troops
were sent to defend." In a news release he announces, "I am not in
favor of spilling American blood for oil." "What we need in the Middle East," he tells constituents, "is United Nations intervention, not
American intervention."

In the time between the doctrine's approval and the operations
in Lebanon, Morse despairs that his own Democratic party has gone
the way of the Republicans. He expresses his frustration to his old
ally Herbert Lehman, now retired from the Senate. "Herbert," he
writes, "it is my judgment that the Democrats are fumbling the foreign policy issue."

> I attended the Democratic caucus at the beginning of this
> session and I listened to . . . reports on the investigation
> being conducted by the Senate Preparedness Subcommittee.
> It was a chilling experience. The emphasis was on military
> force. Nothing was said about a peace offensive; no stress was

placed upon disarmament.... Now we have news today that
Dulles once again has surrendered to the international
blackmail of the Arab dictators. You can be sure that Lyndon
Johnson et al will back him up. How we can avoid war is beyond me if the Democratic Party too refuses to face the ...
fact that might has never made right.

VIETNAM, 1954–1964. Although few will know the facts until years
later, the United States is heavily assisting the French in their effort to
retain control of Vietnam. In addition to financial aid, Secretary of
State Dulles offers the French the use of atomic weapons, then tries to
persuade the British to participate in a joint military undertaking
with the U.S. to send troops in support of the French army. Eisenhower decides not to intervene directly when the British turn Dulles
down. After the defeat of the French, the United States refuses to accept the final declaration of the Geneva Conference, which calls for
an orderly cessation of hostilities in Laos, Cambodia, and Vietnam.

In the mid- and late 1950s, while the CIA is involved in numerous secret operations in Southeast Asia, the United States provides
massive support for the Saigon government and training for the
South Vietnamese army. Early in 1962 the American Military Assistance Command (MACV) is installed in South Vietnam; by midyear
the number of American military "advisors" is increased from seven
hundred to twelve thousand. In 1963 American officials authorize the
overthrow of the Ngo Dinh Diem government in Saigon; by the end
of the year the U.S. military force reaches fifteen thousand. In 1964,
before the Tonkin Gulf incident, the Pentagon formulates plans for
bombing North Vietnam.

MORSE'S RESPONSE. In 1954, ten years before Tonkin—when few
Americans had ever heard of Vietnam, let alone thought of Indo-
china as an area of importance—Morse tells an Armed Forces Day
audience at the Umatilla Ordnance Depot in Oregon that "the potentialities of the Indo-China problem are even more grave than the
dangers of Korea." On May 7, 1954, the day the French are defeated
by the Vietnamese at Dien Bien Phu, Morse—replying to colleagues

pressuring the government to assist the French—predicts that the "next time we go to war we will find that we were plunged into it by events, and then the Congress will be called upon to draft a declaration of war, simply to make it legal." He warns a California labor official that to support certain Republicans is to support the "Nixon machine and the Fascist elements it represents. . . . [A] check must be placed upon the Republican party in this country which has come to be dominated by military and reactionary leaders, whose policies . . . threaten to involve us in an Asiatic war without justification." In a "Capitol Cloakroom" interview the following January, he repeats an earlier call to make all of Indochina a UN trusteeship.

In a 1960 pre-election letter to campaign supporter Jason Lee, Morse states prophetically, "It is my judgment that with Kennedy as President, we will be in a war by the end of his third year."

In a September 1963 statement signed by twenty other senators, Morse calls for withholding aid to the Diem government in Vietnam; he refers to that government as "the most tyrannical, dictatorial and atrocious regime on the face of the earth outside the communist world." Later in the year, in what *Newsweek* magazine describes as "a three-week engagement of the swing-along-with-Morse budget-chopping show," Morse leads a senatorial revolt that results in a severe slashing of appropriations for the U.S. foreign-aid program. Morse insists that such action is necessary because instead of going toward national development, money from the program is being funneled "into numbered accounts of Swiss banks," thus serving only to make "the oligarchs richer and the poor poorer."

In 1964, in the months leading up to Tonkin, Morse crisscrosses the country speaking against American involvement in Vietnam; in the Senate, from March 4 through June 18, his remarks on Vietnam policy fill 203 pages of the *Congressional Record*, prompting General Nguyen Khanh, Diem's successor in South Vietnam, to call him a "traitor." According to columnists Rowland Evans and Robert Novak, "What is getting under [LBJ's] skin is the carping criticism of Sen. Wayne Morse of Oregon, who is systematically undercutting the administration's resolve to control the Communist threat in South Viet Nam."

Robert McNamara (shown here at a news conference in 1963) indicated in 1995 that he regretted having accepted Morse's characterization of the Vietnam conflict as "McNamara's War." (AP/Wide World Photos.)

In March, Secretary of State Dean Rusk labels critics of U. S. policy on Vietnam "quitters." To which Morse replies, "The most helpful quitting the Secretary of State could do would be to quit being Secretary of State." He tells a Philadelphia audience in April that the "foremost history lesson of the 20th century is that the white man is through in Asia and Africa. White Americans can no more hope to preserve the remnants and vestiges and fringe benefits of colonialism than white Frenchmen could in . . . Vietnam. American military power and American manhood will be sapped and drained by this war every bit as much as French manhood was sapped and drained."

Morse has been referring to "McNamara's War" since 1961. In an April 1964 press conference, Secretary of Defense Robert McNamara says he is "pleased" to accept Morse's designation. (Thirty-one years later, McNamara will describe his retort as "an impulsive and ill-considered statement that has dogged me ever since.") In a press release that same day, Morse remarks that "aside from the illegality of our intervention, there is the sheer stupidity of a unilateral American land war in Asia, whose only promise is to bog us down there indefinitely. President Johnson may cry 'Peace, peace,' but he will not have peace until he changes what we are doing in Vietnam."

In a speech at Utah State College, Morse castigates narrow-minded legislators for dwelling on the trivial while yielding to the White House on the issues that really matter:

> Having abandoned its responsibilities for the big things, Congress falls back on making the most of the small things. Frustrated members who fear to question the Pentagon brass, the State Department, and the Central Intelligence Agency, concentrate on the full exercise of their more petty powers. ... Having swallowed the camel, Congress strains at the gnats. And the sad thing is that nearly all the proposals for Congressional reform do not treat this major source of sickness.

FOR MORSE, CONGRESSIONAL IRRESPONSIBILITY WAS REVEALED nowhere more than in the 1964 debate over the Tonkin Gulf Resolution. So much has been written about the resolution, the events preceding it, and Morse's resistance to it that it is difficult, looking back, to select the most clearheaded way of discussing it. Rather than reconsider the entire history of the period, I have chosen as a point of departure the argument made by Robert McNamara in his remarkable 1995 book, *In Retrospect: The Tragedy and Lessons of Vietnam.*

What is most striking about *In Retrospect* is McNamara's willingness to admit how "terribly wrong" he and his colleagues were in the decisions they made at critical junctures before and during the Vietnam War. One suspects that had he been alive, Morse would have been astonished and gratified at the sight of the former whiz kid of American defense admitting that he had helped lead the country into one of the greatest disasters in American history. Morse's prediction that those supporting the war would live to regret it is certainly fulfilled in the person of McNamara, and one feels that Morse would have kindly left unnoted the fact that it took the former head of Defense thirty years to deliver his heartfelt *mea culpa.*

But Morse might have been less charitable when it came to the details in McNamara's account of what actually transpired at the time. For all its candor and effort to set the record straight, there is throughout *In Retrospect* a running defense of self in which mistakes, however grievous, are presented as the result of honest misunderstanding, critical misinformation, or unanticipated misadventure, rather than the products of hidden agendas or deliberate attempts to deceive. We are meant to see McNamara not as a G. Gordon Liddy in diplomatic raiment, but as a perspicacious Jimmy Carter in the guise of anguished apparatchik. But the Liddy-like element is ever-present, especially visible in the confrontation over the Tonkin Resolution.

Before reaching the Senate on August 6, the resolution came first to a joint Foreign Relations–Armed Services meeting, during which Morse hotly disputed McNamara's version of what had happened in the Tonkin Gulf. Morse had no reason to question the administration's assertion that North Vietnamese torpedo boats had, a few days earlier, fired on the U.S. destroyer *Maddox,* one of two incidents that presumably had prompted the submission of the resolution to Congress. However, on the basis of a tip from a secret contact in the Pentagon, he felt he had every reason to question the legitimacy of the *Maddox* (and its sister ship, the *Turner Joy*) being in the gulf to begin with—and question it he did, in a speech which McNamara quotes at some length in his book.

> I think we are kidding the world if you try to give the impression that when the South Vietnamese naval boats bombarded two islands a short distance off the coast of North Vietnam we were not implicated.
>
> I think our whole course of action of aid to South Vietnam satisfies the world that those boats didn't act in a vacuum as far as the United States was concerned. We knew those boats were going up there, and that naval action was a clear act of aggression against the territory of North Vietnam, and our ships were in Tonkin Bay . . . standing as a cover for naval operations of South Vietnam.

McNamara uses *In Retrospect* to argue that the United States did *not* oversee the South Vietnamese attacks on the North, nor, he insists, did it act as cover for these attacks: "Our Navy played absolutely no part in, was not associated with, [and] was not aware of any

South Vietnamese actions." "Senator Morse," he continues, "knew
these facts, for he had been present on August 3 when . . . I briefed
the senators." Morse had indeed been in the committee room three
days earlier when McNamara had delivered his belated briefing,
months after the first South Vietnamese attacks had taken place. But
with a maverick's innate suspiciousness, Morse had not accepted
what he was being told as fact. Unlike Foreign Relations chairman
Fulbright, he had a strong feeling he was being lied to about the
South Vietnamese espionage / hit-and-run forays in the North (code
name "OPLAN 34A") and about the U. S. Navy spy ships monitoring
the waters off the North Vietnamese coast (code name "DESOTO").

McNamara's own recollections suggest that Morse had good
cause for suspicion. In describing 34A less than ten pages earlier in
his book, McNamara tells us that the "CIA supported the South Vietnamese 34A operations, and MACV maintained close contact with
them, as did General Krulak of the Joint Staff in Washington." In addition, he states that 34A, like all covert activities involving the CIA,
was approved by the infamous 303 Committee, made up of the president's National Security Advisor (McGeorge Bundy), the Under
Secretary of State (George Ball), the Deputy Secretary of Defense
(Cyrus Vance), and the CIA's Deputy Director for Plans (Richard
Helms). Apparently, McNamara's position is that he was not being
untruthful when he said 34A was not administered by the *Navy*—he
never denied that 34A might have been managed by *other* parts of
the U. S. military. Whatever else such a position is—and it is clearly
an evasion of Morse's charge that the United States was in fact running the show—it is entirely in keeping with the sort of duplicity
that characterized McNamara's congressional testimony throughout
much of the 1960s.

McNamara himself is forced to admit that at least part of his
1964 report was misleading: "I went on to say the *Maddox* 'was not
informed of, was not aware [of], had no evidence of, and so far as I
know today had no knowledge of any possible South Vietnamese actions in connection with the two islands that Senator Morse referred
to.' That portion of my reply, I later learned, was totally incorrect.
. . . My statement was honest but wrong." While meant to demon-

strate *post hoc* veracity, such an admission raises further doubts about McNamara's concept of honesty. The former Defense Secretary conveniently leaves out of his citation his complete response to Morse at the joint-committee hearing. What he actually said was that the Navy ". . . played absolutely no part in any South Vietnamese actions, *if there were any*." McNamara had suddenly cast doubt on the existence of the South Vietnamese raids, the very raids he had outlined to committee members in his previous briefing. Perhaps he thought the senators had extraordinarily short memories. Whatever he thought, his offhand equivocation could only have been meant to cause confusion over events that were not clearly understood to begin with, and it is not surprising that such a remark is omitted in the secretary's 1995 retelling of the story.

Nor is it surprising that in the second part of his quote, McNamara, though he now admits he was wrong about the Navy's awareness of 34A, chooses to omit his arrogant insistence in 1964 that his statement was absolutely indisputable. Originally, when he said the Navy had ". . . no knowledge of any South Vietnamese actions in connection with the two islands that Senator Morse referred to," he added, "*I say this flatly. This is a fact.*" We now know that reliance on such flat assertions—made over and over by McNamara, Rusk, et al. —carried the nation into a decade of agonizing warfare; this is a *truly* unassailable fact, and qualified admissions of inexactness thirty years later do little to mitigate its appalling consequences.

Elsewhere in his book, McNamara recalls that he was sometimes "less than candid" with the media about Vietnam. He might have offered the Tonkin incident as a case in point. In a press interview—not cited in the book—on August 5, the day after the Tonkin Resolution was placed before the joint committee, McNamara was asked the following:

Q. There have been reports that South Vietnamese vessels were . . . taking some sort of action against North Vietnam approximately at this time.

A. No, to the best of my knowledge, there were no operations during the period I was describing last night.

In light of such clear mendacity, it is small wonder that Morse had difficulty swallowing McNamara's artful briefings. The larger wonder is that so few in Congress had a similar problem. Seven years after Tonkin, Senator Paul Douglas would write, "Along with my colleagues, I erred in believing McNamara instead of Morse."

One last observation on *In Retrospect*: McNamara attributes much of the blundering of American policy to ignorance on the part of the policymakers. "I had never visited Indochina," he reports, "nor did I understand or appreciate its history, language, culture, or values. The same must be said, to varying degrees, about President Kennedy, Secretary of State Dean Rusk, National Security Adviser McGeorge Bundy, military adviser Maxwell Taylor, and many others. When it came to Vietnam, we found ourselves setting policy for a region that was terra incognita. Worse, our government lacked experts for us to consult to compensate for our ignorance."

Nowhere is there a plainer indication of what Fulbright meant by the "arrogance of power." Despite an almost complete lack of knowledge or understanding of the area they were dealing with, the military and diplomatic experts, led by McNamara, unhesitatingly "set policy" that would make war inevitable—a brutal war that would, as Morse had predicted, involve hundreds of thousands of casualties. And while it may have been true that the security elite within the administration lacked the requisite expertise, there were, outside the White House, State Department, and Pentagon, innumerable authorities who might—if they had been regarded with anything other than contempt—have provided the necessary comprehension and judgment.

One such authority was Morse, who, with the help of Phyllis Rock, had steeped himself in the recent history of Southeast Asia, studied and mastered the terms of the Geneva Accords ending the French-Indochinese war, and appeared before the National Security Council earlier in the year (on April 3) to offer a viable, nonmilitary solution to the area's problems. But as others had been, Morse was given his few minutes, then immediately ignored by a militantly anticommunist NSC impervious to reasonable opposition. A similar fate would befall Morse in the Tonkin Resolution "debate."

"Ignored" is in reality an imprecise term to describe the NSC's response to Morse. Two months before Tonkin, when the White House had already worked up a resolution and was looking for the most propitious moment to present it to Congress, McGeorge Bundy sent a memo to President Johnson stating that "[CIA director] John McCone has been telling everybody in Government that you can easily get a Congressional Resolution if you want one. . . . I have told him that he should convert Morse first."

There was in fact no real debate over the Tonkin Resolution in the Senate. After refusing Morse's request for committee hearings, Fulbright put the motion on the calendar for August 7. Morse threatened to filibuster unless discussion were allowed on the evening of the sixth; Fulbright relented, and Morse spoke for roughly two hours —mostly for the record, since few senators bothered to attend. His equally long speech the following day was, as previously indicated, also largely for the record, even though on this occasion the chamber was nearly full.

Once again Morse deplored the fact that the resolution granted the president unconstitutional powers, repeated his conviction that the North Vietnamese attacks in the Tonkin Gulf had been reprisals provoked by South Vietnam and the United States, and, echoing his words of the previous day, prophesied that "future generations will look with dismay upon a Congress which is now about to make such a historic mistake." As it had with the Formosa and Middle East resolutions, the Senate allowed Morse his discourse, then scurried to give the president the free hand he had requested. One or two senators—e.g., Democrats Frank Church of Idaho and Gaylord Nelson of Wisconsin—were unsettled by Morse's allegations, but as expected, only Alaska's Gruening joined him in voting no. (The House had already unanimously passed the resolution.) If other members were at all uncertain, they undoubtedly followed the comfortable path taken by Maurine Neuberger, who explained, "When it came to foreign policy, I did whatever Bill Fulbright said I should do."

Over the next year and a half, as the U.S. military force in Vietnam grew to two hundred thousand and the saturation bombing of North Vietnam became a routine news item, Fulbright himself began to question what he and his colleagues had wrought. But since the Foreign Relations chairman was hesitant to condemn administration policy, it was to Morse that the growing antiwar movement looked for inspiration. The *Mamaroneck* (New York) *Daily Times* described a scene at the Westchester Jewish Center that was repeated in lecture halls and meeting rooms across the country: "Sen. Morse entered the crowded hall like a hero, applauded as he walked down the aisle." George H. R. Taylor, working at the time for the AFL-CIO, recalled arriving in New Haven on the same plane with Morse: "We got off, and my god, there was this crowd of Yale students waiting for Wayne that seemed to go on for miles. And there was a band playing. They hoisted him up, and he waved as he was borne away by these adoring students."

For his own part, Morse was slow to become involved in public demonstrations against the war of the kind that had become commonplace at Yale and elsewhere, confining himself initially to speaking out in the Senate and other more traditional venues. He could not, however, say no to joining Dr. Benjamin Spock, Coretta Scott King, and other antiwar principals in June 1965 to lead a massive march through the streets of New York to Madison Square Garden, where a throng of seventeen thousand "roared its approval" as Morse decried America's involvement in "a hopeless war." Thereafter, Morse readily joined such protests when he could, and eagerly called upon others to participate. "What is needed in America," he declared from the floor of the Senate, ". . . is the tramp, tramp, tramp of marching feet in the communities of America, of free people protesting; non-violent demonstrations against the course of action of the United States."

While Morse caused the administration many uneasy moments in 1965 by the sheer relentlessness of his antiwar speech-making, he produced far more than uneasiness with a midyear diplomatic proposal. Because he worked closely with Johnson on education and labor matters, Morse had the president's ear more than many members of Congress, and he used his access whenever possible to try to persuade Johnson to turn the Vietnam problem over to the United Nations. Johnson—more to get Morse out of his hair than because he was truly interested—relented at one point so far as to tell Morse

to send Secretary of State Rusk a written proposal which he, Johnson, would then read and consider.

Morse may be described as America's last great apostle of international law. Unlike the security elite, which, along with most members of Congress, saw the United Nations as an arena for diplomatic one-upmanship or a repository of enemy intrigue, or both, Morse
still retained hope that the UN could become the forum in which
disputes among nations could be debated, settled, and ultimately accepted by contesting parties. With this aspiration in mind, he produced a five-page memorandum for Rusk detailing how perfectly the
Vietnam problem fell under the auspices of the UN Charter and especially the authority of the Security Council. Johnson was due to
speak in San Francisco on the UN's twentieth anniversary,
and at "the risk of being presumptuous," Morse appended a page
of language for LBJ to use in his speech to announce a dramatic shift
in American policy. He wanted the president to tell the world that
the United States stood "ready to be judged by the conscience of

*Because of his important work for the administration on education and labor mat-
ters, Morse had the ear of President Johnson. He continually lectured Johnson on
Vietnam, but the President seldom seemed to listen. (George Tames,* New York
Times *Pictures.)*

mankind as represented in the United Nations." Johnson must have choked on the idea.

Rusk turned Morse's proposal over to McGeorge Bundy, who found it prudent to give it his immediate attention. In a note to LBJ, he wrote:

> I think Morse's memorandum is tightly argued and complex, and if we answer it point by point at this stage, we will be almost sure to trip over ourselves as we make tactical decisions in the coming months. So it seems to me better to give him the soft answer which is suggested in the attached draft. And just because his paper is so well argued, I am sending a copy to [Under Secretary of State] Harlan Cleveland so that in anything we do we can take account of the possibility of flanking fire from Morse.

What Cleveland would do to counter Morse's "flanking fire" is unclear, but the "soft answer" Bundy had in mind consisted of LBJ speaking personally to Morse, presumably to mollify him somehow —without committing the administration to any change in policy, so that all avenues could be kept open for whatever "tactical decisions" the security elite might wish to take.

Bundy's attached draft makes clear precisely how the administration and Morse differed on how to best utilize the United Nations.

> The Morse memorandum makes the tightest case I have seen for taking Vietnam to the UN. . . . As you know, I myself think that we can and should take further initiatives to see what the UN can do about Vietnam. I think this is primarily a tactical matter, designed to show that the Soviet Union is not prepared to desert other "socialist" countries on this issue. The trouble with this tactical approach, of course, is that a man who holds Morse's basic view is likely to denounce it as a fraud unless we take it all the way through and actively work for a resolution which would get us out of there. . . . So I think the underlying difference between us and Morse is not whether we should take the case to the UN,

but what we take it there *for*. I would take it there in order to pin the rose of aggression on the Communists. I think Senator Morse would take it there in order to cover a withdrawal and a Communist takeover.

While Bundy's draft to Johnson was dated June 24, the question of how to respond to Morse was still unresolved on July 7. Secretary Rusk, who had by this time reentered the picture, seconded the idea of a personal conversation, but now Bundy had changed his mind and offered his "own educated guess" that "a confidential letter might have more effect in keeping Morse quiet." Johnson chose the personal approach; and while his conversation with Morse is unrecorded, the evidence suggests that it did not go well. It certainly failed to quiet Morse, who not only maintained his vigorous assault on administration policy, but also went public with the details of his memo to Rusk. That Johnson was more than a little shaken by Morse's attacks is demonstrated by the fact that the president ordered reports on Morse's next Senate speech—which reiterated the call for UN intervention—from both Bundy and Vice President Humphrey. (Johnson also appealed to UN Ambassador Adlai Stevenson to reason with Morse and remind him that it was LBJ who had named him to the Foreign Relations Committee in the first place.)

Humphrey's comments on Morse's Senate remarks reveal that the administration was considering taking Vietnam to the UN *just* to get Morse off its back. It was Humphrey's view that such a move would be unproductive. "Wayne Morse," he warned, "would not modify his position even if we did place the Vietnam issue before the Security Council."

Humphrey was, of course, correct: Morse would never have bought an approach to the UN à la Bundy intended solely to engineer a tactical advantage. And since there would in fact be no sincere effort by the administration to involve the Security Council, and since over the next eighteen months the bombing of the North would intensify even as the number of American troops in Vietnam approached four hundred thousand, Morse, far from modifying his position, would step up the level of his opposition. During 1966, in addition to his almost daily attacks in the Senate, he gave antiwar speeches on sixty-seven separate occasions in twenty-one states. He was being closely followed not only by Johnson, Bundy, Humphrey, and Harlan Cleveland, but also by America's internal-security establishment.

The FBI, the CIA, even Army and Navy intelligence kept Morse under surveillance. His staff was convinced that their office phones had been tapped, and according to Judy, the family residence was similarly bugged. To point out his lack of patriotism, the CIA regularly sent Morse translations of Radio Moscow broadcasts that applauded his criticisms of American policy—including one, for example, in which Morse, referring to the June 1966 bombing of oil depots near Hanoi and Haiphong, was accurately quoted as saying that "American flags all over the world should be lowered to half-mast to deplore this step by the Johnson Administration." In response to the CIA's tactics, Morse publicly condemned the agency's long history of illegal and immoral activities and called for it to be overseen by the Senate as a whole, or at least by the Foreign Relations Committee, and not just by the spinelessly collusive Armed Services Committee.

When in 1966 Morse inserted into the *Congressional Record* ninety-three antiwar letters from citizens who had written to him, LBJ secretly ordered FBI agents to "seek derogatory information" on all ninety-three. If Johnson hoped to frighten Morse's supporters into silence, he would need a thousand FBIs to do the job. Although he did not place every one into the *Congressional Record*, Morse received over twenty thousand pieces of mail on Vietnam between February 22 and March 22 and another forty thousand over the next three months. So heavy was the influx that local Democratic party volunteers had to be called in to help sort through the letters and telegrams.

With few exceptions, the incoming deluge was supportive of Morse and helped to sustain him against attacks from the administration and most of the media. He was especially pleased to receive a note from the AP's South Vietnam bureau chief, Malcolm Browne, who wrote from Saigon to say, "Your voice has been one of the very few retaining the courage of dissent. Thank God there is still Wayne

Morse in the Senate." Occasionally, criticism from a constituent reached his desk and might rankle slightly, as, for example, when a Salem voter wired, "You are wrong about Viet Nam. You should resign now." Morse wired back, "You will be no more successful in removing the blood from your hands than Macbeth." Normally, however, when Morse responded personally, he typically thanked hawkish correspondents for their views and tried to convince them of how wrong they were and how deeply he felt on the matter.

Few understood the depth of Morse's emotion on Vietnam. The war was not just another controversial policy matter, but a tragedy of epic proportions which he had dedicated himself to overcoming. And if Macbeth (or, more correctly, Lady Macbeth) was on his mind, Morse saw such a role embodied in the person of Rusk, acting "the innocent flower" but living "the serpent under it." And yet, while he might revile Rusk, McNamara, Bundy, and the rest of the Washington establishment for their part in the tragedy, the administration figure he felt worst about was the man whose job it was to defend the U.S. position to the rest of the world: America's ambassador to the UN, Adlai Stevenson.

Next to Bob La Follette, Stevenson had been Morse's political hero—his man in 1952, the one he had left the Republican party to support; his man again in the 1956 election; and, as "one of the greatest minds in American public life," still his man in 1960, despite Stevenson's refusal to take on Kennedy at the Democratic convention. After the 1960 election, while Stevenson was considering the UN offer from Kennedy, Morse wrote him a long letter of advice in which he cautioned, "If you are to accept the United Nations assignment, you must insist . . . that the jurisdiction and nature of the job be changed." Morse argued that the "position should be that of Secretary of State for United Nations Affairs," a cabinet slot equal in rank to that of the traditional Secretary of State. He continued:

> If this job is left on an ambassadorial level, then you are performing a great disservice to the country. . . . You have an opportunity and a duty to insist on raising this post . . . as a condition precedent to your accepting it. If you don't do it,

Adlai Stevenson had been Morse's political hero, and Morse could not understand why Stevenson was willing to defend McNamara's policies on the war. (Oregon Historical Society, OrHi 93521.)

you will never be able to make a success of it, but what is much more important, great harm will be done to our country within the United Nations. . . . You should insist on . . . being protected from Pentagon Building interference with American foreign policy decisions.

Morse added that it was particularly urgent that Stevenson demand "such a blue print" because Kennedy's first Secretary of State could turn out to be someone as repugnant as, for example, Dean Rusk or J. William Fulbright.

When Stevenson accepted the UN ambassadorship from Kennedy, he did so with no preconditions. He agreed to stay on at the UN when Johnson became president and, as a well-behaved diplomat under both administrations, defended whatever policies were set by his superiors in Washington. Finding it increasingly hard to accept Stevenson in such a position, Morse wrote to him in 1964, making no effort to conceal his irritation: "I realize that your position as United States Ambassador to the United Nations is a delicate one. Nevertheless, I think the American people are entitled to know whether or not you agree with the policy of our Government in sending American boys to their death in South Vietnam in absence of a declaration of war. If you do, I think you should say so publicly so that those of us who disagree with such a policy can take your position into account." As he would whenever Morse pressed him, Stevenson replied with evasiveness. "It goes without saying," he wrote, "that the questions you have raised are serious and thoughtful, and deserve a thoughtful answer. I shall get around to this as soon as the situation lets up a little here at the United Nations."

Contributing to the UN "situation" was a speech on Southeast Asia Stevenson had delivered the previous day advancing the positions of McNamara and Bundy. For Morse, that speech marked his hero's final fall from greatness. To a Portland correspondent he wrote:

> One of the great tragedies in the whole affair has been the conduct of Adlai Stevenson. . . . He should have resigned his position as Ambassador to the United Nations before he loaned his lips to reading before the Security Council the speech that was written for him in the State Department. When I said . . . on the floor of the Senate that by reading that speech he extinguished his light of world statesmanship and became Humpty Dumpty, I, in fact, described a great personal tragedy. Why Adlai Stevenson, I will never be able to understand.

Morse would never fully grasp the fact that for all his wit and intellect, Stevenson was, like most of his peers, a Cold War ideologue, ready when asked to proffer the most self-serving of policy rationales in defense of anticommunism.

If Morse could not comprehend Stevenson's motivation, he would have no such difficulty understanding that of another, more outspoken Cold War protagonist, General Maxwell Taylor, former chairman of the Joint Chiefs of Staff and for more than a year the

American ambassador to South Vietnam. Although it had taken a considerable time for Fulbright to reverse himself on Vietnam, he had begun in the months following the Tonkin Resolution to understand that he had been lied to by the administration, and, like Morse, he had come to view White House responses to questions from Congress primarily as exercises in propaganda. In an effort to get straight answers, his Foreign Relations Committee held five days of public hearings on Vietnam over a two-week period in February of 1966. Watched on television by up to thirty million viewers, the hearings featured, along with Secretary of State Rusk, retired General Taylor, no longer ambassador to South Vietnam but still one of Johnson's chief advisors on the war.

Taylor, known as "Mr. Attack" for his aggressive maneuvers during World War II, read a prepared statement stoutly defending American policy—particularly the bombing raids, which, he assured the committee, were giving the North Vietnamese no "enjoyment." Shortly thereafter came the following exchange:

> MORSE: I happen to hold the point of view that it isn't going to be too long before the American people will repudiate our war in Southeast Asia.

> TAYLOR: That, of course, is good news to Hanoi, Senator.

> MORSE: I know that is the smear . . . that you militarists give to those of us who have honest differences of opinion with you, but I don't intend to get down in the gutter with you and engage in that kind of debate.

Morse's remark produced a burst of applause in the hearing room. It also generated another onslaught of mail, some correspondents wondering whether it was wise to lose one's temper against such a luminary with much of the nation watching. Morse replied that he had no choice but, in his words, to "nail General Taylor's smear," for to do otherwise would be to acquiesce in the use of "McCarthyite tactics" against opponents of the war. To his old rhetoric master Smiley Blanton, he explained that he had in no way lost his composure, but had reacted "very calmly," under the circumstances.

What Blanton and others did not know was that Morse had, as the result of previous experience with the Taylor family, come prepared to deal with broadside assaults on his loyalty. When he had opposed Taylor's ambassadorial appointment in 1964 and had said so both in the Foreign Relations Committee and on the floor of the Senate, he received the following handwritten letter:

Sir

So now the sage of Oregon counsels that the appointment of Gen. Maxwell Taylor would be a national calamity. Senator, if you possessed one half of the wisdom, one quarter of the intelligence, or one eighth of the selfless patriotism of General Taylor, you would [direct] such utterance to the Communists.

Sincerely,
Capt. Thomas Taylor
(his son)

To which Morse replied:

It is obvious from your letter of July 1 that you do not possess either the sagacity or the brains of your distinguished father. . . . The extraordinary situation that exists in South Vietnam made it more desirable to appoint a civilian experienced in diplomatic relations as our Ambassador in South Vietnam rather than a military man. . . . I think it was a great mistake to make him our Ambassador in Saigon.

All that had happened since Taylor's appointment had only lowered the general in Morse's estimation. Now, there would be no recognition of sagacity or distinction. Taylor had become, as Morse informed Blanton, "one of the most dangerous men in the country."

While Morse's attitude toward Taylor and the rest of the security elite could not have been more explicit, his feelings about Johnson, especially in the earliest days of Vietnam, had been ambiguous. It had been McNamara's war first and foremost, with the complicitous involvement of the Rusks, Taylors, Bundys, et al., abetted by the fervent hawks and mindless camp followers on the Hill. The president, Morse had said on several occasions, had been getting poor counsel from those he relied on for guidance in foreign policy. But by the spring of 1966, with Great Society funding showing signs of diminishing, Morse could no longer avoid the obvious. Taking direct aim at the Oval Office, he said, "I blame nobody but Johnson for our predicament in Vietnam—not his advisers, not anybody but Johnson." And if at last LBJ could be tagged with full responsibility for Vietnam, it might also be the right moment to look for someone other than Johnson to move the nation in a new direction. Morse already had that someone in mind.

In March, Morse startled the Oregon state Democratic convention—as well as Democrats around the country—by announcing that if Bobby Kennedy continued to intensify his opposition to the war, he would back RFK for president in 1968. Later in the year he declared that Kennedy, who despite being critical of the war had been unwilling to repudiate his party's leadership, had "a duty to go after the nomination." It was not that Morse saw Kennedy, with whom he had never felt especially collegial, as the best possible option, but, as he told innumerable correspondents, he knew of no "other person on the political horizon that could take on Johnson and beat him in 1968. I . . . have my reservations about him, but I would much prefer him to Johnson [and] his policy of slaughtering American soldiers in South Vietnam."

Other antiwar activists wondered at Morse's determined support for Kennedy, an avowed noncandidate who, for all his dissatisfaction, was plainly reluctant to break with the administration. Morse's resoluteness may have been partly an effort to force the issue and bring pressure on *both* Johnson and Kennedy, but it may also have been the result of his conviction that shortly before the assassination, John Kennedy had been ready to overhaul American foreign policy and de-escalate U. S. involvement in Vietnam. If JFK had in fact been prepared to make such a drastic change, mightn't his younger brother, a growing critic of the war, be even more prepared to follow suit? Morse could consider the second part of this question because he firmly believed there was no "if" involved in the first. Not everyone shared his certitude.

Indeed, Morse's conclusion, repeated many times over the years, that President Kennedy was about to reverse himself on Vietnam gave rise to a historical debate that is still alive today. Morse strolled with JFK through the White House Rose Garden ten days before Dallas. During the walk, Kennedy reportedly said, "Wayne, I want you to know you're absolutely right in your criticism of my Vietnam policy. Keep this in mind. I'm in the midst of an intensive study which substantiates your position on Vietnam." Writing in 1978, Kennedy insider Arthur Schlesinger used this statement, along with those of others close to the scene, to suggest that JFK would have brought an early end to the war. Certain later historians have relied on the Rose Garden conversation to come to a similar conclusion.

To support the idea that Kennedy might have laid down "peaceful" footsteps which his brother could fruitfully follow, Morse would have had to assume that the same McNamaras, Rusks, and Bundys who had set policy under both JFK and LBJ would have moved with Kennedy in an opposite direction in 1964. There is, however, no conclusive evidence that either they or the president were ready to effect such a dramatic reversal. The best one can say is that John Kennedy seemed deeply ambiguous in his public statements, simultaneously maintaining that the struggle was at heart a Vietnamese problem *and* that the U. S. had a moral obligation to stay in Vietnam to the end— while, behind the scenes, planning for a much-enlarged conflict proceeded apace. Even Schlesinger admits that President Kennedy left a "hopelessly divided legacy" on Vietnam; and it seems clear today that had Bobby lived to become president, he would have had to find a path to peace entirely his own. Right or wrong about JFK's intentions, Morse would have been happy to help point Bobby in the right direction.

Meanwhile, as the war escalated, so did the need for money to finance it. Thus, the administration returned again and again to Congress for supplemental appropriations, over and above the funds already budgeted for defense, to pay for the manpower and matériel requested by the Pentagon. Most senators, even most of those opposed to the war, were invariably persuaded that "our boys" had to have whatever they needed on the front, whether we wanted them there or not. Though subjected to considerable abuse for their stand, Morse and Gruening (and on certain votes Gaylord Nelson) refused to accept this argument. Morse, at his maverick best, proclaimed that he would "vote against every Defense appropriation request of this administration until it changes American military foreign policy. I shall not sit in the Senate and vote one single dollar to continue to kill American boys in southeast Asia.... Only when Congress begins to use its check of the purse strings on the President of the United States will we stop the killing."

Morse had another ploy which would, if successful, force a change in policy. Against the wishes of confederates in the small but growing antiwar faction in Congress, he insisted in February 1966 that the Senate formally reconsider the Tonkin Gulf Resolution. Most doves felt that reconsideration would result in a resounding defeat and be interpreted as a victory for Johnson. Their fears were largely realized when Majority Leader Mansfield's motion to table and thereby kill Morse's proposal to repeal the resolution carried 95 to 5, with only Gene McCarthy, Stephen Young, and Fulbright joining Morse and Gruening in opposition.

While many in the peace movement wondered why Morse had persisted in a tactic so clearly doomed to failure, it seems probable that the vote itself was not his first priority. His motion accomplished two things. Because of Morse's skillful manipulation of parliamentary rules, the Senate was compelled to debate the issue for a full two weeks—the two weeks immediately following the televised hearings. This gave many senators, including a few who had previously been silent, an opportunity to voice their concerns about Vietnam, even though they could not refuse, in the words of Democratic whip Russell Long of Louisiana, "to unite behind the President in time of war." Furthermore, the issue served to force Fulbright's hand. With his vote, the reticent Foreign Relations chairman finally and totally repudiated his part in the Tonkin Gulf Resolution and moved irrevocably into the camp of the doves. Those who, like Maurine Neuberger, had automatically followed the powerful chairman's lead in 1964 could be expected to ponder their support of the war in the future.

Fulbright's vote to rescind Tonkin also put an effective end to what was left of the chairman's relationship with the president, a relationship that had been badly deteriorating over the previous two years. Ironically, while communication between LBJ and Fulbright came to a halt, the Morse-Johnson connection seemed to grow stronger. As late as March of 1967, Johnson could drop the following note: "Dear Wayne, I am leaving for Guam in a few minutes to try to get your peace in Vietnam"—this despite the fact that Morse had begun wondering aloud whether the president should be impeached. No such note would be sent to the Democrat from Arkansas—"Senator Half-bright," as Johnson had taken to calling him—nor could Fulbright, uncomfortable as rebellious outsider, engage in the following sort of persiflage with the president. When, at the White House one day, Johnson asked him how he managed to stay so healthy-looking, Morse replied: "Well, Mr. President, I'll tell you. Every time I read in the papers what you're doing about Vietnam, it makes my blood boil. That purges me, it keeps me fit."

The special nature of the tie between Morse and LBJ did not go unnoticed by those who saw it firsthand:

JOHNSON AIDE JOE CALIFANO: If the Johnson-Fulbright relationship is the how-not-to of presidential personality politics, the Johnson-Morse relationship is the how-to.

JOHNSON AIDE GEORGE REEDY: I'm absolutely convinced that there was genuine affection between those two men. And yet Morse did the most outrageous things. . . . Wayne would constantly implant his foot right in Johnson's groin, and yet a few days later they would be bosom buddies.

JOHNSON AIDE JACK VALENTI: At midday, the irascible senator from Oregon would rise in the Senate Chamber and in the most furious and virulent manner attack the President for a multitude of sins, and denounce him for an impressive number of shortcomings. The next morning, Morse would be sitting at breakfast with the President discussing, at the President's request, a labor problem, and giving counsel to the president on how it could be solved. Before the meeting would end, they would invariably chide each other in high humor about the quality of the bulls they raised and the off-spring sired by their masters of the herd.

While such colorful stories about how the two men got along were legion—similar tales were told about earlier quarrels and rec-onciliations in the Senate—the truth was that, as Valenti implied, Johnson needed Morse, just as he had needed him in 1964, and as leader of the Great Society he could not afford to break with him, however damaging Morse's foreign-policy attacks might be. And while it may be too much to say that Morse also needed Johnson, it was certainly the case that he reveled in the role Johnson helped create for him on the domestic scene. This unusual mutuality would be put to the test, not only in the debate over the war, but in the area of national labor negotiation, where Morse's expertise was in heavy demand.

MORSE MAY HAVE BEEN CONTENT to remain out of the education-al spotlight in the 1960s, but he had no such choice when it came to the high-profile field of labor. Early in 1963, he reluctantly left a For-eign Relations Committee hearing—Rusk was reporting—to an-swer a phone call from President Kennedy. JFK persuaded him to head a three-person team to settle a strike of sixty-two thousand longshoremen that for thirty days had paralyzed every major port along the East and Gulf coasts, causing shipping losses into the bil-lions. Morse, the first sitting senator ever appointed to such a panel, was suddenly thrust back into his old job as waterfront arbitrator.

It was as if he had never been away. Immediately, he informed the press that there was no such thing as "a labor case that could not be settled by good-faith negotiation," and after the first day's session he could report the "splendid cooperation" received from both parties—a reason, he said, for "really inspired optimism." By the end of the second day of nonstop, nonsleep negotiating, Morse and his fellow mediators—both from the private sector—had a proposal ready; by the end of the fifth, an agreement. Suddenly the strike was over, demonstrating that even in the most intractable of cases, Morse still had his uncanny touch for bringing labor and management together.

Twelve months later almost to the day, Morse helped settle another strike on the East and Gulf coasts, this time returning 65,000 of the 75,000 dockworkers who had been out for thirty-three days, one day less than in the previous year's stoppage. Unlike in the earlier case, however, Morse was in effect co-opted directly into the administration, serving at the behest of Johnson on a panel alongside Labor Secretary Willard Wirtz and Commerce Secretary John Conner. By the time the second strike was settled, it had become clear that, the separation-of-powers doctrine notwithstanding, whenever the president had a difficult labor dispute on his hands, he would not hesitate to turn first to the legislative branch for the intervention of the senator from Oregon.

Morse was herding cows in Poolesville when the next call came, in late August 1965. An anxious Johnson wanted to fetch him from the farm via White House helicopter so that, with Under Secretary of Commerce LeRoy Collins as his partner, he could begin working at once to head off an impending nationwide strike by 350,000 steelworkers. Morse declined the chopper ride, but he spent the next twenty-four hours looking into the situation. He quickly became convinced that normal collective bargaining between the steelworkers' union and the industry had become hopeless: the two parties could be brought together, he believed, only if the president himself became involved in the proceedings. Morse argued that Johnson, with a government-backed set of recommendations in hand, should bring representatives of both sides into his office for an extended negotiating session. Against the advice of Wirtz and Conner, who felt that for political reasons the president should keep his distance, Johnson decided to follow Morse's suggestion. When it worked and an agreement was reached, he and Morse proceeded to engage in a bouquet-throwing contest that had to amaze those who saw the two solely as obdurate combatants over American foreign policy. Johnson: "If it hadn't been for you, Wayne, we might have a steel strike on our hands right now." Morse: "Don't kid yourself, Mr. President. It was you who did it."

The following year would see fewer congratulatory exchanges, as both the administration and Congress sought ways to meet the stubborn demands of the airline-machinists' union. In what had become routine procedure, Morse received a call from the White House in April of 1966. This time, however, Johnson didn't bother to ask. "Wayne," he said, "my ox is in the ditch and I want you to help me get it out. I am appointing you as head of the mediation panel to prevent a strike on the airlines. I just wanted you to know it before you read it in the papers."

Morse's charge was to seek an agreement between the International Association of Machinists and Aerospace Workers (IAM) and five of the nation's leading airlines (Eastern, National, Northwest, TWA, and United) that adhered to the 3.2 percent inflation limit placed on wage and benefit increases by the administration. Morse and his two colleagues had two months to complete their work, Johnson having invoked a sixty-day no-strike provision of the Railway Labor Act, a statute understood to cover airline as well as railroad employees. The panel issued a report on June 5 proposing an annual increase of 3.5 percent, close enough to administration guidelines for an eager Johnson to endorse it without hesitation. One day later the IAM, which had been asking for 5 percent, rejected the proposal, and its thirty-four thousand members went on strike the moment the sixty-day period was over.

Morse had anticipated a possible union turndown, but had expected workers to stay on the job pending a further round of vigorous negotiating. He contended not only that the "strike cannot be justified on any basis whatsoever," but also that it was "not reconcilable with the patriotic responsibility of the Union to its government, and to the people of our country, including our troops in Vietnam." To counter the strike, he proposed government seizure of the airlines. But he got no support for such a move from Wirtz, who, whatever he thought privately, said in public that he did not believe the strike— which had stranded thousands of travelers at airports throughout the country—constituted a national emergency. Morse then recommended congressional action to seek a court order forcing machinists back to work for a specified length of time while negotiations resumed. He issued a press release stating: "It is the clear duty of the men to go back to work at once. The national interest, the national health, safety and defense, and their own civic duty require it."

The union retaliated. Pugnacious IAM president P. L. (Roy) Siemiller declared that "Sen. Morse is wrong again, just as he is wrong in Viet Nam." In its house publication, *The Machinist*, the union designated its longtime ally a "strikebreaker" and noted that his stand on Vietnam indicated a suspicious lack of anticommunist zeal. In Oregon, the *Labor Press* accused him of "leading the pack of congressional wolves" out of sheer "vanity." Morse was convinced that the latter piece had been planted by AFL-CIO president George Meany, his former colleague on the War Labor Board. Thus, when AFL-CIO lobbyists had him paged from a Senate session to express their views on another matter, Morse exploded. Standing on his maverick's creed, he said: "Because you supported me, don't get the idea you own me. Tell Meany," he added, "I'll fight for labor when it's

Morse in a 1966 White House meeting with Johnson aides (from left) David Ginsberg, Cyrus Vance, and Joseph Califano and Attorney General Nicholas Katzenbach. Under discussion was the 1966 airlines strike. (Wayne Morse Collection, CN 1311, Special Collections, University of Oregon Library.)

right and I'll fight against labor when it's wrong. . . . Don't call me off
the floor again," he concluded, "and tell Meany to go to hell."

Morse had been placed in the awkward position of criticizing an
action of his traditional backers in organized labor, an action he defined as unpatriotic because it was detrimental to a military effort he
vehemently opposed. This argument gave the AFL-CIO, undeviating
hawks on Vietnam, an opportunity to attack *his* antiwar actions as
unpatriotic for similar reasons. Morse was forced to prepare an
eight-page, single-spaced form letter in an effort to explain himself
to a multitude of confused constituents. Contained in the letter was
the following paragraph: "Don't forget we are at war. Although I
think it is an unjustifiable war, nevertheless, as long as we are in it, all
of us here at home have a clear duty to follow an economic course of
action that will promote the public interest, not injure it." In light of
their senator's repeated votes against appropriating funds for the war,
it is unlikely that Oregonians found such an argument convincing.

Meanwhile, after one settlement had been accepted by IAM leaders but then vetoed by the union membership, an agreement was finally reached, just as Congress, under Morse's direction, was about
to enact mandatory back-to-work legislation. The strike had lasted
forty-three days and had ended in victory for the machinists, who,
with White House acquiescence, got nearly everything they had demanded, leaving Morse to grumble that the "inflationary spiral" had
become "an inflationary tornado."

Given that he had emerged from the airline strike with something less than distinction, and that in the process he had alienated
the machinists' leadership, it came as a surprise the following year
when Morse was called in yet again by the administration to deal
with a labor issue, especially since that issue involved threatened action by those very same machinists. In late January 1967, Johnson
again invoked the Railway Labor Act to block for sixty days a strike
of 140,000 railroad maintenance workers—including members of
the IAM—against the nation's major carriers. A mediation board
then recommended a settlement, but its terms were rejected by the
unions, most vociferously by the IAM. Morse introduced and floor-
managed an administration bill he had helped to write requiring a

ninety-day strike delay, during which a mediation team would issue a report whose terms would, failing an agreement, become compulsory for up to two years. The bill passed the Senate but stalled when a House conference committee refused to accept the Senate's version. After a standoff between the two chambers ran on for several weeks, the unions, led by Siemiller and the machinists, went on strike.

With national railroad traffic at a dead stop, and with McNamara and the Pentagon complaining that the war effort was being seriously impaired by the disruption, it took Congress but two days to enact Morse's bill. Then, to the surprise of nearly everyone concerned, Johnson appointed Morse to head the team that would mediate the dispute. Even though Meany was among the other four panel members, many labor officials cried foul. "We're speechless," said one. "This is like giving us the back of the hand." Another echoed Siemiller in labeling Morse "the biggest strike breaker in the nation." When the panel finished its work, however, the annual 5 percent increase for two years stipulated in its binding report was far closer to the unions' figure than that offered by the carriers. It was thus not surprising that Meany signed off without comment, while the big-business appointee, Frederick Kappel, former board chairman of AT&T, did so only under protest. Despite the fact that Morse had met the railroad workers more than halfway, his legislation had in fact broken the strike, and for his efforts he had earned the heated animosity of some of the country's most powerful unions.

Which raises the question of why Johnson had appointed him to head the mediation team and why he had accepted the job, particularly since he had been steadily in labor's line of fire since the airline strike and since other, more publicly neutral mediators were readily available. In naming him, Johnson told Morse he had gotten the "black bean." Joe Califano recalled that when Morse had asked LBJ what he was talking about, Johnson related a story about members of a nineteenth-century Texas military expedition who were taken prisoner by Mexican soldiers. Since the jails were too small to hold all the captives, a kind of lottery was held in which each Texan had to close his eyes and pick a bean from a plate. White beans went to a jail cell; black were executed. "In late 1968," wrote Califano, "Morse would understand what LBJ had meant by [getting] the black bean."

Supreme Court Justice William O. Douglas gave a firsthand account of what the president had indeed meant. Douglas met with Johnson shortly after the strike was concluded and the settlement had become law. After derogating Morse, Fulbright, and other opponents of the war, Johnson explained why, in his words, "I decided to make Wayne chairman."

> First I told him that I had read in the paper his statement that it was too bad Goldwater had not been elected in 1964, for [then] the Republicans would [have been] saddled with Vietnam. I said that if Goldwater had been elected I would not be honoring Wayne Morse with this call. Wayne is a vain man, and when I told him I had drafted him for the railway labor job, I said, "Wayne, all the labor law I ever knew I learned from you. You are my teacher." With that buttering up, Wayne took the job. Now, I knew it was a decision he'd have to make against labor. He's coming up for re-election in 1968. I knew his assignment would defeat him in that election. You just wait and see. And then tell me who the smartest one is—Wayne or LBJ?

When I showed Douglas's recollection—recounted in his 1980 autobiography—to congressional and executive personnel who had worked in Washington in the sixties, most tended to discount it as exaggeration or intentional distortion on Douglas's part. After all, they argued, Johnson depended on Morse in both education and labor and could not afford to lose him; and besides, everyone knew that whatever their differences, they got along well and were certainly not personal enemies. While theoretically valid, this analysis misses real-life factors that influenced both men.

There is at the outset no cause to doubt either the accuracy of Douglas's memory or the possibility that Johnson could engage in such intrigue. Though a man of acknowledged passions, Douglas was noted for descriptive exactitude, and in any event he would have had no reason to invent such a story thirteen years after the fact. As far as Johnson was concerned, we know from any of several LBJ biographies that he was capable of the most ornate and vengeful plotting.

That Morse had been berating him without letup on Vietnam Johnson could tolerate, as he could Morse's conjecture about why it would have been better to have had a Goldwater victory in '64. According to Califano, LBJ could even shrug off Morse's talk about impeachment. But to carry antiwar sentiment as far as an endorsement of Bobby Kennedy—that smart-assed, Harvardized, Back Bay Irishman, whose family had for three years treated him like dirt—this was surely more than Johnson could stand. However much affection he had harbored for Morse in the past—and one suspects that for all its public display, it was never more than necessity required—that affection ceased when Morse joined the camp of the enemy.

Furthermore, Morse had lost much of his usefulness to what might be left of Johnson's domestic program. Because he had, partially at Johnson's instigation, become *persona non grata* in important labor circles, Morse could never be the functionary he had been in the past, someone able to act simultaneously as a neutral arbitrator *and* a protector of union rights. As for education, Morse had by 1967 begun earnestly attacking the administration for shortchanging the academic needs of America's youth, for caving in to the demands of the military at the expense of the Great Society. Morse, in short, had become a liability. Whatever benefit he could bring to the president no longer outweighed his obvious negative impact as a self-proclaimed Kennedyite assaulting administration policy at every turn. Johnson would not think twice about getting rid of him.

And Johnson's observation about Morse's vanity was also to the point. Typically oblivious to what others thought of him, Morse was always vulnerable to flattery, and even the most trivial of compliments, if delivered from on high, could at times be enough to turn his head. In 1962, for example, he wrote to future Oregon governor Bob Straub to tell him, among other things, how rapturous he was over a note he had just received from President Kennedy. "I am still walking on clouds," Morse exulted, "because in his letter [JFK] says: 'Your explanation of the position taken by the United States at Punta del Este was the clearest and most concise yet put forth.'" Johnson, the past master of all flatterers, who liked to address Morse

By playing on Morse's ego, Johnson was able to persuade Morse to be his primary troubleshooter in management-labor disputes. Here Johnson attempts to work his wiles on Morse aboard Air Force One. (Wayne Morse Collection, CN 1314, Special Collections, University of Oregon Library.)

as "Professor," knew far better than Kennedy how and when to play on Morse's ego to achieve a desired result, even to the point of getting Morse to position himself on labor issues so that he contradicted his deepest feelings about Vietnam.

Journalist Ken Johnson recalled a moment in 1962 when LBJ, as vice president, appeared in Medford at a Morse campaign event. "Johnson said all the usual nice things—Wayne Morse is a great senator who understands foreign policy, and so on—nothing terribly elaborate, but the Senator was really ecstatic that he was getting this praise. He was almost awestruck, his eyes nearly glazed. I had never seen that before." Knowing that Morse, for all his toughness, was susceptible to a fulsome application of Oval Office eyewash, it is clear that Johnson, from his elevated station as "Mr. President," could set the Professor up in 1967 for a fall in 1968. It seems equally clear that Johnson tried to engineer precisely such a setup.

Could it work? Could Johnson bring Morse down after twenty-four years in the Senate? That question would be answered in less than a year.

14

A Maverick's Dénouement

IN THE ANNALS OF AMERICAN HISTORY, 1968 will be remembered
as a year of uninterrupted political turbulence: the year Lyndon
Johnson declined to seek a second term after Eugene McCarthy
nearly beat him in the New Hampshire primary; the year Robert F.
Kennedy embarked on his own presidential quest, only to be shot to
death in Los Angeles upon capturing the California primary; the year
civil-rights leader Martin Luther King, Jr., was assassinated in Memphis, causing rioting and unrest in major cities throughout the country; the year police violently attacked antigovernment demonstrators
during the Democratic national convention in Chicago; and, with a
turbulence of its own, the year a campaign was launched to win a
fifth consecutive term for Senator Wayne Morse of Oregon.

Because Oregon was insulated from much of the general turmoil
in 1968, only some of what happened nationally—the Eugene Mc-
Carthy phenomenon in particular—bore directly on Morse's reelection effort. More important were events that had occurred two
years before, when Maurine Neuberger decided not to run for another six years in Washington. To succeed her, Oregon's Democratic leaders, with Neuberger herself in the forefront, promoted a hawk
for the Senate: tough-talking, two-term representative Bob Duncan,
a forty-five-year-old attorney from Oregon's fourth congressional
district. His opponent was Mark Hatfield, who, having served two
sessions as governor, was eager to become the first Republican U. S.
senator since Guy Cordon lost to Dick Neuberger in 1954.

Appalled that his party had put up a prowar candidate, Morse
talked his old confrere and fellow dove Howard Morgan into running against Duncan for the 1966 Democratic nomination. Together,

they launched what the *New York Times* called the "'Wayne and Howard' show," a hard-hitting, well-financed primary effort that greatly annoyed party regulars and their supporters in organized labor, who believed that only by unifying behind Duncan could they defeat the popular Hatfield. For his part, Morse took it as a personal affront that labor continued to support Duncan even after Morgan entered the contest. He told Building and Construction Trades president C. J. Haggerty that by endorsing Duncan, "you undercut me and engaged in an act of trying to pull the political rug out from under me." He warned the AFL-CIO's Andrew Biemiller that union leaders had every right to "weaken my hands if they think that is what should be done, but when they do it, they should understand that they picked the fight and I did not."

Morse also fell out with state and local party leaders, nearly all of whom stayed with Duncan. He wrote to Democratic functionaries from Multnomah and Lane Counties, accusing them of unfairly fronting for Duncan; and with similar accusations, he refused to make his annual fifty-dollar contribution to the party's state organization. Democratic leaders responded in kind. One told the *New York Times* that Morse "was at the lowest ebb in his career" in Oregon; and in an effort that failed to get very far, others tried to mount a recall petition to expel him from the Senate. However great the vexation of Democratic chieftains over Morgan's race and Morse's attitude, it was minimal compared to the fury they felt when, even before Duncan's comfortable victory in the primary, Morse publicly announced that in the event of a Morgan defeat, he would be voting in the 1966 general election not for his party's nominee, but for his onetime enemy, Republican governor Mark Hatfield.

Morse was supporting Hatfield for one reason: Hatfield was opposed to the war. Whatever else he was or might have been was beside the point. Except for his pro-Pentagon posture on appropriations, Hatfield's public statements on Vietnam could have been written in Morse's office; and with his election to the Senate, Morse would have a valuable antiwar ally in the upper chamber, the first from the other side of the aisle. If Oregon Democrats could not understand Morse's position on the election, then they could not understand how transcendent Vietnam had become for him. As Morse explained to International Woodworkers president Al Hartung:

> I consider the foreign policy issue of greater significance than all other issues facing the American people combined. ... What a good many Democrats don't like to face up to is that most of the Democrats in Congress have failed their country in carrying out their Congressional obligations in stopping Johnson from continuing his unconstitutional and immoral war. I am not going to be a party to it [and] I would rather have a Hatfield in the Senate than a hundred Duncans.

Morse could, of course, have remained silent on how he planned to cast his vote, contenting himself with criticizing Duncan's Vietnam stand while applauding Hatfield's. The fact was, however, that quite apart from their affinity on the war, Morse and Hatfield had grown politically closer since the infamous events of 1958. This increased intimacy had been helped along by the redoubtable Glenn Jackson, chairman of the Oregon Highway Commission and head of the state's largest private utility. Though Jackson was widely regarded as one of Oregon's most powerful leaders, he had no specific political leaning, and he made it a point to back those who, in his view, could best advance the interests of his state. He had long been a Morse supporter (and yet another cash customer for a choice head of Devon) as well as a Hatfield booster, going back to Mark's days as Oregon's secretary of state. Acting as intermediary between the senator and the governor, Jackson had used his powers of persuasion to help bring the two together in the early sixties.

So far had the relationship developed that sometime in 1963, during his second term as governor, Hatfield could make free to send Morse the following handwritten note: "Would it embarrass the Sen. in the least if a request were made for an auto[graphed] picture for me? In all the years of assoc[iation] I have never had one. Would assure you no political use would ever be made of it." Morse, who duly provided the asked-for photo, had again become an elder statesman for Hatfield, someone he could look up to and work with to the benefit of their common constituents. With the relationship thus

Credit for easing the tension between Morse and Mark Hatfield went to pipe-smoking industrialist Glenn Jackson (pictured here with Morse and Jack Travis, a Morse supporter from Hood River). (Wayne Morse Collection, CN 1313, Special Collections, University of Oregon Library.)

improved, Morse was not only eager to vote for the younger man as a potential antiwar colleague in the Senate, he was truly pleased to make his intention known to anyone who cared to listen.

Not everyone did. Indeed, many wanted to know why Morse was opposing a fellow Democrat—one who, excepting Vietnam, voted his way on every important issue—while doing such a radical about-face on Republican Hatfield. Typical of letters from critical constituents was one inquiring how Morse could "justify backing . . . a man who you said: 'is thoroughly, intellectually dishonest [and] cannot be relied on.' These remarks were made by you in 1958. Now, eight years later, this same man is the person you said you would personally vote for. . . . I find I have mixed emotions with regard to my admiration for you and my faith in your judgment."

In response to such letters, Morse tried to both defend himself and take the offensive. Somewhat disingenuously, he said he had attacked Hatfield in 1958 only on the narrowest of grounds, and only because he had been asked to by Governor Holmes's campaign manager. "If I had it to do over," he confessed, "I would not have agreed to do even what I did do." Furthermore, he added, his respect for Hatfield—who, he said, was more liberal than many imagined—had greatly increased because the two men had been able to work as a team for Oregon on a thoroughly nonpartisan basis. Finally, advancing his most fundamental argument—the only one that really mattered—he insisted that resistance to the war outweighed all other considerations. As he informed another correspondent who had denounced his Hatfield endorsement, "It is one thing for politicians here at home, safe in the security of their political offices, to vote to send young American draftees to die in an unconscionable war in Vietnam, but it is another thing to be one of those boys. I do not intend to put their blood on my hands." From Morse's perspective, a vote for Duncan in 1966 would be a vote to increase the blood quotient from Vietnam, and no Oregonian should cast a ballot for such a despicable purpose.

With arguments like these, Morse sought to explain why he had once again defied the norms of convention, exercising, as he had in 1952, the maverick's prerogative to support whomever he chooses, regardless of party label or political repercussions. Morse had survived and overcome the backlash in 1952. Would he be able to do so again sixteen years later? Would his arguments prove convincing? He himself wondered about such questions, especially when Hatfield emerged victorious over Duncan in a very close election. It is doubtful that his opposition contributed significantly to Duncan's loss, but there were certainly Democrats who felt that it had. "It may be," Morse wrote in the letter to Al Hartung, "that in 1968, I may not have the support of labor, and I may not have enough support to be reelected, but I am perfectly willing to let the people of Oregon be the judges of that issue. I am also willing to let history be the judge of my position on foreign policy." As 1968 approached, it appeared that history might be easier on Morse than the Oregon electorate would be.

ON MAY 18, 1967, A YEAR AFTER THE 1966 PRIMARY, Oregon's Democratic National Committeeman Norm Stoll wrote to Morse expressing concern about "the bitterness that has followed in the wake of the last campaign. I haven't seen any signs of it in the principals, but it certainly is kept alive by both Morse and Duncan partisans." Others did see such signs in at least one of the principals. On June 12, Joe Califano informed Lyndon Johnson that Morse was angry over a Lane County Democratic dinner that had in part honored Duncan; because National Committee people had been associated with the event, Morse felt that "the clear implication" was a preference by the party's leadership for Duncan over Morse. On the following day, Johnson aide Marvin Watson, having consulted a contact in Oregon, reported that there had been no such implication and that Morse had simply overreacted. He quoted the contact as saying, "Morse is crazy. He's always been crazy. You know he's crazy. Everybody knows he's crazy."

But while Morse may have impulsively read more into the Lane County dinner than was actually there, given the ceaseless political maneuverings in Oregon over the previous twelve months, he was far from crazy in thinking that opponents were seizing every opportunity to put him at a disadvantage. Foremost among such opponents was Duncan himself, who, as *Time* put it, had "never stopped running" since his loss to Hatfield and who, the magazine suggested, could "expect at least covert help from the White House" in his anticipated challenge to Morse in the 1968 primary. Whatever his hopes regarding White House support, covert or conspicuous, Duncan's candidacy—officially announced near the end of 1967—would rely far more heavily on the good offices of organized labor.

The International Association of Machinists would, of course, rise to the occasion. This was their chance to get back at Morse for his positions on the airline and railroad strikes; and Duncan would never have taken him on without their promise of heavy financial assistance. As early as mid-August, under a headline reading "Machinists Plot Defeat of Morse," the *Eugene Register-Guard* reported that Machinists president Roy Siemiller was trying to line up the Teamsters and the International Woodworkers behind the idea of ousting Morse from Washington. His plan showed signs of success when a September straw poll at the Oregon AFL-CIO annual convention gave Duncan 269 ballots to Morse's 101. Moreover, Morse's own opinion polls indicated that labor's anti-Morse sentiment had spilled over into the general public: one taken in October 1967 showed Duncan ahead 51 percent to 40 percent. For the first time since his initial race in 1944, Morse was in serious trouble in a primary. Lyndon Johnson, whose people were closely watching the Oregon scene, must have felt smugly optimistic about his prediction to Justice Douglas that Morse would go down at the hands of labor.

Then, an occurrence in January threw both the Machinists' and LBJ's hopes into disarray. Lister Hill unexpectedly announced that he would not seek reelection. Benefiting from the sort of serendipity that had characterized the 1944 and 1956 elections, Morse suddenly found himself heir apparent to the chairmanship of the Senate Labor

Having lost the U.S. Senate race to Hatfield in 1966, former Oregon congressman Bob Duncan (shown here with family and supporters) went head-to-head with Morse in the 1968 Democratic primary. (Oregon Historical Society, OrHi 93520.)

and Public Welfare Committee, one of the most powerful positions on the Hill, *the* most powerful when it came to the interests of labor. However many trade unionists had previously considered joining the Machinists' campaign—the Oregon Steelworkers and the Marine Cooks and Stewards had announced for Duncan, as had a few county labor councils—all would now think twice before alienating such a potentially formidable figure. Thus, while the state AFL-CIO organization remained neutral, it surprised no one when most of the larger unions—the Longshoremen, Retail Clerks, Building Trades, Sawmill Workers, *and* the Teamsters—not only endorsed Morse, but backed their endorsements with significant contributions.

With the big-labor scales thus rebalanced and with a huge campaign treasury at his disposal, Morse steadily gained on Duncan. By election eve he held a lead of 49.2 percent to 45.7 percent, with most of the remaining support going to a thirty-nine-year-old Portland real-estate mogul and superhawk named Phil McAlmond. The lead gave the Morse campaign reason for optimism, but the percentages were so close that commentators correctly labeled the race a toss-up. Though the result remained in doubt for days, Morse was finally declared the winner toward the end of election week, garnering 48.8 percent of the vote to Duncan's 46.4. He had squeaked through, but the thinness of his plurality showed that he was still in trouble.

Just how much could be assessed by looking back at what had transpired. While Morse had carried the state, he had lost Multnomah County, his longtime stronghold, by 3,500 votes. Furthermore, it was apparent that without two key advantages—money and McAlmond—he would have been beaten. As in 1962, Morse had little trouble funding his campaign, raising $312,000 and spending $294,000. By contrast, Duncan spent a mere $90,000, of which he raised only two-thirds, ending up with campaign debts totaling $29,000. Even with such a massive budgetary edge, however, it took the votes for McAlmond—who almost dropped out in midcampaign—to gain Morse the nomination. The contest had turned on a variety of issues—logging, jobs, political seniority, candidate personality, government spending in Oregon—and had not, as some had predicted, been a clear-cut referendum on the war. The currency that Vietnam did have as an issue had been somewhat devalued when Johnson, after he became a lame-duck president in March, instituted a partial halt to the bombing of the North and then turned down a request for adding still more American troops to the fray. Yet the war remained an important topic, the views of the candidates were well known, and everyone understood that in a two-man race, the promilitary support for McAlmond would have gone entirely to Duncan.

If winning the primary depended on such an adventitious variable as McAlmond, what, Morse's backers wondered, would it take to carry the general election? How could they defeat the thirty-six-year-old Bob Packwood, who, through years of tireless organizing, had risen from a no-name legislator—at one time the youngest in Salem—to one of the more widely recognized and better-financed Republican politicians in Oregon, one who, according to the polls, could provide Morse with a realistic challenge? One thing was clear: given Packwood's momentum and the need to heal the wounds within the Democratic party, Morse would have to wage the campaign of his career. And it soon became equally clear that to wage a *successful* campaign, he would have to overcome a myriad of problems.

PEOPLE PROBLEMS. The image Morse had employed in one of his 1961 "cowboy" letters to Gene McCarthy—"death stalks the range"—might well have described his own situation in 1968. Bill Berg had come out from Washington after the first of the year to get the campaign off to a smooth start. He was hospitalized with cancer in February, and would be dead before the campaign ended. Suddenly deprived of the steady hand that had helped him through so many storms in the past, Morse seemed dispirited at times, uncertain of how to proceed most effectively. This problem was exacerbated by the fact that Charlie Brooks's wife had also contracted cancer and also lay dying in a hospital. As a consequence, Brooks was often distracted, and less the consummate aide-de-camp than he had been in the past.

Mix-ups like the following may have been attributable to such distraction. For campaign recruiting purposes, the Washington office was supposed to forward to Brooks the names and addresses of everyone from Oregon who had written to Morse in support of his stand on Vietnam—a very large number. But Charlie received only the names of those who had explicitly offered their assistance in the reelection effort. The rest remained buried in Midge's constituent file, unexploited by a campaign that suffered at critical moments from an absence of capable volunteers.

Getting an adequate workforce had been a serious issue early in the primary season, especially because many younger activists had committed to working on McCarthy's presidential campaign (whose manager in Oregon was, ironically, Howard Morgan). The volunteer pool further diminished as the number of liberal office-seekers competing for unpaid workers became larger. As Midge wrote to a friend in late March, "Things were complicated enough before Kennedy decided to come in. You can't imagine how difficult things are now with all the cross currents and rip tides. It's a bad year to have to run for office."

As far as accumulating campaign workers was concerned, the bad year grew worse when Morse alienated McCarthy adherents by announcing even before the beginning of the Democratic national convention that after the initial balloting, when all Oregon delegates were required to vote for McCarthy, he would back Hubert Humphrey for the nomination—this despite Humphrey's dogged support of the war and despite the fact that McCarthy had won a stirring victory in the state's presidential primary. Morse argued that McCarthy, whom he otherwise liked and admired, could not be taken as a serious candidate; that Humphrey (who had written privately to Morse promising a quick settlement in Vietnam) was the only serious candidate and was, for all his past mistakes, infinitely preferable to Nixon. But such arguments found little sympathy among McCarthy diehards, many of whom stayed away from the Morse reelection office even after McCarthy dropped out of the contest and stayed away as well from the general election in the fall, thereby withholding votes that would otherwise have gone to Morse.

PLANNING PROBLEMS. "Bob Packwood," observed a UPI wire story in July, "is an example of a candidate going full-bore during the summer dog days." Senator Morse, the story continued, "is currently tied up in Congress. . . . Morse, unlike Packwood, will attend his party's presidential convention in Chicago. Packwood didn't run for delegate, feeling he couldn't spare the time from campaigning." Nothing could have kept Morse from the convention—a convention where he might, given the new possibilities on Vietnam with Johnson out of the race, actually make a difference. As it turned out, his six-minute speech in behalf of a serious peace plank in the Democratic platform produced "deafening applause" as well as a lengthy floor demonstration; but it was, predictably, defeated by a coalition of conservative delegates, 1,567 to 1,041.

If staying away from the convention was unthinkable, being "tied up in Congress" was a matter of choice, a choice made in favor of promoting education legislation on the Hill over campaigning back home. Indeed, Morse believed that it wasn't an either-or situation, that pursuing education legislation was in reality an effective way of campaigning. In late June he informed a valued supporter, crusty Hood River farmer (and Devon customer) Jack Travis, that he couldn't "do anything with the campaign until after August 1. I just have to get the education bills through the Committee and ready for floor debate. . . . In my judgment, there is nothing more important in my campaign than these education bills." We know, however, that passage of the 1968 education package occupied Morse's attention throughout much of the year; thus, August 1 came and went without his presence in Oregon, and in the end he spent only six days out of that month in the state. While his campaign schedule picked up in September and October, there were notable periods even in those months spent rounding up legislative votes in Washington rather than electoral votes in Coos Bay, Klamath Falls, or Oregon City.

It is possible that after the bruising battle with Duncan, Morse truly believed he could refocus just enough to give Senate achievement priority over Senate campaigning. Perhaps he regarded Packwood as a less formidable opponent than Duncan. (Packwood was, after all, the second choice of many Republicans, who would have preferred the better-known Tom McCall, Hatfield's successor in the statehouse, as their standard-bearer.) An August poll gave some credence to this view, showing Morse leading Packwood by a comfortable 49 to 40 percent. A closer look, however, revealed that of those who had supported Duncan in the primary, a whopping 50 percent said they would vote for Packwood in the general election, while 31 percent felt that Morse had grown too old for the job. The warning signs were clearly there, but Morse apparently felt they were not that ominous.

HOSTILITY PROBLEMS. Once the primary was behind him, Morse worried most about improving his standing with labor, considerable parts of which had gone for Duncan. As far as financial backing was concerned, he needn't have bothered. As one Oregon AFL-CIO officer put it, "We'll all rally around Morse in November, despite the mixed feelings in the primary. It only makes common sense." Even the Woodworkers, who had remained neutral during the primary, eagerly contributed to Morse's coffers.

But while Morse could confidently count on most unions for funding, he could not similarly rely on the recalcitrant Machinists, whose support he still had to win back. To this end, he sent numerous letters to IAM officials, suggesting that they had misunderstood his positions on the airline and railroad strikes and unblushingly reminding them how much they had to gain by a Morse victory or lose by a Morse defeat. To union vice president Charles West he stated:

> As you know, if I am reelected in November, I will automatically become Chairman of the Senate Committee on Labor and Public Welfare. I need not tell you how important that is to the legitimate interest of organized labor. . . . The existing balance on the Committee between liberals and ultraconservatives is too close for comfort, and I think that labor leaders should think a long time before they decide to either oppose me or sit on their political hands during my oncoming campaign.

Eventually, the Machinists came through with a modest contribution; they were not, however, persuaded to eschew political handsitting, at least as far as the Morse campaign was concerned. They might be officially supporting Morse, but along with other labor activists throughout the state who remained ambivalent about his candidacy, they were doing so without their usual degree of personal involvement. Many, in fact, chose to work elsewhere, either for Humphrey or for labor-oriented candidates on the state and local levels.

As with labor activists, so with party activists. State Senator Don Willner, an avid Morse supporter, wrote Wayne in early June to say that he had "never seen a primary in Oregon in which the feelings were so deep.... I would urge that efforts to heal the wounds within the party be the very first ... priority." Morse chose not to put such efforts at the top of his agenda, but even if he had, he could not have overcome the problem of the 1966 Hatfield endorsement, an issue which refused to die among party functionaries (even though among the electorate as a whole, those who said they approved of the endorsement were equal in number to those who said they disapproved of it).

Morse had never worried much about building a political organization, still less about the attitudes of party functionaries. Typically, he preferred to go his own maverick way, confident that he could attract sufficient support every six years to conduct a viable campaign. But since he lacked a consistent organization of his own, and since he could not rely on county committees and precinct captains to deliver quotas of bankable votes, he could not count on such votes being cast his way in a tight election. However imperfect and unpredictable the party's influence had been in the past, that influence —those bankable votes—could be essential in a 1968 election that promised to be very tight indeed, and Morse might come to wish that for once he had the party securely in his corner.

FORENSIC PROBLEMS. Like a handful of others around the country, the Morse-Packwood race drew the attention of the national media —in part because of Morse's potential for committee advancement, but mainly because the contest promised a dramatic dove-hawk confrontation. However, as the New York Times's Tom Wicker quickly discovered, the contest was one in which "the gut issues are local," meaning that Morse-Packwood was even less a referendum on the war than Morse-Duncan had been. Only on appropriations for Vietnam and bombing of the North was there an easily seen difference, Packwood insisting that the extension of both was vital. More generally, Packwood took a kind of middle ground, which called for continued support of South Vietnam but on the condition that South Vietnamese rulers institute a program of land reform. What such a program would look like and how it might work was left largely to the imagination. Perhaps Morse might have a chance to force Packwood to be more specific on this point if the two were to meet in a campaign debate.

Packwood had long wanted such a debate. As soon as the primary results were in, he began hammering at Morse to meet him face to face before a live audience and the media. Following the conventional wisdom of the day that incumbents never provide a public forum for lesser-known challengers, Morse for several weeks refused Packwood's demand. But there were those in his campaign who, moved by the closeness of the polls, thought he could gain considerable advantage by showing his superior rhetorical skills in one of his favorite formats; and when Humphrey toured the state charging Nixon with evading a similar debate in the presidential campaign, Morse felt he no longer had a choice. A meeting was thus set for October 25 at the City Club in Portland. Everyone wanted to see it.

And not just Oregonians. The debate would not only be televised live by two Portland channels and then replayed by major stations throughout the state, it would also be excerpted on CBS news and the Voice of America. The already considerable press attention would be intensified, with national coverage provided by *Time*, *Newsweek*, the *New York Times*, the *Los Angeles Times*, the *Chicago Sun-Times*, and the *Christian Science Monitor*. Reporters had even flown in from Thailand for the occasion. So enormous was the interest that the venue had to be changed to the ornate Masonic Temple ballroom in downtown Portland. An audience of eight hundred sat at crowded dining tables, two hundred standees swarmed into all remaining spaces, and nearly three hundred hopefuls were turned away for lack of space. This would be Oregon's version of the Nixon-Kennedy showdown of 1960.

Morse had every reason to feel confident. Just a few days earlier he and Packwood had appeared, seriatim, at a local high school, where Morse had, according to the *Washington Post*, "put on an oratorical show that made his young rival seem pallid." A mock election following their two speeches gave Morse a 429 to 402 victory—this despite a simultaneous 416 to 173 vote for Nixon over Humphrey. But before a clearly pro-Packwood City Club audience, it was a different story. Garbed in a conservative gray suit, which seemed to accentuate his age, Morse sounded hesitant, ponderous, old—"Let me say this . . . ," "If I may comment . . . ," "May I make it very clear . . ." —compared to the youthful, more agile Packwood, who had prepared an assortment of quick and easily digested responses to whatever the audience might ask. Morse's frequent mention of his seniority added to the perception that his best days might be behind him.

Many observers felt that the 1968 debate between Morse and Republican Bob Packwood (left) turned the Senate race in Packwood's favor. (Oregon Historical Society, OrHi 93519.)

A question period followed ten-minute presentations, mostly on Vietnam, by each candidate. Several of the questions seemed especially intended to give Morse trouble, and this, as it turned out, was no accident. Packwood had packed the ballroom with supporters primed to ask Morse why Oregon, compared to its neighbors, seemed to fare so poorly in terms of federal dollars spent in-state. The plan, which was at least partially successful, was to make Morse look like a legislator who couldn't bring home the bacon for his constituency. "We set Morse up," crowed one Packwood backer. "Sandbagged" was the word used by Ed Conklin, who knew that on a per capita basis, and taking into account its lack of in-state military expenditures, Oregon did as well as or better than most states.

Morse's task was made infinitely more difficult by the fact that he had to complete his answers within a two-minute time limit. Surprisingly, such a time constraint had been suggested by Morse's staff (and eagerly agreed to by Packwood's), apparently because they were afraid their boss would run on too long to maintain audience attention. However legitimate such a fear, the remedy was a catastrophe. Packwood had mastered the ninety-second sound bite required by the age of television, while Morse, as Ed Conklin observed, "couldn't give you the time of day in two minutes," let alone explain the complicated ways by which government money was allocated to various Western states.

Substance aside, Packwood was awarded the debate on style points. As one editorial put it, "It was Packwood who amazed everyone by his composure under fire, his verbal facility . . . and his deftness in handling questions." Using excerpts from the debate, Packwood would display such attributes in prime-time TV ads that ran from the day after the City Club confrontation until the eve of the election.

THE PACKWOOD PROBLEM. When Packwood resigned in disgrace from the Senate in 1995, Mark Hatfield, in an effort to say something positive about his colleague, recalled that Packwood had been his best political science student at Willamette University. He remembered as well Packwood's effectiveness as a campaigner, noting especially the brilliance of his initial run for the Senate against Morse. With a straight face, Hatfield suggested that such brilliance could best be seen in the campaign's slogan, "People for Packwood"—a slogan which, Hatfield took pains to note, Packwood had contrived without the help of advertising agents or PR professionals. (Hatfield charitably left out the fact that Packwood's other slogan, "A strong new voice for Oregon," had been lifted directly from the campaign of Republican senator Charles Percy of Illinois.)

It was somehow fitting that Hatfield should think first of campaigning as Packwood's most praiseworthy accomplishment, and then offer sloganeering as the best example of that accomplishment. For the truth is that in an otherwise undistinguished career, Packwood's reputation as a campaign virtuoso—the words "genius" and "wizard" were frequently applied—far exceeded his actual abilities. His much-touted use of lawn signs, neighborhood coffees, and precinct-saturation methods—as well as his rigging of the audience at the Masonic Temple—certainly stood him in good stead, but such techniques scarcely constituted original breakthroughs in the art of electioneering. In the end, Packwood probably owed his success in 1968 more to difficulties experienced by the Morse camp than to any displays of brilliance of his own.

Where Packwood did have a talent was in overall campaign supervision, an area in which Morse had always been weak. Tom McCall would describe Packwood's as "one of the best organized campaigns I had ever seen," an assessment shared by activists in both parties impressed that a thirty-six-year-old could accomplish so much while acting as his own campaign manager. Behind such organizational acumen lay years of nonstop political spadework: being helpful to other Republicans in the way that Morgan and Sweetland had been to Democrats in the forties and fifties; lining up loyal supporters so that favors could be called in precisely when needed. With Morse's campaign under so much stress, such efforts were bound to pay off.

Morse was not oblivious to Packwood's organizational edge, and during the last days before the election he sought to make up ground by increasing both his television advertising and his appearances in the Willamette Valley's larger cities. Judy, described in the press as "the pretty 'brownette' with the singer's voice," came out from Connecticut to give five to six speeches a day in the smaller, outlying communities. Such exertions unquestionably served to improve Morse's standing—both father and daughter drew large, enthusiastic crowds—leaving Morse on election eve precisely where he had been just before the primary: at a virtual standoff with his opponent. An October 24 poll showed that among those most likely to vote, 47.4 percent preferred Morse, 47.7 percent Packwood. The poll declared the race deadlocked and implied that every vote would have to be tabulated before the decision of the electorate would be known.

The vote would in fact be one of the closest in Oregon history, and getting a complete tally would take even longer than it had in the primary. Although Packwood took an early lead in the counting, Morse's total continued to mount as ballots dribbled in from Multnomah County and some of his other strongholds. But when it became apparent three days after the election that the three thousand remaining absentee ballots would not change things regardless of how they went, Packwood claimed victory.

But Morse refused to surrender. The difference between the candidates was 3,445 votes, less than 1 percent of the more than 814,000 cast, and it seemed conceivable that a recount could alter the outcome. Though there was division within the Morse camp on taking such a step, Morse himself decided to proceed, demanding that the results in several precincts be reexamined. Around sixty thousand ballots were recounted in a protracted process that in the end changed the margin of victory by fewer than two hundred votes. Morse's defeat was official. And though he considered prolonging the issue by asking the Senate for further investigation into alleged irregularities, he finally conceded just after Christmas. As he wrote to Conklin, "I don't want to drag myself through a Senate contest and end my Senate career by having the Senate turn me down."

Which is certainly what the Senate would have done. The question is, did Lyndon Johnson bring Morse to the brink of such indignity; had the soon-to-be ex-president tricked him into creating the inevitability of his own defeat? The answer is a qualified yes.

In a defeat so narrow, any number of causes could have played a decisive role: Bill Berg's illness; Charlie Brooks's distraction; the lack of competent volunteers; the resentment over Morgan's race in 1966; Morse's endorsement of Hatfield in that same year; remaining too long in Washington during the summer of 1968; supporting Humphrey instead of McCarthy; the poor showing in the debate—looking back, all seem important. Add to the list the candidates' stands on gun control—Morse was for modest regulation, Packwood opposed all controls—an issue which, according to Packwood, voters raised at every campaign stop; the fact that other antiwar liberals were also turned out in '68 (Gruening never made it past the primary); and, perhaps most telling, the fact that Nixon and George Wallace together received nearly 100,000 more votes in Oregon than Humphrey. With that kind of margin, even the shortest of coattails could have worked in Packwood's favor.

Nevertheless, had Morse not allowed Johnson to talk him into the middle of the railroad dispute, had he refused the mediator's post once he had written the strike-cessation legislation, had he instead worked to mend fences with labor after the airlines stoppage, one imagines that the meager 1,800 votes needed to reverse the election might have been his. Insofar as Johnson's strategy deprived him of these votes, that strategy may be said to have worked. Thus, one also imagines that even as the already repudiated president was licking his own political wounds, he must have taken special pleasure in receiving the following from Joe Califano on November 19: "Wayne Morse called me today informing me that while he was going through a recount procedure, he thought the odds were against overturning his defeat. Assuming he loses, Morse says he has to find something to do since he is not self-sufficient and would not be happy without some kind of a job. He asked me to alert him to any jobs I heard about."

Had he known about it, Johnson might also have found a measure of satisfaction in Morse's reaction to being beaten. Although he tried to put up a cheerful front, Morse was devastated. Campaign coordinator Phil George noted that he "was a different person after he lost. He was not the kind that could take very much rejection." For twenty-four years Morse had lived on the political edge, maintaining always that he would rather suffer defeat than violate deeply held principles, insisting that Oregon voters should be the final judges of his actions, however popular or unpopular a particular action might appear at a given moment. Now, because of the electorate's judgment, Morse was, as he indicated in the letter to Conklin, feeling "very blue." He became uncharacteristically reclusive, canceling at the last minute and without explanation a series of November and December personal appearances, including one in Seattle—where he was to receive a distinguished-service award from the National Association for Public School Adult Education—as well as others in Detroit, Salt Lake City, and Elizabeth, New Jersey.

Morse's constituency had not only removed him from the Senate, it had also left him in the unhappy position of being out of work. What, everyone wondered, would Senator Morse, at age sixty-eight, do with the rest of his life? What would Senator Morse be now that he was no longer Senator Morse?

IN PORTRAYING LYNDON JOHNSON in his post–White House period, biographer Doris Kearns Goodwin provides a description which, with appropriate modification, could be applied generically to veteran political warriors whose fighting days are brought suddenly to an end. Johnson, Kearns writes, "had no inner resources left to commit himself to anything once the Presidency was gone. So dominant had politics been, consuming all his energies, constricting his horizons in every sphere, that once the realm of high power was taken from him he was drained of all vitality. Retirement became for him a form of little death."

As with LBJ, so with Morse, and the depletion of vitality was in Morse's case exceedingly painful to behold. Writing to Drew Pearson's wife on the occasion of the famous columnist's death, Midge remarked that the "only comforting thing I can think of is that Drew will never know any diminution of power; this, for a man, is an agonizing experience." Said Amy in 1984, "I guess we never really knew how much being a senator meant to Daddy until he was no longer in the Senate."

One might have thought that for Morse, at least, retirement could be something less than agonizing, since it afforded an opportunity to give himself at last to the farming and ranching ventures that had so occupied his time in the past. But the fact was that his interest in such enterprises had greatly diminished—he would have sold both Edgewood Farm and the Poolesville property if the right offers had come along; and perhaps the Verona-style life had always been so beguiling precisely because it provided a recreational diversion from his main concern with politics.

There were prospects beyond farming, but while well-paid speaking and arbitration opportunities came Morse's way, no regular vocation seemed to capture his fancy. In 1969, Abe Fortas raised the possibility of a law partnership. Things had greatly improved between Morse and Fortas since their bitter disagreement over the coal miners' strike during World War II. Indeed, Morse had, according to White House staff, been "one of the few tough, stand-up fighters" supporting Fortas's nomination as Supreme Court chief justice in 1968. Having resigned from the court and, like Morse, looking for something to do, Fortas hoped to start a new practice in Washington, with Morse as a full partner. But the thought of doing law, with Fortas or anyone else, held no appeal for Morse, and he quickly turned the invitation down.

He also turned down a Washington law firm that wanted to hire him for a sizeable retainer to lobby in behalf of selected interests before Congress. Refusing to pass through what has come to be known as the legislator-to-lobbyist revolving door, Morse stated that in his opinion, "it would be both unprofessional and unethical for me to make use of the confidential information . . . I had acquired during my twenty-four years in the Senate." He did not, he said, "intend to commercialize on my service in the Senate." Going even further, he ultimately refused *all* requests to testify before congressional committees, even those concerned with foreign policy.

Morse toyed with the idea of writing his memoirs—more than one publisher had contacted him—but in truth he was no author, and even if he had been, he could not get himself sufficiently motivated to undertake such a project. The same was true of teaching, in which he had long since lost interest; possible positions at Notre Dame and the University of Hawaii would not be seriously pursued. In fact, it soon became apparent that intellectual life of any kind held little attraction. In 1969, Morse spent three days at Robert Hutchins's Center for the Study of Democratic Institutions in Santa Barbara, the result of which was an offer of an appointment as a regular staff member. Morse declined, explaining to Ed Conklin that while "it pays well, it is not my forte."

Not only was Morse not attracted by the possibility of working in what he called an "intellectual monastery," but he would find undesirable any situation that emphasized thought over action. As he confessed unembarrassedly to Michigan State University professor Albert Blum, he had always been essentially a "non-reader," and as he approached seventy, he could find, in his own words, "little enthusiasm" for launching himself afresh into the life of the mind. Remarked Phil George, "He didn't read at all. I don't know how in the hell he knew anything, if you want to know the truth."

It was politics, and politics alone, that held Morse's interest. Though saddled with debt from the 1968 campaign and deteriorating somewhat in health, he began contemplating possibilities for 1970 almost as soon as Packwood's victory was made final. Since neither of Oregon's Senate seats would be up that year, he considered, like Florida's Claude Pepper, stepping down a rung to run for the House in either the third or fourth congressional district. If, however, he chose to make the race, he would do so without the blessing of Midge. "I know he wants to run," Midge informed a friend in Eugene, "but . . . I can give him no encouragement. For one thing, I can't bear to see him hurt again." But Midge knew that if he set his mind on it, Wayne would run even without her reassurance; she was therefore greatly relieved when he decided against doing so, limiting himself instead to an endorsement of Edith Green's opponent in the Democratic primary.

In 1972, however, nothing could prevent Morse from running. So great was the desire, so powerful the ambition, that even an opponent's resistance to the war could be regarded as a dismissable virtue. Thus Morse was prepared to take on his old antiwar ally, Mark Hat-

*Morse remained a hero to the antiwar movement. University of Oregon
freshmen Ann Robinson and Peggy Mansfield listen intently to his views in
1972. (Photo by Wes Guderian, Oregonian.)*

field, who, he argued, had in every area except Vietnam become an
irredeemable Nixonite. In the primary, Morse managed once again
to defeat the ever-hopeful Bob Duncan; but he was no match for
the better-financed Hatfield, who carried the general election by a
margin of nearly eight percentage points. Nevertheless, as Morse's
425,000 votes (enough to have beaten Packwood in '68) demonstrated, the Morse name still carried considerable weight in Oregon.
On the strength of his 1972 showing, Morse would—contrary to the
counsel of most advisors, and the heated opposition of some—seek
to avenge his ouster from the Senate in a return engagement with
Packwood in 1974.

Thus, five months short of his seventy-fourth birthday, Morse,
having defeated state Senate president Jason Boe in a low-key primary, found himself again slugging it out with Oregon's now well
entrenched junior senator. And despite a campaign short on organization and shorter still on funds, he seemed to be holding his own
against Packwood, with a few pundits giving him an outside chance
of staging an upset. Then, in a late July development that caught the
entire state by surprise, Morse was admitted to Good Samaritan
Hospital in Portland, diagnosed with what was described at first as a
form of pneumonia, then as a more serious urinary-tract infection.

Still a powerful orator, Morse began to show his age during the 1974 senatorial race. He is pictured here delivering the last speech he gave at Oregon State University. (Wayne Morse Historical Park Corporation.)

After two days, he was said to be responding to antibiotics and generally improving, and it was thought that he would be back on the campaign trail in less than a week. Three days later he was dead.

In 1967, Morse had told a constituent: "Of one thing you can be sure and that is that whenever my medical examinations do not show me to be in full vigor, I shall retire from public life." However, when medical exams revealed a body far from vigorous, one that was in fact in dangerous decline, Morse could not make himself hold to his promise. He kept from the voting public both his gravely anemic condition and the fact that he had to have periodic blood transfusions to keep himself alive. Proust, who knew something about poor health, wrote that "illness is the doctor to whom we pay most heed." But so strong was Morse's urge to return to the Senate that he paid that doctor no heed whatever. Ten days before he entered the hospital, Morse ran a three-legged race tied calf-to-thigh to an athletic young girl at a campaign picnic.

Everyone, except for those few in the know, was stunned by Morse's death. Oregon longshoremen put down their unloading hooks for thirty minutes in his honor. "It's kind of like losing a father," said one campaign worker, reflecting the feelings of antiwar activists who continued to see Morse as their steadfast champion. Contacted on location in Rome, Burt Lancaster, a part-time Oregon rancher (and with Robert Vaughn, Harry Belafonte, and many other Hollywood performers a devoted Morse supporter), voiced the frustration felt by those who had hoped to see Morse returned to the Senate. "It is difficult for me to express in words what his loss means," said Lancaster. "I thought it would be great for him to give them hell for another 10 years."

Morse had died as he might have preferred, trying to persuade voters to send him back to Washington for another term of salutary hell-giving. But his prodigious effort to both run a comeback campaign and keep a terminal illness totally secret was based on more than the hoped-for satisfaction of political ambition. It represented the maverick's attempt not just to vanquish the "little deaths" delivered by retirement, but also to assert a kind of masterlessness in the face of death itself. Morse would look the grim reaper in the eye and exclaim, "Don't think you own me." If he had to die, he would do so on his own maverick terms, a political actor *living* his role to the last. Wesley Nicholson, pastor of Eugene's First Congregational Church —which Morse attended from time to time—reported that just before he died, Morse, in a semicoma, imagined himself before a group of supporters at the end of a long day's campaigning: "I want to thank you all for coming. Thank you for such a beautiful day. Thank you, everybody. Thank you."

THOSE INTERVIEWED FOR THIS BOOK offered a variety of memories of Morse's life and what it meant to them. A retired teacher suggested that without his Great Society education work in the sixties, her school would have closed and she would have been out of a job. A Bay Area longshoreman felt that Morse's arbitration efforts in the thirties and forties had been vital to the survival of his union. The

favorite memory of a part-time actor who supported Morse on Vietnam was of his senator, astride a chestnut quarter horse, throwing
himself into eight consecutive takes of a ten-second cameo role in
the movie version of "Paint Your Wagon," the Clint Eastwood mu-
sical filmed in Oregon in the middle of the 1968 campaign.

But it was foreign policy above all, and Vietnam in particular,
that most people recalled when they thought of Morse: his resolute
defense of the United Nations and international law; his unrelenting
attack on the abuses of executive power and the reliance on military
force; his maverick conviction that fighting an imperialist land war
anywhere in Asia was "not worth the blood of a single American boy."

Memories of what Morse had stood for were also central to the
letters and wires that flooded in after the defeat in 1968. An Oregon
constituent expressed her "heartfelt regret that, not only will you no
longer represent the state of Oregon in the U. S. Senate, but also that
the Senate and the country will be deprived of your voice which has
so often awakened our conscience, spurred us to action, and reminded us of our goals." A Eustis, Florida, man, describing himself
as "just a lowly citizen," said he had to write "in this hour of disappointment" to assure Morse "that yours is not the only heart that is
bleeding." A Forest Hills, New York, dissident voiced the thoughts of
1960s protesters for whom Morse remained a stalwart hero: "You cut
through the bullshit like a knife. Your politics was real. Your stand on
Vietnam was, and is, magnificent. . . . I am 24 years old, and bored
with political processes, for I think they are not enough to save America. . . . But I will never forget *you*."

From a less partisan perspective came those like A. Robert Smith,
who when interviewed said he simply found the Senate an uninter-
esting place once Morse was no longer at his desk. "We don't have
mavericks like Morse anymore," he remarked, "and we're the worse
for it. Whatever one thought of him, he could be counted upon to
generate excitement on the floor and in the gallery. I looked forward
to covering the Senate when he was there."

In *A Political Education*, Harry McPherson put it a little differently. Describing Morse as "brilliant" and "tireless," McPherson wrote
that he

lectured on Southern racism, District of Columbia parking fees, and whatever else had recently aroused his displeasure. A gadfly, insensitive to obloquy, he was nevertheless extremely effective when given a leadership role—when managing a labor or education bill he was tolerant and skillful, knowing when to give way and when to resist amendment. He could easily be the most irritating man in the Senate. Yet he was also indispensable: he would fight a bad bill when others wanted to but were afraid.

Observed Burt Lancaster, speaking for everyone who saw Morse as indispensable, "I don't know how we are going to find another man like that." The truth is, we never have.

Notes

PROLOGUE: MORSE AS MAVERICK

PAGE 1   "I am perfectly . . .": "Making Democracy Work," *Interracial Review*, Aug. 1947, p. 8.

"I am seventy-nine years old . . .": interview with J. William Fulbright, Apr. 12, 1984.

PAGE 2   "I believe that . . .": cited in Anthony Austin, *The President's War: The Story of the Tonkin Gulf Resolution and How the Nation Was Trapped in Vietnam*, J. B. Lippincott Co., New York, 1971, p. 102.

PAGE 4   "As long as I . . .": to Ralph D. Moores, Feb. 19, 1945, Wayne L. Morse Papers, Special Collections, University of Oregon Library, Series S, Box 5.

PAGE 5   "Senator Wayne Morse's . . .": *Kansas City Times*, July 8, 1947.

"puzzling behavior . . .": *New Republic*, July 1, 1957.

"eccentric"; "bundle . . .": Irving Bernstein, *Promises Kept: John F. Kennedy's New Frontier*, Oxford University Press, New York, 1991, p. 230.

PAGE 6   "the Typhoid Mary . . .": Stanley Karnow, *Vietnam: A History*, The Viking Press, New York, 1983, pp. 374-75.

"The answer to your question . . .": letter from William Proxmire to author, Dec. 15, 1983.

PAGE 10   "certain of . . . *biographie romancée*": Vladimir Nabokov, *The Real Life of Sebastian Knight*, New Directions, New York, 1941, pp. 52, 20.

CHAPTER 1: PROGRESSIVE BEGINNINGS

PAGE 11   The confrontation with Principal Barnes is described by Morse in one of a series of tape-recorded interviews he did with his longtime associate Phil George beginning in the late autumn of 1973. The last tape was made in February 1974, approximately five months before Morse's death. Use of these materials, hereafter referred to as "Morse interviews," was made possible by Special Collections, University of Oregon Library. The tapes are *not* included in the *Inventory of the Papers of Senator Wayne L. Morse, 1919–1969*, prepared by Martin Schmitt and published by the Library in 1974.

Unless specifically indicated, materials for this chapter and the next are drawn from the Morse interviews, plus the following: (1) Interviews with Caryl Kline, in person, Apr. 19, 1984, and Aug. 13, 1985; by telephone, Oct. 5, 1985. (2) Interviews with Mildred M. Morse, Apr. 6, 1983, and Mar. 31, 1985. (3) Interview with Ralph Axley, Apr. 21, 1984. (4) Responses by Morse to a questionnaire from Professor Neil Sabin. Sabin, then of the Lewis and Clark College Speech Arts Department, put a series of forty-six questions, which Morse answered on Feb. 15, 1954. Use of this material was made possible by Professor Sabin.

"There is a young Junior . . .": Morse Papers, unprocessed.

PAGE 12   "feet never . . .": interview with Mrs. T. Garvey and Mrs. A. Holmes, Apr. 6, 1985.

"Please excuse me . . .": Kline interviews.

PAGE 13   "blue-belted Yankee": Axley interview.

"Oh, you Johnny Bull!": Kline interviews.

PAGE 14   Madison's hospital situation: David V. Mollenhoff, *Madison: A History of the Formative Years*, Kendall/Hunt Publishing Co., Dubuque, 1982, pp. 400-402.

PAGE 15   "He is a farmer . . .": Beryl Markham, *West with the Night*, North Point Press, San Francisco, 1983, p. 156.

"All things shall . . . strong navel development": cited in George William Rankin, *William Dempster Hoard*, W. D. Hoard and Sons Co., Fort Atkinson, Wis., 1925; reprinted in Justus F. and Barbara Dotts Paul, *The Badger State*, William B. Ersmans Publishing Co., Grand Rapids, Mich., 1979, pp. 279-81.

PAGE 16   "the outside of a . . .": quoted in A. Robert Smith, *The Tiger in the Senate: The Biography of Wayne Morse*, Doubleday & Co., Garden City, N.Y., 1962, p. 165.

PAGE 17   The argument between Jessie and Wilbur is recounted in the Morse interviews.

PAGE 18 "devil's trinity" and the data on Madison saloons: Mollenhoff, pp. 311-12, 321-22.

PAGE 21 "would interrupt . . .": quoted in Smith, p. 33.

Wayne's religious views: Sabin questionnaire.

PAGE 22 "a complete snow job . . .": quoted in Smith, p. 23.

"grasshopper mind . . . stupid": Kline interviews.

"where ideas counted . . .": quoted in Smith, p. 23.

PAGE 24 The Madison flu epidemic: Mollenhoff, p. 417.

PAGE 25 The Hi-Y incident: Smith, p. 34.

Wayne's poolroom prowess: Mildred Morse interviews.

PAGE 26 Midge's early love for Wayne: ibid.

PAGE 27 "One boy . . .": Morse Papers, Addendum.

PAGE 28 "wonderful, liberal political . . .": Mildred Morse interviews.

La Follette's Shakespearean reading: Morse interviews; see also Smith, p. 35.

PAGE 29 Madison's female workforce: Mollenhoff, p. 376.

PAGE 30 On Progressive change in Wisconsin, see Edward Newell Doan, *The La Follettes and the Wisconsin Idea*, Rinehart, New York, 1947; and David P. Thelen, *Robert M. La Follette and the Insurgent Spirit*, Little, Brown & Co., Boston, 1976. For a treatment of the philosophy of Progressivism, see Mason Drukman, *Community and Purpose in America*, McGraw-Hill Book Co., New York, 1971, chap. 9.

"where the poor shall . . .": quoted in Mollenhoff, p. 294.

PAGE 31 Description of the Bunch: ibid., p. 303.

On changes in Madison, see Mollenhoff, chap. 6.

PAGE 33 "Christian Capitalists": William Appleman Williams, *The Contours of American History*, Quadrangle Books, Chicago, 1966, p. 423.

CHAPTER 2: A MAVERICK'S EDUCATION

PAGE 35 On Progressivism and education, see Rush Welter, *Popular Education and Democratic Thought in America*, Columbia University Press, New York, 1962, chaps. 15-16. See also Frederick C. Howe, *Wis-*

consin: An Experiment in Democracy, Scribner's, New York, 1912, chap. 9; and Robert S. Maxwell, La Follette and the Rise of Progressivism, State Historical Society of Wisconsin, Madison, 1912.

PAGE 36   "Sold shoes to . . . Bet with Mother . . .": in Morse's account records, Morse Papers, Addendum.

PAGE 37   "You owe me a box . . .": ibid.

"Well turned out" is Axley's phrase (Axley interview).

PAGE 38   "I'm your prey . . .": Kline interviews.

"three large young men": Mildred Morse interviews.

PAGE 39   "Rec'd from Folks": Morse Papers, Addendum.

PAGE 40   Finances had improved sufficiently for Morse that he was able to spend part of the summer of 1921 at Camp Knox, Kentucky, doing advanced ROTC training. "I was," he reported years later, "so much interested in the course that my work resulted in my being elected to the honorary military fraternity, Scabbard and Blade." He completed the four-year requirement and upon graduation received a reserve commission as a second lieutenant in the field artillery (Sabin questionnaire).

"an official dipping . . .": Morse Papers, Series V, Box 1, Vol. 1.

PAGE 41   "My personal conviction . . .": ibid.

Accounting 181 episode: ibid.

PAGE 42   Morse's association with La Follette: Morse interviews.

Morse's campaigning for La Follette: there is only a brief mention, without reference to date, in the Morse interviews. A. Robert Smith suggests that Morse campaigned for La Follette while still in high school (Oregonian, Jan. 14, 1955), but there is no corroborating evidence of this. Axley was not certain, but thought it more likely that Morse would have campaigned in the 1924 election (Axley interview).

In The Tiger in the Senate, Smith quotes La Follette's son, Philip, to the effect that Morse had not defended the elder La Follette during and just after World War I (p. 87).

PAGE 44   "Sleepy-eyed Axley": Kline interviews.

"The interest taken . . .": Milwaukee Journal, Oct. 22, 1922.

PAGE 46 Weaver's assistance to Morse apparently did not include the use of his car. Weaver was afraid he would use it to transport livestock and return it reeking of manure (Kline interviews).

"Forensic Yankee": Morse Papers, Series V, Box 1, Vol. 2.

Visit to La Follette: Morse interviews; Sabin questionnaire.

PAGE 47 "He was a very . . .": Morse interviews.

PAGE 48 "Thanksgiving 1921 . . .": Morse Papers, Addendum.

"in recognition of . . .": ibid., Series V, Box 1, Vol. 1.

PAGE 49 The Morses' arrival in Minneapolis: Morse interviews; Sabin questionnaire.

PAGE 51 Belle La Follette's book did not appear until long after her own death in 1927 (Belle Case La Follette and Fola La Follette, *Robert M. La Follette*, 2 vols., Macmillan, New York, 1953).

"every cow in the township . . .": Morse interviews.

"I hardly saw . . .": Mildred Morse interviews.

"We wanted a human . . .": Frank Rarig to Emery Hildebrandt, July 9, 1955, Papers of Frank M. Rarig, University of Minnesota Archives.

PAGE 52 "be encouraged to . . .": Frank Rarig, "Report on the Teaching of Mr. Morse," ibid.

"He liked to see them . . .": from some uninventoried research data belonging to Sabin, hereafter referred to as "Sabin, unprocessed," on deposit in the Lewis and Clark College Archives. One of those to benefit from Morse's enlarged speech team was an "awkward" young student named Harold Stassen, who would go on to become governor of Minnesota and a perennial presidential candidate (Morse interviews).

For Morse's approach to mental hygiene, see Wayne L. Morse, "The Application of Mental Hygiene Techniques in Teaching Speech," *Mental Hygiene*, Apr. 1929, pp. 336-42.

PAGE 53 Midge's reaction to life in New York: Mildred Morse to Mrs. Frank Rarig, Sept. 12, 1928, and Dec. 26, 1928, Rarig Papers.

PAGE 54 "Midge & I spent . . .": to Frank Rarig, Sept. 9, 1928, ibid.

"more than a philosopher . . . droll fellow": to Frank Rarig, Oct. 8, 1928, ibid.

"His appearance . . .": to Frank Rarig, Oct. 29, 1928, ibid.

"had a good chuckle . . .": ibid.

PAGE 55   Morse's Columbia University grades: Morse Papers, Series S, Box 1.

PAGE 56   Morse actually began exploring the possibilities of teaching in a law school as early as February 1928 (to Justin Miller, Feb. 21, 1928, ibid., Box 3).

"I liked the guy . . .": Sabin, unprocessed.

"Glandular": to Frank Rarig, Apr. 9, 1929, Rarig Papers.

PAGE 57   "Mrs. Morse was a crack . . .": John Gunther, *Inside U.S.A.*, Harper & Brothers, New York, 1951, p. 111.

CHAPTER 3: VAULTING AMBITION

PAGE 59   "almost idyllic": diaries of John Laurence Casteel, 1931–1942, Oregon Historical Society, entry dated Sept. 6, 1931.

"The campus . . .": ibid., Sept. 7, 1931.

"is the kind . . .": ibid., Oct. 14, 1932.

"can be called . . .": ibid., Oct. 29, 1934.

PAGE 60   "found no . . .": Sabin questionnaire.

Morse negotiated with Columbia through an exchange of letters with Professor Edwin W. Patterson (Oct. 18, 1929, Feb. 16, 1931, Feb. 27, 1931, Mar. 4, 1931, Morse Papers, Series S, Box 1).

PAGE 61   "while the preachers . . .": to Frank Rarig, Nov. 8, 1929, Rarig Papers.

PAGE 62   Morse's version of the student strike: Morse interviews. The students' side: interview with Judge William East, Aug. 8, 1984.

PAGE 63   "a position which . . .": to Edwin W. Patterson, Apr. 9, 1931, Morse Papers, Series S, Box 1.

"dear little . . . Sometimes I wonder . . .": Mildred Morse to "folks," Jan. 2, 1931, Rarig Papers.

Carpenter's analysis of Morse: Charles Carpenter to Arnold Bennett Hall, Mar. 23, 1931, University of Oregon archives.

PAGE 64   "too unfavorable . . . has been a . . .": Charles Carpenter to Arnold Bennett Hall, Apr. 8, 1931, ibid.

"your friend will . . .": from Arnold Bennett Hall, May 5, 1931, Morse Papers, Series S, Box 1.

PAGE 67   "the Grab": Paul L. Shim, "Eugene in the Depression," *Oregon Historical Quarterly*, Winter 1985, p. 353.

On Morse's connection to Neuberger, see chap. 9.

"the goddamnedest . . .": undated tape recording, University of Oregon archives.

On Kerr's academic credentials, see the exchange of correspondence between Morse and Joe Smith, Nov.-Dec. 1933, Morse Papers, Series S, Box 1.

PAGE 68   "self-appointed few . . .": cited in Smith, p. 39.

PAGE 69   "Orlando, I'm . . . Only when . . .": interview with Orlando Hollis, Dec. 20, 1983.

"insulting, insinuating . . .": *Eugene Register-Guard*, Nov. 4, 1933.

"The meeting ended . . .": Morse interviews.

"No one knows . . .": Casteel diaries, Nov. 4, 1933.

PAGE 70   "encroachment of . . .": *Today Magazine*, Nov. 19, 1933.

"You take . . .": from A. M. Kidd, Dec. 13, 1933, Morse Papers, Series S, Box 3.

PAGE 71   Morse's constitution was such that he could react unpredictably to any drug that affected his nervous system. Seven years after the whiskey-and-morphine incident, Morse wrote to his friends Paul and Ruth Washke about treatment he had received for an ear infection: "Monday they brought me to the hospital and gave me gas and lanced my ear. I acted like a fool under gas. Of course, I don't mean to imply that that is the only time I act like a fool. However, under gas I jumped out of bed without saying a word, socked the nurse in the jaw and knocked her into a corner, hit young Dr. Norton and sent him in the other direction. The third nurse ran out into the hall and got the orderly. All I can remember about it is that they had me down on the floor, and I did not want to be operated on the floor" (ibid.).

"Today brought . . .": Casteel diaries, Jan. 17, 1934.

"I am with you . . .": from Charles A. Brand, Dec. 7, 1933, Morse Papers, Series S, Box 1.

PAGE 72   "a masterful orator . . .": undated tape recording, University of Oregon archives.

           "No gangster's funeral": to John M. MacGregor, Apr. 20, 1934, Morse Papers, Series S, Box 3.

PAGE 73   "Now what would . . .": quoted in Studs Terkel, *Hard Times; An Oral History of the Depression*, Pantheon Books, New York, 1970, pp. 253-54.

           Midge's train incident: to Joe Smith, Feb. 8, 1934, Morse Papers, Series S, Box 3.

PAGE 74   "in my own . . .": to Arnold Bennett Hall, Sept. 27, 1934, ibid., Box 1.

           Morse's opposition to a third child: to Margaret Thompson Hill, Jan. 10, 1945, ibid., Series A, Box 57.

           "moral vigor": to Arnold Bennett Hall, May 6, 1935, ibid., Series S, Box 3.

           "I am doing . . .": to Mrs. Arnold Bennett Hall, Feb. 22, 1935, ibid., Box 1.

PAGE 75   "would provide . . .": to Justin Miller, Mar. 5, 1935, ibid., Box 3.

           "Things are going . . .": to Margaret Read, Dec. 6, 1935, ibid.

           "the best one . . .": to John Rae, Dec. 14, 1935, ibid.

           "I am satisfied . . .": to Justin Miller, Nov. 27, 1935, ibid.

           "the Brotherhood . . .": to John Rae, Dec. 14, 1935, ibid.

PAGE 76   The barn's priority: to John Rae, Jan. 31, 1936, ibid., Box 2.

PAGE 77   "I am not . . .": to Stephenson Smith, Jan. 19, 1937, ibid., Box 3.

           "If you are . . .": to James Gilbert, June 10, 1937, ibid., Box 1.

PAGE 78   "throw my hat . . .": to Orlando Hollis, ibid., Box 2.

           "Let me whisper . . .": to Giltson Ross, June 15, 1937, ibid., Box 3.

PAGE 79   "plenty scared . . .": to Paul Washke, June 17, 1937, ibid.

           "interests [would] . . .": to Paul Washke, June 19, 1937, ibid.

           While Morse was away, Hollis sent him lengthy letters detailing every decision he had taken and every aspect of law school life, including information about individual grades, law school dances, law school baseball-team results, etc. Morse in turn offered extended opinions on every faculty committee: who should be on which, who should not, and why. For an example of such a letter, see to Hollis, Apr. 4, 1937, ibid., Box 2.

"be very careful . . .": to Eugene Allen, Aug. 28, 1936, ibid., Box 1.

PAGE 80   "I am exceedingly . . .": to Cornelia Marvin Pierce, Oct. 16, 1937, ibid., Box 3.

Tugman's views: William Tugman to Patricia Haight, Mar. 22, 1944, William M. Tugman Papers, Special Collections, University of Oregon Library, Box 1.

PAGE 81   "the most vigorous . . .": to William Tugman, July 2, 1937, Morse Papers, Series S, Box 3; see also to Orlando Hollis, July 8, 1937, ibid.

PAGE 82   "I shall be . . .": to James Gilbert, May 5, 1937, ibid., Box 1.

"I have decided . . .": to Paul Washke, July 3, 1937, ibid., Box 3.

"more than one . . .": to C. Valentine Boyer, July 16, 1937, ibid.

PAGE 83   "Too often absent . . .": ibid.

PAGE 84   "As the years . . .": East interview.

PAGE 86   "I have been . . .": to Paul Washke, Dec. 14, 1938, Morse Papers, Series S, Box 3.

"That makes me . . .": to Orlando Hollis, Dec. 19, 1938, ibid.

CHAPTER 4: ARBITRATOR SUPREME

Unless otherwise indicated, Morse's arbitration experiences are taken from Morse Papers, Series V, Box 1, Vols. 6-12; interview with E. D. Conklin, Apr. 10, 1983; and Morse interviews.

PAGE 88   "Bloody Thursday": *San Francisco Chronicle*, Mar. 31, 1990 (article on the death of Harry Bridges). See also Jeremy Brecher, *Strike!* South End Press, Boston, 1972, p. 153.

PAGE 92   "He had to . . .": interview with Norma Frazee, July 3, 1984.

"a kind of . . .": Charles P. Larrowe, *Harry Bridges: The Rise and Fall of Radical Labor in the United States*, Lawrence Hill & Co., New York, 1972, p. 205.

PAGE 93   "collusive": *San Francisco Call-Bulletin*, Oct. 8, 1939.

PAGE 95   "consent of his . . .": *San Francisco Chronicle*, Oct. 12, 1939.

Morse's thirteen-page letter to Erb is dated Oct. 23, 1939 (Morse Papers, Series S, Box 1). In her interview, Frazee contended that Morse was less than forthcoming in describing his secretarial arrangement. She argued that Morse's arbitration fees included money for her time, and that she rarely, if ever, saw any of it.

Even when Morse was away, his personal affairs intruded into the office, occasionally generating a jocular but pointed rebuke from Hollis: "Your secretary found it necessary today to request a slight lengthening of her noon hour so that she might attend to some 'errands' for you. I am wondering whether you could arrange to handle the sale of your horses and livestock during your absence through a recognized auctioneer instead of through the Law School secretary" (Oct. 24, 1941, ibid., Box 3).

PAGE 97   "charged with emotionalism . . .": *Oregonian*, July 24, 1941.

PAGE 98   "Dictator . . . he doesn't know . . .": *Oregon Labor Press*, Sept. 20, 1940.

"do an honest . . .": from Floyd Healey, Dec. 12, 1940, Morse Papers, Series S, Box 1.

"He is a sound . . .": memorandum, Frances Perkins to President, Oct. 8, 1940, Franklin Delano Roosevelt Library, Hyde Park, N.Y.

"always been a . . .": to Wayne Stewart, Aug. 6, 1940, Morse Papers, Series S, Box 3.

PAGE 99   "Wayne L. Morse . . .": William Flynn, "Waterfront Boss," *The Coast*, Feb. 1941, pp. 15-16.

PAGE 100   "suffocating . . . As I . . .": to Orlando Hollis, Sept. 23, 1941, Morse Papers, Series S, Box 3.

The "striptease" incident: to E. D. Conklin, Sept. 18, 1941, ibid.

The other members of Morse's board were James C. Bonbright, Professor of Finance, Columbia University; Thomas Reed Powell, Professor of Law, Harvard University; Huston Thompson, a Washington, D.C., lawyer; and Joseph Henry Willits, Director of Social Sciences, Rockefeller Institute.

"new evidence": Morse Papers, Series V, Box 1, Vol. 12.

PAGE 101   "It is all . . .": to Walter J. Monro, Dec. 18, 1941, ibid., Series T, Box 13.

"entirely different . . .": to Orlando Hollis, Dec. 18, 1941, ibid., Series S, Box 3.

"Keep the fences up . . .": to Elma Doris Havemann, Jan. 30, 1942, ibid., Box 4.

PAGE 102 "keep your own . . .": to Elma Doris Havemann, Sept. 17, 1941, ibid., Box 3.

"One with your . . .": to Elma Doris Havemann, Oct. 2, 1941, ibid.

PAGE 104 "czar": ibid., Series V, Box 1, Vol. 13.

PAGE 105 "Coordinator . . . This is . . .": memorandum, FDR to Jerry Land, Mar. 20, 1942, FDR Library.

"this is a . . .": to Orlando Hollis, Feb. 21, 1942, Morse Papers, Series S, Box 3.

PAGE 106 On the importance of membership maintenance, see Foster Rhea Dulles, *Labor in America: A History*, revised edition, Thomas Y. Crowell Co., New York, 1960, p. 335. See also Brecher, pp. 222-23.

PAGE 107 "Following this war . . .": to Henry S. Fraser, June 2, 1942, Morse Papers, Series T, Box 23.

"Congress can pass . . .": Notes by Mr. Morse on his visit to the White House and his conversation with the President, Aug. 21, 1942, ibid., Series S, Box 5.

"in defiance of . . .": *New York Herald-Tribune*, May 8, 1942.

When the government took over a company because of *employer* noncompliance, it did not in fact send in personnel to run day-to-day operations. It merely "raised the flag" over a facility, whose management continued to perform their normal tasks under federal direction. For the companies involved, however, a takeover was frequently inconvenient, always embarrassing, and to be avoided at all costs. When the government decided to take over an operation because of *union* noncooperation, it usually had to send in military personnel to do most of the unskilled labor.

PAGE 108 "drastic action . . .": *New York Herald-Tribune*, July 22, 1942.

"Mr. Morse talked . . .": *Memphis Commercial Appeal*, July 23, 1942.

"Mr. Morse is everlastingly . . .": *Evansville Courier-Press*, July 26, 1942.

"To the sentiment . . .": *Knoxville Journal,* Morse Papers, Series V, Box 1, Vol. 14.

"a costly mistake . . .": *New York Times,* July 23, 1942.

"as a teacher . . .": to Editor, July 29, 1942, Morse Papers, Series T, Box 23.

PAGE 109 "we will respectfully . . .": ibid., Series V, Box 1, Vol. 15.

"illegal and unsound . . . one of the most . . .": ibid.

PAGE 110 "It was an inspiring . . . the best thing . . . a peach": to A. W. Metzger, Dec. 17, 1942, ibid., Series S, Box 3.

"without further delay": *Sunday Star* (Washington, D.C.), Dec. 13, 1942.

PAGE 111 "particularly if I can . . .": to Colonel Alexander Heron, Oct. 21, 1942, Morse Papers, Series S, Box 5.

"I got a letter . . .": to Orlando Hollis, Mar. 23, 1943, ibid., Box 4.

For more on the Little Steel Formula, see *First Monthly Report of the National War Labor Board,* Jan. 12, 1942–Mar. 31, 1943 (issued May 10, 1943), Washington, D.C., p. 3.

"no parallel . . . serious threat . . .": summary of letter to FDR, June 2, 1943, FDR Library.

"unnecessarily foolish and . . .": quoted in Laura Kalman, *Abe Fortas: A Biography,* Yale University Press, New Haven, 1990, p. 93.

PAGE 112 "I am not bothering . . .": this and subsequent letters in this exchange are in Morse Papers, Series S, Box 4.

PAGE 114 Morse apparently had no regrets about the intercourse with Fortas and Ickes, but he seems to have been concerned that he might look bad if the letters were made public. When a journalist inquired about them six months later, he insisted that the exchange "is not a matter of public record, and is not a matter that I care to have discussed. . . . it not only would be exceedingly bad taste, but in my judgment, very unethical of me to disclose at this time the contents of the communications" (to Margaret Thompson Hill, Jan. 10, 1945, ibid., Series A, Box 57).

"I suppose that . . .": to Monroe Sweetland, July 7, 1941, ibid., unprocessed.

"What do you . . .": Presidential Memorandum for the Attorney General, Sept. 22, 1943, FDR Library.

PAGE 115 "both father and . . .": to Orlando Hollis, Apr. 9, 1942, Morse Papers, Series S, Box 4.

"How is your . . .": to Lowell Miller, May 28, 1942, ibid., Box 5.

"certainly is a . . .": from Levitt Wright, Feb. 8, 1942, ibid., Box 3.

"first real vacation . . . We leave . . .": to Mrs. Paul Washke, Aug. 11, 1942, ibid., Box 6.

PAGE 116 "law widow . . .": to Justin Miller, Nov. 14, 1939, ibid., Box 2.

"I have worked . . .": to L. O. Wright, June 21, 1940, ibid., Box 3.

"Call Midge . . .": to Orlando Hollis, Dec. 11, 1941, ibid.

"Keep in touch . . .": to Elma Doris Havemann, Feb. 12, 1942, ibid., Box 4.

"yard full of . . .": to John Rae, Feb. 14, 1941, ibid., Box 3.

PAGE 117 "I don't mind . . .": to Orlando Hollis, Oct. 15, 1941, ibid.

"one of my . . .": to John Anderson, Dec. 3, 1940, ibid., Box 1.

PAGE 118 "We are very . . .": to Margaret Hoffman, July 29, 1942, ibid., unprocessed.

PAGE 119 "a very negative . . .": to Miss Hoffman, July 25, 1942, ibid.

"over compensates for . . .": to Mrs. (*sic*) Hoffman, June 29, 1943, quoted in Smith, p. 163.

"I am afraid . . .": to Miss Hoffman, July 21, 1942, Morse Papers, unprocessed.

CHAPTER 5: RUNNING PAST RUFUS

PAGE 120 "would sound kind . . .": from Stephen Kahn, June 17, 1937, Morse Papers, Series S, Box 3.

PAGE 121 "there is nothing . . .": to Warren Smith, Dec. 2, 1943, ibid., Box 7.

Morse did have one possible fallback position in case he lost the election. Before entering the race, he became a partner in the Eugene law firm of O'Connell and Darling (Kenneth O'Connell had been a colleague in the law school). O'Connell recalls that the partnership "gave him the benefit of an image of being in a practicing firm. It gave us . . . the benefit of having a prestigious name attached to our stationery" (interview with Kenneth O'Connell, Oct. 17, 1984).

"Wowie! I have . . .": to Ruth Washke, Jan. 29, 1944, Morse Papers, Series S, Box 3.

PAGE 122   "Rattling . . . Right Honorable . . .": ibid., Series V, Box 2, Vols. 21-24.

"mind our . . . maneuvered us . . .": *Oregon Voter*, Feb. 19, 1944.

PAGE 123   For an analysis of Oregon Democratic party problems in the 1930s and 1940s, see Robert E. Burton, *Democrats of Oregon: The Pattern of Minority Politics, 1900–1956*, University of Oregon Books, Eugene, 1970, chap. 5. For Multnomah County voting percentages, see Burton W. Onstine, *Oregon Votes: 1858–1972*, Oregon Historical Society, Portland, 1973, pp. 62, 359.

PAGE 124   "we need liaison . . . I have had . . .": to Steve Kahn, June 19, 1937, Morse Papers, Series S, Box 3.

"interested, of course . . .": to Gus Solomon, Nov. 21, 1936, courtesy of Judge Solomon.

PAGE 125   "I have always . . .": to Harold Stassen, Nov. 21, 1938, Morse Papers, Series S, Box 3.

"good, swift kick . . .": to John W. Anderson, Nov. 8, 1940, ibid., Box 1.

PAGE 126   "I have not . . .": to Monroe Sweetland, July 19, 1941, ibid., unprocessed.

Morse used the term "middle of the road" among other places in to William Berg (Mar. 23, 1944, ibid., Series N, Box 2).

PAGE 127   "The New Deal . . .": this and other extracts from the Lincoln Day speech are cited in Smith, pp. 93-94.

"the greatest godsend . . .": to Ruth Meyer, Sept. 26, 1944, Morse Papers, Series A, Box 85. See also to Geo. W. Rochester, Mar. 23, 1944, ibid., Series N, Box 2.

PAGE 129   The $7,500 figure is mentioned in the Conklin interview.

"although of course . . .": to E. D. Conklin, Feb. 12, 1944, courtesy of Mr. Conklin.

PAGE 131 "curtain call": *Oregonian*, Mar. 11, 1944.

"matter how soothing . . .": Morse Papers, Series V, Box 2, Vol. 20.

"high-handed and . . .": *Oregonian*, Apr. 30, 1944.

PAGE 132 "Steve, I need help . . .": to Pvt. Stephen B. Kahn, Mar. 10, 1944, Morse Papers, Series N, Box 1.

"I must get . . .": to William Berg, Mar. 11, 1944, ibid.

The letters to George Meany and Philip Murray are dated Mar. 11, 1944 (ibid., Box 2).

"I can't accept . . .": to H. Michele Olsson, Mar. 7, 1944, ibid.

PAGE 133 "Tell them that . . .": to Almon Roth, Mar. 11, 1944, ibid.

"My greatest opponent . . .": to Otto J. Formayer, Feb. 11, 1944, ibid., Box 3.

PAGE 135 "It certainly is . . .": Rufus Holman to Henry M. Hanzen, Dec. 3, 1943, Henry M. Hanzen Papers, Special Collections, University of Oregon Library, Box 1.

"Anti-Semitic?": *The Economist*, July 15, 1944.

"Undoubtedly Wayne Morse . . .": to Henry M. Hanzen, undated, Hanzen Papers, Box 1.

PAGE 136 For Holman's attacks on Morse, see *Portland Journal*, May 2, 1944; and *Oregon Statesman*, May 21, 1944.

"the Halitosis of . . . ": Morse Papers, Series V, Box 2, Vol. 23.

"trouble with Holman . . .": ibid.

PAGE 137 The Multnomah County poll is mentioned in to William Berg, May 4, 1944, ibid., Series N, Box 1.

"Relocate all Japs back to Japan": quoted in Smith, p. 100. A second variable, which at least had to be considered, was the simultaneous campaign that was being waged for Oregon's other U.S. Senate seat, left vacant by the death of Republican Charles McNary. But that contest seemed to occupy separate turf from the Morse-Holman race, and as the November tally would show, voters had little trouble distinguishing the two sets of candidates in their minds.

PAGE 138 "audit will show . . .": cited in *Oregon Voter*, May 6, 1944.

"the Jews contributed . . .": to E. B. McNaughton, June 12, 1944, Morse Papers, Series S, Box 5.

"yet to give . . .": to Gertrude Bellis, July 27, 1944, ibid., Series N, Box 1.

PAGE 139 "at a loss . . .": to William Berg, Jr., July 7, 1944, ibid.

"I think that . . .": to Ruth Meyer, July 21, 1944, ibid., Series A, Box 85.

"partisan of unquestioned . . .": cited in Smith, p. 104.

PAGE 140 "a vicious smear . . .": to Margaret Thompson Hill, Mar. 3, 1945, Morse Papers, Series A, Box 57.

"an unusual departure from . . .": from S. Eugene Allen, Oct. 2, 1944, ibid., Box 14.

"bureaucratic professor": *Oregon Voter*, May 13, 1944.

"because I am . . .": to Joseph F. Smith, Oct. 4, 1944, Morse Papers, Series N, Box 2.

PAGE 141 "There are a thousand . . .": Mildred Morse to Clifford H. Noyes, Nov. 17, 1964, ibid.

CHAPTER 6: STORMING THE SENATE

PAGE 144 "god-damned deficit": to James Landye, July 16, 1945, Morse Papers, Series S, Box 5. Eddie Sammons offered advice (which Morse chose not to follow) as to an easy way to overcome the campaign shortfall: "Pardon the back seat driving but re the deficit the thought occurs you could put Mrs. M. on the payroll as an advisor ala [*sic*] John Garner, Harry Truman and many others and the net tax could clean it up without embarrasement [*sic*]" (from Sammons, Mar. 27, 1945, ibid., Box 6).

"fat cats . . .": to Paul R. Washke, Feb. 21, 1945, ibid.

"go-to-hell . . .": to Dr. M. M. Allen, Oct. 9, 1945, ibid., Box 3.

"as long as . . .": to Ralph D. Moores, Feb. 19, 1945, ibid., Box 5.

"I am not . . .": to Paul and Ruth Washke, Oct. 11, 1945, ibid., Box 6.

PAGE 146 "He has bearded . . .": *Washington Post*, Aug. 5, 1945. The quantity of Morse's speeches is the more impressive when one considers that other members of the freshman class were far from shrinking violets. Some were skillful orators who would go on to make names for themselves in the upper chamber. They included Homer Capehart of Indiana, J. William Fulbright of Arkansas, Bourke Hickenlooper of Iowa, Leverett Saltonstall of Massachusetts, and Glen Taylor of Idaho.

PAGE 147 "cheap little politicians . . .": *Chicago Tribune,* July 9, 1945.

"Wayne Morse has . . .": Morse Papers, Series V, Box 2, Vol. 28.

"Mary had a . . .": ibid.

PAGE 148 "a matter of . . .": to Charles Watkins, Dec. 29, 1945, ibid., Series A, Box 122.

PAGE 149 On American postwar atomic policy, see Gregg Herken, *The Winning Weapon: The Atomic Bomb in the Cold War,* Alfred A. Knopf, New York, 1980. See also James P. Warburg, *The United States in the Postwar World,* Atheneum, New York, 1966, chaps. 1-7.

PAGE 150 On Vandenberg, Connally, and Lucas, see Herken, pp. 28-32.

"the atomic bomb . . .": to Charles Watkins, Dec. 29, 1945.

"opportunity . . . adopt the policy . . .": *Oregonian,* Nov. 28, 1945.

"Never before in . . .": to Paul R. Washke, Nov. 14, 1945, Morse Papers, Series S, Box 6. Unless otherwise indicated, all quotations in this section are taken from this letter. See also to Paul and Ruth Washke, Dec. 10, 1945, ibid.

PAGE 151 The reference to war within fifteen years is in to Professor P. M. Brandt, Nov. 13, 1945, ibid., Series A, Box 5. Morse was generally concerned that the military was overstepping its bounds in attempting to dictate public policy. Earlier he had informed Washke that there was "a great fear here in Washington, well backed up by supporting evidence, that the Congress . . . must be constantly on guard against the War and Navy Departments' encroachment upon the civilian life of this country" (to Lieut. P. R. Washke, U.S.N.R., Apr. 27, 1945, ibid., Series S, Box 6).

"Right now we . . .": to Dr. and Mrs. Adolph Kunz, Dec. 28, 1945, ibid., Box 4.

PAGE 154 "That was one . . .": *Eugene Register-Guard,* June 2, 1946.

PAGE 155 "unkind in the language . . .": cited in Smith, p. 131.

"what you said . . .": from Harry Truman, Mar. 15, 1947, Morse Papers, Series A, Box 146.

PAGE 156 "the man in . . .": *San Francisco Chronicle*, Sept. 22, 1946. Looking toward the 1948 election, Morse told Jim Landye's partner, B. A. Green, that he would prefer any kind of Republican to four more years of Truman: "I believe that Truman has no political philosophy except that of political expediency. . . . There is no hope for a sound program or for any stability in the country under such a charlatan course" (to B. A. Green, Sept. 25, 1946, Morse Papers, Series A, Box 51).

"demonstrated in a . . .": *New York Times*, Jan. 5, 1946.

"a grand flop . . .": Morse Papers, unprocessed.

"better things to . . .": ibid., Series V, Box 3, Vol. 31.

PAGE 157 "Harry Cain will . . .": cited in Richard L. Neuberger, "Jekyll and Hyde in Politics: Oregon's Wayne Morse," *Frontier*, May 15, 1950, p. 3.

On Morse's campaigning for conservatives, see *Salt Lake City Tribune*, Oct. 7, 1946; *Oregonian*, Oct. 10, 1946; *Oregon Journal*, Oct. 8, 1946; *Christian Science Monitor*, Oct. 17, 1946; and *Nation*, Nov. 2, 1946.

"prostituting": *Idaho Evening Statesman*, Oct. 7, 1946.

"worry about . . .": to Dr. and Mrs. Paul Washke, Nov. 5, 1946, Morse Papers, Series S, Box 6.

"in each instance . . .": to Richard Neuberger, Nov. 8, 1946, ibid., Series A, Box 95.

PAGE 158 "some of my . . .": to C. C. Chapman, Oct. 17, 1946, ibid., Box 105.

In 1953, after bolting the Republican party, Morse saw fit to acknowledge the earlier error of his ways: "We all make mistakes from time to time, and I wish to confess that in 1946 . . . I made a very serious political mistake involving Hugh Mitchell. My mistake was to give first consideration to party regularity by carrying out a request of the Republican National Committee to make a speech in Tacoma, Washington, in support of Mitchell's Republican opponent" (to Western Oregon Jefferson-Jackson Day Banquet [Mitchell was guest speaker at the banquet], May 15, 1953, ibid., Box 33).

"very much disappointed . . . for the most . . .": to James Landye, Mar. 9, 1947, ibid., Series S, Box 5.

PAGE 159 "the most concentrated . . .": cited in Brecher, p. 228.

"an almost complete . . .": Joel Seidman, *American Labor from Defense to Reconversion* (1953), cited in Brecher, p. 228.

"but a maverick . . .": *Newsweek*, May 12, 1947.

PAGE 161 One newspaper counted more than seventy-two thousand words in Morse's filibuster (*Washington News*, June 23, 1947).

PAGE 162 "to eat jack rabbit": *Oregonian*, June 20, 1947.

"until the democratic . . .": Morse Papers, Series V, Box 3, Vol. 33.

PAGE 164 "We Westerners can't . . .": ibid., Vol. 32.

Morse's own recounting of the history of the Morse Formula appears in a long letter to Senator William Proxmire (June 6, 1969, ibid., Series S, Box 1). Among other places, the term "grab bag" is used in to Robert Condon, Mar. 18, 1954, ibid., Box 74.

PAGE 166 "the pressure and heat . . .": to the President, Sept. 19, 1950, ibid., Series A, Box 74.

Morse was uneasy that as a result of the Truman Doctrine, a reactionary government had been established in Greece. But he believed that the reactionaries had popular support and that the alternative would have been a takeover by the Communists, who did not, in his opinion, have the public behind them. He admitted that the United States had no theoretical right to interfere in Greek affairs, but argued that in this case "theory must give way to facts" (to J. D. M. Crockwell, Feb. 2, 1948, ibid., Box 27).

PAGE 167 "we will be . . .": *Oregonian*, Apr. 13, 1948.

"I am opposed to. . .": to Don Cooper, Aug. 8, 1949, Morse Papers, Series A, Box 7.

For the rumor that Morse would become Secretary of the Interior, see Morse Papers, Series V, Box 3, Vol. 34.

"The Elephant's Future": Dec. 4, 1948, ibid., Box 4, Vol. 35.

Morse's mail count: ibid., Series S, Box 5.

"great men," "Joe Palooka": undated, ibid., Series V, Box 4, Vol. 39.

PAGE 168 Morse as vice-presidential material: ibid., Vol. 37.

"those who know . . .": ibid., Vol. 36.

Morse's talkativeness is documented in *Salem Capital Journal*, Sept. 1, 1949.

PAGE 169 "moral obligation . . . meant that we . . .": *Salem Farmer Union*, Aug. 15, 1949.

PAGE 170 Drew Pearson's column appeared in the *Salem Capital Journal*, Aug. 3, 1949. See also a similar piece by Tris Coffin, Morse Papers, Series V, Box 4, Vol. 36.

For the story of Morse's accident, see *Oregonian*, Sept. 9, 1949; *East Oregonian* (Pendleton), Sept. 24, 1949; *Salem Capital Journal*, Nov. 11, 1949; newspaper accounts in Morse Papers, Series V, Box 2, Vol. 29; to Mr. and Mrs. Paul Washke et al., Sept. 28, 1949, ibid., Series S, Box 6; and to Dr. P. M. Brandt, Oct. 20, 1949, ibid., Series A, Box 15.

"as though it . . .": to Cape Grant, Sept. 24, 1949, ibid., Series S, Box 4.

PAGE 171 "I hope you . . .": from Harry S. Truman, Sept. 12, 1949, ibid., Box 5.

CHAPTER 7: IN THE DAYS OF MCCARTHY

PAGE 175 "My welcome throughout . . .": Douglas MacArthur, *Reminiscences*, McGraw-Hill Book Co., New York, 1964, p. 405.

"When an ex-national . . .": quoted by Smith, p. 223.

"son of a . . .": cited in David M. Oshinsky, *A Conspiracy So Immense: The World of Joe McCarthy*, The Free Press, New York, 1983, p. 194.

"God help the . . .": *Eugene Register-Guard*, Apr. 16, 1951.

PAGE 176 "Every time we . . .": to E. D. Conklin, July 16, 1951, courtesy of Mr. Conklin.

"goes far afield . . . There is no . . .": *Military Situation in the Far East: Hearings before the Committee on Armed Services and the Committee on Foreign Relations*, U.S. Senate, 82d Cong., 1st sess., 1951, pp. 65-66.

For Cain's statement, see *Military Situation*, pp. 3561-605.

PAGE 177 "have done so . . .": *Eugene Register-Guard,* Apr. 16, 1951.

"of the twenty-six-member . . .": Smith, p. 227.

For other discussions of the Senate hearings, see J. Lawton Collins, *War in Peacetime: The History and Lessons of Korea,* Houghton Mifflin Co., Boston, 1969, chap. 11; and Richard H. Rovere and Arthur M. Schlesinger, Jr., *The General and the President, and the Future of American Foreign Policy,* Farrar, Straus & Young, New York, 1951, chap. 4.

"My mail on . . . come to understand . . .": to E. D. Conklin, July 16, 1951, courtesy of Mr. Conklin.

Morse was joined in requesting an investigation into the China lobby by Senator Brien McMahon, Democrat from Connecticut. For discussions of the China lobby, see Thomas C. Reeves, *The Life and Times of Joe McCarthy,* Stein & Day, New York, 1982, pp. 219-22; *Washington Star,* Apr. 20, 1952; and *St. Louis Post-Dispatch,* Apr. 28, 1952.

PAGE 179 "in good faith . . . Red as a . . . the No. 1 item . . .": *Chicago Tribune,* Sept. 29, 1951; see also *Chicago Tribune,* Sept. 30, 1951. An anti-Morse editorial by Colonel McCormick entitled "Republican in Name Only" was reprinted (along with an answer from Morse) in *East Oregonian,* Sept. 27, 1951. For more on the investigation of IPR, see Ellen W. Shrecker, *No Ivory Tower: McCarthyism and the Universities,* Oxford University Press, New York, 1986, chap. 6.

"we should not . . .": to Jesse Gard, Feb. 14, 1951, Morse Papers, Series A, Box 49.

"freeing Chiang . . . the life of . . .": to A. E. Brettauer, July 11, 1951, ibid., Box 16.

PAGE 180 "secret information . . . the highest levels . . . strongly prejudiced": *Congressional Record,* Apr. 10, 1952, pp. 4021-24.

The *New York Times* story appeared on Apr. 10, 1952.

"Chinese Dragon . . .": *St. Louis Post-Dispatch,* Apr. 28, 1952.

PAGE 181 "It's my only . . .": Morse Papers, Series V, Box 2, Vol. 27. See also to Mr. and Mrs. William Oswald, Jan. 24, 1945, ibid., Series S, Box 5.

PAGE 182 Jenner's collection for hay: Samuel Shaffer, *On and Off the Floor: Thirty Years as a Correspondent on Capitol Hill,* Newsweek Books, New York, 1980, p. 150.

"It is surprising . . .": to E. D. Conklin, Sept. 17, 1951, courtesy of Mr. Conklin.

On the accident and its aftermath, see also *Oregon Journal*, Aug. 10, 1951; *Eugene Register-Guard*, Aug. 12 and 27, 1951; to Midge and Amy, Aug. 16, 1951, Morse Papers, Addendum; to William Tugman, Aug. 18, 1951, ibid., Series A, Box 147; to James Landye, Aug. 18, 1951, and Sept. 15, 1951, ibid., Series S, Box 5; to Mr. and Mrs. G. E. Bible, Aug. 23, 1951, ibid., Box 3; and to William Berg, Jr., Aug. 23, 1951, ibid.

PAGE 183   "new approach . . .": Truman, memorandum, Dec. 26, 1951, cited in Robert H. Ferrell, ed., *Off the Record: The Private Papers of Harry S. Truman*, Harper & Row, New York, 1980, pp. 221-22. See also Smith, pp. 132-34; and Robert J. Donovan, *Tumultuous Years: The Presidency of Harry S. Truman, 1949–1953*, W. W. Norton & Co., New York, 1982, pp. 375-78.

PAGE 184   "a Democrat could . . .": to Honorable Harry S. Truman, Dec. 22, 1951, Morse Papers, Series S, Box 6.

"Dear Wayne . . .": from Harry S. Truman, Dec. 24, 1951, Harry S. Truman Library, Independence, Mo.

PAGE 186   "isolationist wing . . . it is about . . .": *Madison* (Wis.) *Capital Times*, May 28, 1952.

Discussion of the Salem meeting is based in part on an interview with Clay Myers, Jr., Apr. 3-4, 1984; see also *Oregonian*, June 8, 1952; and *Oregon Journal*, June 8, 1952, Morse Papers, Series A, Box 159.

PAGE 187   "you may be . . .": to Richard M. Nixon, July 28, 1952, Morse Papers, Series A, Box 96.

PAGE 188   For the argument about massaging Morse's ego, see Smith, pp. 140-54.

"I deeply appreciate . . .": to General Dwight D. Eisenhower, Morse Papers, Series A, Box 36. Eisenhower's thank-you letter was dated Aug. 20, 1952 (ibid., Series V, Box 6, Vol. 49).

PAGE 190   "Taft lost the . . .": cited in a letter from Senator William Benton (D., Conn.), Sept. 16, 1952, ibid., Series A, Box 14.

"I Liked Ike": ibid., Series V, Box 6, Vol. 49.

"The Eisenhower I supported . . .": *Oregonian*, Oct. 19, 1952.

PAGE 191   "morally dishonest": ibid., Oct. 17, 1952.

"Judas . . . recent kicks . . .": ibid., Oct. 19, 1952.

"egomaniac . . . blatant . . .": cited in Smith, p. 148.

"snide . . . calumnious": cited in letter to Midge from Tom Stoddard, Oct. 26, 1952, Morse Papers, Addendum.

"the senator felt . . .": *Oregon Journal,* Nov. 27, 1952.

"The only thing . . .": from B. A. Green, Nov. 7, 1952, B. A. Green Papers, Special Collections, University of Oregon Library.

PAGE 192   "Keep calm . . .": from B. A. Green, Oct. 22, 1952, ibid.

The letters from Morse to Sammons are dated Sept. 19, 1952, and Oct. 14, 1952 (Morse Papers, Series S, Box 6).

"a lying sonofabitch": from a tape-recorded interview, University of Oregon Archives. In 1984, ten years after Morse's death, thirty-two years after he had left the Republican party, I tried to set up an interview with Sammons, who was by then in his nineties. He said he wanted nothing to do with that "no-good bastard" or with anyone writing about him, and hung up the phone.

PAGE 193   "punitive measures . . .": Morse Papers, Series V, Box 7, Vol. 51.

PAGE 194   "gutless wonders": to James Landye, Jan. 30, 1953, ibid., Series S, Box 5.

"Wayne I want . . .": from Hubert H. Humphrey, Feb. 12, 1953, ibid., Series A, Box 59. Morse's response to Humphrey is dated Feb. 13, 1953 (ibid.).

PAGE 195   "garbage can": *East Oregonian,* Jan. 19, 1953.

"Glum but Game": *Washington Daily News,* May 26, 1953.

"You silly jackass . . .": *Los Angeles Examiner,* Mar. 25, 1953.

PAGE 196   "goddamned big . . .": to Irving Ives, Mar. 11, 1953, Richard L. Neuberger Papers, Special Collections, University of Oregon Library, Box 30.

"want the public . . .": to Richard Neuberger, Apr. 2, 1953, Morse Papers, Series A, Box 95.

PAGE 197   "the most outstanding . . . embroiled in State . . . on a subject . . .": to A. T. Weaver, Jan. 28, 1941, ibid., Series S, Box 3.

PAGE 198   "communists and fellow . . .": *Oregon Journal,* Apr. 3, 1949.

"What I fear . . .": to Arthur J. Freund, May 17, 1949, Morse Papers, Series A, Box 46.

Morse's and Rusk's ideas on investigating universities were reported in the *Chicago Daily Tribune*, Mar. 6, 1953.

"Morse Truckles to . . .": *I. F. Stone's Weekly*, Mar. 14, 1953.

On McCarthyism and academic freedom, see Schrecker.

PAGE 199 "a lot of . . . My answer to . . .": Memorandum for Dr. Graham, June 20, 1942, Papers of A. Robert Smith, Oregon Historical Society, Portland.

PAGE 200 "demanding the return . . .": from Judge C. D. Nickelsen, Apr. 20, 1944, Morse Papers, Series N, Box 3.

"spread out very . . .": to Judge C. D. Nickelsen, Apr. 26, 1944, ibid.

"the prejudiced bigoted . . .": to Lt. W. W. Wyatt, June 2, 1945, ibid., Series A, Box 159.

PAGE 201 Morse deplored the appearance of witch hunts as early as 1947 in an article in *Cross Sections*, published by the Republican Open Forums (ibid., Series V, Box 2, Vol. 28).

Smith's "Declaration of Conscience" is discussed in the *Christian Science Monitor*, June 2, 1950.

PAGE 202 On the "Mr. X" story, see *Oregon Journal*, July 26, 1950.

"kangaroo courts": *Washington Post*, June 25, 1950.

"I do not . . .": to Dorothy A. Robinson, Aug. 17, 1950, Morse Papers, Series A, Box 83.

"It is my . . .": to W. C. Ludders, Mar. 27, 1950, ibid., Box 110. See also to Mrs. E. B. Sampson, Apr. 11, 1950; and to Henrietta Rice, Aug. 1, 1950, ibid.

"since the bleakest . . .": Oshinsky, p. 173. See also Robert Griffith, *The Politics of Fear: Joseph R. McCarthy and the Senate*, University of Kentucky Press, Lexington, 1970, pp. 117-22.

PAGE 203 "I would be . . .": to Edward Sammons, Sept. 14, 1950, Morse Papers, Series N, Box 8. See also to Mark and C. Chamberlain, May 26, 1952, ibid., Series A, Box 25.

"the great work . . .": to J. Edgar Hoover, Mar. 17, 1947, ibid., Series S, Box 4.

Information from Morse's FBI file was obtained through the Freedom of Information and Privacy Acts. As is typical in such cases, a considerable amount of material was censored or withheld by the bureau, which cited the usual list of reasons for so doing. Although I am sure that useful materials were withheld for unjustifiable reasons, I did not feel it worth the time and expense of a lengthy lawsuit to pursue the matter further.

PAGE 204 "is a police . . .": FBI files.

"I am shocked . . . lazy policeman's tool": ibid.

"real subversion of . . .": Morse Papers, Series V, Box 7, Vol. 56. On the need for a warrant, see to George B. Holmes, Sept. 21, 1954, ibid., Series A, Box 158.

PAGE 205 On the Communist Control Act, see Griffith, pp. 292-94; and Carl Solberg, *Hubert Humphrey: A Biography*, W. W. Norton & Co., New York, 1984, pp. 157-58. During the Vietnam era, Morse used his cosponsorship of the Communist Control Act to deflect criticism from those who questioned his patriotism. See, e.g., to Richard Mason, Sept. 16, 1968, Morse Papers, Series U, Box 89.

The Morse-Lehman proposal was released in the form of a reprint from the *Congressional Record*; see Morse Papers, Series A, Box 83.

PAGE 206 "MORSE. Does the . . .": quoted in Smith, pp. 268-69, 270.

"hard to believe . . .": *I. F. Stone's Weekly*, Mar. 14, 1953.

On Anna Rosenberg, see Morse Papers, Series V, Box 5, Vol. 44.

PAGE 208 For a full picture of the problems with Russell Duke, see to Henry Hanzen, Apr. 11, 1950, ibid., Series N, Box 5; *Congressional Record*, May 6, 1953, pp. 4758-61; *Portland Journal*, May 5, 1953; *Oregonian*, May 8, 1953; from R. W. Duke, Jan. 7, 1954, Morse Papers, unprocessed; to R. W. Duke, Jan. 8, 1954, ibid.

"The Loneliest Man . . .": Samuel Grafton, *Collier's*, Apr. 4, 1953.

"ideological Socialist . . .": Jack Lait and Lee Mortimer, *U.S.A. Confidential*, Crown Publishers, New York, 1952, pp. 53, 128. The FBI saw fit to include excerpts from this book in its files on Morse.

PAGE 209 "political thuggery": *Christian Science Monitor*, July 31, 1954.

"I realize that . . .": to Jim Landye, Aug. 9, 1954, Morse Papers, Series S, Box 5.

PAGE 210   "the fairness of . . .": *AFL News-Reporter*, Apr. 17, 1953.

"nice little boys . . .": *Oregonian*, Aug. 17, 1954.

Regarding McCarthy's "liberal" background, the *Milwaukee Journal* stated on November 6, 1946: "In talking with McCarthy one gets the impression that he will make a record as a liberal Republican, and that he will be closer to Republicans of the type of former Gov. Harold E. Stassen of Minnesota and Senators Wayne Morse of Oregon and Joseph Ball of Minnesota than he will be to Sen. Robert Taft of Ohio" (cited by Reeves, p. 107).

PAGE 211   The Senate dining room incident is recorded in the Myers interview, Apr. 4, 1984.

On the swapping of neckties, see *Oregon Journal*, June 1, 1951.

"there is no . . .": cited in Griffith, p. 294.

"the Senate remained . . .": ibid.

"insulting": *Washington Times-Herald*, Feb. 17, 1949.

For Morse's views on communism in 1961, see Morse Papers, Series B, Box 156.

"transfixed by . . .": Griffith, p. 294.

CHAPTER 8: LEADING THE REVOLUTION

PAGE 213   "on principle": *New York Times*, Jan. 23, 1953.

Between Labor Day and election day, Morse gave 110 speeches for Democratic candidates, an average of nearly two a day (Morse Papers, Series A, Box 102).

PAGE 214   For more on the rise of the Oregon Democratic party, see Burton, chaps. 6-7.

"At various times . . .": Howard Morgan, unpublished memoir, Jan.-Feb. 1985.

Sweetland's Pacific activities: interview with Monroe Sweetland, Apr. 30, 1984.

PAGE 216   "The party was . . .": remarks of Howard Morgan to the state Central Committee, Multnomah Hotel, Portland, Aug. 2, 1959 (printed copy courtesy of Beulah Hand, then acting state chairman).

PAGE 218 "unfortunate . . . responsible member": *New York Times*, Nov. 21, 1954. Morgan and Sweetland had had a serious falling out in 1954 when Morgan opposed Sweetland in his wish to run for Congress.

"I didn't even . . .": interview with Charles Brooks, Apr. 26, 1984. All quotations of Brooks in this chapter are taken from this interview.

PAGE 219 "This is Morse's . . .": quoted in *St. Louis Post-Dispatch*, Oct. 10, 1955.

Morse's fainting spell: *Oregon Journal*, Jan. 27, 1953.

"I am tip-top . . .": to James Landye, Feb. 26, 1953, Morse Papers, Series S, Box 5. For the horse-kick incident, see chap. 7.

PAGE 221 "Robert A. Taft . . .": *New York Times*, Apr. 25, 1953. Morse might have had himself to blame for some of the strict limitations imposed upon him. It was clear from the outset of his speech that one of his intentions was to provoke the Senate majority leader:

> MR. TAFT. May I ask how long altogether the Senator expects to speak this time?
>
> MR. MORSE. I had a rather bad meal last night, which is going to handicap me somewhat, but I think I am good for from 8 to 12 hours. [Laughter.]

(*Congressional Record*—Senate, Apr. 24, 1953, p. 3906)

PAGE 222 Caryl's view of Morse's bladder control: Kline interviews. Bernstein's opinion on the same topic: interview with Merton Bernstein, Apr. 20, 1984. All quotations of Bernstein in this chapter are taken from this interview.

"there is much . . .": to Neil Sabin, Sept. 21, 1954, Morse Papers, Series A, Box 81.

"The Presiding Officer . . .": quoted in *Oregon Statesman*, May 1, 1953.

The origin of the rose in Morse's lapel: interview with Dorothy Berg (Bill Berg's widow), Dec. 31, 1983.

PAGE 223 "never had a . . .": Morse interviews.

PAGE 224 "What he wants . . .": *Washington Star*, Nov. 6, 1954.

"the most important . . .": Alfred Steinberg, *Sam Johnson's Boy: A Close-up of the President from Texas*, Macmillan, New York, 1968, p. 343.

"I can't reconcile . . .": *Houston Chronicle*, Feb. 2, 1954.

"way down here . . .": from Lyndon Johnson, Oct. 18, 1955, Lyndon Baines Johnson Library, Austin, Texas. The impact of Morse's Texas speech on Johnson's reelection campaign is difficult to assess. In his biography of Johnson, Robert Dallek first argues that it helped far more than it hurt. But on the very next page, he suggests that it may have contributed to a sizeable drop in Johnson's popularity, as measured in a Texas Poll taken just after the speech (Robert Dallek, *Lone Star Rising: Lyndon Johnson and His Times, 1908–1960*, Oxford University Press, New York, 1991, pp. 448-49).

PAGE 225 "one of the very . . .": from Lyndon Johnson, Jan. 14, 1955, Morse Papers, Series A, Box 67.

"have difficulty . . .": quoted in Dallek, p. 471.

For an example of Raymond Moley's criticism of Morse, see Morse Papers, Series V, Box 8, Vol. 58.

On Morse's problems with A. Robert Smith, see to William Tugman, Nov. 24, 1952, ibid., Series A, Box 147; to W. L. Beale, Jr., Apr. 23, 1953, ibid., Box 7; to Robert Ruhl, July 21, 1953, ibid., Box 128; *Eugene Register-Guard*, Feb. 15, 1954; and A. Robert Smith to William Tugman, Tugman Papers, Box 2. On the Associated Press, see to Josh Horne, Aug. 11, 1953, Morse Papers, Series A, Box 7; *Oregonian*, May 29, 1953; to William Johnston, Oct. 5, 1953, Morse Papers, Series A, Box 66; and Nick F. Cariello, "Morse and the AP," *Frontier*, Jan. 1954, p. 23.

PAGE 226 "Always Polluted": quoted in Smith, p. 195.

Morse's primary-campaign expenditures: *Oregonian*, June 1, 1956.

PAGE 227 "We were absolutely . . .": Bernstein interview.

PAGE 228 The July poll: Morse Papers, Series V, Box 9, Vol. 65. The August poll: ibid., Series N, Box 14.

"the Oregon Senate . . .": *New York Times*, Oct. 14, 1956.

PAGE 229 "by outside influences . . .": *AFL-CIO News*, Sept. 22, 1956.

For Morse's campaign contributions, see *Roseburg* (Ore.) *News Review*, Sept. 21, 1956; *Oregonian*, Oct. 28, 1956; *Medford* (Ore.) *Mail Tribune*, Nov. 5, 1956; Morse Papers, Series N, Box 20; and Smith, p. 325.

PAGE 230 "come out and . . .": from Lyndon Johnson, Aug. 4, 1956, Morse Papers, Series A, Box 67.

"shocking abandonment": *Oregonian*, May 6, 1953.

PAGE 231 "I represent the . . .": *New York Post*, Sept. 13, 1956.

"You'd think I . . .": *Wall Street Journal*, Apr. 25, 1956.

PAGE 232 "a wonderful speaking . . .": *New York Post*, Sept. 13, 1956.

"He was on . . .": *New York Times*, Oct. 10, 1956.

"with the benign . . .": *New York Post*, Sept. 13, 1956.

PAGE 233 "to choose between . . .": *Oregonian*, Mar. 10, 1956.

On *The Documented Record of Senator Wayne Morse*, see *New York Times*, Aug. 9, 1956; and Smith, pp. 317-19.

PAGE 234 On the cropped-photograph episode, see *Eugene Register-Guard*, Oct. 24 and 30, 1956; *Oregonian*, Oct. 28 and 30, 1956; and *New York Times*, Oct. 28, 1956.

"A high-level . . .": from Mike Mansfield, Aug. 10, 1956, Morse Papers, Series A, Box 31.

PAGE 237 "Windbag . . . from W. B.": Brooks interview.

"It's the votes . . .": undated memorandum, Morse Papers, Series A, Box 82.

"the issues don't . . .": ibid. To McKay's credit, when Morse pointed out during the campaign that Interior had been issuing gas and oil leases after the secretary had supposedly banned this practice, McKay took the blame even though responsibility belonged to someone else (oral history of D. Otis Beasley, Dec. 15, 1969, John F. Kennedy Library, Boston, Mass.).

"not surprised . . .": Morse Papers, Series V, Vol. 65.

PAGE 238 A. Robert Smith's description of the Morse-McKay debate: Smith, p. 326.

The October poll: *New York Times*, Oct. 6, 1956.

"Well, we did it . . .": to Bud Welker, Nov. 15, 1956, Morse Papers, unprocessed.

PAGE 239 Neuberger's press release, Nov. 14, 1956: ibid., Series A, Box 95.

"extend to President . . .": to Nellie Crystal, Nov. 15, 1956, ibid., Box 45.

CHAPTER 9: DICK AND WAYNE

PAGE 241 The introduction by Hoyt is mentioned in a letter from Morse to Russ Sackett, Nov. 21, 1950, Morse Papers, Series A, Box 95.

The column on Hoover is from the *Oregon Daily Emerald*, Oct. 22, 1932.

PAGE 242 "He had a gift . . .": this quotation and some of the other material on Neuberger's activities at Eugene are from an interview with Stephen Kahn, Sept. 20, 1984.

PAGE 243 "Oregon Daily Emerald plan . . .": *Oregon Daily Emerald*, from Feb. 21 to Apr. 4, 1932.

"detrimental to the . . .": ibid., Feb. 24, 1932.

"the meaningless . . .": ibid., Mar. 2, 1933. Earlier, Neuberger had referred to fraternities as "childish and pathetic," and said "they flaunted their prejudice and bias" (ibid., Feb. 28, 1933).

"Roscoe Pound . . .": cited by Smith, pp. 335-36.

"sing together . . .": to Neuberger, June 21, 1934, Morse Papers, unprocessed.

PAGE 244 The grade-change request was dated Sept. (day unknown) 1933 (ibid.); the wire from Neuberger to Morse was dated Sept. 21, 1933 (ibid.). As the following quotation from Morse indicates, his connection with Neuberger was more than a little friendly: "I want you to know that I sincerely appreciate the spirit which motivated you to present me with the lovely key case gift. . . . I know that you realize that I cherish our friendly and argumentative relationships and I want to assure you of my sincere desire to befriend you whenever I can" (to Neuberger, Oct. 10, 1933, ibid.).

"I only want . . .": from Neuberger, June 19, 1934, ibid.

PAGE 245 "face facts . . .": to Neuberger, July 30, 1934, ibid.

"I cannot begin . . .": to Neuberger, Aug. 23, 1934, ibid.

"If you do . . .": to Neuberger, Sept. 24, 1934, ibid.

PAGE 246 "you had to . . .": Kahn interview.

"Those sons of bitches . . .": ibid.

"like a Philadelphia lawyer": ibid.

"absolutely honestly . . .": "Transcript of Record," Nov. 19, 1934, Morse Papers, unprocessed.

"yielding to sentimentality . . .": "Minority Report," ibid.

PAGE 247 "Dean, what are . . .": from Neuberger, Nov. 20, 1934, ibid., unprocessed. This quotation and, unless otherwise noted, all remarks by Neuberger and Morse cited in the next few pages are taken from correspondence between the two men during the period of Neuberger's honors case. These letters were kept in a sealed box by the Special Collections department of the University of Oregon Library until more than ten years after Morse's death. Permission to open the box was granted by the Senator's widow, Mildred M. Morse, in 1985. Ironically, Neuberger's difficulty with Spencer's course could have been predicted. The previous summer Neuberger had told Morse (in one of the later-sealed letters) that his parents were permitting him to return to Eugene only on the condition that Morse would be staying on. "If," Neuberger said, "I should start at Oregon law school and then you should leave after a year or so, I would be up a tall tree. Because I will not study law under the Hon. Mr. Spencer—UNDER NO CONDITIONS" (from Neuberger, July 31, 1934, ibid.).

PAGE 249 Nelson's letter to Pierce is dated Nov. 29, 1934 (C. Girard Davidson Papers, Special Collections, University of Oregon Library, unprocessed).

"stop tormenting that boy": Kahn interview.

PAGE 250 "After Dean Morse's . . .": "Special Staff Meeting," Nov. 27, 1934, Morse Papers, Series S, Box 3.

"I do not intend . . .": from Neuberger, Nov. 29, 1934, ibid., unprocessed.

PAGE 251 "Any gentile who . . .": to Roscoe Nelson, Nov. 30, 1934, ibid., Addendum III.

"studying now as . . .": from Neuberger, Dec. 9, 1934, ibid., unprocessed.

"had unloaded . . .": to Orlando Hollis, Dec. 20, 1934, ibid., Series S, Box 3.

"I hope you never . . .": from Neuberger, undated, ibid., unprocessed.

"cheap dramatics": Kahn interview.

On the lowering of Neuberger's grade, see Smith, p. 338.

PAGE 252 "safe, sane and conservative . . .": to Arnold Bennett Hall, May 7, 1934, Morse Papers, Series S, Box 1.

PAGE 253 "a very adept . . .": Kahn interview.

PAGE 254 "University honors . . .": to Neuberger, Nov. 26, 1940, Morse Papers, unprocessed.

PAGE 255 "With his movie-villain . . .": *Progressive*, Dec. 10, 1945, p. 4.

"He used to stand . . .": quoted by Morse in a letter to Neuberger, Dec. 26, 1945, Morse Papers, Series A, Box 95.

"I don't object . . .": ibid.

PAGE 256 "a swell campaign": to Neuberger, Mar. 4, 1946, ibid.

Morse's advice two years later: to Neuberger, Feb. 7, 1948, ibid.

PAGE 257 "Off the record . . .": to Neuberger, Jan. 8, 1946, ibid.

"brilliant in debate . . .": Neuberger to Charles Angoff, Mar. 25, 1947, Neuberger Papers, Box 30.

"To what extent . . .": Richard Neuberger, "Morse versus Morse," *Nation*, Jan. 14, 1950, p. 29.

PAGE 258 "an interesting piece . . .": Morse quoting himself in a letter to Andrew T. Weaver, Feb. 18, 1950, Morse Papers, Series S, Box 5.

Morse's "convivial" letter to Neuberger: Feb. 3, 1950, ibid., Series N, Box 7.

"one of those . . .": to Andrew Weaver, Feb. 18, 1950, ibid.

PAGE 259 "no Parisian *roué* . . .": Neuberger, "Jekyll and Hyde," p. 3.

"did not care . . .": Morse quoting himself from earlier correspondence in a letter to Russ Sackett, Nov. 21, 1950, Morse Papers, Series A, Box 95.

PAGE 260 "I swing back . . .": Neuberger to Robert W. Ruhl, Apr. 1, 1953, Neuberger Papers, Box 30.

"but he is . . .": Marquis Childs to Neuberger, June 30, 1953, ibid.

"indulged . . . 'diatribes' against me": Neuberger to Helen Fuller, July 8, 1953, ibid.

PAGE 262 "Where in the world . . .": to Neuberger, Oct. 26, 1953, Morse Papers, Series A, Box 95.

PAGE 263 The Democratic dinner incident: interview with Howard Morgan, Nov. 11, 1984.

"outright indorsement . . .": from Neuberger, Mar. 23, 1954, Morse Papers, Series A, Box 95.

PAGE 264 "May I say . . .": to Neuberger, Mar. 25, 1954, ibid.

"Really, I don't . . .": from Neuberger, Mar. 30, 1954, ibid.

"I only believe . . .": from Neuberger, Apr. 10, 1954, ibid.

"the simple fact . . .": to Neuberger, Apr. 14, 1954, ibid.

PAGE 265 "when you are . . .": ibid.

The high estimate of the number of speeches Morse may have given for Neuberger appears in a letter to Maxene Dungey, Mar. 15, 1961, ibid., Box 31; in 1959, *Time* enlarged the figure to "more than 300" (June 15, 1959, p. 27).

"The Senators from Oregon": "Two for the Show," *Time*, Jan. 17, 1955, pp. 24-28.

PAGE 266 "reaching a different . . .": to Maurine Neuberger, Feb. 28, 1955, Morse Papers, Series A, Box 95.

PAGE 267 "very fine working . . .": to Mr. and Mrs. Hibberd Kline, July 6, 1955, ibid., unprocessed.

PAGE 268 On the Friends of Wayne Morse, see *Medford Mail Tribune*, Jan. 13, 1957; Neuberger to Herbert Lundy, Jan. 8, 1957, Neuberger Papers, Box 30; from Neuberger, Jan. 10, 1957, ibid.

PAGE 269 "People ask if . . .": Richard Neuberger, "Morse for President," *Progressive*, Apr. 1957, p. 19.

PAGE 270 "saw possible challengers . . .": interview with Lloyd Tupling, Apr. 13, 1984.

"there is no . . .": "Open Letter to the People of Oregon," Mar. 15, 1957, Morse Papers, Series A, Box 89.

PAGE 271 "Dick Neuberger . . .": to C. Girard Davidson, July 20, 1957, ibid., Box 30.

"a snide attack . . .": Neuberger Papers, Box 30. All quotations from the Morse-Neuberger correspondence of Aug. 5-13, 1957, are taken from this source.

PAGE 274   A. Robert Smith's account of the correspondence appeared in the *Oregon Statesman*, Aug. 15, 1957.

"served a very . . .": from Neuberger, Aug. 27, 1957, Morse Papers, Series A, Box 24.

"civil rights . . . sucked in": *Oregon Journal*, Aug. 29, 1957.

"bewildered": press release, Morse Papers, Series V, Vol. 68.

"a shame that . . .": Neuberger to C. Girard Davidson, Sept. 3, 1957, Davidson Papers, unprocessed.

"Lately, there has . . .": Neuberger Papers, Box 30.

PAGE 275   The list of twenty-five roll-call votes is in Neuberger Papers, Box 30.

"Mr. Eisenhower is . . .": Neuberger to Harold Warner, Dec. 23, 1959, ibid., Box 19.

PAGE 276   "Admiration for Neuberger . . .": *Bend* (Ore.) *Bulletin*, Sept. 23, 1957.

"You tried to . . .": to Merton Bernstein, Jan. 3, 1958, Morse Papers, Series A, Box 14.

PAGE 277   "We used to . . .": Tupling interview.

"amused . . . rumor stories": *Eugene Register-Guard*, Jan. 15, 1958.

Morse's memorandum to the delegation was dated Jan. 14, 1958 (Morse Papers, Series A, Box 102).

PAGE 278   "who spent approximately . . .": cited in Smith, p. 350.

"and their word . . .": to J. W. Forrester, Jr., Feb. 7, 1958, Morse Papers, Series A, Box 57. Neuberger's comments on Morse's exchange with Forrester are in a letter to Morse dated Mar. 29, 1958 (ibid.).

"Al, Charlie, Edith . . .": to Neuberger, Mar. 31, 1958, Neuberger Papers, Box 30.

The interview with A. Robert Smith took place on Apr. 17, 1984.

PAGE 279   "In the political . . .": Smith, p. 349.

"Neuberger may not . . .": ibid., p. 364.

PAGE 280   The exchange of letters between Morse and Porter is alluded to in Porter to Morse, Aug. 6, 1958, Neuberger Papers, Box 30. The Douglas County Historical Society had not made the situation easier by talking tough to Morse. In a letter written the previous December, they said: "Senator Morse, we are determined to claim, without any outlay of funds, the return of the remainder of the Lillie Moore Estate. . . . Your thinking, it seems, applies your 'Morse Formula' to this matter. We flatly state that it does not apply" (from Cristina Micelli, Dec. 30, 1957, Morse Papers, Series S, Box 89).

PAGE 281 "there was ample . . .": from Neuberger, Aug. 5, 1958, Neuberger Papers, Box 30.

"You have a . . .": to Neuberger, Aug. 6, 1958, ibid.

"regretted . . . abusive . . .": from Neuberger, Aug. 6, 1958, ibid.

"in keeping with . . .": to Neuberger, Aug. 7, 1958, ibid.

PAGE 282 "abusive nature . . . Neither Charlie . . .": from Neuberger, Aug. 7, 1958, ibid.

"I understand . . .": to Neuberger, Aug. 8, 1958, ibid.

"I am completely . . .": from Neuberger, Aug. 8, 1958, ibid.

PAGE 283 "for hours . . . two supposedly . . .": interview with Phyllis Rock, Apr. 7, 1984.

"I swear to god . . .": Tupling interview.

PAGE 284 "Your letter of . . .": to Neuberger, Aug. 11, 1958, Morse Papers, Series A, Box 89.

PAGE 286 "very sad this . . .": to Al Ullman, Jan. 31, 1957, ibid., Box 148.

"an already heavy . . .": from Al Ullman, Jan. 31, 1957, ibid., Box 110.

"I do have . . .": from Charlie Porter, Jan. 31, 1957, ibid.

"I have, on thorough . . .": from Charlie Porter, Aug. 12, 1958, Charles O. Porter Papers, Special Collections, University of Oregon Library, Box 23.

PAGE 287 "I am glad . . .": from Neuberger, Aug. 12, 1958, Morse Papers, Series A, Box 89.

PAGE 288 "I am amused . . .": to Neuberger, Aug. 13, 1958, ibid.

PAGE 289 "I read it . . .": oral history of George Reedy, Feb. 29, 1984, 13, pp. 12-13, LBJ Library.

"Dick would write . . .": ibid., Dec. 14, 1968, p. 10.

"Is it morality . . .": this quotation and the following material on this issue—including quotations—are taken from a story by A. Robert Smith, *Oregonian*, July 2, 1958.

PAGE 291 "political window dressing . . . jockey politically . . .": *Eugene Register-Guard*, Nov. 14, 1958.

PAGE 292 "During your six . . .": to Merton Bernstein, Nov. 21, 1958, Morse Papers, Series A, Box 14.

"political prostitute": William McClenaghan to Neuberger, Nov. 19, 1958, Neuberger Papers, Box 30.

"Senator Morse ventilates . . .": Neuberger to McClenaghan, Nov. 20, 1958, ibid.

"very unsatisfactory . . .": to Tup, undated, ibid.

PAGE 293 "carried away . . .": *Coos Bay World*, Dec. 16, 1958.

"I was not . . .": *Oregon Journal*, Dec. 11, 1958.

"Morse Leaks Senatorial . . .": *Oregonian*, Dec. 12, 1958. The responses from Morse and Shaffer: ibid., Dec. 13, 1958.

"Since then, Neuberger . . .": *Newsweek*, Dec. 15, 1958, p. 30.

The *Oregonian* poll appeared on Dec. 21, 1958.

PAGE 294 "political thuggery": *Chicago Tribune*, July 19, 1959.

"nothing short of . . .": Tom Enright to Neuberger, Dec. 18, 1958, Neuberger Papers, Box 30.

PAGE 295 "I trust we . . .": from Neuberger, Jan. 2, 1959, Morse Papers, Series A, Box 95.

PAGE 296 "Dear Senator Neuberger . . .": to Neuberger, Jan. 5, 1959, ibid.

"very distressed": from Neuberger, Jan. 2, 1959, ibid.

"*This is not . . .*": Neuberger to Drew Pearson, Jan. 14, 1959, Neuberger Papers, Box 19.

"old law school . . .": to Mary Kelly, Jan. 27, 1959, Morse Papers, Series A, Box 20.

"act of legislative thievery": to Byron Brinton, Feb. 12, 1959, ibid., Box 35.

Neuberger's Apr. 13, 1959, letter to Morse is in Neuberger Papers, Box 30.

"I am sorry . . .": to Neuberger, Apr. 14, 1959, ibid.

"point out to . . .": *Oregonian*, May 28, 1959.

PAGE 297 "Morse has the . . .": Neuberger to Herbert Lundy, June 9, 1959, Neuberger Papers, Box 19.

On Neuberger's interest in maintaining Morse's opposition, see Smith, p. 380.

On renaming the Green Peter Dam, see Neuberger to Sam Allen, Aug. 5, 1959, Neuberger Papers, Box 19.

Charlie Brooks's report appeared in a memorandum to William Berg, July 28, 1959, Morse Papers, Series A, Box 103.

"My opinion of . . .": to Arthur Freund, June 8, 1959, ibid., Box 46.

PAGE 298 "We will all . . .": cited in Smith, p. 383.

PAGE 299 "Never before have I . . .": from Neuberger, Jan. 10, 1957, Neuberger Papers, Box 30.

PAGE 300 Shaffer wrote to Morse on Jan. 12, 1959 (Morse Papers, Series A, Box 89).

"when one suffers . . .": to Samuel Shaffer, Jan. 14, 1959, ibid.

CHAPTER 10: ONCE A MAVERICK . . .

PAGE 301 "geared to the best . . .": cited in Dallek, p. 468.

PAGE 302 On the Dave Beck contretemps, see *Medford Mail Tribune*, May 29, 1957; *Oregonian*, May 27 and 30, 1957; *Philadelphia Inquirer*, May 23, 1957; and *Washington Post*, May 21, 1957. The quoted statements of senators Hickenlooper and Wiley are taken from these sources.

PAGE 303 For the exchanges between Morse, Johnson, and Mansfield, see to Lyndon Johnson and Mike Mansfield, May 23, 1957; from Lyndon B. Johnson, May 24, 1957; from Mike Mansfield, May 25, 1957; and to Lyndon B. Johnson, May 27, 1957, all in Morse Papers, Series A, Box 67.

PAGE 305 "Lyndon Johnson made . . .": Solberg, p. 179.

"unconscionable compromise": to Frank Rarig, Jan. 6, 1958, Rarig Papers, unprocessed.

PAGE 306 "a pallid little . . .": quoted in Solberg, p. 180.

"a piece of . . .": interview with Joe Rauh, Apr. 11, 1984.

"compromise is not . . .": quoted in Solberg, p. 180.

"It disgusts me . . .": to Herbert Lehman, Feb. 10, 1958, Morse Papers, Series A, Box 3.

"laughing up . . .": *Oregon Journal*, Aug. 29, 1957.

"Oregon's Lone Ranger": *New Republic*, July 1, 1957.

"I think we . . .": to G. Mennen Williams, July 11, 1957, Morse Papers, Series A, Box 157.

PAGE 307   "I would point . . .": to Frank Rarig, Jan. 6, 1958, Rarig Papers, unprocessed.

"hoax and a sham": *Oregon Journal*, Aug. 29, 1957. For a view advancing the utility of the 1957 Civil Rights Act, see George E. Reedy, *The U. S. Senate: Paralysis or a Search for Consensus?* Crown Publishers, New York, 1986, pp. 178-80.

"The 1957 Civil . . .": Paul H. Douglas, *In the Fullness of Time: The Memoirs of Paul H. Douglas*, Harcourt Brace Jovanovich, New York, 1971, p. 293.

PAGE 308   For accounts of the Schwartz episode and the House Commerce Committee investigation, see Tyler Abell, ed., *Drew Pearson Diaries, 1949–1959*, Holt, Rinehart & Winston, New York, 1974, pp. 425-65; Jack Anderson with James Boyd, *Confessions of a Muckraker: The Inside Story of Life in Washington during the Truman, Eisenhower, Kennedy, and Johnson Years*, Random House, New York, 1979, chap. 11; Drew Pearson and Jack Anderson, *The Case against Congress*, Simon & Schuster, New York, 1968, chap. 7; Oliver Pilat, *Drew Pearson: An Unauthorized Biography*, Harper's Magazine Press, New York, 1973, pp. 222-25; Bernard Schwartz, *The Professor and the Commissions*, Alfred A. Knopf, New York, 1959; and Smith, pp. 28-29.

PAGE 309   "honeycombed with immorality": *Oregonian*, Feb. 15, 1958.

"erect and pugnacious . . .": Anderson, p. 295.

PAGE 311   For the Hatfield accident and its ramifications, see *Eugene Register-Guard*, Nov. 1 and 25, 1958; *Oregonian*, Nov. 9, 1958; and Smith, pp. 370-78.

PAGE 312   "I don't intend . . .": *Oregonian*, Nov. 1, 1958.

PAGE 313   "deplored," "regretted," "goofy," "Sen. Morse was . . .": ibid., Nov. 2, 1958.

"ill-timed . . .": interview with Keith Skelton, Dec. 1, 1983.

On the Salem Chamber of Commerce, see *Oregonian*, Nov. 3, 1958.

"for the mother ... inexcusable ...": ibid., Nov. 2, 1958.

"No regrets ...": Smith, p. 378.

For Morse's constituent letter, press release, and TV address, see Morse Papers, Series A, Box 56.

"Not even Edith ...": to Merton Bernstein, Nov. 21, 1958, ibid., Box 14.

PAGE 314 "heartsick over ...": to Robert Holmes, Nov. 12, 1958, ibid., Box 57.

The possibility of a plot to oust Holmes came up in an interview with former *Oregonian* columnist Gerald Pratt, Oct. 11, 1984.

PAGE 315 Harry Hogan was interviewed on Feb. 27, 1985. Whether they believed it or not, all parties accepted that Holmes had no knowledge of the discussion between Hogan and Morse; he was, to use today's political idiom, able to retain deniability on the issue.

Mark Hatfield was interviewed on Dec. 30, 1983.

"when Wayne Morse ...": Jebby Davidson to Helen, Aug. 27, 1958, Davidson Papers, Box 4.

"In my speeches ... ": Morse Papers, Series A, Box 56.

"one prominent ...": to Robert Thornton, Nov. 12, 1958, ibid., Box 146.

"When you were ...": to Neuberger, Aug. 13, 1958, ibid., Box 89.

PAGE 317 For accounts of the Clare Boothe Luce nomination, see Ralph G. Martin, *Henry & Clare: An Intimate Portrait of the Luces*, Putnam Publishing Group, New York, 1992, pp. 349-53; Stephen Shadegg, *Clare Boothe Luce: A Biography*, Simon & Schuster, New York, 1970, pp. 279-87; Shaffer, pp. 147-53; Wilfrid Sheed, *Clare Boothe Luce*, E. P. Dutton, New York, 1982, pp. 119-24; Smith, pp. 48-53; and W. A. Swanberg, *Luce and His Empire*, Charles Scribner's Sons, New York, 1972, pp. 396-99. See also to Gwen Coffin, May 18, 1959, Morse Papers, Series A, Box 97.

PAGE 318 "abolish Bolivia ...": quoted in Swanberg, p. 397; and Martin, p. 350.

"if it proves ...": quoted in Martin, p. 350.

"grave consequences ...": quoted in Swanberg, p. 346.

PAGE 319 "globaloney": for this quote and Fulbright's response, see Haynes Johnson and Bernard M. Gwertzman, *Fulbright the Dissenter*, Doubleday & Co., Garden City, N.Y., 1968, pp. 64-66.

"the only American . . . mortal enemies": *Nomination of Clare Boothe Luce: Hearing before the Committee on Foreign Relations*, U.S. Senate, 86th Cong., 1st sess., pp. 5-6.

"There are all . . .": ibid., p. 8.

"wholeheartedly": ibid., p. 17.

PAGE 320 "in the form . . . I think the Senator . . .": ibid., pp. 25-26.

"My difficulties . . .": quoted in Shaffer, p. 150.

"That explains me . . .": quoted in Shaffer, p. 150.

"an old, old pattern . . .": quoted in Smith, p. 50.

PAGE 321 "thinking left": Sheed, p. 124.

"the climate of . . .": quoted in Shadegg, p. 286.

"Why beat on . . .": quoted in Martin, p. 351.

"What a nice . . .": quoted in Swanberg, p. 398.

"In truthful numbers . . .": Shadegg, p. 283.

PAGE 322 On Morse's defense of his call to Luce's doctor, see to Frank Rarig, May 21, 1959, Rarig Papers, unprocessed.

PAGE 323 On the arsenic incident, see Martin, pp. 331-32; Shadegg, pp. 262-66; and Smith, p. 52.

"I was quite . . .": Sheed, p. 121.

"For twenty-five . . .": *Time*, May 11, 1959.

PAGE 324 "no regrets for . . .": Neuberger to Clare Boothe Luce, May 27, 1959, Neuberger Papers, Box 5.

PAGE 325 "Investment(s) in . . .": undated note, Morse Papers, Series A, Box 46.

For Edith Green's queries to Morse regarding the 1960 primary, see *Oregon Journal*, May 17, 1960.

PAGE 326 On Gary Neal, see Smith, pp. 399-400.

"Morse back-knifers": to Merton Bernstein, May 26, 1960, Morse Papers, Series A, Box 14.

PAGE 327 New York and Los Angeles contributions: Brooks interview.

On Morse's labor film, see *Washington Star*, Jan. 7, 1960.

"political opportunism . . .": quoted by Smith, p. 401.

PAGE 328 "an exceptionally good . . .": *Eugene Register-Guard*, Apr. 13, 1960.

"like an alderman . . .": *Washington Post*, Mar. 3, 1960.

"if our campaign . . ." to Hibberd Kline, Jr., May 5, 1960, Morse Papers, Addendum II.

PAGE 329 "Why, in God's name . . .": from Merton Bernstein, Feb. 18, 1960, ibid., Series A, Box 14.

"You seem to be . . .": to Merton Bernstein, Feb. 25, 1960, ibid.

PAGE 330 "constant repetition . . .": oral history of Walter Spolar, June 9, 1966, p. 3, JFK Library.

"They sent in . . .": Sweetland interview.

For the primary-campaign expenditures, see *Eugene Register-Guard*, June 1, 1960.

PAGE 331 "fighting chance": ibid., Apr. 13, 1960.

"dead serious . . . Even a Wayne . . .": *Oregonian*, May 16, 1960.

PAGE 332 "It's a long shot . . .": interviews with Raoul "Joe" Smith, Mar. 18 and July 24, 1984.

The write-in poll appeared in *Oregon Statesman*, Jan. 20, 1960.

"second best . . .": *Washington Star*, Feb. 10, 1960.

Porter's poll appeared in *Albany Greater Oregon*, Apr. 22, 1960. Even as superficial evidence made it appear that Morse's campaign was making headway, those monitoring events closely knew otherwise. Thus, Harry Hogan wrote Morse on March 31, 1960, to tell him how much "it breaks my heart that things in Oregon are going so badly for you. Please slow down, ease off, get some rest, and then take inventory" (letter courtesy of Dan Sellard, former reporter, *Eugene Register-Guard*).

PAGE 333 "Don't forget . . .": *Eugene Register-Guard*, Apr. 13, 1960.

PAGE 334 "Jason, I serve . . .": to Jason Lee, June 2, 1960, Morse Papers, Series A, Box 75.

"let me assure you . . .": to Merton Bernstein, May 26, 1960, ibid., Box 14.

"Neither Kennedy nor . . .": to Merton Bernstein, July 26, 1960, ibid.

PAGE 335 On Morse's preference for Humphrey over Kennedy, see to William Evjue, Jan. 23, 1960, ibid., Box 35.

"Wayne thought he . . .": Mildred Morse interviews.

On Kennedy's absence from subcommittee meetings, see oral history of Alexander K. Christie, Dec. 6, 1966, p. 6, JFK Library.

For Merrick's observations, see oral history of Samuel V. Merrick, Oct. 16, 1966, pp. 24-25, JFK Library.

PAGE 336 "phony liberals . . . Morse couldn't . . .": *Washington Post*, Oct. 27, 1959. Privately, Morse complained to United Auto Workers president Walter Reuther that "on seven different issues I moved that the Senate conferees stand in disagreement and go back to the Senate for instructions. On each occasion Kennedy voted with the Republicans and prevented further Senate consideration of these seven issues. . . . if Kennedy had supported me in my motions . . . we would have prevailed in the Senate on several" (to Walter Reuther, Oct. 13, 1959, Morse Papers, Series A, Box 69).

"willing to shake . . . no matter how . . .": telegram to William Evjue, Nov. 10, 1959, William T. Evjue Papers, State Historical Society of Wisconsin, Box 94.

"a tremendous admiration . . . the liberal who . . .": to Merton Bernstein, Aug. 23, 1958, Morse Papers, Series A, Box 14.

"we are certainly . . .": to Arthur Bone, Aug. 10, 1960, ibid.

PAGE 337 "This guy is . . .": Clinton P. Anderson with Milton Viorst, *Outsider in the Senate: Senator Clinton Anderson's Memoirs*, World Publishing Co., New York, 1970, p. 306.

Chapter 11: A Matter of Character

PAGE 338 "Character is always . . .": Carol Brightman, "Character in Biography," *Nation*, Feb. 13, 1995.

"very little . . .": interview with Phil George, Dec. 5, 1985.

PAGE 339 "dirt farmer": Morse interviews.

"hair flying . . .": Frank Rarig to Anne Kelsey, Aug. 28, 1955, Rarig Papers, unprocessed.

"I have always . . .": to Margaret Thompson Hill, Jan. 10, 1945, Morse Papers, Series A, Box 57.

"last Saturday afternoon . . .": to James Landye, Sept. 15, 1951, ibid., Series S, Box 5.

PAGE 340 "as tickled about . . .": to Lee Everly, July 27, 1946, ibid., Box 4.

PAGE 341 "hard, fast and . . .": Anita Holmes, "The Senator Is a Horseman," *Old Oregon*, Mar. 1948, p. 10.

"The Senator has . . .": *Washington Post*, Aug. 6, 1953.

"howled and yipped . . .": *Oregonian*, Oct. 11, 1950.

PAGE 342 "induced": this word was used by Senator Eugene McCarthy in an introductory memorandum sent to me on July 6, 1984. Included with the memorandum was the senator's file of 1960–62 correspondence among Humphrey, Chapman, Morse, and himself. All quotations concerning the cattle partnership venture are taken from this file, courtesy of Senator McCarthy.

PAGE 344 A note from Morse's secretary dated Oct. 17, 1960, indicated that when then-outstanding checks cleared, the Morse bank account would read $16.57 (from Mildred McCullough, Morse Papers, Addendum II).

"Wayne was a . . .": Mildred Morse interviews. Unless otherwise indicated, all quotations from Midge Morse in this chapter are taken from these interviews.

"to Mrs. Paul . . .": Morse Papers, Series S, Box 6.

On Morse's financial shortages, see to Nancy, Aug. 10, 1953, ibid., Addendum II.

"we thought very . . .": interview with Gladys Uhl, Mar. 29, 1985.

PAGE 345 "burning with . . . for two cords": to John Kennedy, Feb. 8, 1958, Morse Papers, Series A, Box 70.

On the D. F. Pickert incident, see *Eugene Register-Guard*, Dec. 16 and 17, 1958.

"The cornfield is . . .": cited in interview with Hugh Cole, Jr., Feb. 29, 1984.

PAGE 346 "I lived on . . .": cited in Uhl interview.

"And then we'd . . .": Cole interview.

"a job in a . . .": July 20, 1961, Morse Papers, Series A, Box 100.

PAGE 347 "sweatshop . . . hardship . . .": Smith, pp. 177-78.

"Morse was unmerciful . . .": interview with Lawrence Hobart, Mar. 28, 1985.

PAGE 348 "There was an attitude . . .": interview with Juliane Johnson, July 25, 1984.

"It was the kind . . .": interview with Penny and Hal Gross, Apr. 15, 1984.

PAGE 349 "planning a tour . . .": *Eugene Register-Guard*, June (day unknown) 1948, Morse Papers, Series V, Vol. 34.

"This isn't unusual . . .": *Raleigh News & Observer*, Nov. 28, 1954.

PAGE 350 "even when he . . .": Brooks interview. All quotations from Charlie Brooks in this chapter are taken from this interview.

PAGE 351 "would pull away . . .": interview with Judith Morse Goldman, Sept. 4, 1985. All quotations from Judy Morse in this chapter are taken from this interview.

"have a good time . . .": to Andrew Comrie, Feb. 10, 1951, Morse Papers, Series S, Box 4.

"volatile Judy": to James Landye, Sept. 24, 1949, ibid., Box 5.

PAGE 352 "I am sorry . . .": to Amy, July 7, 1953, ibid., Addendum II.

"no doubt about . . .": to Mr. and Mrs. Paul Washke, Mar. 19, 1953, ibid., Series S, Box 6.

"a very possessive . . .": interview with Nancy Morse Campbell, Nov. 11, 1982. All quotations from Nancy Morse Campbell in this chapter are taken from this interview.

PAGE 353 "took matters into . . .": *New York Daily News*, Dec. 11, 1954. On Morse's attitude regarding Nancy's previous engagement, see to Andrew Comrie, Feb. 10, 1951, Morse Papers, Series S, Box 4.

"Eta says if . . .": Frank Rarig to Bower, Oct. 27, 1958, Rarig Papers, unprocessed.

"Mother and I . . .": to Nancy, July 25, 1942, Morse Papers, unprocessed.

PAGE 354 "It was . . .": ibid., Series V, Box 3, Vol. 33.

"understand the relationship . . .": to Margaret Thompson Hill, Mar. 28, 1945, ibid., Series A, Box 57.

"The Morse stables . . .": to Paul and Ruth, Oct. 3, 1939, ibid., Series S, Box 3.

PAGE 356 "Housekeeping is just . . .": *Eugene Register-Guard,* Dec. 7, 1955.

PAGE 357 "Your father came . . .": *Washington Post,* July 31, 1957.

"Midge has had . . .": Frank Rarig to Al, Jan. 14, 1955, Rarig Papers, unprocessed.

"I have long . . .": *Oregon Daily Statesman,* Dec. 3, 1956.

"Mrs. Morse sometimes . . .": Penny and Hal Gross interview.

"Not once in . . .": Hollis interview. All quotations from Orlando Hollis in this chapter are taken from this interview.

"Wayne never even . . .": interview with Charles Porter, Nov. 10, 1983.

"I don't think . . .": Smith interviews.

PAGE 358 "get the hell out . . .": Midge quoting Morse, as told to Penny and Hal Gross, from interview.

PAGE 359 "*One time when . . .*": Conklin interview.

"*I don't think . . .*": to E. D. Conklin, Dec. 17, 1973, courtesy of Mr. Conklin.

"The Loneliest Man in Washington": Samuel Grafton, *Collier's,* Apr. 4, 1953.

"I honestly think . . .": Cole interview.

"I seldom use . . .": to Henry Corbett, Apr. 12, 1951, Morse Papers, Series S, Box 4.

PAGE 360 "that gravel voice . . .": Stephen Wasby to author, Sept. 3, 1984.

Landye referred to Morse as "my best friend" (from Jim Landye, Mar. 12, 1945, Morse Papers, Series S, Box 5). Regarding reservations about Washke, Morse reminded Judy, who was in Eugene at the time, "I play my cards very close to the chest as far as giving any information to the Washkes is concerned, and I hope you are doing the same thing" (to Judy, May 20, 1953, ibid., Addendum II).

"true blue": Juliane Johnson interview.

"as if . . .": Edward Fadeley, from a 1975 collection entitled "Wayne Morse Remembered," Sabin, unprocessed.

PAGE 361 "Wayne, you've just . . .": interview with Tom Enright, Aug. 16, 1984.

"that wonderful steak . . .": interview with Gerald Robinson, Feb. 1, 1984.

"on an entirely . . .": Cole interview.

"what the hell . . .": from Orlando Hollis, Mar. 4, 1965, Morse Papers, Series B, Box 53.

"I really have . . .": to Orlando Hollis, Apr. 22, 1965, ibid.

"You don't call . . .": Juliane Johnson interview. On a related subject, one year Morse's staff gave their chief a "Name Remembering Award," complete with a certificate and blue ribbon. "It's very seldom," the document stated, "that a union as humble as ours can give an award to a great labor mediator, but we give this award for the Senator's never having called one of the file clerks by his correct name" (Dec. 22, 1966, Morse Papers, Series V, Box 13, Vol. 94).

PAGE 362 "never played marbles . . .": William Tugman to James Hamlin-Howard, July 16, 1947, Tugman Papers, Box 1.

"disgusting . . . that psychologically . . .": to E. D. Conklin, June 24, 1947, Morse Papers, Series S, Box 4.

"total attention . . .": Smith interviews.

"Wayne's shit list": Rauh interview.

PAGE 363 "One thing we . . .": J. Girard Davidson to AHP, June 8, 1959, Davidson Papers, Box 7.

"the silly bastard . . .": interview with Pat Holt, Mar. 26, 1985.

PAGE 364 "sheer, absolute brilliance . . .": Hatfield interview.

"long periods of . . .": William Tugman to Robert Frazier, Dec. 5, 1952, Tugman Papers, Box 1.

"next to T-Bone . . .": to Kathryn Cravens, Nov. 3, 1959, Morse Papers, Series A, Box 85.

"greasy pastry shelf": interview with Mike Kopetski, Apr. 24, 1984.

PAGE 365 "a layman trying . . .": Hatfield interview.

"Wayne Morse . . .": *Atlanta Constitution*, Morse Papers, Series V, Box 7, Vol. 51.

"his strength came . . .": Smith interviews.

PAGE 366 "I realized that . . .": Penny and Hal Gross interview.

"each of us ...": Howard Morgan memoir.

PAGE 367 "It is extraordinary ... The Senator from ...": from a compilation of tributes to Morse dated Oct. 1966, Morse Papers, Series O, Box 18.

CHAPTER 12: STRONG MAN OF THE SENATE

PAGE 368 "the one domestic ...": cited in Bernstein, p. 224.

PAGE 369 "emergency situation ...": Senate speech, Aug. 2, 1955, reprint from *Congressional Record*, Morse Papers, unprocessed.

"Morse ... was eager ...": Bernstein, p. 231.

"move onward and ...": to Lister Hill, Dec. 3, 1960, Morse Papers, Series B, Box 118 (italics added).

PAGE 370 "cantankerous and irascible ...": oral history of Samuel Halperin, July 24, 1968, p. 13, LBJ Library.

"We all hope ...": from Caryl Kline, Jan. 1, 1961, Morse Papers, Series W, Box 3.

"all alone on ...": to Ken Johnson, Jan. 17, 1961, ibid., Series U, Box 38.

PAGE 372 "suffused with triumph ...": Harry McPherson, *A Political Education*, Little, Brown & Co., Boston, 1972, pp. 195-96.

"the year 1961 ...": Bernstein, p. 234.

"not want to weaken ...": to Lister Hill, June 26, 1961, Morse Papers, Series B, Box 29.

"the biggest surprise ...": *Washington Post*, May 28, 1961.

"the great skill ...": *Oregonian*, May 28, 1961.

"in 1961 Morse ...": oral history of Mike Mansfield, June 23, 1964, JFK Library.

PAGE 373 "In round one ...": Bernstein, p. 237.

"the second successive ...": *Oregonian*, Feb. 12, 1962.

PAGE 374 "Is this clipping ...": memorandum, Phyllis Rock to Charlie Brooks, Dec. 21, 1961, Morse Papers, Series N, Box 21.

"The boss refuses ...": memorandum from Phyllis Rock to Charlie Brooks, Dec. 5, 1961, ibid.

PAGE 375   "For Wayne Morse . . .": ibid., unprocessed.

"Get that the hell . . .": Rock interview.

"character assassination . . .": *Oregonian*, May 9, 1962.

PAGE 376   "if we really . . .": message from Ernest Swigert on Hyster Co. stationery, Oct. 19, 1962, Morse Papers, Series B, Box 120.

"Unless steps are . . .": to John F. Kennedy, Sept. 1, 1962, ibid., Series N, Box 24. Earlier Morse had written JFK a nineteen-page, single-spaced letter demonstrating, item by item, how Oregonians were suffering as much from federal neglect under Kennedy as they had under Eisenhower (July 7, 1962, ibid., Box 23).

"I don't like . . .": *New York Times*, Oct. 20, 1956.

PAGE 377   "eating breakfast one . . .": interview with Joseph McCracken, Oct. 17, 1984.

PAGE 378   "set-aside": interview with Robert Wolf, Apr. 10, 1984.

"We had begun . . .": McCracken interview.

"unlocking": *Oregonian*, Mar. 7, 1962. (A board foot of timber is one foot square by one inch thick.) See also *Medford Mail Tribune* piece by A. Robert Smith, Morse Papers, Series V, Box 11, Vol. 78.

PAGE 379   "a walk in . . .": Brooks interview.

"So far as . . .": *Washington Star*, July 31, 1962. For a brief discussion of the communications-satellite issue, see Lewis J. Paper, *John F. Kennedy: The Promise and the Performance*, Da Capo Press, New York, 1980, pp. 271-72.

PAGE 380   "As I gather . . . brooding silence . . . a word in . . .": Morse Papers, Series V, Box 11, Vol. 79.

"Morse Uncorks . . .": *Washington Post*, Apr. 6, 1962.

"Oregon's new . . .": Morse Papers, Series V, Box 11, Vol. 77.

"Morse water": *Oregonian*, May 24, 1962.

PAGE 381   "Lee had a . . .": Norman C. Thomas, *Education in National Politics*, David McKay Co., New York, 1975, p. 133.

"If Senator Morse . . .": interview with Edith Green, June 17, 1984.

PAGE 382   "next to Senator . . .": Halperin oral history.

"She simply didn't . . .": oral history of Jim Grant Bolling, Mar. 1, 1966, JFK Library.

PAGE 383 "people *do* learn . . .": quoted in Bernstein, p. 238.

PAGE 384 "in round three . . .": ibid., p. 237.

PAGE 385 "Sen. Wayne Morse . . .": *Oregonian,* Jan. 5, 1964.

"Morse was a master . . .": interview with Charles Lee, Nov. 29, 1983.

PAGE 386 "had a cast-iron . . .": Bernstein, p. 241.

"I conduct my . . .": address to American Association of School Administrators, May 13, 1965, quoted by Stephen K. Bailey, *ESEA: The Office of Education Administers a Law,* Syracuse University Press, Syracuse, N.Y., 1968, p. 28.

PAGE 387 "Mrs. Green's stand . . .": from Carl Perkins, Dec. 18, 1963, Morse Papers, Series B, Box 32.

"You know, the . . .": oral history of George Reedy, Feb. 29, 1984, p. 9.

PAGE 388 "On [an] education . . .": oral history of Joseph A. Califano, June 11, 1973, p. 25, LBJ Library.

"If *impacted* could . . .": interview with Stewart McClure, Mar. 9, 1984.

PAGE 389 "What is past . . .": "Excerpts from Address to Convention of the Nebraska State Education Association," Oct. 30, 1964, pp. 4-5, Morse Papers, unprocessed.

"massive investment": quoted by Solberg, p. 267.

PAGE 390 "We made the decision . . .": quoted in Eugene Eidenberg and Roy D. Morey, *An Act of Congress: The Legislative Process and the Making of Education Policy,* W. W. Norton & Co., New York, 1969, p. 108.

"Morse had commented . . .": Mike Manatos to Larry O'Brien, Mar. 1, 1965, LBJ Library.

PAGE 391 "this tenuous alliance": Douglas, p. 420.

"Let us not . . .": quoted in Eidenberg and Morey, p. 127.

"unanimous vote . . .": ibid., p. 159.

PAGE 392 "one of the year's . . .": *New York Times,* Apr. 10, 1965.

"the stakes are . . .": Lyndon Baines Johnson, *The Vantage Point: Perspectives of the Presidency, 1963–1969,* Holt, Rinehart & Winston, New York, 1971, p. 211.

"the Wayne Morse . . .": *Washington Star*, Apr. 11, 1965.

PAGE 393 "a great innovation . . .": *Washington Post*, Apr. 15, 1965.

"ESEA was the . . .": McClure interview.

"accepting the encomiums . . .": *Oregonian*, Sept. 12, 1965.

"If I left . . .": quoted in LeRoy Ashby and Rod Gramer, *Fighting the Odds: The Life of Senator Frank Church*, Washington State University Press, Pullman, 1994, p. 199.

PAGE 394 "We may find . . .": Morse Papers, Series B, Box 121.

"Morse will never . . .": Mike Manatos to Barefoot Sanders, Apr. 27, 1968, LBJ Library.

PAGE 395 "Congresswoman Edith Green . . .": Douglass Cater to the President, May 1, 1967, LBJ Library. See also Ralph Huitt (HEW Assistant Secretary for Legislation) to Douglass Cater, Henry Wilson, William Cannon, and Herbert Jasper, Feb. 13, 1967, ibid.

"Green was pulling . . .": McClure interview.

"When the smoke . . .": Thomas, p. 84.

PAGE 396 "political reunion . . .": *Oregonian*, July 13, 1967.

"fine record . . .": ibid., June 28, 1967.

"on the Teacher Corps . . .": Joe Califano to the President, June 27, 1967, LBJ Library.

"deep admiration for . . .": from Douglass Cater, June 29, 1967, Morse Papers, Series B, Box 31.

"get down on . . .": ibid., Series V, Box 14, Vol. 98.

PAGE 397 "more a tribute . . .": Thomas, p. 89.

PAGE 398 "the never defeated . . .": *Corvallis Gazette-Times*, Dec. 22, 1967.

PAGE 399 "of a serious . . .": Thomas, p. 98.

PAGE 400 "God-awful bloodbath": *Oregonian*, Nov. 15, 1967.

"engulf the resources . . .": press release, Apr. 24, 1964, Morse Papers, Series B, Box 57.

"reduce the domestic . . .": press release, May 12, 1968, ibid.

Chapter 13: Vietnam

PAGE 401 "the blunt directness . . .": Austin, p. 101.

PAGE 402 "Many people seem . . .": Morse interviews.

PAGE 403 "the armed forces . . .": quoted in D. F. Fleming, *The Cold War and Its Origins, 1917–1960*, Doubleday & Co., Garden City, N.Y., 1961, vol. 2, p. 707.

"blank check authorizing . . .": ibid.

"a completely dictatorial . . .": *Jewish Standard*, Feb. 25, 1955.

"satellite": *Oregonian*, Jan. 24, 1955.

"preventive war . . . trigger happy . . . we could not . . .": reprint from *Congressional Record*, Jan. 26, 1955, Morse Papers, Series A, Box 45.

PAGE 404 "requesting assistance against . . .": quoted in Fleming, p. 847.

"under the domination . . .": quoted in Fleming, p. 922.

"I am not going . . .": quoted in Paper, p. 64.

"unconstitutional and authoritarian": *Senator Morse Reports* (newsletter), July-Aug. 1958, Morse Papers, Series A, Box 86.

"is oil our . . . I am not in favor . . . What we need . . .": press release, July 15, 1958, ibid.

"Herbert, it is . . .": to Herbert Lehman, Jan. 31, 1958, ibid., Box 76.

PAGE 405 "the potentialities of . . .": May 14, 1954, ibid., Series N, Box 13.

PAGE 406 "next time we go . . .": quoted in William Conrad Gibbons, *The U.S. Government and the Vietnam War, Part I, 1945–1960*, Princeton University Press, Princeton, N.J., 1986, p. 226.

"Nixon machine and . . .": to Joseph DeSilva, June 16, 1954, Morse Papers, Series A, Box 31.

The "Capital Cloakroom" remarks: ibid., Series R, Box 14.

"It is my . . .": to Jason Lee, June 2, 1960, ibid., Series A, Box 75.

"the most tyrannical . . .": ibid., Series V, Vol. 82.

"a three-week . . .": *Newsweek*, Nov. 25, 1963.

"into numbered accounts . . .": *New York Times*, Nov. 13, 1963.

"traitor": quoted in Nancy Zaroulis and Gerald Sullivan, *Who Spoke Up? American Protest against the War in Vietnam, 1963–1975*, Holt, Rinehart & Winston, New York, 1984, p. 17.

PAGE 407 "What is getting . . .": *St. Petersburg Times*, Apr. 16, 1964.

"quitters . . . The most helpful . . .": file note, Morse Papers, Series B, Box 57.

"foremost history lesson . . .": address at Temple University Downtown Club, Apr. 20, 1964, ibid., Series O, Box 17.

"McNamara's War": ibid., Series B, Box 50.

"pleased . . . an impulsive . . .": Robert S. McNamara, *In Retrospect: The Tragedy and Lessons of Vietnam*, Times Books, New York, 1995, p. 118.

"aside from the . . .": press release, Apr. 24, 1964, Morse Papers, Series B, Box 51.

PAGE 408 "Having abandoned its . . .": remarks at Logan, Utah, July 7, 1964, ibid., Series O, Box 17.

"terribly wrong": McNamara, p. xvi.

PAGE 409 "I think we . . .": quoted in McNamara, pp. 136-37 (from *Joint Hearing before the Committee on Foreign Relations and the Committee on Armed Services*, U.S. Senate, 88th Cong., 2d sess., Aug. 6, 1964).

"Our Navy played . . .": McNamara, p. 137.

PAGE 410 "CIA supported the . . .": ibid., p. 129.

"I went on . . .": ibid., p. 137.

PAGE 411 "*if there were any*": quoted in Austin, p. 68 (italics added).

"*I say this* . . .": ibid., p. 69 (italics added).

"less than candid": McNamara, p. 105.

"Q: There have been . . .": quoted in Austin, p. 70.

PAGE 412 "Along with my . . .": Douglas, p. 610.

"I had never . . .": McNamara, p. 105.

PAGE 413 "John McCone has . . .": quoted by Kathleen Turner, *Lyndon Johnson's Dual War: Vietnam and the Press*, University of Chicago Press, Chicago, 1985, pp. 266-67.

"future generations will . . .": for Morse's remarks during the two days of debate, see *Congressional Record*, Aug. 6, 1964, pp. 18398-430, and Aug. 7, 1964, pp. 18441-71.

"When it came . . .": interview with Maurine Neuberger, Apr. 12, 1984.

PAGE 414 "Sen. Morse entered . . .": *Mamaroneck Daily Times*, Oct. 12, 1966.

"We got off . . .": interview with George H. R. Taylor, Mar. 28, 1985.

"roared its approval": *Binghamton Press*, June 9, 1965.

"a hopeless war": *New York Times*, June 9, 1965.

"What is needed . . .": *I. F. Stone's Weekly*, Oct. 25, 1965, p. 3.

PAGE 415 "the risk of being . . . ready to be . . .": "Memorandum for the President on United States Policies in Vietnam" (undated, but delivered to White House before June 21, 1965), LBJ Library.

PAGE 416 "I think Morse's . . .": memorandum, McGeorge Bundy to President Johnson, June 21, 1965, LBJ Library.

"The Morse memorandum . . .": memorandum, McGeorge Bundy to President Johnson, June 24, 1965, LBJ Library.

PAGE 417 "own educated guess . . .": memorandum, McGeorge Bundy to President Johnson, July 7, 1965, LBJ Library.

The July 18, 1965, *Oregonian* carried an Associated Press dispatch quoting Morse's description of his memo to Rusk.

Johnson's effort to enlist Adlai Stevenson to talk to Morse is noted in Stevenson's diary, Jan. 5, 1965 (Walter Johnson et al., eds., *The Papers of Adlai E. Stevenson, Ambassador to the United Nations, 1961–1965*, Little, Brown & Co., Boston, 1979, vol. 8, p. 667).

"Wayne Morse would . . .": memorandum, Vice President Humphrey to President Johnson, Aug. 13, 1965, LBJ Library.

PAGE 418 "American flags all . . .": Morse Papers, Series B, Box 54.

"seek derogatory information": *Eugene Register-Guard*, July 17, 1988. Ironically, as his FBI file reveals, Morse was forced to call upon the bureau throughout the 1960s to investigate the numerous threats from extremists against his life and person. According to Judy Morse, such threats were not taken lightly by Morse or his staff.

On the huge amount of mail coming into Morse's office, see to Mrs. Charles Davis, May 17, 1966, Morse Papers, Series B, Box 55; and to Mr. and Mrs. Tom Chatburn, Sr., July 13, 1966, ibid., Box 54.

"Your voice has . . .": from Malcolm Browne, Apr. 8, 1966, ibid.

PAGE 419 "You are wrong . . .": telegram from Don Peterson, Mar. 26, 1966, ibid., Box 55.

"You will be . . .": telegram to Don Peterson, Mar. 28, 1966, ibid.

"one of the greatest . . .": reprint from *Congressional Record*, May 23, 1960, ibid., Addendum II.

"If you are to . . .": to Adlai Stevenson, Dec. 9, 1960, ibid., Addendum I.

PAGE 421 "I realize that . . .": to Adlai Stevenson, May 14, 1964, ibid., Series B, Box 49.

"It goes without . . .": from Adlai Stevenson, May 27, 1964, ibid.

"Of course, one . . .": to Remy Fulsher, June 5, 1964, ibid.

PAGE 422 "enjoyment . . . I happen . . .": *Time*, Feb. 25, 1966.

"nail General Taylor's . . .": to Joseph Maloney, Mar. 4, 1965, Morse Papers, Series B, Box 55.

"very calmly": to Smiley Blanton, Mar. 1, 1966, ibid., Box 53.

PAGE 423 "Sir . . .": from Thomas Taylor, July 1, 1964, ibid., Box 49.

"It is obvious . . .": to Thomas Taylor, July 9, 1964, ibid.

PAGE 424 "I blame nobody . . .": quoted in A. Robert Smith, "Senator Morse's Advice and Dissent," *New York Times Magazine*, Apr. 17, 1966.

"a duty to go . . .": to Thomas Holahan, Dec. 3, 1966, Morse Papers, Series B, Box 121.

"other person on . . .": to George Rochester, June 27, 1966, ibid., Box 55.

PAGE 425 "Wayne, I want you . . .": *Boston Globe*, June 24, 1973. See also *New Haven Register*, Mar. 19, 1967; and to Esther Hendrickson, Mar. 17, 1967, Morse Papers, Series B, Box 56.

Schlesinger's argument appears in Arthur M. Schlesinger, Jr., *Robert Kennedy and His Times*, Houghton Mifflin Co., Boston, 1978, pp. 755-56. See also oral history of Peter Lisagor, Apr. 22, 1966, p. 64, JFK

Library. For more on the historical debate, see John M. Newman, *JFK and Vietnam*, Warner Books, New York, 1992, pp. 423-24; Tristram Coffin, *Washington Spectator*, Mar. 15, 1986; and several columns on the subject by Alexander Cockburn, *Nation*, 1994–95.

"hopelessly divided legacy": Schlesinger, p. 756.

PAGE 426 "vote against every . . .": reprint from *Congressional Record*, Mar. 20, 1967, Morse Papers, Series B, Box 56.

"to unite behind . . .": *New York Times*, Jan. 30, 1966.

PAGE 427 "Dear Wayne, I . . .": from Lyndon Johnson, Mar. 18, 1967, LBJ Library.

"Senator Half-bright": quoted in Ashby and Gramer, p. 220.

"Well, Mr. President . . .": quoted in Austin, p. 152.

"If the Johnson . . .": Joseph A. Califano, Jr., *A Presidential Nation*, W. W. Norton & Co., New York, 1975, p. 209.

"I'm absolutely convinced . . .": oral history of George Reedy, Dec. 14, 1968, LBJ Library.

"At midday, the . . .": Jack Valenti, *A Very Human President*, W. W. Norton & Co., New York, 1975, p. 185.

For a characterization of the Morse-Johnson relationship during their Senate days, see Booth Mooney, *LBJ: An Irreverent Chronicle*, Thomas Y. Crowell Co., New York, 1976, pp. 105-6.

PAGE 428 "a labor case . . .": *Washington Post*, Jan. 17, 1963.

"splendid cooperation . . . really . . .": *Newsweek*, Jan. 28, 1963.

PAGE 429 "If it hadn't . . .": *Washington Post*, Sept. 12, 1965. See also *New York Times*, Aug. 28 and 30, 1965.

PAGE 430 "Wayne, my ox . . .": *Washington Post*, June 2, 1966.

"strike cannot be . . .": ibid., July 8, 1966.

PAGE 431 "It is the clear . . .": press release, July 25, 1966, Morse Papers, Series O, Box 18.

"Sen. Morse is . . .": *Oregonian*, July 23, 1966.

"strikebreaker": *The Machinist*, Aug. 4, 1966.

"leading the pack . . .": *Oregon Labor Press*, Aug. 5, 1966.

"Because you supported . . .": *Washington Post*, Sept. 8, 1966.

PAGE 432 "Don't forget we are . . .": Text of Letter Written by Senator Morse Concerning Airlines Dispute, Sept. 2, 1966, Morse Papers, Series V, Vol. 93.

"inflationary spiral . . .": *Oregon Journal*, Aug. 3, 1966.

PAGE 433 "We're speechless . . .": *Washington Daily News*, July 19, 1967.

"the biggest strike breaker . . .": *Eugene Register-Guard*, July 26, 1967.

"In late 1968 . . .": Joseph A. Califano, Jr., *The Triumph and Tragedy of Lyndon Johnson: The White House Years*, Simon & Schuster, New York, 1991, p. 195.

PAGE 434 "I decided to . . .": William O. Douglas, *The Court Years, 1939–1975: The Autobiography of William O. Douglas*, Vintage Books, New York, 1981 (first published 1980), p. 317.

PAGE 435 "I am still . . .": to Robert Straub, Feb. 9, 1962, Morse Papers, Series B, Box 120.

PAGE 436 "Professor": Conklin interview.

"Johnson said all . . .": interview with Ken Johnson, Oct. 19, 1984.

CHAPTER 14: A MAVERICK'S DÉNOUEMENT

PAGE 438 "'Wayne and Howard' . . .": *New York Times*, May 2, 1966.

"you undercut . . .": to C. J. Haggerty, Apr. 21, 1966, Morse Papers, Series U, Box 76.

"weaken my hands . . .": to Andrew Biemiller, Apr. 21, 1966, ibid., Series B, Box 121. The White House was also anxious to see a Duncan victory in the primary. A memo from a Humphrey aide to a Johnson aide noted that "Duncan is a key figure in terms of the vindication of the President's policy, and I should think we would want to give him every bit of help that we can possibly muster" (William Connell to Marvin Watson, Apr. 19, 1966, LBJ Library).

"was at the lowest . . .": *New York Times*, May 2, 1966.

On the effort to recall Morse, see *Oregonian*, May 4, 1966.

On the differences between Morse and Hatfield on military appropriations, see telegrams from Hatfield, Mar. 1, 1966, and to Hatfield, Mar. 2, 1966, Morse Papers, Series B, Box 55.

PAGE 439 "I consider the . . .": to A. F. Hartung, Apr. 22, 1966, ibid., Box 121.

"Would it embarrass . . .": note from Mark Hatfield, 1963 (month and day unknown), ibid., unprocessed.

PAGE 440 "justify backing . . .": from Mrs. D. E. Carlson, Nov. 10, 1966, ibid., Series B, Box 121.

PAGE 441 "If I had it . . .": to Mrs. D. E. Carlson, Dec. 16, 1966, ibid.

"It is one thing . . .": to Thomas Roe, June 29, 1966, ibid.

PAGE 442 "the bitterness that . . .": from Norm Stoll, May 18, 1967, ibid., Box 122.

"the clear implication": memorandum, Joe Califano to the President, June 12, 1967, LBJ Library.

"Morse is crazy . . .": memorandum, Marvin Watson to Mr. President, June 13, 1967, LBJ Library.

"never stopped running . . .": *Time,* Jan. 5, 1968.

"Machinists Plot Defeat . . .": *Eugene Register-Guard,* Aug. 18, 1967.

PAGE 443 For the AFL-CIO straw poll, see *Oregon Journal,* Sept. 20, 1967.

The October opinion-poll results, as well as later primary polls, are in Gerald E. Robinson Papers, Oregon Historical Society, Box 1.

PAGE 444 McAlmond had not only cost Duncan the election, he had done so in an almost offhand way. After Morse's victory, he indicated that "if he [Duncan] had asked me to withdraw, I would have. A lot of other people came to me, but Duncan never did" (Morse Papers, Series V, Box 16, Vol. 109).

PAGE 446 "Things were complicated . . .": Mildred Morse to Lowell Mason, Mar. 28, 1968, ibid., unprocessed.

Humphrey wrote to Morse before the Democratic national convention promising "a negotiated settlement—a political settlement" (from Hubert Humphrey, June 27, 1968, ibid., Series N, Box 27). Later in the year, in a letter to a GI who had written that he could see little difference between Humphrey and Nixon on Vietnam, Morse wrote that "Mr. Humphrey, if elected President, will not perpetuate the misguided policies of the past but will face the issues freshly, energetically, and honestly, with an eye toward immediate cessation of the conflict. It is my firm conviction that a victory for Richard Nixon in November will spell disaster for this country" (to PFC Joseph Shirley, Oct. 14, 1968, ibid., Series B, Box 57).

"Bob Packwood is . . .": *La Grande Observer*, July 11, 1968.

PAGE 447 "deafening applause": *Salem Capital Journal*, Aug. 29, 1968; see also *Medford Mail Tribune*, Aug. 29, 1968.

"do anything with . . .": to John Travis, June 24, 1968, Morse Papers, Series B, Box 133.

The August poll: ibid., Box 122.

PAGE 448 "We'll all rally . . .": *Oregonian*, May 30, 1968.

"As you know . . .": to Charles West, July 20, 1968, Morse Papers, Series B, Box 123; see also to Jule Sweet, July 20, 1968, ibid.

PAGE 449 "never seen a primary . . .": from Don Willner, June 7, 1968, ibid.

"the gut issues . . .": *New York Times*, Oct. 1, 1968.

PAGE 451 "put on an oratorical . . .": *Washington Post*, Oct. 22, 1968.

"Let me say . . .": for the complete debate text, see *Oregonian*, Oct. 26, 1968.

PAGE 452 "We set Morse up": quoted in Mark Kirchmeier, *Packwood: The Public and Private Life from Acclaim to Outrage*, HarperCollins, New York, 1995, p. 105.

"Sandbagged": Conklin interview.

"couldn't give you . . .": ibid.

"It was Packwood . . .": *Oregon Statesman*, Oct. 27, 1968.

PAGE 453 "genius": ibid., Oct. 6, 1968.

"wizard": Kirchmeier, p. 87.

"one of the best . . .": Tom McCall with Steve Neal, *Tom McCall, Maverick: An Autobiography*, Binford & Mort, Portland, 1977, p. 108.

PAGE 454 "the pretty 'brownette' . . .": *Oregonian*, Nov. 9, 1968.

The October poll: ibid., Oct. 24, 1968.

"I don't want . . .": to Edmund Conklin, Dec. 23, 1968, courtesy of Mr. Conklin.

Packwood's assessment of the gun-control issue: interview with Robert Packwood, Jan. 7, 1984.

PAGE 455 "Wayne Morse called . . .": memorandum, Joe Califano to the President, Nov. 19, 1968, LBJ Library.

"was a different . . .": interview with Phil George, Dec. 3, 1985.

PAGE 456 On the appearance cancellations, see Morse Papers, Series O, Box 24.

"had no inner . . .": Doris Kearns Goodwin, *Lyndon Johnson and the American Dream*, St. Martin's Press, New York, 1976, 1991, p. xviii.

"only comforting thing . . .": Mildred Morse to Luvie, Sept. 8, 1969, Morse Papers, Addendum II.

"I guess we . . .": interview with Amy Morse Bilich, Apr. 6, 1983.

PAGE 457 "one of the few . . .": quoted by Kalman, p. 333.

"it would be both . . .": to Arthur Melville, Oct. 18, 1971, Morse Papers, Addendum III.

PAGE 458 "it pays well . . . intellectual monastery . . . little enthusiasm": to Leonce and Ed, Mar. 7, 1969, courtesy of Mr. Conklin.

"non-reader": to Albert Blum, Oct. 5, 1971, Morse Papers, Addendum I.

"He didn't read . . .": George interview.

"I know he wants . . .": Mildred Morse to Dorothy Leeper, Jan. 19, 1970, Morse Papers, Addendum II.

PAGE 460 "Of one thing . . .": to Jeanette Morser, May 25, 1967, ibid., Series B, Box 121.

PAGE 461 "It's kind of like . . .": *Oregonian*, July 23, 1974.

"It is difficult . . .": *Oregon Journal*, July 23, 1974.

"I want to thank . . .": Sabin, unprocessed.

PAGE 462 "heartfelt regret that . . .": from Lynn Franklin, Nov. 6, 1968, Morse Papers, Series B, Box 123.

"just a lowly . . .": from Floyd Irvin, Nov. 8, 1968, ibid.

"You cut through . . .": from Thomas Frenkel, Nov. 6, 1968, ibid.

"We don't have . . .": A. Robert Smith interview.

PAGE 463 "lectured on Southern . . .": McPherson, p. 47.

Sources

ARCHIVES

The collected papers of Wayne Morse are located in the Special Collections department of the University of Oregon Library. An invaluable guide to all but a small percentage of these papers is Martin Schmitt, *Inventory of the Papers of Senator Wayne L. Morse, 1919–1969*, University of Oregon Library, Eugene, 1974 (addendum, 1981). Special Collections also has available a transcript of interviews of Senator Morse conducted by Phil George in 1973 and 1974, as well as the papers of C. Girard Davidson, B. A. Green, Henry M. Hanzen, Richard N. Neuberger, Charles O. Porter, Robert W. Sawyer, and William M. Tugman.

At the Oregon Historical Society in Portland are selected papers of Gerald E. Robinson, A. Robert Smith, and Monroe Sweetland (plus tape-recorded interviews with Sweetland) and the 1931–42 diaries of John Laurence Casteel. Materials bearing on Morse's Wisconsin years can be found at the State Historical Society of Wisconsin in Madison.

The following presidential libraries contain relevant documents: Dwight D. Eisenhower Library, Abilene, Kansas; Lyndon Baines Johnson Library, Austin, Texas; John F. Kennedy Library, Boston, Massachusetts; Harry S. Truman Library, Independence, Missouri; Franklin Delano Roosevelt Library, Hyde Park, New York.

Along with back issues of the *Oregon Daily Emerald*, the University of Oregon archives in Eugene has among its holdings official and unofficial law school documents and miscellaneous tapes and papers. The Frank M. Rarig papers are housed at the University of Minnesota archives in Minneapolis. Selected research data by Neil Sabin on Senator Morse can be found at the Lewis and Clark College archives in Portland.

Books

In addition to the books listed here, readers may consult U.S. Congress, *Congressional Record*, vols. 91-114, 1945–68, as well as *Executive Sessions of the Senate Foreign Relations Committee*, an ongoing series published by the U.S. Government Printing Office, Washington, D.C. Significant material can also be found in files on Wayne Morse that were kept by the Federal Bureau of Investigation and by other government agencies. Periodical and newspaper references are listed in the notes to each chapter.

Abell, Tyler, ed. *Drew Pearson Diaries, 1949–1959.* Holt, Rinehart & Winston, New York, 1974.

Anderson, Clinton P., with Milton Viorst. *Outsider in the Senate: Senator Clinton Anderson's Memoirs.* World Publishing Co., New York, 1970.

Anderson, Jack, with James Boyd. *Confessions of a Muckraker: The Inside Story of Life in Washington during the Truman, Eisenhower, Kennedy, and Johnson Years.* Random House, New York, 1979.

Armstrong, Robert C. "Four Communication Problems concerning the Constitutional Liberalism of Senator Wayne Morse." M.A. thesis, University of Washington, 1980.

Ashby, LeRoy, and Rod Gramer. *Fighting the Odds: The Life of Senator Frank Church.* Washington State University Press, Pullman, 1994.

Austin, Anthony. *The President's War: The Story of the Tonkin Gulf Resolution and How the Nation Was Trapped in Vietnam.* J. B. Lippincott Co., New York, 1971.

Bailey, Stephen K. *ESEA: The Office of Education Administers a Law.* Syracuse University Press, Syracuse, N.Y., 1968.

Bernstein, Irving. *Promises Kept: John F. Kennedy's New Frontier.* Oxford University Press, New York, 1991.

Brecher, Jeremy. *Strike!* South End Press, Boston, 1972.

Burton, Robert E. *Democrats of Oregon: The Pattern of Minority Politics, 1900–1956.* University of Oregon Books, Eugene, 1970.

Califano, Joseph A., Jr. *A Presidential Nation.* W. W. Norton & Co., New York, 1975.

———. *The Triumph and Tragedy of Lyndon Johnson: The White House Years.* Simon & Schuster, New York, 1991.

Collins, J. Lawton. *War in Peacetime: The History and Lessons of Korea.* Houghton Mifflin Co., Boston, 1969.

Dallek, Robert. *Lone Star Rising: Lyndon Johnson and His Times, 1908–1960.* Oxford University Press, New York, 1991.

Doan, Edward Newell. *The La Follettes and the Wisconsin Idea.* Rinehart, New York, 1947.

Donovan, Robert J. *Tumultuous Years: The Presidency of Harry S. Truman, 1949–1953.* W. W. Norton & Co., New York, 1971.

Douglas, Paul H. *In the Fullness of Time: The Memoirs of Paul H. Douglas.* Harcourt Brace Jovanovich, New York, 1971.

Douglas, William O. *The Court Years, 1939–1975: The Autobiography of William O. Douglas.* Vintage Books, New York, 1981.

Drukman, Mason. *Community and Purpose in America.* McGraw-Hill Book Co., New York, 1971.

Dulles, Foster Rhea. *Labor in America: A History.* Revised edition. Thomas Y. Crowell Co., New York, 1960.

Eidenberg, Eugene, and Roy D. Morey. *An Act of Congress: The Legislative Process and the Making of Education Policy.* W. W. Norton & Co., New York, 1969.

Ferrell, Robert H. *Off the Record: The Private Papers of Harry S. Truman.* Harper & Row, New York, 1980.

Fleming, D. F. *The Cold War and Its Origins, 1917–1969.* Doubleday & Co., Garden City, N.Y., 1961.

Fulbright, Johnson William. *The Arrogance of Power.* Random House, New York, 1966.

Gibbons, William Conrad. *The U.S. Government and the Vietnam War.* Part II, 1961–1964; Part III, January-July 1965; Part IV, July 1965-January 1968. Congressional Research Service, Library of Congress, Washington, D.C., 1985-1994. Reprinted by Princeton University Press.

Goodwin, Doris Kearns. *Lyndon Johnson and the American Dream.* St. Martin's Press, New York, 1976.

Griffith, Robert. *The Politics of Fear: Joseph R. McCarthy and the Senate.* University of Kentucky Press, Lexington, 1970.

Gunther, John. *Inside U.S.A.* Harper & Brothers, New York, 1951.

Herken, Gregg. *The Winning Weapon: The Atomic Bomb in the Cold War*. Alfred A. Knopf, New York, 1980.

Hodgson, Godfrey. *America in Our Time*. Vintage Books, New York, 1976.

Howe, Frederick C. *Wisconsin: An Experiment in Democracy*. Scribner's, New York, 1912.

Johnson, Haynes, and Bernard M. Gwertzman. *Fulbright the Dissenter*. Doubleday & Co., Garden City, N.Y., 1968.

Johnson, Lyndon Baines. *The Vantage Point: Perspectives of the Presidency, 1963–1969*. Holt, Rinehart & Winston, New York, 1971.

Johnson, Walter, et al., eds. *The Papers of Adlai E. Stevenson, Ambassador to the United Nations, 1961–1965*. Vol. 8. Little, Brown & Co., Boston, 1979.

Kalman, Laura. *Abe Fortas: A Biography*. Yale University Press, New Haven, 1990.

Karnow, Stanley. *Vietnam: A History*. The Viking Press, New York, 1983.

Kirchmeier, Mark. *Packwood: The Public and Private Life from Acclaim to Outrage*. HarperCollins, New York, 1995.

La Follette, Belle Case, and Fola La Follette. *Robert M. La Follette*. 2 vols. Macmillan, New York, 1953.

Lait, Jack, and Lee Nortimer. *U.S.A. Confidential*. Crown Publishers, New York, 1952.

Larrowe, Charles P. *Harry Bridges: The Rise and Fall of Radical Labor in the United States*. Lawrence Hill & Co., New York, 1972.

MacArthur, Douglas. *Reminiscences*. McGraw-Hill Book Co., New York, 1964.

McCall, Tom, with Steve Neal. *Tom McCall, Maverick: An Autobiography*. Binford & Mort, Portland, 1977.

McNamara, Robert S. *In Retrospect: The Tragedy and Lessons of Vietnam*. Times Books, New York, 1995.

McPherson, Harry. *A Political Education*. Little, Brown & Co., Boston, 1972.

Martin, Ralph G. *Henry & Clare: An Intimate Portrait of the Luces*. Putnam Publishing Group, New York, 1992.

Matusow, Allen J. *The Unravelling of America: A History of Liberalism in the 1960s*. Harper & Row, New York, 1984.

Maxwell, Robert S. *La Follette and the Rise of Progressivism.* State Historical Society of Wisconsin, Madison, 1912.

Moley, Raymond. *After Seven Years.* Harper & Brothers, New York, 1939.

Mollenhoff, David V. *Madison: A History of the Formative Years.* Kendall/Hunt Publishing Co., Dubuque, 1982.

Mooney, Booth. *LBJ: An Irreverent Chronicle.* Thomas Y. Crowell Co., New York, 1976.

Newfield, Jack. *Robert Kennedy: A Memoir.* New American Library, New York, 1969.

Newman, John M. *JFK and Vietnam.* Warner Books, New York, 1992.

Onstine, Burton W. *Oregon Votes: 1858–1972.* Oregon Historical Society, Portland, 1973.

Oshinsky, David M. *A Conspiracy So Immense: The World of Joe McCarthy.* The Free Press, New York, 1983.

Paper, Lewis J. *John F. Kennedy: The Promise and the Performance.* Da Capo Press, New York, 1980.

Paul, Justus F., and Barbara Dotts. *The Badger State.* William B. Ersmans Publishing Co., Grand Rapids, Mich., 1979.

Pearson, Drew, and Jack Anderson. *The Case against Congress.* Simon & Schuster, New York, 1968.

Pilat, Oliver. *Drew Pearson: An Unauthorized Biography.* Harper's Magazine Press, New York, 1973.

Reedy, George E. *The U.S. Senate: Paralysis or a Search for Consensus?* Crown Publishers, New York, 1986.

Reeves, Thomas C. *The Life and Times of Joe McCarthy.* Stein & Day, New York, 1982.

Robinson, Archie. *George Meany and His Times: A Biography.* Simon & Schuster, New York, 1981.

Rovere, Richard H., and Arthur M. Schlesinger, Jr. *The General and the President, and the Future of American Foreign Policy.* Farrar, Straus & Young, New York, 1951.

Schlesinger, Arthur M., Jr. *Robert Kennedy and His Times.* Houghton Mifflin Co., Boston, 1978.

Schwartz, Bernard. *The Professor and the Commissions.* Alfred A. Knopf, New York, 1959.

Shadegg, Stephen. *Clare Boothe Luce: A Biography.* Simon & Schuster, New York, 1970.

Shaffer, Samuel. *On and Off the Floor: Thirty Years as a Correspondent on Capitol Hill.* Newsweek Books, New York, 1980.

Sheed, Wilfrid. *Clare Boothe Luce.* E. P. Dutton, New York, 1982.

Sherrill, Robert. *The Accidental President.* Grossman Publishers, New York, 1967.

Shrecker, Ellen W. *No Ivory Tower: McCarthyism and the Universities.* Oxford University Press, New York, 1986.

Small, Melvin. *Johnson, Nixon, and the Doves.* Rutgers University Press, New Brunswick, 1988.

Smith, A. Robert. *The Tiger in the Senate: The Biography of Wayne Morse.* Doubleday & Co., Garden City, N.Y., 1962.

Solberg, Carl. *Hubert Humphrey: A Biography.* W. W. Norton & Co., New York, 1984.

Steinberg, Alfred. *Sam Houston's Boy: A Close-up of the President from Texas.* Macmillan, New York, 1968.

Stone, I. F. *The Haunted Fifties, 1953–1963.* Little, Brown & Co., Boston, 1963.

———. *In a Time of Torment, 1961–1967.* Little, Brown & Co., Boston, 1967.

———. *Polemics and Prophecies, 1967–1970.* Little, Brown & Co., Boston, 1970.

Swanberg, W. A. *Luce and His Empire.* Charles Scribner's Sons, New York, 1972.

Terkel, Studs. *Hard Times; An Oral History of the Depression.* Pantheon Books, New York, 1970.

Thelen, David P. *Robert M. La Follette and the Insurgent Spirit.* Little, Brown & Co., Boston, 1976.

Thomas, Norman C. *Education in National Politics.* David McKay Co., New York, 1975.

Truman, Harry S. *Off the Record: The Private Papers of Harry S. Truman.* Edited by Robert H. Farrell. Harper & Row, New York, 1980.

Turner, Kathleen. *Lyndon Johnson's Dual War: Vietnam and the Press.* University of Chicago Press, Chicago, 1985.

Valenti, Jack. *A Very Human President.* W. W. Norton & Co., New York, 1975.

The Vietnam Hearings. With an introduction by J. William Fulbright. Vintage Books, New York, 1966.

Walth, Brent. *Fire at Eden's Gate: Tom McCall and the Oregon Story.* Oregon Historical Society Press, Portland, 1994.

Warburg, James P. *The United States in the Postwar World.* Atheneum, New York, 1966.

Wells, Tom. *The War Within: America's Battle over Vietnam.* University of California Press, Berkeley, 1994.

Welter, Rush. *Popular Education and Democratic Thought in America.* Columbia University Press, New York, 1962.

Wilkins, Lee. *Wayne Morse: A Bio-Bibliography.* Greenwood Press, Westport, Conn., 1985.

Williams, William Appleman. *The Contours of American History.* Quadrangle Books, Chicago, 1966.

Zaroulis, Nancy, and Gerald Sullivan. *Who Spoke Up? American Protest against the War in Vietnam, 1963–1975.* Holt, Rinehart & Winston, New York, 1984.

ORAL HISTORIES

John F. Kennedy Library

D. Otis Beasley, December 15, 1969

Jim Grant Bolling, March 1, 1966

Bernard L. Boutin, June 3, 1964

Alexander K. Christie, December 6, 1966

Mary Kelly, February 12, 1966

James Kirwin, March 1960 (no day given)

Peter Lisagor, April 22, 1966

Mike Mansfield, June 23, 1964

Samuel V. Merrick, October 16, 1966

Joseph Rauh, Jr., February 12, 1970

Walter Spolar, June 9, 1966

Lyndon Baines Johnson Library

Joseph A. Califano, June 11, 1973

George E. Reedy, December 14, 1968; May 23, 1983; February 29, 1984

Samuel Halperin, July 24, 1968

Harry S. Truman Library

C. Girard Davidson, July 17-18, 1972

Library of Congress

John W. Bricker, October 2, 1978

J. William Fulbright, March 5, 1979

Edith Green, November 18, 1978 – March 18, 1980

Maurine Neuberger, April 5 – May 15, 1979

INTERVIEWS

Ron Abell	E. D. Conklin	Penny Gross
Jack Anderson	Travis Cross	Charles Grossman
Steve Anderson	C. Girard Davidson	Marko Haggard
Ralph Axley	Sylvia N. S. Davidson	Beulah Hand
Lois Baker	Walter Dodd	Mark Hatfield
Scott Bartlett	Lyndon Duke	Elma Doris Havemann
Wickes Shaw Beal	Bob Duncan	Herman Hendershott
Dorothy Berg	William East	Wally Heyden
Merton Bernstein	Tom Enright	Lawrence Hobart
Amy Morse Bilich	Bud Forrester	Harry Hogan
Charles Brooks	Norma Frazee	Orlando Hollis
Windsor Calkin	J. William Fulbright	Mrs. A. Holmes
John Callahan	Mrs. T. Garvey	Pat Holt
Nancy Morse Campbell	Phil George	Hallie Huntington
Henry Carey	Arthur Goldberg	Juliane Johnson
Jack Churchill	Judith Morse Goldman	Ken Johnson
Tris Coffin	Edith Green	Aaron Jones
Hugh Cole, Jr.	Hal Gross	Stephen Kahn

Henry Kaiser
Mary Kelly
Ed Kienstra
Caryl Kline
Wayne Kline
Mike Kopetski
Tom Landye
Charles Lee
Dorothy Leeper
Jean Lewis
Hans Linde
William Lubersky
Eugene McCarthy
Stewart McClure
Joseph McCracken
George McGovern
Hobart McQueary
Carl Marcy
Joseph Miller
Howard Morgan
Mildred Morse
Clay Myers, Jr.
Gaylord Nelson

Roscoe Nelson
Leonard Netzog
Maurine Neuberger
Wesley Nicholson
Gus Norwood
Warren Nunn
Kenneth O'Connell
Laura Olson
Robert Packwood
Nels Peterson
Charles Porter
Gerald Pratt
William Proxmire
Joe Rauh, Jr.
Floyd Riddick
Gerald Robinson
Phyllis Rock
Maurice Rosenblatt
Neil Sabin
Dan Sellard
Mary Jane Sills
Keith Skelton

A. Robert Smith
Raoul "Joe" Smith
Richard Smith
Gus Solomon
Ben Stephansky
Norman Stoll
Bob Straub
Monroe Sweetland
Elwood Taub
George H. R. Taylor
Hale Thompson
Seth Tillman
Lloyd Tupling
Gladys Uhl
Al Ullman
Jim Weaver
Blaine Whipple
Don Willner
Mort Winkel
Robert Wolf
Wendell Wyatt
Ron Wyden

Index

AFL-CIO, *229, 431, 432, 438, 443, 444, 448*

AFL-CIO News, 228-29

Acheson, Dean, *177, 180*

Adams, Sherman, *289-90, 310, 317*

Aiken, George, *160*

Allen, Robert S., *273, 292*

Allen, S. Eugene, *140*

American Association of University Professors, *70, 72, 74, 75*

American Bar Association, *204*

American China Policy Association, *178*

American Civil Liberties Union, *124, 199-200, 248*

American Federation of Labor, *103, 108, 128, 132, 210*

American Mercury, 257

Americans for Democratic Action, *218, 259, 267, 306*

Anderson, Clinton, *337*

Anderson, Jack, *309, 310*

Angell, Homer, *123-24*

Angoff, Charles, *257*

Anti-Defamation League, *306*

Ascoli, Max, *318*

Associated Press, *226, 320, 418*

Astorian-Budget, 138

Atlanta Constitution, 365

Atomic Energy Commission, *163*

Austin, Anthony, *401*

Avery, Sewell, *109-10, 131-32*

Axley, Ralph, *40, 41, 42, 44, 46, 48*

Baker, Edward Dickinson, *169-70*

Ball, George, *410*

Barkley, Alben W., *146, 153, 159*

Barnes, Volney G., *11, 24, 28, 33*

Beck, Dave, *302*

Belafonte, Harry, *461*

Bend Bulletin, 219

Berg, Bill, *132, 139, 221, 235-37, 345, 348, 360, 445, 455*

Bernstein, Irving, *5, 369, 372, 373, 384, 386, 393*

Bernstein, Merton, *221-22, 227-28, 235-37, 265, 276, 292, 298, 313-14, 317, 329, 334, 347-48, 358, 361*

Biemiller, Andrew, *438*

Blanton, Smiley, *52, 422-23*

Blum, Albert, *458*

Boe, Jason, *459*

Bolling, Jim Grant, 382

Bonneville Power Administration, 172

Borah, William, 3, 255

Bowles, Chester, 147, 154

Boyer, C. Valentine, 74, 75, 77, 82, 252

Bradley, Omar, 167

Brand, Charles, 71

Bridges, Harry, 9, 93-94, 97-98, 126; photograph, 96

Bridges, Styles, 178

Brokaw, George, 317

Brooks, Charles, 218, 227, 235, 297, 327, 330, 350-51, 357, 358, 359, 374, 379, 445-46, 455

Brotherhood of Locomotive Firemen and Enginemen's Magazine, 255

Browder, Earl, 179

Browne, Malcolm, 418-19

Brownell, Herbert, 204

Brown v. Board of Education, 304-305

Bryngelson, Bryng, 56

Bundy, McGeorge, 410, 412, 413, 416-19, 421, 425

Burgess, Nan, 358, 365-66

Cain, Harry, 157, 158, 176, 178

Califano, Joe, 388, 396, 427, 433-34, 435, 442, 455; photograph, 431

Campbell, Hugh, 352-53

Capehart, Homer, 168, 302, 317, 342

Capital Press, 370

Carpenter, Charles, 57, 60, 62-64

Carter, Jimmy, 409

Casteel, John Laurence, 59, 69, 71, 83

Cater, Douglass, 395, 396

Chapman, C. C., 158

Chapman, Oscar, 342-43

Chase, Bruce, 352

Chester, Colby, 154

Chiang Kai-shek, 178, 179, 180, 324

Chicago Sun-Times, 450

Chicago Tribune, 178, 198, 199, 322

Childs, Marquis, 256, 260

China, 174-81 passim, 266, 283, 402, 403

China lobby, 177-80, 190, 324, 403

Christian Science Monitor, 450

Christie, Alexander, 335

Church, Frank, 296, 366, 413

Churchill, Jack, 326, 331

Civil Rights Act of 1957, 271, 305-308

Civil Rights Act of 1964, 387, 397

Clark, Joe, 306, 402

Cleveland, Harlan, 416, 418

The Coast magazine, 99

Cohen, Wilbur, 382, 388

Cold War, 154, 167, 275, 283, 402, 421

Cole, Hugh, Jr., 345-46, 359, 361

Collier's 208, 359

Collins, LeRoy, 429

Columbia University Law School, 53, 54, 55, 60

Columbia Valley Authority, 171-72, 173, 257, 258

Communist Control Act, 205, 210, 211

Congressional Record, 148, 155, 168, 406, 418

Congress of Industrial Organizations, *103, 108, 128, 132, 139*

Conklin, Ed, *129, 135, 138, 144, 176, 177, 182, 359, 364, 452, 454, 456, 458*

Connally, Tom, *146, 147-48, 149, 150, 153*

Conner, John, *429*

Cooper, Genevieve, *191*

Coos Bay World, 293

Corbett, Henry, *191*

Cordon, Guy, *143, 158, 166, 209, 229, 256, 257-58, 437*

Cranston, Alan, *366*

Daniel, Price, *224*

Davidson, C. Girard "Jebby," *172, 314, 315, 326, 363*

Davis, Willam H., *105, 110*

Deal, C. W., photograph, *91*

The Delineator, 53

Department of Labor Conciliation Service, *95*

Des Moines Register, 309

Dewey, John, *54*

Dewey, Thomas E., *140, 167*

Dirksen, Everett, *321*

Dixon, George, *195, 196, 356-57*

Dodd, Thomas, *367*

Douglas, Donald, *154*

Douglas, Paul, *229, 271-72, 273, 305, 307-308, 320, 391, 412*

Douglas, William O., *434, 443*

Downer College, *14*

Drummond, Roscoe, *290*

Duke, Russell W., *208*

Dulles, John Foster, *168, 169, 324, 403, 405*

Duncan, Robert, *437-38, 439, 441-45, 447-48, 459*; photograph, *443*

Dworshak, Henry, *157, 158*

Eagleton, Thomas, *322*

East, William, *62, 84*

Eastland, James, *197*

East Oregonian, 278

Eastwood, Clint, *462*

Economic Opportunity Act, *387*

Edgewood Farm, *76, 82, 85, 96, 116, 117, 142, 144, 345, 457*; photograph, *84*

Eidenberg, Eugene, *391-92*

Eisenhower, Dwight, *8, 9, 125, 187-89, 190, 195, 196, 212, 213, 228, 230, 233, 238, 239, 263, 266, 267, 274, 275, 301-302, 304-307, 309-10, 317, 321, 324, 345, 369, 403, 405;* photograph, *227*

Eisenhower Doctrine, *404*

Elementary and Secondary Education Act, *389-93, 394-95, 396-98*

Elwell, Fay S., *41*

Enright, Tom, *294, 360*

Erb, Donald, *79, 80, 95-96, 99, 121*

Ervin, Sam, *397*

Eugene, Ore., *59, 67, 243*

Eugene Hunt Club, *84, 116, 355*

Eugene Power Board, *84*

Eugene Register-Guard, 67, 80, 126, 349, 442

Eugene Rotary Club, *84*

Evans, Rowland, *406*

Evansville Courier-Press, 108

Fair Employment Practices Commission, *162*

Federal Bureau of Investigation, *203-204, 211, 418*

Federal Communications Commission, *308, 310*

Federal Trade Commission, *310*

Ferryboatmen's Union, *75, 89, 90*

Fisher, Earl E., *137*

Flanders, Ralph E., *209*

Fleming, D. F., *403*

Formosa Resolution, *266, 271, 402, 403, 413*

Forrester, Bud, *278*

Fortas, Abe, *112-14, 457*

Fountain, L. H., *397*

Frank, Aaron, *128, 138, 144, 228*

Franklin, Yvonne, *389*

Frazee, Norma, *92, 96*

Freund, Arthur J., *198*

Frontier magazine *259, 260*

Fulbright, J. William, *1-2, 3, 6, 7, 318, 319, 401, 410, 413-14, 420, 422, 426-27, 434*

Fuller, Helen, *260*

GI Bill, *371*

Gardner, John, *397*

General Motors, *107-108, 159*

Geneva Accords, *8*

George, Phil, *338, 455, 458*

Gilbert, Charles, *375*

Gilbert, James, *67, 69, 77-80, 82, 333*

Ginsberg, David, photograph, *431*

Goldwater, Barry, *209, 294, 342, 389, 434, 435*

Goodwin, Doris Kearns, *456*

Gore, Albert, Sr., *229*

Graham, Frank, *199, 203*

Great Depression, *61, 66, 85*

Great Society, *9, 371, 389, 393, 399, 424, 428, 435, 461*

Green, B. A., *191-92*

Green, Edith, *214, 217, 269-71, 277, 278, 285, 292, 311, 313-14, 325-26, 361, 375, 381-82, 387-98 passim, 458*; photographs, *215, 270, 294, 383*

Griffith, Robert, *211*

Gross, Hal, *357, 366*

Gross, Penny, *348*

Gruening, Ernest, *2, 402, 413, 426, 455*

Gunther, John, *57*

Haggerty, C. J., *438*

Hall, Arnold Bennett, *45, 46, 57, 63-67, 72*

Halperin, Samuel, *370, 382*

Hamilton, Roulhac, *225-26*

Hanzen, Henry, *135*

Harris, Oren, *308-309*

Hartley, Fred, *160*

Hartung, Al, *439, 441*

Hatfield, Mark O., *187, 291-92, 311-16, 326, 363-64, 365, 376, 437-41, 442, 449, 452-53, 458-59*; photograph, *312*

Havemann, Elma Doris, *101-102, 116, 130*; photograph, *102*

Head Start, *399*

Health Professional Educational Assistance Act, *385*

Hells Canyon, *230-31, 267, 268, 285, 302*

Helms, Richard, *410*

Hickenlooper, Bourke, *302*

Higher Education Facilities Act, *382-85, 393, 394, 399*

Hill, Lister, *369, 372, 443*

Hiss, Alger, *179*

Hitchcock, Phil, *226*

Hoard, William Dempster, *15*

Hobart, Lawrence, *347*

Ho Chi Minh, *8*

Hogan, Harry, *315, 334*

Hollis, Orlando, *57, 66, 69, 78, 79, 83, 86, 100-102, 105, 111, 116, 117, 249, 251, 252, 333, 357, 358, 361*

Holman, Rufus C., *121-23, 131, 135-37, 139, 163, 214, 216*; photograph, *122*

Holmes, Robert, *277, 278, 311-16, 345*

Holt, Pat, *363*

Hoover, David, *173*

Hoover, Herbert, *98, 125, 241*

Hoover, J. Edgar, *203*

House Commerce Committee, *308, 309-10*

House Committee on Un-American Activities, *178*

House Education and Labor Committee, *372, 394*

Houston Chronicle, 224

Hoyt, E. Palmer "Ep," *122-23, 126, 128, 129, 241*

Humphrey, Hubert, *194, 203, 205, 231, 273, 306, 320, 321, 324, 326-28, 330, 331, 335, 342, 389, 417, 418, 446, 449, 450, 451, 455*

I. F. Stone's Weekly, 198-99

Ickes, Harold, *98, 111-12, 113-14, 119*

Idaho Power Company, *230, 302*

Institute for Pacific Relations, *178-79*

International Association of Machinists and Aerospace Workers, *430-33, 442, 444, 448-49*

International Court of Justice (World Court), *149, 151-53, 154*

International Education Act, *394*

International Harvester, *106*

International Longshoremen's and Warehousemen's Union, *89, 92, 93-95, 98-100*

International Longshoreman's Association, *97-98*

Interstate Commerce Commission, *156, 310*

Ives, Irving, *160, 195, 196*

Jackson, Glenn, *439*; photograph, *440*

Jackson, Henry, *8*

Javits, Jake, *367*

Jenner, William, *182, 190, 206-208*

John Day Dam, *268*

Johnson, Edwin, *150*

Johnson, Hiram, *3, 255*

Johnson, Juliane, *348, 361*

Johnson Ken, *370, 436*

Johnson, Lyndon, 9, 193-94, 205, 213, 224-25, 229, 275, 289, 301-307, 331, 334-35, 367, 380, 384, 391-98 passim, 405-406, 420, 428-36 passim, 442-45, 454-56; and the Vietnam War, 1-3, 6, 393-94, 339, 401, 407, 413-18, 422-25, 427-28; photographs, 383, 415, 436

Joint Committee on Atomic Energy, 150

Judge Advocate General, 110-11

Kahn, Stephen, 124, 132, 241-42, 246, 249, 251, 253; photograph, 242

Kaiser, Henry J., 136

Kansas City Times, 5

Kappel, Frederick, 433

Karnow, Stanley, 6, 401

Katzenbach, Nicholas, photograph, 431

Kearns, Carrol, photograph, 381

Kefauver, Estes, 229, 231

Kelty, Paul, 255

Kennedy, Edward, 330

Kennedy, John F., 9, 205, 283, 320, 324-37 passim, 345, 367-69, 373, 376, 379, 380, 384, 387-88, 393, 404, 419-25 passim, 428, 435-36; and the Vietnam War, 406, 412; photographs, 329, 371

Kennedy, Robert F., 424, 425, 435, 437

Kennedy, Rose, 330

Keppel, Francis, 386, 388

Kerr, William Jasper, 66-72 passim, 75, 77, 129, 197-98; photograph, 68

Kilgore, Harley, 161

King, Coretta Scott, 414

King, Martin Luther, 437

King, William, 97

Kiwanis Club, 131

Kline, Caryl Morse, 12, 22, 28, 48, 86, 130, 222, 267, 370, 381; photograph, 31

Kline, Hibberd, 328

Knowland, William F., 178, 209, 403

Knoxville Journal, 108

Kohlberg, Alfred, 178

Kopetski, Mike, 364

Korean War, 175-77, 180, 186, 371

Ku Klux Klan, 123

Kunz, Adolph, 151

La Follette, Belle, 51

La Follette, Robert, 3, 13, 19, 28, 30, 32, 35, 42-43, 46, 47, 51, 149, 193, 197, 221, 255, 325, 419

Lancaster, Burt, 461, 463

Land, E. S., 104, 105

Landrum-Griffin Act, 327, 335-36, 369

Landye, Jim, 128-29, 135, 158, 191, 209, 220, 339, 360

Langer, William, 327, 403

Lapham, Roger, 105, 108

Larrowe, Charles, 92

Latourette, Howard, 173, 239

Lattimore, Owen, 179

League for Industrial Democracy, 215

Lebanon, 404

Lee, Charles, 347, 381, 385, 386, 388, 390; photograph, 381

Lee, Jason, *334*, *406*

Lehman, Herbert, *194*, *205*, *231*, *306*, *403*, *404*

Lewis, Jean, *235*

Lewis, John L., *111-12*, *114*, *126*

Liddy, G. Gordon, *409*

Life magazine, *234*

Lilienthal, David E., *163*

Linde, Hans, *276*, *284*

Lipmann, Walter, *393*

Lodge, Henry Cabot, *168*

Loeb, William, *178*

Long, Huey, *72*, *73*, *161*, *222*, *255*

Long, Russell, *426*; photograph, *189*

Longfellow School, Madison, *20*, *21*

Look magazine, *154*

Los Angeles Times, *450*

Lucas, Scott, *150*, *159*, *173*

Luce, Clare Boothe, *178*, *182*, *317-21*

Luce, Henry, *178*, *317*, *323*, *324*

Lundy, Herbert, *297*

McAlmond, Phil, *444-45*

MacArthur, Douglas, *175-77*, *179*, *182-83*, *324*

McCall, Tom, *447*, *453*

McCarran Act (Internal Security Act), *202-203*, *205*

McCarthy, Eugene, *342*, *343*, *437*, *445*, *446*, *455*; photograph, *343*

McCarthy, Joseph, *175*, *178*, *190*, *199*, *201-202*, *205*, *208-11*, *302*, *324*

McClure, Stewart, *388*, *393*, *395*

McCone, John, *413*

McCormick, Robert, *178-79*

McCracken, Joe, *377-78*

McGee, Gale, *8*

McGrory, Mary, *332*

The Machinist, *431*

McKay, Douglas, *186*, *187*, *213*, *226-34* *passim*, *237-38*, *258*, *268*, *297*, *379*; photograph, *227*

McKellar, Kenneth, *146*

McNamara, Pat, *369*

McNamara, Robert, *407-11*, *419*, *421*, *423*, *425*, *433*; photograph, *407*

McNary, Charles L., *143*

McNaughton, E. B., *128*, *138*

McPherson, Harry, *462*

Madison, Wis., *11*, *13*, *14*, *18-20*, *24*, *30-32*, *43*, *48*

Madison Capital Times, *336*

Madison Central High School, *11*, *19*, *22*, *23-24*, *26*, *30*

Mamaroneck Daily Times, *414*

Manatos, Mike, *390*, *394*

Mansfield, Mike, *234*, *303*, *304*, *372*, *379*, *380*, *392*, *426*

Mansfield, Peggy, photograph, *459*

Marshall, George C., *170*, *190*

Marshall Plan, *166*

Meadowbrook Saddle Club, *181*

Meany, George, *132*, *133*, *431-32*, *433*

Medicare, *380*

Meier, Julius, *144*

Memphis Commercial Appeal, *108*

Mental Health Facilities and Community Mental Health Centers Construction acts, *385*, *387*

Merrick, Samuel, 335

Middle East Resolution, 402, 404, 413

Miller, Justin, 63, 74-75, 76, 79

Milwaukee Journal, 44

Minneapolis, Minn., 49, 50

Mitchell, Clarence, 306

Mitchell, Hugh, 157

Moley, Raymond, 55, 60, 70, 72, 73, 85

Mollenhoff, Clark, 309

Montgomery Ward, 109-10, 131

Moore house, Roseburg, 280-81, 284, 286, 296

Moores, Ralph, 130

Morey, Roy D., 391-92

Morgan, Howard, 214-18, 235, 263, 366-67, 437-38, 446, 453, 455; photographs, 215, 219

Morse, Amy Ann, 75, 96, 117-19, 349, 350, 352, 353, 456; photograph, 118

Morse, Caryl, *see* Kline, Caryl Morse

Morse, Grant, 12, 14, 16, 17, 19

Morse, Harry, 12, 14, 16, 17, 19, 24-25, 38

Morse, Jessie Elnora White, 12-19 *passim,* 22, 25, 29, 33, 38, 40, 86-87; photograph, 31

Morse, Judith May, 74, 96, 117-19, 191, 339-40, 349, 351, 352, 353, 418, 454; photograph, 118

Morse, Mabel, 12, 14, 19

Morse, Mildred "Midge" Downie, 25-29, 35-40, 44, 47-53, 57, 63, 66, 71-77 *passim,* 82, 115-19, 129, 140, 141, 183, 191, 330-35, 344, 349-60 *passim,* 446, 456, 458; photograph, 27

Morse, Nancy Fay, 66, 72, 96, 117-19, 181, 191, 349, 352-54, 357; photograph, 118

Morse, Wayne Lyman; becomes political Independent, 190-91, 213, 216-18; birth, 14-15; children, 66, 74, 75; death, 460-61; farming, 13, 20, 23, 76, 339-45; horses, 16, 61, 76, 82-85, 116-17, 140, 170-71, 181-82, 339-41, 354-55; joins Democratic Party, 219; marriage, 49; maverick quality, 3-7, 33, 45-46, 144, 158, 211, 304, 308-11, 337-38, 370, 449; parents and siblings, 12-14; personal finances, 36-40, 344-45; presidential candidacy, 325-33; religion, 21; temperament, 85-86, 101-102, 120, 235-36, 362; World War II service, 110-11; photographs, 15, 26, 31, 39, 49, 50, 65, 91, 102, 134, 141, 145, 171, 184, 189, 201, 219, 230, 232, 270, 279, 294, 340, 343, 356, 363, 371, 381, 383, 415, 420, 421, 436, 440, 451, 459, 460

Morse, Wilbur Frank "Wib," 13-21 *passim,* 24, 28, 29, 33, 38, 40, 46, 61, 76, 86, 163; photograph, 31

Morse Formula, 164-66, 280-83, 296, 317

Murray, Philip, 132, 133, 154

Myers, Clay, Jr., 186, 210-11

The Nation, 253, 257

National Association for the Advancement of Colored People, 166, 196, 306

National Defense Education Act, 371, 372, 385

National Defense Mediation Board, 102, 105

National Education Association, *198*, *373*, *383*, *388*

National Friends of Wayne Morse, *268-69*, *325*, *327*

National Lawyers Guild, *125*

National Teacher Corps, *393*, *395-96*

National War Labor Board, *9*, *103-16 passim*, *119*, *121*, *126*, *131-33*, *162*, *199*, *236*, *254*, *431*

Neal, Gary, *326*, *330*, *331*, *334*

Nelson, Gaylord, *413*, *426*

Nelson, Roscoe, *68-69*, *70*, *249*, *251*

Neuberger, Maurine Brown, *255*, *261*, *265-70 passim*, *292*, *372*, *413*, *426*, *437*; photograph, *261*

Neuberger, Richard, *67*, *70*, *124*, *157-58*, *214-17*, *229*, *231-300 passim*, *313-16*, *323-25*, *347-48*, *366*, *374*, *437*; photographs, *230*, *242*, *244*, *261*, *270*, *279*, *294*

New Deal, *85*, *123*, *125*, *127-28*, *131*, *132*, *135*, *136*, *163*

New Frontier, *337*, *368*, *371*, *380*

New Republic, *5*, *260*, *306*

Newsweek, *159*, *292*, *293*, *300*, *406*, *450*

New York Daily News, *353*

New York Post, *232*

New York Times, *108*, *156*, *180*, *194*, *221*, *228*, *232*, *253*, *308*, *376*, *392*, *438*, *449*, *450*

Nicholson, Wesley, *461*

Nixon, Richard, *187-89*, *190*, *212*, *223*, *229*, *237*, *309*, *324*, *336*, *337*, *406*, *446*, *450*, *451*, *455*, *459*

North Atlantic Treaty Organization, *169*, *188*

Northern Oratorical League, *47*, *52*

Novak, Robert, *406*

O'Brien, Larry, *390*

Office of Price Administration, *147*, *148*

Office of War Information, *128*

Ohling, Charles, *130*

Onthank, Karl W., *249*

Oregon Commonwealth Federation, *125*

Oregon Daily Emerald, *67*, *241*, *242-43*, *245*, *247*, *254*

Oregonian, *122-23*, *126*, *241*, *254*, *255*, *292-94*, *297*, *313*, *373*, *377*, *385*, *393*, *396*

Oregon Journal, *226*

Oregon Labor Press, *140*, *431*

Oregon Law Review, *73*

Oregon State Board of Higher Education, *66-72 passim*, *78*, *80*, *128*, *139*, *197*, *249*

Oregon State College, *66-71*

Oregon Statesman, *332*

Oregon Voter, *158*

Pacific Coast Maritime Industry Board, *104*

Packwood, Robert, *445-55 passim*, *458*, *459*; photograph, *451*

Patterson, Paul, *226*

Pearson, Drew, *170*, *273*, *296*, *308*, *309*, *310*, *342*, *456*

Pepper, Claude, *458*

Percy, Charles, *453*

Perkins, Carl, *387, 389, 391, 394-95*

Perkins, Frances, *92, 95, 98, 99*

Perlman, Selig, *45, 46, 89*

Philadelphia Bulletin, 193

Philadelphia Inquirer, 302

Pickert, D. F., *345*

Pierce, Cornelia Marvin, *249*

Poolesville, Md., Morse farm, *339-44, 350, 363, 457*

Porter, Charles, *270, 271, 276-83 passim, 289, 311, 313, 326, 332, 357*; photograph, *270*

Posniak, Edward G., *202*

Powell, Adam Clayton, *372, 382, 387, 391, 394*

The Progressive, 255, 268-69

Progressivism, *19, 28, 29-33, 35, 43, 45, 89, 125-26*

Proxmire, William, *6-7, 8, 336*

Railroad Emergency Board, *100-103, 116, 117*

Railway Labor Act, *100, 430, 432*

Rarig, Frank, *51-56, 307, 339, 353, 357*

Rauh, Joe, *306, 328, 362*

Rayburn, Sam, *309, 310*

Reader's Digest magazine, *253*

Reedy, George, *289, 387, 427*

Reichert, Lorena, *21, 25*

Reporter magazine, *318, 320*

Republican National Committee, *156, 157*

Robinson, Ann, photograph, *459*

Robinson, Gerald, *361*

Rock, Phyllis, *235, 283, 348, 374, 375, 412*

Rock Creek Park, *181, 350*

Roosevelt, Eleanor, *229, 232*; photograph, *232*

Roosevelt, Franklin D., *95, 98-110 passim, 112, 114, 120, 123, 125, 126, 128, 131, 135, 141, 146, 147, 149, 186, 319-20*; photographs, *104, 127*

Rosenberg, Anna, *207*

Roth, Almon, *133*

Rusk, Dean David, *199, 407, 411-25 passim, 428*

Russell, Richard, *397*

St. Louis Post-Dispatch, 180, 219

Salem Capital Journal, 191

Salem Chamber of Commerce, *313*

Saltonstall, Leverett, *187*

Sammons, Edward C., *67, 72, 128, 191, 192, 203, 228*

San Francisco, Calif., *88-89, 92-94*; photograph, *88*

San Francisco Chronicle, 98

Saturday Evening Post, 354

Schlesinger, Arthur, Jr., *425*

Schwartz, Bernard, *308, 309-10*

Scott, Owen, *342*

Senate Armed Services Committee, *164-66, 176, 186, 193, 195*

Senate Banking and Currency Committee, *225*

Senate Committee on Government Operations, *280-81*

Senate District of Columbia Committee, *193, 195, 225*

Senate Foreign Relations Committee, _1_, _147_, _148_, _168_, _169_, _176_, _225_, _318_, _321_, _336_, _361_, _403_, _410_, _414_, _417_, _418_, _422_, _423_, _428_

Senate Interior Committee, _267_, _268_, _377_

Senate Interstate Commerce Committee, _156_

Senate Labor and Public Welfare Committee, _156_, _159_, _160_, _164_, _193_, _195_, _303_, _347_, _369_, _388_, _391_, _443_, _448_; Education Subcommittee, _369_, _382_, _391_

Senate Public Works Committee, _193_, _195_

Senate Select Committee on Small Business, _225_

Shadegg, Stephen, _323_

Shaffer, Samuel, _293_, _300_

Sheed, Wilfrid, _323_

Siemiller, P. L. (Roy), _431_, _433_, _442_

Signalman's Journal, _255_

Skelton, Keith, _313_, _314_

Small Business Administration Act, _377_

Smith, A. Robert (Bob), _177_, _188_, _207-208_, _225-26_, _238_, _274_, _277_, _278_, _293_, _313_, _315_, _347_, _373-74_, _396_; comments on his biography of Morse, _278-79_

Smith, Edgar W., _139_, _141_

Smith, Joe, _67_, _140_, _332_, _345_, _357_, _362_, _365-66_

Smith, Margaret Chase, _201_; photograph, _201_

Smith, Raoul, _332_

Smith, Stephenson, _125_, _197_

Smith, Woody, _226_

Smith Act, _202_

Solomon, Gus, _124_, _134-35_

Sorensen, Theodore, _368_

Sparta, Wis., _48_

Spencer, Carlton, _63_, _64_, _245-46_, _252_

Spock, Benjamin, _414_

Spolar, Walter, _330_

Stassen, Harold, _125_, _213_

Steelman, John, _95_

Steinberg, Alfred, _224_

Stevenson, Adlai, _190_, _212_, _235_, _238_, _268_, _324_, _328_, _331-33_, _417_, _418_, _419-21_; photographs, _230_, _420_

Stoll, Norm, _442_

Stone, I. F., _207_

Straub, Robert, _435_

Stuntz, George R., photograph, _91_

Sundquist, James, _383_

Swanberg, W. A., _318_

Sweetland, Monroe, _126_, _172-73_, _214-16_, _218_, _235_, _314_, _326_, _330_, _453_; photographs, _184_, _217_

Swigert, Ernest, _376_

Symington, Stuart, _331_, _333_

Taft, Robert A., _146_, _152_, _156_, _159-60_, _161_, _168_, _173_, _178_, _187_, _190_, _193_, _194_, _195_, _221_

Taft-Hartley Act, _160-63_, _171_, _221_, _222_

Taiwan, _179_, _180_

Taylor, George H. R., _414_

Taylor, Glen, _157_, _158_, _161_, _162_

Taylor, Maxwell, _412_, _421-23_

Taylor, Thomas, _423_

Teagle, Walter, *105-106*

Tennessee Valley Authority, *172, 258*

Thomas, Elbert, *168*

Thomas, Norman, *324*

Thomas, Norman C., *381, 395, 397*

Time magazine, *178, 265, 318, 324, 442, 450*

Toledo, Peoria and Western Railroad, *108*

Tonkin Gulf Resolution, *1-3, 401-402, 405, 408-13, 426*

Travis, Jack, *447*; photograph, *440*

Truman, Bess, photograph, *184*

Truman, Harry, *9, 149, 153-69 passim, 175-79, 182-86, 202-203, 230-31*; photograph, *184*

Tugman, William, *67, 77, 78, 80, 126, 225, 361-62, 364*

Tupling, Lloyd, *277, 283, 292, 293*

Uhl, Gladys, *342, 344-45, 346*

Ullman, Al, *270, 271, 277, 278, 285-86, 311, 326, 361*; photographs, *270, 294*

Unander, Sigfrid, *374, 375-76, 379*

Union of Soviet Socialist Republics, *149, 150-51, 154, 166, 169, 176, 283*

United Automobile Workers, *159-60*

United Mine Workers, *100, 111, 114*

United Nations, *147, 149, 151-53, 166, 179, 336, 343, 402-404, 406, 414-17, 419-21, 462*

United Press International, *446*

U.S. Department of Justice, *76-77, 81, 83,*

U.S. Department of Labor, *94, 95*

U.S. Department of the Interior, *111-*

12, 378

U.S. Information Agency, *275*

U.S. Maritime Commission, *98-99*

U.S. News and World Report, 342

University of Iowa, *121*

University of Minnesota, *49-50, 52-53, 55-57, 255*

University of Oregon, *57, 59, 66-72, 74, 77-79, 82, 84, 95-96, 103, 121, 197, 241, 242-43*

University of Wisconsin, *14, 16, 35-36, 40-45, 48*

Upward Bound, *388, 399*

Valenti, Jack, *427*

Vance, Cyrus, *410*; photograph, *431*

Vandenberg, Arthur, *149, 150, 153, 166, 168, 169, 173*

Vaughn, Harry, *290*

Vaughn, Robert, *461*

Verona, Wis., *13, 14, 15, 19, 21, 43*

Vietnam, *2, 3, 6-8, 379, 394, 398, 400, 401, 405-36 passim, 438-41, 445, 450, 452, 462*

Vocational Education Act, *385, 399*

Wage Stabilization Act, *148*

Wagner Act, *190, 159*

Wallace, George, *455*

Wallace, Henry, *3, 319, 324*

Wallace, Mike, *302*

Wall Street Journal, 231

Walsh, William, *173*

War Labor Board, *see* National War Labor Board

War Manpower Commission, *146*

War on Poverty, *387, 389*

Warren, Earl, *167*

War Shipping Administrator, *104*

Wasby, Stephen, *360*

Washington Daily News, *195*

Washington Post, *146, 290, 328, 372, 380, 451*

Washington Star, *224, 392*

Washke, Paul, *79, 82, 86, 144, 150-51, 157, 237, 344, 352, 354-55, 360*

Washke, Ruth, *121, 157*

Waterfront Employers' Association, *89, 92-95, 99, 100*

Watson, Marvin, *442*

Weaver, Andrew T., *46, 47-49, 258*

Webber, Lynda, *22-23, 25, 40, 49*; photograph, *23*

Welker, Herman, *195-96, 209*

West, Charles, *448*

West, Oswald, *144*

Western Forest Industries Association, *377*

Wherry, Kenneth, *163, 173, 178*

White, Flora Dickerman, *14, 20, 21, 25*

White, Myron Renaldo, *14, 21, 115*

White, Stephen, *14*

White, Wallace H., *146*

Wicker, Tom, *449*

Wiley, Alexander, *303*

Williams, G. Mennen, *306-307*

Williams, John, *309*

Williams, Rolland F., *44*

Willkie, Wendell, *125*

Willner, Don, *449*

Wilmington News, *108*

Wilson, Charles E., *220*

Wilson, Leah, *22*

Wirtz, Willard, *429*

Witte, Edwin, *45, 46, 89*

Wolf, Bob, *377*

Workers' Alliance of America, *81*

Works Progress Administration, *76, 81*

World Court, *see* International Court of Justice

World War II, *85, 99, 103, 122, 149-50, 186*

York, Frances, *354*

Young, Stephen, *321, 426*

Zorn-MacPherson bill, *66-67, 122, 124, 130*

THE TYPEFACE USED FOR *WAYNE MORSE: A POLITICAL BIOGRAPHY* is Minion, a contemporary face based upon classical, old-style type-faces of the late Renaissance, created for electronic composition by Robert Slimbach. The book was designed by John Laursen at Press-22. The text was edited by Nancy Trotic and indexed by Jean Brownell. The dust jacket photograph was retouched by Mohamed Zuhairy at Oscar Photo Restoration, and all of the images were scanned by Precision Digital Imaging. Printing and binding were done by Publishers Press, and the dust jacket was printed by Martin Curtis at CME Printers.